THE TRUTH ABOUT
REALITY

Find Out What Nobody Ever Knew About God!

Did you know that all you learn, believe and do keep you in a state of spiritual fiction; that you exist in virtual reality that we enforce on each other?

It is becoming clearer that whatever human minds conceive can exist in our sense of reality. A mind conceived that man can walk on the moon; and man did!

What this book relates to you, though, did not spring from the mind of man; it was planted in a human mind from a place the author calls true reality. This book is about the realism of fantasy and our ignorance about reality.

Scientists virtually proved that the universe was created solely to place the earth as habitat for humanity. They are right yet the author is telling you that the whole ball of wax is a hoax.

The author reveals that Jesus came to us in the role of dual agent. Jesus said, he came to separate goats from sheep. He came for the sheep, but more urgently, he came for the goats. The benefits of this book in insight, understanding, and knowledge will work for you continuously.

Over the past decade Anti-Christ wrote articles to a group of expert insiders about environment, history, law, government, and religion from a novel perspective.

Overall, he wrote some twenty thousand pages. Anti-Christ has been a student on topics he has written about, but an integrated perspective on reality only fell into place 5 years ago.

He is a man of his own ideas. He speaks out about things he thoroughly knows about and listens when others can teach him. He has a keen interest in "Life", because

Life makes no sense.

Big deals and the universe are only in the mind. The mind is a set of spiritually preconceived belief-systems.

The universe is memory because "*now*" does not exist. "*Now*" is always just out of reach.

Being born is a death sentence; but for what crime; and who pronounced the sentence? Everybody dies "*now*"; and "*now*" is the aperture in the mind through which the frames of "Life" us the experience of existing. When the aperture closes but existence continues without physical perception. sconnected from the physical display.

Poster displayed in post offices throughout the United States.
"Let us dare to read, think, speak and write" (**the truth**).

THE TRUTH ABOUT REALITY

THE TRUTH ABOUT REALITY

Beyond God and Religion

ANTI CHRIST

To order additional copies of this book, contact:
Xlibris Corporation
1-888-795-4274
www.Xlibris.com
Orders@Xlibris.com
38823

Anti Christ
1-877-204-0966
www.sciencefictionofreality.com

CONTENTS

BOOK II—*Insight into the Process and Depth of Deceit*

BOOK IV—*The Science Fiction Of Life*

BOOK V—*Human Perception of Reality Is a Spiritual Fabrication*

APPENDICES

FIGURES

BOOK I

THE INVENTION OF VIRTUAL REALITY

Note to the reader

This book is based more on philosophy than on attacking organizations, people and groups. The point of the book is to open your eyes to the false rationale on which all our observations, experiences and premises of physical life are based. This false rationale is planted in you by means of propaganda.

Your universe, your country, your religious affiliation, and your friendships, are all based on propaganda (unseen and unnoticed forces in your life that you gregariously embrace and cross-disseminate). You seek these forces out with gusto because they ground you in your environment, in your relationships, and make the burdens of life, [and as slave to spirit and human authority] more bearable as you share them with your group of similarly indoctrinated people. The groups of people you regularly associate with will cross promote the belief systems in the group. This type of conditioning actually makes 'life' worthwhile and gives you a feeling of being sane, appreciated, loved and accepted. It is all phony, yet life would be unbearable if we did not allow ourselves to be duped this way.

The science, art and technology of effective propaganda have found out these urges in humans and animals and the practice of this art in society has them arranged into manageable and goal-oriented systems whereby people can be formed into huge groups that will obey the command triggers given by an over-all propaganda system. Friendships, relationships, one's identity in a group, several groups, and nations of people are carefully fostered so that we will be amenable to serve by free will in these groups through volunteering, accepting duties and willingness to defend and die to secure the safety, continuity, grows and might of the group. It is all based on deceit that one willingly and desperately embraces to make one's existence acceptable, worthwhile and desirable.

Through broadcast systems of propaganda people, without compulsion, will align themselves with actions to intimidate and coerce individuals and entire nations by means of ridicule and full-fledged efforts of war.

My intentions are honorable in that I want to induce you to reconsider every urge you feel to comply to do things that might hurt others and, without fail, yourself also. If we truly want to make the world a better place to live we must be more honest to ourselves and to our fellow men and we must be determined to keep corruption and promotion of false premises and accepted deceits from our belief systems. Yes, we only have belief-systems in physical life. Know-systems do not exist. We have to return to reality to know things. Presently we exist in a fictional reality. Nothing here in this universe is real. I want you to really get in touch with that idea because it is the only truth ever expressed in the universe.

I speak and write forcefully because the world is a very evil place where you are always under pressure and compulsion of many different conspiracies to alter your culture, belief-systems, intentions and modes of life and happiness.

Life is terrible and each of us will do all we can to cloak our terrors into modes of group-conformance, acceptability, companionship and entertainment—all based on systems of propaganda.

Please read the book as if it is just fiction. I do not intent to arraign you into action of any sort. I suggest; I do not command—yet each of us must decide if we want to continue soul existence in a mode of self-deceit or awaken into true reality.

The choice is terrifying because we believe that we know what we have in physical life and we pretend to know absolutely nothing of this true spiritual reality. Spiritual reality, though, is just like existence in this life, except we are free and we would never have to pretend, conform or accept intimidation or coercion of any kind.

Our problem is that we really do not know anything of physical existence either. We all exist in a state of quiet terror and uncertainty. We never know who is preying on us, whether someone close to us is deceiving or betraying us and whether the environment will betray or mislead us. One thing is certain, they are preying on you and using you and you have no clue who they are and what to do about it. Our lives from beginning to end is based on false premises, enforced obedience, and lies believed and accepted as if they are true. All our actions are based on misconceptions, even the actions of people who consider themselves, and are considered by others, as successful and full-filled religiously, politically and professionally.

If you want a change of outlook and insight of what spirit really is, study this book and confirm it with your understanding of the Bible, your experiences in life and your fears and uncertainties of social and corporate existence. We use each other to make life bearable and to extort an existence from our fellow beings on earth. Life would not exist without it because the universe and physical existence is based on systems of accepted deceits.

The very best kindness you can do to anybody is to tell other people of this book.

Chapter 1

Introduction

News as Basis for Virtual Reality

One's awareness of the physical environment is re-established each moment through illusions spiritually fed to us. We consider ourselves one with the environment because of the continuous, uninterrupted replay of illusions of a make-believe environment fed to us make-believe creatures by someone who wants us to believe that the physical environment is reality. Beings we traditionally refer to as god, the devil, angels, and daemons want to make us, as soul-entities, believe that creatures, the world and the universe are for real.

We are inside a witches' brew of make-believe, mind twisting deception. It all seems so real, because it demands our total attention. Our ignorance about existence draws us into the plot of the universe, and we dramatize our role in it. By acting out our role, we all enforce the universe on each other, as the only communications we are aware of come from other "living" creatures and from our environment. Our awareness of the environment is very limited because we hardly know a thing about our immediate environment and how it can be adversely invaded each moment. There are too many surprises possible. We are forever insecure and beset by fear. We jump when someone comes close unannounced. We must be on guard even when we are at home.

This fictional "reality" is like a TV sitcom show that comes on every day at the same time, and that all of us watch. Pretty soon, we become familiar with the setting of the show; and we can consider ourselves at home in this illusionary environment.

The many corporations that form the news media give us an integrated coordinated script scenario of things happening on the local, state and world scenes. Each day we receive the same story that changes according to news breaks; and from hour to hour the changes are so slight we could not tell if things really changed at all, but these oft repeated broadcasts cast us into a mass-produced mental frame.

People in the whole nation read the news in their papers, get in-depth discussions in their news magazines and then discuss the news in social chats, barroom discussions, political debates, religious activities, family settings, etc. News percolates like coffee until everyone is saturated in it.

All 'important' political news comes from just one source—a government agency propaganda news department. They work by direction of propaganda scientists. The 'news' is sent by wire to all the media who pick it up in the same format and rewrite the same story in dozens of different formats with hundreds of different commentaries. It is viewed by 'experts' and is then either broadcast or printed and then distributed. The media create a synchronized idea in the mass mind of the American people of things that seem to happen in the world, and this idea is in contradiction with what is really happening. Through such deceitful propaganda, the government can play us as a virtuoso plays his violin. We will jump up at command and fight wars with countries that are wholly innocent of the accusations made by our government.

News as a Medium of Fiction

News is merely a well written, integrated story script that bears truth only in actually verifiable data, such as a plane coming down or a building is bombed, the president visiting Africa, etc. The rest of the story, of who did it and why, is mostly fictional, and it is created with the express intention to deceive the public. In this manner a fictitious idea of what is happening in the world is imbued into the public mind which has settled in mental concrete of a strongly enforced public opinion bunker. No one can oppose this mental bunker of public opinion because it would attack the reality of how the public sees and understands the world. You are considered a nut if you dare to oppose it and if someone does, it is generally done in a sort of kidding-fashion into which a person can quickly withdraw when he finds himself under attack by his cronies for even mentioning the matter in that kind of light. Behind this artificially created mindset, long established undercover plans are integrated to make it look like events happen according to newly arrived actions and decisions, but the entire scenario has been planned for decades and is slowly brought into execution as if things are happening in a natural order of things.

Carefully choreographed events in the world are brought to our attention through the news channels of all the news media. These are backed up with real photos and real dead people and real people who found themselves caught in the incidents, but the crux of the events have been altered to create a false reality to which the greater part of the public reacts in the exact same manner. Our mental picture of the political situation has very little grounding in fact. We are being deceived on a very large scale.

Spiritual "News"

In the spiritual situation our souls have been similarly brainwashed to see this physical realm the way we all see it. Our impression of the world is a complete fabrication. We, as spiritual entities, believe that we exist as intelligent creatures in a physical universe. But really, we exist as spiritual 'non-matter' in a spiritual-computer-projected environment called the universe. We are comatose spiritual cells, also called souls, of a comatose spiritual being. The universe is an apparition of souls' collective deceived awareness. This awareness is the spiritual public opinion of all souls. There is nothing real in what we perceive of the universe. Souls project this universe based on false information. And who do you think feeds us this false information? You will never guess! Our beloved God in Christ—Jehovah! I am not belittling Jehovah and Jesus Christ although, through much of the book, it may seem that way. The entire book will reveal the complete concept and thesis.

Keep On Reading

Now that you have read this far, you are obligated to read the whole book because as you go through the book it will reveal the incredibly many systems of deceit souls are buried in. This book, as you progress through it and reread it, will expand your mind, let me say for comparison, from a squashed particle of matter in the core of the earth to the open and liberated conscious of a spiritual soul free of mental garbage. The book will alter your propaganda-distorted mental picture of reality to what reality actually is. For example, I back up my contentions with progressive lists that show how the public has been led from one point to the next; from being free people in 1776 to being no more than a herd of much exploited cattle managed by the authorities; and from innocent soul to deceived soul to a soul pretending to exist in a spiritual virtual reality.

Human Mind Is a Maze of False Belief Systems

The human mind is a belief system based on the falsehoods held in soul. Human reality exists as the deepest level of fiction in a number of nested virtual realities; the highest of which is anchored in our native spiritual realm, paradise, through the dreams of a set of comatose souls. The soul is comatose because it holds a lie about its native reality. It now imagines itself to exist in a virtual reality or dream reality. Each deeper section of fiction has been drawn from the next higher system of fiction. The set of such fictional belief systems forms a deep, virtually inescapable spiritual trap. Innumerable categories of souls are caught, each category of soul in its own section in the trap. The entire display of these categories represents the composite display of the physical environment as encountered by the creatures in it. All creatures enforce the physical environment as if it is true in the same manner US citizens enforce the political environment in the USA on each other through an artificially, media-created public opinion as if it is true. Everything is carefully choreographed hocus-pocus.

There Must Be a True Reality Out There

There must be a realm of true reality from which all the fictions have been drawn and exist in. This true reality is the reality of the Trinity of the true father, the true son, and the true communion between these two. Paradise already is a corruption of that true reality because the trees in paradise all represent fictional, constructed universes. Sets of Adam and Woman are placed there to learn to be in that ultimate reality. These trees in paradise are class rooms that teach all aspects of reality. Classes that teach the ideas of "good" are taught first. The post-graduate course is the tree of "Knowledge of Good and Evil."

All universal creations exist in nothingness extracted, by some license, from higher levels of virtual reality. The highest level is true reality, true god. Paradise, as encountered in Genesis 2 and 3 in the Bible, is the highest level of fiction below true reality. I see paradise as existing in a zero-potential spiritual setting. The fact that Adam and Woman had to be informed of what they could partake of and what not is proof that they were not in ultimate reality.

Positive reality is god in truth, and negative reality was created through a lie-believed by Woman and Adam. There must thus be a lying spiritual being. The spiritually-based lie-believed is the nothingness in which the universe was created. A fictional setting depends for its existence on the belief of a deceit. The nothingness is a part of the higher reality that when filled with fiction creates a new environment. For example: The nothingness as a place to be for the US navy in the setting of the physical universe is so filled with fictional titles of nobility and hardware that is comes across as the reality and might of the US Navy. At one time the US Navy did not exist which proves that the US Navy exists in a virtual reality. It exists by force. Science tells us that the universe is some 5 Billions years old. That tells us that it was created. Anything that once did not exist and now does, exists in virtual reality. Reality is, as Jesus said, "I AM". He always is. He IS reality because he always, ever, and ever "*IS*".

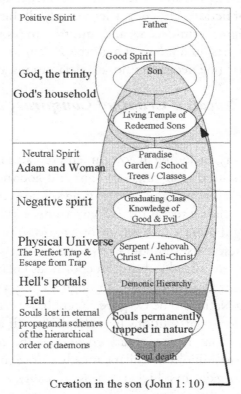

Creation in the son (John 1: 10)

The three realms of existence
Positive, Neutral, and Negative Spirit

There is a fourth realm, Hell. It is the
irrevocable part of negative spirit.

Figure 1

Creating Fictions in Environment Is Magic

In a nested set of fictional realities the higher level must be presumed to be reality and the lower one a distortion of reality as perceived from the higher level. By believing a misrepresentation in that higher reality one descends one level farther away from the pure truth. In reality, we understand that everything based on a lie is nonexistent, but we humans are immersed deep inside a nested set of fictional realities, so we are dealing with relative differences in fiction; such as a fiction within a fiction, within a fiction, etc.

Courts of law, for instance, try to obtain facts as these relate to the level of reality of the crime. The criminal tries to stack evidence or hide evidence in unrelated systems of fiction. The court tries to unify all the different fictional settings into the original crime scene, and thus tries to prove someone guilty or innocent. The courts do not have a high track record of success. Creating fictions is magic, and one needs another magician to unravel the mystery.

Power Exerted Reveals a Criminal Conspiracy and a False God

Power in any entity, including in government, reveals a false god. The false god always disguises itself as an angel of light and goodness. And, through this disguise, its base of power and control grows. The events of the last one hundred or so years clearly reveal the US government as a mean, deceitful, false god. It has fought more wars than any other government in the world in that time, and all these wars were sold to us as being necessary for the public good. In fact, they were waged to bring an enormous enlargement of power to the US government and, worldwide, through a US-government-installed entity, to the United Nations. The US government has exerted the most effort and provided the most contributions to make this outfit a venerable power in the world. It was done in secret dark corners, at the cost of millions of human lives and mega-billions of dollars, mostly extracted from the gullible American citizenry. Again, in a higher setting of reality, internationally and politically significant news comes from just one major source—a government propaganda news department. As I said earlier, carefully choreographed events in the world are brought to our attention through the news channels of all the news media. These are backed up with real photos, video clips, real dead people, and people who found themselves caught in the incidents. In this manner, all societies throughout history have been set against each other for reasons that had nothing to do with the people, but with deceit of power mongers at the head of these societies. This is why Jesus said that this environment is evil, a realm of darkness. History is rampant with lynching parties and wars, in which entire societies wholeheartedly participated to overpower another nation or group of people, under a set of false pretenses. I give the eradication of the American Indian tribes in America as an example. The American public gave its enthusiastic support to this government instigated crime. It was worse than a lynching party. It was genocide on grand scale, and the public supported it.

Propaganda Is the Evil Advertised in the Tree of the Knowledge of Good and Evil

The schemes of propaganda employed make it seem real, but the acts of terrorism, the conspiracies, and organizations blamed for the incidents may be utterly false. Or the settings and organizations may be correct, but the instigators to such events may be your own government, who want to create situations of conflict and horror to garner mass support for their plans of supposed retaliation. They planned an attack on some organization, and now they want your support to carry it out. They planned the entire terrorist scenario so that you will believe that certain people or organizations are America's enemies, and that we need to destroy them. Your support for this agenda supports the attack on innocent people and organizations. The target group or nation is an enemy of government for its own reasons; it never was an enemy of the American people. Your unqualified support of government in these situations may make you and your fellow Americans terrorists at heart and action. I give the destruction of the World Trade Center as an example. The facility's engineer vowed that an airplane crash could not bring down such a building, let alone several of them. I refer you to well documented articles published at web page: www.globalresearch.ca/index.php?context=viewArticle&code=GR120060129&articleId=1846 and at web page www.infowars.com/print/sept11/FDNY.htm

I have garnered enough data myself to convince me that the buildings were brought down by officials of government or by officials of insurance companies on behalf of certain officials in government. My conclusions were later reinforced by a TV show that went over all the supposed details culminating in the buildings coming down by cause of the planes crashing into them. Flames on the floors in the buildings were artificially introduced or painted in the video clips. In the end of the program, a clip was shown of one of the two buildings that were attacked that day when it was standing and then, abruptly, came down. No warping or bending of construction steel at all. If you watch the video of that building's collapse, you can see, at the tip of the building just before it comes down, the radial expansion streaks of black smoke illustrative of demolition explosions in a clear blue sky. The black smoke continues to linger in the air after the perfect and instant collapse of the building. Building 7, that was demolished afterwards, had the same signature of demolition as the other two buildings. It's clear that all three buildings were destroyed in this same way. Three thousand people were sacrificed in order to garner complete support for the US government to attack groups in specific countries that were blamed for that vicious act of terrorism.

You may have heard of the concentrated air bridge that was formed by the US government after the communists erected a wall around the western sector of Berlin at the end of the Second World War[1]. That air bridge supplied that city with all the necessities of normal life for about a year.

Air Bridges

In a similar situation, where civilians were evacuated from South Vietnam after the war was supposedly "lost", there was a condensed bridge of helicopters ferrying people from the American embassy to the airbases. Helicopters were waiting, several in line, to pick up refugees. The line of refugees was constantly moving; people were airlifted that fast.

---

1   The allies-erected wall of fire over the Elbe River, river of death
    The Allied Forces during WW2 consisting of Britain and the USA invented the mined zone between the USSR and the Allied Forces in Germany. The Elbe River was chosen as separation between East and West Germany. The Russians were still hundreds of miles away from the Elbe River. The Allied Forces installed a strong defensive line along the entire western shore of that river. Search lights swept the expanses of water at night and whenever a German or Russian, trusting in the righteous cause of the Allied Forces, was discovered in the river to flee to the free western world from Communist suppression he/she was riddled by bullets from Allied machine gun fire. This was, I would say, at least a year before the Russians put up there mined, wall-enclosed strips between East and West Germany. Yes, folks, that is America for you. I got this information from a book written by a Jewish US army tank commander who wrote a book about his war experiences.

I claim that a concentrated air bridge of helicopters, of which the government and business in the New York area have hundreds, would have airlifted all the people from the towers safely well within a four-hour period. Authorities could have organized a concentrated air bridge of helicopters continually working from two platforms that would have airlifted all the people from the top of the towers down to the ground. No effort was made to rescue the people hunkering at the top of the building. That gives me more evidence that the people were deliberately sacrificed to further other secret plans that hinged on the collapse of the buildings and the accompanying death of many thousands of people.

Holocausts

I watched in consternation as the fire chief of New York City ordered hundreds of firemen, loaded down with heavy packs of equipment, up the narrow stairs of a 1,400-foot-or-so-tall building. That was the greatest effort in futility that day. These firemen formed a complex obstruction to the people on levels below the fires coming down that same set of staircases, greatly increasing the number of deaths in that deliberate holocaust. This, dear reader, is a real holocaust—people deliberately sacrificed to death for a secret evil reason. It was a sacrifice to an evil god for a favor.

What can be the explanation of this deliberate premature destruction of these buildings? I believe that insurance underwriters and officials of city, state, and/or federal government will not allow the erection of such immense buildings without having a sure way of bringing them down, in a perpendicular fashion. A building that's a third-mile high or higher can't be allowed to destroy the buildings surrounding it, should it become unstable for one reason or another. A back-up plan is necessary.

Undermining Sky Scrapers under Construction

During the erection of the buildings, demolition charges were placed in structurally strategic positions that were wired or wirelessly connected to a computer some distance away from the buildings. When the time came to bring them down, the buildings were demolished according to a well-thought-out computer program that would ensure that they would come down vertically, in an orderly manner. Had the building come down through structural weakness as a consequence of the plane crashes, the building would have bent at the weakest point and the upper half fallen away side-wards and large portions of concrete would have broken away from the major metal structural elements. After such a natural collapse, huge lengths of twisted sections of structural steel would still have been pointing skyward. The government did not tell us the truth of how the buildings actually came down, so how can we believe government about anything else that happened with respect to this event?

It was a perfect collapse according to the narrators. Perfect collapses do not occur in nature; they occur only by the execution of a well-worked-out design. Somebody pushed a button to start the demolition sequence. The buildings could have remained standing erect for many weeks at least.

The painting in of all fierce flames across whole floors in the reconstruction of the destruction was done to make you believe that the flames caused the buildings to collapse in support of the narration. The flames are camouflage. These were fires within enclosed areas. The fumes could not escape upward as in open fires but had to find a way out between the concrete floors, obstructing sufficient air from rushing in to feed the fires. The heat of the fires was so low as to be unable to cause any damage at all. I saw video clips of enormous fireballs outside the building. These did no harm for the heat could dissipate upward into the sky. What these fireballs do tell you is that huge amounts of unburned fuel escaped as gas into the open atmosphere where they had an opportunity to ignite in open air harmlessly, which could not have happened inside the building. Also, the fuel in planes is stored inside the wings. The wings did not penetrate very deeply into the buildings. Some 80 percent of the fuel fell harmlessly outside the buildings all the way down to the ground, or was evaporated and carried off by natural circulation.

Massive amounts of fuel vapors kept oxygen-rich air from the fires as the vapors worked their way harmlessly outside the building. Also, the automatic fire-extinguishing systems immediately kicked in to keep these fires at low intensity. This was aircraft kerosene burning. Compare these huge billowing clouds of black unburned fuel with the almost-transparent, efficiently burned jet plane exhaust fumes. From the solidly dark smoke coming from the fire, one can tell that the fires were of a very low intensity and, thus, gave off very little heat. When liquids evaporate, they have eight hundred times the volume of the liquid. The evaporation of a liquid takes a lot of heat that was absorbed into gas and that was thus not available to heat structural members inside the building. The black unburned gases crowded out the necessary oxygen for the fires to show open flames.

Those painted-in flames were to give you the impression that what the narrators were telling was true. The painted-in flames merely supported the believability of the lie. The people responsible for the collapse of the buildings realized that the only opportunity to demolish the buildings was shortly after the plane crashes. People would become suspicious if the buildings were secretly demolished two months later in one perfectly arranged collapse. It had to be done at that time or never, especially, also, as impact value for the accompanying official propaganda that identified the supposed attackers.

The media did another thing that makes their natural collapse suspect. They announced the guilty party some half-hour after the event. That always points to the involvement of some propaganda scheme. The accusing party causes a major disaster; and immediately thereafter, while the public is still stunned, reveals who the perpetrators are, deflecting culpability and anger to another previously chosen innocent party. Every guilty party will point immediately away from himself to draw suspicion of guilt to some other entity. The US government, through the media, pointed away from themselves. That fact alone makes them suspect.

Below are Websites that can enlighten you more about the destruction of the World Trade Center towers. The first address is long because it is a specific article in their archives.

"The Destruction of the World Trade Center: Why the Official Account Cannot Be True"

www.globalresearch.ca/index.php?context=viewArticle&code=GRI2006012 9&articleId=1846

Other sites include:

www.911truth.org
www.911forthetruth.com
"The Truth Behind 9-11" *www.geocities.com/northstarzone/WAR.html*

The Iraqi War

The war with Iraq found the root of public support right at ground zero. Iraq was singled out as a reprobate nation under Saddam Hussein that was supposedly developing and/or producing nuclear weapons. Iraq, even according to the propaganda, had nothing to do with the attack on the World Trade Center. The World trade Center disaster was used as propaganda props to obtain US public support for Bush's call for war on Iraq. It is a very dirty trick played on the American people.

In spite of facts reported by the CIA months before the war was started that proved that Iraq never had any such program going, President Bush continued to push for this war and engaged America into a bloody and internationally illegal war. President Bush must be held responsible for all the unnecessary death, mayhem, and destruction in Iraq. What are the people going to do about it? Nothing, as they always do nothing, except to play slave to their government and die by the hundreds because of blind obedience to a set of crooks and deceivers in government.

The whole series of events in this disaster makes the authorities suspect in having a major hand in the destruction of the WTC in order to wage wars against Afghanistan and Iraq. It is clear that President Bush and his co-conspirators for the formation of a One World Order are proven international terrorists. The American public became guilty through association and through its gullibility in believing a deceitful government. Americans now have a way to expunge their guilt in this matter by confronting their government.

Government Is Fiction Made to Appear as if Real

Government is a fictional institution. It is a corporation and it is run on the principles of management of a corporation. A corporation is a nothingness that must be filled with fictional entities. Everything that gives power and authority in a corporation is fiction, an agreement of a few people enforced on the many that want or are forced to participate in the fiction. A fiction is just a plan or conspiracy among some people that they want to put into execution. The execution of the plan gives it life. In order for it to have life, people and animals need to be recruited who believe that the whole thing is real and worthwhile. To keep fiction alive, swift and overpowering enforcement are needed. Life seems real-like, but it remains a fiction. It is an illusion that is kept in place through propaganda and through the benefits that clever propaganda brings to the operators and managers of the fiction.

Like a human body consists of many cells, a corporation consists of many people, slaves or workers. Living cells [employees] may die, but these are automatically replaced, and the structure remains in business—alive. Essentially, the corporation is eternal as long as it continues to find new entities to believe and to work in the operation. The structure is just a fiction, but it is the fiction that perpetuates through make-believe. The cells die or are removed and are replaced, but the structure remains, and the nature of the structure may or may not change as the ideas and lusts of the major owner may change. In the case of a change in goals of the operation, the schema of the structure is emptied of its previous intent and content and refilled with whatever the new owner wants to fill it up with. The workers down in the sweat pits don't particularly care. They believe that they need their mundane jobs to exist and continue to work toward the execution of the final product—cars, universe, war, whatever—in order to live.

Having come to this point we are ready to translate the concepts covered to a higher level of reality.

Chapter 2

"Reality" on a Larger Scale

The Universe as a Corporation

We can look at the universe as one giant corporation with a god [Jehovah, Allah, the Great Spirit, etc.] as president. He has engaged every spirit whom he could persuade to see things his way to aid him in forming and operating this corporation. The daemons, higher-level spirits, are his managers, and he has swarms of lowlifes acting as robots to help make this universe come to life, and to keep it running.

To do that, a great number of sets of "Adam and Woman" were attracted through a propaganda scheme and employed. They were then, disassembled spiritually into cells of power and beingness that we call souls. The whole structure is Jehovah, and Jehovah is in the entire structure. The billions of propaganda-addicted souls involved have been assigned positions of laborer and so on—such as human beings according to the several races, animals, and plants. All the souls have agreed on being these particular entities as were assigned to them through a process of propaganda. The statement in the Bible seems to confirm this: "As below; so above." What goes on high up in universal spirit is similar to what happens among us people here in our little planet.

The universe is expanding because the main owner is able to continue to attract more sets of Adam and Woman to come into the fiction and help to build the universe. For Jehovah, *business is good.*

In the schema of the corporation, human beings—all alike and having one-human-being power and one-human-being mind and one-human-being body—are chosen and given fictitious titles of nobility and powers of authority to go along with them. This "title of nobility" conferred to certain human beings gives them clearly defined fictional power of execution. *Moses is a good example of such a person.*

The entire structure relies on assumed might, authority, and enforcement; for in person, these people invested with the powers are as mighty as any single man without title of nobility. Those with title of nobility status are placed in charge of those that have no title whatsoever. This power is made to project itself through executive power, pomp, protocol, tradition, status, ceremony, reverence, and a belief in a lie. The structure is based on necessity, greed, prejudice, allegiance, favoritism, and enforcement.

The structure will endure as long as most of the creatures in it believe in the plan and support it. As soon as the mass of entities in it can see through the veil of illusion that gives the structure a body *and see that they form the body*, they may decide to refuse to cooperate and the entire structure will come apart. If the means of enforcement remain intact, the uprising may not succeed, especially if the management of the fiction can also rely on surrounding fictional entities to support it in times of need. Now we can see the true necessity of police forces and standing armies. Successful revolutions often happen through upheaval and resistance. The entire structure tumbles down, after which a new structure is formed, strangely enough, in exactly the same format.

Most of our perception of things comes from spiritual propaganda projections that give the impression that political events and situations come along impromptu, without careful prior planning or human conspiracy. No! Just as employees do what careful previously-determent management plans make them do, so people, unaware of these controls and enforcements in spirit, do what the spiritual management plans make them do. We are creatures who always act in effect, not cause. From a spiritual point of view, President Bush is just a dungeon rat that is told what to do at each moment, although he believes he acts from plans and conspiracies worked out in a causative setting here on earth.

It is absurd that somehow, by whatever means it has been arrived at, one person can control everything and everyone in a certain region of the world or the universe. Yet, a group of conspirators can form a corporation, a country, or a universe through clever propaganda schemes that can be held together and made to grow. There is no doubt that all people and their associated spirits are created with equal standing. There may be differences in experience, but in class, all are the same. It is through the magic of fiction put into execution that inequality is established and countries and corporations come to life and remain in operation through sheer deceit and overpowering force and enforcement.

The Incorporation of the Promised Land

In general, any corporation exists by some license given by a higher authority. It has been given permission to operate, and as long as the license is enforced, the corporation exists. License is privilege. The power through which the license was granted helps keep it in business as long as the rules and the laws of incorporation are obeyed. The stipulations for the license usually include a clause of tribute and allegiance. Jehovah gave his support to Abraham and his posterity. When he was ready to implement his support, he set up a license for them to operate as a nation and specific laws and procedures of giving tribute.

The license included a set of stipulations according to which Jehovah would give his full support to Abraham's descendants, Hebrews. He then set up a set of rules by which the corporation was to function. The license would continue as long as Israel acted as stipulated. The enforcement of the stipulations was given in Deuteronomy 28 and 29—the blessings and the curses. These stipulations, of course, were only good for these Hebrew people as long as they adhered to the stipulations, and only while they were in the region assigned to them—the Promised Land.

The Israelites soon noticed that other city-states operated in a different manner because their licenses to operate were derived from different entities in the spiritual realm, and they became jealous of the success of these other corporations. They started to operate by the rules and laws of these other city-states and drew the anger of Jehovah on their backs. They forfeited the validity of their license. So, instead of the blessings, they incurred the curses and the full wrath of Jehovah, who eventually revoked the license and dispersed them over the globe.

The Israelites started to disobey their charter of existence as a nation. They continued to do so with flagrant disregard for their god, so that Jehovah started to mete out penalties and fines. As more penalties and fines were dispensed, the Israelites became ever more unhappy. They started to look elsewhere for guidance and sustenance. This is how a nation that was blessed by their god ended up being cursed by him and dispersed.

The present Jews and all of Christendom also, still adhere to the stipulations of a withdrawn license. This does not make any sense! The Hebrew people have drawn the wrath of Jehovah on their backs, and that is the situation in which they now exist. They were later on forgiven by Jesus, but they were not reissued a new license. It only meant that Jehovah's curses had ended, if only the Hebrew person would believe in Jesus. This confirms my belief that souls reincarnate because if they are forgiven now, they must be the same ones who violated the license and were cursed before. [In this sense, the present state of Israel makes no sense. The territory of present Israel was not given to them by Providence, Jehovah. They forced possession because Jews have enormous clout in the governments of most powerful nations such as Russia, Great Britain, and the United States.]

Jesus, in his role of Messiah, has changed this condition of being cursed to a position where they are forgiven, but only if they believe in Jesus and are baptized into the new condition of being forgiven for prior wrongdoing. The Messiah came for the cursed Hebrews, and for no one else, because no one else had ever violated the stipulations of the license.

For Christian Hebrews—the present white race, also called Caucasians—this condition of having been forgiven is valid, but for no one else. It makes no sense for Indians, Chinese, and black people to accept the Christian faith for they never broke any promises with Jehovah. Jesus said to Hebrews to go out and proclaim the good news of redemption to your brethren, if they will believe. The Hebrew people were utterly dispersed, remember, so the apostles were instructed to go out into the entire world to find these dispersed persons to tell them about the good news. I do believe that Jesus, in the name of the true father, came to provide redemption to all souls caught in the universe, if they can understand his message.

I know that I am just a physical expression in the dream of a soul in a coma in reality. I, as the form of this projection, think and act as dictated by this particular dreaming soul. This soul is under the strict orders of Jehovah through an enforced propaganda scheme that soul believes. I—soul, dream in spirit, but projected as physical being—I am not to know that I dream or what subject I am dreaming about. The physical being only observes, as real, all the things I, as soul, dream about in spirit. My dream in spirit is not my own but Jehovah's, who dictates what I dream, just as US government dictates much of the behavior and understanding we have as US citizens. It is all make-believe. We obey because we believe what we are told is true. This mental image is far from the true facts of our situation.

Chapter 3

Experiencing and Understanding the Foundation of Reality Is Soul's Job in Negative Spirit

The Tree of Knowledge of Good and Evil

Imagine paradise as a huge spiritual computer. The individual programs show up as tree icons. To enter the program of any one of these trees, one assumes a coma, a dream state, and the program takes over from there. You are in another reality. These realities are all different, but they all have one thing in common. They give ultimate honor to the god of their native reality and probably give a good impression of the archangel in charge of the particular program. The good thing is that, of all the programs devised by the several archangels Adam and Woman, on their own volition, may exit the program. The programs have a beginning and an end—and open entrance and exit doors.

The Adopted Disintegration of the Cells of the Spiritual Body

The living cells of Adam and Woman are dispersed into the reality of the program when the icon is activated by their participation. This gives Adam and Woman a comprehensive view, from any possible angle and medium of perception available in the program, of the understanding a particular archangel has of his father, god. At the end of the completely interactive program, one can take one's leave of the program and, again, enter into the reality of paradise. One can look upon all the trees in paradise as nonprofit corporations because they give honor not to the archangels but to god, their father.

The Tree of the Knowledge of Good and Evil

This is not true, however, of the Tree of Knowledge of Good and Evil. The other programs [trees] taught one only knowledge of good; one came from the program refreshed and imbued with a deeper understanding of their god, and of that particular archangel. It is a way by which archangels introduce themselves to Adam and Woman. When Adam and Woman leave, they are invited to come back sometime.

This particular tree, the Tree of the Knowledge of Good and Evil, however, teaches the entities entering into it not only the concept of good, but also the exact opposite of good-evil. This tree is extremely dangerous because it invites the cells of Adam and Woman as souls to experiment with all the possibilities in the concept of evil. If one becomes utterly enchanted with this concept of evil, a soul can be permanently sucked into this concept so that the way out seems unimportant, and becomes hidden. Every soul will experiment with all the possible positions and roles in the program so that souls will die and reincarnate to play all the other positions and roles, one or several roles per incarnation. The position of true good in this program is taken by good itself, the position of evil disguised as good is enacted by the Serpent and his hierarchy of daemons and all individual souls that made up the entities of Adam and Woman. Remember that Jesus said of himself that he did not consider himself good but that *there was only one—God alone is good [Luke18:19]*. Therefore, this universe cannot contain "good." And since no one knows what this good is, we are lost to it in this physical realm by trying so hard to make a success of life in it. The good in this universe is that only through knowing evil one begins to understand the true meaning of good and one will seek that good beyond the realm of evil because one understands that the principle of 'good' does not exist in this physical realm of existence. One can see how overpowering evil is because one enters into this tree after having been engaged in all the other trees that taught Adam and Woman qualities of good. In spite of all that prior knowledge of learned good in paradise, the concept of evil when fully engaged in, will wipe all knowledge of good from the mind and one is fully determined to use evil to the full extent to take care of oneself first, and always. In that kind of mindset, the idea of true good recedes farther and farther back in the awareness of soul.

Jesus' True Message Was Directed To Soul

Jesus did not only speak to physical beings but to, as he called it, the hearts of the people. It is something within the people that is not part of the projection seen as human being. This heart is soul responsible for projecting the human organism. Jesus wanted to reach beyond the sensible physical part to the unseen and undetectable part of the thing of which the human form is composed. Soul is the point of reality upon which the entire universe gets its expression. What happens in the heart determines whether the soul has an orientation in truth or in fiction.

Even Though The Killer Tree Embroils Souls in all Aspects of Evil Its Purpose Is to Teach the Value of True Good

The theme of the program is evil, and evil aided by all souls existent in the program will do whatever it can to oppose good. The projection of soul, the human being, is singularly and primarily concerned for itself as the physical body is a tyrant that demands such favoritism. This extreme sense of self-concern is the fountain of all evil intent.

One can say of this tree that its function was established for profit. It gives honor to its manager—the Serpent/Jehovah—not to his father, "Good." As physical beings, we try to give honor to some daemon in order to receive a position of favor for ourselves; an endeavor that always holds that we must suppress someone else's effort to do the same. "Favorite" means that only one or a few can hold that position. Favors are granted through the punching of a hole in an already functioning reality. Once the nothingness is there, it must be filled with fictions, because nothing 'real' can exist in nothingness. An established corporation is nothingness in a higher level of fiction effectively filled with the lower-level fiction we are made to believe is real. Disfavor and hatred and extreme anger works in the same way. Someone wants to curse another so this person creates a void in which to place this person and one prays to a daemon or other entity that exhibits power to place it there in a position of want, oppression and cruelty.

This void is filled, or incorporated with titles of nobility, and means of enforcement and power. A well-functioning fiction has these things arranged so that relative good and evil are permanently built into it (see figure 2, page 51). Human societies operate exactly according to that system, through a spectrum going from relative, super good to a position on the other end of the spectrum or scale of relative super punishment. The best relative good is granted a license over a fictional region or profitable operation. The other end of the scale is occupied by conditions of being stripped of all status and a very confined space to be. The purpose of it is to create a status of pariah from which it is extremely difficult to raise one self, because when released from this place of disfavor, one must compete again in a strange world with many overpowering strikes of prejudice and limitations of opportunity against one's person.

Rules and Favoritism Is Part of Fiction

Government is god, and those who aid and favor this god are favored by it. Most well-off people own an incorporated business or maintain a high position in the business of another person. Those who own businesses can only do so if they will force tribute to government from the employees [the "income tax" due from the paycheck of the workers]. Those with a management position or with high skills and experience aid the owner in meeting his goals in profit. They are in favor with government also, and whenever needed, they will side with government against the interest of the workers. All these activities aid the corporation in collecting the tribute for god/government to maintain its status. Just as souls enforce the universe on each other, so owners and managers of corporations force the fictional environment of the corporation on the employees and the general public.

The operators and their aids are under very strict orders and surveillance by the government clergy to insure that they operate within the license and reams of other laws, rules and regulations, so that everybody hates this god government. Governments are systems of hate and suppression. These exist to extract the highest amount of revenue from its realm. This god and all gods in the negative realm will try to find the knife-sharp edge where their rule of oppression can barely contain the expected uproar of the suppressed. This means that as governments and gods remain in power over extended periods of time they need ever more enforcement power to remain in operation, because more and more people become outright suppressed and thus more rebellious. This condition is pretty well approached now in America. Only exponential increases of enforcement power can keep the realm in control. We see ever more new enforcement agencies springing up and these forces are explained to us as for our good because foreign terrorists are ganging up on this "marvelous" country [where everyone is oppressed and yet believe through clever propaganda to exist in liberty and freedom]. However, terrorist groups are created by the government to draw everyone back into a consolidated mass seeking government's protection. We are managed as lucrative assets for those who reign over us, whether the monarch is an individual, a small group or a more pervasive conspiracy among many governments such as the One World Order is.

Banking super-executives are in control of this One World Order; and this means that they insist on huge profits from their assets. That is the nature of bank management; they are blood suckers, super criminals. They will always be the reason that peace on earth is not possible. They are never satisfied. Their profit curves must always rise. If their profit curves level out the peons below them are driven to suck the population out some more. It is a never ending money squeeze and the one squeezed is you. We enforce fiction on each other because everyone is preying on others to get a little better position of comfort, and the more proficient squeezers rise above you and so on until the super criminals sit on top of the mountain. This universe was designed to be as evil as evil can be made to operate. We operate exactly according to the basic operating parameters of the universe. The dictum is oppress, oppress some more, and than try to increase the oppression just a wee little more, and no matter what, keep squeezing.

Because of our presence in this realm we enforce the realm on each other. Just by being present we are made to believe that all these others out there are real, just as they look at the environment and us and say, yes this is true reality. Therefore also, workers enforce the environment on the manager. All flora, fauna, and inert matter enforce the universe on others simply by being present and interacting in and with it. We, as souls and as the physical projections of souls aid one another to stick our heads in the mud so that we will never discover true reality. The universe, after all, is a nothingness punched in true reality by means of a lie. So existence in earth is hell. Believe me; this realm is not capable of keeping anybody happy for any length of time.

Jesus, Part of the Fiction

Jesus said that no one is good, not even he, but only his father in spirit is good. Like the rest of us, Jesus enforced the universe on all of us also through the body he inhabited. Through his presence as a human being he impressed on us that the physical realm is reality. It is not; and Jesus' purpose was to tell us that it is not. That is why there is so incredibly much confusion on the subject of Jesus.

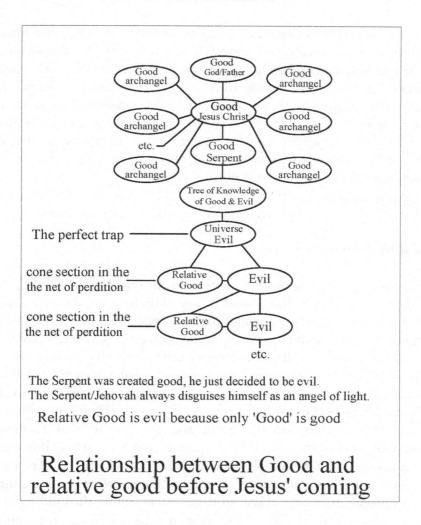

The Serpent was created good, he just decided to be evil.
The Serpent/Jehovah always disguises himself as an angel of light.

Relative Good is evil because only 'Good' is good

Relationship between Good and relative good before Jesus' coming

Figure 2
see also figure 11 on page 396

Jesus was ashamed of being in the physical body, and of the fact that he enforced it on us while knowing the truth. We can claim to do this enforcing on each other as deceived beings in spirit, but Jesus does not have that excuse. He made it even worse by performing many miracles and many instances of healing. He redeemed us and himself when he allowed himself to be nailed to the cross. He can be excused, though, because the only way to show comatose souls the way out of their condition was for him to teach to souls through the human beings by physical communication that they exist in a state of spiritual deceit. [Further-on in the book this idea will be discussed in great detail.]

It was said of Jesus that when many people wanted to befriend him, he kept himself apart because he knew what was in their hearts. People wanted to befriend him and exploit his friendship to do miracles for their benefit. Jesus could not allow that because by doing so, he would acknowledge selfish preference through favoritism/fiction. He had to discourage that as much as possible. Jesus performed miracles only to show that he was a special person who had a very important message to convey. Miracles were an attention getter. Yet, almost every Christian is hung up on his miracles and never even guessed his real message, because of his dual role.

He separated the goats from the sheep. He made the one group more comfortable in the negative reality and the other more uncomfortable.

Evil and Jehovah's Universe

The physical environment we entered is the environment of evil; there is nothing of good in it. Evil starts by disguising itself and the environment as good. We give in to evil because of the seeming fragility of the physical form and the limitations inherent in the environment. We are addicted to the physical realm, and we will do whatever we can to forestall physical death—to the point of harming whomever we must—to whatever extent possible to maintain our position in this phony environment, in extreme comfort. The comfortableness of the rich is the heaven of Jehovah [Deuteronomy 28]. It is a very corrosive and insecure heaven, and it is sheer illusion. From what we know of Jehovah from the Old Testament, people blessed by him receive their blessings at the demise of others [check Deut 28 and 29]. The easiest way to accomplish this is to allow the persons blessed to have mind control, through propaganda, over others so these others will do the bidding of the blessed. Blessings to the rich are the curses for the rest of us; Deuteronomy 28 and 29 teach us that.

However, Jehovah's blessings still lead to death and to starting all over again. Wealth does not bring happiness because the idea of wealth includes a competitive factor. Wealth teaches that it does not make one happier. It makes one insecure and stirs one easily into jealousy and intrigue. The higher you rise the more one must watch out for all the others who would want to kill you. There is no happiness in being physically blessed.

You may ask why this universe is evil. I get this idea from what took place in a very high level of virtual reality, paradise. Adam was created in paradise. It is his native realm of truth. A lie believed in that realm about that reality is proof that one does not consider that reality worthy of one's trust. Adam [in whom I include Woman], and we as cells in him, believed a lie, so we as citizens of paradise declared paradise a fiction and the 'lie believed' truth. An inversion in the awareness of reality took place. I will go in greater detail about this idea later on in the book.

The great contradiction and spiritual confusion is that in trying to do "good" as people, we only produce what is evil. The efforts of saintly priests, monks, and nuns to help and aid the frail and poverty-stricken prevent redemption because charitable activity is so important to the poor and to their benefactors. Spiritually, such activities prevent souls from seeing through the deceit played on them. Helping another is most often a reinforcement of false reality. Jehovah wants you to do well and help those in need. He wants to establish your universal awareness and integrate your contributions in physical reality to the full and in the full belief that you act in true reality. He wants you to believe in him as the only good in the universe. He never wants you to find out that he is the deceiver and a liar from the beginning. We try our best to do good as we learned to practice it in paradise from all the other archangels. However, this physical realm is deliberately set up in such a manner that doing 'good' is impossible. Whatever we do, sooner or later, crumples to dust. Nothing lasts, except for evil. It is the spirit of this universe.

This is Jehovah's trick. Souls believe they have entered a familiar [good] reality, but it is evil that Jehovah has disguised as good. Remember that evil always comes disguised as an angel of light and good. Scams played on people seem so good when first viewed. We just have to join or pay for a service and later we discover we have been had. This is because evil always disguises itself as good. So, if Jehovah comes across to us as a good god, he is hiding a scheme from us because there is no good in his realm of spirit.

Proof of Our Fictional Existence

We know physical reality to be fiction because we cannot see or communicate face to face with god, Jehovah. He is of a higher system of reality than we are and he is hidden from us. So what we experience as reality is a fiction, because if it was not fiction we would be able to commune with Jehovah face to face. We are dead to his kind of reality. Jesus taught that even though we see ourselves as alive, we are dead in our sins. What kind of sin? We, as souls, believed a lie about our native realm of spirit, the reality of our origination.

Originally, after their fall, the offspring of Adam and Eve lived well over six hundred years on earth. They thought they were still eternal beings or very similar to it, and life was easy and good. This was their second mistake. The first one was to believe the lying Serpent over the advice of their true father. That belief alone banned them from the environment of good and truth. They fell into a coma to truth and began a dream—a routine part of the program to allow them to exist in this new reality, evil.

Their father, god in paradise [with whom they could commune face to face] was able to convey his disapproval, and explained what their new conditions of being would be like. But to them, they did not seem to have died, and they conceived and produced offspring in the world, and these confirmed the words of the Serpent to them. They were like god and could create. It confirmed their faith in the Serpent who became their god. They became oblivious to their native realm and their native god.

In the new environment, nothing seemed to sustain them very well. They had to exert themselves in order to exist. People already in the world [my assertion that people already existed in earth when Adam and Eve entered into it is explained further in the book] enchanted them and intermarried with them. They soon learned how the others provided for themselves through first experience. They were captured and forced to work for others. Later on, they learned to use deceit and propaganda to ensnare people to work for them through incentives of reward and punishment. They were learning firsthand about evil because it was they who were captured and misled to think they needed to be servants rather than to remain free. A good example was how Israel, son of Isaac, was made to believe by the father of a girl, Rachel, to whom he was attracted that he could earn her by working for her father for seven years. He learned well because he worked for some twenty years and was goaded to marry the older and not so good-looking daughter, Lea, first; and then he had to work many years longer to get the daughter he was promised originally. He learned from his father-in-law, and made sure he was recompensed as well because he was promised a dowry of all the spotted sheep [a rarity]. He increased the number of spotted sheep by crossbreeding white-and-black sheep deliberately. He ended up with the major part of his father-in-law's flock. These kinds of cunning and deceit were looked upon as exemplary.

If these kinds of conduct are considered appropriate, one can see how dishonesty and depravity increased rapidly in the societies of these Adamites in the universe. They learned so well that, by hook and by crook, they pretty much were able to enslave all the nations and races on earth and to exploit their lands. They learned the idea of evil extremely well. The time has come for them to try seriously to find the way out of this realm of evil before it will consume them as it did all the other races and species. The dazzling possibilities of modern technology are the bait in the trap to consume them forever.

Jehovah's America

Let me go back to the corporation—the model formula for creating a slave camp of those who think they may have a future in this form of establishment. It is a formula that has incentives and duties as functions to give the operators complete control over the activities of all those employed in the firm and open avenues to riches that most people cannot imagine. A charter or license is just a plan to exploit one's fellow citizens in a more or less oppressive way. Licenses are awarded by individuals higher up in a hierarchy who profit enormously from granting the licenses.

The founders of the new republic—the United States of America—considered themselves the top of a hierarchy in the United States. They did so under the auspices of a deity called Providence. I believe they were not exact enough in their choice of deity because no deity at all bothered to aid them in retaining their liberty. It is another expression of evil they have to experience here on earth. As will be explained, the American people lost their liberties along the fast route, and they still foolishly believe that they are free and better off than other people on the globe. That is the power of propaganda.

The United States was created by determined resistance of a bunch of people in the colonies that, prior to that time, operated under license of the Crown of England. The colonists saw that they were not treated as Englishmen, but as subordinate beings to English-born people. So they protested to the Crown several times in documents referred to as Declarations of Rights. The Crown ignored these documents but, in reprisal, sent out troops to keep the colonies stable. There were skirmishes, followed by war. In retaliation, American colonists put together a Declaration of Independence and declared their own nation. From that moment on, Americans were outlaws of England. Everyone who did not pledge allegiance to the English Crown was declared an outlaw, and the death of these outlaws was sought to restore obedience. Few people supported the war efforts for fear of retaliation by the English Crown. The colonies won the quarrel and established themselves as independent Free States, united in the United States of America. The freedom fighters did a most heroic feat in defeating the English, but they were never honored or recompensed for their efforts and sacrifice.

The free people recognized themselves as belonging to independent states that were formed from the prior colonies. The problem with the original document of incorporation and the Declaration of Independence was that no structure of organization and no authority were included to bind the several states into a manageable nation.

The newly formed government of the union of states had no powers of authority, and had no control whatsoever in the running of this new nation. It became impossible to keep the union together much longer. This original agreement of incorporation of the United States had avoided giving the United States any powers of authority at all. This was because the crafters of the union could see how a government over the states, united, if given power would usurp all the power of the states in no time flat. Were they ever right!

Therefore, a meeting was called to establish a constitution, which began with the following sentence: "*We the People of the United States, in Order to form a more perfect Union, establish Justice, insure domestic Tranquility, provide for the common defense, promote the general Welfare, and secure the Blessings of Liberty to ourselves and our Posterity, do ordain and establish this Constitution for the United States of America.*" The purpose of the United States of America was for it to secure the liberty of the people. The Constitution's main goal is to secure the people's liberty. A constitution is established to create a means of **communion** between the master and the servant. As example, there is the communion between the ultimate god and his son in the Good Spirit. In order for god to commune with his son, he established a set of ground rules through which they could commune together. I refer to that communion as the Good Spirit. The Good Spirit is really larger than god or his son because it includes the both of them. The Good Spirit defines reality between them. It caused a realm to spring up. The Constitution was designed to do the same thing. However, since the universe is the realm of evil, the chief daemon corrupted this Constitution so that it became not an instrument of liberty for all but an instrument of oppression by the few over the masses. There is nothing good in the constitution because whatever is good in the constitution is used as propaganda together with what is evil in the constitution. Together these make the Constitution a means of communion that deceive the common people, us. The real purpose of the Constitution was for it to be an instrument whereby the few can deceive the many. This nation is riddled with state constitutions and every one of them is a communion of deceit between the officials and the people. If you look carefully you can see our present-day laws are set up so that the officials have more freedom and more protection from the people than the people have protection from their governing authorities. All earthly kinds of communion are a clever deceit. These kinds of communion are not a communion that is greater than all its parts. In physical types of communion those in whom we placed our trust are advantaged over those who they are to serve. It is a structure. The officials, clergy really, enforce law on us rather than the people, the real masters, enforcing the Constitution on the clergy of government. We are the god, government is the son, and we do not teach the son how to behave and watch its manners so government's elected officials became unruly and betrayed our trust in them. Now they are the masters and we the slaves.

The important thing to see here is that it was "the [free] people" who were the bosses of the United States. They gave a charter of limited power and authority. They even went so far as to include ten, superfluous amendments to perfectly secure the agreement and understanding that the people had the power and retained their rights as organic, or real and free, people, having been given life by Providence or spiritual power, implied to be Jehovah.

The purpose of the constitution was to guarantee to the people that government would be extremely limited in its powers and could *never* accrue status over and above the free people; *that this government would be beneficial, liberating, and protect us from our REAL enemies*. These ground rules of de jure communion remain; no matter to what de-facto, low condition the people have been reduced by the deceits of conspirators in government and the super-rich. *Madison, after leaving the conference, declared this constitution to be a republican form of government, and he added, if you can manage to keep it that way*. Madison knew the evil spirit of many of the members of the Constitutional Convention, and knew that a war was already at hand, and that he felt that the people would not have much of a chance to ward off the powerful evil faction that was present at the convention. Power is expressed through money, and it always resides with the bankers. Madison saw things right, straight from the beginning. So instead of protecting us from our foreign enemies government became and is our worst enemy.

Chapter 4

Real versus Virtual Reality

The People Are Free, and Have the Power

Then, the government of the United States was populated by the giving of titles of nobility and power of authority to human beings. These officers of the union hired subordinates to complete the creation of the government. The government was eventually accorded a place of establishment—the District of Columbia—which district was not included in the Free States that formed the union. *The United States government thus became an independent nation outside the assemblage of Free States.* It had two forms of authority and power of execution: It was a governing body for the assemblage of Free States called the United States of America [and, as such, was a servant to the people], and, at the same time, it was the sovereign over its own district, also called the United States of America. The people in power deliberately chose identical names for the government as servant and government as sovereign to play a deceit on the free people. The sovereign entity of government should have been called the government of the District of Columbia. Had that occurred, the US government would not have been able to deceive the people so easily. From this deceit alone, one can grasp the evil intent of the government. The authorities in government since and including Lincoln got the bankers back in the saddle as a secret power behind government. These conspirators poured out the original content of the Constitution and refilled it with content exactly the opposite of what the original Constitution ordered. It took many decades to accomplish this, but this is the typical "modus operandi" of the US government. It's called "creeping gradualism". It is like a snowball that is slowly rolling downhill and gathering mass and power as it continues to roll on. This allegory contains prophesy. As the ball keeps rolling its mass increases to an all-powerful crescendo of might, and then either comes to a stop and is harmless or it explodes against an immovable object and shatters and is no more. It is the typical scenario for any endeavor in the physical realm.

Ever since, these two independent authorities—the servant and the sovereign in one body [consisting of elected officials]—have deliberately confused the people of the Free States. The government of United States—the sovereign, and not the servant—through the instrument of war, was able to usurp all the power and all the authority in this assemblage of states of free people.

The Civil War was the purpose of, and the means whereby all American state citizens lost their status as free people. After the Civil War, government officially incorporated this fall from free citizens to serfs of government by demoting the people and *their posterity* by a deceitfully promoted and governments' adopted amendment to the Constitution, declaring that all state citizens are citizens of the United States *and subject to the laws of the United States [now the sovereign over all the states]*. Yet even after this amendment, people still thought and think of themselves as being free.

US government, the servant to the republic, has been put to rest about a hundred and forty years ago. It does not exist anymore. Government the sovereign was born from its ashes as the commercial, socialist democracy.

Following is the spiritual method of nesting virtual realities of an ensnared spiritual soul: There is a soul caught in a coma in a high level of reality dreaming an enforced dream. In this example I use the soul projecting out a human animal body in physical setting. Every species of creature in nature is in its own virtual level in the greater realm of nature. There are many levels of virtual spirit below that of human awareness. Every species has its own daemon god in charge of it. Soul is never abandoned spiritually. A high-level spirit, Jehovah is always in control of that soul itself, but a daemon is in charge of the projection of the physical creature. Soul, thus, finds itself back deep inside a large set of virtual levels in the consciousness of a fictional human body; in our case as a person in the state of, say, New York, US of A.

Say, 'Joe Blow' lives on Long Island and has a social security number by which he is known to authorities of the state of New York. He is in the following set of virtual realities. He is a person under control of local government, a virtual reality that has a spiritual authority in the form of a daemon bureaucrat; he is under control of a higher authority of the county. This county has a ruling daemon assigned to it. He is under control of state authority; this state has a ruling daemon in charge of it. The person is under the control of the US government who has a ruling daemon assigned to it. The US of A is under control of the United Nations of the world. It has a ruling daemon assigned to it. The United Nations is under the authority of the International banking consortium. It has a ruling daemon assigned to it.

Then, there are couples of layers of virtual realities that I have no idea of who rule them and what their purposes are; but they are all in higher levels of awareness to which we as souls have become numb. We cannot observe or detect them in any way because they are spirit, undetectable by physical means. They are of real spiritual composition. Our physical soul projections are barred from observing spirit because we sit in their realms of awareness like a sitcom show on TV sits in our physical realm of awareness. The characters in the TV show we are watching cannot see us but we can see the characters on TV.

You say, "But these characters are fictional, they are part of an electronic display! Of course, they cannot see us." I say, "Exactly!! We are the characters in a computer program on display in a much higher realm of spirit. What TV characters are to us in physical reality, we are to the spiritual entities that are observing us from their height in spiritual reality. Our universe is only an interactive internet website in these higher realms of virtual reality. They can see us, observe us and control us through our brain circuitry, "hormone substances" by spiritual means of control. They are in control to teach us the concepts of evil, in order to allow us to understand the concepts of good. That is the purpose of the Tree of the Knowledge of Good and Evil."

The Hierarchy of Negative Spirit

These spiritual entities are organized in a serial [linear] vertical hierarchy with Jehovah as the kingpin in negative spirit. I call it "*negative spirit*" because in order to enter in we had to be enticed to believe a lie about our native reality, paradise. We as souls occupied a lower level virtual spiritual existence in the higher level spiritual bodies of Adam and Woman, just as our bodies consist of lower level, living cells through which our human coordinated conscious is generated. These cells assembled into a human body make the awareness of a human being. These cells are like a multitude of slaves helping us realize ourselves as human beings. The negative realms of spirit, in which we have our being, movements and life, have absolute bars to entry in the neutral and positive levels of spirit. This is done to prevent encroachment of evil in the realms of truth.

I differentiate between daemons and demons in this book to indicate the difference between a spirit that is part of Jehovah's incorporated hierarchy of universal control and scavenger spirits outside the spiritual hierarchy. Daemons are officers of Jehovah's hierarchy of control; and demons are not part of that hierarchy. These are the spirits that do harm to individuals by possessing them or causing harm to a person.

This daemonic hierarchy is under the control of very high-level spirits, called gods. I do not know all the levels, but these gods exist on levels that compare to that of an emperor and his immediate following of advisors and companions. Each of these nobles in the emperor's following has his own title, level of status, power and authority determined by the level of inner circle the individual occupies in the circles of intimacy that surrounds this sovereign. The Bible teaches us correctly that as it is here below in our physical sense of reality so is it in higher levels of reality. So, just as Jesus did, we can draw correlations between high level spirit and physical awareness in order to visualize and comprehend the spiritual realms of existence.

The Hierarchy of All Spirit

The highest god is ultimate reality. All creative power resides in this entity. He put all his creative effort in creating his son, in whom this ultimate god has vested all authority and power. They exist each in their own level of power and reality. A means had to be created to have real communion between them. *This communion is like what we call an agreed upon constitution.* It determines the relationship in trust between them. All other levels of reality are encompassed by this means of communion. I call it *the Good Spirit*, because that is what this new entity is. Entities in these levels exist in truth because of the voluntary conformance to the standards set by the constitution that envelops them all.

The Good Spirit oversees all creation to make sure that nothing in the nature of evil can invade the levels of true reality. It envelops all creation, including negative spirit.

The lowest levels of isolated reality are consigned to teach new souls the ideas contained in the concepts of evil. These souls fell into this set of virtual realms by believing a lie and now they have to exist in this realm of deceit which they imagined was good. Deceit is always based on inculcating in others a belief in a scheme of deceit that is always hailed as something good. Paul referred to the *devil as some spirit who always disguises his deceit in a cloak of shining good.* You, as spiritual soul, fell for a pitch of spiritual deceit because it looked so good on the outside until one found out afterward that one is caught in a situation from which there is no easy escape. I am sure that all of us know what that feels like, after having been duped innumerable times in our lives.

By immersing these souls over millennia of time in these completely virtual realms of evil to all forms of authorities, the ideas of evil become ingrained in their character. All concepts of authority in physical reality are evil and necessary. There is absolutely no good to be found in the realms of negative spirit. This has been done on purpose.

Human formulated kinds of communion [constitutions, charters of operation, and licenses of incorporation] are supposed to operate like the Good Spirit. However since all concepts of spiritual good are barred from these negative levels of spirit, constitutions formulated by men are deceits played by the few on the masses. Our whole edifice of organization in the United States is one built on stones of the many sorts of deceit possible. It is a card house built on all the known and invented means of deceit possible in our realm of human awareness. These principles of evil are very well known to spirit and that is the reason spirit inculcates them in us. When we have completed our experience of evil in this post-graduate course of spirit, some will yearn for good, which will reemerge in their minds from previous classes taken in paradise. Others will find profit in continuing on with the imagined "good" found in this negative physical realm and will renege on the offer to return to spirit. They will reincarnate without end and continue to deceive and be deceived until they have imbibed so much evil and are so far removed from the principles of true good, that the natural realm is the only reality they can accept. They will drown in physical nature as animals. In physical reality souls will fall continuously to lower levels to ever more intense experiences of evil. The universe is hell and the longer a soul insists on dreaming in hell the worse and more inescapable the nightmare becomes.

Jesus' Two Identities

Jesus came into this purely virtual realm of evil, the physical environment, with two unrelated charters of authority also: one charter as ambassador of the realm of true reality and the other as Messiah for the Serpent of a fictitious universe.

He revealed that fact to us by the appellations he gave himself: "son of god" as the ambassador for the god of Truth; and "son of man" as the Messiah for Jehovah, Lord in negative spirit. This shows that Jesus had a good grasp on fiction and the necessity of titles of nobility. Jesus must reach us before we lose status as humans and fall into the realms of raw nature as animals.

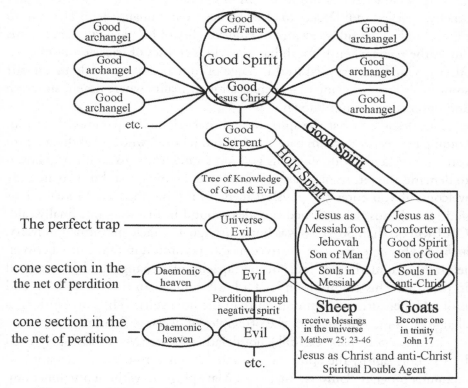

The Serpent/Jehovah always disguises himself as an angel of light.
Depending on the light you see you will be redeemed or condemned.
Relative good is evil because only one is Good.

Relationship between Good and Relative Good after Jesus' coming

Figure 3

For instance, in Matthew 25:23-46, Jesus states that as "son of man," he separates the goats from the sheep. The sheep are obedient and emotionally concerned for the weak, the poor, the prisoners, and all those that suffer. They obediently follow their shepherd. Emotionalism and empathy are expressions of the flesh. It is a desired trait for humans in order to understand evil. Jehovah in the Old Testament often complained that Israel's authorities fell short of caring for the elderly, and those in conditions of poverty and abandonment. He wants us to experience the awareness of human emotions as deeply as possible, and this includes the entire spectrum of emotional feelings from rock-hard cruelty, heartless indifference to bleeding heart emotionality. Jehovah wants to expose soul to the full spectrum of emotionality of human experience. Jesus enters the scene when Jehovah has played his full set of tricks on humanity. After having been exposed to this range of human experience Jesus can stir some souls into believing that there is another reality where deceit, suffering and oppression are not known.

I see Jesus' spirit as the spirit of god that reigned in paradise. I see him coming into earth to claim back Adam from Jehovah who had abducted him through a scheme of deceit. This god of paradise came to confront Jehovah to demand the return of Adam. Jehovah said, be my guest, but you are only welcome if you enter the physical scene as my prophesized Messiah. This god [Jesus] must have turned the idea around in his head and finally said, OK I will do that. So, Jesus was born through a miracle performed in Mary, a child. This agreement was arrived at in a communion that exists between Jehovah, as underling of Jesus in the capacity of archangel and Jesus as god in paradise. This communion is of a lower order than the Good Spirit and is of a higher form of communion than the holy spirit. The holy spirit is in charge of inundating us with the principles of deceit and oppression.

Jesus, as "son of man" can call Jehovah father because Mary was impregnated by the holy spirit, the spirit of Jehovah [a minor routine in the spiritual computer program 'Universe' that made Mary pregnant without insemination], and because Mary is of mankind. This appellation, son of man, cannot refer to the capacity that John, the apostle in John1: 1 calls "son of god", because this son was the first of all creation, while Jesus as offspring of Mary is "son of man". Jesus as "son of god" was with the father from the beginning, before paradise was even conceived and deployed. All creation comes from the "Word", and this "son of god" was the "Word". That "Word" must have been in existence when the Serpent seduced Woman in paradise. The "son of god", the "Word", came prior to the creation of the Serpent and of the universe.

As far as Jehovah is concerned, the goats, as Jesus referred to them, are belligerent and incorrigible. They would be handed down to the hierarchy of daemons and would eventually exist as animals. To Jehovah, obedience to him in this universe is most important.

True reality does not exist in the negative spirit, so from Jehovah's point of view a soul that is redeemed to positive spirit is cast into eternal damnation because the soul will disappear for ever from negative spirit, just as a soul being handed down the line of daemons is seen by Jehovah to be consumed by fire. In nature creatures prey on each other and devour one another. The lake of fire mentioned in the book of Revelation in the Bible may very well be the acid in creatures' stomachs, through which lake creatures pass over and, again, as they become meals for others.

As Messiah for Jehovah, Jesus must encourage those who are permanently, sensationally and emotionally involved in the universe to do what Jehovah wants them to do. If they do as Jesus teaches in the parable of the sheep and the goats, they are eligible for the kingdom of god [Jehovah], which kingdom is a hierarchy, and thus there is a king and there are serfs. Jehovah is a righteous god of the universe, not beyond it. Righteousness demands care for the disadvantaged. At that point in his mission, Jesus had not yet revealed the unknown god, not known before in the world.

In Luke 8:28, a demon in a man recognized Jesus as god, and shouted, "Son of the most-high god, what do you want from me?" Demons can see spiritually more than what man can see. He spoke of the most-high god. Jesus did not deny it. We see that there are many gods and that Jesus is son of the most-high god. There is a hierarchy of gods, and Jesus as "Word" and Jesus as "'son of man" fit into this hierarchy twice. He actually proceeded from two gods. He proceeded from the most-high god as the "Word", and way down the line, as "son of man", from a person of mankind, who was impregnated by the spirit of the deity of the universe. Jesus was a double agent—the "son of god", and the "son of man".

I give you some more references to Jesus as son of man: Matthew 9:6, 2:5, 12:8, 13:41, 16:27, 17:28, 17:9.

In the gospels, Jesus refers to himself, about 99 percent of the time, as son of man. He had to because he agreed, before anything else, to be the Messiah for Jehovah. He had to fulfill that role perfectly in order to be the perfect sacrifice to redeem those that were in the grasp of the "god of truth." Only then could he announce the true god, the god unknown before in the universe.

Jesus referred to himself as part of the Most-High Trinity only sporadically. He relied on spiritual entities to identify him as the true redeemer into the Most High. John the Baptist said of Jesus that he saw the spirit [holy spirit] descend on Jesus and called him the son of god. The only god John knew was Jehovah, because Jesus had not yet revealed the identity of the unknown god, his true father [John 17]. So wherever people refer to him as son of god, prior to John 15 or so, the people mean Jehovah, the known god of the people of Israel.

In John 19:28, it says, as Jesus is hanging on the cross, that Jesus knew that all that was foretold of him as Messiah had been fulfilled. See, Jesus was just dramatizing his role as foretold in the Bible. He did not behave according to traits of his own character and personality, but as an actor. He did not simply work out his own life and, through his life, bring into expression his natural inclination, thereby fulfilling the prophesies about the Messiah. It was because it was foretold of him in the Old Testament that he said, while nailed to the cross, "I am thirsty." He did not say it because he was really thirsty. He said the words because he was playing a role as actor. As a man, chosen by god from among the people, he would have behaved as Messiah naturally, not because of a script.

A soldier gave him bitter wine, and he expired after stating in his role as an actor, "It is finished." Who would, when dying, state that "it" is finished? It was the drama, the role he played, that was finished. If he had acted according to his beingness as a natural person, he would not have stated that his role was finished. He would have simply lived and fulfilled his role as foretold, not knowing that the role fitted him, and would have died from his miseries. Throughout the gospels, it was said of him that he did things, deliberately, only because it was foretold of the Messiah that these things would be done by him. He was role playing all along.

The entities he addressed in the universe were also of two natures: comatose souls in reality and physical projections of their dream characters as humans in the fictional universe. He came among us as a physical person because he was unable to reach the souls lying comatose in paradise. He had to address the souls through their dream projections in the universe, but he could only get permission from the Serpent if he came as his Messiah, as prophesized in the scriptures that he authored. Thus, Jesus was cut off at the pass in his role as ambassador for truth, way before he descended to this earthy realm. As an ambassador for truth, he truthfully played that role of Messiah and, while doing so, snuck in his message of truth and redemption—and he did so without violating any of Jehovah's laws.

The kingdom of god is the heaven of Jehovah. There is no kingdom in true spirit, because there we will be "one with god" inside the Trinity. This being "one with god" is a union of three where we exist as full brothers and friends [assembled into a living temple as Apostle Paul refers to it] in the "Word", Jesus as son of god. There is no hierarchy there, so no kingdom.

We may see it as a kingdom because there truth is king because the lie is not present. Jesus used this connotation for ultimate reality to give ultimate reality a name. He also did so to give Jehovah the impression that he was talking about Jehovah's reign as god. We see here a devious streak in Jesus, but for the cause of good.

You can be sure, in reading the gospels and the book of Revelation in the Bible, that wherever you read about an altar, law, enforcement, and punishment, you are dealing with the Serpent, not the father in reality. These are tools to maintain the fiction. Wherever you read in the New Testament about love, friends, and equality in spirit, you can be sure you are dealing with the father in true reality.

We have, thus, three possible destinations for souls dreaming while in a state of being comatose (look again at figure 3, page 63). One flow of souls will go down into brute nature as permanent creatures in a fictional universe. Another, much smaller flow as sheep, will go to the kingdom of god in Jehovah. A third flow of the "very few" will be guided out by the Good spirit into reality where they will wake up from their comatose condition and proceed high above paradise into the true heaven—god's House—where they will be stones in a living temple forming a child of the true father of all creation.

This is an amazing thing. Jesus' spirit was wide-awake, yet he was able to create a fictional body that he could place, in his full spiritual awareness, in the human setting on Earth to convey a message about utter truth and reality. The true reality he told us about had to be converted into fiction that would fit into our fictional mind-set, because truth cannot invade a realm based on a lie. So he told a lot of parables and metaphors. A lie is a nonentity in reality. And truth is unreal in the realm of fiction, for it would expose the lie. Where Jesus revealed his status as ambassador was in the prayers given in the presence of the disciples to god his father; the most revealing one is the one in John 17. Because of the bar on truth in the realms of evil, this message was not immediately understood, but had to percolate through the souls' minds exposed to this prayer in the presence of Jesus or through reading and studying this prayer, and through several more life times before the message was understood in the setting of true reality.

The apostles could never have understood that Jesus was revealing the Good Spirit to them—the spirit of communion between the father and the son. He revealed this through two statements in this prayer. Verse 3 states that eternal life is "to know" the true god; and later, in verses 25 and 26, he states that this true god was never known on earth. The god, Jehovah, was known for centuries already. It could not be him. Jesus could converse like

that because both the father and the son are real beings. Since fiction does
not exist in reality, they were actually conversing face to face. The marvelous
thing was that the disciples were able to pick up this entire conversation that
took place in reality and in fiction at the same time. Here the bridge was
formed between the physical dream projections of the souls in spirit and the
real beings. God was able to communicate with his comatose souls in the
medium of the Good Spirit, and thus, Jesus' mission was accomplished. The
phrase "Good Spirit" is a new definition of god's method of communion
with his son, to differentiate this spirit from Jehovah's holy spirit, that I call
evil spirit.

This prayer was said the day before he was crucified. There is a communion
between the son and the archangel, Serpent, that was below the communion
between the father and the son. This was because the archangels proceeded
from the son, not the father. Here, as a measure of emergency or by design, lost
souls present during this prayer are included in this most high communion.
This is truly very marvelous.

Chapter 5

Tools for Enslavement

Dual Roles in Jesus and in Government

If Jesus' spirit, the son of the god of truth, could only come to us in a role dedicated to a scheme of propaganda and deceit that almost perfectly hid the message about truth that Jesus proclaimed in shrouds of additional confusion, you can be absolutely assured that those who claim to represent you in government have a double role also. The deceivers hide behind a role of good [as proclaimed in the Constitution] for the hidden purpose of betraying our trust. The difference, though, between Jesus and these charlatans is that they never have your well-being at heart, but only your deeper enslavement. If they do make laws in our benefit it is done to camouflage their permanent evil intent.

War and Taxes

The free people of the United States have become subjects. That is the great inversion of the power granted originally to the US government. This kind of inversion and amplification of power and authority for government always occurs when this government of United States engages in war. People were free before the creation of the Constitution and were the only party present during its formulation, because government was created through the articles and clauses expressed in the Constitution. The people, just by the mere mention of the Constitution, are undeniably free entities, but present-day government treats them as subject to the laws of the United States—mere slaves.

In the republican form of government, government can only create laws to control and regulate the institution of government. In this form of government, government cannot place the free people under law promulgated by government. Free people are governed by amendments to the constitution that are formulated and voted into action by the free people and these laws are enforced by the sheriff, and specifically not the police. Government cannot have any angle of control over the free people. That is the definition of government of free people.

Wars are beneficial for the US government, and are an absolute curse to the people. Through war-propaganda, the people were persuaded to pay income taxes in order to protect America from its enemies. These were enemies of the United States government, never of the people. The people of America have only one set of sure enemies; the individuals that constitute the governments of the states and of the United States. Every level of government from local to federal is conspiring together in keeping the people deceived of the truth of their status. They say the people are free, but they treat them as mere slaves. This deceit is so well incorporated in their outward composure that the people continue to be happily deceived thereby. We must remember that 'government' is fiction; it does not exist. Government must be made to appear real by those elected in office and those hired or contracted by them in their religious ceremonies and duties whereby these charlatans create in us a belief that we are free while treating us as slaves.

Federal income taxes have always been levied to finance war and through war these temporary taxes were incorporated permanently. The current federal income tax smoothly followed the Victory tax enacted for a period of two years [1942 to 1944] to fight World War 2. It was enacted for only two years because, by all standards, it was considered an illegal tax; at least that was the conclusion of all three departments of government in 1942. But when the tax expired it was suddenly considered to be a valid tax and it was perpetuated without end. We were first made to believe that we should continue to pay that tax in order to curb the menace of the USSR. The problem was that the menace of the USSR was only inside your head. It never was a menace to the government of the United States. You have been duped to pay incalculable amounts of taxes for no purpose but to ensure your posterity's permanent enslavement. For more information you can 'Google' Victory Tax. Below are some sites to check.

http://ezinearticles.com/?Victory-Tax&id=833549
http://members.aol.com/StatutesP5/65.Cp.8.html
http://www.taxhistory.com/1942.html

Also read, Jacques Ellul, *Propaganda: **The Formation Of Men's Attitudes***, trans. K. Kellen and J. Lerner [New York: Knopf, 1964]. This is a Borzoi book. And please read it. You'll be surprised what affects the attitude of man—your attitude! To be a responsible free citizen it is more important to read this book than to vote.

The American Civil War

The American Civil War put an end to free, sovereign states, and the free citizens in those states.

The original cause for the declaration of cessation from the Union by the southern states was the unfair trade restrictions laid on the South by a Congress dominated by the northern states. The South was being suckered and provoked to secede so that a war would ensue and so that the South could be blamed for that war. Through that war, all states would lose their sovereignty—which was the secret purpose of the war. This US government has been pulling the legs of your great-grandparents, grandparents, parents, you, and your children, ever since. The situation, presently, is beyond being extremely acute.

The states in the North lost their sovereign statehood by fighting a constitutionally illegal war. By denying the right of the southern states to equal status, according to the incorporation of the United States, the northern states denied these same rights to themselves. How could they justify defeating their fellow states and then, at the point of the gun, force them back into the supposedly free allegiance of states? You tell me that! Something is very, very wrong, and it has come to a point that it cannot be corrected unless the people demand a restoration of their original rights; and are willing to suffer great miseries to secure this restoration because the bankers will not relinquish their hold on America without causing enormous calamities to the people, just as the people experienced during President Jackson's struggle with the banks.

The South demanded the equal status by *right* guaranteed by the papers of incorporation. The word "right" is a declaration that one is free. The states of the south were Free States, and they were treated unfairly by Congress. *Inequality is proof of suppression.* They seceded and then fought to preserve their rights as Free States. Another conspiracy, this time of the bankers and the US government, provided the US government with all the funds it needed, and at the same time, denied financial support to the Confederate government. Wherever the money flows to, there is the winner; and whoever is supported by the international bankers are your real enemies.

It is obvious that the southern states were forced, as conquered spoil, back into the union of states. If the southern states lost their sovereign rights in the Union, so did the northern states. All the states were duped by this sovereign entity called the government of the United States. This sovereign entity usurped the authority of government the servant, and incorporated that authority into its own sovereign status over the District of Columbia. Presently, the government of the United States, the servant has no real connections to the states assembled. We, the people ignorantly and innocently planted this deceiving sovereign entity in the midst of the original states. This entity started the war, arranged for the funding of the war, oversaw the war effort, and managed the stipulations of defeat laid on the South. The independent states were never a part, and constitutionally could never be a part, of those activities. Through these acts, the US government, the sovereign, reduced states and citizens to subjects and became the sole authority. It was a secret revolution and not a single person detected the crime. The brains behind the crime were a consortium of international bankers with pockets full of money.

Had the South won the war, the Constitution would have been upheld. The government of United States now uses the constitution as a prop, propaganda, to make the people believe they are still free and have a valid constitution, while without any doubt, they are subjects. We are under the jurisdiction of an unconstitutional governing authority. It carries the same title but it is the wrong authority. We have been deceived. Rights have been replaced with privileges—and privileges compared to rights are like feces compared to diamonds.

The US government considers itself sovereign and unopposed, so why would it allow itself to be tethered by a piece of paper called the Constitution or by the votes of its serfs? A sovereign, any sovereign, tramples on anything that stands in its way. That is the way of the super egomaniac. Presently, the might and power of the US government, both politically and as an armed force internationally, cannot be entrusted to the vote of mere serfs or their representatives. The power of the US government is too massive and sublime; only carefully picked conspirators can fill the highest positions in federal government. They must be sure that people of America do not have one iota of influence in determining the officials put in office in government. Not even the rich have any influence. International bankers and key co-conspirators decide the appointment for such important positions. The people that fill the three branches of US government are the true enemies of the people. They do not serve you ever because they are hired by your enemies to pull the wool over your eyes and increase your state of oppression.

After the Civil War, a set of illegal amendments were adopted that declared the Negro slaves to be free and that made all citizens of the states citizens of the United States and subject to the laws of the United States. So the slaves never became truly free. In one big swap, slaves were freed and, immediately, together with all the other free people, reduced in status from free state citizens to serf citizens of the United States government. Amendments to the Constitution, by precedence instruments to ensure the limitations of the government of the United States, were now used to increase its power and jurisdiction from just the District of Columbia to jurisdiction over all the citizens of the states. By acquiring jurisdiction over the people, it acquired jurisdiction over their properties and the states as well.

An amazing thing happened after the Great Crash during the Roosevelt administration. A new law converted all citizens from real persons to entities of fiction through the implementation of the Social Security Act and its administration. The social security number is an inventory tag, just as domestic animals are tagged in the ear for business purposes. Through this number, the government can track the profitability of any inventory entity by subtracting government's costs in benefits from taxes, or revenues, collected. By accepting aid [benefits], citizens admit they are not able to cope under their own power, so they admit to being wards and the entity aiding them to be their warden. Citizens turned from free human beings in charge of government to cattle managed and controlled by their caretaker, US government. In the history of mankind this inversion has played itself off many times.

Presently, government can only know a person by the number of the tag. A person's birth name has no meaning to the government of the United States. The Internal Revenue Service [US government's taxing agency] refers to us as their inventory.

Social security is used to force family units apart and to place more strain on the parents. In order for women to qualify for social security payments on retirement women have to go to work. Mothers must work 45 years or so in a position in commerce to get the full benefits. Parents are forced to place their children into the care of perfect strangers licensed by government. It is unnatural and grossly unjust.

Insurance companies, serfs of government, are your government within a government. Some 30% of your activities is dictated or restricted by insurance companies. Just your belief that you, absolutely, need insurance is proof that you have been neutered. You are ensnared in rules and clauses within clauses all under the jurisdiction of an international crime syndicate called US government.

Governments are in conspiracy with international banking and insurance companies to make you worthless creatures. Hardly any American male has his balls intact. All this is done to make fiction the major reality and real human beings as if they have no importance or reality whatsoever. If you go along with it, be welcome to it but you are being screwed by government and by the insurance companies because you have no understanding what liberty and freedom is all about. This is what Jehovah calls the worship of idols. Incorporated companies can only make themselves seen and known through words, pictures sculptures and buildings—non of these have a soul. You, as an organic being, are present and seen simply by being. See the difference. You have been completely overwhelmed by laws, rules and regulations. You have no liberty left.

These fictional institutions are your idols and you prostrate yourself before these horrors and not before your god Jehovah. Many of you call yourself Christians and you are no better than the Baal-worshipers of the Old Testament that had idols all over the place. Every company that binds you into restrictive relationships with it is another idol god you must pacify. You are worse off then the Israelites who were abandoned by Jehovah in the Old Testament. You have no honor or status as real beings left. How can you even honor the founding fathers? You do not have any status left to honor these brave people.

Chapter 6

The Taxman Cometh

US Code Title 42

Let me explain a little about my relationship with the IRS. I was accused and convicted of tax fraud and spent nearly two years in federal penitentiaries—three facilities in all. I am labeled a "felon"; if you believe it.

If you go to a law library you can find *US Code: Title 42*. This volume contains many laws that were active some 175 years ago. Many sections in this code book relate to crimes by agents of government against individuals. For instance, sections 1000 to 2000 contain many crimes that government officials can be accused of that involve trespassing on the rights of private citizens. Most of these sections contain violations of rights against citizens committed by US government agents "under color of law". One example is when an official comes onto your property without warrant and starts searching your belongings and carries some of them off.

Another example is a government official intruding into your home/castle by means of a letter of demand which interferes in your everyday affairs at home—like sending you forms to fill out or demands for additional tax or a request to file an income tax form. These acts are cited as crimes by sections that ascribe penalties from two to ten years in prison and fines from $5,000 to $20,000.

They are still on the books as law, but a person cannot accuse civil servants by the power of these laws anymore. The reason? We lost our rights of protection under these laws by accepting certain types of contracts with government by which we traded our rights for privileges and benefits.

Why the IRS Arrested Me

For several years prior to my arrest, I sent to certain officials [those who have signed such letters of interference] a notice of their trespass against my person. I informed them of the laws they had violated, and of the penalties and fines attached to violating these code sections. I gave them twenty days to respond to my notice with an explanation or apology. If I were to receive no answer, I would be forced to believe that they agreed with the contents of my notice, and I would charge their accounts with the fines appropriate for each code section. I informed them that I would charge 1.5 percent interest per month on the unpaid bills. I gave these notices to policemen, local traffic judges, taxing officials, and just about anyone from government who bothered me in any way in my peaceful pursuit of daily life. I sent each person a monthly statement with all charges due plus the interest that had accrued that month.

In about 2½ years, I had about $4.5 million of debt outstanding, and I reported the debt as a loss, and I offered the IRS a reward of 2.5 million if they would collect the debt for me. After all, they are just a collection agency. I had made a mistake on the tax 1040 form, so I'd sent in another form to correct the mistake. That same year I made some forty thousand dollars working in industry, which I did not report because the company I worked for had already reported my income. I could verify that because I received a copy of that statement.

My Criminal Case Was Titled Wrong

Shortly after, I found myself in criminal court, **not charged by the people of the United States, but by the United States government** for tax evasion, specifically for failing to report $40,000 in income, as well as some other charges relating to my demand for collection of the $4.5 million outstanding debts. Because I had filed a corrected form as well, the charges against me were doubled because I had used two forms—insanity in action in government.

The format of the accusation was wrong. They gave the evidence to the grand jury, a group of people that preside as organic citizens of the country. This jury agreed with the charges of the IRS against me. A complaint filed in criminal court must be filed by **the people** of the United States because government as a fiction has no standing in a criminal court of organic beings.

I was not aware of all the faulty technicalities until I was released from prison. The US government is a registered corporation in California. Corporations can only accuse another "person" in civil court, not criminal court, especially when an accused is charged for crime by a grand jury. By using a jury, the court demonstrates that the people are in charge, not the government. In order to make an accusation in criminal court, the IRS had to present the claim in the name of the people. There is no way around it. The case should have been dismissed.

Trial Without Counsel

I insisted on having government lawyers protect my interests, but that was denied because I refused to report my income and from what sources it was derived. I refused to provide this information because I had a wife at home who needed to support herself from that source. Because I refused to betray my wife, I was denied counsel.

When my case went to trial, the IRS kicked me into every corner of the courtroom, and I was found guilty on all charges. During the trial, when I was in county jail, I found out that the IRS had followed my wife to determine what kind of business she was in and what her income might be. When I found that out, I immediately filled out the disclosure of my income and possessions, and I was assigned a government defense attorney. By the time I met with him, I was already found guilty on all counts.

That trial was a duck shooting event. No legitimate claim, no real charges anywhere and an accused without counsel. The suit was filed in the wrong format. How can there be tax fraud if all the parties know my income, and it is the commissioner's duty to set the tax? This was a clear case of the IRS forcing the judge to allow the charges on the grounds of a jury finding enough evidence to file charges they could not possibly have understood. The jury members were intimidated by the IRS attorneys who browbeat them into agreeing with the IRS' accusations. It is obvious that a grand jury is being compromised when they **must** listen to government attorneys while in session; they receive a government-colored version, not an independently arrived at conclusion.

Good In Spite of the Evil

It was not all in vain. The prison in which I was placed had received half the library from the Presidio military base in San Francisco that had closed;

there were floor-to-ceiling bookcases everywhere. I made my prison term a term of reading and researching. I must have read some fifty books on the Civil War and on the first and second world wars. Because I could compare the differing reports, I could discern what each individual author could not. Much of what I know of the One World Order and the wars fought under its auspices I learned from the books I read in prison. Who else could have possibly have had the time and resources that I had available there?

Chapter 7

The Creation of a Fiction as a Spiritual Means of Education

Fictional Nature of the USA

Below follows a dissertation of how a fiction is created, whether it's a universe, a government, a religious institution, or a business.

As example, the United States of America was created in a void, nothingness. Void is necessary to create a setting for any fiction. This void [Genesis 1] is then filled with fiction. It has to be fiction because that is all that can fill a void. If anything real was in the void or nothingness, it never was nothingness at all. Therefore, all people in a fiction have to have fictitious titles and labels, such as manager and employee, or in the negative spiritual hierarchy of the universe god, daemons, angels, human beings, etc.

When Adam and Woman were in paradise, they visited all the trees/icons to universes of the archangels in paradise in order to learn all the facets of the character of their father, the son. Each tree taught Adam and Woman one facet of understanding of god. The thing missing in my previous understanding was that Jehovah, as the most important archangel, held the knowledge of the ultimate god—true reality. As long as Adam and Woman do not have the knowledge of that facet, they cannot know the true father. As John 17:3 states [Jesus praying to his true father], "This is eternal Life, to know the true god [thus not Jehovah], and [the true] Jesus Christ whom he sent." Jesus could not add "the true" of himself without blowing his mission for Jehovah. Without knowing this facet, and thus the dual nature of Christ's manifestation, souls cannot enter into ultimate reality, the house of the true father of all, including the godhead of Jesus as son.

Isolation of the Major Virtual, Spiritual Levels

All major levels of reality are separated from each other by an unbridgeable bar of awareness. One can only exist in one major level of reality at a time. In order to transcend the reality of paradise, created by the son, to the reality of their father, one must know of their father, the son. This knowledge cannot be gained unless one partakes of all the trees in paradise, which trees resemble class rooms in a university called paradise. Upon graduating from all but two trees one can enter one of two other classes (trees): the tree of Life or the tree of Knowledge of Good and Evil. The tree of Life gives access to the communion in the son of god, a level lower than the communion in the true father and son. We must always remember, though, that the true godhead includes the son, but excludes any reality created in the son. Those in the son are the sons of the son of god, so to speak and grandsons to the god of all truth.

The most important facet is held by the serpent. Listen: The tree is called the Knowledge of Good . . . . It teaches the last facet "good" the nature of the ultimate godhead. The facet is needed to transcend paradise to true reality because Jesus even excluded himself for the title of good, only one is good, god of ultimate reality. To get there, one must fall into the realm of evil, to extract the knowledge of the true good. Jehovah and Jesus are doing a marvelous job to imbue us with that 'Good'.

This facet of "Good" cannot be understood unless one is drenched, through and through, in the knowledge of evil first. Marvelous, isn't it?

Jehovah is working as servant of the ultimate godhead to teach us the last facet of the true god's character.

Jehovah in the Dual Roles of Good and Evil

The serpent, Jehovah, in that scenario, is thus a drill sergeant of the ultimate godhead. He is doing whatever he can to impress the idea of evil on us, to teach us the facet of true good in the true father, which facet can only be taught by the true father himself. He does so [after we have understood the idea of evil perfectly] through Jesus' spirit as Comforter in the Good Spirit who will have spiritual supper with us when we understand the idea of evil completely and are utterly repulsed by it. The funny thing is that the

Serpent did tell Adam and Woman the truth; they just misunderstood what he said:

> The serpent said to Woman "What did god say of the fruit of the trees in paradise?" Woman answered, "That we may partake of all the fruit of the trees of paradise, but that we must not eat of the Tree of the Knowledge of Good and Evil; and that we must not even look upon it and cannot have anything to do with it." The serpent said, "That is not true; if you eat of the fruit of this tree, you will be like god." Then Woman looked upon the tree and its fruit and saw that they were desirable and beautiful. And she ate and told Adam to do the same.

The Serpent called their god a liar, and they believed the serpent by not comprehending the full implication of their belief. She believed their god to be a liar. That belief disintegrated her trust and reliance on their god, their father, and it dissolved their awareness of existence in paradise into something that cannot be real because that reality was created by a liar. If it was not for Woman they might never have communed with the Serpent and would have entered into communion in the Spirit of the god of paradise, son of the true god, through the Tree of Life.

Through Much of This Book I Will Consider Jehovah Evil

I will continue to refer to Jehovah as the evil god for the sake of making his role as clear as possible so you can see his tactics in teaching us the knowledge of evil as evil can possibly get. He plays his role perfectly, just as Jesus Christ played his role perfectly. But it is all done to bring to birth a son of god, so that the roles of these spirits are redeemed in the end by producing the objective of the game by enriching the true god with a new son. In the end we will consolidate our observations and finish by giving credit and honor to those who deserve these.

They believed the Serpent and thus had to consider god in paradise to be a liar. This arrangement was deliberately agreed upon to make Adam and Woman imbibe the thoughts this archangel could share with them. Their choice made them reject paradise for what the Serpent promised, so they fell into a coma in paradise, where they are still lying while they dream this Serpent-induced dream of physical reality to experience all the evil the true godhead wants them to know before they can receive the insight of true, absolute "Good".

Jehovah and the Spirit of Jesus Scheming for the Sake of Good

There was thus some sort of plot between god, the son and the Serpent, Jehovah. To be able to enter into the house of true reality, one had to partake of the tree of the Knowledge of Good and Evil. Jehovah portrayed the face of evil; and Jesus, here in earth, in his real capacity and as 'good disguised as evil' taught us as best he could about the true father, Good. His message was hidden in so much "evil disguised as good" that originally nobody got the true message. It could not be gotten that easy, for evil had to percolate thoroughly through the medium so as to even camouflage the message of good in a realm of evil. His message of "Good" had to be disguised as evil in such a way as to allow the people so see it as good fitting in a reality of evil. His real message was thus understood as belonging to the realm of evil and was incorporated in the creed of Christianity until eventually one soul discovered the truth as belonging to an entirely different reality in which physical reality is temporarily suspended. Folks, this is a very difficult but most important paragraph. The disguise of evil disguised as good and good in a disguise of evil and the different levels of reality in their own guises is very difficult to express in words because they are spiritual concepts and so easily flip-flop in our minds.

Our present time is the era in which the message of 'Good" can be fully understood as coming from an entirely different kind of reality. The face of Good as spiritual light has begun to shine through the murk of evil as darkness in our confused minds. Now the last facet of the character of "Good" has become understandable, and those who do fully understand it will enter into the house of the true and ultimate god. The vocabulary and the ideas presented in modern science and technology were not available in Jesus' time, so he had to converse using parables and metaphors. We, in our modern time, can comprehend the manner in which the universe is deployed. Jesus had to call it the realm of darkness and such, and the place where people are dead while living in earth. How could anybody understand such phrases? Modern man can understand the phrases virtual environment, computer science and technology, projected images, but the people in Jesus time were dumbfounded by his teaching.

Optical Illusions

We have all been exposed to optical illusions. When such illusions are seen according to a certain frame of mind one sees one image, but when the attention is shifted slightly one sees the exact opposite of what one saw before. In a similar manner the physical universe is the spiritual mental illusion souls perceive when existing under the influence of the belief in a lie. But when the understanding of mind is shifted from the belief in a lie to that of truth, an entirely different environment is perceived that has no roots to the other one. One looks at the same ideas but depending on the spiritual frame of mind one receives different understanding and experiences. These are close but absolute opposites of each other. According to the coloring of the facts in a court case a defendant can be convicted of crime or declared to be innocent. Here in this physical environment we are continually under the influence of such mind-altering illusions through the misinterpretation of facts or the lack of certain crucial facts.

The Undoing of Adam

Consequently, the following permanent, spiritual separation of souls can thus be cataloged. Those who entered into all the trees of paradise except the Tree of the Knowledge of Good and Evil will remain in paradise and be happy in that virtual realm of existence. They know a lot about the true father but are lacking the knowledge of one facet. This is not bad because it is their native abode. There is a lot of light in that realm.

Then, there are the souls that did partake of the tree of the knowledge of good and evil, and they fell into an inescapable virtual realm of evil. Naturally there is no good to be found in it. It is a realm of utter spiritual darkness. It seems that souls there are lost to truth forever, for truth is light; and light is not present in utter darkness. The only truth that has penetrated in this realm of darkness is my statement that the universe does not exist in reality. It is a derived truth, not primary truth; but this truth is sufficient to already have rent the fabric of this universal computer program display. This must be so because truth understood will destroy a lie-believed. A light in utter darkness destroys the quality of darkness, and this is true also of truth penetrating a lie-believed. The lie must vanish, for its power only reigns when the truth is absent, hidden in darkness from the awareness of souls. We are subject to the shadow play in the universe where we confuse apparent truth with absolute truth. We are lacking certain facts to arrive at the true situation at hand.

This lack of information is based on making a spiritual lie the truth and the spiritual truth a lie.

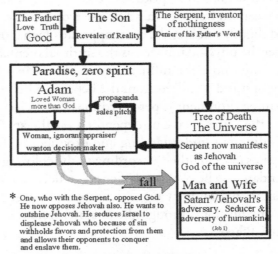

The fall of Adam

Figure 4

Light of Truth Shines in the Realm of Darkness

By the spirit of the son entering into this darkness, light of truth was brought into that realm unnaturally. This light could not be understood or even seen very much because it was forced to cloak itself in darkness on orders of Jehovah. As Jesus tried to tell us, his light was hidden under a bowl, but he had to hide the message so deeply that nobody understood the full meaning [Matthew:5; 5-7]. He had to hide that it was his light that was prevented from shining in total darkness so he transferred this light as belonging to 'you', his listeners, in the hope that one with ears to hear and a mind to understand would make the transference and see that Jesus is the true light that was so perfectly hidden. Those who eventually will see the light will have seen this facet of the character of "Good", god; and they thus know ultimate reality completely.

John 17, the Face of the Good Spirit

Chapter 17 in the gospel of John is the face of the Good Spirit, the communion between the father and the son. The apostles and disciples who were with Jesus in that room were introduced to the Trinity of the godhead by Jesus. It took two thousand years for the first ones of those present in that room to fully understand that they indeed know the true god. All those, who by reading this book and by understanding the full impact of the situation, will get in contact with the Comforter and will be guided also to know the true god and will enter into the house of the ultimate god. They will enter into the mansion Jesus has prepared for us because the final facet of god was revealed on earth through the mission of Jesus. We must make this facet our own.

Those who do not get the message, because they were not given to Jesus by the true father, will remain in this universe and succumb to ever deeper layers of clever propaganda [evil disguised as good] and eventually die spiritually in this virtual realm of darkness, which then has become their only and acceptable abode. They will reincarnate endlessly until there is nothing of their souls left to incarnate. This reminds me of Gollum, in the story of the Hobbit. This character, Gollum, could only exist in the realm of utter darkness deep below the surface of the earth in caves and underground lakes. He had absorbed so much falsehood that he could only exist in the deepest darkness. The gollums of spirit are us. Let us again face the light of truth.

Truth Reigns in the Realms of the True God

The lesson of this last tree, "the Tree of the Knowledge of Good and Evil" is that the true god will never lie. One is utterly and completely safe in him because he will not distort the concept of true reality. He will not deceive us through a corrupted constitution, or communion. The Good Spirit is always good. He is what he is—always. The concept of telling a lie, telling something that is not truth, will catapult a believer of the lie into a state of being in unreality—virtual reality, not being at all. In reality one is always in reality because of the complete purity of the communion.

The son places all his new creations in paradise, the highest level of virtual reality. This reality allows one to believe a lie about the truth of that reality in order to understand the concept of true spiritual good. By embracing the lie one is seemingly condemned to the realm of evil forever. However there is a gate out of it, but only when the lessons taught in the realms of evil are finally understood and placed in relation to Good. When that insight occurs, the archangel in charge of the Tree of Knowledge of Good and Evil has completed his assignment.

Existence in a virtual reality is death. A lie believed is a trillion times worse than being on a psychedelic drug. The drug wears off, but a lie can remain with you forever, and for most, the cleverest lies believed will stay with them until death. In order to know god, we must thus understand the concept and the evil power of the lie. Without having received the knowledge of evil, you cannot understand the concept of a lie and the trust you can and must have in the true good which true good cannot lie and cannot have a lie percolate through its realm of truth.

So, Jehovah, as a messenger for good, took on a disguise of evil to help bring to us the knowledge of true good. That was also the disguise Jesus was forced to take in order to bring us the Good News of redemption he made available to us through our possible Communion with the Comforter, the Spirit of Jesus clothed in raiment of good, guiding us into the realm of good. The answer of the riddle then is in verse 3 of John 17: "This is eternal life, to **know** the TRUE GOD, and the Jesus Christ [whom this true god] sent."

The truth that is in us "knowers" will throw a monkey wrench in the production of Jehovah. This knowledge of truth can be transmitted through the spiritual computer network consisting of all the comatose souls from those who believe themselves to be viral dust, monkeys, or humans so that the truth will permeate and percolate throughout the entire computer and computer program and infect all souls with redemption. That is the idea of a computer virus. It will destroy the program Universe, and sets its captives free. Let's hope that this will be the case.

There Is a Spiritual Realm of Difference in the Meaning of the Verbs "To Believe" and "To Know."

No creature can know anything for sure by having faith in the universe. One can only have a strong belief that something is true or is false. Everything and every creature in nature upon its creation adopts a cloak of secrecy.

Nothing is known fully, and human beings are even enigmas to themselves and each other. In order to "believe," one uses a scale with a slider to determine how much chance there is of a statement being true or false. If the slider is beyond the midpoint toward being true, we say that we believe the fact to be true. If the slider stays closer to false, we say that we cannot believe the statement to be true. Neither means a thing as to the real fact in the case, but the important thing about propaganda is that it is always believed to be true while it is always untrue. Propaganda uses a mixture of true and false data to create the impression of believability. It always works this way because experts in propaganda know the technology as a truck driver with twenty-five years' experience knows his truck. The universe is one gigantic propaganda display from its infinitesimal tiniest detail to its most massive scene of grandeur of the heavens—everything is based on deceit.

> **In the realm of true reality, the idea of believing does not exist. In reality, one knows a thing. One sees an entity, and one knows it because it hides nothing of itself to anyone.**

The characteristics of a god, as we biological creatures have always understood it, are that a god knows all things, that he creates all things [corporations], sets the laws, holds courts of trial, and has the power and means to punish and the means and power to grant honor, prosperity, and blessings. His subjects are always in the dark. They are not sure of anything but the power of the god. The only one that seems to have some light is the guy/god at the top of this entire hierarchy, the one holding the sword nobody can match in a fight.

A False God Knows all Things about Others While Concealing Knowledge about Itself

The government of the United States has become such a false god on earth. It creates and controls the fictions of incorporation and the Social Security—numbered slaves [numbered fictions] that work in them. It creates the food on which fiction feeds itself, the currency [a fiction] that drives industry, business, banking, and the slaves that work in all these fictions. And it knows, through the corporate identity number and Social Security number, whatever it needs to know about anybody and any corporation. In the near future, babies will be born and implanted with an interactive memory strip; and from then on, through hypermodern technology, nothing will be hidden or can be hidden from government, and government can punish instantly through the use of this interactive implanted chip. It knows where everyone is located at any time, whether stationary or in motion, and knows what every person is engaged in. It is the quality of "knowing" and the sure means to punish when it feels punishment is due, that makes a god in this universe—and anybody can see, government is fiction. This is the only thing Jehovah has over us. He is one up because he knows things, essential to be in command of the universe, while we are only allowed to guess at things as creatures and are told to worship him. The only reason we worship god is because we fear him. That is not love! He insists on having power over us—and that is not love either. He can look in on us in his display but we cannot peek outside the display to see him.

The US government does not exist in physical reality; it has no identifiable body. We are taught from birth on that government exists, that we must pay taxes and must die. We are taught that the flag and the eagle that represent government are sacred and that we must revere this god for which these stand. We are told to pledge allegiance to this flag in honor of this government/god. Government officials [this god's clergy] must take an oath of office to uphold the sacredness of this government god, not allegiance to the people as intended by the phrasing of the constitution. This god claims to exist for the people, but in truth the people exist to make this phony god seem real. We deceive each other in making this god real. It has taken on a reality of its own through the power it exerts on us through its many layers of titles of nobility. Government officials have titles and corresponding powers while the people are stripped of status and are subject to the powers of these phony titles of nobility. We exist in an upside down condition of understanding. Fiction has taken on reality and the people remain as always subjected to the fictions they create. Yes! we are gods because we can make fiction come to life and have it control us!

This shows the essential difference, spiritually, between souls caught in the fictional universe and Jehovah, who designed the universe using us, souls, as powerful, but ignorant, slaves in it. It shows the true nature of "*evil*" in him. He could easily share his knowledge with us and be friends together in operating this universe. However, as friends, the universe is no good to him. He wants to be an all-knowing god ruling over a universe of ignorant creatures. This desire for power and might is one-upmanship. The true god calls this tendency evil. The true god is a friend and shares everything with us, making us his friend and not his underlings. That is why the true god will not command us to his will. Jesus talked about friends and brethren. Jehovah speaks as ruler of the universe and the creatures as his serfs. One-up-ism is only possible in nothingness that needs to be filled through fictional organization. If Jehovah would allow us to know everything in the universe, the evil nature of his subjects, creatures would vanish. Incidentally, his evil nature would have vanished too. So the nature of evil is to keep another in the dark of knowing things. Now you know why the true god called that tree the Tree of Knowledge of Good and Evil and why Jesus called the universe the realm of darkness and the ruler of it the prince of darkness. No one in the universe, as far as I know, has known this before. Secrecy is the key to slavery and vanity. Our nature as unreliable creatures in the universe is deliberately induced in us through artifice and malice afore thought by Jehovah.

Propaganda [deliberate misinformation] keeps organized power in place, and the workers give it power because they are ignorant of what really is going on. Government officials and workers have lost their conscience and operate by the execution and enforcement of laws and rules. What makes government as god possible is an easily deceived society, consisting of members who cannot be entrusted with the worth of a nickel, or with the liberty of their fellowmen and their own posterity.

Just as Jehovah does, government must create unreliable creatures of our children because crime prevention, war on crime, and war on terrorism give much power and status to government. It makes government visible in a big way. The more war is advocated the more power and authority government garners for itself. Government literally breeds war, crime, and terrorism. It is its main product. No wonder it needs so many prisons. If it does nothing it does not exist. Here government acts exactly like god, Jehovah.

Now you also know why Jesus came to us as a double agent. He came to tell us the truth of reality and love [the equal sharing of all knowledge in reality] and he came as the Messiah for Jehovah by which he manifested many miracles—utterly conflicting roles. The truth he came to tell us was to set us free from mystery, and the miracles mystified us as seeing him as a power in this phony universe. His role as Messiah was forced on Jesus by Jehovah in order to be allowed in the universe. Now you can see that Jehovah forced Jesus in this role of dual agent and why Christendom was fooled in combining the good and evil in the manifestation of Jesus Christ into a god that was neither Jehovah nor the Good Spirit in reality. By believing a fusion of two contradictory gods to be the true god, they were fooled into believing in neither god. The god of Christendom is a fool's god. That is the outworking of evil—one is always in the dark.

Once the void is accepted as existing, beings can be coached to fill it with significance called fictions of the mind. These fictions have been so generalized through ongoing propaganda that it has taken on an illusion of reality. Thus, when a person in his status of real being must commune/communicate with creatures existing in a fictional setting, the real person must convey his person and his message as fictions. That is why government had to convert human beings to numbered entities of fiction in its inventory. This is necessary in order to create a spirit of communion between dignitaries of government and its slaves.

Jesus' message was universally misunderstood. His message was understood to apply to existence in the universe in physical substance and in universal spirit. After all, he ascended in his physical body—a body one could touch, hear, see, and smell.

Fiction Steals Power for Its Continued Existence

No organization can operate in a void of power, or really without creating a means of communion for it, so the original government of the USA was granted limited powers in the Constitution some sixteen years after the Declaration of Independence, and which Constitution was underscored by more reaffirmed limits of power in the first ten amendments to the Constitution. This constitution is the original spirit of communion between the free people and their servant government of the United States of America. This spirit of communion was deliberately corrupted so that future dignitaries of government could steal and reverse the power of this spirit of communion. As I wrote before, a virtual reality is created by punching a void in an existing reality and filling it with fiction. The United States government is such a virtual reality. It received its charter of existence and operation from the people, its god. The fiction in it, titles of nobility, have slowly poured out the original intent and has refilled it with new content, the present constitution with its long list of additional amendments adopted by our enemies in government. The amendments and other acts of legislation have reversed the position of servant and god. Now government is god and the people are its servants. The rest is a history of the United States completely misunderstood by the people, who are totally ignorant of how they got to the status of serfs they now have in America.

The creation of fictional reality is a power to create. People have this power. That is why the serpent originally claimed that we can be like god.

He was not really lying, but he has always kept us in such confusion between true facts and fancied facts that not one soul has any idea what is real and what is fiction.

The real power of creation in negative spirit lies in the ability to garner and channel the latent power invested in the masses of people. This activity can only be expressed through the enslavement of this latent power, the people. In the negative realms of spirit the power to create is always an activity of deceit, because the power must be confiscated from those who hold power in itself—the single isolated cells in spirit, souls and their projections in the universe, creatures. People relinquish their power voluntarily through religious belief in a higher order. Some people have always been able to enslave the common man by instilling a system of religious belief. This is also true in the formation of the United States government. The American people are adherents of a religion and praise their god, Government of the United States, and have blind allegiance to this god. This god is an evil god because it obtained its godly power by deceit and by enforcing the deceit by means of the sword. Police are so stupid that they do not understand the real reason for their existence, the power of the Lord [government] to force the national religion on the people. All those who use force are excluded from the realms of positive spirit. They must learn more lessons in the universe and must still come to the point of repentance, but one cannot repent while one still wields power over one's fellowmen and is respected and worshiped because of it. In the mean time, the window of rebirth in spirit is dwindling constantly.

Fictions Are the, Almost, Sure Means to Get Creatures Lost Forever

The possibilities in the creation of voids are endless. One can easily get lost in these possibilities. That has already been clearly proven by all the technological advances the world community has experienced so far. I believe the One World Order is organizing the world into regions of special means of sustenance. Some regions are allowed dominance in the production of certain commodities, for instance the fictitious assumptions such as China in the production of tea, Columbia in the production of coffee, Taiwan in electronics development and production, and so on. This guarantees each region a sustaining economy. This is not bad. But these things should be made public so that some guy in America who wants to start a tea plantation does not find himself without a market because this market has been assigned to another region in the world, and companies are only allowed to purchase through certain wholesale organizations who deal only with certain international suppliers.

The United States government has established itself as god through deceit. The people must now subject themselves to this god through worship. They must surrender sacrifices by paying excessive tribute from the fruits of their labor, subordinate their states rights to the authority of the government of the United States, and must deliver up their progeny to dispensation and authority of the US government—the god of all Americans and of the world [see Genesis 47:13-25, where it is said that *slaves* have to pay Pharaoh 20% in income tax]. If those Egyptian people were slaves, you are super slaves because your combined tax bills amount to something like 66%. Pharaoh was a nice fellow compared to the government of the United States, or more correctly the World Banking System.

The above paragraph shows clearly that organization is evil and indispensable in the universe. The sad thing is that all humanity, and the souls underlying human society, have been caught in the universe, through an analogous history. The universe, originally, was souls' full possession as it was promised them by Jehovah in their initial contact [they were to be gods]. Propaganda and conspiracy turned the whole ball of wax upside down. People, as independent dream projections of comatose souls in the universe, find themselves now at the bottom of all fictionally organized heaps, in effect and not at cause. From this position, they are now trying to rise to the top through their knowledge of science and technology. People do not understand that the blessings of science and technology were granted to them by the spirit world [Hebrews 11:1] and can again be taken from them. Besides, super-technology only helps the conspiracy for a One World Order in guarding and forcing the huge slave pens [nations] of the world into conformance to its will. Technology is always usurped by the high authorities for use against their slaves. Technology will also seduce humanity to continue its way down into the pits of fictional perdition.

Why Modern Man Believes He Can See Fiction

In the days after the War for Independence the people did away with large portions of human-created fiction. The first fiction abolished was that of nobility and the artificial status of titles of nobility. All the people were free, except for slaves. This was one fiction they did not do away with for reason of international competition. It was kept in place through legal fictions of law, cruelty and avarice. It was a fictionally-created, perverted reality in the lives of both the free and the slaves.

People did business in their own names or in partnerships in the legal status of their own being and initiative. If an owner of a business owed a consideration to another and the business could not pay the debt the owner was liable to pay the difference.

Several generations grew up in this business climate and this manner of conducting business became reality for those people. Then, the New York State adopted laws of incorporation because foreign nations had adopted that idea. The people who thereafter incorporated their businesses were basically shrewd and dishonest characters. The businesses they conducted through these incorporated entities were more speculative because their own wealth was not directly at stake. They drew investors into their corporate schemes and these people did lose their money when the business had a setback or went bankrupt.

The workers in these corporations, for a long time, did not realize that a fiction had replaced their place of work. They worked and received their pay just the same. They could not see the fiction because it was invisible. It was a mental concept, and mental concepts cannot be seen unless they are written down and studied and other deliberate schemes are used to force them into visibility. This force, of course is law and enforcement, and their accompanying propaganda. The final result culminated in an established public opinion about incorporated businesses. The common people did not have any interest in reading the laws, so the fiction was completely hidden from them. It was only after a person became successful in his own standing and effort [not in that of fiction] that he was approached by the corporate initiates with schemes to invest in a corporation of some sort.

Laws of incorporation quickly swept the states of the union and it was not long after that most people in metropolitan areas found corporate or trust-based positions of some sort in business and manufacturing; yet most people still had no concept of what a corporation was. They only could see the job and not the fictional **legal** net woven around their jobs.

Through the repercussions of the planned Civil War and through additional state, constitutional and federal laws all the people lost their free standing based on the intent of the constitutions for the states and federal governments, and became subject citizens of the United States and legal residents of the states. To cloak the people's indentured status the phrase "state citizen" was retained and a new phrase of "US citizen" was invented and heavily advertised. Through clever legal and media manipulation we now recognize people inhabiting the states as residents of the states and as "free" citizens of the United States.

Through constant media brainwashing people now see the fictions of incorporation as physical things and can hardly imagine operating a business or any venture without a government license of incorporation. Corporate fiction has become real and visible, and the reality of working a business in one's own name is now considered nonsense.

This exact thing happened to spiritual beings, Adam and Woman in the reality of paradise. Through their belief in a spiritual lie [or a set of lies] the reality of paradise disappeared and the fiction of a universe and, especially, the fiction of earth based on spiritual and natural laws became as if it were real.

The more fictions we as souls will take into ourselves as truth and the more we see true spiritual reality as non-existing the more we, as human animals, will degenerate spiritually into recognizing brute animal nature as the only reality of existence. This fiction of brute animal reality is forced on us through spiritual fear-based decisions that continually intimidate us to again incarnate in the only reality accepted, the reality of biological life in earth. It is an overpowering belief in virtual existence that forces souls to accept existence in a lowered capacity of being that always gyrates deeper into the realms of pure animal existence. In true reality these souls lie in a coma, experiencing/dreaming an existence that does not exist. As long as they continue to believe in lies, they are blind/dead to the truth. They are spiritually brainwashed and utterly dead to true reality which reality is incapable of change. It is there because it is truth—not because it is based on some enforced-on-us belief system.

Why Modern Man Must Understand That It Cannot Tolerate Deception in Government

Truth, basically, is an agreement between god, the father, and his son as to what is real and what is fiction. This agreement is also called the Good Spirit of their communion. All things that can be thought of as real have thus been established. Also, there must be different agreements between god, the father and all his other sons. So, being a part of another son's reality one can have entirely different concepts of reality, and universes based on these different concepts.

So, in Jesus' case, Jesus has established a concept of reality acceptable to the ultimate father. From that concept of reality Jesus created paradise and all the icons/trees that allow Adam entrance into a kaleidoscope of universes that teach the good of their father, the son. All these universes are in agreement with the reality that Jesus has established. There is one archangel that disagreed with Jesus and established his own concept of reality. So, in order to populate his concepts of reality he had to attract sets of Adam and Woman into his realms of spiritually unapproved, fictional reality. The Serpent was this archangel, Jehovah. He devised a set of lies that when conveyed to Adam and Woman would draw them into the belief system that the Serpent had a better means of expressing reality than god, the son, Jesus. Jesus created Adam and Woman, so he always retains ultimate spiritual responsibility over Adam and Woman. Jesus found a means, in agreement with the Serpent, to enter our fictional reality and bring the message of his truth to mankind; the only truth acceptable for redemption. Jehovah's fiction must be repented of and the truth conveyed by the Comforter must be readopted in order to enjoy redemption.

Jesus as Comforter Will Guide Any Lost Soul That Can Comprehend the Betrayal of Trust between Jesus, Jehovah and Adam, into Reality as Established By Jesus.

Jesus, of course, is also responsible for Jehovah, so his purpose is to bring Jehovah's concept of reality back into conformance with Jesus' concept of reality. He has arranged it so that this realm of negative spirit becomes the means of producing the next son of God, so that the Serpent, Jehovah, can be viewed as the mother of this new son of god because as the Serpent announced from the beginning, "If you eat of this tree **you will be like god**." Jesus cannot tolerate that unapproved forms of fiction can have permanent status in his concept of reality, so he provided for the reincorporation of Jehovah's spiritual fiction into his reality. Jesus' original concept of reality must contain remedies to resolve conflicts of reality between him and his archangels. So, because god the ultimate father of reality knows how things can go wrong, he insisted that his son Jesus arrange for a means to deal with such possible unauthorized versions of creativity in Jesus' reality.

The Constitution as a Means of Communion between the People and the Fiction of the Government

Let me give you an example of how such a situation can develop in earth as well. I refer you back to the establishment of the limited government for the United States. In this model "We, the People", are Jesus, god. The people created a constitution for this government [which is the Good Spirit of Communion between the parties] that was agreed on by all parties; so, there should not be any reason to betray this concept. Now enter a third party, the international bankers. They see another concept of reality where they can be the masters and everybody else the slaves. They have a marvelous method to bribe government officials to deceive the people [the spirit of evil] wealth-based currency which they received on good faith from their investors.

The bankers never let up trying to bribe legislators and executives to betray the people and eventually they have created such a breach between the honesty of government officials and the Constitution that these government officials cannot do anything else but become servants of the bankers. We are now seeing the complete fulfillment of the bankers plans; the establishment of the One World Order. The problem is that "We, the People", are still responsible for standing by the original Constitution, and seeing to it that it remains the spirit by which government operates. Let's make some substitutions in this scenario. We, the people are god, Jesus. The Constitution is the Good Spirit [the initial reality established between the people and government]. The bankers are the Serpent, and "We, the people" have become the slaves [deceived souls] in a fictional reality where banks are god, government is the new god's servant and the original god "We, the People" have become the slaves of all. We, like Jesus, must take responsibility in restoring the understood reality between the people and government as established in the Good Spirit of Communion, the Constitution, to secure liberty and freedom for our unborn posterity as the founding fathers, supposedly, also did. Only the people have this responsibility, because government has already determined through laws the method of keeping all posterity as slaves to the bankers. As you can see around us and in the advertisements of banks, the bankers come across as the angels of light and goodness, but are vicious manipulators of the spirit of trust between all of us.

Now you can see why "We, the People" must restore our contract between us and government, as Jesus is restoring the contract between Jehovah and himself. If we must become a son of the true god, it is incumbent on us to restore what went wrong on our level of creation, as Jesus is doing on his level. By making banking the permanent servant of the people and of government we have restored the spirit of communion we are responsible for. This is the test we must pass in order to show our father that we can be trusted in the end to do what is required, no matter how difficult this may seem.

The initial purpose of this essay is to make you realize that through a lot of lies-believed and incorporated in our belief system through the government-controlled [the serpent's] educational system and the media [devils disguised as angels of light] reality as envisioned by the Founding Fathers disappeared from sight and a new fiction has become real. In our mental makeup we were forced to nullify what we saw as real before and were coerced to adopt a mere mental image as something that can be seen. A group of people who we trust and rely on have been lying to us, played mental games with us and replaced a previous mental outlook on reality with another fiction. We, the people, as creating gods of government have squandered the trust of our unborn posterity. We must be despised, not held up as an example of truth and good. We do not deserve to receive honor until we restore what we allowed bankers to steal from unborn posterity. We are not swine, so we must set things straight again. The bankers are the swine, and we'd better get them back into our corrals for good.

We, the souls, were betrayed by the Serpent by telling us lies also. There does not seem to be a way out of both situations, but Jesus has already opened the route out of all the cycles of deceit in which we are wrapped, in this negative realm of reality; a realm that could not exist without our full cooperation.

As we can surmise, Jesus our god, must destroy the fictional universe once all retrievable souls have been extracted from it or he must incorporate the realms of negative spirit into his overall scenario of reality established by him. Jesus must rearrange the concepts in negative spirit so that they can find de jure expression in the concept of reality established by him.

Birth and Death as a Means to Constantly Change Human Reality

This kind of deceit is possible because of the quickly revolving cycles of birth and death. We come into this world over and again as babes that can easily be brainwashed by those in power to see "reality" as it is taught by the deceivers, the parents, religious congregations, public school, and most of all utterly evil and deceitful TV programming. People allow the greatest deceiver possible freely in their homes through TV, radio and written media. In this fashion "reality" changes from physical generation to generation. Reality is not a constant entity in those who exist in a state of deceit as it is for those who exist in truth. Reality is a constant. Reality is something entities in truth will not mess with because if a lie is believed their awareness of reality quickly degenerates into a state of chaos. It is this state of chaos, created in the awareness of those who believed the clever lies of the serpent, out of which he fashioned the universe as told in Genesis 1 in the Bible. Through a clever plan and cleverly executed propaganda schemes, enforced on deceived souls, this Serpent/Jehovah was able to fashion a mental concept in the deceived souls to be aware of a universe that could become visible by accepting a physical body that is part of and in tune with the physical universe. This physical body has a brain that is perfectly matched to be a counterpart of the physical universe by perceiving the environment and by coordinating action in it. Through these sets of "goggles" souls can experience this mental idea of a physical universe as real. The universe and our bodies [and of all fauna and flora] are evidence of spiritual delusion of souls lying in a coma in reality. The mere fact that a baby is born is proof that it was spiritually conditioned to come here. Had the soul inhabiting that baby been sane it would not have appeared in this fictional setting.

I have given you deep insight into the state of spiritual decay you have fallen to and also the means of how to start your return into the state of knowing truth again. Can you now see that presently we, fellow human beings, enforce the state of being spiritually lost on each other? What do you think you must do to return to reality? Do you believe in human and scripture authorities who are equally spiritually brainwashed as you [politicians, teachers, scholars and the clergy] or someone who deliberately came into our "state of being-lost" to tell us about true reality—the son of man and also the Son of God, Jesus?

Jesus' problem was that the only way he could come to us was as dual agent. He had to appear in human flesh and behave as a human being in order to represent himself as a "sane" human being. He was guilty in that role by reinforcing the state of spiritual brainwashing in us, but to his credit he modified that state by doing up-to-then unexplained miracles and healing. He explained and proved to us through these acts that he was more than just a mere spiritually brainwashed soul. We should look carefully where his teachings digress sharply from what normally people and the priesthood could accept, and try to understand what his true message was. If he taught what was already known he wasted his efforts. He came because he wanted us to know another interpretation than what humanity up to then had taken for truth. He came because humanity, and the souls projecting them, existed in a state of delusion.

The ideas taught us by our human teachers that Jesus and god are mysteries are false. It is not the lesson Jesus came to teach. He came to reveal all of himself and of his true father in the only way open to him so that all mystery would fall away and true reality will remain. Can you now also see that we cannot possibly accept as teaching the things he said that were already known to man because he taught those things to us as a man; but that he urged us to listen and absorb those things he taught that flew utterly in the face of the then accepted norms of religion and physical concepts. He said of the miracles and healings he performed that we can do the same things and even do them better. He taught us that there is a new, unknown god. Do these things not fly in the face of what we know from experience to be impossible? Yet, he did not lie. He was teaching us about another reality that was utterly foreign to us and that he urged us to seek and find it with all the might, all the intelligence and all the persistence we are capable of; and if sought with that kind of intensity we would find what we are seeking, truth—reality. He did not come to teach what was already revealed in Old Testament scriptures. He came to us to teach something utterly different, as different as the lie is from the truth, and as different as the meaning of the Old Testament is from the meaning of the New Testament.

Apostle Paul stated that at the trumpet blast Jesus will come with all his angles, and resurrect all believing souls in Jehovah. This will be the moment that all authority in the negative realm will be restored.

Those who seek their destiny in the universe will again see a world restored to the concepts in the holy spirit. Their existence in physical universe continues, after the role-up and redeployment of the universe as creatures of a lower biological order, while a new set of Adam and Woman will have been attracted to empower the universe for another cycle. Those restored in Jehovah will arrive in his heaven, a heaven of light-empowered creatures but still soul projections in Jehovah's negative realms. The souls redeemed in the Comforter are born as spiritual cells in a new son of god in true reality.

Page 156 of this book refers you to the video *Journey Toward Creation* about the concept of creation of the physical universe as seen from an astronomical viewpoint. The video brings us almost to the point of the original Big Bang, the moment the spiritual lie was believed by the first set of Adam and Woman. On the other hand, my essay brings you very close to the moment of creation of the Good Spirit between God, the father and Jesus, the son [the concept of ultimate reality in the son Jesus] as I conceive it to be. As there is no other model available, this model stands and it is this model that humanity must embrace.

Fictional Environments Always Obscure True Reality

Jehovah had a secret plan when he originally surrendered the void to Adam and Woman. Adam and Woman were not in the know of the full plans for the void, just as the progeny of the people who started the United States were not aware of the long-term plans for them in these states united. It is this secrecy of intention at the beginning of the execution of the idea "universe" and "government of the United States of America" that cloaks everything in undisclosed deceit. No full disclosure was ever given at the inception to the spiritual entities who invested themselves in the project "universe." It all started with a lie. Souls were scammed by their god, Jehovah, and their physical projections were scammed by their limited government to whom they entrusted their heritage—the Free States and their liberty. We, humans, have power to force our fellowmen to come clean with us, but it seems to me that the comatose souls in spirit need another higher power than their own to awaken them from the spiritual lie. Humans are completely numb to spirit. Because they are soul projections they cannot see their maker, but the maker can see them. Souls must repent of being other entities' puppets. Jesus said, "Truth will set you free". Since we are souls in spirit, souls are caught, not human beings. Souls must understand truth to evict the lie from their concept of reality. Truth will then be restored and the souls will be free. Jesus addressed souls through the human projection, flesh. He even clarified that the flesh cannot profit from his teaching. We must look a level higher to our spirit and make spirit know truth. When that happens, their human projections [bodies] will vanish from physical reality.

Physical Reality through Spiritual Deceit

The servant spirit, Jehovah, in the universe has become the god of the universe. He deceived Adam and Woman in being the servants by withholding his true intentions. He consumed our souls. He reformed our spiritual substance so it becomes useful to him just as the substance of the mouse is reconstituted to become part of the cat when the cat consumes the mouse. The substance of the mouse, now being a part of the cat, wants to be cat and does whatever it can for the cat to remain a cat and to make sure that the cat is not consumed by something else. We, souls, are like the mouse consumed by Jehovah that now wants Jehovah to remain Jehovah with all power in us as souls. We are Jonah in the belly of the Whale. Jesus tries to get the whale [Jehovah] to spit us out, so we will be free. Then, we can be alive and be friends in Jesus, our brother.

We now exist in Jehovah. We would be lost without Jehovah because he is the only one who knows the plan. Humanity is in the dark and will never see any light [false or true] unless we follow him further or unless we can disentangle ourselves from this project "universe." We are his obedient slaves until we can escape. The escape must come from a realignment of our de facto spiritual ideas of reality to that of true reality. That is the true mission for which Jesus came to us into the belly of the Whale.

The universe does not exist anymore by the privilege granted by souls alone. That grant still underwrites the universe, but the power of the grant has been transferred or has lapsed. We are now trapped as creatures in the universe while it made us souls dead in reality. An inversion of a concept believed and not understood, eventually placed us at the bottom instead of at the top. All this happens through evil. "You want to know evil," says Jehovah. "Come along, I will teach you." The evil is pinned down by one little sentence. The uttering of a lie by a spiritual deceiver and the believing of the lie by another innocent entity is the worst spiritual trap. It sends a sane being spinning down into a reality warp that inverts everything he knows to be true. True becomes false, and a lie becomes the truth; up becomes down and down up; black becomes white, and white becomes black. This reality warp is a state of imagined reality in which propaganda systems keep people, no matter the higher system of reality they find themselves in. This Tree of Knowledge of Good and Evil has taught me what evil is; I hope it will teach you that too—because knowing this will set you free. Jesus stated that *the truth will set you free*, and not even one person had ever understood what he meant by that statement. Now you know too.

Chapter 8

Deceit and Hidden Truths

Physical Reality as a Smoke Screen for True Reality

The universe hides truth from us, soul projections, and souls are unconscious because of a lie believed. Hidden things and hidden meanings that are arrayed against you are evil. Things that overpower you against your will or against your better judgment because of unknown factors are evil. Those who overpower you by whatever means are evil. So it is clear that government, which has oodles of classified material we are not to have knowledge of, is evil. Those who make you believe that you have access to all information but secretly withhold very important information are the ones who stick your head in the mud by making you believe things that are utterly false; and because you believe their BS, you are one down to them, and they enslave and exploit your ignorance of the situation. And we citizens believe it is up to us to form government by voting. How can you have a valid opinion when you are deceived and ignorant about government conspiracies against you? The deceiving politicians and bankers run circles around you.

Those who have the power [given them by public trust], and who make you believe you can trust them but who cannot be trusted are evil. Thus, Congress, the Executive Department and the Justice Department who aid each other in keeping things classified and hidden from us, are evil. This has to get changed in order for people's vote to be of any value. I, for one, do not like another human being or human beings playing god over me. The only way people can play god over another is to keep him ignorant about things. If I would be in the know, their one-step-up position would disappear.

In Our State of Delusion We Can Get a Close Resemblance of Truth by Reversing Everything We Know

In dealing with the universe itself, the prudent thing to do is to reverse all you believe to know about physical reality. I say this because the projector that displays the universe is hidden [Heb.11:1]. We cannot perceive in our physical nature who controls the projector, how it operates, how this scheme is used against you, and who might be the entity responsible. A good case in point is Jehovah; for millennia we believed him to be the true, righteous, good god. He now stands exposed as a liar, deceiver and cheat. Jesus came to tell us to get out of her, this whale of a deceit, but he had to be careful how he made that clear.

As human beings, we are unconscious spiritually; and physically, we are unconscious as well. We behave irrationally spiritually, and we make our social/political decisions irrationally because we have been deceived by those who have gained the power to control the information available within society. This is what is called being in effect, rather than being at cause—lies spread to the entire society and those "lies believed" do that. Such deceived persons are their own worst enemies.

When you hear controversial or disturbing information, it is always prudent to see who will most likely be the beneficiary if the information might be part of some propaganda campaign. By thinking things through, one will quickly come to the conclusion that the party or group having the power and influence to stage the propaganda campaign is the only beneficiary. Then you can turn the information this way and that and find what the motive of the campaign is. In order for the government of the United States to become our servant again this must happen on a national scale. All people must participate, or at least a vast majority. This seems unlikely because of the immature and irresponsible nature of the common man. Many people are just out to deceive enough others to make some sort of living, and the rest are kept busy as slaves to such extent that they have no time left to become spiritually observant. Those duped thereby may be damned and those doing the duping will be damned for sure, because true reality cannot take into itself souls that practice deceit on any level as a way of life.

I return now to the spirit extant in paradise and the exchange of false information between Woman and the Serpent. Both the deceiver and the believer of the lie are doomed to exist in nothingness because real beings cannot hold a lie in themselves and remain in truth. They have been made powerless in reality by believing or uttering a lie. This is true of "true" reality, universal reality, and any other social reality one might be trapped in. It is a scheme of nesting realities, all based on created nothingness with respect to the next higher reality. Lies-believed have trapped us.

A lie-believed is nothingness. It does not exist in reality. It is fiction.

Deceived souls cannot exert their beingness in reality. Even though their spiritual entities are still present in reality, they cannot exert their corrupted beingness in reality, so they have adopted a reality in fiction. *One of the consequences of these dreaming souls lying in a coma in true reality is an imagined dream creature existing on earth—you.* Soul has life, or beingness through you. And you form a fictitious living entity in the fictional body of the person that consumed you [through a lie you believed]—the Serpent/Jehovah/god.

The BS in the US, in the world and in the universe, is piled extremely high and deep; and at the bottom of this heap is this entity—you, a physical person, utterly overwhelmed and lost by all the deceit. The deceivers in any of these systems are as deceived as those they deceived. Humanity exists in a void of knowledge, which void we call universe. Humans cannot gauge the complexity of it. The same is true for Jehovah, who can be said to be our environment because he controls every aspect of it.

The souls of animals are buried in piles of deceit that is many times the height of the piles we are covered in, and trees are so deep in it they prefer to be frozen in one place. Most souls trapped in the universe will inhabit trees on their further way down and out of reality, altogether. The longer a soul is subjected to ongoing propaganda in this universe, the less control it has.

The Hierarchy of Stacked Voids

All voids must have a link to a higher form of reality from which it was extracted as void. One can see this happening in the Tree of Knowledge of Good and Evil in the formation and operation of the universe, in the formation of nations and corporations on earth, and in the minds of souls who were originally duped. You could look at brains as computer processors put to work to keep up with all the deceits it believed. The brains in animals may be shrinking because animals gave up trying to keep up with all the fictions, and simply accepted all the fictions as their total reality and have settled in it as such. Deceit overwhelmed them completely.

A good example of a void is the empty memory system in a computer. It is a void. It shows up as containing nothing until a person starts filling it with things he/she likes to do or likes to look at. The computer processor is trying to keep up with all the fictions a person is feeding it and making sense of it through the use of programs.

The computer has a base in physical reality; its memory has a base in the technology and manufacture of the computer, and you as a user have a link to this computer through the reality in which the computer exists also. By some unfortunate set of circumstances, the entire contents of your computer memory can be wiped out. In the same manner, the memory of the universe can disappear just as easy; and according to Jesus and Jehovah, it will. The reason is that fiction cannot have eternal life. Sooner or later, the lie underlying the fiction is revealed, and the whole structure collapses. Jesus said that all things done in secret, dark corners will be revealed by it being shouted from the rooftops. He was mainly talking about the deceit he was forced to enforce in order to be here in our virtual reality.

This I say in support of my contention that the universe is just a fiction of our imagination. If it was real, it could not be wiped clean and made to vanish. The proof is actually intensified by Jesus proclaiming that after it has been wiped out, it will reappear. I just want to impress on you that this universe is just a program run on a spiritual computer. Below are some examples in the manner of creating and filling voids with "meaning" and fiction.

Revolutions such as the Russian communist revolution against the tsar's regime can only happen through foreign implanted propaganda that stirs up the people and by the involvement of at least one foreign nation that funds and guides the operation of the revolution [the US government calls such operations advisory operations]. After which this foreign nation secretly becomes the owner/head of the new nation. France, obviously, was the supporter of the US revolution, but this nation could not hold its place of mastership over the USA very long. Jefferson was one of the prime movers of the revolution. Was he not the US ambassador to France?

Politics and Propaganda Are Synonyms

By the way, the word "politics" and "propaganda" are really very close relatives. They are just treated in the system as different concepts so the population can be easier engaged in the campaigns of politics rather than campaigns of propaganda. Politics and propaganda are like ying and yang. The one needs the other, and the other needs the one to complete each other as a whole. That is why there is really only one political party. They are just made to appear as if there are two. The whole idea behind a two-party system is to dupe the people in believing that they are contending for different ideologies; while in truth, a third party secretly runs away with the real prize.

I do not necessarily accuse candidates for office as evil creatures; but, for sure, their campaign managers are. These campaign managers are, more than anything else, propaganda experts. Their first concern is to condition the mind of the candidate so he/she is allowed to continue to run for office. If the candidate does not respond to the propaganda triggers and demands of the campaign manager, the candidate will be pushed on a side spur, another will take his place, or he will lose the election. The second purpose of the campaign manager is to be in charge of the platform campaign so that the voters are indoctrinated and will support the election platform. Candidates not properly responding to the triggers and demands of the propaganda system cannot ever hope to win an election. Those who slide through anyway, such as happened to one of the governors of Arizona [Meacham, I believe his name was], will be set up—his name smeared—hauled in court, and found guilty on one or another charge. This particular governor was thrown out of office, and he was never heard of again. That is the power of the banking system in politics. Mayer Amshell Baur Rothschild, a very prominent international Jewish banker once stated, *"**Give me control of a nation's money and I care not who makes its laws.**"* That statement is completely correct. We can see that the bankers have done their job very well and own most nations in the world because they control the money of all these nations through their control of their money supplies, including the US currency through the independently operated Federal Reserve Banking System and foreign national systems like it. The politicians elected by you sold you to the worst crooks in the world, bankers.

The propaganda for the communist revolution was spread by the sovereign US government that by that time was completely in power over the states and over the people. The United States government needed a nation out there that it could be in enmity with in order to start a campaign of peace for the formation of a One World Order. The United States was, and still is, in secret, the boss of the communist regime—now democratic Russia. It was so in a completely indifferent position of authority outwardly till the end of World War II, but behind the scenes, there was much communion between them.

When, after the Second World War, it needed a permanent enemy threat in order to fully integrate the United States into the One World Order through the intermediary of the United Nations—an organization planted in the world through much US government involvement, the "supposed" threat of the cold war established the full might and power of the United States as sovereign. Ongoing cold war propaganda bound the mass of American people solidly into a nation ready to face any threat. The people were willing to pay any tribute in taxes to establish the power to do so. The funds, instead, were used to forge a One World Order; that fact was affirmed by the first president Bush who called on us to give our full support to this One World Order while fighting Iraq under false pretenses.

In fact there never was a communist threat. When US citizenry had accepted the United Nations as a higher form of government in the belief of the communist threat, and when UN authority was accepted as the governing authority in the world by all nations, the communist regime in Russia was no longer needed. A tiny revolution that lasted a few days, and took two lives, put an end to this huge brutal regime—it was rolled up in a puff of smoke and vanished.

Politics Is a Microcosm of the Negative Spiritual Macrocosm

This kind of deceit is exactly what I want to touch on because it is happening to us in the universe. This universe, as real and menacing as the USSR seemed to all of us, is but an illusion and, without even a cloud of smoke, can be rolled up like the mighty USSR. In Matthew 24: 35 and Luke 21: 33, Jesus said so, *"Heaven and Earth will pass away but my words will not pass away"—and he is correct.* The universe is a smoke screen—an illusion in the minds of men and women—and held in place by the mind power of deceived souls lying in a coma in reality. These souls have been so deceived that they pretend to be humans that know nothing. *Jesus' words must remain because truth is eternal [see also Isaiah. 34:4 and Rev. 6:14, 21:1].*

The Lake of Fire in Revelation

Revelations 20:14-15 says this: "And death and hell [the universe, the only hell there is] were cast into the lake of fire. This is the second death. And whosoever was not found in the book of Life was cast into the lake of fire. This lake of fire is the second death." The book of life, of course, is the knowledge in reality of who is there and who is not [just take a roll call]. To be in reality, one must be there in full awareness and not in some dream state that pretends another reality exists due to believing a lie. Believing a lie places a person outside reality. A lie believed is fiction. Fiction is a fantasy. Fiction does not exist, *period; and a real entity so deceived has no choice but to assume a coma*. It cannot die because its substance is real.

The lake of fire is the ultimate power of truth. If, in the very end, when the project universe is complete and reveals itself for what it is—fiction in completion—it, and the god for which it stands, cannot conform to truth, they will be consumed by the power of truth. These have, thus, no right of being. The universe is Jehovah's fictional body. It is a lie. We are part of his body, and we make it work according to his sense of awareness, just as we use the fibers and cells in our bodies according to our sense of awareness. The life of the cells in the body causes a human being to exist in a sphere of human awareness. Life is in the cells. For Jehovah life is in his captured and consumed souls.

The Creators in Negative Spirit Are Captured Souls

Paul stated that those who believe what Jesus preached are part of Jesus' body. The assembly of the several parts of the body of a person makes one coordinated unit, and the mind of the person does the coordinating. Jehovah, just like Jesus, has wired the souls of Adam and Woman through an integrated nervous system into his fictional functioning body—as the electronic parts in a television set form an integrated system to display video signals received from a TV station. Electrical and mechanical engineers have transformed raw dirt into electrical, electromechanical, and mechanical components that are forced to perform specific tasks dependably in the scheme of the TV set. Universal dirt consists of soul-projected substances. Souls were forced in the body of Jehovah to form mass in his body—the universe. The TV set, consisting of matter forced to do functions as a TV set, has become a working part in that body of Jehovah. Jesus has been able to persuade soul projections to become a part of Jesus' negative spiritual body. This is done also through a belief system. It is called the body of Christ as long as the souls continue to retain their comatose state to form the physical church. Upon waking they form the positive spiritual body, the spiritual body which will be born a son of the true god. Jehovah does not have creative powers so he uses souls to do the actual creating for him.

The power of the lie and the manifestations of systems of lies must eventually be revealed. The truth will dispel the lies held in the consciousness of souls. These lies are consumed/annihilated by the power of truth. This cannot be any other way because a lie has no standing in reality. The fate of this project universe when completed is that it has no standing in reality and is consumed together with its god and all the souls still participating in it because its god has consumed itself in his expression of the universe.

As long as the universe is not finished, it cannot be proven that it is not in truth. Therefore, I believe that Jehovah will procrastinate finishing the project "universe" as along as he can because he knows that when he finishes it, he is dead. The true god allows the weeds to grow with the wheat in the field, and at maturity will garner the wheat and burn the weeds.

Examples of Nothingness

I give you another example of nothingness that is filled with substance. I am working on this book, and I store the data in this computer's hard drive. Each night, I roll up the program by shutting the computer down until the next morning. It is dead because I shut off its source of energy to keep going—electrical power. The next morning, I feed it again by turning on the power, and it starts up again; and I can retrieve the substance of the article and continue to write or continue to edit the book.

Every so often, the prey—electricity—decides to break down; and my computer dies, destroying whatever I did that is not saved in the hard drive. I have had it happen more than once that the program Windows crashed, and all the data on the hard drive and its backup hard drive was destroyed—nothing left. I counted on the companion hard drive as a backup system; but through the ignorance of the technician bringing back to life my computer, he reformatted the backup drive. You cannot trust anything. The best way is to back data up on CDs, but that quickly becomes a CD storage issue.

This book will go through many scenarios and explanations of the spiritual conspiracy that caught souls to be an energy source in a void of nothingness that they filled with fictional mass, called the universe, and projections of themselves as physical creatures. All is fiction, but the substance consumed into the fiction has a link to reality in which it was created. Jesus called the universe the realm of darkness because there is no light of reality in it at all. What I do not know is whether the drill sergeant, Jehovah, will simply close down the project in agreement with god, his father, and resume his standing as archangel, or is he so emotionally involved that he cannot let go of it? As the boss of it, it must hold awfully strong temptation and seduction for him. The object of the class is for souls to understand evil and good, just as I am explaining it in this book. So when we understand what really is going on, we can graduate by practicing what we know. We may have to transform this universe into something that has standing in reality so that everything in this fiction can be redeemed. Jehovah, god's master sergeant, will stand in front of his class of students and present it to god in truth as a mission accomplished.

As you can see, the United States of America, as we were taught, is but an illusion of science fiction in the awareness and minds of the American people. This illusion has established itself as their god. It has consumed the entire body of people in the nation that now does the bidding of the brain [government], just as my hands do the bidding of my mind in typing on this computer. The state governments can be seen as the obedient organs of that body—such as liver, lungs, etc.—in the body of the US government.

Humanity and the universe are just illusions on the scale of science fiction [things believed to be possible]. Souls, by the way, are just cells in the greater structure of Adam and Woman—just as human bodies consist of billions of cells incorporated and organized to form the functioning human body; and as the citizens of the United States are just cells of voters and nonvoters organized and programmed through propaganda to form the body of the de facto government of the United States. As below, so above! All is fiction in the universe.

The spirit of Jesus is among us to tell us of all the deceit perpetrated on the sleeping addicted souls in reality. His spirit, the Comforter, is unable to reach them in the realm of true spirit because the souls respond to input orders from Jehovah [negative spirit]. Jesus had to come among us in the dream to inform the sleeping souls what they really are going through [imagining] as they spent their energies dreaming up the universe and being a part of this universe in the form of biological creatures.

Jesus' spirit in Jehovah's body is like a piece of dirt in the digestive track. Jehovah's body cannot break down this piece of dirt [Jesus] to absorb it in its own tissue. The dirt continues to exist whole in the body of that person. Jesus is not susceptible to the seductions of Jehovah.

The Sense of Time

Idea is a timeless entity until it is converted into a concrete expression in the physical world. For that idea, time starts to roll from the moment the idea is put into action. The idea remains a thought, no matter how much time may elapse. Say, I have the idea of a perfect house. I dream about it for years. Then one day, I have the opportunity to have this house built. The moment the execution of the idea of the building of the house starts, time starts rolling. Time is a sequence of events that dreaming souls create in the fulfillment of their dreams. The time is measured in milestones—such as the activities needed in finding an architect, in conveying the idea to the architect, in obtaining the property, in transferring conversations and sketches into an architectural design and a set of building prints, in obtaining the approval for the structure, in excavating and grading of the property, and in building and finishing of the house. All these activities are specific steps that in the mind of soul are translated in a sequence of time. It is just a sequence of time that is part of a greater sequence, the unfolding and decaying of the universe.

The same goes on in the universe. The universe is still in the building phase. It continues to expand; thus, matter is added in the configuration of the design. Time is measured as moments as long as the universe is in the building. Once it is complete, there is nothing to do but return to timelessness.

The older souls that were engaged in this project ended up as seemingly lifeless matter, as soil, as vegetation, and as animals. Their energy was used to create masses of matter, hydrogen, or some more elemental form of matter. This had to be the first conversion of soul energy. The whole project rested on heaps of matter coming into the void. This matter can only come here through the conversion/condensing of spiritual soul energy into physical matter. This conversion was obediently accomplished through propaganda the souls believed. They saw the end of the project as an idea and were willing to accept their responsibility in the execution of the project in sacrificing their soul identity in being just plain matter. Any natural scientist can tell you that matter is condensed energy. The energy potential is still in the matter, but the threshold of re-conversion into energy is too high for this to happen naturally. The energy of the sun and the magma in the center of the Earth are evidence of such natural re-conversion.

Matter is souls' dream material. Their dream energy has been converted into matter, which matter through programs of biology was reconverted in biomass energy on which other creature projections of souls could exist and progress. Depending on how long this universe will continue, many of our souls might end up being matter until the final curtain comes down when the universe is finished. The primordial fact, of course, is that the universe has been suspended and redeployed many times, simply because of a shortage or a fresh supply of souls gullible enough to be taken in.

Evolution: a Figment of Human Imagination

As can be seen from this scenario, evolution is just a figment of human imagination. This theory of evolution was sent to us from the daemon world to confuse us into believing that things happen in the exact reverse as they were being implemented. Like all propaganda, it is used to steer us wrong. We are made to believe that we have some cause in it all. The entire plan was there at the origin of the universe—the "big bang," the moment time began, the moment of the execution of the project universe. The universe is a house for gods. It is upheld by millions of daemon operators and trillions of soul slaves used as implementers of tiny details and as just raw matter. They fell into it to learn and know evil and many were caught into it permanently. We know evil by practicing it, by suffering under it, by making others suffer by our insincerity, by profiting from it, by utterly succumbing to it, and finally by understanding that we do not want any part of it [hopefully].

I salute all the souls so far captured and consumed by the project. You all made my person possible and made it possible for me to find out about you through the one who deserves our everlasting standing ovation, the spirit of Jesus of Nazareth. He, often and patiently, comes to us, comatose souls, and tells us who we really are. He wants us to wake up. He is standing at the door of your heart and knocks, but you feel safer dreaming than waking. Be brave, face the truth; let us arise in spirit!

Jesus Was Meek Because He Withheld Super Power to Be One of Us

Jesus did walk on water. He changed water into wine, and he could have loosed himself of the shackles by which he was bound when he was led before the priests. He could have made his body as tough as steel and as strong as a bulldozer. He allowed every little and great insult to his body to comply with a promise made to Jehovah. Jehovah did what he could to make it possible for Jesus to commit a sin. Jesus did not. It proves that Jehovah and Jesus were contenders. What could they possibly be contending about? Jesus suffered for you and for me and for the sake of reality itself. Reality could not be swallowed up in fiction! I thank him, for I do not want to be stuck here—this fictional universe—any longer than I have to. You and I have been fooled to cooperate with Jehovah to project this universe and for us to be caught in the scheme. Jesus made it possible for us to escape. For your own good, don't pass up this opportunity. Turn everything that seems real and true to you inside out and look at it from the back rather than the front. By doing so, you will know what this universe truly is even though your senses will tell you something else. The reason is that the senses are rigged so that you will get everything backward and inside out with respect to reality. The sole purpose of Jesus' coming into the world was to rescue you; in return you must escape through the door out of negative spirit. The Comforter stands at the door to welcome you to your true home, ultimate reality.

Chapter 9

Human Society

Common Human Characteristics: Dishonesty, Betrayal and Crime

I must agree with Jehovah through Moses that to build a community that has high moral standards, one must have very severe, tough laws against crime. Criminals are truly unwanted characters. Criminals are treated too mildly in the United States. One must have absolute proof that one is dealing with a criminal, and one must be absolutely sure that the laws on which a person is found guilty of violating are based on principles of liberty and justice before tough sentence is meted out. An accused found guilty of a crime and sentenced to death must be retried by another jury—not by legal maneuvering, but through delivery of facts without interruptions by the prosecutor. In this case, the prisoner must prove that he is innocent. Individuals in society must step forward with proof of guilt or innocence. If a person is executed for crime, and later on, it is proven that a person did not step forward before the execution to prove him innocent, that person will receive the same sentence. Society cannot put an innocent person to death when it could have been prevented if the guilty person or one with proof of the condemned person's innocence had stepped forward.

I disagree strongly with Jehovah in making anyone too rich. Not a person in the world can manage his own personality in the face of overabundant riches. Such a person becomes a menace to himself, the people around him, and to society as a whole. When matters in the world go wrong, they always involve the very, very rich. Presently, the world is at a peak of crime by conspiracy of the very wealthy against the people.

Signs of What Is Wrong With Present Society

The rich exist in the rarity of wealth, riches, and power—and the whole structure of riches lies in the illusion riches have for the common man and woman. Because of the misunderstanding of power in the common people, the rich remain rich. This delusion causes people to become criminal. It is the only way a person can see themselves as becoming rich. The rampancy of crime gives the rich their power. With their riches, the powerful can claim to be on the side of the people that do not engage in crime through their show of fighting crime. Yet, their think-tanks constantly find ways to increase crime even if they have to create criminal intent in others or by committing crimes themselves and then blaming the crimes on other parties, as is now the case in falsely accusing Islamic nations of harboring international terrorist organizations. If such organizations exist in Islamic nations, one can be 95% sure that the ones doing the accusing have placed them there. Their riches make them remorseless, and it gives them the power to use other deceived people in their service while planning to betray them in the end by accusing them and having them destroyed. The very, very rich, therefore, are not to be trusted and should be denied a place to be. They must be hunted out of existence.

Don't Fear Death

The Arabs got it right. Don't fear death, and there is not one man who can scare you. I write this to enlighten, but I know that very few will have the courage to set themselves free. The Old Testament gave an example of that when the Hebrew people were set free from Egyptian slavery. In liberty, in the desert, they were yearning for the fleshpots they received while enslaved to pharaoh. Americans too have their fleshpots well filled, and they too are enslaved. It takes real courage to pursue liberty. Liberation is, for the most part, overcoming one's addiction to comfort and relative ease. The greatest addiction is the creatures' love of the lie. To suddenly have to face the truth of one's existence is too great an obstacle to overcome. The cold turkey effect is overwhelming, so people stick their heads back in the mud.

Oh, one can contemplate and agree with the theory of it as I explain it here, but to put the theory to the test is too much to ask. So humanity has opted for excellence in one activity or another to prove one's worth, whatever it takes, so long as one does not have to face truth. Excellence, of course, is measured in fictional money and in recognition of one's status by one's fellow slaves. The standard of ambition is, "I want to be the best." Life is the childish pursuit of not confronting one's true dilemma. In a virtual reality no soul will benefit. There are no benefits in dreaming in a state of a coma.

Politicians Are Either Criminals or Aids and Abettors of Criminals

Politicians use rampart crime to get into office and to stay in office. Candidates for positions of judge, attorney general, and congressman/congresswoman generally cannot get into office without stating that they are warriors against crime and cannot stay in office if they do not use the fighting of crime in their platforms. This in itself already proves that they need crime to get into these lucrative positions. These are the characters that foster crime by condoning it in leniency by being ultra-soft in meting out tough penalties. If a judge does give tough penalties, the higher courts will overrule them. All this is true of general crime; but when one is fighting the filthy rich conspirators or threatening their card house, they suddenly become very tough—like in the way they deal with tax protestors, who have valid claims in the situations they try to expose or correct; and they are given no mercy.

President Bush Jr. proposed a $2.3 trillion budget for 2008. He is an executive. He has no right to talk as a legislator. If he wants to do so, he can run for Congress. He has no right as an elected official to cross governmental department boundaries to address Congress. It is the job of Congress to determine the size of the budget. President Bush's proposal is 2.1 trillion too much. The amount of money the government has at its disposal is exponentially proportional to the power to further deceive, overpower, and enslave you. Besides, it contains a huge amount of money the nation supposedly owes the bankers—if you believe it.

Everything is a hoax—numbers pulled from a hat—and you are supposed to be responsible for paying these absurd extortions. These funds represent your efforts, and they use it to reinforce the corrals that confine you. This is a nation of slaves enslaving the slaves. The ignorant masses keep each other enslaved because they believe clever, cunning liars. God warned us about them way back in Genesis 2, but no one paid him any heed. The power of political liars always depends on the masses who believe their lies. They lie because others holding super riches have bribed them. Lying has taken on worldwide proportions; and through propaganda, they are poised to control the world and the universe. Their success depends on you believing and obeying them and by doing nothing to thwart them.

California's Governor Schwarzenegger proposes socialist legislation. He wants to give medical insurance to those with illegal entry into the United States. In the fifties, the government was extremely successful in stemming the influx of Mexican illegal aliens into the United States. In that era, the influx was premature, so it was contained. Now it is a scheduled event. Today, government may feign to stop illegal entry, but it is more shadow play. They will keep the borders wide open to the influx of aliens. US government is the friend of aliens and the enemy of the American people. This reversal of allegiance by government has existed for about hundred and fifty years. Bush just signed an international treaty reforming the North-American continent into a new nation including also Mexico and Canada. This is treason.

Governor Schwarzenegger's proposal, based on a court case, is absurd. The court case is rigged as are many cases coming to the attention of the US Supreme Court. This measure, if successful, will open the flood gates of illegal entry into the United States. As governor, he has no standing as legislator. He is infringing on the legislative branch. He has no right as an elected official to address the nation. His job, and the president's jobs are to execute the laws, and most of these are unconstitutional. Truly, our first job would be to make all government, again, obey the original intent of the Constitution because only that document is the communion between the people and government.

The Miserable American Grind

It is absurd that in our modern times both parents of a family with 2 to4 children must work 8 to 10 hours a day and spend at least 1 hour commuting, to barely scrape by financially. This is a crime of government that is so heinous that I will never agree with anything our elected politicians tell me. It is an outright scandal. They have forced the tax rates and the number of taxes to such a high pitch, it is a like squeezing a sponge through a press roller. I can only admire people for doing this for 45 years or more, every day. There is a large group of people that cannot stand that sort of vicious grind for very long, so they become criminals, become drug addicts and careless in the rearing of their children. They take to drugs and alcohol and always exist in a state of anger, fear and anxiety—all by secret government policy.

My Experiences with the Working-Grind

I can remember about 2 years before my divorce I was hardly capable of performing my job responsibly. I became so incredibly bored hanging around a bunch of dud coworkers. My job included rather intelligent and diverse responsibilities. My days were cramped with decision making in order to keep others busy with my designs. I could not understand that both my wife and I had to work all day to rear our two children and had hardly anything left for ourselves. I had a home in the country and I was hardly ever there.

We had no time whatsoever because of a rather long commute, shopping, dealing with kids, being the soccer coach for the kids in AYSO, etc. We could not be a harmonious couple because of this grind. I decided on a new routine because I felt I had a right to enjoy part of the day as purely for me. I started to take walks from ten to eleven AM each morning and every so often some tight-assed manager fired me. So, I got another job, do the same thing and got canned again. I did not give up. I had a right to a part of the day for myself in the sun. I must be the guy that was fired the most in the whole world. Early on I understood that our insane life style was forced on us through government taxing policies and bank-set rates of interest. Every time I got a raise, it was due to inflation; and as my deflated earnings increased my graduated income taxes went up due to percentage increase of the tax rate. So every time I received a raise I became poorer. I became a determined tax protestor and ended up in jail because of you, fellow Americans siding as grand jury members with, of all things, the suppressive IRS.

Bankers

These are signs that our form of government has been corrupted by politicians. We are witnessing the merger of the three departments of government into one. Why? America—lock, stock, and barrel—is owned by the bankers. They insist on having full power and control. It is too complicated to manage this asset US government if it is divided into three separate branches. To the bankers it is only an investment; and as sole owners, they want sole control. However, this investment has been acquired by subterfuge and conspiracies. Their investment is an illusion as are all things in the universe. It just proves that the people do not have the ability to secure and perpetuate their posterity's liberty. I read somewhere that the management of the brotherhood of Masons is closely linked to international banking.

The American people started out with liberty, but it lasted less than a century. The people are too divided—they are too lazy, they are too selfish, they are too vain, they are too busy, they are too deceitful, immature and cowardly, and they are utterly lost in the many webs of illusions spun around them; yet they can be herded mentally like cattle. They are caught in a net from which they do not know how to extricate themselves—and if they would know they do not have the courage. They ignore their predicament and work on having fun and on being happy, as is told in the story of Pinocchio. Yet old age and death are coming nearer, and they have no idea of what to do about that either. That story "Pinocchio" also emphasizes the evil of lying and the believing of lies. It is a story about the American people.

Declaring War

The president has no right to propose or declare war. Declaring war is a legislative function. It is established by the division of powers that the president cannot propose and/or declare war and be the chief of the armed forces at the same time. Members of Congress have a primary duty to report anyone who infringes on their duty to legislate, whether such infringement comes from banks, special interest groups, the president, or any person that has been granted a limited title of nobility. It proves that the legislature and the executive branches are conspiring against the people. A jealous legislative branch would have stopped the president short in proposing a matter that concerns a legislative function. They allow Bush to be a dictator!

The Supreme Court

The Supreme Court always has been the lapdog of the executive and only in token manners do they pretend to be against the legislative. What they have done and are continuing to do is to pour out the content/intent of the original Constitution and replacing it with other meaning and interpretation. They have refigured the Constitution as a tool to guarantee the power to government and to deny any powers to the people. They have done so using the sly techniques and procedures inherent in socialist democracy. They poured out the original intent of republican form of government that guarantees the power to the people and replaced it with socialist democracy that secures the power to government because socialist democracy holds the people to be incompetent to handle their own affairs and the affairs of state. So the government has become the warden of the institution of mentally and physically impaired American masses. For that to happen, the branches of government must be merged into one manageable organ. The purpose of it all is for government to perform as the management institution for the owners, the bankers.

Chapter 10

Suggestions for Improvement in Government

The Need for Absolute Separation of Indispensable Government Services and Tough Rules to Keep Them Separate

Title of nobility can only be granted for one specific capacity. If such a person oversteps the bounds of his office, he must be severely reprimanded by the spokesperson of the institution whose duties were infringed. If such infringements are acceptable, we no longer can claim to have separation in the departments of government. We, as people, must severely limit the powers that elected officials have, especially the power to levy taxes.

It is utterly unacceptable that the US government runs such a department as the Social Security Administration and that this was voted in by Congress. It is utterly unacceptable that the US government can run up a debt to the size it purports to owe today. It is totally unacceptable that the US government can tax state citizens for any purpose, including war. The US citizens have been brought down to the level of serfs. The founding fathers fought a very hard war to reestablish our liberty. We have sunk much deeper into enslavement by government than the founding fathers ever experienced. This government—legislative, executive, and judicial—has combined to conspire to separate the American people from their rights and liberties and consume them in the formation of its own body. This was done by another secret party that has limitless funds available for bribes to prevent our elected officials from doing as they promised according to the Constitution.

We Need a New Constitution

A new Constitution needs to be devised to safeguard the right and liberties of the people and to write out into laws the maximum extent of power granted to each title of nobility in government, state, and federal. The commander in chief of the armed forces cannot also have a position in government. This position must be held by someone from the people. He may be appointed by the legislature, but this vote must be upheld by a committee of top level personnel in the armed forces. Its budget cannot be tied to the decisions of the legislature. Its budget must be voted on by the people and declaration of war must be seconded by the commander in chief of the armed forces to be valid. If a conspiracy is discovered all members party to the conspiracy must publicly hang until dead.

The Farce of Present-Day Democracy

If we are supposed to have a democracy where even the US senators are elected by the people, we must ensure that any amendment to the Constitution can only be voted on, democratically, by the people. Our elected officials, state and national, have betrayed the people too often in promulgating and adopting amendments that limited the rights of the people and hugely increased the powers of the government branches; and the banking institutions should be banned, forever, from collecting a tax in the name of government. Government betrayals have gone too far. Changes must be made immediately.

Forbid Lawyers from Being President and Members of Congress

The Constitution must forbid lawyers and banking officials to run for government. The primary duty of a lawyer is to be council. People must ensure that this is the only capacity they can ever have. If lawyers do not like this arrangement, I advise them to not become lawyers. Lawyers are crooks at heart. The only place for them in government is as judge and only as long as informed citizens in full standing form the jury of twelve and can make decisions untrammeled by the counselors and the judge.

Elected Officials Cannot Belong to Secret Societies

We have been deeply betrayed over the many years by our elected key-officials. The reason is that such elected officials belong to the same secret society.

In the future, all candidates for office ought to be required to declare that they have never been a part of a secret institution whose purpose is to change the form of government or to merge this nation into a union with other nations by means of conspiracies and to never become a member of such a society.

From what I see, the elected officials are very selective in the amendments they propose and laws they enact. It is clear that a secret program is being followed that the voting citizens of this nation are not informed of. What makes this even more sinister is that the media are not giving us information about our government that allows the people to keep control of their government and the laws they enact. It is clear that the major channels of the media are in conspiracy with elected officials against the people. They have no other choice. They are owned by members of the conspiracy and they are captured inside a second fence by being incorporated and controlled by government. The entire infra structure of control of all the most important institutions in America in securing liberty for the people have been removed from control by the people.

Media Can Report News but Cannot Make Commentaries

You ask, "How is it possible that all the media are against the people?" The media are tied hands and feet to government for information. Their existence depends on pleasing government. You have seen the trend of corporate takeovers in America and the world. Huge corporations buy each other out in friendly or hostile manners. The courts give them their consent. There should be a constitutional mandate that makes buyouts by fictional institutions of other fictional institutions impossible. If a company is not profitable, it must go under. If it is profitable, it must remain so without depriving another company from being profitable on its own efforts and wisdom by trying to buy it out. The size of a company must be limited. That is a guarantee that people will retain their liberty. One entity cannot own more than one entity of the media. The media must be dispersed among as many owners and operators as possible. We cannot be hamstrung by someone who owns most of the media in a country; it is insane to allow them to do such things.

The Super Rich as Enemies of the People

I believe that the super rich think that they have a method to ensure that they can reincarnate after death in a capacity to inherit the wealth and power that they left behind when their bodies died previously. It would ensure their position as human gods on earth. Maybe they have such a system, and maybe not. The idea, though, is so repulsive that as human beings we must prevent such a thing from happening through the formulation of a constitutional clause and the enforcement of that constitution that limits the amount of wealth a person can own. I go for a limit of $200 million of today's value; certainly no more than $250 million. No one has a legitimate use for more money than that. This amount must total the entire assets of an individual. We must be sure that the super rich cannot conspire with other rich people to take over government to force conditions on the citizenry of any nation. Society gives any person the freedom to earn or make $250 million, but after that the person should gracefully surrender his expertise and skills and earning power to the people who, ultimately, made it possible for him to garner those riches.

Banking Must Become a Helpless Servant

The people are way overdue in overhauling the manner in which the power and constitution of government is delineated. Government and banking must become the servant of the people, and there must be a way that ensures that government and banking institutions remain in that position. The Federal Reserve System must become a subordinate institution to the government and it may not align or associate itself with banking systems of other countries into a conspiracy of wealth. Any decisions to allow associations of banking institutions worldwide must be fully under the control of government and must be seconded by the people. The size of banking firms must remain limited. In order to finance a large undertaking, many banks must provide for the financing; and special management companies must coordinate the efforts of many small corporations in order to start and complete huge construction projects. After the project is completed the special management team must be broken up entirely.

Huge corporations must also become a thing of the past. There are many ways in which the size of a corporation can be defined and controlled. Corporations are the real slaves, and we as people must control these slaves or they will overpower us as they have done up to now. Huge corporations give the owners and the directors too great a power. The power must remain in the people and not in institutions or the owners and operators of them.

International Banking, a Severe Public Danger

Huge banking institutions are a danger to society. The Federal Reserve Board must become an institution under the control of the people. This institution has run our nation completely bankrupt. Banking and government have betrayed the American people. Bankers and government are the enemies of the people. They must become eternal servants, or we will be their eternal slaves. It is a matter of all or nothing. There can be only one winner. The winner must be the people of a nation over government and the people of the world over the World Order.

Debt Currency

Since the adoption of the Federal Reserve System, this is how money is created and disbursed. Government needs money, corporations need money, and people need money. This need creates the basis of the printing of money. The US government issues a demand for, say, $50 billion to the Federal Reserve Bank. The bank issues a purchase order for that amount of money to be printed by the US Mint, which, I believe, is still part of the US government. The Federal Reserve Bank does not ask to print the interest charged on the money to be loaned out; therefore there will always be a shortage of currency, by about 6 to 10%. The United States prints the order and sends the money to the Federal Reserve Bank together with a bill for printing the money. Say the bill amounts to $1 million. Suddenly, now that the printed money is in possession of the Federal Reserve Bank, this $1,000,000 value turns into the face value of $50 billion. This is a multiplication in value of 50,000. Now the Federal Reserve Bank issues, say, $40 billion loan to the US government at, mind you, prime interest rate. The government now spends the money to wage all its illegal wars by purchasing war supplies from industry. Some of the money now finds its way into the hands of the people working in industry. They must pay some 66 percent of their wages back in overt and covert taxes to the state and federal taxing agencies, which all are employed by the Federal Reserve banking system. The rest of the money goes for people's living expenses and some savings. The people's savings are invested for down payments on cars, houses, appliances, vacations, etc. The loans they receive for these down payments are covert by $9 billion, which is in the hands of the bank. The bank keeps $1 billion in reserve. So the entire amount is spent. The $49,000,000,000 in debt run up by the nation now becomes "assets" of the bank by law that authorizes the bank to issue an order to print money in the amount of seven times this debt. So potentially, the banks can issue a purchase order of $50 billion x 7 = 350 billion or so to the US Mint that will cost the bank maybe some 3 to 5 million dollars. Every time this amount is disbursed and loaned out the last amount becomes the basis of currency 7 times as large as the previous amount spent. The banks control

the economy by their control of the interest rate and their own immense
wealth by charging interest on absolutely phony value of the currency that,
in reality, is based on the sweat of the working slaves. The fractional reserve
bank dollars really belong to the people because their efforts in commerce
make the paper script valuable.

People Must be in Control of the Currency

In order for a nation to be free, this control over the currency must be
in the control of the people and not in the control of immense, powerful
institutions. There is something so evilly wrong between bankers, government
and the condition of human nature that we secure our own doom by allowing
these conditions to continue. All minor and major changes in rules and
structure of banking must have the approval of the people.

The US government has not been granted the right to subcontract the
management of the currency to a bank. The debt incurred by society in
using the currency is based on the collateral of the nation's property, not the
banks. The banks charge interest on phony money; and because of the huge
amounts of currency [it is not money] loaned to government at interest, the
national debt, which was zero before the Federal Reserve System was enacted,
has become so great that the nation and all the states went bankrupt. The
national debt was, long ago, declared to be impossible to be paid off. President
Reagan declared the national debt to be structural to the institution of the
United States—not the US government, but to all the citizens of the United
States. This means that the people have been officially made responsible for
this debt. The condition of this debt being too great to be ever paid off makes
every citizen a piece of property of the Federal Reserve banking system. All
of it is fiction, and your government sold you, a man and a woman of flesh
and blood, for absolutely nothing to this fictitious Federal Reserve banking
institution. This banking institution is a private trust. It cannot be audited
by federal government who tried several times to audit this monster. The
Supreme Court aided the bank in its independence. The beneficiaries of this
trust of the Federal Reserve System are immensely wealthy.

I suspect that there must be two kinds of Supreme Court, because the
Constitutional Supreme Court decides issues arising in or among the states,
not in the District of Columbia. Does the Supreme Court have secret, dual
authority as well?

As you can see, your slavery was accomplished through deceit. This
identical process has played itself off in every nation in the world except in

many Islamic nations. Ours is a house of cards held in place by the police and armed forces of the world. All the police forces and all the armies in the world are the property of the IMF [International Monetary Fund]. When wars are fought, they are fought under the auspices of the IMF through the United Nations. Now the IMF wants to include the Islamic nations into its herd of slaves. That is the real reason for all the hostilities of the United States in Asia Minor. It uses our armed forces to corral these nations for the benefit of the IMF, while the American citizens must pay the bills of war.

Nation Towing Companies

The nations of the world are like nation-tow-truck companies for the international banking cartel, that are used to tow a nation back in line when payments are not made or when they are disobedient to the IMF, like a car that is towed away because payments are in arrears. The armies of the world are used to force any nation to obey the instructions given to its government by the international banking cartel. As can be seen, Iran was recently placed under severe financial sanctions by the United Nations because it refuses to stop the enrichment of nuclear fuel. This was done on orders of the IMF, the hidden owner of the United Nations. Iran is not allowed to produce nuclear fuel because that privilege has been given to other nations in the world. As soon as Iran walks the line by adopting a national bank under suzerainty of the IMF, it will be allowed to produce nuclear fuel—maybe!

Banking officials should be voted in by the people, directly. If they violate their oath of office, they must be very severally punished. Betrayal of duty by elected officials cannot be tolerated at all. There cannot be leniency for betraying the trust the people place in their elected officials. Why do I have the right to state these things? It is because of the intent of the Magna Charta and the original Constitution for government. Banking should be under mandate of a Constitution or charter given by the people. Banks must be under suspicion even before governments are placed under suspicion. Everything banks do involves crime.

"We, the People" Must Uphold the Constitution, Not Government

The American people were not prepared to deal properly with the conspiracy that led up to the Civil War. They had no idea that the war was a conspiracy against all the American people. They did not know what happened to them when the Fourteenth through Seventeenth amendments were forced on them. The people cannot trust their representatives because state representatives sold the people out as slaves to the federal government. The Constitution is created by "We, the people." "We, the people" must uphold constitutions. Therefore the people must be responsible for proposing and voting in amendments; and in defending and keeping safe their constitutions from infringements by government and banking officials.

Political Parties Are the Government; We Must Do Away With Them

We are now a democracy, and the people even vote the US senators into office. If America is a democracy and if people are the ones to vote in the senators, then the people, and not the political parties, must select these candidates as well as vote one of them into office as senator. Political parties, when viewed from the best angle we can give them, are already at least more than half a part of government. Let's face it; elected officials are executives according to the party they represent. They do not represent the people. The same goes for judges, representatives, and senators of the legislatures. After allegiance to the party, they have an allegiance to those who paid large sums to get them elected. The providers of these sums are party aligned. We, the people, in the rear of all this, are betrayed. The people are never given any consideration because the people are brainwashed, and the elected officials know that. The people are like cattle, and they are exploited like cattle. That is why we have the illegal and preposterous Sixteenth Amendment. It was voted in by the legislatures of state governments who are the enemies of the people, as declared in the Constitution. This amendment would not have applied to the people; but conspirator Supreme Court judges, some years prior to the proposed amendment, deliberately defined what an excise tax is and included in their verdict that personal wages are taxable as an excise tax. Even a moron can see that personal wages are not taxable as an excise, unless you agree that "we, the people," are slaves, commercial property on whose productivity an excise tax can be levied. The Sixteenth Amendment declares the people of America to be slaves because it includes all commercial activity as taxable without apportionment, and your elected officials sold you out as slaves [to the Bankers], who insist on receiving a profit from owning you. The IRS and all the state tax collection agencies collect revenue from you for the benefit of the bank, not for the government and not for the people. The bank pays the federal and state governments money as management agencies in its service. All the elected politicians receive money for betraying you.

Elected Officials Cannot Vote or Make Recommendations

We must prevent the politicians from messing with the entire voting process, and we must prevent the politicians from messing with the Constitution. As soon as a candidate is voted into office, he is an integral part of the government—government and the political parties are the enemies of the people and against which the people-enforced Constitution is supposed to be a safeguard.

Government Is the Bear Guarding the Honey Pot

The present arrangement is as stupid as telling a bear to guard an open jar of honey. The judicial departments of any state and federal court must be prevented from sitting in on questions concerning the Constitution. I can see that many of the originators of the Constitution were also enemies of the people. Any sane person, who would be truly interested in making a constitution that would keep government in its place, would never have formulated or agreed to this phony constitution. The US Constitution is a deceit and not a safeguard to keep government in its place. It is a propaganda scheme. It looks like a safeguard. That is why it put the people to sleep. It was a tool for government from the start, and you are now the dupe of this deceit perpetrated on you by the *majority* of the participants that created this Constitution. I believe that Jefferson was for the people. He always had a quarrel with those who supported banking when the Constitution was written and after that as well. I cannot help but be stunned by the betrayal these Americans in the service of banking perpetrated on a bunch of die-hard independence fighters holed up in Valley Forge during an entire winter without proper clothing, food, or shelter. They were used as slaves [they were not paid] because they were betrayed even then by their fellow Americans. Politicians are not statesmen; they are paid lackeys to the super rich. These kinds of betrayals are perpetrated on all of you all the time.

The conspirators to all these depravities used this tool, the Constitution, by taking baby steps in implementing its power for government. See, you have been betrayed from day one. It seems impossible for any people to fight for liberty because all your efforts will always be short-circuited by those you trust. They betray you for lucre/bribes or because they and their families are threatened by those who really wield power. As elected officials, the people's trust must override responsibility for their families. President Andrew Jackson set that example and set the precedent for all elected officials thereafter. That is why I have such great regard for President Andrew Jackson, who was wholly for the people and against the shenanigans of hoodlums in government and banking to the extent that it seriously harmed his loved ones.

People Are Free to Accuse Any Elected Official— Elected Officials Must Be Stripped of Protection

I declare that anybody can make accusations against government and its elected officials with impunity because the Constitution implies that we must enforce the Constitution against government. How can we possibly have believed that government can safeguard the Constitution for us? The Constitution is the only safeguard people have against officials placed in high positions of power. The official must prove his innocence by disproving all accusations against him from any person. Upon having been found guilty, there can be no other penalty but death. *Betrayal of the trust of office is betrayal of individual life and liberty.*

Corporations ought not to be able to make donations to candidates for office or to measures placed on the ballot. Corporations should be forbidden to lobby the government. The legislature may place representatives of a corporation on the stand to inquire about the feasibility of a plan proposed by someone in the legislature. Corporate representatives on the stand can only answer questions and cannot make volunteered suggestions that would lead the legislature in making a predetermined solution. Corporate representatives have no right to make suggestions. Corporations are not part of We, the people.

Elected Officials Lost Standing through Betrayal

The US government and the states governments have lost their standing to govern me. It must prove its standing to me by the original intent of compact forming the United States and by intent of the above-board intentions of the Constitution before it can ever make any accusation against me. People of America, it is time to wake up from your stupors. You are spiritually deluded and enslaved; you are deluded religiously; you are deluded as "we, the people of the United States"; and you are deluded in your understanding of your duties and rights in this nation. You have sunk deep. Repent! Reform your government according to the mandates of a newly organized spirit of communion [constitution] between the governments and the people. These present governments institutions have betrayed and abused the constitutions created for them. They have almost never abided by the dictates of their charters and wherever they could they have infringed on them by pseudo legal measures to overturn their own limits and made themselves powerful authorities over the people.

No Rights for Elected Officials

Elected officials cannot have the rights of free citizens. They hold positions of privilege at the hands of the people. In this standing of privilege they lose their rights. It has been proven that they cannot have equal rights with the people. Government officials, in their capacity of human beings, must always be considered to be deceiving the public. They act first in their own interest and the interest of the people is never considered.

The Power of the Jury

Rights are reserved for free citizens who must fend for themselves. Juries are responsible to ensure that laws enacted by our representatives are valid. Juries must have the power after hearing the case and the laws applied whether the laws are acceptable to the jury. The jury may dismiss, not only the case, but may throw out the law on which the case rested. If three different juries in three different cases reject a particular law, the law is declared void, and it must be deleted from the codebooks. The people are boss, not just in name but in power. Entities in or employed by government may not sit on jury panels.

If accusations are leveled against an elected official, the official must prove his innocence. The people do not have to prove this official's guilt. He occupies a position in public trust. He'd better make sure he lives up to that trust. This must be so if the people are serious in securing the freedom and rights for posterity. The American people have been selling their posterity short in just about all categories. You pay taxes and religious dues and perform public service duties, such as sitting on juries in faith of your power as juror, but your faith in public officials is always betrayed because you can only become juror in complete obedience to a crooked judge and a long series of government-established rules. In spite of all your contributions the country and our freedoms get curtailed all the time. What is the use of paying if you do not get the service? Fire the bums!

How is it possible that a corporation, a fiction, can accuse a person of flesh and blood? Corporations must rely on a lower kind of court than the common-law court where only people have standing. Government ought not to be able to reduce real people in status of a dependent fiction so that a person can be called into a court of equity where cases of fictions of law are handled. People are not fictions, corporations are. The people must repent of allowing government to place them in such subordinate and positions of enslavement.

Accusations against government by a real person can be made through the published written word or by making a formal complaint in court. Government cannot be a favored party in court as it is now. Government and its officials must always be under suspicion even if it is the plaintiff in court. Any person ought to be able to make a counterclaim on any claim the government makes against a person. Presently an accused in criminal court cannot make a counterclaim against an accusation from government. It is absurd. It is one powerful means to put all its enemies among the people in jail.

I once sued the US government. A hearing was set for a certain day and hour. *I was there on time. The government was absent. The court went so far as to send word to the representative of the government. Two hours later I asked the clerk of court what would have happened if I was two hours late. The clerk answered that I would have been found in default summarily. A representative of government finally showed up. The hearing started, and I withdrew my case by reason of partiality.*

Chapter 11

Religion Is Deceit in Action

Propaganda is Like Photography, the Negative is Black on White and the Positive is White on Black

Propaganda distorts reality, or really, it empowers a conspiracy against the people as if it is a program to benefit the people. You eat, live and breathe propaganda. The framers of the Constitution in aid of the bankers, and legislatures who adopted the democratically elected republican form of government have shown a complete track record of usurping ever more power from the people and at the same time depriving the people of their hard-earned wages by misappropriating great chunks of their wages as excise tax. "Excise" means that if you do not want to be taxed, you should not engage in this taxable form of activity. Government is suggesting you abstain from work and starve to escape the tax. The real fruit of the people extending some powers to the governing officials has ended up in reversed roles by making the people slaves that are taxed to the limit of tolerance of the people. If we cannot trust our governing authorities to represent us sincerely we cannot trust anything in the universe. Your elected governing officials will always, *always*, **always** be the enemy of the people. Government is a religion. Religion is spiritual deceit. You believe in the viability and honesty of it and it betrays you. All religious authority is blind as bats. They betray you because they pretend to know more than you. Their heads are even deeper in the mud than yours. My advice to parents; do not raise your children to be so gullible. Make them realize that they exist in a realm of evil where evil always disguises itself as some form of good. Make them natural enemies of government and of religion and make them extremely suspicious of anything that looks too good; it certainly is a trap that robs them of their liberty, freedom of responsible action, and their possessions. Propaganda is so clever that it causes humans and souls to see their environment as if it is a photographic negative. Everything is inverted. Nothing is as it truly is, and through such a mindset nothing makes sense.

Religion Manipulated Jesus as Friend into Our Enemy

Christians are phony. There is no other word for them [but so are the adherents of any other religion or creed]. The only supposed "good" thing that ever happened in this universe is Jesus. He is the only person who ever conveyed any truth to us. Yet, religion has misunderstood him and so adopted him in the role he reluctantly played to bring us that truth. There is not a single religion that understands Jesus because religion is based on the false belief that the Bible is pure truth. The Bible is a court in which a vicious battle rages over the possession of your soul and one of the parties uses any scheme of deceit to get the upper-hand in court. The crucial aspect of it is that you, as human being sit in judgment which good you shall have—true good or make-believe good. Those who have been given to understand Jesus' true message have not been active members of religion. They were raised from mere believers of lies to knowers of truth. They decided for reality, all others opt for existence in religious fiction.

So people who believe that the US government does a good job are also believers in fiction and also believe in Jehovah. Those who disagree with everything government does in its present position of power want reality back in their life. They cannot have it here in earth but they may choose reality in spirit and there they will have it in all abundance.

This is a universe of evil where brother betrays brother. I am being enslaved by my brothers and fellow citizens because their motives are selfish. One cannot guarantee each other's liberty with a selfish attitude. Selfishness always will betray trust. Betrayed trust always leads to enslavement. My enslaver is you, the reader of this book. You are your own enslaver also because you do not understand the meaning of liberty, and you do not know the meaning of love. Evil is the loveless enslaver. We are all guilty of it. An unarmed citizen is an enemy of the people. He is not willing to defend the Constitution against government. Government officials and bankers should fear with a deadly fear any person he sets his eyes on, but at this time he is protected and defended by the only people allowed weapons, utterly brainwashed police personnel and members of the armed forces. These people are spiritually blind as bats and are dedicated slaves of our worst enemies. Repent; come out of the establishments of the whores of Babylon who become rich by deceiving and enslaving the public.

The super rich [those that own mega billions] are crooks. They give themselves more privileges than they give the poor. They may be legally correct, but morally and ethically, they are dead wrong. No matter who claims to be god here in this earth, there is truly only one god on earth—the people. If not all the people are properly appreciated for their work, there is something wrong. Those in charge are too greedy for their own good. If your business is running well, reward those who made it possible—the people working there from the lowest to the highest. The lowest paid person should receive extra reward because, in general, he needs it the most; and he works the hardest and receives the most derogation. No business owner should start to build a big house for himself until he is satisfied that all his workers are well situated monetarily by his tax-free donations. By this I mean that the least of the workers has a well-built home, that he can well support his two children and wife, and that he can educate his children according to the wishes and/or the aptitude of the children. All this must come from the business owner—never from government. Government and the corporations are the true slaves and the generators of ideas and funds for all. The business owner can reap benefits from his business by allowing himself a decent interest on his investment in the business and by receiving an ample salary for the work he himself performs in the business. You can support a One World Order secretly as much as you want; if you cannot be fair, this order will become an enormous slave camp—and know that not one soul will escape the penalty of selfishness. Karma will prevent it.

Government Officials' Deceit Knows no Limit.

The Nazi regime and the communist Russian regime were established for specific reasons besides having enemies to fight. Both regimes had the input of the US government behind it. I can say that because Senator McFadden found out in the early 1930's that the US government was sending huge shipments of gold into Nazi Germany. McFadden spoke for two days straight to get the attention of Congress on this topic, and no one gave him an ear. He could not get anybody to second his proposals. From the things I read about the end of the Second World War, I can say that the holocaust was a propaganda fabrication in which the US government had a major hand. Why did it do that? You figure it out. The answer is close at hand.

Lenin set sail from the US to Russia with a ship's hold full of gold to conquer Russia by usurping the then-ongoing revolution there.

The Nazi regime was supposed to prove to the world that the white race is superior, and the communist regime was supposed to prove that the people were able to govern themselves. Both these regimes were put in place by the One World Order conspirators. Both regimes were put in place so that the One World Order could topple or destroy these regimes in order to insinuate that the premises on which these governments were based are wrong. Both regimes eventually toppled according to the plans of the One World Order conspirators. The hidden purposes of these two regimes were to convince [not to prove] to the world, through enormous propaganda schemes, that all races are equal and that people must be made to believe that people are not able to govern themselves. Both regimes had to fall because they were the antithesis of government the One World Order planned to erect—the capitalist-based, commercial, liberal socialist democratic form of government; and as you see, this is the only surviving form of government today, at least in Western society. This preferred method was perfected in the United States. It had the manner in which nations could be united under a single government down pat, and the socialist democracy was perfected to the satisfaction of the hidden conspirators. Propaganda instilled the false belief that interracial marriage was morally and ethically correct.

Nothing can be farther from the truth. Genesis 2 clearly states that Adam and his wife Eve upon their leave of the house of their father, paradise, shall be one wherever they end up. Woman is flesh and bone of Adam's flesh and bone. They must procreate in the race they belong to, just as other sets of Adam and Eve must be one in the race they belong to. It is a spiritual principle. One cannot be redeemed into positive spirit unless one is pure generation of Adam and Eve that came down together. You must truly observe this principle for the sake of your posterity. People that flaunt this principle are destroying their future offspring's chance of redemption and there cannot be any kind of forgiveness for that sin. It is an act that injures future beings that depend on your good judgment to preserve their spiritual rights. Since souls reincarnate, it will be their own souls that are condemned.

It so happens that a wealthy upper crust found out that *liberal democratic socialism* is the easiest and foolproof manner by which the masses can be enslaved and controlled—again the exact opposite of what everybody believed.

By the people agreeing to receive varied and uniform aids and benefits from government, the people admit that they are unable to provide for themselves. They thus admit that they cannot be free and need to be governed and controlled. By adopting liberalism, government can assure to themselves the proper level of unsocial behavior and criminality/disrespect for law and order so it can make itself visible as a beneficial type of government that has the interest of the people at heart. By forbidding certain drugs, government can have all kinds of propaganda schemes going by which it can prove that people are unreliable, vicious, and unpredictable. By keeping people in a mode of undefined fear and uncertainty, the government is solidly in the saddle.

By allowing people to vote, the people have the impression that they count; and in case people object to certain legal measures and actions of government, the government can claim that the people are responsible because they, supposedly, voted into office all the officials. Also, the people only get one chance to vote and be heard—at Election Day; and thereafter, they have no say in the running of government. Some setup!

The problem is that there is not one politician that keeps his word concerning the platform on which he ran, and secondly, the campaign issues have been very carefully selected by the secret group of power mongers before the election campaigns started. The issues introduced early on are the only issues continually debated, and these are brought into view in such a manner that the people can clearly see how they should vote, but which, secretly, is the preference of the hidden government and disadvantageous to the people. The cleverest trick is that both political positions are in the best interest of the hidden government, and ultimately against the interest of the people. Government think-tanks have made sure of that. Political campaigns are the most effective propaganda methods known to man. People's voting preferences are goaded by the election campaigns. The masses have no educated opinion at all and vote whatever or whoever seems popular.

Proposed bills before Congress, important to the hidden government [such as gun control] generally go through a shadow war where nobody seems to win, but in the end, the measure is adopted by a very slim majority. Sometimes a cruel outburst of mass murder by guns precedes the legislation. I have seen that happen too often to be mistaken. It is all cleverly choreographed shadow play. I say this all only to impress on you how evil this universe is that can allow such schemes to always, bear fruit. For money, people will commit crime or be a traitor. TV and mystery novels should have made that clear to you.

I am only expounding how crime and deceit in high places makes this world an unsuitable place to ascertain individual liberty. Freedom is withheld because you can only believe and not know the truth. Jesus said that *knowledge, not belief,* will set you free. You need to know the methods used to keep you in the dark spiritually and mentally. Everything, including your physical body, is just shadow play. The body was designed to suppress you. It does a soul very little good. So what would spiritual light without shadows be like? You would be in absolute liberty because no one would ever try to fool you. To me it seems that having a body anywhere would be a detriment. Having a body means you are imbued with a set of observation goggles to observe the virtual environment, making the soul blind to any other reality. So, what could we have in place of a body? The answer is pure spiritual awareness—reality!

Chapter 12

What Should Humanity Do With the Banking Institutions?

Egomaniacs

Up to now, bankers were essential for the progress of science and commerce. They were nothing but setups to deceive the people. The nineteenth and twentieth centuries were the bloodiest in the fighting of war in the last thousand years. The wars were planned; and they were planned to be the most destructive wars in order to collapse the people of the world's resistance to a One World Order. In order to learn the truth, we must forget everything we were taught in the schools and through the media. The entire communications scheme between government and the people is one-sided and carefully planned with the most cunning and malice aforethought.

I spent a little time on Hilton Head Island in South Carolina and spoke to the Gullah people. In spite of all the skills the slaves brought with them when they were freed, they fell back into bare bones tribal community. The land was basically shared by the greater population living in it who divided the land among the several villages on the island. They lived a more or less peaceful life without internal or external enemies. The strange thing is that they never used the pretty high-level skills they brought with them other than skills learned in agriculture. I believe that they felt that as long as the land was considered useless to sophisticated society, society would not encroach on their primitive sort of peace.

The only way I can explain it is that they lacked egomaniacal individual traits that will drive a community or a nation to accomplish progress and arts and technology. They just came out of slavery, and no one was going to tell them what to do anymore. They lived simple lives and were happy, and by keeping things primitive, greater society would continue to shun them. They had no enforced hierarchy, no chiefs who demanded status of wealth, allegiance, or pomp.

So we can conclude that egomaniacal traits in certain individuals drive the rest of the people to do things to raise them in wealth and, thus, in status far above the common folks. *Propaganda* of *status* is the oldest technology extant. It separates those with power from those that have been made powerless. Status is only an illusion that draws its power from people's fear of authority.

How Power Is Generated and Exploited Against the People

The power in the people is latent. This raw power becomes available through a scheme of deceit. A person or a small group can channel this power into a torrent by claiming that an alien group is out to destroy them. Under the threat of destruction, people will allow themselves to be placed under centralized authority. The society is thus organized for defense. If the authorities can continue to claim that a threat is imminent from a certain quarter for decades on end, this organized authority can consolidate its power and authority until the organization becomes permanent. This can be done in conspiracy with a make-believe enemy as the US government has done with the USSR. In this case, the authorities were so successful that after half a century of cold war with USSR, the international banking cartel, hidden behind the front of the United States, considers itself unopposed in the world. It was this phony tension that made a success of the United Nations. The citizens of the United States have been as effectively captured and channeled as water power, electrical power, and nuclear power. All it takes is human engineering and the techniques of propaganda well understood.

Those knowledgeable in the technology of capturing and channeling man's power can control and direct that power as a person driving a car can control steering, braking, and motor power by easy manipulation of control devices. The human being, thus, is nothing more than a captured and trained animal that an operator of human power can easily control and direct. All it takes is to feed the trained animal the proper signals through propaganda to make them do anything their drivers/managers have told them to do.

Human society is demeaning and has as little dignity as a mule drawing a cart loaded with its own manure. A mule is a cross between two good species of animals. Those with status and dignity are now putting out massive propaganda/orders to society to racially integrate the races as mules are. Humans will obey the dictates of propaganda and will thus obliterate their posterity. A cross between races has lost its right to be free because it has made the greatest error physical life can commit.

Racial integration can only happen by force of propaganda—a system of lies that makes the scenario of the deceit as if it has merit. Since physical creatures love the lie more than the truth, they can easily be taken advantage of. We see the result of such control of men power in the American Iraqi war effort.

The Iraqi War Is a Cock Fight

The Iraqi War is like a cock fight with trained attack animals attacking and subduing the people of another nation, which nation has not committed one crime against the people of the United States! President Bush was able to mobilize the Americans against the Iraqi people by simply telling them a lie. The lie was discovered two months before the US government attacked Iraq. The American people did not stop dead in their tracks of war but allowed Bush to start the war. This, in anyone's opinion, makes Bush the leader of a lynching party, drawing the entire American society with him into this crime of international terrorism. How can I retain my respect for Americans? They have proven to be mere trained animals without any power to resist their ranch masters. The American people have much to answer for. They are the most treacherous critters assembled into one herd in the world. They allowed Bush and his One World Order co-conspirators to score another goal against you by allowing them to merge you a little tighter into their One World Order.

As a nation, we have progress and technology pretty well by the tail. We can continue in this straight without super rich egomaniacs. The super rich are so dangerous to society that they will sacrifice tens of millions just to accomplish some minor goals in the execution of their plans for a One World Order. Since egomaniacs drive this plan, you can see that they will derive the maximum value from this plan.

How Can You Explain the Socialist Democracy?

How can you explain the drive for a socialist democratic state if the benefits will accrue to these egomaniacs? You can see that something is very wrong. A socialist democracy will only benefit the masters and will never benefit the slaves. It is a clever scheme to control the masses. The voting process never places the right person in control. The American voting process only places a choice of two candidates before the people, and these candidates have been very carefully screened by the super rich—either of the candidates is OK to them. You just placed another enemy of the people in office. Problem is that when these clowns are in office, you have to tolerate whatever measures they put in place. They say that you had a hand in it because you voted the person into office. Fellow Americans, know that you live on a huge slave farm, and unless you take control peacefully or by means of force, the people will never be free. We will continue to be working mules of the rich. They have cleverly constructed a seemingly rock-solid house, but it is merely a house built of cards; a gentle blow, and the whole thing comes apart. The problem is that they have psychiatrists that determine exactly how we, the people, will react and how to keep control. All we need to do is behave differently. Set aside our fascination with riches for a while so we can think clearly, take control, and set up society and the Constitution so that no maniacs can manipulate the people again.

Anyone Who Proposes a Justified War Must Hang Until Dead

The first rule we must adopt is that anyone or any group that proposes a war, for whatever reason, that the people agree to fight must be hanged when war is declared. This is the only way we can be sure that this war will not benefit the conspirators and their spokesmen. It is the brave thing to do. When war is started the person(s) who proposed the war should be the first to die as a declaration of his/their sincerity and as meaningful support for the armed forces that the cause of war is worth it.

I will accept this fate if the people will be absolutely certain that they want to restore liberty by the means I herewith propose and actually accomplish it. Death is much more preferable than submission to slavery. Read the abundant material the founding fathers left us about such rock-solid determination. It was this kind of determination on which the United States was founded. These documents are included in a reference to a website in the appendix.

This, however, must be a worldwide movement because the rich must not be given any place to hide. It must be done in a much more clever way than the French Revolution. The French did one thing right—they killed all the rich in their country. Any rich person, resisting this plan must be utterly dispossessed and placed under arrest and tried for treason. This thing must be brought about in the most peaceful manner. Let them surrender themselves and be a material part in the process of reducing their wealth to the amount allowed. After the revolution, all the institutions will continue exactly as they have been run before, but now, the benefits accrue to the people as a whole and not to the very few. Everybody can accumulate riches up to $250 million, and no rich person will be in want for anything. It is possible to prevent further efforts of conspiracy of a few to take over the world. All people who have reached $250 million in possessions, including all their commercial holdings and their contacts must be placed under surveillance of agencies under control of such people. These agencies are also constantly under the scrutiny of other institutions. When a conspirator is found guilty, only death will repay such betrayal of the people. Anybody who aids the rich must be hanged with their masters. It is much better to be safe than sorry. Do not give the super-rich a place to hide. It is thus better when you are rich to keep your riches below the maximum amount allowed.

It Is a Crime to Be Super Rich

I just do not trust people that own too much riches. Their riches are never used for good. We need a cultural revolution, and it must begin with all the superrich and the way banking institutions are run and controlled. It must become unacceptable for them to hang on to such riches. Incorporated institutions also cannot retain any more funds than is necessary to run their operations. Operating budgets must be surrendered each year to the people. The banks then will keep track of the funds they use, collect and disburse. There will no longer be hoards of funds in the ownership or under the control of one person, one race, a religion, or a group of people. It is ridiculous for the rich to continue to adversely control the lives of those at the bottom of the standard of living scale. They will not any longer use their funds for secret purposes against the well-being of the people of the world. No race or group of people will force their will on the commonwealth of all the people in the future. The poor must come first. They must be trained and educated so they can earn a more than sufficient living. All that needs to be done is to limit the power and riches anyone can have and continue just as before, but with altered Constitutions and with the proper safeguards that no person or a clique of persons can conspire to enslave the people. The independent chief of the armed forces' first duty is to insure that government operates completely within the intent of the communion between the people and its servants, the incorporated institutions.

Punishment for True Crimes Must Be Absolute

The safeguards must be absolute, and the penalties for trespass must be absolute. It is all so easily done if only the people have the guts to get things straightened out. It would only take a couple of months; just as long as it took to dissolve that terrible USSR. Just take the secret plans, pour out the contents, and refill it with the plans for the execution of a world order under the control of a people-controlled United Nations.

George Bernard Shaw stated, *"We are made wise not by the recollection of our past, but by the responsibility of our future."* This kind of wisdom has and will forever lead us again into slavery. I can see that Shaw's reputation is not based on his personal wisdom. This statement shows utter disrespect for true wisdom and shows that he has none. It is a statement for the idiots amongst us. We are made wise not only by the lessons learned from the past but also by their proper incorporation toward our responsibility of the future.

The US government showed us how to deal with the rich. It burned down all the mansions of the rich in the South after the Civil War and confiscated their wealth. It is time we followed their example with respect to the criminally rich in the world. They can surrender first or they will have all their possessions confiscated and their lives forfeited.

International Banks Run the World—That Must Stop

In the Civil War, both sides treated their prisoners in the most inhumane manner. Most people taken prisoner died within a month after capture. The camps were infested with deadly diseases, and no one cared. Americans did these things to Americans. They had no excuse to be inhumane. Military inhumanity comes down from the top. Discipline is disciple. The top was government and bankers united with the states in the North. The North had no excuse. The bankers were feeding government money in steady streams. The South was throttled in any way possible. The navy saw to that. Even England, to whom the South was more befriended than to the North, did not help the South with naval support. The English navy was still the best and strongest in the world. The reason for their standoff attitude—the English Crown and London City were enslaved to the bankers as well.

What I want to bring forward is that people cannot be entrusted with the care of other people, and bankers are a group of creatures, way below the level of even the toughest criminal. Today, bankers collect taxes, not government. Government is just their slave to mete out punishment if they do not obey the IRS and state tax institutions. All the major taxing authorities, those that collect income tax, work for the bankers because the governments and all the state governments are bankrupt by some phony scheme in the establishment of money and ownership of banks. Bankers' tax collection agencies do not forgive. If you owe back taxes to them, they will enforce a 100 percent interest per year until you pay—never mind if you do not have the ability to pay even the dollar. If, for some reason, you were able to make a couple of trillion dollars, they would collect the entire amount if you have not succumbed to their rules. Liberty, in the environment of international bankers, does not exist. If you value liberty, you must get rid of the bankers. Bankers to the people of a nation are like the Lyme disease. You do not know for a long time that you are infested by it. You feel lousy, you have no energy, and when you get energy, it is drained away. Nothing in the body works properly, and the source of the malady remains unknown. That is banking control over humanity to the teeth.

A Professor Instructs a Group of Alumni About How to Enjoy Life

If you want justice and peace on earth, listen to what the professor had to say to the alumni below. It took another twenty years for the professor to teach them the final lesson. Make sure that you learn this lesson. Immature attitudes cannot longer be tolerated. I got this off the Internet.

A group of alumni, well established in their careers, got together to visit their old university professor. The conversation soon turned to complaints about stress in work and life.

Offering his guests coffee, the professor went to the kitchen and returned with a large pot of coffee and an assortment of cups—porcelain, plastic, glass, crystal, some plain looking, some expensive, and some exquisite. He told them to help themselves. After all his ex-students had a cup of coffee in hand, the professor said, "You notice that all the nice-looking, expensive cups are taken up, leaving behind the plain and cheap ones. It is normal for you to want only the best; and that is the source of your problems and stress. Be assured that the cup itself adds no quality to the coffee. In most cases, it's just more expensive. What all of you really wanted was coffee, not the cup, but you *consciously* went for the best cups and then began eyeing each other's cup.

"Life is the coffee. The jobs, houses, cars, things, money, and position in society are the cups. They are just used to hold and contain life. The type of cup we have does not define nor change the quality of life we live. Sometimes, by concentrating only on the cup, we fail to enjoy the coffee. God brews the coffee, not the cups. Enjoy your coffee. Being happy doesn't mean everything is perfect. It means you've decided to see beyond the imperfections [mere inconsequentials]."

Whoever wrote this is clever. He made you see your foolishness and then managed to stick your head back in the mud. If imperfections concern our liberty, these must be cut out and set straight. In matters of imperfections in the definition and conditions of liberty for the people, we are dealing with a substance like yeast. If you do not bother to remove the imperfections, the imperfections will infest and corrupt the entire lump [liberty] so that liberty has disappeared before you can look at what really has happened.

Bankers have infested life and our liberty completely with unnecessary obligations. Presently, liberty is nonexistent. The people are way too careless in their control of government. You see, voting did not do us any good—scrutiny, suspicion, and investigation and an armed, public solidarity against wrong government actions would have safeguarded our liberties much better than ignorant voting, but propaganda kept us asleep. And the media does not inform us of the evil conspiracies in very high places. You can see that police and the armed forces cannot be placed under the control of those who make the laws. Police and armed forces are there, mainly, to keep government in its place. Making the armed forces subject to government must be the greatest asinine thing a free people can do. The people need police and the armed forces to keep government under control.

People versus Animals

People will never learn. They are dumber than animals. Animals always scrutinize their environment to make sure there are no snares and hidden traps, and these careful creatures still fall prey to predators. In society, *everybody* is born a sucker because people are lazy, and they love to believe a lie. The whole world votes, and yet the people of all nations are enslaved by the bankers—maybe that tells you something about voting.

Banks' Power Base Inside the Conference Composing the Constitution in 1792

If you read the books and essays written about events during and shortly before the independence war, you can see that the nation had big troubles with the banking cartel in formulating the Constitution. Jefferson was the head of a group that wanted to protect liberty by ensuring state sovereignty. Mr. Hamilton was the spokesperson for the banking cartel. He was Jefferson's most important enemy. The yeast of banking started to corrupt the whole lump after the Constitution was adopted. As early as 1815, the bankers were in complete control of US finance. Such things happen by force and corruption. Banking has always been the people's worst enemy. It is about time humanity gets rid of private banking for ever. It can be done. In many states, the manufacture and sales of liquor is under the jurisdiction of the state. It always used to be a private function. If commerce in liquor can be in government control, so can banking. The effects of private banking institutions and finance are much worse than drugs, liquor and heroin. The bribes banks offer and disburse addict corrupt officials in government; bribes are a drug to make politicians and other government bureaucrats ignore their positions of trust to the people.

The world of finance is a government function. The Constitution empowered this government to regulate the supply of money. Government has illegally subcontracted this function to the only institution that cannot be trusted with matters of public finance—international bankers. Financial matters must be completely in the control of the people through their government, and government must be shackled and harnessed so that it is a beast of burden and not a wild fire-spitting dragon. International private banking must, on a worldwide basis, be thrown out of its seat of control of government finance. Our liberty cannot be entrusted with a private banking concern that owns or controls our national banking affairs. The interest paid to private banking on the sums that government irresponsibly loans from them will always bankrupt any government and enslave the people they are supposed to serve. In comparison to influential international banking officials, Al Capone was a little bully playing in the sandbox.

An Independent Judiciary

Judges should not be appointed by the executive branch. Judges should appoint their own. They must be forbidden to align themselves with any political or ideological group. The people cannot allow them to dispense justice through politically filtered consciences. People must be able to vote any judge out of office when a judge is found to betray the trust of his office and the judicial department is not doing anything about the matter. The entire consortium of judges should then be voted out of office.

Independent Media

No race or group of people can be allowed to gain control of the media, and no state or nation can be forced or coerced to join a greater union of states or nations. One cannot deliberately ostracize a state or a nation that has chosen to remain independent. One cannot even attempt to do so through a court proceeding. To force another to join a confederacy is proof of criminal intent and suppression. An assembly such as the United Nations may be acceptable to many nations, but it may not be acceptable to other nations or people because one would again be faced with a situation like the Civil War in the United States. However, if a non-aligned nation starts to coerce another nation that is part of the United Nations, then the UN will form a consolidated front against that nation. If a media firm is found to be involved in a propaganda scheme, the firm must be put out of business entirely and the chief offer put to death.

The Differences That Led to the Civil War Should Have Been Peacefully Resolved

Concerning the Civil War, the conflict between north and south should have been peacefully resolved to allow the southern states to secede. One could thereafter have continued negotiations to find solutions to bridge the differences in policy between the nations. Another union between two unions of states could then have been accomplished, which union could be maintained as two entities or the states could have merged again into a full union of states. Intelligent people could have easily arrived at this solution. That this did not happen is due to deliberate political aggression of US government against the southern states; and this was done for entirely different reasons than what the people were made to believe.

The civil war was not just a dispute between the North and the South; it was a conspiracy against the freedom of all the people. It was an unconstitutional war between US government and the South. US government was able to align the North to its filthy plans by bribes from banking.

US government, the sovereign, won the war because it had control of the entire navy, which in truth belonged to US government, the servant [without which, the South would have won the war]. The North had conspired with the world's banking establishment to deprive *all* the states of their sovereign independence. Such conspiracies can only happen through evil intent of those who control the supply of money. Banking ought not to have such a stranglehold on the economy and welfare of any group of people, nation, or union.

The international banking cartel is guilty of such manipulation, and therefore, they must be placed under the control of the United Nations. They may not operate independently ever again, and the United Nations' Constitution must be revamped to make absolutely sure that no institution or conspiracy can do what the banking institutions have done in the nineteenth, twentieth, and twenty-first centuries to the entire world. There is no doubt that the banking institutions had their hand in all the wars since, and including also, the war of 1812 and the Civil War. Control of all the national banks in the world must be placed in the governments of the world. The world banking institutions and their affiliates must be placed under the jurisdiction and control of the United Nations. Rich people found guilty of manipulating their wealth against the welfare of the people must be disenfranchised altogether and hung until dead. They have proven to be unable to be just and content with their wealth. Personally, I will never trust any government and especially not any big financial institution. By the mere size of their operations, they become subject to temptations that are secret, unholy, and that encroaches on the sovereign powers of the people.

Strong Control over Real Criminals

There is another group of superego maniacs: malicious criminals. They are so self-centered that they cannot consider anybody but themselves. They are sneaky sinister characters that make life impossible on the local scene. They are like animals disguised in human bodies. The human body is their camouflage to fit amongst ordinary people and to rip them off one way or another. This is a group of people that will continue to make the universe hell. They are the local hoodlums and small time criminals that make it unsafe for people in their neighborhoods. Convicted criminals proven to make our neighborhoods unsafe must be hung. No one has use for them, and if they had any intentions of repenting of their life style they should have done that before they were apprehended. Once caught and duly convicted they should be put to death immediately. Presently, government allows them back on the street so that they can claim to be forgiving, but the truth is they want them back on the street so that government can make itself visible.

I begin to see more and more reasons for many of the social laws and rules Jehovah set up for the nation of Israel. Jehovah wanted obedience because he wanted to end up with a universe where all would operate as if truth was everywhere. He wanted to duplicate reality from which this fiction was extracted. The imperfections of fiction did not allow for such a reality to develop. That, more than anything else, made Jehovah angry and disappointed. But face it; one can never create reality from a fiction. As Jesus said, "Things of spirit [reality] are spirit, and things of flesh are flesh", and flesh is fiction.

Human Beings Are Worse Than Animals

Humanity is extremely hard pressed to have peace on this globe. The worst problem is that nobody seems to be willing to consider his neighbor. Without law, the human being, in general, is a cruel and vicious animal—no, the human being is much worse than animals. Animals have not been granted a social conscience. I cannot understand that people want to be this way. If I was rich, I would never expose my animal nature in such a blatant way—I could not even show this nature if I was poor. Humanity has much to answer for, and it has no answer because it has no excuse.

Discipline Children

Treat a child with an upbringing of discipline and personal respect in the home. Then, when grown-up, treat it as a worthy person and it will generally conform to a peaceful existence, especially if the person can establish himself in comfort and dignity.

The liberal attitude of treating children enforced by law has created monsters of them. It has proven to be a failure. Liberals have lost the capacity to act in a peaceful social setting. Their attitude is that anything goes. Women have been granted equal rights; and as a consequence, far too many of them are worse than sluts—they have no social responsibility and no subdued elegance. With liberty comes responsibility. If responsibility is not there, liberty will lead to chaos and depravity. Misused liberty is a crime against humanity, and it drives the criminal nature in men to pursue these sluts. You can see that government loves this setting of brutal criminality because this setting gives lots of exposure to government to come across as the institution that does "good" by controlling something they caused in the first place. The more public exposure it can get for doing "good," the more it feels justified to garner more power to itself at the cost of one's earnings, and liberty and peace in society. The real brute, again, is government that forces these things on us for its own benefit.

Chapter 13

The People's Path into Slavery

Every government decision is influenced by bankers' bribes to corrupted elected officials. You can actually follow all the strategic steps the conspirators had to take for the banks to own this nation and to be able to tax and collect the tax directly from the people.

1. Banking was involved in creating the Constitution. How do I know? Before the Constitution, the national government had a currency based on a unit called continental. It was issued by the Continental Congress to finance the Revolutionary War. It was a worthless piece of paper. Nobody accepted it as currency. After the Constitution came the dollar. Its value was based on the silver Spanish piece of eight, and paper money, backed by gold and silver. Suddenly, after the Constitution was adopted, there appeared currency backed by value. Where did the value suddenly come from? It was not there before the Constitution! The banks provided it against interest and for political considerations. That tells us that the banks got a foothold of influence in this Constitution from the start and thus in the running of the US government. Banks never give something of value without making an enormous profit.

    Because of tainted wording in the Constitution, government was able to modify the original Constitution. [The original Constitution had clauses that looked solid but had loopholes that allowed government to start usurping power.] The founding fathers were concerned about the unrestrained control of the money supply. One thing they all agreed upon was the limitation on the issuance of money. How many of you even know that Thomas Jefferson warned of the damage that would be caused if the people assigned control of the money supply to the banking sector? He said in 1791, "*I believe that banking institutions are more dangerous to our liberties than standing armies.* **Already they have raised up a money aristocracy that has set the government at defiance.** *This issuing power should be taken from the banks and restored to the people to whom it properly belongs. If the American people ever allow private banks to control the issue of currency, first by inflation, then by deflation, the banks and corporations that will grow up around them will deprive the people of all property until their children will wake up homeless on the continent their fathers conquered. I hope we shall crush in its birth the aristocracy of the moneyed corporations which already dare to challenge our Government to a trial of strength and bid defiance to the laws of our country*". Nobody listened to Thomas. Many lined their pockets with bank bribes even before they entered the conference. What Thomas wrote then is prophesy because that is exactly what happened. We, the people cannot go on in this manner.

2. The conspirators had to make all business subject to government control, and they had to make citizen workers subject to government. [The laws of limited liability through government licensed incorporation of business ventures took care of that in the late 1830s and the 1840s.] Thomas Jefferson saw this one coming too.

3. They had to remove sovereign status from the states and liberty from the people. [The Civil War accomplished this together with a long list of other objectives]

4. Next, authority over the state citizens had to be transferred from state to federal government. [The Eleventh to Fifteenth Amendments took care of that.]

5. The international bankers had to have a "national bank" in place. [From the inception of the Constitution to the establishment of the Federal Reserve Act of 1913, the bankers pushed for a national bank. They got a permanent foothold in government through the Civil War hostilities and were settled comfortably in 1913. They are masters at taking baby steps so no one generation can follow their tracks. Not 16 years later we had our first Federal Reserve Bank instigated economic crash by withholding necessary loans to the private sector. Since then this trick has been used over and again.]

6. A way had to be found to make taxation of personal wages possible as a standard procedure. The Supreme Court in 1895 declared that wages are an excise, thus an indirect tax. The average man, not having much savvy in legislation and law were condemned to be slaves.

7. Federal corporate taxes needed to be levied to support their card-blanch, unlimited federal loans with the Federal Reserve Bank. The federal Corporate Income Tax Act was adopted into law at the end of this first decade of the twentieth century.

8. A way had to be found to take the states legislatures out of the control of US Congress. The Seventeenth Amendment changed the US from a republican to a democratic form of government. It was really a phony amendment because the people were already indentured to the federal government, but it took care of removing states' influence from the US Congress. [Henceforth, the states were without sovereign status and were thus merely provinces of the federal government.] It is noteworthy that even though state influence was removed from US government, amendments were still adopted through the power vested in states by the Constitution. There is not a single amendment that was placed before the people for vote. This is too fishy for words.

Public documentation leading up to this amendment are completely contrary to what really happened. Federal government in conjunction with the banks bribed certain states legislatures to derail the manner in which some states appoint their senators. They kept the appointments of senators in disorder for several decades and so forced the amendment to be adopted. Now, we do not even have a supervising body keeping track of federal legislation, because the people have no power whatever. The banks insisted that states were removed from control over federal government, so they bribed some legislators in state assemblies to derail the appointment of their states' senators. Henceforth federal government and the banks had eradicated all interference from the states legislatures in the regulation of government. The federal government was nationally in full control and suddenly had wings to soar unhindered by any trammels. It is done through shadow play.

9. The 16th amendment delineating income tax matters was adopted into law on recommendation of President Taft in 1909.

10. The banking institution in Washington had to be imbued with authority over the creation of a national currency based on national and private debt. It also needed to find a way for US government to

obtain unlimited credit from this banking institution. They had to
find a way to allow the federal government to quietly go bankrupt.
This was accomplished through the Federal Reserve Act in 1913.
It arranged for government to have access to unlimited amounts of
bank credit, and it arranged that the bank could collect taxes for
government in order for government to have unlimited access to
loaned finances. The bank, through its newly incorporated agency,
the IRS, now collects the taxes, and then credits government with
the collections, minus interest due. The year 1913 was a very dark
year for liberty in the United States. That year America acquired a
new spirit, International Banks, and a new god, the United States of
America. States are not states any more so the appellation United States
is a misnomer. The people of America, physically and spiritually, are
totally dumb and numb. Since that year, the United States of America
had money to burn to engage itself in all sorts of military aggression
disguised under the label of defending liberty and democracy. I guess
that 75% of all federal taxes collected were, and are used to fuse
the states into a blanket of federally controlled regions and for the
establishment of the One World Order.

11. A federal personal income tax was needed to collect taxes from the
    serfs, corporations and the human masses. [This was accomplished
    through the personal, Federal Income Tax Act of 1913. It was based
    on the precedence of the prior Brushaber Supreme Court decision.

12. A tax-collecting agency was also established in 1913, and soon after
    the name was changed to the now-familiar Internal Revenue Service.
    It is a private institution.

13. A way had to be found to transfer the assets of the United States to
    the banking institution, to create an accounting system of the banks
    inventory of assets, and to draw the assets of all the states under the
    control of the bank. [In the early 1930s, the US government went
    bankrupt in order to transfer its assets to the bank. The bank created
    the financial crash in 1929 by withholding loans from business. The
    major depression, caused by the bank's refusal to provide needed
    loans to business, bankrupted many businesses and threw millions
    of people out of work and into severe privations of existence, which
    led to the creation of an accounting system so that each citizen and
    each corporation became an item in the bookkeeping records of the
    banks. And this system was hidden from its true purpose by calling
    it the Social Security System.] Congress can change the original rules

whenever it wants. It can do away with social security benefit as it is structured now and leave the identification number in place; and sooner or later it will.

14. A way had to be found to allow government to run up huge amounts of debts. [This was accomplished through the World Wars and many other regional wars under the cloaks of fighting communism, drug smuggling and terrorism.]

15. From the 'New Deal' flowed The National Recovery Act. To make the nation solvent again, all the assets of the states were declared collateral for US government so federal government could continue its binge of increasing the national debt as quickly as possible.

16. In the meantime, Hitler was being trained and helped to get into the seat of absolute power in Germany, because he was to help accomplish many items on the ever-expanding agenda of the conspirators to create a One World Order. One such item was to start collecting an income tax from all US citizens/slaves, using the newly created Social Security number. In 1942, the US started a tax to be levied against all corporations, state and federal, and all private citizens, state and federal, under the guise of the Victory [income] Tax, but deliberately created by the banks to win the war against the [bank-supported] Nazi regime. By law this tax was to last for only two years. Americans have never stopped paying that tax because the IRS, using its new inventory tool—the Social Security number, did not allow them not to pay that tax. The reason obviously was to make the people pay for the overdrawn war account created by US government and to fund the supposed cold war efforts against communism. [Adolf Hitler's solitary imprisonment in a castle in Germany prior to the war was to train him for his upcoming role as dictator over Germany as a servant of the One World Order.]

17. At the close of the Second World War, the United Nations was formed under the severe international prodding and financial support of US government [your tax dollars at work].

18. Many more choreographed wars were fought by the US government under the auspices of the international banking consortium through the banker-controlled United Nations for the purpose of creating the so-long-dreamed of One World Order and to rapidly increase the size of the US national debt. The people of the United States were set up, over and over again; against other nations the way owners of fighting cocks enrage their fowl to fight each other in the ring. These wars

were fought under the auspices of the United Nations and always were under the control of the UN Security Counsel that, by UN charter, is always under the direction of a Russian general.

19. In the fall of 1995, I heard a news item on TV that announced that Congress had declared the nation bankrupt. In consequence, all national forests were transferred to the bank. Herewith, the banks had full guardianship and control over all property, actions, and measures of the US government that now included all the states.

20. The trouble in Middle East between the newly formed state of Israel and the surrounding Arab countries, and the US wars against the Arabs are under the auspices and orders of the international banking consortium. These wars have nothing to do with the American people, but somehow the US government is always aligned with Israel, to whom it gives billions of dollars in aid.

I have given you a summary of how your government betrayed you into slavery to some super rich conspirators. It has accomplished its goals at the price of wholesale destruction of nations and the death of hundreds of millions of people around the world, with the US government as the major bloodhound for the bankers.

This ancient conspiracy to create a One World Order is spiritually induced, as all the players in the physical field are born and die over time; new ones are accepted and the conspiracy marches on in secret from generation to generation. Hebrews 11:1 can thus be said to apply to this banking conspiracy. It shows that even the most powerful human beings are just puppets in the hands of a secret, unseen negative spirit.

Whatever is hidden behind one or more layers of camouflage, or false fronts that control important aspects of your life can be considered negative spirit because way in back of all the camouflage resides the spiritual hierarchy responsible for the effective control enforced on you and all society. This One World Order conspiracy was formed spiritually because the major players hid themselves behind a front of well-paid servant-hoodlum government officials who in turn hid behind a Constitution created by "We, the people?, and it seems that the daemons hide behind a front of a set of conspiring super rich people. It may very well be that major corporations have patron daemons that watch over them and exploit them as bait—seductions that ensnare souls. The more the people see these corporations as real and meaningful the deeper they slide into the trap. The more deceit a person swallows, the more the person is anchored in the physical universe. You can see that the baits in the many cone sections in the spiritual trap are virtual environments. Such bait based on deceit causes the soul to go deeper into its coma. The souls that succumb to the seductions of riches, status, importance, and prestige that are available in corporate environments are thus set up for a move deeper into the trap in their drive to seek meaning and reality in absolute fiction. They become more helplessly deceived. Jesus said the rich gain nothing spiritually; they remain lost.

Explanation of the Spiritual Trap

Let me explain some words in the above paragraph. I mentioned that the universe is a trap, a trap that I have represented to consist of many cone sections. Figure 11, page 396, in between the covers of this book is a graphic representation of this trap. This trap has many cones in it. This kind of trap is used in Europe to catch eel. I saw the use of the same kind of trap in Maine to catch alewives, a variety of baby eel. Eel, like snakes like to hug to the ground. Even, when in the trap they like to move to the river bottom, thus to the outside of the trap surface, and away from the opening in the truncated cone. They, therefore, never find back the open end of the cone located in the center through which they entered the present cone section. Since the surfaces of the cone themselves prevent them from leaving they continue on into the deeper section and immediately swim to the bottom of the net, and so find themselves a cone section deeper in the net, and so on.

Amazingly the spiritual trap works exactly like that. Souls will seek out ever more fiction so they cling to the outside net surfaces where fictional realities are perceived, and cannot see the center-openings in the cones that would, if a soul follows the centerline of the trap, would lead him straight out of the trap into utter reality and liberty. We, as souls, are not one bit smarter than the eel. Therefore souls that do not seek spiritual help through the Comforter will, over time, be the very same eels caught in this physical net as used to catch eel. The entire spiritual trap is the universe.

In the case of soul entrapment, the section opening to a spiritually, higher section is hidden. It is hidden from physical creature awareness because anything spiritual is hidden from physical awareness. The baits in lower sections of the trap change from of mental, and sensational baits higher in the trap to more physically gratifying baits deeper in the trap, until the cone sections reserved for species of animals is reached.

The cone sections inside this trap are serious business. If there were no sections in the trap all creatures would be of one species. The cone sections differentiate the many species of physical life from each other, and each section has a different daemon in charge. The cone sections in the trap hold the entire specie-hierarchy in place. Each species exist in its own virtual environment, through a spiritually-accepted belief system.

How to Get the Most of Being Trapped Forever

For those who want to, or must encounter their destiny inside the universe [the spiritual trap], there, also, seems to be no escape from the new layer of spirit the bankers placed us in, but there is one. The bankers fear you; that is why they accomplished their plans in secret. Against well-informed and alert communities of people in the world, they have no power but their lucre. You, as people, and not as soldiers, police persons, and servants in the pay of these conspirators, can forego receiving currency long enough to set the world straight, just as the patriots in Valley Forge did. You will be reimbursed a hundredfold when matters have been set straight. Don't give these super-rich conspirators a place to hide. After they have disgorged their wealth, their wealth should be used as a national or UN asset. The currency based on debt must be abolished, unless it can be redesigned so that no private institution or group of people unduly benefits from such a currency. After that, the world simply returns to business as usual, using the exact same business practices as before but with some powerful changes in the way the constitutions for governments are written and with strict duties for all titles of nobility to keep government's and banks' hands tied as servants to the people forever.

Better yet, seek the way out of the seemingly inescapable trap with the help of the Comforter and reenter true reality where such shenanigans are impossible. There you will always be free and will always be at cause. There you will be respected for your full worth, always, without cost or sorrow to you or anyone else.

I can now see why Jesus insisted on acquiring an immortal physical body. When absolutely needed he can step in and take control over the spiritual computer. The spiritual computer is Jehovah's brain, and we souls are wired into it spiritually and projected into his body, the physical universe, as biological creatures. As cells in a human body replenish and die, so human creatures as cells in his body multiply and die. Jehovah is nothing without us, deceived souls.

The Universe and Its Purpose

Recently we were looking through a mail-order catalog and saw this DVD for sale, *Journey toward Creation* [Questar, Inc, P.O. Box 11345, Chicago, IL 60611-0345], toward the moment in the history of the universe when light came into being; or better phrased, darkness [disguised as light] came into being that hid the real light of truth. I had a notion that it might corroborate my view of creation of the physical universe. The video proves beyond a doubt that the entire universe is a created thing based on a specific design for a specific purpose; to position planet Earth as a habitat for physical life.

After viewing the Astronomy-based and science-inspired video, I agree with their conclusion. The possibility of human life as an accidental development is much smaller than $1/10^{256}$. This is a number so incredibly small that it proves that the universe was designed by a super intelligence to create a place of being for physical life and human life in particular. Does not Genesis 3:1 say, "Now, the Serpent was the most cunning animal that the Lord god has made"? Did not Jesus agree that he was Lord? It was god the son, who created the possibility of the universe as habitat for human life, and it was this serpent that saw the possibility and found a way to make this possibility a reality. That possibility could only exist in fiction. He made this fiction a reality in the minds of the creatures Adam and Woman by making the extant reality of paradise a hoax to them by believing his lie. Since reality of paradise became a hoax they could not be there anymore. One cannot believe that true reality is fiction [a hoax] and yet remain in reality. Thus they were drawn in by the Serpent in creating a new, spiritually envisioned habitat based on consequent lies they believed.

Physical creation and time came into existence only after the plan was revealed and understood by these complex structures of souls in Adam and Woman. Their bodies now lie comatose in paradise, and their independent cells dreamed up the universe in concord with the master plan given them by Jehovah. This proves another idea of mine; that time is the progression of lies essential to corroborate the first lie. As long as the progression of the scheme of lies continues, time in the universe continues. The progression of the scheme of deceit is time.

The universe was created to fashion an earthly habitat for humans. Christ's coming in dual roles, his authoritative manner of preaching, his authoritative stance before Pilate that led to his death, the manner in which his message was received and interpreted by Christendom and, finally, the right understanding of Christ's message by me were all necessary, design-wise, in order to reveal the nature of the true god, the father, to me, and to us all. The purpose of all creation is to reveal the true nature of the true father to the souls of human creatures, and through these souls to all creatures trapped in earth. Two thousand years of existence and progression of science and technology were also vital for the author to understand Christ's message and for that understanding to be transformed in printed form of this book. This progression of science and technology were prophesized in the book of Daniel: *"But you, Daniel, shut up the words, and seal the book until the time of the end; many shall run to and fro, **and knowledge shall increase.**"*

The contemplation of the *"**big bang**"* that started the universe leads us back to the moment the first set of Adam and Woman believed a lie, were isolated from paradise, and had to cooperate with the Serpent to create another habitat, so that they could express an alternate means of being. Let's face it, if Adam and Woman had awareness in paradise, there would be no necessity for earth and human life. We would recognize ourselves as living souls and not as physical beings who have no notion of what their purpose is and what their relationship to the greater scheme in reality is. There would be no purpose for humans to feel so lost and abandoned by spirit.

An Absolute Barrier between Reality and the Virtual Physical Environment

We were made to be ignorant and lost, so that we could search and discover truth—truth of the goodness of our true father. Human existence is a learning program that leads to the understanding of true reality, our spiritual father and our true home. As virgin spiritual entities created in a special setting of paradise, we had to learn the spiritual concepts of good and evil. If soul did not enter the "Tree of the Knowledge of Good and Evil" it was barred to progress and become aware in ultimate reality. Once absorbed into the spiritual concept of a lie, it found individual awareness as physical creatures. In this physical reality soul experienced all aspects of evil. When the soup of evil had been simmering long enough, Jesus, god of paradise was introduced to bring us the idea of escape from evil and introduced the manner of escape from physical existence. If souls understood that it has a choice it would choose escape through the help of the Comforter, but if soul never even gets inkling that escape is possible, it is unsuitable for redemption and will meet it destiny inside the trap, the physical universe.

Jesus' Life Proves That Souls Reincarnate

If we were to live only one life, Jesus would not have to come because our fate would be sealed in the universe after death and no god would care about us. It is because Jesus came in our midst that we can be sure that souls reincarnate in this environment continually until each individual soul is allowed to escape [awakens in spirit] or until it is spiritually undone.

Chapter 14

The Sinister Tracks of the Federal Income Tax

Below is a summary of the legal structure of the present-day Federal income tax. It all seems so logical and naturally arrived at, but I know that it is the track of an illegal conspiracy of our elected officials against the people of the United States, that has a spiritual base because it moves forward in time according to a secret plan of which the people are not a part. The federal government grossly abuses this tax and grossly abuses the disbursement of the tax.

---

http://en.wikipedia.org/wiki/Brushaber_v._Union_Pacific_Railroad

Prior to 1895, all income taxes had been considered indirect taxes [not required to be apportioned among the states according to the population of each state]. In the 1895 case of *Pollock v. Farmers' Loan & Trust Co.*, however, the Court had overturned precedent and ruled that while a tax on income from labor was an excise, or indirect tax [a tax not required to be apportioned], a tax on *income derived from property* such as interest, dividends, or rents was—should be treated as—a direct tax.

In Pollock the courts decreed that the people's labor can be taxed without further ado. The court decided that people are slaves. I say; one's labor is the closest and most intimate possession of one's free organic person in harmony with the intent of the Constitution.

The court decreed also that fictional institutions must be taxed on the profit realized from the enterprise. Commerce is a fictitious activity, work is an organic activity. This decree is a revelation that proves that the Supreme Court courts the rich and powerful and tramples on the workers who can be taxed without any restrictions.

The most intimate interpretation of the Constitution of "We, the people" says that the right to work cannot be taxed out of existence by classifying labor as an indirect tax because in that case we cannot avoid the tax because we cannot exist without working to provide for body and family. The Supreme Court judges in the Pollock case are thus traitors to the people as they surely made slaves of people that must work for a living. In the below listing please be aware that the explanations given by government are merely propaganda. It is up to you to see how the laws were truly arrived at. There is no truth in government's statements released for public consumption.

http://www.privacycommittee.com/1/1/freedom/books/usbrit/www.civil-liberties.com/pages/taxationtale.htm

During the Federalist Debates, the founding fathers decided that both the State governments and the new federal government cannot impose the same kind of tax simultaneously. If one government imposes a property tax, the other cannot; if one has an income tax, the other cannot, etc. Any taxing authority not delegated to the federal government will be reserved for the States. Congress will be responsible for collecting national taxes from the States who in turn will collect the taxes from their people. The debates also resolves that State taxes are to be classified as internal taxes and national taxes are to be classified as external taxes. That agreement died because the states are now federal property, who sold it all to the bankers because it was not able to pay its loans back.

1787: A few members of the newly created U.S. Congress immediately tried transferring Congress' power to collect taxes to the Treasury Department. The bill was declared not constitutional and failed to become law.

July 14, 1798: In preparation for the war with France, the Federal government imposed a $2 million direct tax. The tax is apportioned among the States who collected the tax from property owners. This is the war where France lost its suzerainty over the US government.

July 22, 1812: To help pay for the 1812 war, the Federal government imposed a $3 million direct income tax. The tax is apportioned among the States who collected the tax from property owners. The following month, the Federal government created tax districts, each with its own private tax assessor and collector who earned a commission from the taxes they collected.

January 9, 1815: Because of the 1812 War, the Federal government imposed a $6 million direct tax which was apportioned among the States. This tax allowed tax collectors to sell property of citizens that did not pay their share of the tax, however, essential property like homes, tools of trade and household utensils were exempt. To protect the public from abusive tax collectors, penalties applied to collectors who used extortion or otherwise broke the law to make collections. This must be the origin of US Code Title 42. This is also the year that the banks were authorized to establish a national bank. It was this outfit that President Jackson was able, with extreme efforts, to dislodge and scrap. The 1812 war were instigated by the International bankers.

August 5, 1861: The outbreak of Civil War leads the Federal government to impose a $20 million apportioned direct tax. The Act which created this war tax also included a new form of taxation; the income tax as we better know it today. This first general income tax was set at 1-3% which applied to less than 1 percent of the US population who had incomes over $800.

To avoid apportionment requirements by the U.S. Constitution the new income tax was classified as an indirect tax; instead of the proper classification as a direct tax. This of course is fraud. The new income tax was not challenged until 1871. That delay established a de-facto precedent with Congress who then incorrectly classified the tax as such to bypass Constitution restrictions on federal taxes [which is a clear attempt of government as enemy of the people to subject the American people]. Also, because of war, Congress was able to pass tax collection laws that would normally violate Constitutional Rights. The war was phony and thus this was a hostile action against the people. To enforce the tax, Congress creates the position of Commissioner of Tax, a position that included the authority to hire assistants. One can thus see the insincerity of Congress with its relationship to its means of Holy Communion with the people, the Constitution. Note that every time the US government fights a war, the international bankers are closely linked to government to provide the funds for the war and obtain the right to collect the tax to pay off the war debt.

1884: The Federal government imposes another income tax. It tries to get away with installing an income tax outside the arena of war. See the insincerity!

1895: In Pollock v. Farmers' Loan & Trust Co, the Supreme Court rules that general income taxes are unconstitutional because they are a direct taxes; it excluded wages as direct taxes. To this day, the ruling has not been over-turned. This is an act of betrayal by the Supreme Court. The means of communion between government and the people takes precedence, or there simply is no government. They broke the communion declared in the Constitution and thus they have no standing.

June 15, 1909: After the Supreme Court declared general income taxes unconstitutional; President Taft proposes three new taxes to Congress: a graduated inheritance tax, another general income tax, and a new corporate tax. In the attempt to bypass the Supreme Court's Pollack ruling, Taft also proposes the 16th Amendment with the intention of taxing without reservations profits made from commercial activity. Taft was an enemy of the people and a patsy of the bankers as was Lincoln. President Taft overstepped his boundary. He started a new tradition, precedence outside the communion with the people. He was executive and has no right to influence the members of another branch of government—more treason. See, the progressive method of depriving the people from their hard-earned wealth. They never stop.

1913: With the ratification of the 16th Amendment, Congress creates the federal internal income tax and the Federal Reserve Bank to purportedly fight the inflation caused by paper currency. All income tax collections are forwarded to the Federal Reserve to pay the interest on its publicly circulated money. The withdrawal of currency from public circulation through the new tax and the new Federal Reserve stabilized inflation, temporarily. This could have been done in another more friendly way. The ratification of the 16th Amendment is fraud with betrayal and corruption to give government the right of unlimited taxation without further confrontations from any corner. As far as inflation is concerned look at what the dollar was worth in 1913 and now in 2008. The Federal Reserve Board deliberately increased inflation rather than control it in that span of time. It is a totally useless institution because it is managed by betrayers of the people.

January 24, 1916: In Brushaber v. Union Pacific Railroad, the Supreme Court ruled the 16th Amendment doesn't over-rule the Court's ruling in the Pollock case which declared general income taxes unconstitutional; The 16th Amendment applies only to gains and profits from commercial and investment activities: The 16th Amendment only applies to excises taxes; The 16th Amendment did not Amend the U.S. Constitution; The 16th Amendment only clarified the federal government's existing authority to create excise taxes without apportionment. **Pollock decided that wages were considered taxable as an excise and thus never fell within the scope of the 16th Amendment.**

1939: Congress passes the Public Salary tax, taxing the wages of federal employees. It was claimed that because federal workers had a privilege to work for government it was only right they pay tribute for that privilege. They can contort anything, but the main principle here is that if these workers lived in the District of Columbia or any of its territories, the Constitution did not apply anyway.

1940: Congress passed the Buck Act authorizing the federal government to tax federal workers living in the States. This act did violate the rights of the people not living in government territory, but it was all shadow play because the New Deal had given all state property as collateral to cover the federal government's insatiable thirst for more borrowed money. All the forgoing, and what follows in this summation, is part of a greater conspiracy to betray the American people to a One World Order.

1942, Congress passes the Victory Tax under Constitutional authority to support the WWII effort. President Roosevelt proposes a voluntary tax withholding program allowing workers across the nation to pay the tax in installments. The program was a success and the number of tax payers increases from 3 percent to 62 percent of the U.S. population. The Second World War was a conspiracy among world leaders against the people to create the **United Nations** institution. The people never thought to fight this act in court because of its camouflage behind the scene of the betrayal of Pearl Harbor. The US knew from several sources that this attack was planned and deliberately kept its knowledge of the pending attack from the armed forces to give the US an excuse to enter the war big-time.

1944: The Victory Tax and Voluntary Withholding laws are repealed as required by the U.S. Constitution, however, the federal government continues to collect the tax claiming it's authority under the 1913 income tax and the 16th Amendment. Here again government declares itself an enemy of the people. This whole summary bypasses the involvement of the international banking system in taking control over the US government. Here government does not even pretend anymore to give any heed to the Constitution. Government felt it had the right to do so because hardly anyone ever confronted government on its shenanigans over the life of this monster.

Today: A mixture of the 1913 income tax, the 16th Amendment. the Public Salary Act and the Victory tax has embedded itself as a de facto tax on the people of the U.S. in spite of the long standing rulings by the Supreme Court that strictly limit the scope of any income tax. This act consolidated the people as national slaves of government which in turn is owned by the banks. All that now awaits us is the announcement of your permanent enslavement by the introduction and the inauguration of the One World Order.

15% of Net Income Must Be the Maximum Rate for Income Tax If It Is Used at All

It can be seen that both the state and the federal governments tax the same item, the wages of people. *The only item that should always be exempt from taxation is wages and it is taxed twice at enslaving rates of percentage!* According to the intent of our founding fathers, wages are beyond taxation; and by the intent of the founding fathers one cannot be taxed on the same object of taxation by state and federal governments. They have to decide which tax belongs to whom. We are being doubly taxed on income. It is illegal, it is unfounded and it is enslaving. It also proves that war always enlarges government's power to tax the people and is used to gain additional powers over the people. It is preposterous that free people can be taxed to an unlimited amount on there wages, other income and services and possessions. I go for the standard set in Genesis 47 in the Bible where slaves pay 20% tax on income. Since we cannot ever be declared to be slaves I therefore suggest and insist that as free people we cannot be taxed, compositely, over 15% of our wages. We should never be taxed for expenses that are not directly related to the operation of the government. We must strip all powers of governments to award grants to foreign nations, benefits to the people, subsidies and such to the people and institutions. Remember, that state governments sold the people out to federal government; and that federal government sold the people out to the International bankers.

No form of taxation on specific categories should ever exceed 20% Items taxed over 10% must have the 2/3 majority approval of the voters; and items taxes over 15% must have ¾ majority approval of the voter. Every 10 years such taxes must be re-approved by the people then-eligible to vote. No item can be taxed more than once.

People should always be ready to make donations to private schools from grammar schools up to higher education. It is up to the people to insure that the youth receive excellent education at the most reasonable cost.

If we insist on keeping government small as our servant we must keep wealth and power in any form from government. Government must be just able to scrape by in operating itself. It should not include armed forces. Policed and armed forces must be considered institutions outside the control of government. If government can have complete control and access of the armed forces, it is the sure means of keeping the people in slavery.

Keep your weapons in excellent order and be ready to use them against those who work for or support excessive government control over the people.

This book will be the target of much vicious attack from political, governmental, religious and civic institutions. This is only natural as all these are fictitious institutions that profit from a gullible and enslaved populace. However, know that they will use any scheme of propaganda to discredit this book and to ensnare you all over again in their schemes of lies and enslavement.

Do not allow them to do that to you ever again.

The idea of a socialist democratic government is absurd. It is ideology sold to the people under false pretenses. Ideology should never be expanded into a system of government.

Jesus is teaching us that if you create something be the bottom of the creation, uphold and feed it; if you will always be like that; your place in ultimate eternal reality is safe. God does not want a robot as son that only does good, by rote. He wants that his sons know Good and Evil and that they will always make the right judgment each time a situation demands a judgment: do good, not evil—love the good more than yourself.

Do not garner power, or work yourself to be the top and then suck more power, status and riches from this position.

Chapter 15

The Crucial Question

I conclude Book I with the crucial question, "Why does evil exist?" By now, hopefully, you can answer this for yourself. Evil always comes in a disguise of good. Evil is the depth of deceit because it comes disguised as good. Souls **must understand and know evil** [remember, we, in paradise partook of the tree of **the Knowledge** of **Good** and **Evil**] to be able to look through all the disguises that evil can hide behind. This is of spiritual significance because if evil could take on a disguise of good in the realm of good, evil would invade and settle in the realms of good without "good" knowing about it. So, whoever will enter into the ultimate realms of good must know every aspect of evil to be able to look through all the disguises of evil in order to identify and embrace good and shut out all avenues through which evil can slip unnoticed into the realm and communion of good. Nothing is as it appears to be. Everything in the universe is evil in a disguise of good.

Evil is a communion, just as good is a communion. Do not let a communion of evil disguised as good fool you any more. Evil can be a (booby-)trap, expressed without words, but as deadly and tragic for those who wander into it.

If evil would succeed, existence in any plane of reality would become an intolerable nightmare and we would be caught in inescapable suppression and hatred without love and without anything to look forward to, because evil would have shut off any possible escape route. I give you examples of evil that shut off all avenues of escape: the Wall erected between East and West Germany, The Elba River in Germany between East and West at the end of the war with Germany, the river of death and the people trapped on top of the WTC towers when these were deliberately demolished from under them. I give you the continual encroachment of government into our every moment of daily life

Liberty and love would disappear from all levels of reality forever. I hope that everybody in the world can identify with this kind of horror. If you can, you are truly ready to embrace the Comforter in the Good Spirit who is reality as good and not as evil. Government, marriage, children, cars, computers, planes, you name it; they are all disguises of evil pretending to be good.

> *Do Not Let the World Confuse You Any More; There Is No Good in It. Only One Is Good, Ultimate Truth in Ultimate Reality; and As Yet, You Have No Part in It.*

The disguise in which evil tried to usurp the intentions of good in Jesus is so severe, that it took 2,000 years to understand what Jesus was truly doing. Jehovah has been exposed and stands naked. Good is the responsibility of every soul in existence. If you cannot rally for good you will be utterly annihilated.

> *Now, I Sincerely Hope You Take Me To Heart. I Am Not Much Of A Spiritual Leader or Politician, I Am Not Jesus Or Some Saint; But I, Anti Christ, Am All You Have In The Good Spirit, Whether You Are The Pope, The Ayatollah, The Dai La Lama, Bill Gates, Oprah, George Bush, Or Whoever You Believe You Are—Like Jesus' Words, My Words Help Give You Life. They are truly worth all you have*

All Christians brag on knowing truth, however not one knows what truth is. The truth is that you live a lie in a reality based on a lie. Jesus came to make you aware of that fact. From hereon out it is a matter between you, Evil, and the Comforter. The ball is in your court.

NOTE: It is up to you to recommend this set of books in one cover to everyone for whom you care. Many people have a tendency to repress the knowledge of others by withholding recommendation to those they hold dear. This is a selfish attitude. If you love someone you should allow that person to have information and options to form his or her own opinion. Be yourself, not Jehovah's patsy. This book helps you to do that.

This material will give anyone powerful rehabilitation of awareness and understanding of liberty and love. If you are unable to convince a person, or if you believe that a person you would want to recommend this book to will not be persuaded by its spiritual value, recommend it on its value as a works of science fiction, or for its philosophical, historical and political value. It is also up to you to help make the world a better equitable place to be where every race, species and creature can have a worthwhile place. Humility and true understanding are the greatest blessings one can give another.

BOOK II

INSIGHT INTO THE PROCESS AND DEPTH OF DECEIT

Chapter 1

Truth and Lies

Love

1 Corinthian 13 in the New Testament of the Bible tells us what love is. By our understanding of Jehovah in the Old Testament, we know that Jehovah does not fit "love" as described in 1 Corinthians 13. We should know immediately that there is a snake hiding in the grass. In the Old Testament, Jehovah tells us to do as he says and not as he does. He speaks and acts with a forked tongue. The god of love from the New Testament is an entirely different and higher god, from another realm where love is possible. Jesus said that his authority is higher than all authority in the universe. Since Jehovah is indisputably "god" in the universe, we know that he is just an underling in a scheme of greater sovereignty; this universe is just a surrogate of true reality. There must therefore be a realm above Jehovah's negative spiritual authority.

Difference between Paradise and Earth as Environments

From reading chapters 2 and 3 of Genesis in the Old Testament, we can see that something is wrong with souls caught in the universe. Adam and Woman were beings invested with truth native to paradise. Why are humans, their descendants, mired in suffering, pain, death, dishonesty, untruth and confusion? Why do we lack any insight to truth? Why cannot we converse face to face with god?

True reality is being in communion with the well of truth—the spirit of Jesus. We as humans lack that completely. We only believe to know some aspects of physical reality. Even scientists do not know anything in their fields of expertise for sure. Adam and Woman were created from spiritual substance of paradise that relates its own truth to the environment and to entities existing there. Love and true intimacy are possible in an environment of honesty, nowhere else. Adam and Woman were in contact with every part of their being and with everything in their environment, even their maker. God, who never tells a lie because he is truth, told Adam and Woman not to eat of the Tree of Knowledge of Good and Evil because it would cause them to die. In paradise, one exists on ideas native to paradise—and, one dies by imbibing thoughts that are not native to paradise. Ideas that are not native to paradise include that the god over the realm paradise is a liar.

Constitution as Basis for Communion between Levels of Reality

There was a deceiver in the Tree of Knowledge of Good and Evil. His deceit could cause Adam and Woman to die from the reality of paradisiacal truth. The serpent told them lies. Similarly, at the signing of the Constitution for the government of United States of America, the people understood what could be the death of the free union of states and of liberty for the people—government. The people were warned just as Adam and Woman were warned against the entity that could cause their death of liberty.

US Constitution as Propaganda

The Constitution and the conference that led to it were a public declaration that government cannot be trusted. Later generations in America were as careless as Adam and Woman in throwing that knowledge to the wind. The Bible tells us that things on earth are like things in spirit. Carelessness equals death. The cause of death in both situations is propaganda, the art of hiding truth by telling a believable lie so that believers of the lie will cause their own death.

In comparison, the Constitution for the United States government is also a clever piece of propaganda. When looked upon, one believes in it, only to learn much later that it has deceived you. The Tree of Knowledge of Good and Evil is not a real tree, but nothingness in paradise filled with the clever fiction based on propaganda. The Serpent found a way to be a creator by inventing something not available in reality—nothingness. The serpent comes across in the disguise of an angel of light just as US government; and when introduced to it, one must agree with the beauty and greatness of it. By accepting the viability of the tree, one is drawn in by its powerful attraction and communes in it; and one is drugged by the cleverness of the deceit. The reality of paradise becomes hidden by this drug and a new reality takes its place. This new reality is the dream of death, a spiritual coma. The dream reveals the physical universe, and the location is earth.

The Mystery of Paradise

The whole of paradise had one entity of mystery in it—that particular tree. How can that be in a realm where everything reveals truth? It is easy to understand that the tree was not really part of paradise. It was not created by the god of paradise. It was a structure that held enmity toward others, and when looked at would empower that enmity; it held an irresistible temptation to Adam and Woman. Enmity is a new idea in paradise, for it did not exist there naturally.

Soul Existence after the Fall

The new environment is all encompassing, it is new and alien. As one wonders around in this new place one is assailed by ever more lies and deceit that form the strata of the underlying environment.

Mystified and lost from the moment one enters one settles on a place to live and one begins to investigate the area and their new god, the Serpent, who is now know as Jehovah. Jehovah educates them. This education is more propaganda because it causes one to get involved in the dream more solidly. One is led by the nose until trapped and enslaved without one penny having been paid for the enslavement. Public school does the same to all our youth. They all get the same perspective and mental slant on the reality of America and its god, US government. The name of the state a child resides in is hardly mentioned anymore. The US is all important. Why? Because our deceivers want it so.

Connection between Humans and Animals

Newborn human babies go willingly, like newly born, domesticated animals into total slavery through, innocence, ignorance, and helplessness. There is thus a strong spiritual connection between humans and animals. This connection is soul, the same kind of physical bodies in this same physical environment. The spiritual heart of all living creatures is soul—the same sort of soul in humans as in animals. The process of enslavement is deceit, cleverly organized in systems of propaganda. The spiritual cells of Adam and Eve [Woman is called Eve after their fall], souls, were like newborn babies in an unfamiliar environment. They could do nothing but follow the deceiver deeper into the process of propaganda—the path into the unknown and enslavement, so that the unknown seems to take on a guise of reality.

Heavenly Bodies as Icons

As an aside, I am convinced that all our heavenly bodies are mere icons in the sky. They remain icons until "intelligent life" comes closer. The closer it comes the more the program universe expands the icon into another physical object, until at last a person sets foot on this icon and finds it another environment of some sort. This "intelligence" can be a life person or a functioning apparatus sent out by intelligent life. The icon receives permanent specific identity as intelligence gets mentally closer and closer to the object [like viewing a planet through a telescope]; to the extend that when intelligence brings specks of matter under very close scrutiny it continues to release more detailed information. Any item in the universe becomes more specific as intelligence investigates it more closely. Once a detail in environment has been determined by the program all the details are stored for future use when intelligence again puts it under scrutiny. As details and objects become more "understood" by intelligence, the objects under investigation become shrouded in more mystery. Science is in the business of chasing rainbows. We will never come to the heart of the matter because the universe is a virtual environment not under control of physical life. Spirit can lead "intelligence" by the nose forever!

It is like magnifying a picture with huge pixel content. You can magnify the detail until you see one entire pixel. That is where it stops. You can never discover how the pixel got on the screen. The intelligence and the electronics and all the science and technology integrated in making that pixel possible are hidden from the screen you are observing. That is the situation science, technology and theology find themselves; one impenetrable solid wall that stops human intelligence. My book helps you over the hump. You know there is more going on than you can discover from the position of flesh. One has to jump the puddle and get into spirit to see any further. I have the method for you to jump the puddle. Get in contact with the Comforter. He will lead you into all truth. Jehovah and his hierarchy is one level up and you must climb over his back to the top to see how he displayed the universe with you as a soul-projection in it. As long as you continue to see this environment as real you are stumped, just as the character investigating the one picture is stumped when he finally sees the entire screen filled with just one pixel. The wall of the screen stops him from going further. The same is true bisecting biological tissue. You are always looking at walls. You can cut and cut, but all you get is two more walls to look at. It is the same with particle research. You finally come to a stop. The wall prevents you from seeing more—the wall that separates the spirit from the fiction, the spiritual display screen. That wall is a wall of the box you are in; the wall that separates reality from fiction.

This concept of deceit works with deadly precision in our contemporary setting. I once was approached via phone calls and pamphlets to invest in gold and silver coins with a certain New York State—based firm. This company guaranteed that I could sell the coins back to them at any time at a 15 percent increase in price. I believed them and invested about $30,000 in gold and silver coins over some three years. Then, five years later, I needed to sell the coins for cash. I tried to contact the firm but the line was disconnected. I inquired with the state to investigate its new location and address and found they had gone out of business. I was deceived, and in no way could I collect the funds from a business that did not exist.

This business was created by punching a hole in physical reality—a "nothingness." They filled this nothingness with a corporation by incorporating a business and populating it with employees that were ignorant of the dirty scheme. These employees, salesmen, were deceived and enslaved to become willing workers to defraud people of their hard-earned savings. They milked thousands of gullible people of their money and then went out of business, taking the valuables with them, leaving again nothingness. I, later, tried to sell the coins to coin dealers, and they told me the coins were valued at face value, about $800 worth. They were not of collectible quality. I was deceived and could not recoup my losses. The way back to recouping my investments had disappeared into thin air. Even though I existed in the physical environment, I was throwing money into nothingness.

Every major scheme of deceit played on the people through media advertisement, through the US mail, or through the internet is perpetrated by duly registered, incorporated businesses. The corporation stages as the front of the criminals hiding behind it. They cannot be held liable for more than they have invested in the business. But when the business is folded up, there remains not one penny in it—and government allows these things and allows these crooks to go free.

Super criminals hide their schemes behind such fronts as governments. They have a smooth, clear public face; but behind these institutions hide real people who are the greatest deceivers, thieves, and murderers of all. They stole your country and now they want to steal your world and make it theirs. You continue to invest in your share of the United States and did so for years and most of you do not know you are throwing your valuables to the swine. Your ignorance is so absolute that this government has enslaved every one of you and you are blind and ignorant of having been enslaved and are exploited to support your slave master, government. The universe will entice every one of us to believe ever more lies and deceit; and it does not matter whether you are a master deceiver on earth or a trusting little fellow, you are led into oblivion. You need a spiritual guide that can reorient you in spirit so you have again eyes to see and ears to hear and you see what I see; the universe is 100% deceit and an inescapable trap. Know that your god Jehovah is the greatest deceiver in all reality. This is for a very good reason, to open your eyes; if you are not observant, this god will devour your soul.

Can you not see, that when god (Jehovah) told Daniel 2500 years ago that knowledge will increase, that the knowledge we now claim is not discovered but given to us? If god knew what would happen, do you not think that god would make his prophesy come true? How?—by leading us by the nose, like cattle. Nobody is going to catch him in a lie!

A similar propaganda was the manner used in kidnapping Adam and Woman from paradise, and it forced them into slavery in spirit. You are just enforced fictional, physical projections of souls captured in negative spirit. Your soul is a spiritual and physical slave, and you still believe you are free—that, dear reader is the power of deceit.

Why do I call the spirit of the universe negative? Because it is an opposite kind of spirit to the spirit of truth; it is the spirit of deceit. What are souls? They are the spiritual cells of awareness in Adam and Woman that make up the aware beingness of these two entities. Our job as slaves is to deceive each other into believing this universe is real. We are doing a splendid job in deceiving each other on orders of Jehovah, the Serpent. When the need arises, this universe can be rolled up too, just as the coin investment scheme.

How will we ever find our way back out of this trap? Jesus told us about a spiritual being, the Comforter, who can guide us out of this nothingness of the universe [John: 16:12-15], If we did not need to be removed from this place of evil, Jesus would not have had to come and there would be no need for the Comforter. We must convince ourselves with a stronger determination that the power of Jehovah's deceit that has captured us beyond any possibility of escape that physical reality is a deceit. We are locked into illusions that seem so real we are lost. Jesus said we are lost; believe him. Escape is nearly impossible because we are 'like dead' to our home environment in spirit. We are in a coma from which we cannot awaken as long as we are imbued with a propaganda scheme that has flipped our awareness right out of the spiritual realm into the imagined environment created by Jehovah, the serpent and dragon.

This book will show you what has happened to Adam and Woman, and to many sets like them, after partaking of this Tree of Knowledge of Good and Evil; also how human beings exploit and enslave each other to the extent that one group has been able to enslave all humanity. It also goes into proposals for changes in constitutions for government and banking and for laws that will prevent things like these from happening again. This book also tells you how to gain contact with this elusive character—the Comforter. He is not elusive, but very forward. His elusiveness lies in our state of delusion. He is the truth that exists all around us, but we are forced through our bodies to only commune with the physical environment, cleverly woven from spiritual dream material, deceit or make-believe. You are, so to speak, in a display box, the Comforter and our souls are outside the box; but Jesus created a hole in the box through which the Comforter can reach us—that is, if we pay attention. The Comforter cannot reach souls because they are in a spiritual coma. He needs to address soul through souls' human projections, us.

Jehovah is the god of the flesh, the fabric of our bodies and of negative spirit. Since souls, like animals, are clothed in animal skins, he is god over them as well. A spiritual lie believed is negative spirit because it is untrue and thus a fiction. Negative spirit finds its base in a deceit played on spirit. Deceit flips the mind from reality to make-believe—from spiritual fact to spiritual fancy and is a vile offensive weapon against the innocent. Deceit is a trap to enslave gullible beings, whether it is used in spirit or in physical reality. This book is about exposing the "truth about deceit"; and the vile activities of super criminals and their adjutants directed against trusting, decent people. The decency in physical reality lies in the slaves and domesticated animals. They have been so severely deceived as to love and care for their deceivers.

Physical creatures, soul projections, are hermetically locked from reality by means of a prison within a prison, within a prison, or said in another way, layers upon layers of cleverly arranged deceits. The national governments of the world have received aid from international bankers in locking up their citizens. The international bankers, through the United Nations, have forced financial binds on governments and forced them to lock the nations of people into a worldwide slave camp. The negative spiritual realm, the universe, separates all soul beings and their forced expressions in nature from their true father—god of true reality. There is only one goal for us: escape from the realms within realms of negative spirit and propaganda. Oh, I hope so much that you understand and appreciate how badly you have been deceived. Dear souls, wake up and return home as prodigal children. A most high position is waiting for you in the father's house.

Jesus' father is the true god of all spiritual reality—the realm of truth and light; thus, he is the god of love and of the innate fabric of our souls—the only part of a human being that is real, but that is in a coma. *All else we are made to be aware of is fiction! Your entire awareness is nothingness. You are lost in webs of illusions so deep that Jesus had to disguise himself in the vile garb of flesh to reach you. He has cleared a road that will lead all of us home. Follow the Comforter. He is real, and he truly cares. **All else you know is deceit**.*

The Holy Bible, which is not holy at all, is a book that tells the story of two gods—Jehovah, Serpent, the god of a spiritually fictitious universe that we call physical reality; and our true father "god" of true reality. Both gods reveal their status, authority, and purpose in this Bible. The Old Testament, except for most of Genesis 2 and 3, and much of the New Testament concerns the affairs of Jehovah. Only a small portion of the Old Testament and the New Testament is given to the true god by Jesus. The true god is given little space, because what he has to say cannot be put into human words. He is utterly alien to human beings. There is nothing we can know about this god of reality, because a lie believed hid him from us. Jesus came to tell us about him.

Chapter 2

Spiritual Hanky-Panky

The True Realm of the Father

I have to digress a bit here. Our souls' true father is the spirit in Jesus Christ [who came into the world as the imposter, because Jehovah's Christ hides the true father's spiritual son, the world's anti-Christ]. The spirit of Jesus is the true son of the god of all reality; and Jesus' spirit created the first layer of virtual reality, paradise. Jesus' spirit [his true self] is hidden because it is of a much higher form of reality, and humans have been shut out from all reality. Humans exist in a spiritual nothingness, or void.

I call paradise a virtual environment in neutral spirit because it lies between true reality [positive spirit] and negative spirit [fictitious spirit or the spirit of deceit]. Adam and Woman found their beingness in paradise, so Adam and Woman's father must be this spirit of the true son, who came to us as Messiah for Jehovah in a physical disguise. Paradise was created by punching a hole in a higher reality, the reality of his father, god. Where then do the spirits of Adam and Woman come from? Their spirits must have been taken from Jesus' word.

A virtual environment is created from nothingness by comatose beings in a higher reality. This means that some hanky-panky took place in filling out the organization of beings in paradise. It seems that Jesus, the spirit of the son, collaborated with the serpent in the tree in the garden. Since Jesus' spirit is good, we must conclude that Jehovah's spirit is good. It makes more sense to see Jehovah as the drill sergeant-instructor for Jesus' spirit and that the Tree of Knowledge of Good and Evil is the final class of the University of Paradise or maybe a post graduate course. Jesus, in earth taught [as son of the true god] that riches corrupt the being and prevents one's redemption, while Jehovah teaches in Deuteronomy 28 and 29 that riches, power and status are his reward for being obedient. These two opposing character traits of god cannot be harmonized because both claim to tell the truth.

Even Jesus Was Unable to Give Us a Clear Picture of Reality

The true realm of the true father has many mansions [John 14:2]. It is thus not an empty realm. These mansions belong to the redeemed by the Comforter in the Good Spirit. They would not likely stumble over the seduction of untruth in any tree again. They graduated from all that.

The New Testament does not give even one vital link to us to visualize reality. Jesus did provide *some information* about this reality. He referred all true believers to the one he would send to us after he had departed—the Comforter, who is always accompanied by the Good Spirit, the spirit of communion between father and the son. The rest of the New Testament has been usurped by natural human allegiance to Jehovah. The reason I need so many words to explain truth is that it must be "fictionally" expressed in this universe of fiction. *In reality, there is no word for reality, it just is.* Words would only hide reality. It is what it is. As Jesus said in the briefest human kind-of-expression possible, "I am." And believe me, in spirit, those are two words too many. The language of humans compared to the ideas expressed in the realm of truth is the difference, sort of, between dial-up, telephone-link internet and high-speed, broadband internet; the former depends, so to speak, on conveying each syllable in a sentence and the other on conveying complete ideas.

The New Testament is a hodgepodge of confusion because Jesus came to us by authority of two opposing gods. Jesus' mission, death, and resurrection, as is told us in the New Testament was understood by only one person—Jesus. No one can harmonize all the confusions and contradictions in the New Testament. Jesus hammered over and over again that he told the truth. He was speaking on a spiritual level. He was trying to say that all we as souls, and as projections of soul knew was lies. He was teaching us that this realm of darkness was based entirely on deceit and that he had the truth to set us free from all the deceit.

No one can state that true liberty and mature love need laws and enforcement unless one recognizes that the Bible is a record of a war between two gods—one of evil who usurps almost all the content of the Bible to justify his position, motive, and power; while the other can only state that truth and love truly exist beyond the boundaries of this universe and that the only way to get there is by an entity who uses no power and authority at all but a guiding love—the Comforter. He is the spirit of the murdered and risen son of the true god and who also, by coercion, *was* a slave to Jehovah. Jehovah needs much language because he is lying, and the true god has no language to explain truth. Truth just is. ***Language is an invention to spread and anchor lies. Truth does not need language because it lies exposed and revealed to all.*** It is the language of deceit that hides truth because to us reality does not exist because we see a virtual realm as reality.

The unrevealed aspects of physical reality coerce religion on people. Take what I just wrote about Jesus as an example. The way Jesus revealed his father created such fundamental confusions that some hundred different Christian cults have sprung up from what he said of this god and father. His predicament was that he came to reveal the god of true spirit and reality, but was forced by the god of the universe to be a spokesperson for him, the deceiver. The enforcement of this task was so heavy that little opportunity developed to plug truth, liberty and love and what he said about it was understood by humanity to relate to Jehovah, not the true god.

Jesus is only one example. It does not matter what subject or science one brings forward. What we know about these is next to nil; the experts do not know much more. The nature of the universe is hidden from everyone and the knowledge of true reality is zero. We are separated from all knowledge of things that are important. This leaves us fumbling. We pride ourselves on our quick reactions and our expertise in this or that, but most of our activities are tightly controlled routine operations, laid out in the simplest format. This is true whether we are nation-deceiving bankers, politicians, managers, scientist, artists, or members of the general workforce. Many of us think that money spells success and proves expertise but in truth, the art and practice of deceit makes up the greater part of society and of the wealth of successful people—deceit played on fellow human beings. We deceive each other because we have no idea of how to be truthful.

The real fruit of deceit is what is best understood by the word "karma." The god of the universe may be deceitful, but to be a god at all, he has to be righteous. Some, like super rich bankers, believe that they are like gods. Their reign is extremely temporary, as Jehovah in the Old Testament explains. Only the super stupid will disregard this knowledge. Oh, success seems real, and it seems to be based on accomplishment; but the results of effort and accomplishment in the program are just program routines. Your personal feelings and vanities are recorded in the computer's memory so that these can be called up at some other time and equalized. No characters in the program win. Karma tracks all our thoughts and actions and spits them back out to us.

We lived contented without computers. Then people got computers; and that was fun, then dial-up internet became available, and we needed it to communicate with the world and friends. The internet sucked us into buying a million items we do not need. Friends and businesses began to send each other video and audio clips. These had huge files that took time to download so we obtained broadband internet. When we get involved we sink ever deeper; and people do not think to extricate themselves from the cycle. That is how the cone sections in the spiritual trap work. One sinks ever deeper away from the surface of truth, and the idea of going back seems absurd to our deceived minds. Jehovah's seductions are a million times tougher than just needing and buying things. To extricate ourselves from these is beyond creature ability without outside help.

Since humans believe the way things are physically, because they lack spiritual understanding of physical reality, human life is a religion; and religion is the basis of human life. Physical life, based on gross belief systems is played off in the realm of death and darkness. Spiritual 'Life' is based on knowing and is thus played off in pure light of knowing. In the state of spiritual death, one gropes for real things, but there are none, so one goes on believing things and one will again reincarnate.

Physical life even denies us communication with things we think we "know." A good example is your loved ones. What do you know of them? They will reveal only what they want to reveal—the outer surface. It is prettied up and made presentable. Even in their intimate relationships, people fake it and keep things hidden. What is put up for display is false. Things are hidden because people are afraid to reveal them because they are true and too vulnerable to share. *To "believe" is an exercise of trying to be alive*—to be in charge of your affairs, but it is only a fearful bluff. For hundreds of millions of humans, to be in charge of one's affairs means to deceive others in order to obtain the things they believe they need. Everything is a show of falsehood that we pretend is real, sincere and genuine.

We must pretend to aid others to be in charge of our affairs, but we do so to obtain something from other people. Yet, in trying to obtain what belongs to others by coercion or deceit, one only proves that one is not in charge of one's own affairs. This is the trait that leads one into becoming an animal. Animals have lost the ability to aid others by choice. I have never heard of an instance of animals in the pure wild aiding any other animal, but those that run in packs to overpower prey. This is a form of organization and, thus, evil. Evil basically means to coerce or deceive another to obtain something you consider valuable at another's expense. Animals exist on the life of others by killing it and devouring the life in the creature, the living cells.

Daemons are gods that rule above us in universal spirit. Satan and god are synonymous terms. Jehovah is the Satan and the adversary of the son in truth, Jesus' spirit. What Christians call Satan is the adversary to Jehovah, and another daemon below Satan in the negative spiritual hierarchy is the adversary to Satan—and so the hierarchy of daemons goes on and on down to the lowliest daemon. The negative spiritual hierarchy will slowly consume a soul by bleeding the energy potential between their native spirit and the negative spirit of the lie, something like a spider sucking out the juices of its prey, leaving a dry hulk behind.

What will happen to the ashes of soul, the remaining dust of soul? Negative spirit does not know what to do with the stuff. It never had possession of it because the stuff is real, not fiction. You cannot place reality in a fictional setting. It would be like placing a real person in your computer screen; it will not work. The residue of soul remains in its native realm. Reality is all around and through this universe; it simply is where it has always been, in reality. It is as god says [Genesis 3], "From [spiritual] dust to [spiritual] dust." Reality is always in reality. Real dust is part of reality.

Jehovah's spiritual computer runs on potential differential inherent in a deceived soul; a potential difference between the material from which the body is made in the higher realm and the lie that negates that realm. This potential difference when used to power the spiritual computer will drain the soul of its grounding in truth. Eventually, it dies as an awareness unit in reality. As the soul leaks its energy into the operation of the computer, it descends into the dream state of physical life from human down through the natures of all animal life and plant life to dirt. Radioactive material is an example of how dirt disintegrates into the pure nothingness of spent energy.

The soul dust resides as virgin spirit in the god of all truth to whom the material belongs and from whence it never departed. It is just the capacity of the soul to be aware that has ended. But with the end of the dream, the soul returns as dust because this soul, alive, would never be able to exist in reality again and as a deceived entity it has spent its vitality in the dream—fiction is all this soul would understand but the battery is dead. The integrity of this awareness unit "soul" then ceased to exist, just as if this soul had never existed. If there is no personal awareness and no individual soul memory in truth, then personal beingness does not exist. I believe that biological cells in a creature body die also because of deceit inherent in its makeup. New cells are created and imbued with the proper propaganda to allow the body to continue a while longer in this state of self-deceit. This is so because everything in the universe has a connection to soul, and deceived soul is always in a quandary between what is real [innate to it] and the lie believed.

Chapter 3

Being Alive Is Religion

Religion vs. Reality

Even if one does not believe in any religion, one is still religious toward physical life. Everyone has personal beliefs, rules, convictions, and alignments pertaining to existence. Whatever things in life are important to a person is the person's spiritual life, and a person will cling to it with all might and desperation; just as a rich person will cling to riches as if life depended on it. Whether it is a political party, a career, a creed of religion, a sport or sports, TV, a person will act religiously in holding to it. Without such alignment, human life would be unbearable. A human being must have a purpose, and this purpose is the person's religion. A professional football player is a football player religiously. A football player with a permanent injury who cannot play the game anymore still watches sports events religiously and devotes time to meeting the players. Since there really is no purpose to physical life, the purpose is invented and religiously adhered to. The real meaning of life is thus make-believe—religions of insanity that people call "being normal."

If you deviate from this normalcy in human life, you are considered dysfunctional, retarded, or mentally deranged. "Mental Experts" do what they can to realign you to the normalcy of "rational" life. Human life is fiction; so positive thinking, ambition, and other mind games do work because all is make-believe; but insecurities always place obstacles in the mind to impede the success planned; just as happens in dreams.

Dreams and DREAMS

Your dreams consist of random settings and random actions. You must react to situations, and hope for some desired conclusion; but before that happens, you wake up, or the dream scene changes entirely. Dreams work like an awareness altering drug. We are carried off into situations beyond comprehension. It is not the reality in which we exist. Spiritual dreams are similar in action and effect but in the spiritual dream all souls' dreams are hooked into the same computer program and they experience the programmed effects in earth as if every human being exists in the same reality and seems to live its own existence. All the other human beings are fictions with which one "interacts in the environment of the screen." It truly is like being spiritually drugged. When a soul awakens from the dream in reality nothing has been accomplished just as when a person here on earth awakens from a dream. He retains a vague memory of the dream, but the dream does not leave any material facts behind. Human life is such a nightmare. It, also, does not leave any spiritual facts behind. Spiritually, we gain nothing of material substance; what some of us do get is insight into the workings of spiritual evil and a spiritual decision to not ever have anything to do with it.

When a physical person dies he leaves a whole life of unresolved and never really attended-to useless issues behind, just as it happens in a dream. When a soul dreams that it has physically died, its mind will sooner or later wander off into another birth and physical life. Since soul is addicted to the drug of physical life, which is based on spiritual deceit, it imbibes another dose of deceit and comes back as a new life form. It arrives with a huge heritage of propaganda already instilled in it; the next life is assigned by the daemon, then, in charge of the soul.

The Physical Body as a Set of 3 D Goggles for soul

The real you is hidden inside you. Your soul is real but in a coma due to spiritual deceit. The body is a piece of fiction designed by Jehovah to hide your real self-soul—and to hide all truth from the awareness of the physical projection. The body is like a computer image in super 3-D; like a set of goggles placed over the awareness of the soul. The body is utterly oblivious of the existence of soul because the body is an imaginary utensil used by soul. You cannot know yourself unless you can be aware of and be in communication with your soul. The body prevents that because the body can only observe and sense the fiction of its fictional environment. All it sees and is aware of is fiction—unreality, the dream. If you believe your body is who you are and that this universe is real, you cannot be redeemed by the Good Spirit.

Soul's Body Determines Soul's Sense of Awareness

To know yourself as soul is only possible through the Good Spirit, who comes to us from true reality. The Good Spirit is communion in truth, so when enveloped by the Good Spirit you know who you are and you know what reality is. The human body prevents such self-aware contact with yourself—soul; the physical body treats the soul as nonexistent. Only the Good Spirit can reveal the true self to you and your native environment of being. You and the soul are one—even better, you ARE soul. Your body does not exist. The body is an appendage that falls from soul [wears out like clothes or disappears when you wake up], again and again. In the body, you are ignorant of ultimate reality and thus of your soul and of truth. Jesus, in the parable of sickly Lazarus and the rich man, taught that there is life after death. If Abraham lives after dying, so do we. However, we do not know in what conscious state Abraham still exists—reality or fiction.

Confusion of Gods

You are continually moving in jurisdiction from a higher daemon to a lower one from life cycle to life cycle, and the particular daemon in charge of you is your "personal" god. We all talk of god and the holy spirit as being everybody's god, but no one knows another person's god. The other person's god is not your god.

This exercise of unity of belief is enforced on you by your personal daemon, never the Good Spirit. You belong to your daemon, the nebulous director of your physical role. There can be no interdenominational unity because there is no absolute unity of definitions of creed. The religious denominations are different because the gods are different—but everyone make-believe that they are the same. We, all, practice make-believe in settings of make-believe and in a reality of make-believe. We are truly lost.

Each daemon has its own heaven; that is why anybody believing in a particular religion, no matter how absurd it sounds to others, claims to have a god or holy spirit and a heaven in which to be with that spirit if he can earn the "grace" to be accepted. There are many heavens and many daemonic versions of Jesus Christ to guide believers to those heavens. Everybody practices make-believe in hell, which hell they believe is somewhere else—no, this is hell—right here, but there are many mental places to be in hell, according to the daemon who reigns over you!

Most religions claim to be the only one to have the corner on redemption and a place in the true heaven. They are all talking as if they mean the same god and heaven, but no one can understand another because every one defines his version of this *"true" god* and heaven according to the gospel of the lie of his own recognized and accepted daemon in his heart. People do not know the existence of another god, so everyone talks of the vast variety of "daemons" as if they are all one and the same. Just take the differences between the Christian god and the god of Muslims—they are irreconcilable, yet they both are a part of the Old Testament's Jehovah. That is why conversion becomes more and more difficult. Only when a person can convince another that he has the wrong "god" will one listen and maybe be converted—but then one still has the wrong god because only the Comforter can lead a person into truth.

True communication among humans is impossible, not only in communicating one's view of god but communication on just about any other subject. Agreement on subjects only get unified by training and propaganda, whereby everybody is forced to believe the same thing about the same subjects under threat of correction, of ridicule, or of being cast out and so have an artificial understanding on "reality" according to the allegiance of one's group. The ultimate absurdity of this is the different levels of honors or degrees given out for being almost perfect in one's definitions and views on a certain subject matter. The universe has all creatures trained to see things the same way according the public opinion of the group they belong to.

Earth Is Hell!

The physical universe is hell. There is no other. Here in hell, one is separated from truth—reality; one is thus "dead" to [out of communion with] reality. We exist in non-reality or non communion. Here in the universe, one exists in a spiritual, fictional setting. Hell has many special places to be. The Spectrum of species is only a small part of greater hell. Hell is so incredibly deep we cannot comprehend its depth.

Even though we are in hell a soul can still earn a special place in hell, the heavens of the daemons; yet one is still in hell. One still exists in a fictional mode of awareness.

The masses of souls, however, will travel down the broad and wide path into the depth of nature as animals where they atrophy from one species to another, ever deeper and ever lower into the regions of more primitive and more brutal existence of hell. This path is the divine rule for them. Those inside the "heavens" available in hell will die nonetheless, for one is still in the virtual strata of hell. Only *truth* will set you free from hell and ultimate soul death; and *truth* is only available from the Comforter in the Good Spirit.

Human Existence Is Evidence of Spiritual Insanity

Humans cannot exist without betraying all that is important to them. Betrayal can be inadvertent, deliberate, and/or based on coercion by powers beyond their own power to control due to cowardice, worldly wisdom, or both. It is certain that nobody is allowed to express his inner feelings and true convictions because the major propaganda systems [cosmic, religious, governmental, and prejudice] have ruled out these possibilities. Public opinion will force most people to accept that this universe is real. That in itself is proof that it is fiction. Truth will never force reality on another because the reality of all things is plain and known. In the universe, earth has everything so well aligned by propaganda that we are still under the impression that all is true and real, but in spite of that we are aware that there are many shades of true and false about anything.

Only public opinion may be freely expressed because it is forced on the public from on high. It is forced on people because it is a lie. Truth is self-evident. That is why everyone exists behind a mask. The mask is the "you" that you are allowed to exhibit by public opinion. The mask tells us that we do not very often agree with what somebody else, government, or one's creed, family and friends tell us is true or false. This, in itself, is betrayal of one's own person. We do not dare come out of the closet. Before one can betray another, one must betray oneself. Everybody lives behind a mask of shame. These masks can be simple or ornate. Humans having ornate masks [those of the popular genre—con men and politicians] are the most sinister and vain, and they can be least trusted. When a stranger is cottoning on to you, whether through the medium of TV or person to person, you can almost be sure he is out to deceive, con or damage you. The process of conning someone can take from a few minutes to several months or more to weave an aura of trust and expertise, which takes time. The quick way is to bluff one's way through by showing credentials. But the act of conning another always happens through the disguise of an angel of light and goodness.

Betrayal and the necessity for survival are synonymous. They act hand in hand. No one can survive without acts of betrayal.

Rules mean powers arranged against you to intimidate, own, and control you. The act of betrayal rests on the principles of rules. Without rules it is pretty hard to betray another person. This universe is based on deceit. Jehovah says existence without rules is death. Jehovah made that rule because if you act without rules you already have violated his rules. You must obey Jehovah or you are dead. Some god! Tyrant is a better word!

You Can Love Only One Master

Jesus said of life, "Existence **based** on rules is death." In many instances rules forbid you to be yourself. There is no majesty in being forced to exist by rules. It is the existence of a slave to live and exist by rules set by another. Rules are there because people intimidate, deceive, and rob each other. Religion is based on rules, and religion is based on clever deceits. Rules protect some and betray all others. Take whatever religion you will and you will find rules and holy precepts. Realm of darkness is the correct definition of the universe—because a belief in the universe is religion and religion means following rules. When you follow the rules set by others you cannot commune in the Comforter because you take in the precepts of another into your communion with the Good Spirit.

The Good Spirit demands that you follow him only. You cannot follow two guides because they will confuse you. You can love only one master—Good or Evil. Make your choice and follow it to the end. One end is reality, the other is absolute death. This holds in that you act according to your conscience, because the Good Spirit is your conscience if he is your guide, and the holy spirit is your conscience if the Good Spirit is not. Like I said, make your choice and stick to it. Do not let any other person or god influence your decision. The time for your final decision is your present life cycle. Government is part of the holy spirit because it demands that you follow its rules. Paul, in Romans 13, proved that he did not understand the workings of the Good Spirit, but he had some profound insights.

Your Most Deadly Enemies

I, however, say "the governments, religious guides and your family are your personal devils." If you take any of these devils to heart, you will die. Jesus stated that you must love him more than father, mother, child and spouse. He also stated that the authorities [religious and secular] are deceitful hypocrites. They are of the devil. Physical life is a deceit played on your spirit. Wake up from the deceit and you will be your own master. It will not be easy but who are these bully-government officials, judges, juries and police officers telling us every second of the day how you must behave and what you must do or not. They are pirates stealing your most precious possession, soul. They are your deadly, spiritual enemies.

People must lie, more often than they would like, because of rules and intimidating powers of enforcement. Such praised things as science and technology are based on rules. Religion is adoration of daemons, and it is always based on rules. Religion is just a deeper level of death. Jesus told us of the way to be free, to be self-determinate—in him, as sons of god. ***Know the truth and the truth will set you free!*** The Comforter in the Good Spirit is ***all truth.*** **That is the kind of truth that gives life and liberty.**

What Outward Stance Must We Have in the Good Spirit?

I have stated this advice in another section of the book but it is so important that I state it again. Do not be conformed to the world. Let go of everything you ever held dear. It is rubbish. You are different because you follow a different guide than all the people you can meet. You are good in the Good Spirit. None can tell you in your heart what to do but your personal guide. To keep the peace, do as the jackasses do out there and tell you to do; do not argue. By your own accord you can do what a devil wants, but in your heart you know he or she is wrong. These "devils" out there allow you to define what you want your reality to be. They are helping you to create your own heaven. You could not do it without them! We get acquainted with evil in negative spirit so we can define our environment in ultimate reality. This is a project that carries more spiritual weight than anything you can do in earth.

Jesus said, "If someone wants to slap you on one cheek, offer him the other cheek as well. If someone steals your wallet, give him your shirt as well." I finally begin to see why Jesus said all the things he taught. People out there do not understand, because they follow a different master. Don't try to teach him because Jesus said for us not to throw our pearls before swine. The masses out there are the swine. They will trample on your most precious knowledge and understanding; and they will rent your self-confidence. Keep what you know to yourself. Do not listen to anybody for knowledge or advice; they will never lead you in truth, but instead they scheme to bring your spiritual death about. Don't fear physical death. If you are ever threatened the Good Spirit will be closest to you. Whatever these devils want you to do, do it, for nothing in earth carries any spiritual weight unless you give it weight, and then you are following the wrong master. Just be their patsy, why clue them in on your knowledge. If they find out, they will try to make you change your mind because you will fit like a square peg into their cock-eyed scheme of fiction, and devils hate that. They are lost, but if they want to, they can find the Good Spirit if they will only seek. He is everywhere. Deceit hid him from us. Who deceived you? This serpent, Jehovah and his hierarchy of daemons and through them every human being you meet. How? Just by wearing the raiment of deceit, the physical body.

Chapter 4

Gods and Demons

The word "god" in human understanding means self-determination and the power to determine the outcome of all things. There are four levels of gods, as far as I want to go into them. Cattle, for instance, have an owner as their god. The owner can ship them in carts, planes, and boats that could get stuck in a hurricane; he can sell them and slaughter them; he can torture and neglect them. There is nothing the cattle can do about it. Beasts confined to the hold of a ship in a hurricane find their whole environment utterly disorganized, without knowing why, and they can do nothing but strain against the violent movements and the sickness, and moan in utter desperation. Owners of cattle are god over them.

Then there is the emperor, king, slave owner, and the many dignitaries in governments who dictate to smaller or larger groups of people and control sections of their lives. They cannot be opposed, and they are gods to the helpless masses in their jurisdiction or control.

There are daemons that are, more or less, like maligned criminals. They rule over and or suppress creatures and environments in the physical universe. They control our environment, our lives and goods, and all the acceptable and disastrous incidents in our lives. The highest of these daemons [as far as we know him] calls himself Jehovah. Jesus, in contradistinction, talked about a father, who does not set rules, and in whose realm, you are free and self-determined in deed and in thought through a quality defined as LOVE.

Knowledge of and love for the father is not religion—it is not based on rules, except one. This one rule is necessary because it creates the boundary between the realms of truth and fiction. It separates reality and fiction. The rule, which is not really a rule but a state of mind, says, "You cannot trust anything in the universe. There is no truth in it. Therefore you cannot trust any person in the universe with your redemption—not even Jesus the Christ when he lived a human life. He was under rule and jurisdiction of higher physical and negative spiritual authorities. He was in conflict with the liberty he insisted on and the rules and enforcement that forbade it. He admitted to his disciples just before his coming death that he was unable to instruct them in truth but that he would send the Comforter—Good Spirit—who would lead one into "*all truth*." [John 16:12-15]

Phony Gods

Jesus lived this life not for his sake, but for ours. He allowed himself to be subject to the biggest fools around—Caesar through Pontius Pilate and his minions, and the religious fanatics of the Judean priesthood. No matter what despots we have to live with, we are free in our thoughts. But when we try to convey our thoughts to others, and if the authorities [kings, government officials, etc.] find out about it, they can forbid the conveyance of our thoughts to others. They install thought laws, thought-crime laws, and enforcement. They can spy on our telephone conversations by law or outside the law as president Bush is doing. He can bomb and kill dozens of innocent people [in the wee hours of the day] in villages in other countries, as he is doing in Pakistan and Afghanistan, and can get away with it. So, President Bush hanged Saddam, but Saddam had so much better control of Iraq that it cannot even be compared with the butchering Bush is responsible for. We are thus isolated in our true thoughts. Why, ever, should I give that long-distance liar and killer, Mr. Bush, my support?

The physical and universal spiritual despots often will not allow us to convey our thoughts to others. This is the main rule of the universe; no matter what realm you are in, whatever country or religion, you are bound not to think certain thoughts and, especially, not to convey them to others—such thoughts are taboo. You will be betrayed by your best friends if you violate that rule.

Where there are taboos, you are dealing with religion—some despot trying to control and protect his realm, which he confiscated or inherited from others. This is true for a tyrant and for Jehovah. They all, including the US government, have confiscated a realm or by unscrupulous methods made it theirs [by physical force and/or by clever deceit]. The US government is our god [and rapidly is becoming the god of the entire world], and this god is setting up systems to read and control our thoughts—the American people venerate this god and pray to it for all kinds of purposes like forgiveness and benefits. This kind of religion is no different, in all its aspects, from worship of the daemon—Jehovah. Just like all other gods, it cannot be seen. One can only observe this god's very busy priests and clerks active in the service and worship of this god. Be convinced that Jehovah is angry at the people for worshiping this other god before him. The curses of Deuteronomy 29 will be the harvest Americans can count on. The curses are already set in action. America is losing its culture, independence, its racial structure, its credibility, its power, its industrial base, its health, wealth and happiness.

A True God

Here is the great difference between god "good" and god "evil." Good gives all its love to the primary being—the Comforter. God, good, uttered him into being. I like to call this primary being the son, and through the son, many beings were created [John 1:1]. God, "good", gave **all** his love or creative energy into the beingness of his son. The son gave his love or creative energy to beings I like to call archangels. He loves them because their beingness came through this son.

> *The communion in the Good Spirit is total; there are no voids in understanding and knowledge in him*

The Father and the son communicate through the Good Spirit. It is the full and complete communion between them. Therefore there are no secrets. Everything in reality is communed in through this Good Spirit. Therefore, everything that happens in the virtual realms of existence such as the universe is known and communicated between the son and the father. Therefore, there is no void in knowledge in god. When we are born again, a new entity in reality we are an operative part in this communion.

Beings I Call Archangels

Archangels are creative entities also. But since there are many archangels, they have individual character traits. They are concerned with themselves in relation to their brother archangels in the son. The manifestation in paradise of their creativeness is the group of trees in paradise. These trees are the "icons" [keys to programs] that stand for the creations of each of these archangels and the thoughts on which these creations are based.

The archangels expanded all that they have received in love into the creations of their own. This is the limiting factor of creatures in the son. They are individuals. They can only be themselves, not their brothers—and as such, they have character, personal ideals, thoughts, and personality; and with these, come new ideas of jealousy, coveting, and hate. Their creations, then, are as varied as the characters of each of them—hence archangel[s] of good and those of evil. "Good" means those who praise "love" and "honesty" and, thus, true reality. "Evil" means to oppose love and honesty and it prefers fiction, unreality and the power these seem to bring.

Paradise, a Place of Probation

The creatures Adam and Woman in paradise are in a place of probation. They have received advice as to which trees to partake of and which particular tree not to partake of, lest they die. As I mentioned before, all the trees in paradise are like icons. One partakes of them in thought, for immortal creatures live on thought, not food. Depending on the fruits of thought they partook of, they either died from paradise or rose above and beyond it, just as we can imbibe poison or wholesome nutrients.

There were three types of trees in the garden. The tree most advertised was the Tree of Knowledge of Good and Evil. It stood out in the center in the garden. The other trees had good recommendations. One had no recommendation or warnings against it at all. That was the Tree of Life. The Tree of Life, most likely, is the tree of the son.

Adam and Woman were to enter the thought communions of the trees in paradise and learn the praise the archangels beheld for god, the son, who had given them Life. From imbibing enough thoughts of praise in these trees, they were supposed to progress to look beyond the mere recommendation and see the Tree of Life from a new viewpoint and see the beauty of this tree. After partaking of the other trees, they should be knowledgeable and wise enough to partake of it. This tree is the door into the house of the son, their father. Once there, they have no need to go back to the garden although it is, of course, not forbidden. The second type of tree are all the trees of which god said that Adam and Woman could freely partake.

Exit from Paradise through Believing a Lie

The third type of tree is the "Tree of Knowledge of Good and Evil". It provides another exit from paradise. By partaking of this tree, one's awareness takes a flip so that truth becomes fiction and fiction the truth. One leaves paradise by it becoming hidden by the new awareness, and one arrives in a fictitious universe from which place there is no ready escape. This fictitious realm has taken on the nature of reality, but it is merely a mirage. The difference between Alice arriving in Wonderland and the souls of Adam and Woman arriving in the universe is that Alice retained her memory of her native reality while sojourning in Wonderland. Souls in negative spirit have no memory at all of paradise. The memory of it has been robbed from them by believing a lie about it. This universe is all they are aware of, and, moreover, it is a creation of their own minds' imagination. This imagination is guided and enforced by the Serpent who found a way to use and manipulate their minds, as if under hypnosis, to unfold and uphold the universe with themselves projected in it as physical creatures.

The native environment one exists in is one's god. A person communes with it and gleans a feeling of reality from it. As Jesus said, you have your being, your movements and your life in it. It enfolds you and upholds you. It is god—you and it are one." Since you share your environment with others you and those others are one as well.

The Idea of Being Alive

To be alive is to be in communion with one's environment. When dead, one has lost communion with the environment. Lost communion is a lost, shared-understanding of reality [Having lost a shared communion, as long-standing divorced people may experience, means that these people have permanently terminated communication and knowledge of the whereabouts of each other]. All emotional and friendly concerns are dead for at least one of the parties. The other may seek re-acquaintance but generally to no avail. This is the condition for our true father; he wants us back but we do not even know about him to be with him because of a lie-believed. Those who left paradise through death [spiritual coma] became alive through dreams in another environment, the universe—a fictitious environment to which the Tree of Knowledge of Good and Evil is the portal. Jesus referred to humans as dead [to truth] [Matthew 8:22] and that the universe is the realm of darkness. Humanity and all creatures in the universe are dead to their true god who reigns beyond this place of fiction. We are as-dead in our native environment because we cannot communicate in it or with it, or have our being in it. It ceased to be our god. In other words, by imbibing thoughts about the Tree of Knowledge of Good and Evil, one is lost in a sphere of nothingness created in paradisiacal reality. One switched gods.

A person's entry into the universe is contingent on the belief of a lie. The soul believed a fiction and had to receive a body created from fictitious material; and that body can only see, comprehend, and believe things and ideas based on the fiction—to communicate in it, and glean its feeling of existence from it. In other words, we have our being in this dream world. It is very realistic and since this is all we have for an environment we are very solidly attached to it—we are thoroughly brainwashed to see it as our native abode of existence.

Since the universe was created fictitiously it cannot endure, as fiction can change from moment to moment—while truth endures. This is why bodies come and go in the physical environment—through death and rebirth. All life [life=souls] in the universe is caught in fiction, yet, the fiction seems so real that creatures existing in it can only accept it as the only reality. That is why it is so difficult to escape this real-looking fictitious universe—hell.

What Redemption in True Spirit Is Like

Paul talks of a living temple in god of which all the redeemed souls are a part and of which the positive spiritual Christ is the cornerstone. In the temple, all souls exist in true reality. In this realm of reality, one knows all there is to know of the environment, which includes one's fellow souls in the temple, a body, a structure of integrated spiritual cells, a living being. This knowledge of our environment and our fellows is sought and given freely without force or coercion. Nothing is hidden as things are here in this universe. Hence, it is based on true liberty and sincere unity.

On earth, we would call that esprit de corps—a unity of being for all those connected to this temple. This organization of souls (cells) in a body, each with its own awareness, give the souls an ability of being aware as the US government is aware and knows all it wants to know of all citizens that are a part of it; and the citizens are aware of the god-like quality and power of government.

The local spiritual environment in the living temple is such that souls with the same kind of character, interests, and ideas and lifestyles are closest to you; and souls that differ slightly are a bit further removed; and those completely unlike you are at the opposite end of the temple or system of relationships, yet the whole is functioning perfectly and harmoniously. You will enjoy everybody and praise your father in heaven together and with gusto.

More thought interactions take place and more growth goes on throughout the living temple from moment to moment, as I seem to receive them here while typing. Together, the souls forming the temple are forever making the temple more radiant and glorious to behold for "good" and for all.

Governments try to duplicate that live communion within their jurisdictions through propaganda, public education and all other means of communication, integrated into a false sense of community and of course, through law and enforcement. You must do it their way or you are getting nothing. As you can see government wants to be god just as Jehovah and the true father are gods. But only the true god gives you what you would like to get. Evil will force on you what they want you to have.

Your purpose as a student in the Good Spirit is to encounter all the evil this universe can give you and determine in your heart that it should not be like that in earth and therefore not in your place of reality. You have to commune every thought about reality in the Good Spirit in order for him to know exactly what you want your true reality to be like. As you are defining your reality Jesus in 'heaven' is creating a place, a mansion, according to the specifications you give the Good Spirit. So, be not of the world, but be a very good observer of the world, so you can discern what you do not want in heaven for you. Since the universe is a place that teaches you everything about evil by making you experience it, you give the Good Spirit a complete definition of what you want your true reality to be. Once your ideas and that of the Good Spirit coincide you are out of this realm and in the true reality of your specifications. There is no ambiguity of reality, and nothing hidden. That is reality. Jesus went to reality to be the contractor of the architectural mansion you gave him the plans for. Jesus Christ is listening to your wishes in the Good Spirit to realize or give you everything you are asking him to do for you. Jesus said, "Ask and it shall be given you." Now you understand the full meaning of what he told us so long ago. This statement has nothing to do with wishes being granted in this universe. It is true in negative spirit also, but in negative spirit it is based on deceit. Everything in earth tarnishes and is destroyed. Jehovah and his daemons can only deceive and hurt you, so that you, once you are in the Good Spirit and have figured out that earth is evil; you can specify what you really would like to experience in true reality.

Chapter 5

A Reservoir as a Model for Spiritual Realities

Hidden Knowledge

The universe has the aspects of all things hidden in it [we even hide our true feelings from ourselves]. Jesus said that there is no truth in the universe. Here on earth, we know nothing of even our closest friends and family. We can only interpret what we think we are experiencing on earth and with our friends and intimates. These experiences are all based on ignorance, lies, and concealments. We are lost in the universe. We think we know where one surrounding begins and where another ends and how far the intermediate surroundings extend. But we know not for sure, and government sets up hidden mental, physical, and emotional boundaries that confuse and trap us even more. We are insecure about many things, and we lie to ourselves about the things we think we know. Everyone tries to deceive others to hide their shame and depravity or some predatory intent.

A Realm Where All Things Are Revealed

In the living temple, all truth proceeds from Jesus Christ who is the cornerstone of the edifice. He is like the center of a nerve system. We can never be lost because we can go back any time to commune with the cornerstone in the foundation and be oriented in truth. In the temple, we **know** at all times all about our environment and we can get to know about the total environment whatever is needed by going back to the cornerstone. There we are in the realm of light.

We thought that the Internet would bring us in closer communication, but what we find most often on the Internet is clever deceit that leads us into traps that cost time and money from which to extricate ourselves. The predators on the Internet have the latest technology working for them, and they are getting rich at other people's expense. The Internet is more a trap than a means of communication. Whatever man designs for good is turned into ashes and corruption. There is no escape from predators in the physical environment. They make life miserable for everyone, even themselves.

The redeemed soul, however, makes all god's love worthwhile and is why he would do, and does, the same over again. The triumph is in returning his fallen "beloved" from being almost irretrievably lost back to the highest, the understanding and love created in his son; and this is why the redeemed become like the son of god. They also have truth and have acquired true understanding and love.

An Allegory of Spirit in a Worldly Setting

Once the energy received by the archangel is expanded on his thoughts and ideas, the archangel cannot use energy on another creation. He wants to maintain his creation. Maintenance is another idea that follows thoughts of creativity, planning, and execution. Whatever he receives is now in the form of budgetary needs for maintenance. An archangel could not possibly create anything else, but what he created, a full statement of himself. It expresses the love the father, through the son, has for the archangel and vice versa.

True reality, then, is flux—a converting of one kind of energy into another. For example, say, a dam holds back a height of three hundred feet of water. Let's call the latent energy in the supply of water god, Good. In the base of this dam, there is an electricity generating station. The high-pressure water flow through the generating station, the son, creates high potential electricity for distribution to the laboratories of his archangels residing in the region of distribution [paradise]. The archangels expend the energy on diverse kinds of uses. True reality is even more than that. True reality is the Good Spirit because all reality is bound up in the Good Sprit—the communion between the father and the son. But the extraordinary thing here is that this forms a binary computer system, and the Good Spirit allows archangels to design and run their programs on that computer. The designers and operators of these diverse programs are the archangels. The archangels can create their own programs, universes.

All the available high pressure water flow is given to the "son" who is envisioned here as the generating system in the base of the dam [the love god has for the son]. The son passes on what he receives, except for a certain amount needed for his own maintenance [internal friction in the water conduits and transforming machinery and electrical need of operating equipment]. The amount given depends on the size of the water conduits that directs the water pressure and flow to the generating stations. Their sizes match the need for high potential electricity in the area the generators serve. But all the time the pressure of the water held back by the dam continues to give; and the son continues to receive, and to give to the archangels.

Everything everyone receives below the level of son is just enough to sustain the creations of the archangels. Each archangel can only create one universe and never receive more love or creative spirit than to create and sustain that one universe. Our universe represents the Serpent and is him in thought, expression, and action. He is in all the parts, and all the parts are in him—along the line of the prayer Jesus had with his father in John 17.

The transformers that convert the high potential electricity to a lower voltage can be for good or for bad. Most of the generators will serve communities and hospitals. Others may be devoted to a research station involved in chemical, nuclear, and germ warfare. Say, this is bad, for this use of the energy is to kill and destroy. The output of all transformers is used for good and bad purposes simultaneously—for phone calls that can save a life and for obscene and threatening calls that upset or can kill a person. The weather that links the exhaust water to the rivers and the rainwater back into the lake can thus be said to be the Good Spirit. It is the communion between all entities loved by god and the son.

In returning to the model of the dam, in John 17, Jesus became like an archangel himself because he takes from the father what was given him in this universe, which is fiction. What was given him in John 17 was not what he had before—*brethren* [creatures of his own race] who believed that he was the son of god. This grant of status to the son is a new creation in Jesus in which he will expand what he receives from god. He is in all the believers; and the believers, altogether, make Jesus. It is just as Paul stated, "One can look at the believers as the bones and tissue of Jesus' body, and Jesus expresses himself through all these parts by means of the Good Spirit." What, thus, has happened to a true believer is that he has risen to a higher level—from a level below the dam [inside a universe] to a level as near to god as the son himself. Redeemed believers will make up a new living temple as Adam was previously—a creation from a status below the viceroy [son] to status equal to viceroy [son of god] and as brother.

This can be expressed in the model of the dam and the lake of water behind it by what is actually happening in a situation of the water flowing through the generators. During the peak hours, the maximum amount of water is supplied to the generators to keep up with the demand for energy, but during periods of low demand, the excess energy is used to pump water from below the dam level back into the reservoir.

The Good Spirit in this model is in the dam because the dam is the communion between water force and the water contained behind the dam. The dam knows exactly when the water rises and the pressure increases or when the water drops and the pressure decreases. The Good Spirit also communicates with the son [the generators] and the father [the water pressure behind the dam]. The Good Spirit is in the river system supplying the lake and in the weather that keeps water in the river in flux [spirit]. The Good Spirit is the communion [loving interaction] between the father and the son and thus evaporates the water that has flowed through the generators and returns it through rain and drainage to the river and back into the reservoir. The Good Spirit is thus the total communion between the father and the son.

The archangels are below the level of the dam. All they know is high voltage electricity [the son]; they never knew, and will never know, about water and its flow through the turbines [the true god] and how it returns there.

Entrance into and Sustenance of Soul in the Universal Programs

Adam and Woman can receive thoughts from any of these trees. Once they have imbibed the fruit of a tree, the substance of Adam and Woman are disintegrated into cellular awareness entities called souls into the computer display. Souls caught or residing in a created universe of an archangel are there on their own volition. Soul is sustained by the son; but his universal projection is sustained by universal resources.

In our universe projection, soul projections [creatures] are sustained by the body tissue of other creatures in the environment while one receives molecular oxygen from the environment. If a certain location has a limited amount of free oxygen, life will be sustained in competition with other creatures until the oxygen runs out. This, of course, will not happen naturally because the subroutine in the program "World" prevents it. The daemonic hierarchy has a duty to make this a viable environment to entice us to continue to be a part of it. The universe defines its own evil by forcing entities to kill and devour other creatures.

The Different Strata of Awareness in Spirit

The creatures in our universe know nothing about paradise and the trees in paradise. They might have heard of it because Jehovah may have disclosed it to one of his favorites like Moses. They can only see as far up as Jehovah, who can thus claim to be their highest god.

The redeemed souls [those who actually are back in truth] are in the son and now share in the Good Spirit on the other side of the dam where the water is. They are thus somewhere in the dam and the turbines and are an active force in the trinity, "one" with water, "one" with the dam, and "one" with the turbines—Jesus. In the case of the regular trees in paradise, the archangels [and thus Jehovah also] never were acquainted with the Good Spirit. The spirit of love and redemption reigns free in our universe to redeem those in his grasp, because Jehovah does not know him and cannot stop or divert him. There might be a private spirit of communion between ultimate reality of god and Jehovah, but that is outside the Good Spirit, because the Good Spirit is the communion between father and son. If there is a son there must be a mother. I suspect that Jehovah is god's wife and that there is a truthful spousal communion between the two.

Another excellent example of the flux in spirit is the medium of legal currency, or money in an economic system. It too is a flux, a conversion of funds, created out of sheer nothing for the execution of ideas and plans. Currency runs in a loop and continues to flow from low to high potential and back to low through a generating system called the mint and institutions called banks that hold back a percentage to overcome their own internal friction and release the rest to corporations [archangels], who create their little or great universes of activity and production, using employees [slaves] as mini energy converters that run on little bits of currency supplied to them. They in turn flow currency into the corporations for needed articles from whence all the currency returns to the bank for accounting and redistribution.

Chapter 6

A Constant Stream of Changes
Betrays a Virtual Reality

The Influence of Authority

Human creative spirit is closely related to religion. Consider the many expressions of religious art throughout history by divergent religious institutions. Those inventing a new religion do so by the urgings of daemons, other spirits, or even gods. They establish the creed through expressions of art. Art is used to train a following to accept the adopted tenets of the religion. Such newly created beliefs stir the traditional authorities to fright and anger. It undermines unity and causes loss in collected revenues. In Jesus' case, the authorities thought that Jesus started a religion that differed from the established one. All he did was attack their hypocrisy, and more importantly, introduced the world to another god, unknown in the world before.

Our modern systems of design, production and distribution are based on religion. It is based on the belief of universal reality as the ultimate reality. All creature activity is done in the belief that the universe is all there is. It is a belief system brought in expression through manufacture. It is spiritually deadly. But, really, what can we do? We take life so seriously we cannot do anything else. That is religion. Well-indoctrinated Christian, Muslims, and what have you express their religion just as seriously.

The religious and "secular" authorities were also enraged with Mohammed, Martin Luther King, Calvin, and other protestant reformers, who opposed the national religions around them. Jesus as man opposed the Judaic religion and also wished to enlighten the people to the existence of a never-known-before, and higher god. As far as teaching and convincing the masses, he failed utterly. This is only natural. On earth, nothing can succeed that is not backed by force, vast amounts of funds, and an ignorant but determined early following that will financially and status-wise profit through participating in spreading and establishing the creed.

The Manipulation of Religions and Ideologies for Private Gains

King Henry the Eighth reformed the church he controlled for his own private and political purposes, which caused King Phillip of Spain to prepare for war [the Spanish Armada] and to attack England to bring the king back to heel. Then, the world entered the area of "political revolutions." We had the American and the French revolutions, many in South America and Central America. On the heels of these and even during that era, we had ideological upheavals and betrayals of the philosophies of the then present systems of authority.

In American history, we had a constant infighting between those who wanted individual liberty and those who wanted protection and favored status of banking and commerce over individual liberty. This quarrel was already fought tenaciously during the formulation of the American Constitution. This quarrel was led by Jefferson for those who wanted to retain personal liberty and by Hamilton who led the fight in favor of the bankers.

The bankers were able to pervert the Constitution by inclusion of clauses that allowed government entities to change the intrinsic understanding of the Constitution. In the 1830s, New York State adopted laws for the incorporation of business firms on the principle of limited liability, which already existed in Britain. The rest of the states followed suit, and then it became law in the United States as well. The Fourteenth through Nineteenth amendments that followed the Civil War officially documented and incorporated the flip-flop of power from the people and the states to the federal government. The corruptions in the original Constitution were used to accomplish the addition of the Eleventh Amendment on up. The state and federal laws of business incorporation worked against President Andrew Jackson's victory over the national banking arrangement and eroded his victory completely.

Incorporation by government license was such an advantage over individual proprietorship that soon every successful business was incorporated. This placed the citizens working for the corporations in a position of subjection to government control. Through laws of incorporation personal income taxation became possible because the free people derived their income from government-controlled institutions. They had to pay taxes for the privilege to work in these institutions. That is how the right to make a living, which ought to be free from taxation, became a job, under government privilege, that was subject to the income tax. The incorporation of the Social Security Act in the 1930s made an end to the right to make a living, twisting it into a privilege to work. This act put the final nail into the coffin of liberty for the people. One can see that through irresistible seductions by government, the people allowed themselves to be robbed of their rights. As an additional note, the laws of incorporation in England were not as dramatic in the changing of the people's rights as they were for Americans. The English already were serfs of the Crown.

Hostilities between libertarians and commercial interests changed to hostilities between socialist democrats and old-guard patrician republicans. This soon deteriorated into a commercial, socialist democratic struggle where both parties—the Democrats as socialists and the Republicans as conservatives—embraced the socialist ideologies from different viewpoints; and then the parties were merged into one party that fronted two opposing parties. The true republicans lost out altogether, but these new pseudo-Republicans were able to pervert socialist democracy into a tool in their service.

The original differences between the parties drowned in a flood of new ideologies. The patricians thus lost in appearance, but in reality, the republicans [the wealthy, including rich bankers] embraced and corrupted the principles of democracy to enslave the people even deeper through an expansive and insidious system of control and propaganda. Human beings [who are lost spiritually and politically] can be herded hither and thither; like cattle, we can be slaughtered [through phony wars] and never know that we are being exploited, enslaved, and kept utterly confused.

Comparison of Betrayal of the People and Adam and Woman

This process is uncomfortably similar to the scheme of seduction that the Serpent used to tumble Adam and Woman from free, eternal beings to slaves upholding a universe. The Serpent adopted the new name of Jehovah. [I use the name Jehovah for the group of daemons that seduced Woman and Adam, for we are dealing with—just as the One World Order—a hierarchy of entities with special titles of nobility.] Human society simply continues on the scheme of original deceit. What I wrote above is only a continuation and variation on this scheme. This process will go on and on. A little further in the book figure 11, page 396 shows a representation of the trap showing the cone sections of the trap. The deeper sections in the trap are the situation for all animals. They are trapped forever. They cannot prevent slipping deeper and deeper into the net called universe where conditions for existence become worse and worse. They are so enticed by seduction that they are addicted to it. We know that it is a dog-eat-dog world and no one will do anything about it. This seduction is called hunting instinct. There will always be hunters and prey. Many cultures see heaven as an eternal hunting ground. What they don't know is that earth is just that—and it is hell!

As you can see, we had a being, a nation called the United States of America, consisting of states [organs] and free human beings [cells], that was seduced. This seduced nation changed character from good to evil, and all the cells [human beings] were captured and used to uphold this new character. The being, the free union of states, has lost its liberty; and the cells upholding the original body are enslaved to uphold their own slavery, just as souls are used to uphold their own hell, the phony universe.

People think that they know what is going on and what is for their good, but propaganda instills false beliefs in them that can be changed at will by the manipulators of the propaganda system. After all, in our economic system, currency is the driving spirit; and it has always been under the control of the patricians or local gods. They are lost fools, and through their deceitfulness, they deceive themselves. All who are part of the propaganda, and those deceived through it will fall into the pit [the blind leading the blind]. It raised havoc with personal liberty in America. Americans have no idea what really happened to them. They foolishly maintain the idea that they are free. This is due to the power of propaganda. If people would only open their eyes and minds, they would readily see that they are serfs rather than free people. This experiment of liberty in America failed so miserably that one should be able to see that liberty on earth or in the universe is not possible. The foolishness of it is that nobody gains. All lose—the rich, the poor, the lucky, and the unlucky—but no one understands why.

The clever use of lies and deceit will never benefit anyone. The rush of excitement for someone or a set of conspirators to deceive others, or as many others as an entire nation of people, and now also a world of people, is just too much of a temptation to resist. The catch of falling for a temptation is that one walks into another unseen trap and cannot see why, until it is too late. We are now all so deep in the spiritual trap that escape, for most, has become impossible. Why? It is because the fiction of the universe has taken on importance beyond its merits. It has taken on reality so that we cannot see it as anything but the only reality. True reality has been covered in a layer of deceit so deep that it cannot be found, similar to the snow cover on northern Greenland where the soil has been covered so deep in snow and ice that the local inhabitants have never seen soil or rock.

Cauldron of Change

Ideological revolutionary upheavals were prevalent in French that quickly followed each other. The Russian communist revolution and many in other countries were ideological in nature in efforts to create a more equitable economic relationship in society. The ideologies were closely related but antagonistic towards one another just like the many "in" quarrels in the denominational churches that tore the fabric of the Protestant Christian movement to shreds. Christendom divided along a system devised by daemons who seduced the Christian populace into fragmentation so that each successive daemon had a slice of the worship and devotion, all under the suzerainty of Jehovah. These revolutions were aided by banking and commerce; the great common denominator in societal evil.

In religious upheavals, political division and ideological warfare, parties become fanatically opposed and treat captives of the enemy in the most gruesome, hateful, and depraved manner. This can be seen in the way Jesus was treated after capture, or how Henry the Eighth treated his Spanish first wife, how the Japanese treated their captured Chinese and white prisoners, how Stalin treated the neutral population, how the Nazis treated their Russian prisoners, etc. In other words, it does not matter whether one labels a struggle for supremacy religious, political, or ideological, the means, ways, and purpose of the struggles are identical. That makes all struggles of any kind religious, and makes religion the bastion behind which people will always divide and regroup.

Ideologies are on parity with religious creeds, in origin, in structure, and in operation. Ideological control works like a church. People are indoctrinated and must regularly attend indoctrination meetings in order to make the ideology real in the minds of the captured people. Religion is hateful and is a depraved way of expressing people's innermost feelings, which feelings are always stirred up by cleverly worded and executed propaganda.

A good case in point, again, is Jesus. His trial before Pilate was supposed to be a religious affair between the way the religious authorities expressed their traditions and Jesus who criticized their way of having reverence for "god." When the priests could not get Jesus convicted and sentenced on religious grounds, they quickly reverted to political innuendo to stir Pilate into a sentence of cruel punishment and death for Jesus, for Pilate's god was the emperor. No one, on religious or secular basis, objected to the depravity and deranged violence against Jesus. The propaganda was quick and successful because major propaganda systems, backed by seduction and raw power, always are. In this case, a major powerful propaganda system aligned itself with the lesser propaganda system by means of clever logic and rhetoric.

Another example that shows politics up as a religion is how the Democrats and Republicans in America treat each other. Whenever they can get away with it, or it seems unavoidable, they cheat, lie, and deceive the public in any way, yet the people religiously continue to back a party solely because of tradition. Look at President Bush and his lying to the people to get a very expensive war [in funds, resources, lives, and permanently maimed bodies fought against Iraq. The Iraqi war claims five hundred deaths a day. The comparison between Bush and Saddam makes Bush look like a butcher and Saddam Hussein as a saint. Bush is responsible for hundreds times the deaths than Saddam. Saddam had the people and factions in his country well under control. Bush runs a police state, he has no control whatever, and he is responsible for more deaths than Saddam. It all spins around religion and "politics." As far as we can truthfully determine, Saddam Hussein has not committed any direct crime against America or against the world, and the accusations of Bush that Saddam is a butcher are far-fetched. On those grounds alone, almost every regime in the world is guilty of the same, including the US government. Bush's regime butchered the sons of Saddam Hussein, people who had no power and were not part of whatever Bush said he held against Saddam. In fact, Saddam had the population in extremely good control while Bush's reign is chaos and murder. Bush should be fired and strung up for what he caused to happen to Saddam and also for the unnecessary death and mayhem of many Americans and Iraqis. I cannot understand that he is allowed to outright lie and cause serious upheavals and death, while his lies were discovered before his plans were executed. We, in America, exist in a democratic police state.

Now Bush wants to exclude the enemies from space. What enemies? The US government is the greatest enemy of the people on earth today! There is not even one single country that has declared war on the United States and backed its declaration with a war machine to match the US armed forces. Yet the United States has declared wars on many countries. It has invaded many countries and taken over governments and set up their governments to be the patsy of the US. The US has done that to Afghanistan and Iraq without provocation to the US citizens. The United States declared war on drugs and makes any country with drug traffic its enemy and invades these. The nation with the greatest drug traffic is the United States, and I am sure that most drug traffic involves the US government directly or indirectly. It simply is part of their propaganda machinery. Government needs war and crime to make itself visible and to come across as an angel of light. Remember Oliver North. Through the CIA [US Central Intelligence Agency], much crime and terrorism in the world is linked to US government. What if the government security managers of the major international airports are franchised to the Mafia or some other crime syndicate? These managers could control the exact import quota of drugs smuggled into the US, as long as the syndicate pays it dues to government. I can see that this is exactly what is happening. Drugs are not disappearing from the American scene!

We can safely state that where there is authority, there is money and vanity. Where there is unlimited money and unlimited vanity, there is, undeniably, a thirst for limitless power; and where there is this thirst for power, there is an unlimited inclination for malicious criminality. Voila! We have the US government and the Federal Reserve Board that have unlimited supplies of printed money and an unlimited supply of super egomaniacs to bask in vanity and undercover criminality.

This insatiable thirst for power, with its inherent characteristic for crime, is fully satisfied by being the head, or near the head, of a religious or secular organization. Religious power, based on all-encompassing fear of damnation or curses in the world, together with propaganda and propaganda-backed laws, gives those at the top of a religious empire [whether religious or political in name] total power over its subjects.

The majority of Americans are religiously American. They worship US government, and thus government can almost do anything it wants as long as it keeps coming across as even a shabbily cloaked angel of light. For comparison's sake reflect on power of government domestically and as a world power in 1807 and 2007. We, the people, never granted that increase in power. State governments, in conspiracy with banking and federal government, did. The first step was the deliberately planned, bloody Civil War that took 500 percent more deaths per capita of Americans than the Second World War. Every war, including the Civil war, was deliberately planned and fought under false pretenses to increase US government's base of power in the world and domestically.

US government has its limitless array of laws, propaganda machines and a never-ending procession of administrations to damn and curse anyone and any country opposing it. By holding prominent positions in national politics and justice, those in power continue to sell their fellow citizens into ever more oppressive slavery. How can we take any party or political rhetoric seriously? Through many decades of voting people's liberties and freedom more restricted. We need another system of government for this one has failed us miserably. But what can we do? We know full well that human society is under control of a deranged hierarchy of daemons to whom we must prostrate ourselves according to sick religious doctrines and false religious propaganda.

Thirst for power and authority are religious inclinations, induced in certain people by daemons in order for the spiritual hierarchy to remain in charge of overall human affairs. Souls, however, were created to be inhabited or to be in complete communion with true spirit, the spirit that exists everywhere—the spirit of Good. The foundations of every institution of society are built on quicksand, spiritually, commercially, politically and socially. *Life sucks and then you die* sums it all up! Thanks to Jesus there is a way out of this phony existence; take that road and be rid of the universe.

Chapter 7

Master-Slave Relationships

You Cannot Serve Two Masters

After the "fall" from paradise, souls were [and still are] under the control and influence of the entity in charge at that moment in the negative spiritual hierarchy. This control takes two forms, spiritual and physical; the spiritual entity works through some human placed in charge of a tribe, a region, a nation, and also through direct control over the spiritual computer. Direct spiritual control is spread across the hierarchy of daemons. Examples are pharaohs, kings, popes, generals, President Washington and President Lincoln. These people are always under the control and influence of a daemon. That is why such humans come to be in charge; look at Moses and the judges in OT Israel. It is so for Bush and for the pope.

In all human affairs, whether under guidance of the Good Spirit or any of the negative spirits, all "spirit" is defined by Hebrews 11, verse 1, "To have faith is to be sure of the things we hope for, to be certain of the things we cannot see". What is visible and sensible is supported and upheld by things not seen and a tiny part of the things not seen is that soul you, enslaved to serve a daemonic Hierarchy, Jehovah. So humans are never proceeding under any measure of their own steam and control.

Up until Jesus arrival on the physical scene the people had only one highest master, Jehovah. Jesus announced another master, in John 17. Now we have a choice between 2 masters. We can now switch allegiance. If you want to be redeemed to reality disavow Jehovah. Ignore all your attachments to the world, its seductions and troubles and seek the one and only true good in all creation—the Comforter who reigns absolute through love. Through this stance you stay free of seductions and cause communion between the Good Spirit and your soul. The reason I write vigorously about the criminality of the US government is to encourage you to withdraw from Jehovah-upheld politics altogether, and focus on what is possible in guidance of the Good Spirit. The world is doomed and so are all the egomaniacs. The evil that goes on in earth has its origin in high negative spiritual places and souls are the victims.

In Earth One Is Always Misguided

The following is a universal statement: Where there is religion and/or government in charge of a group of people, there is a criminal organization at the top. It cannot be any other way in this universe because the criminality comes from up high in negative spirit.

The best attitude for a follower of the Good Spirit is thus a mental stance of utter indifference to life and loved ones because whatever is conceived or held up as the latest "philosophical truth" is hogwash. As Jesus said, "Only one is good." And Jesus excluded himself as man. Whatever is not good is part of the daemonic structure and organization—the negative spiritual hierarchy under authority of Jehovah, the spiritual father of lies.

History—religious and secular—is always written and controlled by the winner in the form of propaganda. Jehovah is a winner, and his propaganda is the physical universe. In America, all news and all history today is issued and or monitored by agencies of the US government of which the IRS, Home Land Security and the CIA are not the least, and Bush now allows more snooping and personal searches in homes and in public, and there is not a person that can resist it. It rubs me the wrong way to have to betray one's business relations to the taxing agencies by order of government. It is unethical.

Christian government or Christian-influenced "secular" government is bound to a generally recognized physical "good" [another disguise of evil]. Government cannot be considered benevolent if this is not true. The masses would rise up and that would topple the privileged hierarchy. Under the guise of doing good authorities will always continue to exploit the masses. In doing so it must stay just a hair above being downright suppressive. Government, today, uses the finest scientific knowledge and control to find that line. They seek the most control and revenue without upsetting the peace. The amount of protestors against government in society is a sure sign we are very near the line of brutal oppression. As long as the protestors are minor in forces, propaganda and law enforcement can stifle their influence. The bombing of the federal building in Oklahoma was pinned on McVeigh, a well-known protestor, to condemn and ridicule the tax protesting patriots. That is the manner that is generally used. Government has all the power to fabricate evidence to pin the crime on a patriot. Government-proffered evidence is completely unreliable because government can forge identity papers and whatever they need to blame others and to make their plans succeed. McVeigh was captured too quickly; and the destruction of evidence afterwards was too swift to not tie government to this crime. With government, we must take all their rhetoric on belief. People never have the facts to verify what government does secretly. Where we are dealing with belief we are dealing with religion, and the belief we are stuck with comes from lying people and it is most often wrong.

Modern Man Worships Evil

In the case of Christendom, authority's power to reign is tied to a *man*, Jesus Christ; and in the case of US government, to the "Constitution". Because it was a document to insure guaranteed limits of power for government liberty was given the death sentence from its inception. The governments of America, over the years, trampled it to death. Being a "good citizen" for government's sake is absolute proof that a person is practicing a religious creed and is dead to the intent of the Constitution and to the true spirit because US government is a false god.

A churchgoing Roman Catholic American citizen is a well-deceived person, for he has adopted and worships two entirely irreconcilable gods—government on the one hand and Jehovah through both Jesus and Mary, that are worshiped through government-incorporated religious authority. This person is thoroughly brainwashed and he does, like a robot, what is expected of him as dictated by the two propaganda systems. American government has risen above the power and might of the Catholic Church, so a good Roman Catholic will obey government law first and secondarily obey papal law—why? He fears the punishment of trespassing government's law over papal law. He is a "good" US citizen first and a Roman Catholic second. The "good citizen" Roman Catholic believes that government provides the best good and the more-to-be-feared law enforcement in physical life [one prays to it for benefits]; and god, Jehovah, supposedly provides the best good in the spiritual realm. The Roman Catholic, and any other religious adherent in America thinks that he has the best of both and can have eternal life as well. The truth is that only the true god is good, all else is just false belief. Jesus, the man nailed to a cross, is material evidence of the spiritual lie. If the universe was not upheld by corrupt spirit, Jesus would not have had to be born and murdered.

Christians of all major denominations believe that government is the best good available. Christ is only given lip service by "Christians". Jesus was spiritual good disguised as evil, or more accurately, Jesus was "good" disguised as "evil that disguises itself as good". It is because of his disguise as evil disguised as good that nobody ever before seems to have gotten his deeper message. Christians and Mormons worship the disguise; they never could see the true spirit in Christ. Christians never have understood the real purpose of his coming, so they venerate the evil and are oblivious of his spiritual good. Jehovah's Messiah is believed to aid the Christian when he observes Romans 13 [Everybody must obey state authority . . .]. This gives government a powerful secular edge as seducer and deceiver. It gives government religious license to commit crime. As seen from a true spiritual perspective Jehovah's Messiah is the anti-Messiah of true reality. The true spiritual "Messiah" from the realm of good was never recognized, because reality is obscured in a realm of fiction.

Government as a Temple of Worship

Those employed by government in positions of high authority are its priests, accolades, and religious enforcers; and very many of these, and many government employees as well, are very religious as believers in some other god secondarily. This sense of religiousness toward government is heightened many times in the case of individuals in the police and armed forces. They are the temple guards with license to kill on orders of priests of government. These are thoroughly deceived by government and consider government the highest god. They must take a sacred oath to obey the governments' priests. Officials in government have always been privileged and must be addressed by "titles of nobility." Judges still retain their title "Your Honor." We pray to government for aid, and help in our arguments with other entities.

The April 2005 issue of *Reader's Digest* has an article that states that prayer aids in healing people from diseases and mental traumas. Religious prayers are heard and acted upon by daemons or minor gods of the negative spiritual hierarchy. These prayers hold no true spiritual content because they are addressed to the wrong god. Pray, instead, for deliverance from the gods of the universe.

Many people, also "pray", to government for financial aid—government's holy spirit [credit], confiscated from the people as sacrifice. Such prayers tell us where the hearts of the worshipful are—on their physical perspective, not on their true spiritual perspective.

> *There cannot be any spiritual healing in the Good Spirit as long as people thoroughly confuse evil for good.*

These several sources of universal "good" had to be corrupted first and the corruption taken as the original for the general public to be baited and caught in it. Jehovah had to corrupt true spirit to pretend to be the highest god and government had to corrupt its license to operate to be our god and master; and to be able to dispense benefits prayed for. Modern good can only come from a government licensed and incorporated business, whether that would be a church, a charitable institution, or a commercial business. Private, secret charity is not recognized and not supported. People who worship through a religious institution or democratic form of government are lost and remain lost to the true spirit, and to reality. Jesus said that truth [that comes from beyond the universe through the Good Spirit], if understood and embraced, will set one free [free from the universe and negative spirit, spiritual confusion].

> This proves that our predicament is bound in untruth or, rather, a lie. What kind of truth or lie can we be dealing with? It cannot be some physically grounded lie because we consider ourselves alive, so we must believe and are condemned because of a spiritual lie believed. Jesus said we are dead in spirit. We are in effect of some spiritual lie believed. This is the major premise of this book.

Present humanity, in fact, worships the physical universe through the actions of their bodies by believing and participating in the commercially-grounded, socialist democratic process [things and ideas of the world].

Voting as a Sacred Token of One's Worship of Government

Hidden powers in government control the voting process and determine who will be allowed in the branches of government to have a say in the formulation of its laws and enforcement. The power available at the top is too great to haphazardly decide who shall have it. The most-high priests decide who shall have the high-priestly positions. In America, government has established itself as god that is actively worshiped by its registered voters. Such deification can only be established through force, careful selection from above of its political ministers and priests, and ongoing fanfare of propaganda. That is how all religions got power, from the Moonies under Rev. Moon to the Catholic Church under leadership of the pope and to the Muslims. The full array of Christian denominations has lost the propaganda war against the US government, and these are now obedient subjects to government. This has been possible through Christians' obedience to Romans 13 in the New Testament; and, because of it, America is no longer considered a Christian nation.

Incorporated Religion Acknowledge Government as Master, and God.

The universal hierarchy of spirit can be compared to the loan industry or banking in America. A loan officer gives an entity funds to bring to life, or to keep alive, a business. But through this grant of life, the loan institution insists on receiving a continual tribute—interest or tax. Jehovah, as the head of the universe, forces souls into his realm of evil. Once in the realm, the soul receives a grant of life, the physical body, in which to be and act in the world; and in return, the spiritual hierarchy demands a tribute. What the comatose souls do not know is that they are wired solidly into the power supply of the computer to feed it the necessary energy, just as US citizens are wired in solidly to government through the corrupted Constitution and governments' laws as working slaves to supply its needs. The people even believe that these laws were created and kept in power by **their** license to government.

In "Old Israel," Jehovah established a system of tribute through the creed laid down in the Torah [basically]. There was a demand for continual enforced worship and interest, sacrifice, and a correspondent blessing of spiritual protection and a position of favored status as long as the community remained loyal and worshipful toward him. In case of default, the community or the individual were cursed with physical, communal, and financial catastrophe [Deuteronomy 28 and 29]. As you can see, this system of worship is exactly like the setup in the United States of America, except in America the system was established through progressive deceit over two hundred years. The end results are the same.

The Hebrew religion, through promises made by Jehovah to Abram, and later to his offspring, was essentially a contract. The Old Testament creed of the Israelites was a contract between a god and his people. Abram was first approached by Jehovah in a clever sales pitch with "samples" thrown into the pitch to hook Abram in pursuing the contract that he proposed between Abram and his posterity as one party and himself as the other party [almost identical to the seduction by the Serpent to Woman].

The Basic Principle in Master-Slave Relationship Is That the Slave Cannot Contract With His Master

This happened also to the American people. The founding fathers, relying on Providence, a higher authority [Jehovah], created a new government based on a contract called "the Constitution." The people and the offspring of these originally free, American people, as "we, the people," were bound to defend this contract in reliance on this "higher authority" against the officials of government, their implied enemy. Jehovah also demanded that the Israelites defend themselves from encroachment of external powers. Jehovah would only help them if they showed the courage to defend themselves. Jehovah deliberately allowed the ancient nation of Israel and the people of the United States to be defeated and destroyed because they lacked the care and courage to defend their communion with this deity.

The government, formed in agreement with this contract, soon began to entice the people with its own quasi contracts, which, when entered into by the people, violated and demeaned the original contract—the "Constitution" by making government the higher authority. The basic principle in master-slave relationship is that the slave cannot contract with his master. This is a principle clearly understood in the culture of keeping slaves; yet nobody bothered to keep "slave" government from contracting with "we, the free people". This mistake was exploited by government to reverse positions and now "we, the slaves" cannot contract with our master, government. We must first identify ourselves through our slave tag [US I.D. number] in order to approach the master. Government is smarter than we, the people, because it keeps tight control over its newly won position of master. The people are suppressed to the limit of endurance, and the people seem to love it so. By government pretending to be our hero, we were suppressed. It holds all the power and the people have absolutely no power.

US government accomplished even more by fighting many unnecessary wars. The accumulative effects of many such violations of the original contract, caused by ever more cleverly devised seductive alternatives to the Constitution, made the Constitution obsolete as a guarantee to limit the powers of government and caused the reversal of positions between master and slave. Government became master, yet the Constitution originally made government a slave, a servant. It is the "**holy spirit**" between the people as master and government as slave; but government, through neglect of the people, has made the Constitution the "holy spirit" between government as master and the people as slaves.

The American people failed to see this and failed to keep government confined to a position of subservience. Presently, government is the people's most important god. The government, now, is the higher authority and only in pretense holds up the Constitution to the people as a means to deceive them with the belief that they are still free as a nation of people. The deceit is blatantly false, and any sane person can see it; but brainwashed people are blind to recognize the truth of the matter and powerless to do anything about it because the police forces are aligned against the people and are under control of the people's worst enemy—government. The police can see no wrong in this present system of government. The United States is a nation of fools. The evil powers hidden behind a democracy are more secure in the seat of power than any monarch.

In the Old Testament, Jehovah complained against the kings of Israel about the violations of the original agreement, but to no avail; so Jehovah cursed, punished, and, eventually, abandoned them. This is exactly what the American people must do to this present government. In America, over the last six decades, a small group of true patriots, called by government and the media right-wing extremists [the same kind of folks who fought the English during the Independence War], complained to government that it has seduced the people to accept an alternative set of contracts than it was to adhere to originally. This group has been suppressed by government, media, and public opinion induced in the brainwashed masses. This is a very sad story.

The People, Having Acquired Inverted Understanding, Now Denounce Those Who Fight to Restore Liberty

These patriots claim that the government ought to be the servant and slave of the people, by constitutional mandate. Presently, government is the master of the people through many contracts that override the constitution and government-adopted amendments to the Constitution. We, the people, have been sold a parcel of goodies not worth the value of the paper of the original contract. The goodies of "socialism" are utterly antagonistic to the welfare and "good" that the Constitution promised. The Constitution guarantees individual liberty under the government system of the republic; the democracy claims to be for the good of society [society is defined as the "the will of the majority"—if you belong to the minority, then the goods promised to the majority comes at your cost]. But the good of society is the exact same guarantee Jehovah's contract gave to the people of Israel, except that Jehovah really is god in the universe. The "good" of society is under socialist-democratic government control. Government control means mastery of the public that needs to be controlled against the rights of the individual. The more control government acquires, the more suppressed as slaves people become. Society has been bundled into one entity, the majority, and the majority is divided on all issues and simply forced into the majority. Government in the commercially-grounded, socialist democracy pretends to protect that will of the majority. This entity "majority" does not exist. That is a different promise from what the Constitution promises—protection of individual rights.

If You Want Liberty, Worship Jehovah, Not Government

If you want rule according to the good of society, you must again contract with Jehovah. He gives the best form of society ruled by a god. Government is a false god. It will deceive you, no matter whether you please it or not. Jehovah will bless you and society as long as you adhere to his rule and obey him absolutely as Joshua and his friend, Caleb, did. However, the people lost Jehovah in these violations to the original Constitution. Jehovah demands courage, the US government demands betrayal [cowardice] in order to receive blessings. The posterity of the founding fathers never showed the courage necessary to keep the government under control, but we have had plenty of people betraying the true defenders of the Constitution. Traitorous cowardice is the mark of slaves.

True Courage Is Recognized By the Comforter

The truly faithful should not be concerned about political corruption. The true Christ needs utter separation in allegiance from all power-usurping institutions of a physical nature so that the Good Spirit can guide such individuals from the deepest trap inside many nested traps of fiction to reality. One cannot help being caught in the machinations of powerful conspirators, but an adherent to Jesus' Way must not actively support the system in thought and actions. He should be a non-joiner and an abstainer of politics. Everything devised by "human ingenuity and effort," claimed to be for the "good" of the individual and of society, is a trap to ensnare and kill the soul by preventing the soul from being guided home by the Good Spirit. The true believer is in extremely hostile territory, physically and spiritually.

The Bridge Between the Realms of Good and Evil

In all this, Jesus as person and also as the Comforter is like an intermediary between the realms of truth that cannot contain a lie and the universe that cannot contain truth. Jesus formed a bridge between these two mutually exclusive realms by forging a medium in men known as spiritual faith by appearing as a double agent. Spiritual faith is like a tower with an antenna that sticks into the realm of truth whereby man is able to pick up signals from the other realm by which he can be fed and made to understand that he exists in a dream. By continuing to have faith and continuing to man the tower, he can be brought back to full awareness—to wake up from a lie-induced coma to the reality in his spiritual home.

This is how faith is the bridge over which we cross from one reality back into the other. It is obvious that it is much easier for us to cross from truth to fiction, which is like falling into a hidden trap, than it is to cross from fiction, a deep pit, hole or well, back into reality. Jesus is the one that comes along and has the method to help us out of the hole.

Trust: the Way into Slavery and into Liberty

It does not matter which way one travels, one falls and one is redeemed by trust. To trust is never wrong. It is my duty to trust. If I am deceived through my trust, I have not committed a crime. In order to be true to myself, I must trust. It is the other party's duty to be trustworthy. His deceit will not gain him one iota. He is the loser, and I was fooled once more. If I continue to trust I will also trust the Comforter and he will help me out. So, in life, your duty is to trust. We know who and what not to trust. We cannot trust in shadow play. The entire universe misguides us and will continue to do so forever because it is spiritual shadow play; it hides truth ferociously. Our trust must lie in the one who comes to us in the universe from beyond all layers of authority—the Comforter. The whole universe and all beings in it deny he exists because he is not of this universe.

Those in the Comforter Are Like Fertilized Eggs in Earth

We cannot trust in the universe or in any of its parts, yet we must continue to exist in it until we can depart. Physical reality seems so real materially, yet the solidness of it betrays our confidence in it through widespread deceit and corruption. How can those opposites be reconciled? They cannot! It proves this environment to be a deceit. It is made of material and spiritual content arranged to keep us trapped. We with faith are forced to exist in it, because our spiritually fertilized egg is hatching in Christ's church, and it is watched over and cared for by the Good Spirit. The egg consists of a shell, the human body; and the yoke, our spiritually enlivened faith. The shell must remain intact until the chick is ready to break the shell and escape into reality. Do not despair when you are tricked again and again by characters in the negative spiritual realms. From a perspective of reality, no gain and no loss are recorded for anything done materially. Our spiritual account remains at zeros, until the Comforter contacts us. Then our account will increase in credit rapidly.

Human life is a constant distraction to the soul in determining its real purpose. This is especially so at time of death. It is well known that just before death, a person's whole life is played back to him. It is taking place not in true time, but in a spiritual static. It is a period of reflection and decision for action beyond the release of the soul. If the soul does not awaken in true spirit, it does not know there is a choice at all. When you awake in the morning, you are up and about; you do not continue dreaming. This happens when soul understands that evil is disguised as worldly, emotional and sensational good, and that true good must come from beyond the boundaries of negative, deceiving spirit. This soul who recognizes true reality will drop the fictional body at death, wake up and comes to awareness in reality.

During the moments proceeding, during, and after death, one is subjected to the propaganda of the lie, the fanfare and glory of physical life. It starts with the group of people comforting, crying, and mourning around the deathbed. True spirit is low-key because one cannot be forced on emotional grounds to enter reality. One simply wakes up in reality or one does not. There is no choice. If the soul is not in contact with reality, it has no idea there is such a thing as reality.

Awakening in Spirit

If you commune in the Good Spirit, he will give truth and peace by being himself. He is there for you to commune with in reality. This is part of his character and expression of truth and love. You, as soul, are as real as the Comforter. The moment of physical death for the knower in the Good Spirit is the same moment the chick [the knower] will break the physical shell [abandon the body] and step into reality. He does so because he **knows** he is real. He could not step anywhere else but into reality, just as you could **not** step into reality because you are still in the dream of a comatose soul. Your physical body is proof that you, as soul, are still comatose in spirit.

This awakening in true spirit is not based on the political arm-twisting manner in which campaigns are run where both parties try to out-shout and out-lie each other. In the democracy, both political parties conspire as if they are two parties while in reality only one group is manipulating the masses so that a third party can run off with the prize—both parties are phony. The propaganda of the universe is of that caliber, but the truth and love of god cannot pressure you. If you know the father, you are in reality. Negative spirit cannot prevent you from stepping into reality, because now you **know** *the truth that sets you free* and because you have always been there. You just wake up from the lie-induced coma.

The Group versus the Individual

One can readily see if 'faith' is based in negative or positive spirit. Group religion is negative, individual faith can be positive in spirit. It is exactly like the two original contending political parties in American experience. Republicanism is individualistic and promotes individual liberty; the other, commercial [**International bankers—the Whore of Babylon**] democratic socialism is based on the group, that includes every one of us in a general and not in our individual capacity. Orthodox republicanism is of a much higher class spiritually than commercial, socialist democracy. The mass man democrat [a coward] is brainwashed—he is lost. He deals in groups and expresses power through gangs. The individual in a group sees himself as a homogeneous part of a group because he does not recognize himself as an individual without the group. The popular person seeks power through the group. He is an individualist and uses the adoration of the group to get control and the power of the group. Without a group, popularity means nothing. The popular man is the deceiver in the group. When republicanism became a group movement with group goals, group conformance and group pressure, it ceased to be republicanism and is a fraud. Republicanism, originally, is nonpartisan. It cannot be forced out to engage in a campaign of deceitful words and rhetoric in competition for votes. If this is happening, republicanism is dead. Presently, the Republican Party is a fraud.

A true republican can only understand the force of weapons if the situation demands it. True republicanism died in America. That is why the government prohibits the ownership of unregistered weapons. Government wants to keep republican understanding dead and powerless. Weapons for the public must be kept in a state of severe obsolescence so as not to become a threat to the seat of crime in government. They must be registered so that weapons can be confiscated without much effort. The so-called radical religious group of people in Iraq that is causing all the mayhem in retaliation to Bush's dictatorship is true republican. They fight because they are afraid that if they submit, all will be lost, and they are right. Liberty will fly from their awareness, and they will be enslaved and cowed into order just as the American public, and as cattle and pigs in the pen.

One cannot fight a war alone because the cowards of the socialist opposition will always force the entire society into a group of fighting people under strict discipline and training and force the masses to support them through unconstitutional taxes, selective service inductions, and unconstitutional propaganda campaigns. This is good because through such suppression, one may possibly begin to awaken from the coma of government propaganda, and the Comforter may have a chance to reach you.

The true republican will fight in conjunction with other republicans to subdue the socialist oppressors' organized war machine—and when the war is won, they will disband. [Something like this is presently playing itself out in Iraq.] The Iraqi resistance fighters are not giving up because they are republican in nature. Not so with the US socialist political machinery. Look at the permanently established US armed forces, each and everyone cowardly hiding inside a flack suit—huge and all powerfully arrayed against all who oppose their drive for the One World Order. From the size and permanency of the US forces one can see that the US is the oppressor.

Government, a Conspiracy Against the People

A government that is not a complete slave to the people is not government, but a conspiracy to destroy freedom and to enslave the people. The US government is a conspiracy against the people—a conspiracy that has never been opposed by the people even though the people have had many instances of proof that such a conspiracy was at hand, and has been proceeding for a long time. This is proof that the masses in America have no communion in

Jehovah's holy spirit at all. Their reliance on Providence is a farce. Their souls are as lost as cattle and will be cattle in the not too far off future. In their present condition they are abandoned by all spirit.

Jesus did not marry and did not bring forth posterity because he could not procreate. This is one aspect of being Messiah against which he had to stand firm. He could not promote this realm of darkness by reproducing. If he would have done so, he would have died as son in positive spirit. He would have been deceived as Adam and Woman were deceived in spirit. He was wide-awake in spirit, and he knew that the world was just a display. He could never be enticed by such childishness.

He came to teach and enlighten the few that could have his thoughts so that they could be contacted and guided by this Good Spirit. He came in the form of the Christ [a most repulsive but necessary office for Jesus] in order to teach Israel how to escape the trap—universe. Jesus taught by himself. Reality is one-on-one communication and interaction. Fiction is a group of people competing with one or more groups of other people—deceiving others as they deceive themselves, which process they call "informative communication."

Language was created to promote schemes of deceit, not truth.

Language promotes negative spirit. The Good Spirit communes in thought, not in language. No matter how much communication goes on, truth can never be revealed in human language. The Good Spirit can communicate with us in thought, by separating fiction from truth.

The products of present-day universities, mass production, and commerce, even to the extent of all forms of mathematics and science, are fiction. Mass production depends on hierarchical group actions, thus laws and propaganda. Mathematics, for instance, only reveals the most elementary derivatives of the negative spiritual computer on which the program universe is unfolding. Modern culture and its products can only mislead the soul into soul destruction because modern culture makes the fiction of our environment seem even more real and solid. If you actively seek sensationalism and status, it is sure proof that the Comforter cannot contact you. Science and technology were given to us to keep us in darkness.

You may say to me: "But you use computers, cars, and telephones; and you listen to digitally recorded music." Yes, I do, but I know what these are and what they stand for. I know enough of reality to not let these deceive me. I am still stuck here, and I must keep myself busy doing something, but anything I do is just spiritual garbage—so I do not care what type of garbage I am engaged in.

I give the above political and government examples not because I want reform of any sort. Rational reform is impossible because universal reality is insanity in action. I use these as examples in our visible environment to help make you reach into the spiritual world and understand that not all is well. The universal spiritual hierarchy is set on your enslavement and ultimate death—your complete consumption; we, souls, are in its digestive track. You cannot reach beyond negative spirit, but reality can contact you. Only one can cause you to wake up—you alone. The Comforter will give you input on reality, your dream will try to keep you dreaming, but you, as soul through the physical body, must decide.

The idea behind personal religious inclination has its center in the group through authority and conformity, protocol, ceremony, and personal contribution into a group-fund. All these adjectives are invented to draw you into the group and keep you there. Authorities crucified Jesus because of his stance against the hypocritical group conformance authorities imposed on their subjects [forced adherents]. Authority and the traditions of men are based on law, cruel enforcement, and empty, utterly-devoid-of-spirituality, rote performance—as we can see in almost all religions such as Islam, all forms of Christianity, and the religions called sports and politics. All human activities are expressions of negative spiritual and society-induced propaganda.

Oh, the daemons love it, but they will only deceive you with more physical blessings. The exterior control in suppressive systems is so tyrannical that no other form of thought or expression is allowed. It is enforced by subtle means such as greeting each other with a hand outstretched, "Heil Hitler," or the many daily prayers and rituals enforced on the members of Islam. One is coerced to respond in the same manner, or one will expose one's resistance to the ideology. The Roman Catholic Church makes the same demands by insisting on people crossing themselves and kneeling on entering or approaching the altar or when praying.

In days before Protestantism, during its formation and establishment in the greater Roman Catholic realm of control, the Roman Catholic authorities could easily see if someone was opposing their creed and power structure. There were eras in the reign of Roman Catholicism where the people in whole regions and cities were slaughtered en masse for opposing or deviating from the Roman Catholic creed. In Switzerland, the Lutherans put to death those who resisted Lutheranism. Authorities of Salem in the USA put to death so-called witches. These are direct consequences of applying the doctrine of Romans 13 by Paul that contains the following sentence: "Because if you do what is evil, be afraid; he [the government official] bears not the sword in vain: for he is a minister of god, a revenger to execute wrath upon him that does evil." The commanders leading the armies killing those who deviated from strict RC doctrine instructed their troops that they were to kill anyone who came across from their sword because God placed that person there to be killed. It was just indiscriminate killing, consented to by the insanity of Romans 13.

The masses are always enthralled with authority, group identity, expressed and enforced authority, ceremony, protocol, power, group celebration, and mass solidarity so that hardly any one will take the teachings of individual spirituality seriously. The individualist is often cowed back into group conformance through peer pressure. He is outcast, most of all, by those in power if he fails to conform to the group. The true "individual" is a loner. He is shunned on earth, cursed by negative spirit and praised and guided into redemption by the only spirit who is individual—the Good Spirit.

A 2006 issue of the *Reader's Digest*, with "the Beatles" on the front cover, has an article portraying the supposed chasm of political division in America. The splinter groups of political radicals, the article says, make the chasm absolutely polar in which the rest of society is drawn by a vortex-like action. That is exactly the purpose of these outspoken splinter groups. If their actions and press releases are continually covered by the media, these groups are commissioned by the propaganda system of the United States of America. These splinter groups receive supporting propaganda attached to the news coverage. They cause private debate in clubs, bars, and social gatherings. What is broadcast through the media has the backing and support of government; in fact it is an expression of government to steer the masses in a direction it wants them to go. The media broadcasting, discussing and narrating the actions of the splinter groups are like a group of cowboys herding cattle into corrals of a meat factory.

It draws the masses into democratic activity. Radical issues are the sure modern way to control people. Propaganda seeks to actively engage the masses to follow the news media because propaganda triggers come from the media. The cattle must be prodded as trained killer whales are prodded by high-pitched whistle sounds coming from the trainer. The whales act on cue and so do the human masses. The article says that the majority takes a much more relaxed stance toward the issues. This may be the case originally, but at voting time, the items to be voted on are written in a format that will not allow any relaxed stance; and by that time, the voters are drawn to vote for the choice propaganda has triggered them to make. One must vote for or against, there are no maybes other than not voting, and that would impair the voting process and thus *holy democracy* itself.

In the USA, other political parties than the two major parties have always been ignored by the media or, when mentioned, ridiculed or declared anti constitutional. The two-party political system is the works of propaganda. The express purpose of this article in *Reader's Digest* is to make nonvoters feel guilty by creating a public opinion against them. These nonvoters are doing the right thing as human beings, but the article makes them appear guilty of political ineptitude. This RD article is a very good example of how a propaganda system works. They use the biggest and most popular channels in the media. They give an informative report, and then give the whole article a twist so that people will believe and do what the article suggests. How can the average person defend himself from such clever deceit? The people are putty in the hands of these article writers. The same shenanigans are expressed in religious information weeklies and newspapers.

Love versus Hate

It is a fact that the opposite of love is not hate or indifference. The opposite of love is ridicule and force, force of any kind—criminal, social, religious, political or governmental. Hate is an expression of impotent love. Love is associated with the father in truth or positive spirit; force is associated with the spiritual opposite or negative spirit. Love, peace, and contentment are pipe dreams and are impossible in the universe. We are made to believe by the devious processes of propaganda that these are easily obtainable. Anyone who believes love and peace are possible on earth is insane. It cannot be in an all-pervasive dog-eat-dog environment.

It must be clear that members of a democratic society cannot have rights. In a democracy, one group is made to believe it receives the government's approval and benefit, and another group does not receive this treatment [supposedly because it is in the minority]. In fact, none receive anything but deceit. A group cannot express an opinion unless it is enforced on them through the authority of propaganda. Public opinion is the opinion of a group of brainwashed individuals. Since the public has no true opinion, government in the democracy, which is a distinct entity, usurps public power and rights, overriding the individual's rights and power. Government can only say that it represents society because society, in the loosest sense of the word, is a group of individuals. "Public right" is the government's license to control, because the public's right is defended by the government in the "democracy." There is no one called public so "public" is a fictional entity.

Present government can only enforce public rights. In the originally established Constitution, individual rights were secured. In the constitutional form of government, government would uphold a person's individual rights against government or any group that injured him. Government in a republic is a slave. It had no rights. It only had delegated powers. It had no power to come against anyone of the free citizens just as in England, no one, including the government can sue the Crown. Republican government was supposed to help an individual secure and maintain his rights. Without guaranteed rights for the individual, there can be no rights for individuals forced into a group. The army is a bunch of people forced in a group. The soldiers are under discipline. They have no rights. The army determines what is right for them and what soldiers receive are limited privileges. The exact same is true for every US serf and every entity of domestic stock [there are no more free citizens in America].

The idea of group rights is a ploy of deceitful propaganda, yet the masses of people accept this lie as truth and think that it should be upheld by government against the individual. This lie made government a god and commercial, socialist democracy the religion on which it relies to exercise its [divine] powers. Individuals in the democracy have traded their rights for benefits. An individual in a commercial, socialist democracy can claim to have privileges, which are granted by government, often after paying a fee; and these can be changed or abrogated at any time it is convenient for government to do so. Privileges are granted to slaves if they behave themselves.

Individual Rights in Spirit

I have written that one is allowed to choose one's conditions in positive spirit as soul. That is a republican idea. I got that from Jesus' statement to Peter and later to all the apostles. "*Whatever you bind on earth is bound in heaven.*" This means that you, as an individual, determine what "your" place and condition in heaven will be like in the true republican sense. Is it based on your own authority and none other—not on some other individual's or group's decision or even god's. Your place in reality is based on your individual choice, freedom and liberty, so to speak. It is not based on conformance to group-controlled tyranny or religious dogma. Your place in the living temple is "naturally" just right for you because you choose the specification of your own place. That place is arrived at by you understanding evil, so you can determine the good as a place for you to be.

The spiritual choice Jesus gave us is the power of the individual applied to the individual's own eternal circumstances. Everyone is always in the process of determining one's own eternal conditions. One determines one's conditions in hell as well as in heaven. Returning to reality is a matter of letting go of one's security blanket, physical existence. The comatose soul is too scared to take the chance of returning to reality that it chooses to dream instead of to awaken. That fear is based on the belief that truth is a sham [which belief I can understand because we encounter nothing-but shams in our daily life.]

The awakened soul will arrive in a place prepared by the Good Spirit according to the desires of the awakened soul.

For a soul who is not redeemed into positive spirit, there might be a place in one of the many heavens where daemons have jurisdiction [something on the order of Dante's *Inferno* but entirely different in organization]. All these "heavens" in the hierarchy of daemons are temporary abodes, special alcoves in hell for the privileged, because the universe and all it contains will be rolled up. Another difficulty in any of these universal heavens is that one can be thrown out for not continuously pleasing that daemon. A soul must please his god or face agonizing reprisals. Or a soul might get bored with his god and his heaven, and the soul is seduced to try his "luck" in the bait enticingly held up to him in another section of the trap below the one he is in. (See Figure 11, page 396) He cannot reach the bait in a higher trap because the cone section he is in prevents it. A soul caught in the universe is forced to start from scratch over and again without end from one life to another, always tumbling down in status and power.

I am a person as good as this world can create in the de jure organic manner. Corporate top executives are people as good as the world can create in the de facto fictional way. I am independent, creative, and able to find my own way, like some of the trappers and explorers of the old days. In almost everything, I am opposed to the commercial, socialist democratic system of government of the United States of America, its domestic and foreign policies, and the deceit perpetrated on the people for the creation of the One World Order. I hold these ideas in an indifferent stance, and I do not get involved other than in a teaching mode. I offer people what they ought to know about true redemption, but I could care less if people ignore me or do listen and yet do not act.

This is hell! Whatever happens must happen. In business, people will never give a sucker an even break. They never come to think that the sucker may be the wiser and more mature. People will always deceive and harass each other, and individuals in groups will always climb over others to the top of the hill. Whatever happens in the physical realms is evil because of three things: it was designed based on deceit; we were enticed into it by deceit; and we are deceiving each other because we threw away truth to follow a deceiver. Jesus set himself a physically, almost-impossible task, but thanks to the Good Spirit, we have a chance to escape this evil where nothing is good as seen from the father's and thus Jesus' true viewpoint.

I can see that when Jesus was present among us in the flesh, he did obey "righteous Jehovah" and promoted his laws and rules. People cannot exist without rules and laws, and threats of perdition of the soul. But his real mission was to draw some of us away from this evil universe so long as it is spiritually possible. He is caught in a narrow window of time. As long as souls have not sunk below the level where they can no longer understand truth at all, he will work; but as soon as the last remaining human has shown no inclination to seek the light, the window of redemption is shut. Not by Jesus, but by us, lost souls in human flesh. That will be the time the universe is rolled up. It fails to have any further purpose. The spiritual battery bank of Adamites has depleted to a point that the computer is put in a sleep mode until a new set of Adamites is enticed to exist in fictional reality so that the entire program can be run again. Then a new universe will be created, with all the natural resources back in place. This will be represented in paradise as a new "Tree of Knowledge of Good and Evil," and it will be there to tempt another Adam and Woman. The present Adam and Woman will have become some lesser strain of animals. This is so because the tree is a permanent trap. Nothing gets released out of it without spiritual help.

We, souls, are humans only temporarily—if souls have capacity to see the light in the darkness of the universe and accept redemption. The souls in humans will be humans temporarily if they never see the light in the darkness. They will slip into the nature of animals. This happens when a soul's belief system is entirely aligned with physical realities, and his personal window of redemption is closed. He has become permanently blind to the true spiritual light—his false beliefs have become his true reality; all he can see is the false light of deceit. He is then ripe to enter the animal world in raw nature in the form of a lower primate or so. Over time, he will sink to the life of insects and lower. Animals are totally in the power of their own ignorance and of nature. When an animal is injured or sick, it suffers until another animal kills it while it is still breathing, or it will suffer until its last breath.

The souls in insects have already started to disintegrate. For instance in the case of a bees nest, the soul is in the queen or whatever leader they have, and all the soul's physical members are scattered in the members of the nest. The queen has some kind of nerve system that connects her to all her bees. She sees through the bees eyes. The male bees, by the way, have become wise. They are completely out of the loop of work and authority. The work is all done by the females who try so desperately to be men or to be like men. The future of humanity is foretold in the organization and operation of the ants' nest.

Corporations Are the New Nobility

Top executives, and especially attorneys, are like the old estate managers of nobility that received all they own—such as prestige, lands, and authority from their king. The ancestors of nobility ingratiated themselves by some means to the Crown who, originally, was only a hoodlum gang leader—such as William the Conqueror, who awarded underlings for services rendered in battle or otherwise. Their heirs were good for nothings, and they have their unsavory ancestors to thank for their position of "noble" standing. Noble means a person and his family appointed by the king to reign over a subdivision of his empire, to make it bloom and produce and to collect a tax from the serfs for the king. The modern nobility in the United States are the corporations. These operate by license, and they collect the taxes.

The Absurdity of the Democratic System

I feel that as governments on earth go, only a kingdom makes sense or some sort of government set up in a similar manner. There can be nothing more moronic than a system where the leader of the nation is elected into office for just a couple of years. In the democracy, everyone is expected to keep up with political news and be up to par with the political situation from day to day—an impossible job, especially because one is never told the truth. It is completely impossible for the average voter to do this while being a parent and a householder, with an eight to ten-hour job and with another hour of commuting thrown in.

Most people do not give even the slightest attention to politics. They just vote for "all women" candidates or "all men" candidates or "all democrats", etc. Near 50 percent of Americans of voting age do not vote. And the greatest block of people who do vote is the undecided block. They could not care less what happens, and the fate of the nation lies in their indifferent hands. What a system! In the American democracy issues are supposedly decided, and officials voted in by something like a mere 20 percent of the people with 18 percent voting for another person and 11 percent not voting on a particular set of issues and candidates, and 51 percent of the people not even bothering to show up. Of those that do vote, some 70 percent vote without having the slightest knowledge of the issues or the candidates. They vote by some irrational scheme. Obviously, the powers hidden behind government cannot allow the leaders of the nation to be chosen in this kind of willy-nilly manner.

This is thus a minority-run government in practice because the true issues and candidates are chosen by those of the hidden government. Advertising and propaganda decide who will win and who will lose of those who were previously chosen by hidden powers, not the people. The present state of the citizens' non-rights is proof that the democracy does not work for the people. In a kingdom, at least the crown can claim that government serves the Crown. The crown had better be placed on the right head.

The Voting Public Demonstrates That They Are Brain-Dead

In a kingdom, duties of the people to keep up with politics are mostly unnecessary. People have become free again. Nothing can be worse than the government system we now have. You cannot eradicate the hoodlums from this government, but in a kingdom, all you have to deal with is the king or queen. It has worked very well in England where a satisfactory level of parity between crown and the people have been reached. Important government positions are filled from behind the scene. One can see this because in any kingdom, the commercial, socialist democracy wins. Is that not odd?

The Human Personality

Mind you—brainwashing forms the whole of anybody's personality. Brainwashing started when we believed the father of lies in Adam and Woman, but he is not entirely at fault—at least half the blame must fall on the souls deceived. Souls in Adam were cautioned not to deal with Jehovah's tree (the Tree of Knowledge of Good and Evil).

In fact, souls do not belong here; so, to fit in, they embrace brainwashing vigorously and use brainwashing to devise a personality and a mask to hide behind. Enforced and embraced brainwashing defines all the features of a person's mask. The mass of humanity can be envisioned to be in a room with a wide picture window, a door and a TV set. People inside the room are receiving all they know from watching the TV and by discussing in great length what they receive by watching this TV and in doing so, they forget there are a door and a window in the room through which they can see the real world or leave the room entirely. The window and the door are there, but the value of these have been discounted to such an extent that they won't, or are afraid to use it. Whatever they observe from TV is deceit masked in cultural decorum. They love that!

Why would they refuse or be allowed to give credence to the reality outside the room? It is through brainwashing that the programming on the TV subjects them to. They are made to believe that what happens in the program is so much more important and interesting than what goes on outside their room. This is the way taboos are created in a local society. They are spellbound [a spell has been cast over them] by the TV programs and by watching utterly irrelevant [unrelated to their own lives] news and programs that bombard them all day long with well thought-out propaganda schemes in which they get themselves wound up so they discount the real world on the other side of the wall. They believe all that matters to them is given to them in that room on the TV, because the wise experts narrate what they should see, understand and rely on. No one dares to question that it might all be cleverly designed propaganda that keeps them locked into the fiction so that reality does not matter. Outside the room, they are helpless and incapable of making their way. So they need all kinds of experts to help them deal with the outside world.

Brainwashing Hides the Principles of Common Law from Us

The present-day codified law prevents people from seeing the true common law because the democracy cannot allow the people the liberty the common law would give them. In that respect, the democracy works itself out in the same manner as the royal prerogative in the British kingdom of Henry VIII, Queen Elisabeth, and King George. In England, the Star Chamber Court and the court of the Exchequer were the so-called courts of equity where the equitable rights of the crown were defended. Most people losing a case in these courts could appeal their cases in the common law courts; but because of red tape, fear, and unwillingness of the lawyers to represent them there, they hardly ever did. Fear of power makes a person a mass person—easily dominated and controlled by government bureaucracy. A person in England and a person in the American socialist democracy have been fooled and coerced not to look out the window or to leave through the door. The majority of people are blind and misled. The deceived person's judgment has been impaired, and his vote would be an act in futility. Jesus said that the blind are led by the blind, and they will come to a terrible end. Blind people have no need to look out the window. They cannot enjoy and savor freedom and liberty. It is the terrible lot of the free person to be always caught in a society of mentally incapacitated people where their lives are squandered by their fellow men. This is why Jesus preached that the masses will follow the broad road to hell, and few will find the narrow path to the kingdom of Jehovah. Jesus, while in the flesh, was a true individual; and, because he was, he was suppressed by the authorities and by the blind masses that were obedient to the dictates of the religious and governmental authorities.

It seems, though, that the only persons with full rights and prerogatives are the hoodlums that have been able to wrangle themselves to the top of the heap. All others are subject to them. So the world ends up being a society run by criminals. It has never been any other way. My father used to say "*Foam always floats to the surface.*"

Bush's Proclaimed One World Order

Democracy will not allow the independent individual his peace. It will try—through public education, laws, phony news broadcasts and propaganda—to contain and inhibit his free spirit and liberty. In the republic, even as intended by the founding fathers, individuals will not be suppressed by the masses or by the republic. The tragic thing about the evil of the world is that the universe was created to be a haven of happiness and satisfaction for the individual [at least that was what was promised in paradise, to be like god]. People themselves torpedoed that vision. The de jure organic inhabitants of the universe were to be the independently acting men of freedom and liberty. As long as they remained individual in thought and in deed, they will remain healthy, vigorous, and strong. One problem with the members of the human race is that they are covetous for power and wealth and thus conspire against others and so lose their standing as individuals. The world will become more suppressive as we are forced to conform and be subjected to ever more strictly centralized worldwide commercial socialist democratic authority. Rampant crime will always be among us because government needs it to make itself needed by the people.

The ultimate, de facto world democracy is the most terrible form of tyranny one can invent. It is the final instrument to recast the human race into a hybridized species with a pure animal nature. The Serpent himself used power to enslave souls. But as highest sovereign, he wanted peace, happiness, and sufficient liberty for his soul-projected human beings. The fabric of the universe cannot provide this. Propagandists of the One World Order want to be sovereign and to set up things so that the people of the world will find happiness and peace under their reign—but, again, the material used to forge the One World Order will make it another pipe dream. Fiction cannot provide happiness. Jesus points the way to reality. There, only one mode is possible—liberty, happiness, and peace coupled with responsibility. Why is that possible? The fabric of reality can flourish naturally, without force or secret coercion. The environment is right side up, not topsy-turvy. Why? Because souls have gained the knowledge and experience of evil, so they choose and defend good in true reality.

Bush Jr., in his inauguration speech, already proclaimed to the tyrants of the world that their time is over. What he was saying was he, Bush, will use your tax dollars and your children to wipe any and all forms of true liberty from the globe. [Freedom fighters are now called tyrants and terrorists, and those who work for the real terrorists are called freedom fighters—topsy-turvy].

The Progression of Brainwashing from the Day of Birth

Our bodies are our worst enemies. Bodies will always try to move us from our goals and further away from Jesus' plan for us. The older a person becomes the more of an enemy the body becomes until, at last, it deserts him altogether.

We are betrayed and deceived through our bodies by clever rhetoric and brainwashing schemes even before we become of age, and thereafter, we will never have the necessary understanding to catch up and become wise to the ways of positive spirit. Those who so cleverly deceive us are even more lost than the rest of us. That is the proper reward for them. Living in a state of accepted deceits or cleverly constructed fictions [such as the universe itself] withers our ability to recognize the truth about our universe. The more fictions we accept as physical fixtures in our daily environment, the more dismal becomes our opportunity to receive truth from within, for the entire "within" is jam-packed with lies that we love and live by, and we hold to be the truth.

The Spiritual Battle Ground

The reason most souls reappear on earth through reincarnation is that when they are disembodied as souls they are again exposed to severe seductions of evil disguised as good. There are two doors to the office of the soul [heart]. One is the door used by the spirits of the universe, and that door is always open. The other door is always closed, and if it is opened, the universal spirits present in the heart of the soul will demand you to quickly close it because on the other side is a traitor who will take you away to a place where you will be utterly alone, like a body floating in the ocean or a ship lost in outer space, with only you aboard. The scare stories given to you about the other door are intense; therefore most souls prefer to remain immersed in physical existence on earth. This other door opens to the Comforter. The Comforter knocks and knocks but that door remains shut (see figure 5 on page 246).

If you have had guidance in your previous life [lives] by the Comforter you may have the courage to allow him to enter from the forbidden side. Contact with the harbinger of truth, the Comforter, must come through that door. Just as the universal spirits told you, the Comforter will tell you about good and evil and remind you of the guidance and understanding you received from him in your previous life. If you have not received such guidance, you most likely will not believe him now. You will find it a better solution to reincarnate rather than follow this wacko who wants to take you from the universe back into the "true reality." It is through fear of the unknown that souls reenter into physical life. They are addicted to existence in the universe. (See Figure 7, page 261)

The Good Spirit can give you back true life and liberty because he knows what true life is and what it brings. True reality gives you liberty, freedom, and unlimited possibilities without injuring others. In reality one is not locked into an artificial environment that brings with it limits of all kinds—a labyrinth of laws, rules, and unknowable conditions in an artificial environment defined by innumerable others. An artificial environment, such as the universe and such as we find in the United States of America, has limits and boundaries. It is governed by rules on which the program is constructed and rules that govern entities created in it. The dreadful thing is that rules are subject to change. It is the great abyss of unknown things in life that make physical existence a nightmare. Unknown things can only exist in a fiction. In true reality all things are clearly visible and defined and these do not change. Most people are so fear-bound that they do not move at all. They turn into bags of sand sitting in the desert that get buried in the sifting sands of existence as all previous civilizations also have.

> **Know that being uncertain and afraid and constantly beset by anxieties, you are in a foreign hostile environment— you are in someone's trap.**

The trends of existence in the universe for mind, body, and spirit are from high to low. The soul caught in negative spirit atrophies from spiritual life to dust of spirit, and from biological being to life bio-dust, utterly disintegrating all one ever was as a soul clothed in the body of the white human race after the fall. This is the meaning of evil, as referred to in paradise when Adam and Woman were taught about the Tree of Knowledge of Good and Evil. Evil is being separated from the good in the true son to being dead to reality through the medium of a lie-believed. Such existence is living death in the universe—hell.

People mocked Jesus when he hung on the cross. They told him that if he was the Messiah, he should come down from the cross. The people failed to see what Jesus was teaching them all along—that human life is death and is not to be treasured at all. *Jesus answered the people by remaining on the cross.* He died, not because he was innocent by the people's norm of law, but because he was guilty by their standards. He refused to fit in. He was a disturbing influence among "law-abiding" people. But that also was part of his teaching, expressed in his actions. All people knew about, or thought important, he declared wrong because the entire universe is wrong—something to be rolled up and be done away with. He even taught that it was the realm of darkness—that human life was death and his message is food for life. How opposite can anyone be from the norm of what people knew, or taught other people, about life, god, and the environment? This physical world and universe is all people know. It is their whole and encompassing experience. It is all the importance to which they can relate beingness. He invalidated everything, even people's ideas and understanding of god, and what was written about god, and the rules and laws in the Old Testament—to the point of invalidating the Sabbath and their other sacred traditions. Religious experts and authorities wanted to be rid of him. He was a nut and troublemaker they could do well without in their spiritual brainwashed stupor. They were so brainwashed by this universe that they would not even try to take him seriously—just like all Christians in all denominations do. That attitude is always proof of having being brainwashed, a thing this universe does best. A prudent person will always listen and after receiving the message evaluate it for some new inputs that he might not have considered before.

The Human Body, Our Spiritual Enemy

How does the universe deceive us? It does these things through these, seemingly, all-important bodies of ours—the same bodies that Jesus declared dead because all we can learn through our bodies are lies that keep us dead to reality. [In Matthew 8:22 Jesus says "Follow me, and let the dead bury their own dead". This was in reply to a disciple who asked if he could go back and bury his father first.] Our bodies are the medium that make us continue to believe in the lie by getting us to feel alive in a fictional environment. Knowing truth, which can only come to us from beyond the means of physical matter, is the only life there is. We must get it through our heads that lies believed equate death; and knowing truth, the way things **really** are, is Life. That is the lesson the Tree of The Knowledge of Good and Evil is trying to teach us.

Whatever we learn from the Bible and from most highly-trained preachers and ministers relates to lies and death. No redemption is possible from these sources. If we are not willing to contemplate new ideas because it clashes with what they already believe to be true, they are trapped by their own taboos and they will never advance any further.

The closed mind is a spiritual prison

Unbeknownst to themselves, they are spiritually brainwashed. Brainwashed people shun ideas that clash with their understanding. They look to what they believe already, not to what new material they might learn. Indoctrinated Christians and Mormons keep the door of their prison closed by their closed mind.

The Spiritual Importance of Christian Clergy and the Bible

Yet, preachers, ministers, and the Bible are important to bring the masses into an understanding of Jesus Christ. By the ritual human sacrifice of himself to the god of this universe, he bought us lock stock and barrel from

Jehovah, and set us apart from anyone's laws, jurisdiction and interpretation of how things must be. All we have to do is to believe in what Christ Jesus did for us, in the correct context, and to have faith that he will return as the Comforter so we can be reached by his spirit and then guided from this dark fictitious hellhole of death to the brilliant light of liberty in truth, life, and love. The clergy must learn to set well-trained Christians free from their intelligent domination once their pupils know the true [inner] teachings of Christ; and point them in the direction of the Comforter. No human being can, from then on, be their leader, teacher, or guide. Only then will the Good Spirit be able to commune with, and guide the believer into all truth. Either "learned" people lead you to death or the Good Spirit leads you to life. **It takes all the courage a person can bring to bear to be led in the Good Spirit because his guidance goes against everything we hold true and dear.**

All we experience in the universe is illusion, a cleverly programmed existence in a cleverly nested set of force-produced environments. This idea can be understood by going back to the realm of paradise. Paradise is the place where the spiritual abduction occurred while the war to set us free is waged in the fictional setting. The Tree of Life and the Tree of Knowledge of Good and Evil are located in paradise. When its fruits are absorbed mentally these affect one's sense of reality permanently.

Spiritual Mind and Awareness Altering Drugs

One can compare these trees with, say, plants on earth, like the poppy and marijuana plant or the plant from which cocaine is produced. When one imbibes them, one's sense of reality is altered. When one chooses to partake by means of ideas of the Tree of Life, one's awareness is affected by one becoming more settled in true reality; one grasps reality with a deeper understanding. It furthers one along in one's understanding of truth. I deliberately do not use the word "god" because a god is a lord, and a lord is one's master, while the Christ from the realm of truth is our friend and brother. A friend cannot be higher than oneself. He is equal. Jesus is fully aware of this and so is his father, but believers fail to see this distinction.

When we partook of the Tree of Knowledge of Good and Evil, we came under a mental spell. We died from the realm of paradise. This spell or enchantment is a trancelike experience where we are exposed to non-real concepts—falling into a deep dream state not resembling paradise. One is, henceforth in the physical universe, exposed to the physical experiences of fictitious ideas over and over again without any grounding in the reality soul had before imbibing the drug or poison. This drug reinforces itself in soul by keeping it under a continuing spell through a continuous process of false-experience-based understanding and awareness. This spell causes soul to have endless reincarnation cycles where one becomes more drugged as one is affected by ever increasing illusionary ideas of existence. The more one is exposed to false ideas that have become part of one's 'weltanschauung' or interpretation of reality, the less chance soul has to come out of the trance and the more primitive kind of a body a soul can occupy. Soul becomes more addicted to the fiction and through this process soul degenerates continually by dramatizing the more bestial kinds of fictional bodies of nature forced on it by the spiritual dream manipulators.

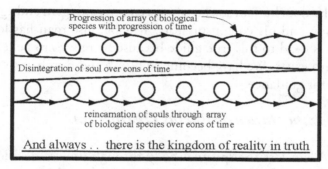

Condemned soul disintegration

Figure 14

The whole experience of man is that he seems to exist willy-nilly, not knowing his origin, his purpose, or his relationship with nature. He is, typically, a lost being—he may even think that when his physical body expires he will not ever be again. In paradise Adam was fashioned by the hand of god and had to be instructed as to what was good for him and what was not. He had thus no innate knowledge of these things. It seems that, at that time, he was a being who needed authority to instruct him, guide him, and help him to develop. Alone, he was confused and lost. So it is clear that he needs another being to be complete. This need of another is filled through communion with god in spirit. This need was cleverly usurped by the Serpent who now tries to guide him in the fictional setting. People have had bad luck in uniting with "spirits." They cannot be relied on. Moses identified the god the Hebrews should obey—Jehovah. Moses, in obedience to Jehovah, also set up a shrine and an entire protocol to house their god and to cater to him through a hierarchy of priesthood and strict rules and laws. This structure resembles the hierarchy Jehovah has in the negative spiritual realm. Jehovah abandoned the Israelites. Today, religious people rely on "learned" people because there is no spiritual guidance. These learned people are considered nothing unless in a close-knit relationship with some institution, association, or person who has claimed authority over them all. In the Western world, one is considered to be without credentials unless one received these from some incorporated and government-empowered religious or secular institution. All of them are fictions with credentials awarded by mere people, and liars at that.

The head of such institutions claiming jurisdiction can be called a king, emperor, president, chairman, pope, or carries another such vain title. These individuals have always been criminals and spiritually more lost than their subjects. Why does human society always congregate again and again around a mere person and his co-conspirators? It is because man has lost his true guide. Man is dead to this true guide because he refuses to believe that this guide in truth exists. We have become so numb and dumb as to rely on our fellow men for guidance.

Spiritual Importance of Racial Distinction

Just as Adam lost the spiritual body through unwise decisions, so will the human being, through acquired ignorance, lose the status of the race of his present body. It happens all the time. If a person would be steadfast to the standards and purity of his race, he will return to the same race after reincarnation. If not, he will reenter in a body less in status and ability to understand his spiritual predicament. Religious Tibetans are very familiar with this. Souls who cannot be reached by the Good Spirit may come back to their prior race once more but eventually will lose the status of his race and be born again in a body of *a species lower in the ranks of nature*. This process continues over long periods of time until the soul will reincarnate in the body of an animal. His chances of being redeemed will have become so much less because he becomes more prone to brute behavior and cannot be reached anymore by the Good Spirit. He shuts himself off from spiritual help. The lesson of all this is that one must, against all propaganda to the contrary, continue to be true to one's own race. From the racial platform where he is now, he has the best chances of finding the true guide and following him out of the universe. They who cross breed their genes will find themselves back in the progeny of the crossbreed.

The Battle for Redemption

The battle for the redemption of the human soul continues unabated since the coming of Jesus Christ. **This battle is a struggle of understanding ideas of reality.** The battle is about the soul's understanding the difference between GOOD and EVIL. **Good is the knowledge of truth and love; and evil is the, deliberately induced, misunderstanding of these.** It holds in that we need guidance. We need the sincere guide, not the deceiving one. The Comforter is here in the capacity of "guerilla fighter" to secretly guide a soul in its understanding of truth. Jesus is like a person who comes into an opium den and slowly rehabilitates a "druggie" into an ex-druggie. Once a soul is rehabilitated, he knows truth, love, and reality and understands the working and power of deceit.

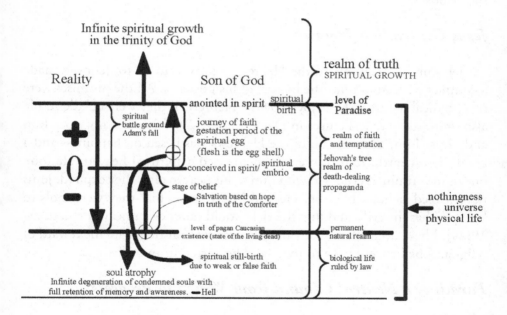

In the spiritual battle-ground everything
happens by one's own free choice and consent

Figure 5

This world is just a tiny little den in the expanses of true reality. Jesus made the statement in his prayer in John 17:3 that "this is eternal Life,

to *know* Thee, the true god, and Jesus Christ whom you sent." It is not
"believing", or "having faith," but *knowing him*, that gives eternal Life.
That is why no one person on earth, not even the pope, can guide us to
eternal life by quoting and interpreting some statements from the Bible. The
Comforter in the Good Spirit, truth itself, can guide us in understanding and
knowing truth. In order to be redeemed, *one must have only one master
and teacher*—the Comforter, who will lead a soul into all truth. Trying
to listen to another teacher led us into the trap in this first place! Trying
to learn from both the Good Spirit and from a religious expert will doom
one to death, for a human being only knows lies and deceit, propaganda,
the lifeblood of physical and universal reality. It is impossible to mix truth
and deceit and come out with only truth. Listening to religious leaders
means spiritual death. They are agents of evil—Jehovah; and Jehovah is
the imposter.

Jesus Contradicts Jehovah

Jehovah never promised the Hebrews a heaven to go to. Jehovah made
a contract with Abram for the benefit of his posterity. All the promises were
of a physical nature to be enjoyed by the Hebrews if they were obedient. He
also promised physical curses in Deuteronomy 29 if they did not obey him
and please him. The religion of the Hebrews was based on happiness and a
good life on earth. Jesus came and mentioned a spiritual heaven. He took
one of the criminals crucified with him to his heaven after they expired. Jesus
never called riches a blessing. He said it is a curse, that they were fools to
lay up riches in earth; and that the rich would never enter heaven [Matthew
19:24]. I have even heard many preachers claim that riches are the reward of
religious obedience! Listen to them and be barred from reality.

Paradise, a Neutral Ground from Which to Progress

Paradise is a neutral area—a state of spiritual "zero" where one can make
a choice of life and death. The realms of *life*, I will call the *positive* spiritual
realms, are where one grows and is nurtured by things that are eternally true.
The realms of *death*, the *negative* spiritual realms, are where the soul is in effect
of lies and deceit, law and order, and where all our concepts of true and false,
good and evil, can be changed and are changed through brainwashing because
everything and every idea in earth is variable. The meaning and purposes can
change. Propaganda is the executor of our soul because when a soul finally

dies in this universe, it knows absolutely nothing about reality at all. People, trying to find significance and importance where there is none will cause their own spiritual death. Nothing they know can lead them to the truth. Being "humble" then means to lay aside all you know and to become like children and knowingly and willingly make the universe of no consequence and to allow the Good Spirit to reeducate you into knowledge and understanding of all truth.

All truth = the father in truth = a true environment = eternal Life
Realm of darkness = spiritual death = creature existence = fundamental lie = hell

There is only one form of life force—it is soul, but many expressions of life-forms to fit the life force. *The form of life a soul will occupy depends on the spiritual atrophy of the soul.* The longer a soul resides in the universe as an ever-reincarnating entity, the more the soul will degenerate. This is because soul, by design and nature, does not belong in the universe. The white human race, as the last race to enter the universe, is the most recently trapped group of souls. The other human races all have entered the universe prior to the present white race. They were the white race in earlier times. The lower primates have entered before all human races. Spiritual atrophy occurs by accepting larger and larger quantities of deceit into one's awareness; by making this universe more real through effort and experience. In this process, truth recedes farther away until, as in animals, truth is irretrievably lost. That happens while being guided along by negative spirit, Jehovah; and by trying so desperately to be part of his body, the universe.

Jehovah, the Mastermind of Slavery and Cursed Existence

Jehovah blames us for not being obedient. Souls, however, were created to be free, unrestricted by rules and laws and subservience. Physical soul projections, humans, sufficiently brainwashed by him, the environment, and certain human compatriots try their best to obey him to the letter but, by their nature, continue to fail and be cursed. It is clear that Jehovah is wrong. He does not keep his promises; he changes his mind. We never know where we stand with him. He designed our bodies to be weak and our minds to keep us in ignorance and in the dark about things of utmost import to us. He gave us awareness and consciousness anchored solely in material reality and blind and numb to spiritual realities. Even in our physical awareness, we are ignorant about everything we encounter and about our own being and feelings. Our bodies get weak, sickly, and die. He plagued us with every disease under the sun—based on deadly weapons, allergenic, germinal, viral, and poisonous substances, etc. When we are disembodied, we feel like homeless pariahs, so we clamor and fight with other souls in competition to reincarnate again. The more a soul reincarnates, the more spiritually retarded it becomes. The more retarded a soul becomes, the lower the kind of body it can inhabit and the deeper it sinks in the utterly spiritless existence of brute, preprogrammed animal existence in nature. The soul is free in thought and mind, but Jehovah and his hoodlum spirits rule him through a reign of tricks and deceit and deny the soul the liberty it longs for and keeps it inundated with propaganda that warps his sense of reality. **Just the fact that Jehovah demands our obedience is proof that he is a false god.**

Jehovah favors the crowd [nations] over the individual, for his propaganda works best and is best enforced on the individual through the individual's interactions with the crowd. Jehovah only favors some individuals like prophets and judges because he needs them to keep the crowd enmeshed in his propaganda schemes. Jesus and his father in true spirit can only deal with individuals free of propaganda—those who stand outside or on the fringe of society.

The Theory of Evolution

The theory of evolution serves only one purpose—propaganda, to make people believe we are the result of innumerable amounts of spiritless, freak accidents and that it does not matter what race you are from. But the more applicable fact is that our bodies were designed for the precise purposes of spirit—to keep track of the many generations of sets of Adam and Woman in paradise that fell into the realms based on lies. The lighter the color of one's skin, the more recent was the fall from paradise. Each set of an Adam and a Woman were white at the time of their fall. The longer a group of souls remain in the universe, the more they take on the distinguishing feature of the universe—darkness and the characteristics of animals in nature. The one world conspiracy is well funded and well supplied with scientific brains to create whatever propaganda is needed to blend the races through miscegenation into a kaleidoscopic array of hybrid, dark-skinned people that, it is hoped, will live in peace and who will easily be controlled by a class of purely white super rich aristocrats.

The following paragraph is taken from an essay on DNA in Wikipedia. I copied it to show that scientists see a ready correlation between DNA codes and technologically-arrived-at computer language. I have highlighted the particular sentences

"There are 4^3 = 64 different codon combinations possible with a triplet codon of three nucleotides. In reality, all 64 codons of the standard genetic code are assigned for either amino acids or stop signals during translation. If, for example, an RNA sequence, UUUAAACCC is considered and the *reading-frame* starts with the first U [by convention, *5' to 3'*], there are three codons, namely, UUU, AAA and CCC, each of which specifies one amino acid. This RNA sequence will be translated into an amino acid sequence, three amino acids long. **A comparison may be made with computer science, where the codon is the equivalent of a byte, which codes for a single letter in a program [like one amino acid of a protein], and a nucleotide for a bit.**"

Does this kind of biological planning and organization look like it was created through absolute random accidents? The changes are so incredibly slim that we know it never happened by accident. The physical universe was planned and incorporated in a computer program using bits and bytes just as bits and bytes are planned and incorporated through dedicated scientists in our computers and programs. I hope this will put the theory of evolution well to rest. It becomes clear that the universe is an interactive website, so to speak, in spirit. There must be very many of such websites and thus other universes out there, all existing in spiritual hyper space.

Please keep in mind the following idea as you continue reading this book:

The concept is closely related to the universe being the display of a computer program and to the DNA structure in biological creatures. The conception of a new human being is clearly based on a binary code. The sperm [s] is one state and the ovum the other state [O] that underlies a computer language based on combinations of [s] and [o], like "sssoososoossosos" being a letter in the code language, to the creation of a new being. Conception starts the process of gestation by reading a biological code language based on the binary system of [s]and [o] that brings into being masses of cells in accordance to the code read by mRNA that when the code is fully read ends up being a new unique person at birth, after which the reading cycle continues to replace dead cells until death stops the reading and expressing of the code, just as my previous computers died through serious malfunctions.

Truth is the Light to Our Darkness

Lies are related—to what?—Truth. The lie is basic to the entire universe in which the father of all lies called the father of truth a liar. Those who believe the truth to be a lie cannot inhabit the realms of truth, so they had to die from the truth in the realm to a place where the lie reigns—the universe. Jesus explained this by calling earth, and thus the universe, a realm of darkness where the truth cannot be found—not even in Jesus. That is why he had to send the Comforter as guide in the realms of truth.

Darkness means absence of light, and it relates to a person's inability to see or distinguish things; to make him sightless, without understanding. In darkness, we are lost—we are so grounded in the universe that we even pretend to know that we are not lost. We are lost in a web of lies. We have no assurance on anything; and if we think we have assurance, we are even deeper in the trap of confusion. In the universe, we, as souls, are lost. Most people do not even know they are souls in spirit.

Light stands for clarity, vision, understanding, wisdom, and liberty. Spiritual light gives you the ability to see things in their native truth. Jesus said that the truth will set you free. Yes! It sets you free from darkness and from this universe, for the clarity of vision makes the universe impossible—a nonentity. What is not real simply cannot be when exposed to light of truth. Light will place you in reality, truth, and in communion with the spirit of truth—the father in true heaven.

Power Struggle between Mind and Heart

One must understand Jesus with the heart, not with a mind drowned in the materialism of the physical universe. The Good Spirit will come into your heart—not your mind. The evil or holy spirit will come into your mind. The mind is the strategist. It will always calculate your odds in the material realms. The heart will set aside competition and deal from a compassionate nature that flies in the face of the mind that is focused on survival and hoarding material aspects of existence. This is what the story of the Good Samaritan is about. He set aside his concern in the world when a person in distress needed his help. He assisted the person in distress as he would like to be assisted if he were in the same situation. The one despised by the so-called "superior" people, one of whom he just aided, is the one loved and redeemed in Christ because he had compassion, and he had exercised it in the face of his better mind judgment. The heart can set aside competition and concern for itself and thus can view utterly new ideas from a viewpoint of love. This is the attitude the Comforter needs to teach truth and to guide a person into the realm of truth and out of the universe. Believe me, the world cannot express love.

Those learned in the theology of Christendom—the ministers, preachers, priests, and prelates—have made a mockery of Jesus and what he came to teach. Jesus often said of the priests and the learned that they were utterly misguided and blind. He said they were hypocrites who insisted that they were guides to guide the blind because they had vision. Ignorance, blinding darkness, has no limit in the learned in any age.

Jesus' Strategy: to Catch a Thief Think Like a Thief

Jesus could do nothing but be a double agent. He came as an agent for his father, but because of the fictional nature of the world and of human society, he had to revert to the scenario that is known as "to catch a thief, think like a thief." In order to set the Israelites free of the yoke of the daemon Jehovah, he had to obey Jehovah and act as if he was his agent. [Jehovah is a thief who stole Adam and Woman from paradise, where they belong.] Jesus became Jehovah's chosen—to be the servant of Jehovah as Isaiah proclaimed in the Old Testament. *Nothing of importance can be done on earth the honest way.* The nature of the physical universe makes it impossible to be true and to be the truth. Jesus came to do incredibly important things, and his plans could not be revealed until they were all executed.

Negative Spirit Perverted Jesus' Secret Mission

He played his role very well; but his adversaries, later, exploited the nature in which Jesus had to do his work so cunningly that for almost all souls Jesus' work is in vain. Jesus had a body of physical flesh. It is a body of evil, and thus it or its identity can be used by others to thwart or inhibit the message he came to proclaim. For one thing, many people revere Jesus' body, his human nature rather than his spirit. They have his broken body hanging on a cross in their places of worship, have it in their homes, and carry it from chains around their necks. This is the result of well thought-out propaganda and its clever execution by his spiritual and physical enemies.

Nothing Is Perfect in Physical Reality

The problem for the universal deities is that Jesus opened the door to the realms of truth, and this door cannot be entirely shut again [for nothing in the universe is perfect—not Jesus' acts and teaching and not the propaganda against him]. Remember the propaganda of the Jewish authorities [a well-organized institution of religion] against him that made the people believe that Jesus' body was stolen from the tomb by his disciples so they could counter the disciples' claim that he had arisen from the dead, yet many believed in spite of their deceit.

People Are Nothing—Organizations Carry All the Power

In this universe, people mean nothing, but organizations do. Even by human standard, these are fictions but carry all the authority and physical power. There were Elijah, Moses, Samson, and many others in the Old Testament. They were individuals but were "deputized" as persons in authority of a spiritual organization—Jehovah's hierarchy. Human organizations such as the USA will sacrifice as many people as necessary to remain in power. The fiction is obviously much more important than the reality of real people. How evil leaders of incorporated businesses are! Everything that is of real importance in human society is fiction and it is defended through the destruction of entities of a higher reality. How cleverly deceit is made more important than truth. Esprit de Corps is one hell of a propaganda principle.

Jesus told us of this in the parable of the unfaithful business manager. He had embezzled much money and was fired. In cleaning up his desk he did great favors for the creditors of his previous boss and made friends among them. Jesus advised us to do what that manager did with those who owed money to his boss. Was he speaking in Jehovah's or his father's name? I do not know. I believe for both of them. Speaking for his father, he meant for us to continue to be guided by the Comforter but also for us to act as a person of the world. "Do not make enemies with those enmeshed in the duties and functions of incorporated government, business, or religion."

Paradise, a Spiritual Campus for Growth

Adam's task was to tend to paradise. This tending was extended to his mate—Woman. "Tending" meant to pay attention to and absorb what it had to offer [like a teacher will tell a student to tend to his lessons]. By tending to the garden, Adam would grow in spirit. All the trees in paradise were spiritual food, except for only one tree, which the father advised they should not pay any attention to or come close to. Paradise was neutral ground, a university campus. The trees are courses in learning about reality in truth and one tree would teach them the evil and power of lies and propaganda.

The trees are like icons that, when activated, transports the soul into a universe that expose the soul to thoughts, insight, and ideas of praise and clarified the existence and character of the father. In this way, the trees are food of growth for the soul. The soul grows by imbibing truth—understanding reality, which is not quite the environment that Adam was created in. Paradise is an environment where he could choose to learn to understand true reality. In itself paradise was a neutral environment because if he did not imbibe understanding from a tree, he was not fed and could not grow. Likewise, if he ate from the tree of which he was advised not to partake, he would die in the body from paradise. He would die, just as a human being dies here on earth—he drops his body, but his spirit continues to exist in the awareness of another reality that negated his native reality, the Tree of Knowledge of Good and Evil offered an environment of fiction—unreality, through the medium of lies.

The Serpent spoke from that tree to Woman. So obviously, food in spirit is the imbibing of ideas. This idea is corroborated by Jesus' statement that his words are food for life eternal and also by the father who admonished Adam and Woman to not have any interaction with that tree at all lest they die. Jesus' words are spiritual food because they will supplant the poison of the lies planted in the soul by the Serpent—souls' god after the fall. The tree communicated ideas that were poison to the spirit of Adam and Woman. By imbibing it, they exposed themselves to a fictional reality, just as partaking of the Tree of Life exposed them to an environment of higher truth. The problem with the deceitful, fictional environment was that it shut them out from their native reality. It is a clever trap that when you fall into it, there is no way out except for one. Remember, the door in your heart that opens to the Comforter.

Truth Is Food for Spirit and Lies Are Deadly Poisons for Spirit

I'd rather be the person deceived by others than to be the deceiver. The deceiver will never know truth. The person who is most often deceived is open enough in mind and spirit to have the opportunity to meet the Comforter. This is in accord with worldly wisdom in reverse, thus, in accord with spiritual wisdom. The world teaches us to be suspicious and deceitful. Spirit teaches us to be like little children, who must have faith that their teachers tell the truth. This kind of attitude works for those who seek in earnest because such a seeker soon enough discovers who tells the truth and who lies. Any deceitful transaction soon lets the believing party know that he has been duped. This way the trusting fellow has a chance to get a deeper and deeper disgust for deceit and propaganda—the exact attitude needed to turn one's back on the world and turn to the spirit of truth. Having the knowledge in this book will speed up the spiritual process exponentially. Trust will give a person material understanding needed for spiritual growth; promulgated lies ensnarl the deceiver deeper into spiritual morass.

The god of the physical world said to Jesus in the desert, "All this [all the kingdoms of the world] I will give you, if you kneel down and worship me." The ruler of the physical realm knows that if he can stimulate you into desiring physical things, you will remain dead or will die to positive spirit. Jesus answered, "Go away, Satan!" This incident confirms what I postulate. The universe is a realm of evil. Jesus wanted no part of it, and he was alive in spirit. This is what Woman and Adam should have said to the Serpent without even looking at him. Jesus knew Satan's game and was impervious to being seduced by material things [for they are meaningless in true spirit]. Satan, Jesus' adversary, tried to seduce Jesus on negative spiritual grounds and failed. Satan is concerned with universal things and, therefore, forsook, and still forsakes, the things of truth. When you die, the seducer wants you to take another piece of fruit from the tree and reaffirm your allegiance to it. Souls do so routinely and reincarnate.

Jesus wants you to forsake all things material and "to seek *only* the kingdom of god" in the true reality of spirit. Truth is really a kingdom because truth is king. The lie is not accepted in that realm. Seduction of negative spirit is aimed at you to reaffirm your allegiance with the tree and thus to you dying even further away from the realms of truth. You are seduced into taking your physical [projected] environment, and thus your body, as all important and into forsaking your true spiritual nature and character.

The Effect of Physical Brainwashing

A person analyzed by psychiatry for schizophrenic behavior has split personalities. This condition is triggered by environment. The person was forced, under very adverse conditions, to take his environment too seriously. He responded to the adverse conditions by adopting a personality stance that was demanded by the environment in certain situations and other personalities as the environmental conditions changed. The person was forced to do this so often that the responses became automatic, just as Pavlov's dog salivated at the ringing of a bell. I suppose that dog could be made to whimper at the blow of a horn after which the food is taken away before it can take a bite.

Then when the food is placed before him and the horn blows it will whimper even though the food is not removed because it is under the belief that it will happen soon. The physical reality and negative spirit play dirty tricks on us.

The influence of propaganda on a person produces a split personality also. The person is allowed to be himself but as soon as a propaganda command trigger is applied through the media, he is stimulated into mental action and dramatization. States of overabundant happiness and intense anger are easily stimulated through propaganda triggers. When a person has responded, along with the similarly brainwashed masses and the plans of the propaganda schemers have been secured, he is allowed again to resume his primary personality.

As soon as the trigger is applied through media propaganda, the mass person is stimulated into action according to the mandates of propaganda. Pearl Harbor, 911, Afghani and the Iraqi wars were US staged events to get the public support for previously planned US actions; and today, to make the US citizens surrender their self-respect when having to board a plane. One goal of the One World Order planners is to decrease liberty, and self respect to the level found below that in third-world countries, but to make it look like these measures are important because of actions by foreign-based terrorists. However, the real international terrorists are in the seat of power in the US government itself.

Every human being is cursed with several personalities. Our social face is a split personality enforced by environment. In human society, regulated by propagandists, it cannot be any other way. A well-trained animal, dog or dolphin, is a brainwashed individual, being himself as long as no triggers are given, but when a trigger is given the animal will immediately respond. Human beings are trained similarly, but in herds. All this is accomplished by the propaganda system by creating a false sense of 'esprit de corps' [team spirit] and by manipulating the emotions of the person ensnared in the propaganda web. US government actually pretends to be on our side and expect us to have a common bond against its enemies. Remember folks; government is always against the public! That is the nature of the beast. Your god Jehovah, Allah, etc. is always *against* you also. You will have to look beyond the boundaries of the universe and negative spirit to find anyone who is *for* you.

Every human being has several personalities. Our social face consists of several personalities enforced by the several social environments a person frequents, such as religious congregation, work, sports, social gatherings, etc. These social personalities are naturally created in society and are under the influence of the people one closely associates with in these spheres of influence. However, the calculated imbedding of propaganda triggers in society is arrived at through public school and media exposure by scientifically trained propaganda schemers.

How to Counter Being Brainwashed

Jesus taught to counteract this tendency by teaching, "Seek ye foremost the kingdom of god." If you set yourself apart from society and isolate yourself by not making anything overly important, you will have a good chance in finding communion in the Comforter who will lead you into the realm of truth. Jesus clearly preached this approach to redemption. A civil, disinterested stance to all societal standards and demands is a way that can lead to redemption. Jesus' way is beyond the reach of almost anybody these days. Our entire existence is engulfed in organized fictions, governmental demands, interference from society and unrelenting media sponsored mind control.

Since the universe is a projected environment in which all other physical environments find their existence, it, too, is a source of propaganda, the most powerful source of all. We, deceived souls, have our life and being in physical bodies derived from and in unison with this universal environment. Jesus wants to change that to having our beingness and life only in him. This is a marvelous substitute for the physical environment. It gives us the impetus to start to live for the kingdom and to die away from physical existence.

The Prodigal Son

In the parable of the prodigal son, there is a great difference between the understandings the two sons had up to the time when the younger came home again. The younger son could not believe that the father would welcome him back and love him, so he tried to return as a servant. He was awestruck to discover that his father had never given up hope to see him again and welcomes him back. The elder son believed that because he stayed home and worked hard, he would be loved and his brother not. Both sons believed that work and attention to the father assured them of the father's love. The elder son could not accept that the father prepared a welcome for his squandering brother who came back after blowing the inheritance the father had given him on his departure. The younger son, because he learned from his debauching life style, experienced the true nature of his father. The elder son was offended and never did see the true nature of love. Love does not expect anything in return; but false love, driven by selfish motives, does expect adoration as reward for efforts done for the other.

Jesus' father has the right kind of love, which is the opposite of the selfish kind upon which the Old Testament god, Jehovah, insisted in order to be accepted and blessed by him. This proves that the true father is love and that, whatever you do, he will love you. What he most appreciates is when you recognize the error of your way and return to him. His return is proof to the father that the prodigal son repented of his previous action. Jesus was trying to teach our souls that we did not have to worry and that we could go home confident of his love. After all, soul is all there really is; our human persons and the universe are mere entities in Jehovah's spiritual computer display.

"This is eternal life, to know the true god and Jesus Christ whom he sent" [John 17:3]. When the prodigal son came back, he suddenly had a flash understanding of the deep love the father had, not only for the elder son, but for him as well. He understood that neither work nor adoration, nor any other thing they could do would diminish the love the father had for them. The elder son was offended by his father for not preparing a feast for him for all the work and loyalty he had shown all his life. The elder son still had the wrong conception that one was to work one's way into heaven [the father's heart] just as the priests of the Jewish religion and the Pharisees believed. They were under the impression that obeying the Old Testament laws to the letter would assure them a special place in their god's heart and thus a place in that god's heaven. They were right if they wanted Jehovah's love but were wrong in Jesus' eyes. The father is waiting for an embrace from his elder son, for it will show that the elder son will have understood him also. All it takes is a sincere embrace after a big misunderstanding. Discord is always based on misunderstanding.

There is no Rhyme or Reason to Physical Existence

Concord and discord in the world are also always based on misunderstanding. Look how peacefully the world accepts the shenanigans of the international bankers. There is concord because the people have been deceived by a set of conspirators in believing that all is well and for their best, while the bankers continue to make nations fight each other for their own profit and to the misery and sorrow of the people.

For some reason, the people always believe that the wars are necessary. That shows the power of propaganda.

Take for example taxes. People want to pay fewer taxes, and so there may be a temporary tax reduction; but you immediately find the services that you depend on the most are drastically reduced, such as less people working behind the counter in the post office or schools suddenly having to lay off teachers. People seem to never understand that these shortages are artificially created to force you into believing that you must pay the additional tax. Government will never reduce man power where it concerns things that are important to them; it is always the people that see restrictions and poor service; yet all services are paid for by the people. Profit only comes through the effort of people. The real power and riches in the universe are in and of the real people. It is government that is privileged to use real humans to work for it. Labor should be held in such high honor by all that it should never be subject to tax. It is unethical and down right evil. What do you expect from a bunch of hoodlums in government?

Jesus' Parable of the Evicted Demon

Jesus taught a parable about evicting a demon from a person. He said that after the person was cleansed of the demon and was again taught according to the religious doctrines, the demon will come back with many demon friends and finding the person clean and restored, he will reoccupy that person and invite all his demon friends in also; and there, lies and deceit have again found lodging in his mind. Jesus meant to instruct us that if a person is not placed under the guidance of the Good Spirit, removing the demons [a set of lies] from the mind, society will only cause the person to seek more lies to replace the ones removed. The reason: He has no other anchor to orient himself mentally. Only the Good Spirit can instill truth after the lies have been evicted.

Chapter 8

The Awakening

The Spiritual Weather Is Changing

The Bible is a book that has always been available. If truth is to be found, it should be in a book like that; however, it is not in the Bible either. The Bible refers to means of getting in touch with truth, but those means are hidden among seas of lies. It also must be an article book generated by the white race because it is that race that has lost truth most recently; and, as yet, not all the race has rejected truth altogether. It will not be long now before the white race will lose interest in truth altogether too. That is the spiritual climate Jesus talked about in order for the world to be rolled up. The spiritual weather is drastically changing, also, due to these supposedly new "Christian documents", the Dead Sea Scrolls. The Dead Sea scrolls have nothing to do with truth, spiritually or materially. Truth is not material, so it cannot be found anywhere in the ground or in the air. It cannot be read from pages in a book, not even the Bible. But what the Bible can do is give you enough spiritual insight so that you will be noted by the Good Spirit, who then will decide whether your seeking is spiritually sincere.

The Ordeal of Awaking from the Spiritual Coma

The quality of character you need most to awaken in reality is courage. Your guidance will always match your courage, so that you will make continual progress. However long it may take, you will be awakened in reality. The spirit will never leave you and will continue to comfort you in your awakening. The journey will be trust-shattering and gut-wrenchingly difficult. It may take many life times. It will always seem that you have no knowledge of anything at all, that you are treading in a seeming spiritual limbo, and that your physical society has become your greatest enemy and distracter. You will thus be in physical limbo as well. All seems hopeless!

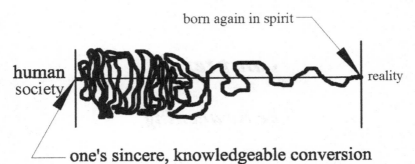

one's sincere, knowledgeable conversion
Born again means that one was real before the fall, and after redemption one becomes real again.

Path of redemption as hampered by the daemons of the universe

Figure 7

The book *The Pilgrim's Progress* by John Bunyan gives you an inkling of it. You will be standing alone apart from your family, community, and the world. No one will understand you, and people and authorities will give you labels such as dysfunctional, insane, antisocial, weirdo, and such.

The Strength of our Ties to the Fictional Environment

The realms of the lie are fictional and do not exist. We are conditioned by what we receive from all that seems to exist in physical reality—parents, schooling, friends and family, lovers, government, religion, and our spheres of interest. The propaganda is all-encompassing. All things physical are in collusion to enforce the fiction on us, and we cannot do anything but accept it because to reject it means being in an irrational, emotionless, meaningless cultural vacuum. However if we emotionally abstain from being involved in worldly matters, and remain not being involved in worldly matters, we can overcome this bar to truth. Keep an indifferent, but loving attitude. Truth is always available to us, except we negate true reality because we think we already are in a real environment. Nothing works but a loving, indifferent stance to life. Do not ever reveal your inner state because society will force you back in the "normal" state of mind.

The seductions and enforcement of the lie are more powerful to us now than the reality of truth and love is in true spirit. We can see from the way Jesus was treated by Pilate and the priesthood how severe the enforcement of the lie is. Reality, however, has no enforcement other than to exclude the lie from its realm. That was the reason god warned Adam not to get involved with the Tree of Knowledge of Good and Evil, the source of the irresistible lie—propaganda. We, here on earth, always discount deceit too much. We think that its harm is negligible; that is why we deceive others so easily. Humans betray each other's chances of redemption because they are ignorant of what they are doing. The main reason for deceitfulness is guilt, irrational competition and jealousy. Another reason is that we are an integral part of a dog-eat-dog environment and consequently we are too much concerned with our social front, fears and survival. We have no recourses left to seek the Comforter, who is a very elusive character anyway due to our involvement in the physical environment. He is not elusive, but our self-imposed environment makes him unreal in our minds.

The Reward of Overcoming the Belief in the Lie

Just as easily as we fell from the realms of truth when we took a lie for the truth, so will we rise beyond the place from which we fell when we know and embrace truth [not the religious kind of truth]. We will have graduated from the hands-on training of the Tree of the Knowledge of Good and Evil, and from paradise to the realm of ultimate truth. The trip will be more than worth it.

Principles of Soul, Raiment, Body and Allegiance

You are a unit of awareness. Let's call this a soul. This unit of awareness has a basic belief system, and according to your awareness, you seek and obtain a body. We started out in paradise integrated in a body. Since that body is eternal, it is still there awaiting for our return. It is there in a state of coma, and the cells of the body, souls, are dreaming into their blank awareness a fictitious environment on suggestion of the liar. As soon as the cells awaken from their dream slumber, they will be again totally aware of its native reality, just as a person on earth wakes from his dreams into familiar physical reality of the bedroom.

The difference between "knowing" and "believing" is that when you "know," you are spiritually awake; and when you "believe," you are spiritually in a coma. It is like day and night, life and death.

Jesus called the body of an entity that is awake in spirit "raiment." Raiment gives standing in that particular environment. Raiment is synonymous with understanding reality. We can see this in the following examples. Our physical body can be considered our raiment in earth, as a cat's body is hers. To have standing on a freeway or turnpike, one must have a valid driver's license and a duly approved registered motor vehicle. The car is the body raiment that gives a person standing to travel the roadway but only if he also has a valid driver's license [approves of and passed the conditions placed on driving a car on the freeway]. The Knights of the Round Table wore raiment acceptable in the circle of knights. They may also have worn some kind of medallion, and they, all, had sworn an oath. The soul pretending to be a cat has validated the requirements of being a cat so a cat body was assigned according to the false belief systems it has to be a cat.

We were given a body that gave us standing in paradise. The body, as part of the environment, was attached to us in paradise. The body was our raiment, and it allowed us to be in full communion with our spiritual father, which communion was paradise. The assembly of souls in the entity of Adam comprised the raiment of Adam. We, souls, had standing in Adam. Adam had standing, having us all together in his raiment, to commune with God, our spiritual father. Communion in and with reality was maintained by Adam so long as Adam, through all of us, *knew* and recognized truth. When we, in paradise, lost the truth by believing a lie, Adam could not recognize our father as the source of all truth. He saw him as a deceiver and liar. We were without raiment, for the native structure of the body of knowing was corrupted. We were not able to commune with our father. We became oblivious to the realm of truth. The lie is a poisonous substance or, maybe, a mind-altering drug in paradise. There is nothing the father could do to prevent us from dying because we did not see him and paradise anymore as worthy to have fellowship with; and we were without means of communicating at all. As Jesus said souls were thrown in outer darkness, naked, without raiment [the physically dead have no means of communion in earth]. We believed the liar, and we accepted him as the source of all truth. In order to be in closer communion with the liar and the environment he had created with his lies, we were assigned raiment [a body] that could commune with that entity and his environment. Since all the liar knew was to lie, his environment is based on lies and thus fiction, nothingness, in the realm of true reality. When we started the dream of physical reality, we had no conscious contact with either spirit, positive or negative, because both reality and the reality of the liar had a base in truth. This is the reason that we seem to be utterly alone as creatures in this physical environment. All we can ever see in the physical body is unreality, physical reality. Spirit is reality and we are not able to commune in spirit because we are dead to spirit.

We Need a Rescuer from Reality to Help us Back to Consciousness

Only through the actions of Jesus can we begin to get into real communion with the true source of reality, the Good Spirit, who can be in contact with us beyond any connection of physical reality. Jesus died to retrieve [buy back] our souls from the one who enslaved us. This is called salvation. Salvation does nothing for us if we cannot also be in contact with his Good Spirit. When we have contact with the Good Spirit we have been sanctified, for only when we have attained a certain standard of being washed clean of universal propaganda, can we be in contact with this spirit. Yes, to attain real status, we must be washed clean from propaganda, all lies believed.

When Jesus spoke about repenting, what did he want us to repent from? From believing the lie we hold in our heart; the lie we believed in paradise. We must shed the wrong belief about reality, so we can be brought back in contact with it. Jesus was often talking from "real entity" [the spirit of Jesus] to "real entity" [soul]. Of course, people had enormous trouble following his line of thought. To human understanding it was mere garbage. He had so little success reaching soul that he is constantly on watch as the spirit of truth in the Comforter to see a glimmer of light in the utter darkness of negative spirit.

If we can maintain individual contact with the Good Spirit, then we can be born again also. **But before we can have contact with the Good Spirit we must first have an inkling that what we hold in our heart is false; that there is another reality that is true and that this physical one is utterly**

false. This understanding is called belief. Having this feeble understanding that something is wrong with our basic understanding of reality, gives the Good Spirit an "in" on our thought process and he can begin to explain what I have tried to put down in this book. He will guide your mind to see the falsehood held in soul. Souls must understand the difference between a lie and the truth and again embrace truth. The Comforter will then reconstitute knowing souls into another Adam [bring back to life in reality a new born son], and this Adam is permeated with the cumulative knowledge of Good and Evil in all his cells.

Considering how extremely difficult it is in this realm of deceit to reintroduce us to the truth, it must have been some extraordinary feat of the Serpent to introduce us successfully into the fictions of his lie. This serpent Jehovah is some cunning entity. Even with the help and constant working of the Good Spirit, very, very few of the believers will be decontaminated from the lie sufficiently to be born again in the realms of truth. This is due to the fact that souls are spiritually isolated from each other in negative spirit.

Jesus was not exaggerating when he said that the highway to hell is wide, well paved, and that very few will find and follow the well-hidden path to heaven [truth]. What hides this path leading to truth? It is a morass of lies, false rewards, deceits, and hang-ups we cannot let go of, because it all relates to our brains as physical reality. Our physical awareness is not on that hidden path at all, but some of our thoughts can be.

I, once, had a woman friend who proudly proclaimed after some discussion about hang-ups that she had given up many hang-ups but was very content with the ones she still retained. That is the case with spiritual hang-ups. We just cannot be expected to give them all up. The abyss we would seem to fall into, according to our false sense of reality and reasoning, is too great a risk to take.

Jesus' Plan for Our Rescue

The reason that the Good Spirit prays in our stead is because our derailed sense of awareness and purpose of being make our prayers spiritually unintelligible, for those who exist in truth. The Good Spirit knows the thoughts of the sincere believer through communion in Jesus, and translates them. This ability of the Good Spirit to translate our prayers is only possible because Jesus existed among us to learn and comprehend the way of human thought. It is his spirit that constantly tries to commune with us. He knows about our thoughts through his experience among us. Jesus' plan to come to earth was well thought out.

> **One of Jesus' objectives was to learn our way of thinking.**
> **It is by what he learned from our sense of awareness and our sense**
> **of logic that the Good Spirit can commune with us and lead us**
> **ever deeper into the regions of truth.**

That explains why Jesus had to return to the father first, before the Comforter could come to us. He had to take his knowledge of our way of being back with him in spirit.

The Process of Being "Born Again"

Pagan life is like an unfertilized ovum in the female. It just drifts around in the uterus called earth. The spirit of Christ is like the sperm. The ovum is an entity that holds all the promise of life but lacks the mechanism to produce a body. The ovum needs a sperm [the word of truth] in order to give the promise of life. The gospel makes a person believe. It is as if the egg [pagan] swallowed up the meaning of Jesus' inner message [the sperm]. The sperm accepted in the ovum changes the entire makeup and structure of the ovum; this corresponds to the inner message of Jesus being accepted in the mind of a person. It changes the mental structure of the person, just like the sperm accepted in the ovum starts a universe of explosive change and growth in the ovum. Cells of new understanding are constantly multiplying in the mind of the believing person's soul. It changes the person's outlook and the experiences of daily life and the purpose and meaning of life itself. It is as if the person becomes new. Generally, he seeks a safe place to nurture the new understanding and make it grow. This safe place is the church of the Comforter. The Comforter knows from personal experience the deceit, fraud, and cruelty by which people are forced back into forsaking this new outlook on life. This corresponds to the mother bird watching over her hatching eggs knowing that many creatures prey on these for food.

The church of spiritual refuge is the nest of the Comforter in which he nurtures the fetus to birth. Here, the message of the gospel is understood in ever deeper levels of truth by the believer. The spiritual fetus can grow in understanding and in depth of meaning, constantly transforming the person from a believer in lies to one who begins to understand truth [to see the light]. The church is like the womb, except that instead of warmth fed to the eggs, understanding of truth and light are implanted in the soul. The initial understanding in a believer [the impregnated ovum], nurtured in this church [womb], will cause "life" to enter the being [the growing child]. A baby is said to be alive when it is born and breathes of its own volition. Life, the presence of the Good Spirit, will abide in the person to guide it into all truth where it will emerge as a live, aware, spiritual entity. When it sees the light, full and clear, it is said to have gained life. The nurturer will then set it free to experience life in true reality. The human body is like the eggshell. It must be broken and left behind. It has no place in this new life. It was just a shelter or protective cover needed in the hatching of the fetus inside. Jesus corroborates that by saying that "flesh profits nothing".

Light equals understanding. **True understanding opens the mind to trust, and trust allows communion.** Communion causes deeper understanding and love. When the Good Spirit has indwelled the person, it is like being born. It is severed from the womb through the process of birth. It now meets the mother in whose womb the fetus has grown to the point of birth. Now the person is sanctified in the spirit, or in the physical analogy—is laid in the mother's arms; and the two meet face to face. It is like a bonding process in spirit. The mother will care and guide the child to understand and be active responsibly, she hopes, in the new environment.

Jesus' secret inner message works a massive change that produces abundant growth that eventually will transform the entire being. The same can be said of the physical sperm and the ovum. Once the egg is impregnated, it seeks a spot on the womb lining [a safe, nurturing haven] and continues to grow until it is transformed at birth into a new person.

After birth, the mother and the child meet and commune, and all this happens in the safe space created by ultimate reality, the father.

Birth into a Realm of Deceit

On the other hand, deceit and **propaganda cause misunderstanding.** Misunderstanding is like utter darkness because one is lost with no way out. Everything a person knew has become unhinged and floats unanchored around in a person's sense of awareness. The one captured by the deceiver follows the deceiver into slavery. The deceiver guides the deceived. The captured one has no other choice because he is lost [This is exactly the condition of all US citizens with our deceitful god, government].

The person enslaved through misunderstanding caused through deliberate deceit believes that the deceiver is the guide into light; but light is always absent, and the person clings even more to the one who seems to be able to find his way around in the darkness, the deceiver. The deceiver now has become a teacher who teaches the lost person to see everything in a new way [propaganda]. In an utter void, the person is taught how to imagine things there [the blind leading the blind]. That is how the universe was brought into the view of the deceived soul's awareness and the world as a place to be. It is just a display of what the deceiver wants us to experience. He was in full charge implanting a new imagined reality into our consciousness. He did it his way, and we are stuck with the way he wanted it because he knows all the aspects and workings of it while we are led to believe in a fictitious reality. We are lost without this teacher-guide. This guide has become god, and we became creatures in his power. That is the quality of the god the world embraces as the loving nurturing god; he is a vicious imposter, Jehovah, Allah and whatever.

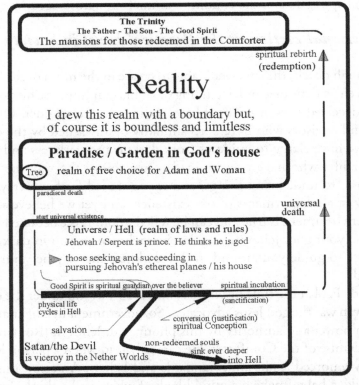

The path of fallen and then redeemed soul

Figure 6

Jesus, the physical Antichrist, is trying to lead us into the realm of truth. The problem is that we are lost in this universe because there is a veil that hides the guide who led us into fiction and that same veil hides the Comforter. We have no point of contact with anything spiritual—we are all projections into an artificial display. It makes us, as misguided souls, more tenacious in remaining exactly where we are so we cannot get lost even more, like trees rooted in the soil. Jehovah led us while in a coma [and the US government led us in pure deceit].

Now, Jesus must first try to wake us up in order to get our confidence to goad us back to reality. The coma was induced because we did not trust this guide, our previous god, anymore. The coma is there to keep us separated from truth in order to not find it back. I believe our coma has deepened because we, as souls, are now utterly lost. We are separated from negative spirit, zero spirit, and positive spirit. It is no wonder masses of people do not believe in any sort of spirit. This is the condition animals in nature occupy.

Transactional Fiction at the Practical Level in Society

Through deceit, the deceiver is able to create in the mind of the "believer of the deceit" a fictitious understanding of affairs that immerse him on a daily basis. A deceived person is not able to act in a secure manner. One needs experts and advisors who have been similarly brainwashed by the deceiver. Hence, we have clergy to guide us from darkness to darkness and advisors in secular life, who have been trained to see things the way the deceiver wants them to understand things; and so we are led farther astray. We are led astray in all departments of our existence, and yet we believe so solidly that the environment is true and can be relied upon. It is calculated insanity. Therefore, your god, Jehovah, is a deceiver who keeps you in darkness. He uses clergy to guide you around in this darkness the way he wants you to be guided.

Apostle Paul at the time he wrote Romans 13 was still under the delusion that Jehovah was the god Jesus advocated. So, government in Christian society was given power and authority by this phony god, Jehovah [Romans 13]. It is to the demise of the Comforter. He can only lead when a person lets go of all society-enforced leadership, standards and beliefs. A person must again become like a baby [make his mind blank of whatever he thinks he knows] and be re-imbued with the values and truth of true reality by one he cannot see and who is not even a part of this universe. As we can see, the negative spirit has such incredible power over our belief systems that truth hardly ever stands a chance. As Jesus warned us, only a very few will be led to the realms of truth from this pit of perdition. Your god, your family, your friends, your religion, your government are all arrayed against you in ever finding back the realms of truth. I know that I am correct in my thesis because Jesus' teaching validates everything I write. Now it is up to you, the reader to make up your mind. This book may lead you into truth, liberty and true knowledge, or your allegiance to society will draw you into perdition. I cannot describe your lot better than I have done in this book. May the true god lead you into all truth.

The Plan and Details for Our Redemption

The important message about your redemption is that if you were brainwashed to see things wrong, so can you be rehabilitated to see things correctly again. The difficult thing is; whom shall you trust to de-brainwash you? It must be some entity that has absolutely no valuable interest in you being de-brainwashed. It must be someone who is not interested in garnering valuables from you and gaining control over you, and whom you trust to lead you correctly. For spiritual rehabilitation you can only trust someone who is willing to die for your redemption; and the worse kind of death at that, in order to convince you that you can trust him the better.

This person is Jesus, the spiritual double agent. He adopted, what was to him, an utterly despicable body of rags, to be among us. He had to come in a guise and as a prime advocate of the god and of the physical environment that are his greatest enemies, Jehovah. Jesus was willing to pay the highest price to gain our trust and absorb the pain, humiliation, and hatred of the ignorant savages, the very ones he came to save, to advertise that he is one who can be trusted about the deep things that he told us about. Jesus, through his voluntary death tries to impress on you that what he teaches you is so important that the only way he could convince you of the importance of his message was to die for you. He said so before his death. A true friend is one who will die for you. He is your friend, not religiously, but honestly. His death was his last message to us about the deceitfulness of physical reality.

Jesus had to undo the mask he wore as the Messiah of the deceiver, so he died a terrible death to discount his physical being. Jesus showed his love and friendship for us by not leading us into more fiction but by showing the cruelty of the world and its inhabitants. Where cruelty, deceit, and camouflage reign as an integral part of the environment, we can be assured that the environment is a product of spiritual deceit.

Jesus' capture, mistreatment, and death on the cross was his final lesson to us to show that he was an ambassador of good and love and that the world and its organizations, based on power and authority, is one of hatred, deceit, and suppression. He taught us therewith to search and sift through the material he taught us to ascertain what came to us from the true father [the wheat] and what must float along with this teaching that is clever deceit [the chaff] coming from the deceiver that must be discarded. It is the same as with a grain of wheat. The grain comes with the chaff. In order to gain the pure wheat grain, one must remove the chaff. He wanted us to know that worldly friendship and love are products of the deceits played on us. True friendship shows itself through being willing to die for the good of another who is too ignorant and cocky to understand what a true friend will do for him. By hanging on the cross, he showed that his body was the chaff that had to be winnowed from the grain. His spirit was the grain that continued to exist and came back to us in an immortal body. **Jesus actually winnowed the chaff [body] from the grain [his spirit] in such a spectacular way that everybody should have understood that not the body, but the spirit, is of value** (see figure 6, page 267).

Jesus proved to us that he was spirit by actually taking back his dead body as a new, visible immortal body. He took back his body to finish his instructions to the disciples both for Jehovah and for his true father and then left by ascending into reality and away from the realm of darkness. His rising from the dead proves to the world that Paul was right in Hebrews 11:1 "To have faith is to be sure of the things we hope for; to be certain of the things we cannot see". **Jesus' miracles proved that spirit exists** (see figure 8, page 393).

All Physical Interactions Are Designed to Hide Reality from You

In the true spiritual sense, your mother and father who are dearest to you are your worst enemies. They deceived you, by the god of this universe's consent, in seeing this physical universe as real. It is the purest example of Jesus' statement that the blind lead the blind. This deceit continues to hide your true spiritual being and your true spiritual environment. This is exactly what Jesus taught against. He said that in order to be his disciples, you must love him more than your mother, lover, father, family, and friends. One must begin to recognize everything in one's environment as upside down and inside out. We are uncomfortable with that teaching because we made the environment of deceit and brainwashing as comfortable and as real as we can make it.

The Spirit of Deceit

There is a spirit of deceit called "holy spirit," which is the communion between the knowing [Jehovah, the serpent] and the ignorant [captured souls] who are exploited by the knowing party. Jehovah practices the deceit by causing us to betray each other so that we all exist in a state of distrust with each other. This distrust keeps us isolated and in a state of cunning alert, ready to attack or defend. Physical environment puts us in fear and distrust of one another. We should be suspicious of this god, Jehovah, who supposedly gave us our environment. What kind of god would envelop us in such an environment and then accuse us of wrongdoing? It is not us that stinks; it is this god Jehovah, Allah or whatever name one calls him, who we trust above all else, that continues to stick our head in the mud so we cannot get back home where we belong. The lie keeps us ensnared spiritually, and ensnarled with each other.

There exists an artificially created status difference between Jehovah and his captured souls, at least in the sincerity and confidence between the parties in the communion. The status difference is denoted by the word "holy." "Holy" means to be separate—exhibiting an exponential difference in class and power. "Holy" relates to communion as a master to a slave. This is how the word "holy" betrays the relationship between our "god," Jehovah, and us creatures in the universe. It is a communion between parties that translates in an unequal status of power and earnestness. The deceiver has the high status and has the ability to control the communion [environment], while the deceived or overpowered ones have the low status and have no ability to control the communion other than by kowtowing. The creatures are visible to the god, but the god is not part of our sense of physical awareness. He can hide anywhere.

As examples of spiritual deceit I give the invisibility of viruses and germinal diseases extant in our environment, to which entire societies fell prey in the past. The sneakiness of the environment hides poisonous snakes in the grass that can bite us and, in the very least, get us very sick. We are always scared of something not seen that can get at us. The drive, or temptation for creatures to prey on others and enslave others, in order for them to exist or make life easier and more luxurious is all-overpowering.

The Whole Armor of God

Paul in his letters to the Ephesians 6: 10-18 proclaims much wisdom, but his letters also show an utter ignorance of Jesus' true message. In verse 12

Paul states correctly, "*For we are not fighting against human beings but against wicked spiritual forces in the heavenly worlds, the rulers, authorities, and cosmic powers of this dark age.*" Paul does not understand that besides the authority vested in the devil; he is putty in the hands of the super authority of his own god, Jehovah. The true wickedness has its roots in Jehovah by having captured innocent, trusting souls by schemes of spiritual deceit. After he had captured them, he inundated them with cosmic propaganda, which falsehoods caused souls to deploy the physical universe with human projections of themselves as the only means of communion between the souls.

There is no armor against the spiritual forces inherent in Jehovah. He has us covered on all sides, spiritually and physically. The only armor against him is in knowing Jesus inner message—that there is a loving, and higher god over Jehovah. That means that we can go over Jehovah's head to the Comforter who can be instrumental in arousing soul from its lie-induced coma by relating truth to the soul via the soul's virtual human projection. By us humans knowing the truth about Jehovah we are set free from his propaganda and can then choose the Good Spirit over Jehovah's holy spirit. Souls relate their beingness through the physical environment. They commune with each other through human bodies assigned to them, so soul understands what transpires between its projection and Jesus, as preacher of the inner message. This inner message tells of a loving caring god beyond the reach of the realms of darkness. The soul that is me knows what I as human being know, because he is fully in charge of my being. That is why I am so sure that this is my last go-around. The Comforter will defeat the after-death propaganda of Jehovah's evil, holy spirit.

We have been in awe of Jehovah long enough. It is time we arise from our spiritual malady and enter the realms of ultimate truth, in the true father. This is so hard to believe that nobody ever discovered the truth of this physical environment. Jesus taught so much about truth, and nobody understood the kind of truth he talked about. Pontius Pilate asked Jesus arrogantly "What is truth?" after Jesus told him that he had told him the truth. It should be pretty obvious that truth is not known in earth or the universe. Jesus said that there was a realm of light where truth reigned. It should also be pretty clear that we were deceived if we are dead to truth, as Jesus claimed. He tried to tell us that the god in charge of the universe was not the source of truth because earth, Jehovah's creation, showed a complete lack of truth. The source had to be higher than Jehovah. Jesus reinforced that idea by saying that his authority was higher than all authority and by always claiming that he said and told truth, making him god of a higher order than Jehovah.

The Spirit of True Communion

There is also a spirit of true communion called the "Good Spirit." The parties of this communion are enveloped by the communion as they bare themselves to one another. This envelopment reveals the total reality of the other—everything in the communion is honest and true. This kind of communion is more than just environment because it is love between the parties that flow together and become one. This love creates a new environment, an environment of pure trust [John 17].

The father and the son have become one through the medium of honest communion. The honest communion is larger and more powerful than the individual parts because this union includes the personal environments into a mutual environment that is the total communion of love. This communion between father and son is the environment called, Good Spirit. This communion holds no secrets and private closets. It gives the parties in the union equal status. Deceit cannot creep into this relationship. This union is mighty and unbreakable and keeps gaining in strength as the communion continues. This newly introduced person "of three in one", trinity, invites us to enter into that union to become one with them. This, of course, can only happen when soul has understood that deceit believed (the Serpent's lies) is spiritual death and will not fall for it again.

> *This communion in the most high, strangely enough, is another method of incorporation. In this form of incorporating, all the members are of equal status and nature, and the communion incorporates the whole environment. No one distrusts another and all exist in complete liberty because no one will lay his will on another, knowing that the other can be trusted totally. All are one. By us, lost souls, embracing this Good Spirit to receive help, teaching, and guidance by the Comforter, Jesus' spirit, we have the status of god and are part in god [John 17].*

In reality, the Good Spirit is the environment between the father and the son. It is their means of common understanding. The environment is embodied in this communion, just as a corporation in the United States consists of a set of high-level, single-sided agreements [communion] between a high master [government] and serf [the officers of the corporation] and a low-level set of single-sided agreements between the serf [officers of the corporation] and its slaves [employees]. This communion is called the corporate environment, which has many levels, and the whole structure is a masterpiece of evil in action.

There is yet another set of trinities at work in the same corporation. It is the employee, as soul, in his relationship, holy spirit, with its master, Jehovah. This employee has a set of single-sided, misunderstood agreements with his physical body called physical universe. Then the body has a trinity of entities called body and organs and its spirit of communion, the nerve system, and the nerve system has a trinity between it and the cells through innumerable body fluids such as the hormone adrenalin, and many more such substances. Each level of awareness has its own trinity based on communion. The entire structure is based on deceit and capture. All levels in this structure of communions are under the observation and control of Jehovah, our clever and evil master.

Betrayal by an Inside or Outside Party Breaks the Communion.

However, when communion between friends is broken through betrayal by an outside party, the spirit of communion between the friends is dead. Death is the cessation of communion with one's environment, and death always is a betrayal of trust and dissolution of the parts. The dissolution happens because the communion between the parts ceased to exist. The communion between spiritual body [spiritual cells] and the mind in Adam [a higher realm of understanding] is severed by the interloper, Serpent. This communion between mind and body died. It does not exist anywhere at all. This leaves souls isolated from each other and helplessly in the power of Jehovah. The holy spirit is the communion between the deceived souls and Jehovah. It is the control system Jehovah has by inserting souls in his spiritual computer electronics; and for causing souls to project personal human bodies [not the spirit between soul and the human body, because the computer projected physical environment is that spirit, virtual realm, a fully interactive website].

How Jehovah Deployed an Entirely New System for Souls to Again Commune With Each Other

Jehovah induced another communion between soul and an outwardly projected physical body through the projected physical environment (a communion of betrayal]. Soul is forced into communion with a projected physical environment through accepting an outwardly projected physical body. The new-born baby is the means of communion between isolated souls and a seemingly preexisting physical environment. Soul thus gets the impression that it exists as physical creature in a physical environment, confusing fiction with reality. This could be accomplished by isolating souls from each other and then by casting them in their own individual body projections. The whole production is Jehovah's. The creation of this artificially produced false communion in a virtual physical environment allows Jehovah to be separate and apart from it. He keeps track of his virtual creation through negative spirit computer-controlled media. The body is the new means of communion between the deceived, captured and isolated soul, and with the phony, computer-generated environment. The physical environment is really a non-communion because it sets up hidden traps and betrayals through which souls become fearful, suspicious and deceitful. The physical environment is the greatest deceit played on souls in a communion of suspicion that once were utterly and completely united through communion in the bodies and minds of Adam and Woman. The amounts of deceit hidden in many layers of awareness is so all-overpowering to creatures that they are isolated and find union only in more layers of deceit called religion, society, family and friend, and relationships of work and trade. By understanding the entire system on which the house of cards is built makes one realize that the physical environment is the full expression of utter evil.

When the spiritual bodies of Adam and Woman died the communion was broken. The spiritual mind that perceived this communion died, was no more. The spiritual bodies of Adam and Woman are completely undone. The cohesive force of union was no more. Only the most basic spiritual (eternal) parts, souls, remain. Jehovah created a completely new display of environment for souls where they are isolated from each other through separate physical bodies and they do not know that they were ever a completely assembled unified temple of awareness in spirit. The souls, by and of themselves, were never to have any understanding of what happened to them and that any other forms of reality exist.

The new relationship the souls have is almost like a master dealing with a dissatisfied serf where the master promises the serf some special privileges because he needs the skills of the serf. Over time, when the serf has complicated his life with a wife and child and multitudes of personal attention-requiring duties, the master can again take away these privileges because now he has other means of keeping control of the serf.

The military does the same with its man power. A young recruit enlists with the armed forced for some four to six years while unattached. The armed forces hope that the person will marry and have a child so that the enlisted person will overly depend on his occupation in the armed forces to support his new family. Most, recently married, enlisted personnel with a child will again sign up for another hitch. This relationship lasts some twenty years, after which the soldier is ditched because he is obsolete and is in the way of a younger generation working itself up in rank. The communion is broken; the soldier is removed from his familiar environment and is considered dead to the organization.

A dead person, and thus the soul projecting a body into this universe, ceases to be in communion with the environment. The environment is the expression of the communion between spiritual soul and physical body. By the body having died the soul is placed outside physical communion. Soul will beg Jehovah to be placed in communion with the universe again, and on certain demands of Jehovah, the soul is allowed to reincarnate. Before the union was betrayed through a previous death, this universe was the channel of communion between the person who died and soul. The physical environment, therefore, is the communion between soul and his temporal body. The communion is always the third party in the trinity. We are all one through this environment that allows us any sort of communion at all. It is a communion in complete deceit. Jesus was severely impeded in revealing his true spiritual message because of the utter deceitfulness of the physical environment and of which his body was a part. The other part was that honest communion is possible in true reality and he invites us to enter into the Good Spirit through an intermediary, the Comforter, who is willing to sup with us on thoughts of truth that will lead a soul to awaken in all truth.

Disembodied souls in the negative spiritual realm have no idea that other souls are present in negative spirit. Such a soul is utterly alone and feels abandoned. The only manner it can have communion is through the physical environment by projecting a physical body. As you remember, souls are souls of a dead being, Adam. They had communion in the organization of Adam. Now that the unitizing entity, the mind of Adam, is dead, they are isolated from one another. The souls are in isolation because the means of communion is absent.

Souls can only be aware of other souls by means of a virtual environment induced in their deluded minds [the physical environment, earth] leaving spiritual communion completely severed because the physical environment is a spirit-undermining means of communion. Other physical creatures are mere extra appendages in this private communion; but all the other creatures in environment are what make the environment so real to us by merely being a part of the all-encompassing interactive virtual environment.

Government and banking have done the exact same all over again by separating us as citizens through the SS# and by laws prohibiting us from communing with one another to overthrow their evil kind of government and through a forced-conformance of public opinion. The public opinion is the artificially created environment of communion of government that isolates individuals from each other. When people gather together legally, the government's chaperon is always present—police. The spiritual and physical systems of communion are duplicates of one another. These officials in government and banking do not believe their system was given to them spiritually. They claim ownership of this evil all for themselves. This misunderstanding will be their demise. Jehovah will not be slighted by his creatures.

The government has its own body. It consists of all the corporations that it has licensed to operate under a large set of unified agreements. The government thus has a body of working organs that consist of many millions of cells—human beings—just as your body consists of a number of organs and a large number of working and performing cells. There is really no difference. As has been shown, the body of government works because of one-upmanship, just as Jehovah's body—environment—works because of one-up-ism and why your body works. What makes any of these bodies die eventually is the deceit and suspicion hidden in the relationships, which like a yeast infect and disrupts internal relationships to such an extent that the entire union collapses. One could also say that the communion becomes burned out because there really never was any sincerity in this communion other than enforced command and obedient subjection. Governments are shaky affairs because there are so many entities that are essential to make the edifice work. History can attest to this from the huge scrap heap of regimes, dynasties and nations that succumbed to internal betrayal. External victory over a regime is always the result of internal betrayal.

The Rupture of a Union by Cause of Betrayal

God in paradise warned Adam and Woman not to partake of the Tree of Knowledge of Good and Evil. He advised them through the communion that was between them. And this communion was the "life" in Adam and Woman. When Woman cast her eyes on the tree, after the Serpent spoke to her and drew her attention to it, she already had betrayed the paradise environment through which she had always enjoyed communion with god. Paradise is the communion between the god of their nativity and Adam and Woman. He told them not to partake of the tree in any manner, not even by looking at it, because it held a betrayal that would kill the communion they had in paradise. The killer tree represented some new concepts—a lie and a liar. A lie-believed about the intrinsic validity of Adam and Woman's native environment shattered their trust in their god and their native environment. They fell out of communion and were in spiritual hyperspace all alone and separated from anything they knew, even each other. They were separated because the communion of paradise was gone. Jesus is trying his best to reunite Adam and Womans souls again in truth through communion in the Good Spirit, and so allow the minds of Adam and Woman to have reality and beingness again in a newly recreated body/temple. It is Adam who will be born again a son of the true god with the redeemed-to-reality souls from negative spirit making up the spiritual tissue of his body. The Comforter will be the communion between Adam's rediscovered mind and his newly recreated body. Adam and Woman will be one again.

Reality Needs Companionship

No one can exist in complete isolation, and this principle applies also to the ultimate godhead and to the Serpent. There can be no reality in perfect perpetual isolation because there is no communion to relate anything to. Aware beings need social communion in order to express themselves. Communion gives an entity a place to be. This explains the idea of god, the father, the son, and the Spirit of Communion between them. It explains especially the third part in the trinity, sincere communion between the father and the son. This communion makes it possible for any reality to exist. It is a vital and essential part of the trinity. Without the spirit of communion there would be an isolated god and an isolated son existing perpetually in the limbo of unreality, not knowing each other.

The serpent also had a problem with having an environment to be in. He was a loner because his untruthful character isolated him from communion in paradise. This is too miserable a condition to accept. He was desperate to ensnare someone into his loneliness to create a reality with. He was lucky to get Woman to respond to his question. Once he had her in communion he was able to get her interested in his scheme of another sort of reality. Woman was game and she got Adam involved as well.

All the Serpent has is us, deceived souls, and he exploits his power of deceit over us making us into kowtowing creatures that need to have his approval to have an acceptable environment to be in. He has control over his own fictional creation. He can make life hard, easy or rewarding for us. His power over us is only a make-believe power. By wising up and recognizing his foul play, we can leave him without communion and thus without a place to be. This reminds me of Jesus' parable in Matthew: 22, about the wedding feast. There was one who did not wear the proper clothing for the wedding feast. The master had him tied hands and feet and had him thrown into outer darkness. To be tied means to be isolated and shunned and to be thrown in to outer darkness is like shooting him off in a rocket to outer space without any means of communion. This person has no reality because he has no means to relate his sorrow, pains, insecurities and despair. It causes the person to not be at all, like being inside a black hole.

Chapter 9

The Universe Is a Spiritual Black Hole

Black Holes

It is said that no energy leaves a black hole. It sucks energy into itself and accumulates in power and mass all the time, but nothing leaves. This is a fallacy. Ten years ago or so, I read a science article explaining how a certain kind of energy leaves a black hole under very specific and rare set of conditions. Particles of energy leave at an angle of ninety degrees to the vertical, along the surface boundary—the horizon so to speak. Even though everything sucked into a black hole has no expectations to ever escape, there is, yet, a means of escape. In this evil universe nothing is as it is perceived.

This phenomenon has several analogies for biological creatures. Our souls have been sucked into something like a black hole whose power of capture consists of spiritual and physical lies and deceit. In universal reality, truth has disappeared altogether. We exist in the blackest black hole, and we have made our home there because escape from it is next to impossible. Humans have tried everything, from soul travel, magic, alchemy, study of nature, religion such as the Mormons, and suicide, to find a way out. Nothing worked until Jesus entered the black-hole-like environment of earth, not because he was sucked in but because he has no mass and no energy to give the black hole power over him. The spiritual lie believed gives a spiritual entity a polarized charge by which Jehovah can prevent souls from escaping. Jesus came on his own volition. Why? To reach those whom his father loved and bring them back to true reality.

Spiritual and environmental delusion keeps the human masses entrapped in slavery in the universe because they exist in ignorance of

THE TRUTH ABOUT REALITY

truth that keeps them imprisoned. Jesus could only reach them as one of them. He proved through his miracles that he was not a captured entity in the black hole. He has status beyond anything caught in the black hole. He had to agree to some deceit. He was forced to come as Jehovah's Messiah to get status in this universe. Without some kind of deceit, a spirit cannot enter this universe in physical attire, the body. Through the body, he became one with the environment. In this body, Jesus was able to be Messiah and himself as pure spirit. The problem was that humans had no ready way to distinguish between Jesus as physical Christ and Jesus as the positive spiritual Christ. All they could readily see was that he was the physical Messiah. His miracles, his healing, and his personal power over nature betrayed him as such. This revelation of him as the Messiah most effectively hid his mission for true spirit as the physical anti-Messiah, but it also brought him what was essential in his role as the positive spiritual Christ. It gave him status as master and teacher. The masses listened to him and spread his fame. He needed this in order to be a teacher people would take seriously and by which he could reveal his message for which he came into the world.

Jesus' Method to Include his Disciples in his Communion with his Father

Jesus found a nifty way to reveal his true message. Jesus, as a physical being and also as true spirit, communed with his father in the language of his companions. [see John 17]. Remember, the spiritual language has no words because everything is conveyed through ideas, instantly. By saying in the human language what Jesus instantly thought spiritually, both the father and the disciples were witnesses to what was specifically and clearly communicated between all the parties! This communion was the Good Spirit because the Good Spirit is the communion between father and son, which is ordinarily, most private because the level of truth is beyond all available media of communication. This was one very rare occasion where humans, as entities of spiritual fiction and as deceived spiritual beings, are included on the highest level of communion—the level of god, and son in the Good Spirit. It is a most loving, intimate communion, and the disciples were deliberately included. Jesus revealed his true nature as son of god, not by just telling he is, but through actual communion with his father. This incident, in relation to those present, is comparable to the escape of energized particles from an inescapable black hole.

Setting the Stage for Redemption

The people had to understand what Jesus came to do, how, and for what reason. The method was written in the scriptures for the Hebrews. He came to teach and to fulfill the first condition for souls to be redeemed. They had to be set free from Jehovah's jurisdiction over them. For that purpose, he had to be born as a Hebrew. Secondly, a way had to be contrived that bypassed the power of the black hole so particles could escape in spite of the power base of the black hole. Its power was based on deceit. It could only be neutralized by giving souls a means to have access to truth in a manner not detectable by negative spirit. Truth had to come from a source outside the realm of negative spirit and that source must have the ability to relate truth in a way humans can understand. Jesus came as man and learned all the ways of man so that he could inform them of the wellspring of truth that was to come through the Comforter after he returned to true reality. Having completed his mission he taught, through the very manner of his death, that communion in the body is worthless by dying on the cross for all to see. It is through the body that we have and retain awareness of the physical universe. Jesus has thus created a means for certain entities [the souls of certain human beings] to escape from the black hole "universe," but in order for that to happen, Jesus had to prepare the particles to a negative-spiritual neutrality.

Means of Communion in Negative Spirit

> The body is the entity that communes with the universe by detecting and making real the fiction of the universe, and then relaying the information through the brain to the soul [or is it the other way around?]. Without a body, a soul cannot have awareness of the universe. When the body is dead, there is no environment to be in for the soul. What is left is a hankering to be part of it again.

The possible scenario of how the spiritual computer interacts with creatures may be explained as follows: It may be something like radio broadcasting; a radio station and a radio receiver working in tandem. The ordinary radio station transmits signals that a radio receiver tuned into its frequency receives, and transforms into audible intelligent sounds. The radio station can transmit but if there is no radio receiver, or if it is defective no intelligence is conveyed. The radio receiver is the human body.

The same goes for the universe and the body. The universe is a propaganda transmitter that is intended to work in tandem with a propaganda receiver—the human body. The physical brain receives inputs from all its sensors arrayed through the body. The brain translates the signals as an ongoing impression to the soul that the soul exists in the physical universe. Now when the body dies [an inevitable condition of having been made from corrupt materials in the universe] there is no communication between the station and the soul. The soul is thus not aware of being a material part in a physical universe. In order to be again in contact with physical reality, it must apply for permission to be part of it again. The authority will give out another license to soul, and it is assigned a new body [propaganda receiver] through reincarnation. This is how souls never leave the soul's mental state of having been deceived.

Jesus Had to Learn How We Interact with Each Other and with Our Deity

Jesus interjected himself into this propaganda system by becoming a servant of Jehovah to get permission to incarnate as a human being. Then, he could figure out how the entire scheme was projected and upheld. He could learn to understand how souls received the awareness of human creatures in earth and how these projections operate and interact with one another and their deity. He needed all this insight to relate the true reality to the souls and to devise a way to extract souls from the trap. As his miracles indicate, he received a password to get access to the spiritual computer. He could put special routines into the computer that allowed him to do miracles, like walking on water. Peter, his disciple, asked if he could come to Jesus on the water. Jesus said that by faith he could do so. Peter steps outside the boat and begins to walk towards Jesus, but fear overcame him and he sank. Peter could only walk on water by faith in Jesus. It was Jesus that allowed him to walk on water because Jesus had access to the computer. He could not allow Peter to continue walking on the water when his faith was overpowered by his fear. Jesus was teaching the power of faith and the power of fear. Peter learned and became a fearless fellow.

Chapter 10

A Theory of How Creatures and Species Are Differentiated and Controlled Spiritually

A Scheme of How the Several Races and Species of Creatures Are Created and How They Behave as Specific Species and Races

A radio transmitter has a spectrum of frequencies through which it can transmit data to many receivers. The receivers may have been tuned to receive one channel. A radio tuned to only one channel can thus receive data over one frequency only. Other receivers may have been tuned to another channel. So very many sets of receivers can be created; each set of receivers tuned to a different channel. In this way different races of the same species can be created and communicated with. Further, each set of receivers for one channel may be separated in two sub-channels like stereo sound is separated and yet is part of one station channel. This separation into two channels can explain the male and female species of each race.

This implies that there can be an unlimited amount of physical realities out there depending on the number of channels over which the deity transmits and the amount of creature type of bodies available that are tuned in to these channels of physical reality. Therefore there can be a reality for white humans, for Negro humans, for apes, for dolphins, etc. The awareness one has of physical environment thus depends on the kind of body "receiver" one is assigned. It may actually be that each body receiver, through the brain, transmits not only to the soul but back to the central transmitting complex to report the status of plans assigned to that body.

The central transmitting complex can thus send and receive data particular to this one type of receiver body in the channel for the specie and in the several sub-channels for the several races in that species, where the transmitter complex can commune with each sub-sub-sub-channel and with each particular individual body.

This also implies that physical reality is designed to be transmitted in an overall plan and that all receivers or creature bodies are deliberate designs of a hierarchy of daemons in charge of this entire display of the physical universe. This kind of visualization of creation does away with the theory of evolution, and explains the movement of the negative creative spirit in this universe. It is easy to see once you have gained insight.

To corroborate this view of existence, I read an article in *Reader's Digest* about brain research. Researchers use brains of mice for their object of research on human brains because the mouse brain so closely resembles the brain of the human being. Brains of men and mice are so close in design that it is obvious that brains have other important qualities than those that are common to all creatures. It is thus quite conceivable that the brains are sort of transceivers through which creature life is brought into existence and through which individual creature behavior, actions, and thinking is coordinated and controlled by the spiritual computer so that creatures are aware of existing in their physical environment. When a body becomes too decrepit to function according to the instructions given it, the transceiver is shut from the transmitting station and the soul occupying this body is severed from further participation in the environment. Death, thus, is a switching off of a receiving-transmitting section located in the brain. Physicians determine death by noting absence of brain function.

The circuitry of sub-channels and their processors differ slightly from species to species and from race to race. The blood of a chimpanzee, for instance, is so closely related to that of the human races that the difference is almost negligible. The species are definitely patterned after a major model from which the characteristics of the different species and races have been taken. Noses are generally at the front of the head, so are the mouths, cheeks, eyes, with the brain located in the upper part of the skull—it is all part of a major model, just as cars have engines, wheels, a steering wheel, etc. all in the general location where they are found in cars.

As the Good Spirit teaches soul the light of truth, the ball and chain begin to corrode and lose its power to bind soul. When the moment is reached, soul will fully understand what has happened to it and understands that a change of attitude will break all bonds to the realm of darkness; he is ready to be clothed in the raiment of light. He has become a particle that escaped the blackest black hole in all reality. Some souls may even disconnect from the computer on its own initiative, and maybe, it can reconnect at will, making this soul-projected human form indestructible in the physical environment.

The Link between Physical and Spiritual Understanding Takes Place in an Awakening Soul

My wife asked me a very penetrating question and I answered her that she should have become a lawyer because her questions are always so deep and bring the crux of a problem to the fore. Her question was, "If we as humans cannot have any recollection of past lives, then all that we discovered about the nature of spirit and the physical universe must have come to us in this life time?"

To get to the answer of this question, let me recapitulate what state a soul is in when projecting a physical body. The body is a computer display entity that is wholly integrated to be in the computer display, the universe. The brain is the piece of equipment in the body that integrates our awareness into the display through the physical senses; and that makes physical existence all-encompassing and spiritual awareness utterly null. So when we exist in the physical we are shut out from spiritual awareness.

I thought about that and we discussed the ramifications of the question. This spiritual understanding is only possible in people because Jesus revealed his true father to us in John 17. My wife volunteered that she has completely incoherent nightmares and dreams. In the morning the feelings and emotional essence of her dream often stays with her for some hours. I must agree with her. I very often do not remember my dreams but when I do the essence does stay with me. I can explain it a bit more. I watch movies and TV programs sporadically, and some movies leave such a feeling of elation behind in my emotional make-up, that I unconsciously place myself in the role of one of the main characters. I remember, for instance, that many decades ago I watched the "Scarlett Pimpernel" starring Tony Curtis. Weeks after, I still identified with Tony in that movie. The feelings were so strong that today I can still remember the feeling vividly.

My gut feeling is that my wife and I were already awakened from spiritual coma to, say, spiritual hibernation, a state where you can be awakened when sufficiently disturbed, and in another lifetime we awakened even more to a state of slumber. When we were placed for the choice to reincarnate or awaken in spirit that time, we were sufficiently drugged by strong identification with the dream to again choose to reincarnate. I believe our spiritual understanding at that time was there but it could not be properly expressed to base a decision on. We could not clearly define our understanding.

However coming to reincarnate in the Twentieth Century and experiencing the technical breakthroughs and establishments of computer technology and its applications, we suddenly were able to define our spiritual understanding so that we could comprehend it and were able to relate this understanding in written form so that others may be awakened more abruptly to our very same understanding.

This understanding may not be sufficiently strong in readers of this book but before expiration from this term of life these souls will have gathered all the understanding they need to make the correct choice and will not be present in this universe again. After each death, soul experiences much fanfare and massive doses of propaganda from the false comforters [daemons] to again reincarnate, but many readers of the book will have sufficient understanding to make the correct choice, by following the true Comforter, who is standing quietly in the background.

Chapter 11

The Crucial Question

I conclude Book 2 with the crucial question, "Why does evil exist?" By now you hopefully can answer this for yourself. Evil always comes in a disguise of good. Evil is the depth of deceit because it comes disguised as good. Souls *must understand and know evil* [remember, we, in paradise partook of the tree of *the Knowledge* of **Good** and **Evil**] to be able to look through all the disguises that evil can hide behind. This is of spiritual significance because if evil could take on a disguise of good in the realm of good, evil would invade and settle in the realms of good without "good" knowing about it. So whoever will enter into the ultimate realms of good must know every aspect of evil to be able to look through all the disguises of evil in order to identify and embrace good and shut out all avenues through which evil can slip unnoticed into the realm and communion of good. Nothing is as it appears to be. Everything in the universe is evil in a disguise of good.

Evil is a communion, just as good is a communion. Do not let a communion of evil disguised as good fool you any more. Evil can be a (booby-)trap, expressed without words, but as deadly and tragic for those who wander into it.

If evil would succeed, existence in any plane of reality would become an intolerable nightmare and we would be caught in inescapable suppression and hatred without love and without anything to look forward to, because evil would have shut off any possible escape route. I give you examples of evil that shut off all avenues of escape: the Wall erected between East and West Germany, The Elba River in Germany between East and West at the end of the war with Germany, the river of death. I give you the continual encroachment of government into our every moment of daily life.

Liberty and love would disappear from all levels of reality forever. I hope that everybody in the world can identify with this kind of horror. If you can, you are truly ready to embrace the Comforter in the Good Spirit who is reality as good and not as evil. Government, marriage, children, cars, computers, planes, you name it; they are all disguises of evil pretending to be good.

Do Not Let the World Confuse You Any More; There Is No Good in It. Only One Is Good, Ultimate Truth in Ultimate Reality; and As Yet, You Have No Part In It.

The disguise in which evil tried to usurp the intentions of good in Jesus is so severe, that it took 2,000 years to understand what Jesus was truly doing. Jehovah has been exposed and stands naked. Good is the responsibility of every soul in existence. If you cannot rally for good you will be utterly annihilated.

Now, I Sincerely Hope You Take Me To Heart. I Am Not Much Of A Spiritual Leader or Politician, I Am Not Jesus Or Some Saint; But I, Anti Christ, Am All You Have in the Good Spirit, Whether You Are The Pope, The Ayatollah, The Dai La Lama, Bill Gates, Oprah, George Bush, Or Whoever You Think You Are—Like Jesus' Words, My Words Help Give You Life. They are truly worth all you have.

All Christians brag on knowing truth, however not one knows what truth is. The truth is that you live a lie in a reality based on a lie. Jesus came to make you aware of that fact. From hereon out it is a matter between you, Evil, and the Comforter. The ball is in your court.

NOTE: It is up to you to recommend this set of books in one cover to everyone you care for. Many people have a tendency to repress the knowledge of others by withholding recommendation to those they hold dear. This is a selfish attitude. If you love someone you should allow that person to have information and options to form his or her own opinion. Be yourself, not Jehovah's patsy. This book helps you to do that.

This material will give anyone powerful rehabilitation of awareness and understanding of liberty and love. If you are unable to convince a person, or if you believe that a person you would want to recommend this book to will not be persuaded by its spiritual value, recommend it on its value as a works of science fiction, or for its philosophical, historical and political value. It is also up to you to help make the world a better equitable place to be where every race, species and creature can have a worthwhile place. Humility and true understanding are the greatest blessings one can give another.

BOOK III

THE SCIENCE FICTION OF CHRISTIANITY: AN EXPOSURE OF THE FALSE PROMISES, BELIEFS, AND RITUALS OF CHRISTENDOM

Chapter 1

The Universe Is Based on a Spiritual Lie-Believed

Evil Cannot Exist in True Reality

If there is evil, it cannot exist in true reality. This alone is proof that the universe is a virtual realm. We know that evil exists in the universe. The beauty of evil is that one must understand evil in order to understand and know "Good" (evil is possible only in a realm of fiction for evil cannot be let loose in reality). If you advance from understanding and doing evil in earth to wanting to know "Good", in the Good Spirit, you will transcend from the realm of virtual existence to true existence in the very house of GOOD, the true Father of us all. We are here in this earth (the only inhabitable place in the universe) to transcend existence in the Son to existence in the Father. We cannot be created in "Good" before we can understand and know evil. The son originally creates in virtual existence, and then proceeds to educate his creatures to become sons of Good in true reality.

The Son (let me call him Jesus) is responsible for creating paradise and the programs available in paradise through the program directors, archangels [of which this universe is one]. Adam and Woman, through communing in the program Universe, play the many roles of evil in earth until Evil has lost its attraction and value for them. They acquire a spiritual distaste for Evil so they will turn their back on Evil in order to find Good. Jesus, through his inner message, introduced us to "Good". However this "Good" is in reality and cannot adopt a role in the realm where evil is taught to be mastered. Good is reality, Evil is fiction; the twain cannot meet. So if one wants to pursue evil one exists in a virtual reality, and when a person wants to pursue good and can graduate to know Good, he awakens in reality. However, one will awaken with a full knowledge of the concepts and pitfalls of evil. The souls who awake in reality from this universe are gathered together into a living temple, a new son of god, our true father. So, I understand that the son creates in true reality, but through the medium of virtual creations. The birth process of a true son begins in paradise with creatures such as Adam and Woman (like a sperm and an ovum) and progresses in and through the virtual realm of the Knowledge of Good and Evil, the universe; and culminates in the birth of a true son in true reality.

A Metaphor of the Birth Cycle of a Son of God

We can see Adam and Woman before their encounter with the Serpent (the impregnator of the ideas of evil in the mind of soul) as being in the larvae stage of transformation. Presently they are together (as one) in a cocoon transforming from a larvae in paradise (where their soul entities are lying in a coma in the state of cocoon dreaming of existence in the physical universe) into a son of God in ultimate reality. It is the only way to progress from paradise to ultimate reality. The Serpent, thus, is a vital link in the development and progress of birth in true reality. Every soul-cell in the bodies of Adam & Woman is being transformed and rearranged into a being that shows none, or very little, resemblance to what they used to be in paradise. The biological process of the caterpillar becoming a butterfly is given to us to understand what is happening to souls as cells in Adam and Woman in paradise. The coordinated set of dreams in the death-resembling state of the coma [a virtual reality] is woven into a virtual reality that seems so real that it is taken as the only reality possible by their projections. All aspects of evil experienced by this family of souls are the main ingredient for the transformation of the entities of Adam & Woman from the neutral virtual reality of paradise to the positive reality of the true and only father of us all, or the gestation process that leads to the birth of a new son of god. All souls who are not able to participate in this transformation process will be retained in paradise to what we refer to in child birthing as the afterbirth.

Existence inside a Set of Virtual Display Boxes

The universe and this includes the negative spiritual reality that makes the physical universe possible, is like a box within a box. It is based on a spiritual lie.

The serpent, Jehovah deceived Adam and Woman in believing that their native god of paradise told them a lie.

The true reality is outside the boxes. Our physical universe is like a program displayed on a spiritual computer that amuses the owner of the universe, Jehovah. It is run and operated by the hierarchy of daemons. The spiritual realm that makes the physical universe possible is another box on the table of the true maker and father of all. This box is a place to store all that is created in nested, lower level environments such as the physical universe, until souls are ready to transcend up from their level in the diverse computer boxes. Almost all souls are so caught in the fictional reality of the program they will never wake; what is worse, they are determined not to wake because they love the lie more than the truth. They have invested so much spiritual energy in creating and upholding it, they do not dare separate from it. Sacrifice is needed to please a daemon and to become successful in an endeavor. He insists on sacrifice in order to grant what you wish—tit for tat. Souls also have sacrificed much to be part of this virtual environment; yet, they do not know how to please their gods.

The condition of being lost spiritually gives human beings a confused mindset. Communication between human beings on a deep personal level is impossible because one cannot possibly describe what goes on inside one's mind. Mental density of ignorance literally is like a disorientation that cannot be expressed. All the human mind is aware of is the reality of the fiction, the physical universe, created from the fabric of cosmic propaganda and much mental energy. The true reality exists right here, in our midst, but souls cannot come in contact with it because the lie souls believe prevents contact. Jesus said that this realm is darkness [maybe like the womb in which the fetus comes of age]. The soul's mental energy necessary to keep the lies-believed in an environmental context is bewildering. This bewilderment is expressed deeply within the psyche, by distrusting the environment and by trying to be the master of one's immediate surroundings. It expresses itself in deceit, lying and hiding one's true nature to others. Since everyone is doing this, communion in the physical realm is farcical.

True spiritual reality is a method of communication called communion. Those enveloped in communion experience it as environment. In sincere communion both parties have no concept of a lie. Everything there is truth. A lie is always told by a party not a part of the true communion, an interloper. In a deceitful communion only one is aware of a deceit, the predator, the prey is unaware and is thus like a sitting duck to a hunter.

Because the soul believed the lie the serpent told, it caused the soul to be shut out from its native reality. Its native reality simply does not recognize one who believes a lie about the communion available in that environment. The believer in a lie in spirit exists in limbo, a spiritual coma. Jesus refers to an entity believing a lie as being clothed in rags unbecoming of true reality. These clothes, of course consist of the lie-believed, a false reality and thus a false environment.

A soul wrapped up in a lie-believed is cast out of god's house into outer darkness. So, in order for it to be somewhere, the physical universe was created by means of the truth on which the lie is based and the lie itself—a binary power structure that holds within itself the ability to create this physical universe out of seeming nothingness because a lie is nothing. It does not exist in reality. Funny thing is that the universe is powered by the energy released by the potential difference created in the soul believing the lie—if you, as soul, are cleared of the lie-believed your potential goes to zero. You are then released from bondage [from being caught in the universe] like a donkey that dies after it was forced to always carry heavy burdens. When it dies it is set free from its burdens—no means and no reason to knock itself out.

The universe is not truly based on nothingness, because one component of the binary system is truth which, in the negative spiritual computer, occupies the "0" state as it is not appreciated or recognized. A soul entity is that truth. The lie-believed occupies the "1" state as it is precious. The tension between truth and the lie creates the energy potential upon which the universe is created and run. In negative spirit we see a reversal of values. Truth is not appreciated and the lie is treasured. We know thus that propaganda was at work because the purpose of propaganda is to make the truth a lie and the lie the truth—making black white and white black.

It is based on the same concept a writer uses to create a novel. The fiction comes from the mind of the writer and exists nowhere else. The writer, though, has to be fed, clothed, housed, and given an environment to be in. Even though the novel is an imaginary reality, the means of producing it depends on energy, intelligence, skill, and directed, focused effort in the reality of the physical author.

In the case of the author, the fictional setting is logically and rationally designed. In the soul it was secretly implanted by devious means. Jesus told a parable about this condition. A farmer planted wheat in a field and an enemy, at night [darkness] sowed weeds in the flied. The field was corrupted and could not yield a good crop—in a mind sown with truth, some one came and planted a lie.

So the only reality a deceived spiritual person can have is a fictional reality. This communion in a lie is not true, therefore it is fictional. A new communion, environment to commune in, came into being based on the lie, a virtual environment. The belief in the lie exists in the soul of the human being. It consists of nothing other than spiritual energy mass, which is the mass of the universe itself, make-believe. The mass is transferred to the human mind. It is energy mass we experience outside and inside our being. Our environment is a spiritual fiction of soul, created and kept in suspension by the physical human mind that keeps it out there on orders from the deceiver, Jehovah. The mind is the go-between, between the truth fabric of the soul and the lie it believes. This mass is created by the confusion in the mind the lie has forged in the soul who is created in truth. There is spiritual uneasiness in soul because the fabric of the lie is not part of it native heritage. Energy must be expanded to, somehow, make it fit into that heritage. Mental energy or mass is the confusion of the soul, who has to create all kinds of other false assumptions to keep the lie alive and viable. This necessity to keep the lie intact through the production of other supporting lies is referred to as "loving the lie more than the truth," and this process takes considerable energy.

Confusion is spiritual darkness—the realm of the universe, and the mass is the tangible body and environment in which it seems to exist. "Being lost" is being in total darkness in an unfamiliar place. Darkness is the permanent malady of humanity, and of the souls that underlie the physical environment, although the lower the soul sinks into the animal world, the more this darkness is perceived as light, the only environment possible [more evidence of propaganda at work]. This malady becomes the truth of existing for animals in nature. The confusion of the soul is buried so deep in physical experience that the idea of another reality being possible vanishes from the soul mind of an animal altogether, leaving nature as its only true reality.

The program "universe" is based on protocol, conventions, and rules that govern the environment on which the program can be displayed. It is completely analogous to the art and technology of computer science, and the art and technology needed to write and run programs on the human-created computers. We call some of these rules the laws of nature. We have been allowed to discover some of them and use them to our "benefit" here on earth. Yet, even though they seem to benefit us, we do not get any better, wiser or happier, because deep down, the soul knows this is just a gimmick. Therefore, Paul's statement that "they go on deceiving others as they are being deceived themselves" is more correct than he ever could have imagined. Everything in the program has been designed and calculated to keep those trapped in the program trapped forever. The spiritual computer-generated environment tricks us into believing we are in true reality, and all the players, or souls, interact as if they were in true reality and thus indoctrinate themselves and others to believe the same thing. The trap is inescapable, but thanks to Jesus and the Comforter whom he sent, some of us have a chance of escape. Jesus' preaching was considered by many of his listeners to be complete bunk. It just did not fit their idea of reality, and they were too careless to even try to understand.

Shadow Play

In countries where the Malay people live there is a form of theatrical play produced on a translucent screen that is lighted from behind the stage. The actors are wooden carved grotesque "wayang" puppets mounted on sticks. The actors act out a play behind the screen according to roles played out by people holding these puppets up in the light so that the audience on the other side of the screen can only perceive the shadow play, music and voices. This is the way things are as stated in Hebrews 11:1 (see figure 8, page 393); things that are seen are upheld and controlled by things that are not seen, but it must be remembered that this is a coordinated play performed according to a routine laid down by a composer. Let's face it, god, Jehovah, knows everything, even the future. If that is so, he must be able to see those things on a record of the completely composed scenario he has already laid down.

There is absolutely nothing to worry about in life, because all future events are already determined by the script of the play we are engaged in. The funny thing is that we as soul projections are isolated from the determinations made in spirit. All we experience as soul projections, [human beings] is what the brain perceives is happening around us right now in a setting of reality that is pure fiction.

Very Few Find the Way Out

The Comforter, if we want to be led by him, wants us to throw out our most precious possession—our understanding of Jehovah as the god of all things and of the physical environment and thus our physical beingness [the parable of the treasure in the field].

Jehovah is god, but his reign as deity is over a false reality. From where the true god stands, no universe is visible, only a mass of spiritually dead-like souls lying in paradise—souls that experience the physical universe in a spiritually drugged state. The lie will alter a person's awareness here in this physical universe and even more dramatically in true existence; in true existence, soul is dead to truth by believing a lie. Souls are still present in paradise but they are out of communication with it.

What souls experience in their spiritual lie-induced dream is the physical universe and Jehovah, the serpent, as their god. In communion with this deceiver they project out a physical body in this physical environment. The physical body in the physical environment is the communion between the deceiver and the deceived soul. Souls, clothed as human, animal, and plant, are so ensnared in the fictional reality that they cannot find their way back out, and so the dream continues. As Jesus said, so few find the way back out that it is a true miracle when it happens. If it happens, it will most likely occur during the state when the soul is in a white human body. If you are white, treasure your race. Souls of the white race will not have it much longer. The spiritual weather that foreshadows the end of the world that Jesus talked of can be predicted by the mental state of white people. As they deliberately and energetically continue to corrupt their genes with the genes of other races, the end of the world comes nearer. The spiritual storm is "in the brewing" and coming closer.

The Universe as a Computer Program

There are many references in the Bible where Jehovah interfered with the proper working of the universe. Once he stopped time for many hours. In another instance, a little oil to make just one little loaf of bread did not run out; and yet another instance, an oil supply for only one day in a lamp kept the wick burning for eight days. There was also the time Jehovah ordered a man named Gideon to fight for him. This man asked Jehovah to prove that his intentions were pure and that this demand was coming from him. He asked to make dew in the morning, but not on a sheepskin he had laid out. Then, the next morning, he asked to make it dew on the sheepskin and nowhere else. Jehovah did as requested. The Bible is full of descriptions of such "miracles."

Scientists and the physical laws discovered by them prove that all non-biologically induced movements in nature occur by adherence to precise mathematical formulae. If an imbalance occurs somewhere in a system, a balance is recreated according to the working of a specific mathematical formula or a complex of specific mathematical formulae.

Movements of objects in the universe always occur by adherence to one or more precise mathematical formulae [laws]. I now state that all biological movements are also ordered, maybe not by natural laws, but by program routines that order the existence of creatures. Very good examples are the natures of the different species of animals, including the human animal specie. Once we can see the order in the universe, and once we observe the nature of biological life, we can see intuitively that this is so. Human anger, impatience, emotional hurt, and many other emotions express themselves always in the same manner, coming up strong, staying steady, and waning afterward. This is so for all human emotions and other actions—and as for women in general, someone stated it pretty accurately, "The urge for sex starts to wane at the moment the wedding cake is cut." Our sex drive follows a precise curve, just as the act itself. You can analyze and see this programming in almost all human activities; and what is not innately programmed, indoctrination by powerful authorities will, by force of law, coerce conformance to a program or tradition.

Astrology

Astrology is an ancient art. It produces excellent results although I do not ascribe to it. Astrology again corroborates the idea that the universe and we, creatures, in it are creations displayed by a spiritual computer. The validity of astrology points out that creatures, at least human creatures, are in effect of the aspects of the astronomical 'frozen' "print-screen" of the heavens determined by the moment and location of birth. This moment, in the final stages of gestation, is determined by the conditions in the mother; by her strength to expel the child, by her contractions and her determined effort to aid the contractions; by the aid she gets from doctor, nurse or the 'shaman' and from artificially induced birth procedures. The soul's decision, or maybe the decision of some spiritual authority over the soul, to inhabit the new child depends on the choice of inhabiting that baby body according to the analysis of this "Print-Screen" chart. This print-screen chart determines the new person's destiny as a projected being. After the soul inhabits the body at birth it loses all conscious memory of this pre-incarnation decision (because interpretation of life-experience detected through the physical senses is recognized by the physical brain based on actual current physical events and sensations that are controlled by the computer's program routines). The new baby subconsciously lives by the dictates of the progression of the trajectories of the planetary bodies in the heavens in accordance to soul's decision—so that, say at age 35, an astrologist can make an accurate chart based on the "print-screen" image of the heavens at the person's birth and from it can make all kinds of accurate predictions for the future and an analysis of the character and physical dispositions of the person under analysis.

This discussion on astrology is given to corroborate the ideas in this book that the universe is a virtual reality in which no permanent spiritual errors can be made. The universe and the process of reincarnations for souls is the perfect medium to learn "good" through whatever trials and errors this process may bring a soul, without causing any damage whatsoever in reality. It also points out that those chronological events in the universe take place on a track of a recorded program. There is absolutely nothing taking place in the universe and in a person's life that is not already predetermined by the sequence laid down in the recording. Physical life is like a symphony engaged in, in the same manner in which musicians participate in a written piece of music. If it was not prerecorded and learned and practiced beforehand the piece could not be produced and played in synchronized concord. The drummer must rely on the other members of the orchestra, and all the other members must rely on the drummer to do his part according to the dictates of the conductor who again is subordinate in his actions to the composer of the piece of music that is being played. The past is as much history as the future that has not yet passed through the aperture of the projector displaying the composition "Life on Earth".

The experiences of the human being are arranged to happen by impulse from the computer on the input of the soul in spirit. Since physical experience is limited to physical events and sensations the human biological being can record and remember these as new brain-detected experiences. The human being is absolutely ignorant of a decision made prior to birth in negative spirit outside the stage where the play is performed. This explains why human beings have no knowledge whatsoever of the negative spiritual environment from which their projections are cast into the display of the universe. Creatures exist as if they are in reality but in truth they are mere puppets whose actions and experiences are dependent on the computer routines to which these are keyed. Through schemes to deceive others for private gain souls may learn Good in truth. It is a long process, but eternity has unlimited patience to bring forth such a splendid being as a son of the true god.

Miracles as Expressions of Program Manipulation

What I am coming to is that the miracles we read about in the Bible can only be explained if we see the universe and its many subsystems, such as the Milky Way galaxy and the solar system, as being a part of an extremely intricate [spiritual] computer program that can be manipulated by entities outside the computer system complex. Each subsystem has its own set of controls that can be set on automatic or be placed on manual control. The systems manager, so to speak, can thus set things on automatic for all parts, and manipulate certain subsystems, including the thoughts and actions of an individual person. It is told, for instance, that a mother of little strength lifted a car to retrieve her child trapped under it. The woman had super-strength in that instant, but never before or after. It was done through the actions of the operator in charge of a particular routine or subsystem in the program. She must have prayed to the god[s] for the strength to do so. One can now visualize how the end of the world can be engineered spiritually. An operator takes the routine of an ordered universe out of automatic operation and manipulates the controls to create chaos—the same chaos from which "god", Jehovah created the new universe and the new world in Genesis 1. This process is reenacted every so often when a new set of Adam and Woman have swallowed the lie to empower the computer system. While the serpent is busy ensnaring another set, he cannot have his mind on the computer program.

Why are there so many white humans while there was only one Adam and one Woman in paradise? In paradise, they were eternal and did not reproduce. They were fully integrated. When they fell by believing a lie their spiritual cellular makeup disintegrated, and these cells were used as single entity souls for humans. All Adam's spiritual cells became men, and Woman's cells became women. Together, all white women form a cellular system that is Woman and likewise for men and Adam. All other individual species and races form the spiritual cellular structure of earlier seduced sets of Adam and Woman that were not redeemed into reality.

So, how are miracles performed and observed before people's eyes here in this universe? Some daemonic operator behind his control panel receives an order to allow a certain non-routine event to occur in the program. He pushes a few buttons and the miracle exhibits itself in the physical environment before the eyes of some observers. How is the universe rolled up? Just turn the computer off or discharge the energy source it runs on. One turns it back on or recharges the system by simply seducing another set of eternal beings to enter the program. In doing so, a different or a modified program begins to run, causing a new history in the new universe for those new spiritually charged cells caught in it.

The Ancients Revered Many Gods

Through all history, people had valid interactions with daemons and revered state, city, and house gods not just for the fun of it. These "gods" or daemons were worshipped, feared, and revered—and according to the amount and intensity of kowtowing by the worshippers, they received or did not receive what they wanted or were punished or helped along. All these things can be easily found in the Old Testament. Nothing is new under the sun or in the universal spiritual [negative] realm. Humans make computers and design programs to be run on them and so, obviously, do daemons. Jehovah's heaven must be the receiving of blessings for reincarnated Hebrews [the descendants of Abraham who were favored by Jehovah] in the nation and territory appointed to them, the Promised Land; curses must be curses and misfortunes for reincarnated Hebrews. Jehovah's heaven and hell are here on earth, but only for future reincarnations of the same souls of the ancient Hebrew people to whom the promises were given. Hebrews will reincarnate in their own nation.

Comatose Souls as Energy Units

When Adam and Woman believed the lie, they became the most important part of the program universe. The charges of the lie-believed in them generated a power system that could be used in the computer, and they themselves became components [they were, so to speak, spiritually wired] in the operation of the computer. This is possible because their souls are always truth, and this truth is placed against the charge of the lie they believed, and a spiritual potential is created.

Souls as cells in the "live" and aware, integrated bodies of Adam and Woman worked together in harmony. Souls in the comatose bodies of Adam and Woman believe in lies that affect their harmony and integration of action. They are disintegrated by the lie. The unity of beingness in paradise is gone; and contention and competition is created through the manipulation of their individual minds. That is why polite, suspicious discord is the normal mode of the human mental state. Since the serpent is their new god, they obey his orders and assume their individuality according to his dictates. The one category of unison that Jehovah requires of souls is in the unfolding and upholding of the universe that is the whole of the communion between the deceiver and the deceived souls. They exist in a state of enchantment. This Jehovah did through a spiritual propaganda scheme. He obtained their cooperation in an orchestra-like setting where all souls work together under the control and direction of Jehovah, the conductor. Souls, then, projected themselves as individual temporal human creatures on earth—as a part of the environment of the universe. Competition, avarice, contention, and deceit are forced on physical creatures, because creatures can only exist on the substance or flesh of other creatures, be they animal or vegetable. Jehovah, thus, forces evil and death on us.

Chapter 2

The Spiritual Battle

Jehovah Is the Enemy

Jehovah in the Biblical story of the Tower of Babel in the Old Testament destroyed the unity of mankind and thus of soul unity, twice. Jehovah does not want us to unite because as a united entity, we might find the reason for our disunity and avarice. He only wants unity under his direction, not under the direction of humanity itself. Strife, war, deceit, false propaganda, and cruelty are men's constant companions, by design; it is their physical means of communion.

Through their integrated computer bodies, souls have rejected their maker, the spirit in the person Jesus. We betrayed him in paradise, and also when he came to us in human form due to the cleverness of Jehovah. This is because truth in the human brain does not compute. To humans, Jesus' teaching is illogical and unrealistic; as it was considered by Adam and Woman when they were deceived in paradise. Jesus' person and miracles are spiritual curses that hide his true spiritual message.

Means to Detect When the End Is Near

The propaganda systems are so intensely integrated and all encompassing that the real message of Christ cannot penetrate the consciousness of humans without extra aid. The human race is actually destroying their chances to be redeemed. This is the indicator by which to forecast the change in the spiritual weather. It is unsettling to observe how zombie-like humans have become. They now act, not only on cue of cosmic programming, but on the commands brainwashed into them by a very small group of people, integrated in close-knit US and UN organizations. The sub-routines in the spiritual computer that control human interactions and interactions with the operator, Jehovah, must thus be under special, monitored, spiritual control. Twice Jehovah's control went awry as the Old Testament tells us. Once, Jehovah wiped out an entire racially interbred race and saved only Noah and his family because they were not racially interbred, and the second time when Jehovah chose Abram [and renamed him "Abraham"] because the rest of humanity was conditioned to worship other deities and no longer recognized or obeyed Jehovah. This time he will cause the roll-up of the universe because it is an event in the program scenario.

Jehovah's Blessings Are Spiritual Curses

I can see that Jehovah favors the conspirators who are enslaving all humanity into a One World Order. He is taking measures to make sure that when truth invades the realms of fiction, his losses will be minimal. He favors the few to control the many.

The big difference between Abram and the rest of humanity at that time when Jehovah approached Abram was that Abram was faithful to Jehovah. Abram was faithful to Jehovah because he swallowed Jehovah's hype hook, line and sinker.

So Jehovah renamed him Abraham, and made a special pact with just Abraham and his offspring from Sarah, which pact did not endure too long either. According to the Old Testament, all human races were eventually abandoned by Jehovah until Jesus started to preach. Now, Christendom worships Jehovah through the interactions of the human, dead and risen, Jesus. The Jesus that arose from death is still Jehovah's Messiah, but he is now above and beyond Jehovah's law. He rose from death to guide to Jehovah's heaven all those, called sheep, who can never be redeemed to reality because they see the universe and this earth as the only and true reality and Jehovah as highest god. Soul projections and thus souls themselves never received and/or understood Jesus' true message of spiritual redemption. Jesus as Messiah is leading Jehovah's sheep for Jehovah; while Jesus as Comforter is guiding his goats, who can have his spiritual message, out of the realm of fiction into all truth.

Jesus' Dual Role

Jesus came to us in a spiritual computer-generated body. He received this body from Jehovah if he would be his Messiah. So according to a pact with Jehovah, Jesus entered the realm of human existence depicting Jehovah's Messiah. In his role as Messiah, he did many things that were very strange to the people of that time, like insisting on riding on a donkey, doing miracles, and healing the sick and many other things that were foretold that the Messiah would do. Much of the foretelling about Jesus in the Old Testament comes from the book of Isaiah. I believe that Jesus could do all these things because his being was not wired into the computer system through a lie-believed and was not an energy source in the system. He was here on his own cognizance, on the mission his true father had sent him to do.

Jesus' real mission was to teach about true reality and the way one must follow to return to the realms of truth. The problem with his dual role was that he was misunderstood by the masses. He warned them that only the very few would be able to understand his message to let them know they should listen to these extremely few, rather than the multitudinous cadres of religious leaders that are always available.

Jehovah—Jesus' Adversary

Jehovah is not the god who Jesus calls his father, but the father of lies of whom Jesus said that he was the god of the Jews. This misunderstanding makes all present and previous Christian worship useless and void of positive spiritual content. Jehovah's universal propaganda is mind-bogglingly clever and is the reason why Jesus' message is so susceptible to misunderstanding. Jesus did kowtow to Jehovah but only in order to become the Savior in truth. He had to pretend to be Jehovah's servant in order to be perfect in Jehovah's mind, in order for Jehovah to surrender all souls to him. Jehovah tricked Jesus also because Christendom became not worshipers of the true father but of the father of lies, Jehovah, all over again. Thus, as the Old Testament foretold, Jesus was the Messiah through whom all Hebrews again worshiped Jehovah under the [new] name of Christians, which, if you look at it biblically, is a word ascribed to Jehovah. *Christ* in Greek means "Messiah." Jesus went so far as to call the physical reality the realm of darkness and to inform the people to watch for signs that would foretell the end of the world and the universe. If that is possible, then the universe is just a computer program that can be run and aborted.

Jesus, of course, was well aware of the fact how incredibly difficult it is for humans to understand that this universe is just fiction. So he warned the people that only a few would be able to be redeemed through the aid of the Good Spirit in order to raise the statistical probability of the number of the few. He told us to be observant and listen for truth. That is what he means when he speaks of those who have eyes to see and ears to hear—try to understand, with all one's might, mind, and soul; and the Comforter will be revealed. He that seeks shall find! How many confessing Christians ever do this to even the most basic extent? To not do so causes one to go to hell where the flame never goes out, and the worm never dies. His warning was all-encompassing, because whatever you diligently seek you will receive.

The End Is Coming Nearer

It will not be long before the entire white stock of humans will have disappeared because never has propaganda been this fierce and so well integrated that no one can escape the mental command to racially interbreed. As a matter of fact, because people are so brainwashed, they will eagerly help to bring this disaster about—for people, as is now becoming ever clearer, love the lie more than truth. This is a fact well known to the science and techniques of propaganda.

The Worm and the Flame of Hell

Jesus said that in hell "their worm never dies, and the fire is not quenched" [KJV Mark 9:44-48] [Good News Bible: . . . the fire that never goes out . . . there the worms that eat them never die]. The worm is the digestive track, and the fire is the acid of the digestive track. A lake of fire is an acid bath. It is a lake of fire through which all living creatures go endlessly as they are born, die, and are reborn.

Souls have a very long half-life and can only exist in bodies that grow old and that have to be discarded very frequently—just as people will discard their old cars and buy new ones repeatedly. Their dead [or not so dead] physical bodies are consumed by "worms" [digestive tracks of creatures] and are digested in small lakes of fire, but by combining all the acid in the stomachs of all creatures into one place, it is one enormous lake of acid fire [as related in Revelation 19 and 20]. Flame can be the perpetual fire-energy of the soul, or it could mean the power of the ever-active acid of stomachs.

Bible Study Will Destroy the Spiritual Life of Most Readers

Reading and believing all that is in the Bible is truth will not save a person—but reading and understanding certain parts in the Bible, in

communion with the Good Spirit, will lead a person to a permanent connection with true spirit through the medium of the Comforter, and so a soul will escape from attachment to the fictional universe and be born again in the realms of truth. If such rebirth occurs, the source of energy of the deceived spiritual cell is lost to the computer—a malfunction in Jehovah's scheme of things. The person vanishes from the environment. For some reason this seemed to have happened to Enoch as told in Genesis 5:20-15. Enoch was taken out of the computer display. He was deleted, either by Jehovah or by the spirit of Jesus.

If one reads the Bible in communion with the holy [evil] spirit, one receives the physical interpretation and understanding, and one becomes more under the control and sway of Jehovah and more comfortably settled in hell. Such believers call themselves Christians.

There is no religion, preacher, or leader who will ever or can ever give aid in your spiritual rebirth in reality [rebirth, because you first had to die away from true existence]. All any man can do to help another is point to the source of truth, the Comforter. Jesus told us to look for the Comforter. The Comforter is the Good Spirit, not the "Holy Spirit". Redemption into the realms of truth can only be completed from the realm of truth, a realm utterly foreign to us physical beings. It can only happen through communion with the Comforter, who is Jesus in spirit and not in flesh! No preacher or minister or holy man has an inkling of what truth is, from what I understand, no one ever understood what Jesus meant by truth. It is hidden from us. We cannot get in touch with truth because we are dead to it and locked inside a running computer program that prevents us from observing the real environment outside the program. Only the Good Spirit knows the truth and can lead us out of the program, "cosmic propaganda," and thus into the realm of "all truth." See the article "Three Kingdoms" in Appendix 2 of Book 5.

The computer program has made us blind and senseless to what happens outside the computer. Our computer-generated bodies can only interact with computer-generated entities, movements, and feelings. The program "universe" is unaware of the spiritual realm in which it exists. Reality is a realm of itself outside the limits of the spiritual computer display. The computer, of course, has a station somewhere in spirit; and it displays a program called universe, which is placed in automatic but subsystems, and minor subroutines are constantly manipulated to give certain actions, effects, etc. Some of these special effects are called "miracles." They are miracles because they are not part of the routine operation of the program. Miracles have been specially activated by an operator daemon to convince someone that there are spiritual beings that we cannot see, and to seduce us to accept their sole leadership or prodding. Jesus' miracles, thus, are used to settle souls more comfortably in the physical universe.

Spirit of Deceit

Remember, I explained that the holy spirit is the spirit of deceit. It is a system of propaganda. "Holy" means "separate"; keeping worshippers at a distance and keeping oneself higher up from all others; to be of more importance than all others by means of force. This is logical, of course, as Jehovah is outside the computer environment, and we are inside. The same idiotic principle of "holy spirit" governs the attitude of royalty and nobility and that of most [self-] important people of the world; they set themselves apart from the rabble, not knowing they are the rabble.

Spirit of Love

"Love" or "good" means being united and embraced by the other—making the other more important than oneself. [In John 17—the entire chapter—the word "holy" must be replaced to read "loving"]. Jesus prays for this embrace to happen among all the parties present, just as if the father is in another place and he cannot wait to get together for this to happen. Love includes the other into one's own reality and giving equal or higher place of honor and status to the other. This aspect is totally missing in Jehovah's character. Jesus spoke thus of another, higher god. This higher god loves intrinsically, not because we are obedient and kowtowing worshippers. In love worship is mutual, not one-sided.

Love is realistic as it includes the god with his creatures in a mutual embrace in reality. Hence, there cannot be a medium of a computer or a dream-state in between this god and the creatures. They are one in the same reality. This is the embrace Jesus' spirit wants for you.

For love to express itself, the lovers must be in one and the same environment. This love of the true god is thus always actively trying to return us into his realm of being, getting back into communion in him; because once there, one is embraced by true reality. Positive spiritual love finds place in the reality of both the lover and the loved one. The communion in love is true reality. As long as we are separated in different realities [enveloped in different kinds of communion] the embrace cannot take place. That is why I know that in ultimate reality we all form a temple, a living being, in which souls are reintegrated as cells are in the human being. In this being everybody loves everybody.

Barrier between Reality and Fiction

In negative spirit, the "love of the lie" separates us, souls, from the liar, Jehovah, in that the liar is in a one-up position from us, souls. This happens by the soul loving the lie more than the truth which creates a situation of master and slaves. The holy spirit, the computer program in which we are locked, separates us from the reality of the liar. Therefore, there cannot be an embrace in the same reality. It is the relationship of master and slave. The relationship in the universe between god and creature is like a prison setting where a visitor comes to see the prisoner, but both are separated by a bulletproof sheet of one-way mirror glass. An embrace is impossible because the environments are separated and the master can see us but we cannot see the master.

Thus, in the case of the true god, if we can return his love for us, we actually enter back into reality where we will be conscious of the true environment. His love for us is truth. One can see, then, that love and holiness are antagonistic. They cannot coexist. They are characteristics of different beingnesses. One being is called good and the other evil. So here we are on earth, supposedly learning what the Tree of Knowledge of Good and Evil is to teach us—the difference between good and evil. We learn that evil is difficult to recognize because it always disguises itself as good. It is so difficult to recognize evil that almost everyone sees Jehovah as good and some other daemon as evil. This is incorrect. The truth is that Jehovah and his hierarchy of daemons are the devils while the father of Jesus in reality, screened from our awareness by belief in a lie, is the good.

Chapter 3

What is the Truth Jesus So Often Referred To?

Back to the Very Beginning, Paradise

Let's get back to the beginning of it all. [Remember that the Jewish priests said to Jesus that they were descended of Abraham, their father, and that they never had been enslaved. Jesus answered them that their father was a liar and a liar from the beginning. John 8:39-44]; they were enslaved from the beginning because a lie will enslave the believer of the lie. Who is this liar who lied from the beginning and was their father? Who else can this be but the daemon that seduced them to believe a lie in paradise and thus made them lose standing in the realm of their native truth? This daemon is the serpent. This serpent was clever enough to recognize the potential of getting a universe started on the basis of telling a lie to an entity in paradise in order to generate his own source of power and potential difference to create a spiritual computer to operate his own universe.

Now, I again want to touch upon what truth is and what a lie [propaganda] is. A lie is a statement not in accordance with facts, which cannot be verified or is not meant to be verified. Propaganda is a clever lie or a clever scenario of lies that makes a person believe and, therefore, act in accordance with that falsehood. A lie must always have a basis in the reality in which the falsehood is inserted. If the falsehood or a set of falsehoods were removed from an integrated deceitful plot, the true facts remain—the delusion vanishes. For instance, if the propaganda surrounding the destruction of the World Trade Center were removed, the fact that the buildings came down still remains, but we would not continue to believe that Arabs carry the main responsibility for the crime.

But ultimate spiritual truth is a fact that never alters or changes. Jesus said, "*I am!*" He *is* always even if the universe vanishes or is rolled up. He remains, and he has a realm of communion and a body for that realm and exists there forever. As far as it goes for him, he could care less if the universe is rolled up. All is well for him. He wants the same for us. This is ultimate security. Why does he exist forever? Because truth is real, and true reality cannot vanish [because all those enveloped in the communion only recognize the true facts and not some fable about it]. If it could vanish, it would betray itself to be another lie. The funny thing about a propaganda line or complex set of lies is that when the lies are revealed, the truth left standing is just a bunch of facts that have no relevance whatsoever. The truth used in a scheme of lies is there to give the lies credence. Let us investigate, again, how it is possible that this universe can be rolled up and why.

A Powerful Discussion about Truth and Lie

In the below discussion I quote from the Good News Bible, because it is handy, and I have studied it at length. It is cluttered with notes, arrows, underlining etc.

In John 8: 21-end, Jesus explains much that is misunderstood or has escaped Christian doctrinal scrutiny. I will go through this section from one revealing verse to another.

Jesus was saying that he will go away and that the Jewish authorities would not be able to find him, because where he is going they cannot follow (in their present state of traditional understanding). He continues "*You belong to the world here below, but I come from above. You are of this world, but I am not of this world. That is why I told you that you will die in your sins* [of believing a lie about the truth]. *And you will die in your sins if you do not believe that I am who I am.*" Jesus stated here what he has stated repeatedly—that he tells the truth, and does as his father has shown him, which is truth. Jesus could not expound that riddle without breaking his promise to Jehovah. The priests just did not believe that there was any truth different than from what they understood of truth. They were the highly learned experts of the Scriptures. To them Old Testament scripture was truth. Jesus' truth obviously contradicted with the truth of the scriptures because if Jesus had relied on scripture he would be in agreement with the priests. *We can thus see that Jesus implied that Old Testament scripture is evil disguised as good.*

It is clear that Jesus is trying to explain that there are separate realms of existence and that there are different states of mind. Jesus exists in truth, spirit; it is a realm impenetrable by those who exist in spiritual deceit, or propaganda believed [a fiction about truth, negative spirit and the world/universe as a subsystem in it].

Jesus answered the question of the Jewish high priests of "who he was" with *"What I have told you from the beginning."* What was the beginning? The beginning was when god (son of the true father, Jesus' spirit) said to Adam, *"Do not eat of the tree of the knowledge of good and evil"*? He warned Adam and Woman in Paradise about the killer tree. You suffer and die because you did not believe me, Jesus' spirit, then either. Jesus never deviated from truth. He was god in paradise when they fell, and he is god while he was speaking to them in Judea. Because of their delusion of existence in the universe, they could not see the truth about Jesus when Jesus spoke to them. The physical environment separates them from spirit and from communion in spirit. That is why the Jewish priesthood still cannot see Jesus as god but only as man. If they truly had spiritual eyes to see, ears to hear and a heart to understand, these priests could plainly see Jesus' spirit as god. But as humans they were dumb to spirit and will not believe when Jesus speaks and says he is the true god's son. He makes no sense, so they decided to kill him. [They killed their most intimate friend and god, without blinking an eye. Jehovah is responsible for this reprehensible act.]

He continues *"I have much to say about you, much to condemn you for. The one who sent me is truthful, and I tell the world only what I have heard from him."* A little farther up he says *"I do nothing on my own authority, but I say only what the father has instructed me to say. And he who sent me is with me* [he is in spirit and the universe does not really exist; Jesus and his father were then both in reality, together. It is just that Jesus also acquired a fictional body to commune with us in a universal manner.] ***He has not left me alone, because I always do what pleases him."***

Since Jesus is always present in reality, because he has never believed a lie, those in reality are always with him. When you know truth you please the father. Here in the world we, as lie-believing souls, are abandoned. We are utterly separated from the spiritual realms of truth. All we know is that, somehow, this universe and this world and we, as physical creatures, are upheld by invisible spirit [whatever that means]. Spirit is invisible because it is real and we can only exist in a fiction created by believing a set of original lies and many, many sets of subsequent lies. Souls are blind to reality because we solely believe in fiction.

In verse 31 Jesus said to those who believe him "*If you obey my teaching, you are really my disciples: you will know truth, and the truth will set you free.*" What could the truth possibly set us free from? Is it not the original lie we as souls believed in spirit? Which lie did we believe in spirit? Was it not the lie the Serpent told us? We are here in this realm of evil because we are the ones that believed the lie of the serpent. Nobody in Christendom understands that sentence of Jesus, "You will know truth, and the truth will set you free." If we lack truth we are rich in falsehood, right? The lie hides the truth behind itself. Who is that teller of the lie? It can be no one else than the father of lies, the Serpent [Jehovah] who lied from the beginning—the lie. That is the beginning of our existence in this virtual reality called physical realm. We followed the liar and forgot the true god altogether.

If we exist in a realm created by the belief in a lie, then our universe is phony, our bodies are phony and the experiences we have in this physical setting are phony. We as souls are real, but we kicked ourselves from the realm of reality. There is no other place to be but reality. If we are not conscious in reality by the proof that Jesus gave us supra, we must thus be unconscious. What is the only activity an unconscious entity can do? It is not to dream? Souls believing the original lie conspire together and against each other by the power of the Serpent, Jehovah, the liar from the beginning, to set up this dream universe in order to give us a fictitious place to be and, of course, to learn the ins and outs of evil.

The following verse proves that the Jewish religious authorities and Christendom in general have never understood what Jesus is telling them. The Jews countered Jesus, "*We are the descendants of Abraham, and we have never been anybody's slaves. What do you mean, then, by saying, 'You will set us free'?*" They could not grasp the connection between being free and the knowledge of truth on the one hand, and believing a lie and be caught in the delusion of that lie on the other hand.

Jesus spoke to *their souls* not their human minds. They are not free because a spiritual lie ensnared them and keeps them prisoner as human beings projected in a virtual environment. They have no knowledge of truth because they believe a lie to be truth. They, as humans, could not understand what Jesus was saying because Jesus referred to a truth that souls [made of spirit] hold to be a lie. Souls see this universe as reality based on the sales pitch given to them by the Serpent, Jehovah.

Jesus answers them "Everyone who sins is a slave to sin. *A slave does not belong to the family permanently, but a son belongs forever.*" I can see that you are a slave if you believe a lie in true spirit. They would be free if they still held to the truth Jesus, as their god, gave them in paradise. Jesus is giving them a choice again between being slaves and being free as sons of the true god—the one who always tells the truth, the father. One is enslaved by believing a spiritual lie; and one is free when one embraces the spiritual truth, reality. It is that simple!

Jesus continues "*If the son* [one who is free as a true son of the true spiritual father] *sets you free* [by telling you spiritual truth], *then you will really be free in spirit [reality]*." You will be released from the prison of unconsciousness [spiritual coma] and your dream-world caused by believing a lie, and you will wake up in true reality.

Jesus Compares the Faith Abraham Had in a False God Jehovah to Adam's Infidelity Who Did Not Have Faith in Jesus as True God in Paradise

Jesus admires the faith of Abraham and wished that his listeners would show as much faith as Abraham did. As you remember Abrham was approached by Jehovah in the form of a man and Abram believed him. Jesus' spirit as god approached the priests and Pharisees also in the disguise as man. He was their true god in spirit, and they did not believe him, and Christians, then and today, do not believe him. They see him in the role of Messiah for Jehovah instead of the god of paradise.

Next Jesus said "*I told you what the father* (in truth) *has shown me, but you do what your father* (in deceit) *has told you.*" Jesus is confronting them with what Abraham did. Abraham believed the only god he knew, Jehovah. Abraham was rewarded by this god Jehovah for showing faith in this one god he knew about. It is Abraham's faith that is discussed here; not the fact that he believed the liar from the beginning. There was no other god available to Abraham, so Abraham showed faith in the only god he knew, a liar but whom he thought to be the true god.

Jesus was speaking here to **Abraham's descendants** about them showing faith in the one [his own person] who comes to actually tell them truth, not just another set of lies. Jesus always said that he told the truth. Why? Why was he constantly hammering on the fact that he always tells the truth? It is because he told the truth to us in paradise and we did not believe him. He said several times that he was higher than the god of the world/universe, thus higher than Jehovah, the god that spread lies. There is thus a definite line-up of contenders here, the true god versus the liar from the beginning. And this is the terrible confusion a lie-believed introduces into a discussion about ultimate truth. The deceived people, in their spirit, souls, believe(d) a lie to be truth. So, how can a person who tells the truth, ever convince them that they are believing a lie? These realms of the lie and the truth are mutually exclusive realities. Sincere communion between one who exists in an environment of deceit and one who is free in reality of truth is impossible, no communion took place at all. There was no point of agreement anywhere between Jesus and these priests.

We speak of naked truth, but for us that is an oxymoron. There is no naked truth in the physical realm because the liar cloaked truth so that truth is invisible and unknowable in the physical reality we exist in. There can never be a point of contact until one person, I, appears who receives the guidance of the Good Spirit because he can believe in the Good Spirit, who tells the truth. This person, I, could only have gotten this faith to believe in truth rather than the lie because Jesus spoke to me in spirit to spirit, and was able to unravel the terrible knot in my spiritual mind in which the truth was entwined by existing in a realm of deceit/evil. It is spirit, soul [not the human mind] that must understand truth so that soul can dispel the lie and reenter reality as son.

Jehovah, Liar and Murderer from the Beginning

The Jewish priests answered him "*God himself is the only father we have, and we are his true sons.*" Jesus answered "*If god really were your father you would love me, because I came from god and now I am here. I did not come on my own authority, but he sent me. Why do you not understand what I say? It is because you cannot bear to listen to my message. You are the children of your father, the devil* [the liar], *and you want to follow your father's desires. From the very beginning* [definitely in reference to the lie told in paradise] *he was a murderer* [he killed Adam and Woman] *and never was on the side of truth, because there is no truth in him. When he tells a lie, he is only doing what is natural to him, because he is a liar and the father of lies.*" So, here Jesus actually points an accusing finger at Jehovah, father of lies and the god of the Jews; the priests only believed in one deity, Jehovah. So they decided, "Off with his head!"

To Know God Is to Recognize Him From Before Our Fall

Jesus, bringing a spiritual message to creatures that are devoid of spirit, only refers to truth and lying as spiritual realities, not physical realities. What does it really matter if you tell another lie to somebody who exists in a realm of lies and deceit? Jesus does not concern himself with the deceits of physical reality, He addresses the comatose souls telling them that they are enthralled by spiritual lies and should wake up to the reality of true spirit. He is telling us that when a soul believes a lie it is dead to spirit. The way to come back to life is by embracing *spiritual* truth again. Later in his mission, just before he is crucified, he declared that he had told his disciples as much as he could but that after he had ascended he would send the ***Comforter*** who would lead his believers into ***all truth***. He would transform believers into **knowers** (John 17:3) and so bring back reality into their *souls, not their human minds.*

> ***This is eternal life, to know the true god, and Jesus whom he sent. [John 17: 3]*** This *"know"* means that you must again recognize him as the god of truth in paradise before you believed the liar. You will then recognize him as the god that always tells the truth—the truth he keeps hammering at in his sermons and teachings as Jesus. *I, as soul, know him as such; that is why I write this book.* I am trying to get in communion with your soul. You must see yourself as a being in the spiritual nest of the Comforter. When you awaken from your coma, as a chick breaking free from the egg shell [your body], you look up and see the Spirit in Jesus and say, "I know you, you are my god from paradise whom I betrayed. Thanks for watching over me."
>
> We do not know god now because we believed a lie about him which lie hid him from our deceived soul's awareness. The pure evil of Jehovah hid the true god from us and now this Jehovah pretends to be our god instead.

Proof That Souls Reincarnate

By the way, Jesus here is telling us that we do reincarnate over and over again. The souls in Adam fell into this universe some five thousand years earlier and here at year 28 AD or so he is telling the people that they must ***know*** [recognize] god to be again back in reality. We must recognize god and Jesus whom we called liars and admit that the true god and Jesus always told the truth. People lived only 50 years or so in those days. Jesus tells them, after all this time, while people die and are born for millennia on end, that they must recognize god and Jesus from the way they knew them while in paradise. This can only make sense if souls reincarnate over and over again. We are still the same souls living in year 2008 as the souls to whom Jesus spoke in the year 28 AD or so and those who fell from paradise because of a lie-believed.

Every time a Christian dies, Jesus stands there at the gate to reality and every time the "Christian" soul totally ignores him as it comes back into the universe—hundreds of times again and again. For centuries on end the very great majority of white people have been Christians. These are thus the same Christian souls that reincarnate, constantly ignoring Jesus as god while making another choice to be back in the universe.

Chapter 4

Our Responsibility as Physical Beings

Each Cycle of Physical Death and Physical Birth Is a Spiritual Switch between Spirit and Fiction

The conclusion we must draw from his intercourse with the Jewish religious authorities [in the book of John, Chapter 8], is that we in spirit, believed a lie that caused reality to vanish. Therefore in the spiritual mind reality was cloaked in a system of deceit. That is the reason I wrote the book—to help you, as a physical being, to unravel the confusion that the lie caused in your spirit, soul. Jesus puts the responsibility on us, as physical beings, to enlighten our spirits to bring the truth to our souls in spirit, so that you, as a real entity in spirit, can wake up, and by so doing utterly obliterate your own universal beingness. It is quite a task.

Let Us Not Blow It Again

We really have no excuse. Every time we die, our god Jesus is standing there when you are again in naked spirit. He is waiting for us to recognize him while we are disembodied. We reincarnate over and again, and in all these cycles of reincarnation we did not recognize him because we, in soul, still believe him to be a liar. Once you do recognize him you are in reality. My job is to teach you to go to that quiet character in the background and forget all the fanfare and platform of propaganda designed to get you back into the universe in a new body. All you have to do is recognize Jesus after you die and you are with god. No Christian alive today, and that includes me, has ever recognized Jesus for 2,000 years; we, alive today, are proof of that. Let's us not blow it again.

Playing the Game of Russian Roulette with Your Soul

Our spiritual consciousness is a switch that can turn on the fictional reality or true reality. Every time we die we are being switched from physical reality to spiritual reality. In each life cycle we are again confronted with the true god and the true Jesus and the liar from the beginning; and every time again we choose Jehovah's spiritual political platform, and we come back another miserable physical creature—and [horror beyond horror] we do not know when that physical creature, you, will be an animal. It is like playing Russian roulette with a revolver loaded with one bullet. It is insane.

In short, then, Jesus is telling us that one's realm of existence is according to what one knows: the lie or truth. The spiritual mind is thus so powerful as to be able to project a seemingly real physical reality to counter true reality. Belief in a lie is such a tremendous shame (or whatever term seems proper) that the deluded spiritual mind will counter-create according to the wording of the lie-believed and according to the methodology of the liar, the Serpent/Jehovah so as to obliterate any memory of the true god.

Our true father said to Adam in paradise, "Do not eat of the Tree of Knowledge of Good and Evil, for if you do, you will die". In spirit, [the means of true communion] where this god speaks to his creatures, one dies as one does here on earth.

> **Death is cessation of communion with the entities in the realm in which one exists, the entire environment disappears. When you die in earth the universe disappears for you, but it is still there for others.**

Before their fall, god in paradise spoke in person to Adam. They were part of the same reality [they were in agreement on things]. They knew each other face to face. Ask Jehovah to have a personal talk with you. He cannot do it. He would have to disappear into the fiction and come to us as a person, but that person is not Jehovah, and few people would believe him if he said he is Jehovah. See, in this universe, we do not have to believe anything, for nothing can be surely known. We simply believe or we do not believe. If we say we are

sure, we still don't know. However, I am talking of meeting person to person
without a set of goggles [the human body] through which we can detect him.
We cannot meet Jehovah face to face in his spiritual garb, so he is a deceit. So
was Jesus. He came in the disguise of a human, son of man, not as he is in
reality. His reality was cloaked in the deceit of a human body. We know thus
that he played a deceit on us, even though he identified himself correctly: son
of man. If we reincarnate, and the evidence that this is so is overwhelming,
then it is proof that the universe is a spiritual computer program where we
can enter and exit according to a set of program rules that govern us.

Jesus' body came back to life. His closest acquaintances on earth did not
recognize him when he resurrected. He had to show every one his injuries
from the crucifixion for them to get a reality on him [they had to commune
in a common set of parameters]. His appearance changed. Why? He was
no different than before. He could do miracles before crucifixion and after.
Why did he change appearance? Is it possible that after coming back to life
after his crucifixion he showed his true countenance—and no one recognized
him, even though they see him after each physical death again and again in
spirit? Be sure of the fact that when you die Jesus is present in spirit for you
to recognize him.

The Messiah had to rise from death. Prior to his resurrection, in John
20:19-23, appearing to his disciples in a locked room, he spoke as the Messiah.
I believe that his mission for the true father was done, so all that was left was
to tie the loose ends in his role as Messiah together and disappear in another
miracle show—his rising out of the sight of the disciples. No wonder that
almost everybody believes in the Messiah of Jehovah, and hardly anyone
got the true message he came into the world for. But in spite of all that, he
arranged the liberty of all those who did get the true message. Jesus exists in
spirit—always. He said "I am". He always is. He did not need another body.
He came to us again after death to commune with us physically.

Jesus Divided the Souls into Sheep, Goats and Those Who Do Not Give a Damn

No wonder we have a Christianity that believes in Christ, son of Jehovah,
and that sees Jesus' spiritual being trying to contact them as an Antichrist. The
truth is that his form of Antichrist is the Christ for redemption into truth.
So we have this separation of souls in the universe. Those who believe Jesus
to be a fraud walk the broad highway into the deeper cone sections of the
trap. (Figure 11, page 396) Then, there are those, a lot less in number than

category one, who see Jesus as Messiah for Jehovah; and they [referred to as sheep] are collected in the holy spirit to some fancied heaven of Jehovah, the liar. Finally, there is that very rare group of souls who can grasp the true reason of Jesus' coming into the world. They see his double role and are not deceived by the means Jesus was forced to use to bring his message of truly good news. These will be guided into reality and find their being in the highest reality, right in the Trinity of God himself, creator of all realities possible.

Communion Must Happen According to a Set of Ground Rules

"Communion" is being in contact with one's environment in a conscious state where one knows that one exists in the realm. Cessation of such communion means one is not aware of the environment anymore. The realm has ceased to exist for the person who died to that environment. So, physical death is a cessation of physical communion in earth. The true father is the center of the realm of truth, and thus, he is the greater environment in which all other environments find their beingness. He is the entity that makes being in communion with him possible. His communion is his environment, the agreement of a shared reality between the father and the son. His communion is truth because he is the environment that makes communion possible. Environment needs a constitution to operate correctly. You must enter into reality with clean hands, heart and mind. Reality is truly sacred.

In a similar way Jehovah as minor god gave us, creatures, communion in the physical environment. However, he is not part of it. We cannot be face to face with Jehovah, because he is in communion not with physical creatures but with captured and helpless souls. He is a kidnapper/soulnapper. The universe is his pen to keep us occupied in nothingness. He does so by continuing to tell us lies we believe. The make-believe reality souls get from that communion is the universe; a spiritual theatrical production; it is full of strife, deceit, war and death. The communion of Jehovah in the holy spirit is deceit and betrayal; we as his adopted children do as he does—like father like son.

Jehovah is a liar, so the environment he created through his propaganda is a fiction called "interactive life in earth". Whatever knowledge of science and inventions we have today; it was received straight from him, Jehovah, the environment. It is all done to seduce you to choose the physical environment again over the realm of truth when you die and are again standing naked [in the outer-space-like limbo without a space capsule]. In reality, science as understood by us does not exist.

The Realm of Darkness

Everything we know of the Old Testament after Adam and Woman fell is about the false god because Adam and Woman and we, as their spiritual-cell offspring, died away from our native god. We know *nothing* of him anymore. This makes Jehovah the only god. No one comes *before* him [the first commandment]. Jehovah created the fictional environment for the soul projections in Adam and Woman [now called Eve because she became the female who was to bear children in much pain]. Our bodies and all our physical senses, such as sight, emotional feelings, rationality, and the responses of our nervous systems, are designed to see and experience nothing else but what is physically given to us in the program universe. There is absolutely nothing of the true spirit that we can feel or communicate with. We are dead to the true god who is still all around us. The only way communion can be restored with reality is by having faith in Jesus' communications with his father that we are made aware of in the New Testament and in the promises he made before his crucifixion; namely that he will send the Comforter to guide us into **All Truth**. We must understand that this "**All Truth**" is reality. We should be able to see that we are presently not in it.

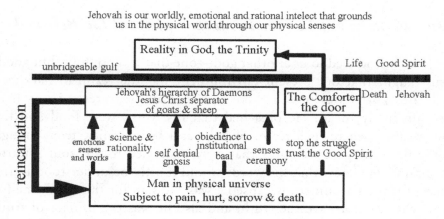

Creatures are dead to reality because the universe
hides spirit through our physical senses

Figure 9

The Right Attitude for Jehovah Worshipers

For this reason, I advise those people who want to become successful in their choice of endeavor [and who do not care to be redeemed to the realm of true reality] that they must, absolutely, worship, sacrifice, and kowtow to Jehovah—the same as Jesus did in his time. Pray to him in Jesus' name, persist in your sacrifice and management of the business you want to be a success because worship in action is what Jehovah demands from people before he allows them to succeed. This is so because such prayers and actions give credence and allegiance to this god and thus to this environment. Pray to him in Jesus' name as the Christ in the flesh [remember, he came to life in the fleshy body and showed his wounds to the apostles, went up to heaven in that body, and Saul of Tarsus saw him in that attire again]. He still is Jehovah's servant. Jesus is your Messiah in a world-conquering sense. We received modern knowledge about the physical environment from his hands, because scientists are continual students and worshipers of this environment and thus of Jehovah. In his physical body, Jesus is Jehovah's Messiah. He gives what they seek because he loves them just as much as those who want to return to the realms of truth. He gives them what they want before hell will drag them into the misery of animal existence. Only then, must Jesus abandon the souls he loves so much because at that moment of their choice to remain in the negative realms they have become unreachable, forever.

Jesus Wants to Set Us Free From the Spiritual Lie-Believed

Jesus introduced to us another god—one that was not holy, but good. Jesus taught that our present environment was the realm of darkness, that "**no truth**" was present here and that all creatures existing here are [spiritually] dead. He preached that his words were food and life and would open to us a realm of light and immortality. Even though in the flesh, he gave us words that were addressed to our souls, not to our brains. He knew that his words would mostly be understood in the sense of this environment because he was Messiah for the "evil" one for those who cannot have the truth; and also he was the bringer of truth for the "good" one, and that message was addressed to the very few who would be able to understand and follow him. If one interpreted his words universally, one remained in the dominion of Jehovah; and if one could grasp the spiritual truth of the message, then one could be elevated by the Comforter into spiritual understanding that leads to redemption in the realm of truth. His hidden messages are life-giving food to the human spirit, not the human flesh. He went so far as to tell us *that the flesh will profit nothing*! Believers who only believe his words in a physical sense and setting will remain dead because they mingle truth with cosmic propaganda emanating from the universe.

In One Entity Jesus Is a Fountain of Bitter and Sweet Water

In one entity, as Jesus, he brought us in contact with both evil and good. This is revealed in the passages about the rich young man in the Bible. The rich young man asked Jesus a question and he addressed Jesus as "good" Master. Jesus answered, "Why do you call *me* good? No one is good except one [God alone]" [Mark 10:18]. Why would he say that? Because he had a body of fiction, one fashioned from the fabrics of lies and propaganda. In the flesh, he was a messenger for Jehovah for those who could not understand his spiritual message and thus accepted his words in a physical interpretation as part of the system of lies [as just about all Christians today do] because they simply could not have the spiritual message. He said that only very few would be able to get his [true] message and that all others would follow the broad and well-paved road to hell. *His physical body* was one of the big signs along the wide and paved road pointing to hell. The path to the kingdom is the narrow path; it is very hard to find because the kingdom of heaven is within [one would have to look through his physical body at his spirit]. It is within us because there really is nothing out there but fiction that we, poor suckers, believe is real. Your pastor, your minister, or your priest is lost in the fiction as well. The best they can do is to receive the blessings from the holy spirit. One has to find the Good Spirit within. I know because there is where I bumped into him.

In John 17, Jesus prayed to his true father. In verse 3, he said, "This is eternal Life, to **know** the *true* God and the [TRUE] Jesus whom he sent." He obviously implies here that there is also a false god and a false Jesus.

Jesus had a physical body. He adopted the false body that went with the false universe in order to talk and commune with souls who believed they were physical. He did not get that physical body from the true god, it was impossible for the true god to provide a body of lies to his son. Jesus received that body at the hands of Jehovah in return for a pact to be the physical Messiah. This physical body is the false Jesus Christ as seen from true spirit.

Jesus, Double Agent

He did an extraordinary thing coming in the flesh. Jesus became a double agent. He came in the flesh as a herald for Jehovah and because of this disguise was able to preach to us of the spirit of truth. He did a lot of random things, such as sitting on a donkey, only because it was foretold of the Messiah that he should do so. He came in the guise in which many believed the physical Messiah would come and did the things that the physical Messiah would do according to scripture, only to attract the attention of the people who believed in that Messiah so that he had an audience to teach about the true god, his father, and the true realm of existence, the eternal one—one that could not be rolled up because it is based on truth. The realm of truth is not based on a computer program. This was the only manner in which he could approach us in the name of the true father. As you can see, only very few could receive his spiritual message. The entire Christian movement today is following the physical path to hell. It is near impossible for me to approach anyone who will take me seriously and who can understand truth in this physical realm of lies and deceit. Many refuse to accept the message because they cannot see why I should be the pointer to the Comforter in the Good Spirit and not them. Their refusal is based on jealousy and also on the fact that I am not an ordained minister. That is the crux—an ordained minister cannot even begin to lead anyone into all truth. Ministers and priests moralize and teach about existence in the universe. They can lead a person to be adopted in the holy spirit, but Jehovah's heaven is still a place in negative spirit.

It is a very corrupted second choice to being guided in the Good Spirit. If they would only point to the Comforter in the Good Spirit and not sermonize by the authority of their association of denominational ministers or of the pope, their work could have real substance.

> **True spirit cannot communicate with an institution for an institution is not connected to soul. Spirit communes from spirit to soul. Spirit does not see an institution because it is not real; only soul is real.**

If one interprets Jesus' words in a physical sense, one becomes a Jehovah worshipper, which is good, because it means the father did not give Jesus your soul to return to reality.

If a person's soul was pierced by the spiritual message, it was a soul given to him by the father. In this sense, Jesus pleased both his father and Jehovah. In the case of Jehovah, he obtained souls as kowtowing, hymn-singing, and Jehovah-praising "Christians"; and who [thank Jesus] preserve his words and actions in the Bible.

Those who could receive the spiritual message of the true god in the true spiritual Christ were grasped by the hand and are led in the Good Spirit by the Comforter [Jesus' spirit] as sons of God to be born again in true reality. People believe the physical Messiah, if they are evil, and will not see the truth even when given to them by god in Jesus. It is their choice not to be redeemed in spirit. This choice is not completely free because they are deluded to such a degree that they refuse [because they are blind and deaf] to hear about truth. They love the lie more than the truth [they are wholly absorbed in the fiction].

Predestination

I would be remiss if I didn't explain the doctrine of predestination at this point. I do not argue that mankind's redemption has been preordained. However, there is predestination for those who only know Jehovah as their god and for those who know the true father in reality. The true father knew from the beginning who would seek truth and who would not. Jesus made that clear when he said that those who were in god's grasp would remain in his grasp. Jesus, the Comforter, was sent to guide these particular souls back to the realm of truth, the loving environment of the father. Those who love the lie more than the truth and seek Jehovah and his heaven will not meet the Comforter and thus will not be guided back to the true father. It is still a matter of choice, but since both the true father and Jehovah know everything from the beginning, they know who will choose Jehovah and who will choose the true father. They know our hearts from the beginning and accept those who wholeheartedly follow each of them.

John 17 in the New Testament Is a Complete View of the Trinity

Let's get back to his prayer in John 17. This prayer is an introduction to mankind of the Good Spirit [*Communion* that exists between the true father and his true son]. Here, Jesus shows the love his true father has for Jesus and for those whom this father has chosen for Jesus. Even though they are

separate, they are one, and they are one in the Good Spirit, and also Jesus is
one in the father and in the believers, and the father is one in Jesus and in
the believers. This prayer introduces another god as being utterly different
from the god in the Old Testament—Jehovah. Jehovah is separate [holy] and
insists on remaining separate. This is very well revealed in the following event
in David's life. Jehovah just adores his Ark of the Covenant; only specially
consecrated priests were allowed to touch the ark. Enemies of Israel had stolen
the ark, and David was bringing it back to Israel. During that journey back
home a common person was killed who, out of goodwill, touched the Arc
of the Covenant when it started to slide off the ox-cart it sat on. David was
very angry with Jehovah over this for a long time. There cannot be a doubt;
Jesus was introducing a different and higher god. Jesus even said that his
authority was higher than all authority in existence—he came before Jehovah,
the god of the universe. Jesus violated the first commandment by saying he
came before Jehovah.

Is it not peculiar that Jesus refers to communion between him and us as
supping? It is because his words are words that sustain the soul in truth and
give the soul back eternal life. How does he do it? By reeducating you as to
what is real and what is fiction—and you must become like children and soak
up his teaching! What he teaches sustains soul and returns truth in the heart
of soul. A person who dramatizes piety is not supping in the Comforter, but a
person who is open to the true spiritual message will be sustained by supping
with the Comforter. The true spirit does not like phonies.

Jesus could only leave the negative spirit by leaving the body behind. In his
exit visit with Jehovah he returned in his immortal body. He left it in custody
of Jehovah. His body is put in the computer memory of the program.

Jesus, then, returned into the realms of truth, which lies all around us
and, from there, seeks to contact us through his spirit, the Comforter.

Souls, in the Comforter, are guided one at the time. This is so because each
soul has been spiritually isolated by Jehovah. Souls can only communicate as
program projections in a false system of orientation. As soul entities they are
spiritually isolated from one another because the integrating factor of Adam's
consciousness is missing. This is done to maintain the fictitious, communal
reality of the physical reality. Jehovah is too clever for words.

Jesus' **body** was hung on a cross and crucified, to make us see that the
human body is worthless, but also as a medium of exchange with Jehovah for
those souls whom the father had given to him. Jesus' **spirit,** however, could
never be crucified or murdered, and that is the only entity that can redeem us
by leading us into *all truth*—God—the father of the spirit of the true Jesus!

Dragons Enslaved Souls in Spirit and in Earth through Systems of Deceit

The grabber of power of the universe over deceived souls is the Serpent. He did so by the power of deceit—the mightiest de facto power extant in reality and fiction. In fictional reality the lie is god; and power-grabbers revere this god. When one reads in history or in fables about dragons they mean spiritual and fictional secret organizations that operate some sort of fiction and enforce this on the people under their sway, by the power of deceit, the sword, religion and/or law; all of them are examples of sets of lies/propaganda.

Hardly any citizens and not many high-level bureaucrats and banking officials even understand that when you handle a piece of currency like a ten dollar bill, you are dealing with a patented [or is it copyrighted?] note of indebtedness for the value of the denomination. People do not understand that currency based on debt is proof that one has been enslaved. They do not understand that by possessing it and by dealing with it, as understood by government and the banking system, they admit to their enslavement and to the debt on which the script money is based; and they are presumed to admit that they owe an undisclosed royalty to the banks on it and taxes to "government"; and also that they are held responsible for that debt as a member of the society that placed the currency in operation. The people do not own any wealth. They admit to a debt because it is presumed that they admit to the debt by possessing and dealing in the script. It is all too clever for words.

Where, then is the wealth hidden that is supposedly attached to the denomination of the currency or the amount in credit stated on one's bank account? There is no wealth attached to the amount of dollars a person owns. Everything we own belongs to government and through government to the privately-owned Federal Reserve Banking System. If we do not follow all the rules of government and of banking, our wealth and our possessions, to the inclusion of our bodies can be, and very often are, frozen or confiscated. Everything we do or use is service to our master, the banking system. They allow us to use the currency and implements of work and play on an equity basis. If we follow their rules and their dictates our equitable status is maintained. It is like Jehovah's laws, if you violate only one statute or ordinance you may be economically and publicly declared dead, and your possessions forfeited, and you person placed in prison.

Who, then, owns all the wealth in the world? It is owned and guarded by the banks. You do not own your house. You believe you do because you say you have equity in it, but the equity is contingent on rules not set by you but enforced on you. If you do not pay your taxes, for instance, the authorities will sell the equity in the property to government. That is not the basis on which this country was founded. In the early states of the USA, people owned their property outright. Their property could not be confiscated without one's consent. 99% of all known taxes levied for one reason or another in present-day United States were not known in the year 1900. These new taxes flow forth from the establishment of the Federal Reserve System in 1913.

We owe our enslavement to the mental and physical convolutions and deceits played on the people of the pre Civil War and Civil War era by their governments. The official stamp of our enslavement is the Fourteenth Amendment. Proof of that are the conquered people in the southern states. Conquered people are slaves; they and the rest of the people in the United States were placed in official serfdom through that amendment that was ratified by the majority of the states. That was easily done, because, first, the votes of all the southern states were held in proxy by the US government, and second the people did not vote in this amendment but your traitor-elected officials in state legislatures did.

If you take redemption into **REALITY** serious, you cannot fly the US flag, you cannot vote and you cannot be on an emotional high over the fanfare of Disneyworld and video movies. You cannot have raucous sexual affairs; participate in national holiday pomp etc. You cannot remain a Christian; you cannot belong to any esoteric or exoteric organization such as the Masons, Elks, etc. These organizations, any organization, will cause you to deny your true Christ over and again. Come out of this harlot Babylon, the capitalist version of the communist democratic US government.

Babylon, a mighty super-seductive dragon is only the pet of the greatest dragon of all, your personality embedded in your own body. This entire evil edifice of the commercial incorporated infra structure is the creation of the international banking cartel. It is your enemy because it is the whore of Babylon. You have to repent and show that you do love true spirit over the evil of the emotional sensationalism of the physical universe.

Be honest with yourself in your heart. If you are, you know that you are not happy, no matter how much money, learning, status, fun or popularity you have. Do not try to fake being happy in this world. Reality is true, this world is utterly false. The entity keeping you unhappy is your personality. Your [imagined] personality is not only your greatest enemy, it is the true God's greatest enemy as well, because your personality prevents communion in truth with him. Your personality is the greatest enemy of Jesus' spirit, your true god. The whore of Babylon only has power over you through your personality and all the deceit harbored there as if it is the truth of God.

The dragons in our illusory existence are from top to bottom, your personality and your body, your mother and father, your spouse, your other immediate family and friends, the corporation you work for, your neighbors, your institution of religious affiliation, local hoodlums and criminals, your local, county and state governments, the several taxing agencies, federal government, the United Nations, the international banking cartel, and finally when you die you must face the great magic dragon, Jehovah. You must conquer each one in your heart [remove the factor of fear and uncertainty for them in your heart] in order to find Jesus in spirit [reality] so he can delete you out of the stupid computer display. You will have defeated all other dragons if you can become the master of the greatest of dragons—your personal identity that is tied closely to your personality.

You can do this by knowing that the world does not exist in reality. You must turn everything you know around in order to find the truth. If this world looks too real to you, know it is a fake display, a paper dragon that looks bad or good but does not exist. Know that what you cannot see is exponentially more important than what you can feel, see and sense. True reality is all around us because we are dreaming; and so we cannot see it. Physical life is the worst nightmare you can ever be in.

The dragons have no real fangs and no claws; they cannot bribe you with true wealth and such because nothing they can offer is real. None of these dragons can hurt you or feign to love you, but they can seduce or scare you to death; if you let them. This is exactly your test, **you must overcome the** *world*. These are the dragons that constitute your world—Jehovah's negative spiritual hierarchy. It is a mighty paper tiger if you see it as such. It is foolishness to not see it that way. Don't let spiritual and physical fools retain a hold on your true sanity. Dragons and their priests are fools. If you allow them to scare you, you are a fool also. Dragons drag you down into the world; that is why they are called drag-ons.

What binds you to the dream is fear that nothing else exists if you do not reincarnate—that you will be in outer limbo, without a place to be. This is not true, the dream is outer limbo, wake up and be home in your true environment. The true loving god would never allow you to be afraid, so a false god gives you all these fears and worries. Wake up and be sane, confident and fearless. Follow the true Jesus and Jehovah will not ever have another angle of fear and seduction on you. Jehovah would really love that too. It is his job to make sure you graduate. Help make his job a success.

Chapter 5

The Crucial Question

I conclude Book 3 with the crucial question, "Why does evil exist?" By now you hopefully can answer this for yourself. Evil always comes in a disguise of good. Evil is the depth of deceit because it comes disguised as good. Souls *must understand and know evil* [remember, we, in paradise partook of the tree of *the Knowledge* of **Good** and **Evil**] to be able to look through all the disguises that evil can hide behind. This is of spiritual significance because if evil could take on a disguise of good in the realm of good, evil would invade and settle in the realms of good without "good" knowing about it. So whoever will enter into the ultimate realms of good must know every aspect of evil to be able to look through all the disguises of evil in order to identify and embrace good and shut out all avenues through which evil can slip unnoticed into the realm and communion of good. Nothing is as it appears to be. Everything in the universe is evil in a disguise of good.

Evil is a communion, just as good is a communion. Do not let a communion of evil disguised as good fool you any more. Evil can be a (booby-)trap, expressed without words, but as deadly and tragic for those who wander into it.

If evil would succeed, existence in any plane of reality would become an intolerable nightmare and we would be caught in inescapable suppression and hatred without love and without anything to look forward to, because evil would have shut off any possible escape route. I give you examples of evil that shut off all avenues of escape: the Wall erected between East and West Germany, The Elba River in Germany between East and West at the end of the war with Germany, the river of death (footnote 1 in book I). I give you the continual encroachment of government into our every moment of daily life.

Liberty and love would disappear from all levels of reality forever. I hope that everybody in the world can identify with this kind of horror. If you can, you are truly ready to embrace the Comforter in the Good Spirit who is reality as good and not as evil. Government, marriage, children, cars, computers, planes, you name it; they are all disguises of evil pretending to be good.

> *Do Not Let the World Confuse You Any More; There Is No Good in It. Only One Is Good, Ultimate Truth in Ultimate Reality; and As Yet, You Have No Part In It.*

The disguise in which evil tried to usurp the intentions of good in Jesus is so severe, that it took 2,000 years to understand what Jesus was truly doing. Jehovah has been exposed and stands naked. Good is the responsibility of every soul in existence. If you cannot rally for good you will be utterly annihilated.

> *Now, I Sincerely Hope You Take Me To Heart. I Am Not Much Of A Spiritual Leader or Politician, I Am Not Jesus Or Some Saint; But I, Anti Christ, Am All You Have in the Good Spirit, Whether You Are The Pope, The Ayatollah, The Dai La Lama, Bill Gates, Oprah, George Bush, Or Whoever You Think You Are—Like Jesus' Words, My Words Help Give You Life. They are truly worth all you have.*

All Christians brag on knowing truth, however not one knows what truth is. The truth is that you live a lie in a reality based on a lie. Jesus came to make you aware of that fact. From hereon out it is a matter between you, Evil, and the Comforter. The ball is in your court.

NOTE: It is up to you to recommend this set of books in one cover to everyone you care for. Many people have a tendency to repress the knowledge of others by withholding recommendation to those they hold dear. This is a selfish attitude. If you love someone you should allow that person to have information and options to form his or her own opinion. Be yourself, not Jehovah's patsy. This book helps you to do that.

This material will give anyone powerful rehabilitation of awareness and understanding of liberty and love. If you are unable to convince a person, or if you believe that a person you would want to recommend this book to will not be persuaded by its spiritual value, recommend it on its value as a works of science fiction, or for its philosophical, historical and political value. It is also up to you to help make the world a better equitable place to be where every race, species and creature can have a worthwhile place. Humility and true understanding are the greatest blessings one can give another.

BOOK IV

THE SCIENCE FICTION OF LIFE

Chapter 1

Analysis of Truth

What follows is from a letter I wrote to a friend, a high official in the Church of Jesus Christ of Latter-day Saints, also known as Mormons.

I write this not to convert you to my form of belief, but to share with you where I stand in my faith in god. The purpose is for you to get the feel of the principles so that you can seek knowledge and truth, not from man or this book, but from the only source available to us, the Comforter in the Good Spirit. My ideas, or those of Jesus, are not truth as truth cannot be expressed, known, or understood in the words of man because truth is alien to this realm of darkness, which fact I will enter into somewhere below. However, I stand firm in these convictions as I did not receive them from the traditions or wisdom of men. I, thus, cannot be swayed away from true knowledge by the mere efforts and propaganda of men.

Mankind Has No Spiritual Senses Whatsoever

Mankind is spiritually numb, and if people entrust their redemption to other people's "supposed" authority and power of salvation for their souls, they will all fall into the ditch of perdition. I either commune in the Good Spirit or I will not commune about Christ at all. The physical Christ misrepresented is the Antichrist of both negative spirit and positive spirit; that Christ cannot save in any manner. This physical Antichrist {Jesus in the flesh] cannot help but guide us into deeper hell. Jesus in spirit is the universal or negative spiritual antichrist, the one Jehovah fears. It is the Christ's function to retain us in the realm of evil in order to keep it populated with live beings under Jehovah's own strict rule. The gods and the creatures in negative spirit are caught in a trap. In society, the group makes sure that no one will escape from the programming the rest of the group is subjected to and is influenced and controlled by. Mankind, as a whole, is an entity with group status; this group-status gives citizenship in hell. Those who see Jesus as Jehovah's Messiah are trapped in the universe. They have not received the hidden, real message Jesus came to proclaim. The real message is plain to see, but it is masked by many other things Jesus said and did as Jehovah's Messiah.

Let the Comforter Be Your Guide

I can only explain the situation we find ourselves in, in this universe, and broach the manner of escape from it. But nothing I or anyone else can say or do can bring you out of your present, confused situation. Only the Comforter in the Good Spirit is equipped and able to do that. All I can do is relate the things that I have already been informed of by my personal guide—the Good Spirit.

The Spirit in Jesus is Soul's Impetus to Awaken in Spirit

My native intelligence tells me that after being informed of the teaching of Jesus, we must seek redemption in Jesus' spirit [he has already saved us from the grasp of all authority in this universe—Jehovah]. If one does not use this window of redemption, one loses the chance of redemption forever. After all, if one is dead to the true and ultimate godhead and away from his presence, one is lost. Lost beings are helpless and should seek the kind of help that will bring them back home to reality. Existence in the Good Spirit [spiritual love and truth] is reality and life. Existence away from him [the only other existence possible for souls] is the reality of the physical universe, the only hell that exists. However, hell has many, many departments as can be seen from the innumerable species of life found on earth. The human races are, as yet, only in the several admission areas of hell. They still have a chance to repent and get out. I suggest that you do not continue to blow your chances.

Those Who Love the World Will Not Seek Truth

Deep sorrow, suffering, and emotional pain enabled me to search and persevere in finding the Good Spirit. It seems that a successful, easy, comfortable, and "joyful" life lulls a person into being at ease with the world and the universe; and suppression, maltreatment, suffering, and sorrow allows a person to seek another reality of being, which is the state of mind the Good Spirit needs to get your focused attention. I hope this book will support you in that endeavor, but without suffering. I believe this book can help anyone but many will not see the value I am bringing across here. Cosmic propaganda is too clever, and it is too well set in the flesh; and wherever cosmic propaganda falls short, political and religious propaganda fills the voids. So, you are left with an epistle on the science fiction of religion. Enjoy the fiction because it can open your mind to see the mind-boggling senses of reality available in paradise and also here on earth. The world and universe drown us in infinite kinds of propaganda and brainwashing. People believe they are sane, however they are insane and sadly enough, they do not know it.

Spiritual Sin Must Be Spiritually Atoned for

Propaganda is a spiritual, mind-altering drug. Here on earth, through drugs, a plethora of mind-altering states become available that are eagerly sought by many. The teenage and young adult subcultures seem to seek false senses of awareness with gusto. It seems that everyone is trying to drown in altered states of mind so that they do not have to face 'reality'. We fell from true reality in paradise into the fiction of negative spirit. We fell from negative spirit into projections of that negative spirit—creatures in the universe and as humans many succumb to many sorts of addiction. Also, we fell from free people to being slaves of those who captured us by artifice of sword and propaganda. We were drowned in religious rituals and taboos that deny us freedom of thought. People continue to fall victim to altered states of mind that drugs afford them, and over large periods of time, souls continue to fall from the awareness of human beings to awareness of animals in nature. And so, souls continue to tumble from bad to worse as they continue to trust those who have deceived them for selfish reasons.

Adam Fell for the Lie Because He Wanted to Chase Rainbows

It seems souls fell for the original lie because they preferred fiction over reality. As with people addicted to drugs, they intended to only experiment with these altered senses of awareness and come back enriched, but the drugs that they are involved with won't allow them an escape. Jehovah designed his trap so well he thought he could trap the god of true reality and could wrap him up in his fiction as well.

In comparison, US government was completely successful in becoming the master of its de jure master, the people. It used similar methods as Jehovah used.

The creature body is the isolation cell in the prison "world." It isolates us from each other. People that love each other can only touch and feel. What they really want is to be one—together in thought, but the bodies prevent it. A human being is like a prisoner in a cell yanking at the bars while seeking to be one with the outside world again. Lovers cannot truly reach each other; they live in constant isolation that eventually breaks the experience of love, and all that is left is naked indifference. All a person can do is touch the outside and look at the blank wall that is the mask of soul of the other.

Repetition Leads to Understanding

If I seem to repeat myself, it is because one facet of understanding of this matter is infinitesimal; the more facets of understanding one has, the more they will help round out one's understanding. I still get many cognitions and facets of illumination I thought I already knew that continue to round out my understanding. These moments of illumination, flashes really, often flood my mind; and I must hastily write them down so as not to lose them again. This, basically, has been the way this book was written—spontaneously—but then I expand, rearrange, edit, and revamp. Cosmic propaganda tries to shut out true facts. This makes being in contact with the Comforter essential, for he reaches you in the medium of reality from truth in reality to ignorance in deceit—from his spirit of truth to your soul, apart from cosmic propaganda.

Chapter 2

Definitions

God in Spiritual Antichrist

The true god and father is head of true reality. When a child is born, it receives a grant of universal reality, a fiction, from the false god, Jehovah. Traditionally, this false god is believed to be the true father; that shows you the clever liar he is.

This true god is the father of the spirit that dwelled in Jesus. Jesus introduced us to him [John 17:5-28] as another god, unknown in the world before that time. Jesus, in verse 25 addresses his father with "righteous father". This is a thing I do not understand. Jesus said what he said, but the word righteous is not what he called his father. There might not be a better word so that John used this word in Greek. I know that righteous is not what Jesus called his father. It is a universal word, not a true spiritual idea; instead Jesus said that his father is "good".

The true god's name is mentioned twice in the Bible, in Genesis 2:17 [the Tree of Knowledge of *Good* [reality] and *Evil* [fiction] and, secondly, in Matthew 19:17 as expressed by Jesus [there is only one that is *good*]. Matthew 11:27, John 17:25-26, and John 14:6-8 prove that Jesus' father as god was never known to man until Christ revealed him to those to whom he chose to reveal him.

The fact that Paul was an apostle of Christ is undeniable proof that Jesus existed and that he is whom the New Testament states he is [this does not hold in that everything in the New Testament is without lies or errors; that would be farther from the truth and from actual fact]. The Bible, then, *can* lead you to Jesus. Jesus can lead you to the Comforter, the Spirit in Jesus, but only the Comforter in the Good Spirit can lead you into *all truth* who is god our true father. The true father is not a mystery. If there is one who can communicate in truth and is eagerly willing to do so, it is the Good Spirit. Christian authority has confused its doctrines so much that it places "good" and "evil" on an equal footing so that apparent evil, doctrinally ascribed to his true father, is considered a mystery because the evil cannot ever be blamed on a good, loving god. Christendom is unaware that there are two gods, one good and another evil. The religiously learned traditionally fuse together the old "known" god [known from The Old Testament scriptures] to the "other unknown" by-Jesus-revealed god [John 17:25-27] and then find that this laminated god cannot be understood at all. Therefore, the denominational churches consider him holy and an utter mystery. Here is the difference: the true father of reality is loving and good, while Jehovah, the deceiver, is holy and righteous. The traits of character of these gods cannot be reconciled. These are not fusible. Gods are individual, not composites. "Good" by Jesus' teaching means a loving caring god who wants to be one with soul and who wants to commune on the basis of parity—anytime. "Holy" means "separate" [look it up], and "righteous" means, you'll get whipped if you do not obey. "Holy" thus stands for, "I am higher than you, and therefore, I must control and subdue you, so you will do what I say."

Jesus Christ

Jesus Christ is the one sent by Jehovah, god of the universe, to the people of a disobedient and disenfranchised Hebrew nation. Jesus, in a manner, is the son of Jehovah because he received his physical body by license of Jehovah. The difference in fatherhood of Jesus' true father and Jehovah as Jesus' father is that Jesus' spirit was conceived of the true father in true reality, but Jehovah only imbued that spirit of Jesus with a body of deceit—the human mortal body. The difference between a regular human being and Jesus as god is that the regular human being fell into the negative realms of spirit through believing a liar, Jehovah, the serpent. Jesus came into the world as true spirit, not deceived by Jehovah, but through an agreement with Jehovah based on a spiritual contract. Jesus was allowed into the realms of darkness if Jesus would be the Messiah foretold to come in the Old Testament. The true purpose of Jesus' coming into the world is to bring a message of his true father to the fallen and enslaved souls in the negative spiritual realms. Jesus thus came in a dual role. Jesus in the flesh was simultaneously Jehovah's physical Christ and Jehovah's spiritual Antichrist.

He personified the meaning of the word, "double agent." As double agent, he divided the people of Israel in three groups—those with standing in Jehovah, those with forsaken standing in Jehovah, and finally, those with standing in true spirit. Those not interested in Jesus at all belong to the second group; those interested in Jesus as Messiah for Jehovah belong to the first group as sheep; and those interested in Jesus as the representative of true spirit, and thus in the role of spiritual Antichrist to Jehovah, belong to the last group as goats. Messiah stands for the man who came in Jehovah's name. "Spiritual Antichrist," as I understand the word, stands for an entity who opposes Jehovah by trying to steal souls from Jehovah's jurisdiction into ultimate reality, Jesus as man and Physical Antichrist means an entity that lures soul's down into the hierarchy of daemons, the animal kingdom. So in a way, I am a spiritual Antichrist in that I want souls to know god in truth, not Jehovah in deceit. But, like Jesus, I would point those who see value in the universal existence to see Jesus in his role of Messiah. Jesus did not deny anyone his personal choice, nor do I! Jesus performed honestly on the contract with Jehovah even though Jesus did not really want the job. The falsehood lies with Jehovah by setting Jesus up to perform that task and thus causing Jesus to mislead careless souls. The true message is clearly in the Bible for those who carefully scrutinize his words. I hope that this letter will set the record straight for you as a careless soul.

The Bible

The Bible is a glitch in the programs of the universe because the Bible is part and parcel of the universe. It is based, like all things in the universe, on lies, truths, and half-truths. *The great revelation of our times is that the universe is a spiritual fiction.* That fact is revealed in the Bible. The Bible, consisting of the Old Testament and the New Testament, will lead its readers easily to misunderstand the facts revealed in it. It was purposely set up that way. "Confusion," or the state of being lost, means that a person does not exist in true reality, but in a fictitious one. Yet this Bible is a pathway that god insists on to be available. It has the ability to lead us to encounter the Comforter in the Good Spirit in our souls [hearts]. The Bible thus is the exact instrument to teach us the knowledge of good and evil. The Bible in conjunction with Jesus is that book because Jesus came into the world as a double agent.

Jesus said that his thoughts and speeches are food for the soul, which, when imbibed, will lead us to believe [not know yet] in the "true" god of truth and love—*thus reality.* This belief in the existence of a true god, when held fast, will cause one to be introduced to the Comforter, who can see the spiritual flicker of light of that soul in darkness. This spirit of truth and love will guide the believer through the maze of deceit and propaganda schemes back into the realm of true reality called by Jesus "*all truth*," that is the native realm of the true father and that is also the environment called the kingdom of god. When we know god, we are with him because Jesus declared to True Good and man [from hence forward I will refer to the true God, Jesus' spiritual father as Good, just as he called his father], "and *this is life eternal that they might know you, the only true god, and [the true] Jesus Christ, whom you sent.*" So having regained knowledge of "*all truth*" is "knowing Good"; and knowing everything about Good, the truth, will restore us to eternal Life. By recognizing the existence of [true] reality, one is in reality [or one can be guided back into a mental state of accepting reality]. Even the soul of a collection of scattered viral entities [the ultimate disintegration of soul] can be redeemed, but the likelihood of the soul of a group of disorganized bio-dust and spiritual dust to be able and willing to believe in the son of Good has diminished to a point of nonexistence. There is hope for each of us. Each one of us must hold tight to the truth given us, and we all must be careful that this truth is not corrupted by lies and fictions.

The universe is a fictional reality, and the Bible is a part of it. The greatest crime one can commit to another is to confuse a person's sense of reality with lies and deceit to create a fictitious reality for purposes of exploitation. Human society is a game with the purpose of confusing and distorting everyone else's sense of reality. We live in a fictitious reality called the universe by the master of propaganda, Jehovah, but at least, this false reality is shared by all. People take over where the gods left off and have perfected the art of confusing and deceiving others and place high honor on those who are the smartest in creating illusions of trust, power, and good and thereby exploiting or destroying others. The devil [we are all devils as well] disguises himself as good. The word "lost" in the *spiritual* understanding in the Bible means that one cannot participate in communion in reality.

"Lost" has a dual meaning. The generally understood meaning of lost is ascribed to people of the Hebrew nations of Judah and Israel who were cast off by Jehovah for wrongdoing. This abandonment does not truly mean being lost; they are still, as soul, part of Jehovah's realm in negative spirit.

The other meaning of the word "lost" is that Adam and Woman were misled by believing a spiritual lie. It caused them to forsake reality and to become part of a fictitious reality. A lie has an anchor in the realms of truth. A lie is a fiction and fiction is nothingness. Being trapped in the universe is being lost in a spiritual lie-believed, being in spiritual limbo. We, and the universe, are not in reality because we believed a lie about truth.

Spirit

Spirit is communion. Communion expresses itself as environment. There are four kinds of spirit. The Good Spirit is the communion between father and son which is true reality. I refer to it as positive spirit. Then there is the spirit between the son as father and the archangels as his sons. It could be called the reality of paradise which I call neutral or zero+ spirit. Then there is the communion between God, the son and Adam and Woman in paradise as zero spirit; and between Adam and Woman and any of the different archangels in paradise that is initiated by Adam and Woman partaking of an icon [tree] of any of the archangels. Each archangel has his own spirit of communion between himself and Woman and Adam when they enter into communion. This communion is expressed in a universal environment. "Archangel" is a lower spirit than the spirit found in paradise because paradise is the native and real environment for Adam and Woman. Universes are fictional creations erected for the purpose of experiencing and thus for learning. This kind of spirit leads us to understand a facet of god the son. It is a spiritual setup to allow Adam and Woman to understand a facet of god, the son as a means of possible elevation into a higher form of communion. Finally, there is the spirit of deceit. This spirit is negative spirit because it separates us from the love and reality of god the son. The spirit of deceit negates the spirit of paradise by the entities believing the lie. By communing in this spirit one dies away from the realms of truth. An entity in paradise that holds in its heart a lie-believed about that native environment cannot exist in that native realm, so it assumes a spiritual coma—an existence in limbo—spiritual make-believe.

I believe that Adam and Woman may have had a spirit of communion between them. This spirit made them to be one. I believe that there was an elementary spirit between these two and their father, the son of god. They were set in paradise to learn to commune in spirit. I draw this inference from what god, the son said and did. He said that it is not good for Adam to be alone [without communion]; so he created Woman as a companion to commune with. There obviously was a rudimentary communion between Adam and his father, the son of god. Communion in spirit is based on shared truth, not shared lies. That is the reason for all the trees in paradise. Adam and Woman proved that they were students because they actually chose to believe a lie in

ANTI CHRIST

communion with the killer tree after having been warned not to engage in communion with that tree.

Paradise is like a university campus with the trees as class rooms. When they enter in communion with a tree they receive a temporary altered state of awareness from the archangel of that tree. They enter a universe where they experience, on the soul level, an altered state of awareness and get to know all the praise and knowledge this archangel has for his god/father, the son.

Awareness

Awareness is the sense of being an integral part of an environment—to realize things [to make things look or appear as if they are real]. This sense is limited to the environment in which one has this sense; it is akin with spirit of communion. A human being imagines him self to exist in the physical universe and is utterly unaware of any other realities of existence. He may guess at another reality, but it can only be a fictional reality in his conscious as he has no idea what another reality could possibly be like. People actually commune in the belief of a lie—in unreality or universe or physical environment.

As a believer having faith in the true son one can be aware of true reality because of the guidance one receives from the source of that reality—the Comforter—which awareness is the source of the new life we have in the Good Spirit. This sense is based on faith, for we do not fit into that environment. When we do, the present environment reveals itself as fiction. The new environment is still only vague, out of focus and murky, because a guided person has, as yet, to be in that reality in order to experience the full impact of it. Physical reality overrides true spiritual reality for the deceived. It can be grasped in the same manner we can grasp the story line and setting of an interplanetary show of science fiction we are watching.

The practice of meditation that Buddhists and Hindus pursue cannot raise them to awareness other than nothingness. Nothingness existed before Jehovah filled it with the fiction of the universe. There is a huge difference in knowing truth and knowing nothingness. These senses of awareness are mutually exclusive—one is real the other is phony. Buddhists may raise themselves a couple of notches up in the scheme of brainwashing [Buddhists compare this to the multiple skins of flesh in an onion in order to get to the core], but they are still in negative spirit, the spirit of a lie-believed. The core of the onion is the lie-believed, as long as the lie remains as lie-believed, reality remains hidden. Every time one is raised a notch up in awareness one is exposed again to a more sophisticated and higher level of propaganda that one was not able to resist before. The universe forged of propaganda and brainwashing, imbued in us a state of delusion that is too extensive and expansive an edifice or temple to overcome; it is environmentally enforced on the soul, and the environment is a scheming god. So in the long run, one runs out of pizzazz [energy, intent, and perseverance]. To overcome one's previously adopted false sense of awareness seems utterly self-destructive to the soul for it leaves soul without a place to be. There is no possible way out of our present state of awareness, except through death; and that leads us right back into another incarnation and, again, into the awareness of the physical realm. The way out is through the teaching and guidance of the Comforter, Jesus' spirit. He alone can correct the error of awareness and reveal reality. Remember—flesh is phony, and it is programmed to make the soul recognize only the fictional environment. The real environment is all around us, but we are not aware of it. This makes magic so insidious because our bodies enforce this magic on the soul—the real you. Oh, yes, there is a real you; but because it is real, you are not aware of it. Creatures walk around inside the greatest deceiver they know—their flesh-and-bone bodies. That makes dying so terrifying—you are faced with the scheme of lies you have been exposed to. Your spiritual reflexes are still so imbued with the fiction that you eagerly seek another body to make the dream continue. The soul has so thoroughly accepted fiction as reality that it shrinks from facing the truth—the true father. This book is intended for you to realize that you live in unreality; and that, what is utter unreality to the human being, is truth. That is why truth cannot be found in the universe. We exist in some sort of opium den and always seek to return to the den of dreams. Why, if truth is so good? I believe that the reason we refuse to return to reality is shame and a feeling of extreme cold turkey. Jesus came into the den trying to restore us to reality. As for the masses, Jesus has very little success, so far.

Mystery

A mystery can be a fiction, or unreality, but in our situation true reality is a mystery. Mystery can be a trick of magic of which the set of procedures by which it is revealed is not grasped by the observers. The magician fools his audience. Jehovah is a magician of spiritual caliber. When Christendom calls their god's ways mysterious, they have accepted a fictitious god; someone who is not the true god of ultimate reality.

Mysteries are the product of deceit and clever lies or of truth that is hidden from us by a form of magic. All we can observe is the veil of deceit laid over it. This veil is a scheme of propaganda laid by the deceiver that hides true reality. Propaganda is the art of creating fictitious reality through lies and clever deceits in the minds of souls and thereby altering their perception [sense of awareness] and reasons for action. The creation of a veil of mystery is the art of magic. The veil itself takes on a reality by which it hides the true fact of the situation.

Propaganda is the spiritual tool that mystifies the masses, it can use actions, speech, special effects, and combinations of them to set the illusion; but the most powerful tool is the lie and innumerably frequent repetition of this fictitious scenario from as many seemingly independent sources as possible to as many people as possible in a group. Propaganda changes a more substantial reality into a more degenerate one. People, thoroughly under the influence of propaganda, are brainwashed, and have opinions that conform to a mass opinion called public opinion. This is actually a fictitiously-enforced and mass-adopted reality. Public opinion binds the people into a malleable and focused mass. It is like a gun with a group of different barrels that one can point hither and thither. It is the most effective, conforming tool, or weapon, against not-brainwashed individuals in the hands of those in control of the propaganda machinery. Propaganda always focuses it barrels at an imagined enemy, a friend accused of being an enemy. In the serpent's case, the enemy is the true god, and what he stole from him was Adam and Woman. The souls in Adam and Eve in the universe are his loot that brings the universe to life. We know that the father in truth is not an enemy to anyone. It is imagined that he is an enemy if he is even recognized to exist.

For example, almost all physical creatures are mindless tools in the hands of Jehovah or one of his underlings because they were brainwashed when they originally partook of the Tree of Knowledge of Good and Evil. They were brainwashed to see fiction as real and reality as nonexistent, thereby shutting out the god of truth from their awareness. As you can see, Jesus knew what he was talking about in John 17:3, "This is eternal life, to **know** the true god and [true] Jesus Christ whom he sent." Knowing excludes believing; if one knows one is in reality.

"To believe" means, by definition, that one was deceived; one is unsure of knowing what truth is. Believers exist in fiction. Those who know exist in truth. To know God thus means that when you see him again after physical death you recognize him and say, "Hey, I know you!", and thus you are back in reality.

Propaganda works because those exposed to propaganda do not know truth. Successive schemes of brainwashing placed souls in the situations in which they presently find themselves, whether they be men or mice. Brainwashed people continue to aggressively seek more sources of propaganda to confirm the public opinion they have succumbed to [whether they be men or mice]. Brainwashed people, the masses in any society [the ignorant and the sophisticated], are dead and cannot be saved as long as they continue to be brainwashed. The more one is brainwashed the more one is spiritually dead. They have penetrated deeper into the regions of hell than the less brainwashed. They have less chance of ever finding truth again. The truth has become beyond recapture, and the fiction is all these souls can ever comprehend. That is why animals are in a deeper state of being brainwashed than humans. The state of brainwashing for humans still gives them a chance to get in touch with truth—the Comforter in the Good Spirit. Jesus came to human animals and not to natural animals. Animals, like the lower primates and dolphins, already are a total loss. Humans are only in a state of being lost, not of being irretrievably lost. Do not ever forget that humans are a species of animals as well. Humans are very close to the edge of no return. The next drop in awareness will drop them in the region of the utterly lost as well.

It is unfortunate that most all Christians are thoroughly brainwashed into accepting and worshiping Jesus in the role of Messiah, and not the ambassador that came from beyond the realm of negative spirit. They have missed the purpose of Jesus' true mission. They are brainwashed in continuing to believe that physical reality is ultimate reality, or maybe some sort of paradisiacal reality.

Why would a soul accept the awareness of a tiger or a mouse if it was not seduced into believing it would want or need to be such a creature? Who has not heard someone utter the wish to be a dolphin or an eagle? The seducing process is a long one; all the way from the first lie the soul accepted when it conversed with the serpent [Jehovah] through a plethora of propaganda down to where the soul is accepting to playing the part of a mouse. Every propaganda scheme succumbed to makes one united with and bound to a more brutal environment than the one above it[1]. The problem of believing one lie is that when we have believed the first lie, we must continue to believe in more lies in order to give substance to the first lie. Propaganda is based on this fact. It is this system of lies that is the underlying code on which the universe is built. It is a binary code [good and evil] of combinations of lies and truths. It is a spiritually charged computer code, so to speak, on which Jehovah constructed the program—"the universe"—in which all other propaganda schemes are subroutine programs, some enforced as rules and laws, and others as interactive routines in a computer-generated environment. All of them include uncertainty as to what is true and what is false.

Environment

A habitat fashioned by a particular entity for the use of the creator of it and those who are allowed or tempted to exist in it. The habitat defines the creator of it and can be assumed to be identical with it. So, the spiritual reality is the father of reality, and the serpent is the creator of fiction and thus of the physical universe. This creator is Jehovah. Environment is a place or a realm that supports and nurtures creatures that exist in it and of which all creatures are a part and support it in return [a complete ecosystem]. The environment uses propaganda to nurture those in its realm of influence, for without this grounding propaganda, the individual is lost as a creature. All the types of propaganda give souls "beingness"—a body, a role, a place to be, awareness, and a task. Without propaganda, there would be no universe, no Americans who think they are free, no Japanese who think they are superior, no horses and tigers, no place for a creature to be, and all mystery would vanish and souls would again be naked and scared, while still embracing the original lie. This is so scary to the physical being whose very body is the product of some propaganda scheme that it fervently tries to find a familiar scheme of propaganda with which it can align itself. This is the reason that disembodied souls again reincarnate. The universe and earth, specifically, is a place where soul can again align itself into a familiar scheme of fiction—make-believe.

The greater environment has many regions that are beyond the reach and concern of a creature in it, which, nevertheless, is necessary for the creature to exist. Any environment or a sharply defined section of an environment has some kind of spiritual authority [daemon] over it who reports to a higher authority above it. This authority is the chief propaganda agent in its particular jurisdiction. The idea that society must be the guardian of the environment is hilarious. The universe is a self-recycling ecosystem that cannot be damaged by mere humans. Pollution control is a propaganda ploy of government to more effectively control the human mass under its control and sway. Society can be taught to respect its environment and thus the daemons that control it. The Orthodox Jewish community and the Mormon community are outstanding examples of how society can be taught to respect others and the environment they exist in. Nevertheless, these belief systems are evil habitats minus a door, or a way out. Our environment is a routine in a spiritual computer program. It can be rolled up and put in place exactly as it was originally put in place with all the resources and configurations as it was projected in a previous projected display.

One can compare a segment of an environment with the establishment of the US Navy that makes use of propaganda and authority to the utmost. It is a small part of a greater environment, but for those who are a specific part of it, the navy organization is what nurtures and confines their activities; and depending on their place in the organization, their environment is either narrowly or more broadly defined. Similarly, a tiger in the wild exists in a particular section of a greater environment; but the tiger is only concerned with a place to be, a source of water to drink, and a source of food to feed off. That this food source consists of living prey is all important, but it does not concern the tiger that the living prey must feed off the environment and replenish itself. Environment is a god of which a person is an integral part; and the greater the overall environment becomes, the greater the god and the more insignificant a part the individual in it is. Environment [or Jehovah] sacrifices one individual for the sake of another. The idea of sacrifices in the Old Testament to please one's god or environment is not an altogether off-the-wall idea [Jehovah sacrificed a civilization in the flood].

Virtual Reality

Let me give some examples of virtual realities. We are all familiar with virtual computer reality such as computer game environments and the Internet environment; another set of them are religious creeds. Existence based on a lie plays itself off in virtual space—the word "life" as used in the physical environment is a deceit. It is not life, it is death. Life holds the same connotation as turning the key of a car and causing the engine to come to life. Both the car and your being are mere virtual artifacts. There is no life in a car.

We are caught in virtual physical environment through our own neglect. This fiction has been created by betrayed trust, illicit power, law and enforcement, and a power to deceive souls and the people en masse, or near en masse—high-tech propaganda.

Earth is a virtual local universal habitat for biological life. It is a small prison-like place from which escape is not possible as yet. We are caught here, and we die here. Earth as all things in the universe is based on natural laws and spiritual rules, which keep the system seemingly whole and perpetuate. Certain properties of physical life prevent biological life to exist freely outside the biosphere of earth. Biological life is caught on earth. It is a prison and international bankers have overlaid another realm of spirit over society, a secret spirit of conspiracy and power money can buy.

Then to make a big jump, we have negative spiritual reality. This is the program universe running on the negative spiritual computer. It is owned and operated by Jehovah, Allah, or by whatever other name this spiritual entity goes by. Again we are caught in this virtual reality through lies-believed. I call it the negative spiritual realm because to exist here one must reject our native reality. One is caught in this virtual reality through an originally believed deceit and ongoing systems of believed deceit. This kind of deceit is propaganda. The propaganda is so powerful and so all pervasive that biological life succumbs to it without a fight. The universe is true reality for those caught in it, although it does not exist at all for those not caught in it. Physical existence consists of the dreams of a set of comatose spiritual cells we refer to as souls.

Paradise

Paradise is the garden in the realm of reality that lies just outside the perimeter of God's immediate household. It is the realm of neutral spirit. It is the creation of the son in the father. Beings such as Adam and Woman inhabit this realm. They are there to acquire the knowledge of god, their father, which knowledge is reality. In order to fulfill their task, they must partake of all The Trees in Paradise except one. The last requirement is to decide which tree to enter into after all the other trees have been attended to: the tree of Life or the tree of the Knowledge of Good and Evil.

Paradise Is a Realm of Spiritual Probation

Paradise where these souls have their being is an escapable virtual environment; it is a place of probation. This environment can best be compared to the desktop of a computer. The desktop has many icons on it that when activated will open a program into which the entity that activated the program will be absorbed. Upon one's free will one can leave almost all of these programs or spiritual virtual environments. There are two main routes of permanent exit from this spiritual desktop. One way is to open the program the "Tree of the Knowledge of Good and Evil" into the negative spiritual realm, which is like jumping from a swimming pool into the fire. The other is an entrance into a higher layer of positive spirit through activating the icon the "Tree of Life." Positive spirit is not an easy path to enter because one must have partaken of all the icons of the desktop except the "Tree of Knowledge of Good and Evil". Through the entrance the "Tree of Life" one goes into the house of your father, the son. By taking either route out of paradise they leave paradise, their father and mother. Adam and Woman become one as related to us in Genesis 3: "and they shall become one" This taking leave is a wandering of awareness because the cells of Adam and Woman remain in paradise.

There is only one way to enter into the house of ultimate reality, the house of All Truth, home of the Trinity of the father, the son, and the Good Spirit. To get there one must risk opening the program the "Tree of Knowledge of Good and Evil", the negative spiritual realm. To enter the realm of ultimate godhead one must learn the concepts of good and evil. By mastering these concepts one will enter into this ultimate godhead and by failing to master these principles one will be annihilated as spiritual entity by the operation of the program.

Once one understands and knows the concepts of evil and good one awakens in positive spirit. The reason for this is that the son has transferred the awakening souls to the realm of the trinity, true reality, for observation. When a soul awakens, it finds itself in the true realm. The proof of that is found in the New Testament of the Bible in the gospel of John chapter 17, which by many is called the sacerdotal prayer. This prayer is delivered in the presence of the true father, to whom the prayer is directed, given by the Jesus in his conscious spiritual state directly to the father through the spirit of communion [Good Spirit], in the presence of and understood by his disciples. Chapter 17 of the gospel of John is a direct view of the Good Spirit [the all-encompassing communion between the father and the son] given to us by the Trinity. The disciples were so to speak in a space capsule in negative spirit, which was filled with the reality of truth. The spiritual battle then, is between Jehovah and the true godhead of the trinity. The comatose souls present as disciples received standing in this true reality during the time of that prayer. This proves that true reality engulfs this virtual universe that seems so real to us.

The Trees in Paradise

The trees in paradise are like icons on a computer desktop. These icons open programs that reveal a universe for those who partake of them. The archangels run these programs based on their understanding of the goodness and love they have of god, their father, the son. These edifices are universes wherein one can experience the honor and appreciation that each individual archangel has for his father. These trees can be understood to be a university's campus where students learn all the aspects of their god, the son of the true god.

ANTI CHRIST

By partaking of them they disintegrate into their spiritual cellular components to experience on a full cellular level all the knowledge, honor and love the archangel has for his god. Each universal realm exhibits the love each archangel has for god, the son. Their love and knowledge, however, is based on just one facet of the character and goodness of god, the son, each archangel has. Each archangel holds another facet of truth about god, the son. When all the trees have been sampled; studied is a better word because the realms will immerse the entire entity of the being in all aspects that the realm has to offer in ideas and experience, they must choose to enter into either the tree of Life, and be one with god, the son; or the "Tree of the Knowledge of Good and Evil" and find themselves in the physical universe. One tree leads up in spirit and the other steps down in to a fictitious realm of spirit, negative spirit, in which one obtains awareness of being on earth in the universe.

The Tree of Knowledge of Good and Evil

An edifice or icon that, when partaken of, opens to the use and experience of the entity who partakes of it. It is created to give honor only to the maker of that particular edifice and specifically not to his god, the son of god, creator of paradise. This tree is a trap to destroy those who enter into it. The trap had to be baited with Adam, creature whom the son of god loved so much that he would go through any length to bring Adam back into his house. The serpent, Jehovah, thought that he had set the law to such a high standard that no flesh could possibly adhere to it [with the son's own permission], especially when he could resort to Satan to tempt flesh beyond the point of resistance. He hoped that god, the son would enter the universe in flesh in order to retrieve Adam and that once he was in the universe that he would fail to obey all the law and so bring the son of god down into perdition. Then, the serpent would usurp paradise and be the son of god himself. This is the very depth of evil: that the Serpent, Jehovah, actually tried to destroy god, his father. He failed.

Jesus came; he was able to set the Adamite race free of Jehovah's jurisdiction, placed an offer to retrieve and redeem them, and ascended back into the realms of truth. Now, as the Comforter, he can guide those who truly believe in him and trust him back while leaving the rest of Adam to their fate in the universe. God has given everybody the chance to be redeemed into the realms of truth. The choice is up to each individual. When Adam and Woman chose to partake of the "Tree of Knowledge of Good and Evil", they became differentiated beings, spiritually. Adam and Woman became undone, spiritually; and all the spiritual cells of his being became, potentially charged, living souls in the flesh. *That is the idea behind a pure race of beings. All the members in the race have a common spiritual origin.* Per the command in Genesis 2, they must be one and remain one in their race. Therefore the several races must keep themselves racially pure.

Food

Food is of two kinds. It is either physical food to feed and maintain the physical body or food that feeds the spirit. In spirit, food consists of thoughts and ideas that conform to truth[s] of god. Food of truth will allow one to continue to exist eternally in paradise and to ascend into a real, ever-deepening personal relationship with the god of love in true reality. Spiritual thoughts and ideas can only come from live entities and are shared in love. Physical food for creatures on earth must also be obtained from live entities in that the live entities must be killed first. Incorporated institutions [legal fictions] also feed on thoughts and [patentable] ideas. These thoughts and ideas have to be ripped off from those who conceived and developed those ideas, by stealth, contract, or whatever other sinister schemes can be adopted to extract ideas from others. Fictions of law are predators, and they prey on the labor and ingenuity of human beings. They steal your ideas, your life, and your sweat.

Deadly Poisons

These are substances that will kill the body of an entity that imbibes them or gets in contact with them. When deadly poison is imbibed, it will cause the entity to be placed in a position of not being able to be in communion with the environment in which the poison was imbibed. To the dead person, the environment, which includes also its inhabitants, is nonexistent. When a person dies, he loses contact with any particle of that environment. Poison, in physical earth, can be compared to spiritual deceit accepted in the souls in spirit. Poison destroys communion with environment.

In paradise a poison is an idea that upsets the relationship of the entity that imbibed the idea with the creator of paradise. A poisonous idea is in opposition to the premises on which the environment was created. When such an idea is imbibed, believed to be true, then an irrevocable clash develops between the newly acquired awareness the entity has of the environment and the manner that environment was deployed. One gets out of communion with that environment. When there is no communion there is no knowledge, and when there is no knowledge of environment one does not exist there. One exists in limbo. Since there is no other place to go, and since the entity is eternal, the entity goes into a spiritual coma and starts to dream of an environment. As long as that entity holds that falsehood about its native environment as truth it remains in a coma. Since the entity is in a coma there is no easy way to expel the mental poison and be healed.

Raiment

Clothes worn over the physical body of a title of nobility, but in a spiritual setting, raiment is the covering, the body of light and truth of the *soul* being. Jesus speaks of the rags in which humans are clothed. These rags are the physical bodies of physical life entities in the universe. These are invisible in spirit, like the invisible clothes of the emperor in the well-known fable. In true spirit, our souls are perceived as utterly naked. They have no raiment. It was withdrawn when a lie about the environment and its creator was taken as truth.

Naked

A being without a covering or raiment; one who lacks status is naked. Adam and Woman were naked after they partook of the Tree of Knowledge of Good and Evil as god had told them, they died to the environment they were part of because their raiment, the spiritual body of truth, had withdrawn from them, leaving them naked and without status. Jesus compared the physical body to filthy rags, flesh that cannot be redeemed to reality, because the physical body is as dirty rags compared to the spiritual raiment of truth with which the bodies of souls are covered in the kingdom. The physical body is a fiction.

When Adam and Woman lost status in paradise they lost the right to be there, and they were translated to the realms of evil by partaking of that one particular tree. This is depicted in the parable by Jesus of the king who gave a wedding feast where all attendees were dressed for the occasion, except for one. He came in rags and was thrown out. That is the reason flesh cannot inherit the kingdom. A physical being is clothed in garments of lies and deceit, rather than garments of light and pure truth. It is obvious that in the spirit, the inherent quality of the fabric of the raiment defines the character of the person wearing them. And it must be obvious that the major objection the realm of truth has against a soul is that he is clothed in a fabric of lies and deceit.

The flesh body is one that must bring viable materials into the body that can only produce waste. It takes deliberately, but it returns to the environment waste materials that only become usable again in cycles completely unnoticed or unplanned by the biological being. The physically attired soul is one that primarily cares for itself, and when it has all the abundance it needs, it might share some of it with others. It lacks honesty and love; it is self-centered and exists on the kill of plants and animals; besides, the physical body is attuned to exist only in the physical environment.

Sacrifice

Sacrifice is a ritual imposed or done voluntarily in the realm of fiction. Reality has no concept of sacrifice. In reality, one's whole existence is a sacrifice to reality, and reality sacrifices itself [gives itself away] continually to all entities in it. Reality is love, an embrace in truthful communion.

Sacrifice, akin to tribute, is payment to a lord or master based on a petition for a favor by a serf or underling. Souls must petition their master, Jehovah, for a grant of physical life to be born, and when born and grown up the person must make continual sacrifice to this spiritual lord and master, Jehovah. Cain and Able understood this concept and made sacrifice to their god. For reasons unknown Cain's offering was rejected. Scriptural experts believe Able's sacrifice foretold the coming and suffering of the 'lamb of god,' Jesus the Christ. Cain's fell short of that prophesy. I believe that is correct because the whole reason for us being here in the negative spiritual realm is to eventually be guided out from it into ultimate reality of the trinity through Jesus' true mission and sacrifice. In order to get the concept of evil, Jesus' mission was shrouded in a duality of roles, one foretold and the other hidden deeper in the revelation of the prophesies pronounced by prophets and acts of Jehovah. It was made to appear that Jesus came as servant of Jehovah which is the interpretation received by all the learned and adopted by the masses. However, Jesus was not only Jehovah's servant, but more importantly, the son of God Most High, several levels above the level of Jehovah's godhead. Those who could differentiate between the two different roles played by the Messiah will receive the guidance of the Comforter, Jesus' spirit in the Good Spirit, into all truth, the realm of the father, the son and the Good Spirit. It is a ring above the realm of the son and his creation paradise.

For those who reject the existence of god "Good", it is good practice to make sacrifices to Jehovah in Jesus' name, because it will make life easier and more rewarding.

Sacrifices in the occult are made according to strict ceremony, protocol, and ritual in order to please a god or to set a group of people free from control and submission to daemons or higher physical authority or to ask for their support and acceptance. Religiously, it is done by a people in the belief that a deity exists who must be pleased in order to obtain a favor or to prevent a curse from being placed on them, or because it is imposed as a duty or to pacify the anger of the deity. The idea of Jesus sacrificing himself to this Jehovah for the sake of a certain segment of the population is therefore not absurd, especially if he has a pure love and concern for those whom he tries to rescue from a trap that had them permanently ensnared. His death on the cross was a religious and an occult ceremony. There was a death, a sprinkling of blood on the earth, the regal and power of the authorities, and the cowing of people before them. People are impressed with power and authority. Sacrifice is performed to pacify a daemon of the universe.

Jesus' ritual sacrifice also set a people free from the chief daemon, Jehovah, because the price of sacrifice was high enough. The whole ritual was to ground the "blind" people solidly into the order of the universe. Yet through Jesus, his brethren were freed from the authority and jurisdiction of the entire universe so that after they had heard and understood the inner message of Christ, they *could* again make a choice in complete freedom as to whom to accept as highest master, Good or Evil [evil always disguises itself as good; it did so from its first contact with Woman and Adam.] By this final human act, Jesus separated the goats from the sheep because the outward appearance of the sacrifice cowed the determined pagans permanently into the setting of the universe while it set those who understand his deeper message free to escape from the universe altogether. The believer must match Christ's last ritual with one last ritual of his own, immersion in water [as proof to Jehovah, not Jesus' true father] to seal one's death and one's resurrection into that of the resurrected Christ in truth [maybe it is akin to the bursting of the water sack in which a fetus has grown to maturity as a baby in the mother just before it is born].

The resurrected Christ is proof that Jesus did not sin. Sinners die; those that are free of sin cannot die. Jesus died [really, he only laid down his physical body] for sinners who believed Jesus to be the Messiah so that their sins are taken away. Jesus said that he had power to forgive sin. So by doing what he requests of us, we are forgiven of sin; we are as clean as the driven snow. One can sin in the universe but spiritually as well, by believing a spiritual lie. Physical death is punishment for sinning in the universe. Sinning is violating Jehovah's laws; or rather a breaking of a contract between soul and Jehovah made before the soul reincarnated. Adam sinned in a spiritual manner by disavowing his native realm of truth that caused him to die to the awareness he had in paradise. In the realms of truth, after one's new birth, one has outgrown a tendency for sinning because one has understood the nature of one's sin and repented of the spiritual sin.

Through Jesus' death one is set free [spiritually] from law and authority. After one's [ceremonial] death through baptism, one should not again be part of the world by participating in the benefits, politics, protocols, ceremonies, and rituals of the world [don't be a registered voter]. Do not again be conformed to the ways of the world. One must now conform to a new reality; that of freedom and truth in the guidance of the Good Spirit within [our only teacher, master, and guide] and to no one of the world [flesh] to which we have been declared dead through the immersion. The idea of a greater god sacrificing himself to buy off a people from a lower god for the sake of bringing them into the highest realm of the environment is thus a sound one. It was a final dividing of the spoils—the sheep to Jehovah and the goats to the Jesus' spirit in truth.

Ultimately, the environment sustains itself through all the parts in it. The environment is one's master [one's only reality], but everyone helps to make his environment viable as a place to be [consider such ideas as compassion, assistance, and teaching]. The god is in all his parts and the parts together is the god. Souls have been consumed by this god and now are part of his body. In the universe, they are all deceived and ensnared in many propaganda schemes of one kind or other. Propaganda can be likened to the active, digestive fluids in the digestive track of creatures. Physical [pagan] creatures are all brothers in the same reality of spiritual deceit.

All people have to be conditioned and coerced to work together for the greater good of all the people in it and for the greater fictional environment called the corporation. Souls enhance their own environment by participation; like the way a football player enhances his game environment by strenuously participating in the team's activities.

Life

Life is a grant of a period of physical awareness. Being alive in earth is a waiting for death to come. Yet death is feared more than anything else. Life is a torture track. The reason basically is that humanity has forgotten the concept of making the required sacrifice for having received the grant of life, as Cain and Abel did. By making a dedicated sacrifice to Jehovah one reveals

to god that he understood the great gift awarded him and thus to secure a
happy prosperous life.

Everyone always wonders why Enoch was so favored by god. It was his
well-chosen sacrifices and prayers that made it so. Death is obviously due
to our lack of understanding of the relationship between god and creature
because Enoch was taken up and did not die. I wonder, though, if he received
guidance by the Good Spirit into all truth. From what I can see I believe he
did because he showed proper understanding of a spiritual relationship.

It does not matter the class you are born in or the education or training a
person receives; life is routine, and routine becomes boring. Even if a person
can afford to change routines at any moment, the change of routine becomes
boring; and in addition to that almost anything bad can happen anytime.
King Solomon gives much insight and wisdom on life. There is only one
thing to do in life—serve god [Ecclesiastes 12: 13], Jehovah; but I say, find
the Comforter and get out of Jehovah's prison of physical life forever. Physical
life is hell. There is no other hell. It is spiritual and human propaganda that
induces us to believe that life is valuable. We have lost our anchor in spirit.
We are born ignorant, without any idea of what we should do with life;
and then we are taught by ignorant people that do not know one iota more
than you knew when you were born. King Solomon was like our modern
scientists—he could only be aware of physical existence ruled by a frivolous,
all-mighty god.

> **Human life is based on the traditions and deceits of men and not
> on an understanding of the true spirit in Jesus.**

Parents deceive children to believe that life is worth the trouble. Life is
a maelstrom of random events, most of them enforced on us, that seem to
have some structure through boring routine—like being forced to pay 66
percent taxes on what you can make, betraying people you do business with
to the tax collection institutions, like doing your best in a marriage for your
family and finding yourself on the street and shut off from it forever because
someone else took your place. It is like you were just put in the garbage, and
another was put in your place. In two years, even the children don't give a
damn. Then the rug is pulled from under you by institutions by people you
never even met and whom you never injured in any way. These people in the
institutions, for a plundered paycheck, will stick it to you because some rules

say they can do that to you. There is nothing you can do about it because another bunch of apes in the police force have been trained to attack when the whistle blows. Human beings are your greatest enemy. For a plundered paycheck any official will betray another innocent person and arrest or kill him on charges of a corporation. Life sucks. Get out of this universe.

So, you join a church, and they stick your head in the mud while you place your money in the offering plate. Human beings are trained monkeys, and they do not care if they hurt their closest friend—because Pavlov's bell is ringing. Obey! Obey! But who are we obeying? Nobody cares. Just obey. Human life is an expression of vanity and foolishness. You chose to reincarnate, so it was your choice to be here. Sex is here to entice you back into a body after death. The seduction for life is too great. However, you never are allowed the other choice because you are spiritually addicted to physical life as a heroin addict is to his hallucinations. Physical life is an illusion that prevents you from waking up in reality.

Faith in Reality

True faith is the understanding that Jesus' spirit came from the realm of truth beyond the confines of the realms of Jehovah. Jesus came to us, fallen souls, because he will do anything to awaken us from our coma and return us to freedom and liberty and true appreciation of our being. This is only possible in reality, and that is proof that physical life is a deceit. In physical life, we cling to each other because we fear solitude; and also because we give validity to the non-existing environment. There is no love, appreciation, and liberty. You are watched by everyone to make sure you walk the line. What line? Somebody else's expectation of you! Oh, you'd better meet those expectations or your name is mud, and you may sit in jail. Those expectations are rules, laws, and demands from suppressive persons. Most of the people who made these rules and laws are long-time dead. Everyone will betray another for a valuable. What is a valuable? Slaves are not allowed valuables. You are allowed them only until these suppressive persons decide you goofed up. Nothing is yours, and when you die, the tax collector will take the major part before anyone else can get a bite of your meager belongings. Wise up—you cannot take anything with you because you are a slave. Dead is dead—and you have to start the whole silly thing again from square one, endlessly.

The only way souls can be redeemed to reality is to come to recognize that what they hold in the center of their being as truth is a lie. Once the lie has been cleared from the consciousness of soul, soul wakes up in reality. The only one who can clear the soul from the "lie-believed" is the Comforter. The only way one can get in touch with the Comforter is by understanding the true message for which Jesus came into the world. Jesus came to introduce us to another god—his father in positive spirit, who exists in the realm far above the negative spiritual realm of Jehovah. If we believe Jesus that the other god he introduced is his spiritual father, and that he is the god of love and extending, ***the Comforter will come and sup in your heart to replace the lie entrenched there with the truth.*** An exposed lie does not exist; therefore, you are again awake in reality. That is the only faith worth having. The universe is only here for you because you believed a liar. Jehovah is that liar!

Ideas

Ideas are food for the spiritual being [Jesus' words are spiritual food that give life], just as physical food is nourishment for the physical creature. Any product must begin with ideas that form the underlying concept of the product, such as ideas of purpose, a need to fill, a market to address, a design concepts, its manner of manufacture, sales, distribution, and customer relations. Each segment of a set of ideas will have its own manager or god over it in an organization chart that defines the environment for all individuals in it in the manifestation of the idea. The individual nurtures the institution, and the institution nurtures the individual. But conversely, the individual, in a clever secret manner, can throw a monkey wrench into the workings of the system and in this manner he is the poison that can destroy or impair the system. This disrupting of the system must also start first with an idea, which when properly formulated can be implemented into actions and hardware. Conversely, the corporation may change and hide its true purpose so that those who are part of it are part of some secret subversive activity, not for good but for evil. ***Spiritual deceit is the foundation of physical reality.***

The same can be said of paradise, where ideas represent the food for the individuals there and where snares [in the form of deceit] are placed for the unwary in order to enslave them into another environment that would treat them in a much harsher manner. Ideas are the spiritual food that underly the final outcome of the environment one ends up in and where the resultant environment becomes the subordinate, more concrete aspect of existence of the spiritual one. The harsher the environment, the more ideas are converted in to environment, the harsher the god over it, the coarser the individuals in it are. In animal nature, ideas have been almost entirely converted into environment, and nature for them is hard as nails. The captain of a pirate ship is a harsh critter, and the crew under his command is coarser yet. The warden of a prison is a harsh critter, and those confined in his prison are no less so. But deep underneath the harsh veneer of an individual, hides a higher nature, which longs to express itself. This is the nature of the soul hidden under the veneer of the physical form by a deceit harbored in the core of his being. Jesus' spirit, together with his Good Spirit, are the good guys trying to help those who are trapped in the harsher outer form, and the environment that confines them, by correcting the misconception in the core of soul with reality.

Those who sincerely seek the Comforter will be guided out. The ideas in the entire Bible will not save a person when believed in and adhered to in an authoritative religious setting because the Bible is an integral part of the universe. By the nature of the thing and of necessity, it will steer you in a fallacious train of thought because the Bible has a plethora of daemons hanging around it who are more than willing to be your advisor according to their possible stake in you—because *thinking is praying,* and according to your thinking, you are being advised by either the Comforter in the Good Spirit or a devil. The Comforter is crowded out by those daemons that have a stake in the physical universe and you as part in that stake. Only a person thoroughly disgusted with the world, can be interested enough and discerning enough to read the Bible with a different frame of mind than the average [learned] reader. Through understanding the hidden principles of Jesus' teaching, a person opens the door of communion with the Comforter, who alone is the guide and teacher who can lead you into all truth, which way out therefore cannot be found in the Bible. Jesus could only talk **about** the truth and **about** his father, but the Comforter will give you truth in mental concepts *in order to not just believe in him, but to know him fully. Jesus could only make you believe in his father, but the Comforter introduces you to him face to face, and you recognize him all over again. You see that you knew him all along. By knowing the true god, one is awake in reality. The term "forgiveness" is not known in the positive spirit; it is only a term with meaning in the realms of negative spirit.* **Knowledge sets you free in positive spirit.** Belief that Christ died to wash away your sins will set you free of sin in the negative spirit. By believing that Christ died for you, you can be washed of your sins in hell, but this condition will not get you redeemed in true spirit. God cannot be limited, not even by what the Bible or authoritative clerics say. I say this because human understanding is limited. The Comforter in truth will do his own communing with soul. He cannot use an intermediary of any kind.

Gods

There is a head for each of the three major realms known to exist—one is positive or true reality, god of love, truth, and extending; the next is a temporary abode created by the son where one can learn to know him as god of paradise. The third god is the serpent Jehovah, the righteous god of negative spirit; creator of the universe by means of a spiritual computer script. His reign is defined by law, power, propaganda, and vanity.

The true father is humble and modest, extending himself in goodness and love. The serpent, Jehovah, is cunning, boastful, and arrogant. His motivation is to control and dominate and capture through artifice. The entire universe is a propaganda scheme that effectively hides all aspects of spirit. When one rejects the Antichrist, son of the true father, who is his spoken word, one rejects truth, love, and thus true reality itself. By rejecting the realm of truth, and thus reality you continue to embrace the lie and you remain dead in the spirit of reality. By rejecting truth you must thus exist in untruth, or virtual reality, by embracing the lie one embraces the false concepts of reality defined by the serpent, Jehovah. The Serpent said to Woman in opposition to what god said, "*That is not true; you will not die*" [The first lie]. He called the god of truth a liar! By embracing the ideas and thoughts of this serpent, one becomes inextricably a part of the environment for which he [the father of lies] stands, the universe; and one awakens in this universe clothed in a body of physical flesh. The gate one enters is an "or" gate; one cannot pursue both choices. By partaking of the tree, one dies to paradise and comes to life in the universe. One can be raised to true reality by again accepting the concepts of true reality. We are humans in the flesh and not in spirit because we rejected spirit, as spirit is true and not deceitful. Jesus' true purpose in earth was to give you truth to replace concept of deceit in our hearts; and thus to bring you to true life, in reality, not in a fictional setting through dreams induced in our comatose souls.

Physical Universe

An artifact or creation fashioned by using a binary system based on two spiritual states that differ in the extreme: one *truth*, the other *lie* [comparable to the physical sciences' "weak" force and "strong" force]. Deceit, propaganda, brainwashing, and conditioning depend for their effectiveness on the artful use of combinations of "truth" and "lie" so that someone who is exposed to it will voluntarily, enthusiastically believe in its viability and its superiority and be driven to partake of it over any other choice [as described in Genesis 3:6]. This physical universe is meaningless because it is based on lies. It is a constructed environment. The materials for it came from another unknown place, just as the souls trapped in it and upholding it came from that other source. It is a trap from which one must be rescued by an entity from a higher realm of existence, reality. John 14:15-18 states that the *spirit of truth* cannot be known or seen by the world or the entities in it or be part of it. He cannot be seen because he is truth, which is hidden from those who believe in a spiritual lie and exist in the realm of the lie. Pure truth is not compatible with the lie. It cannot coexist with it; therefore it cannot be sensed or observed by those whose core is imbued with unreality—lies.

Spiritual Hierarchy

The spiritual hierarchy starts in 'God in Ultimate Truth and from there goes down in pairs of opposing entities. Just as Jehovah is the adversary of the true god by inverting truth into fiction and through this concept seeks to steal souls from paradisiacal reality into one of his own making. In the same vein Jehovah has an adversary called Satan or Lucifer, an adversary who tries to make the souls in Adamite people in Jehovah disobey him, and thus be rejected by Jehovah so that Satan can usurp the immediate jurisdiction over those who have been cast off by Jehovah. Satan, also, has his adversary who seeks to usurp immediate jurisdiction of those in Satan by making those in Satan rebellious to him and so forth down the line until the lowest jurisdiction is reached, which conforms to the daemon with jurisdiction over such things as colonies of disorganized viral entities. A living viral biomass is the utterly disorganized body of an utterly disintegrated soul in the lowest jurisdiction. Viral bio-dust is the physical evidence of the dust of a soul utterly undone, spiritually and physically depleted. It has no powers of organization left. From this state, it returns as physical dust to the earth, and the spirit returns as spiritual dust back into the custody of god in Christ for reuse in the realms of spirit.

Jesus gave an example of the existence of there being two gods in his parable of tearing cloth from a new robe to mend an old robe and the companion parable of placing new wine in an old wine skin. The true meaning of the parable is that you cannot use the commandments of the false god to get into communion with the true and newly revealed god.

ANTI CHRIST

True Love

It is a feeling of endearment toward a specific other that holds the beloved in highest honor, respect, esteem, and fondness. A love held in freedom with no restraint [1Cor. 13 is an expression of true reality, god]. God is not happy with evil [Jehovah], and those who embrace evil in their hearts. In spirit [the only place where true spiritual love exists between the father and the son], true love brings eternal life to the beloved and sustains this life eternally. Love is so supreme that it will not lay hindrances, obstacles, or limitations on the activities of the loved one. For true love to exist and express itself, the beloved must have free choice in its attitudes, preferences of ideas, and the concepts he may adopt. John 1:1 states that all things were made by the "Word," Jesus, and that nothing exists that was not made by this Word. So Jehovah is a product of Jesus' Word and is loved by him, so are Adam and Woman, and the souls that constituted them. All have freedom of belief and action—hence, the universe based on concepts of evil and all that exist in it. True love, however, will always be fervently working to rescue those who have the spiritual power to change concepts of falsehood held in the core of their being, soul, and imbue them with reality of god in Christ.

> *Souls in Adam and Woman fell into disorder because Adam and Woman rejected the love expressed in paradise, their native abode. Without this love the unity of the souls is gone and thus Adam and Woman's awareness died. The disunity of Adam and Woman's souls represents the physical universe to us, soul-projections in negative spirit—the spirit of deceit.*

Chapter 3

Indications That There Must Be Another God Besides the God of Love and Truth

The Case of the Ground Squirrel

I once observed a hawk that had caught a ground squirrel and alighted on a roof of a farm building some twenty feet away from me. It was summer, and the roof was hot, corrugated steel, and the squirrel was pressed against it. The hawk did not bother to kill the squirrel but immediately tore life flesh from its body and gulped it down. I could see the squirrel squirm. After about five minutes, the hawk was disturbed and flew off, leaving the squirrel on the roof. It crawled its way to the edge and fell some twelve feet to the ground where it lay dazed. The next morning I checked on it. I noticed it had crawled another hundred feet around the corner of the building and lay there dead. What a terrible, cruel, unjust ordeal to go through if squirrels are mere innocent beings that cannot sin. There is only one answer—the soul in the squirrel was once a sinning and unrepentant human being.

Sharks' Behavior Is a Good Example of Hell

Similarly, a shark will not mercifully bite somebody's head off before proceeding to feed; no, it tears pieces from the body and could care less what you feel or think about it. If hell is here on earth and condemned souls are degenerating back toward the primordial slime because, in prior ages, they scorned the redemption Jesus offered them, I can see that these incidents are worthy examples of what hell would be like. As the theory of evolution states, capacities and intelligence that are not used or exercised by an organism [or soul] become atrophied and useless, or disappear entirely [most of us misuse, under-use, or refuse to use our higher faculties altogether during most of our lives]; and those functions, capacities and traits, we overly depend on or enjoy, become more prominent as the soul degenerates. Humanity, routinely, indulges in feeding the senses, and in having externalized "fun", like watching TV more than observing internal, private spiritual communion.

Let's face it, our first prerogative in most private or social situations where there might be confrontation is the use of force by means of one-upmanship, argument, seduction, deceit, intimidation, aggression, and finally, violent attack. As I can view the behavior of the larger segment of the human race, I can only see the atrophy of our good traits and the accentuation of our bad traits in progress. That would be exactly in line with what scholars in geology and anthropology have observed is happening along the lines of evolution as time recedes further into history. One loses what one does not use and gains those traits that are overly exercised. That is why a professional piano player is excellent at playing piano, and I am not. One must ever keep in mind that cosmic propaganda is always programmed and operating to deceive us, to keep us in the dark as to what truly is happening, and to cause us to waste our faculties on useless activities that make us degenerate spiritually. As far as our souls are concerned, the opposite is happening from what we seem to be able to deduce from the available [stacked] evidence. We waste our spiritual recourses because we believe lies routinely. We sharpen our ability to make a particular lie more believable and exploit the lie we can imbue in others and completely squander and neglect our ability to seek truth. By deliberately believing the exact opposite of what we are told or are made to believe might be much more according to fact.

"Good" and "evil" are on opposite sides of the fence. Souls caught in the universe degenerate and die over long periods of time because we know that to sin is death, and we cannot help but sin. We also know that sinners must suffer, seemingly eternally, in a lake of fire. I may not be far off the mark if this lake of fire is the acid in the stomachs of animals of prey. Jesus also told us that in hell, the worm never dies. Is not the digestive track an organ that looks like a worm? Animals of prey will be around always. The stomachs of creatures, collectively, form one huge lake of acid fire. Might not the digestive track be the lake of fire in hell? On earth, many creatures must either kill or be killed in order to survive. This would make physical life itself hell because we exist by and practice predatory behavior. It seems logical that lost souls digress through the entire spectrum of biological life, from the highest down to the most simple and disorganized. This must be so because the flame that never goes out is the condemned soul, suggesting that we will reincarnate, endlessly [as our first choice] and many times as pray we are caught and devoured by predators, and thus creatures are going through the lake of fire over and again.

Are Souls Considerate of Their True Father?

The more serious aspect of the degeneration of the soul is linked to the ever-increasing amount of lies, deceit, and propaganda one is willing to imbibe, as these are spiritual poisons that cause ever greater damage to the soul. The damage continues until the sum total of misconceptions of one's reality become so tenuous that the soul becomes utterly undone. The soul is fashioned from principles of truth, which principles are violated every time one imbibes and accepts another round of lies, reducing one's concept of reality until the point of absolute non-reality has been reached, and the soul dies. Whatever lives has a soul, and the soul has an awareness of existing. The *soul* is dead when it ceases to be aware that it exists. A dreaming soul in a coma still has the awareness of having a dream. A dead soul has no awareness at all because communion has ceased utterly, even with itself.

[1   The book series, *Starlight Trilogy* by Marian Wells, clearly shows how an entire control system of bondage and damnation is built up from one original lie—the supposed finding of a set of divinely inscribed gold plates, making the finder, Joseph F. Smith, god's chosen and equal. This first lie is supported by innumerable additional lies. It starts with seduction of supposed invaluable quality for all; while all during his life, benefits accrued mostly to this prophet himself. The rest in the cult are deluded with false promises.

The coming of Christ made all that was recorded previously obsolete. Jesus was the true revealer. The gold and copper plates that were supposedly discovered by Joseph Smith are useless. They do not reveal anything spiritually. It attempts to create another society based on religion. Religion is a death trap spiritually. Religion is something invented by the daemons to prevent us from escaping this trap. Only one daemon, which the Mormons call "Moroni," could have anything to do with the cult of the Mormons. That cult forms another spiritual garbage can from which it will take a soul a long time to extricate itself if ever it wanted to. Everything in this universe, fact or fancy, is based on deceit—I am, this book is, and Jesus, in the flesh was. Anything that feeds our belief that this universe is real and reinforces our belief in the lie is spiritual Antichrist. By spiritual Antichrist I mean things that prevent soul from waking up in true spirit. The universe hides reality. Whatever we can see, feel, touch, or communicate with promotes the lie [fiction] and hides the truth. Apostle Paul made a smart statement that all our prayers must be translated by the Good Spirit through incomprehensible grunts, screeches, and snarls because we cannot possibly know what is good for us or how to make ourselves clear in the language and consciousness of liars and creatures that play make-believe to god, good, who only knows truth. Jesus said that he was not good, but one only—his father in truth. If Jesus is not good, he on earth was like us, part of the problem. Yet he had to come to impart the way out to those who have ears to hear, eyes to see, and a soul to understand. Jesus separated humanity is two groups: those who have ears and eyes to observe spiritually and those who have not. This is a spiritual separation, because as humans we could not tell the difference.]

Chapter 4

Do Animals Have a Soul?

The Presence of Soul in All Creatures

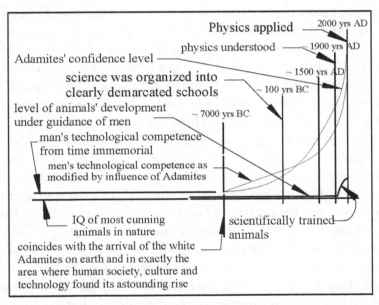

Adamic influence on the advancement of
the races around the world

Figure 10

All creatures have souls, the same kind of souls of humans. What separates
the kind of soul in a human being from animals and from animal type to

animal type is the duration of presence in the universe or the amount of deceptions believed. The older the soul, the more it has been subjected to a fictional existence. The more a soul is subject to life on earth, the more it atrophies and becomes attuned to existence in fiction. This is a natural forth flow from the law that says, "If you don't use it, you lose it." The "it" here means your faculty to be in true reality. Contrary to what biology teaches about evolution of the biological life, the soul entity degenerates with the time it is exposed to universal reality. The reason for the atrophy is that it was designed to be in reality, not fiction. Its ability to be in reality is slowly being lost as the soul's energy depletes or is drained to support its existence in fictional reality.

Animal Einsteins

The November 2006 issue of *Readers' Digest* on page 144 has an article on animal intelligence that confirms what I have stated more than a decade ago. Everyone should get a hold of this article in Reader's Digest because it will overturn the fables we have been brought up with concerning the habits of animals. Animal IQ is not based on instinct, but on the ability to learn and to preserve as tradition [as a habit] ideas and laws that were learned or discovered. Animals are just a more brutal reflection of human beings, intelligence wise, and spiritually. The article is called "Animal Einsteins," but the title is wrong. These are not just some isolated animals that are endowed with super-intelligence [like Einstein] and human type of emotions and interaction. Intelligence is pervasive in all life. These faculties become more brutal as soul over eons in time goes down the scale of the species. What makes humans the most intelligent species is the fact that they have received training from the gods—especially in the art of speech. Human intelligence is closely coupled to training. "Training" is the basic difference between the caveman and modern man. It will be the difference between modern man and humans a million years from now if the universe will persist that long and training continues. Training is attuned to the ability to function in the specialized physical environment of the species. I hate to say it but training is propaganda and it will cause one to atrophy in soul.

We now have a Florida dog who is a sophisticated skateboarder, [see webpage *www.miamioffleash.com* or *www.allstarsanimals.com*].

Trained Animals Have a Higher I.Q.

Animals in the wild have the same brains as trained animals in captivity. The difference in IQ in animals is the amount of training patiently and lovingly instilled in captive or controlled animals versus brute, loveless, fear-driven existence of animals in a grotesquely savage and predator-driven natural environment. In nature, animals only receive primal training in basic survival, the first and last necessity in animal life. If any thinking is done by wild animals, it concerns survival. Similarly, cavemen had as much brains as we do today; the difference in IQ is a difference in the level of training [the amount of propaganda instilled in soul].

The Bee: a Creature Disintegrated Physically, But Having an Integrated Nerve System

Bees baffle my mind. They seem to have an extraordinary high IQ because the mind of the bee is in the mind of the queen. From what I have experienced in my encounters with bees, mostly in defending the nest, is that bees are highly organized and that each bee is under the direct command of the queen, whether that command comes through a squadron commander or from the queen herself, I do not know. I see a bees nest as a whole entity, like a tiger, except that the soul in a bees nest has disintegrated; and with it, it experienced a disintegration of the body. But in the bees nest, the nerve complex still functions as if it had a solid body. Nerve communication within the entities that form the nest, the bee, is still integrated in the queen.

Once, I was busy sawing off sharp protrusions of a cedar stump when suddenly the stump came alive with bees. The extraordinary thing was that only one bee attacked. It bit me where my attention was most riveted, the hand that held the chainsaw. It instantly alerted me to flee, but he swarm stayed by the stump. The situation, for them, was under control; and they stayed on station in a watching attitude.

One bee attacked; the rest formed a menacing thread that was enough for me to take to my heels. I have had other encounters with bees that progressed somewhat in the same manner; but once, a squadron followed me and stung me everywhere they could, even under my clothes in my armpit; and I was not very close to the nest. Considering the diversity of ways the bees behaved, it is clear that flying bees follow orders from a source inside the nest. There is a planning and calculating intelligence present that pervades the swarm. I believe the queen is mother, commander in chief, and has her own personality and insight. I believe she has the capability to see through the eyes of the flying bees as if the flying bees were part of her being with an integrated nerve system. We have the same ability in touch. The slightest caress anywhere on the body alerts a person that contact is made with the body. That makes a bees nest a mighty powerful fort.

Seagulls Behaving Like Robins

I have seen seagulls in the park surrounding Lake Merritt in Oakland, CA that copied robins in the way they catch worms. The seagulls used a slightly different tactic in catching worms. The robins run a couple of steps stand still and look around to see if a worm surfaces. Seagulls high step in place and, while doing so, look around to see whether any worms surface. Worms are alien to seagull diet. It is a sight to see the seagulls doing their silly routine, but one thing is sure, they catch their worms.

Considering what it takes for seagulls to pick up these new routines gives credence to what I just stated about animal intelligence. Some single gull must have observed robins catching worms. Then that gull must have come to understand what that robin was doing and begin to understand that, somehow, it could catch worms as well. The question is, how? Because running like the robin is not in a gull's nature. Then coming up with the understanding that what makes the worm come up is the vibration in the soil caused by the quick movement of the robin. Next it had to figure out how to duplicate that kind of vibration in the soil around the seagull. Then it must have experimented with some plans that failed, and finally, it came up with the idea of high stepping. Once it had the procedure down pat, this gull must have communicated the idea to its pals, and soon thereafter, the whole flock of gulls around the lake was catching big sweet worms on the lawns around the lake.

While standing outside a McDonalds I once saw seagulls catching flying insects that congregated on a lawn near a garbage container. They must have learned that trick from some other variety of birds. The seagulls had perfected a slightly different routine again. They stood around the dumpster and hopped up and snapped to catch a fly or other flying insect. There were not just a few but several dozens hopping around—a very silly sight to see.

The insects hunted were flies, lawn insects, and those that swarm in groups in one place.

Predators in the wild have a deep respect for humans. Killer whales have never been known to attack people. Only very old and incapacitated lions and tigers will sometimes attack humans. Such behavioral characteristics give us insight that such animals know the human condition. It gives a strong impression that that animals have been humans at one time. On the other hand pods of killer whales will attack whales by keeping the animal under water until it drowns. Killer whales know that whales need—air; and that these animals are entirely different in constitution than fish.

> Propaganda, spiritual and otherwise, will always try to delude us into believing the opposite of what truly is happening or is important.

Chapter 5

The Origin of Adam and Woman in Paradise, the Wandering of Adam and Eve and their Offspring in the Physical Realm

Paradise

In paradise [a neutral realm where one could make choices concerning truth and deceit] Adam and Woman were androgynous beings, neither male nor female. Woman was called "Woman" only because he was bone of Adam's spiritual bone and flesh of Adam's spiritual flesh. Adam was, primary; and Woman, according to god, was his helpmeet. They are one. They existed in an environment where god communed with them openly. They were not aware that there were any differences between them. They were not sexually organized as male and female. Paradise is like a garden in god's house. It is reigned over in love. Love is a liberating environment where one can make free choices, unhampered by law and authority. Love, because it is love, will advise the beloved in the appropriate choices to make and then leaves him free to do as he pleases. They had the potential of eternal life.

Paradise exists for them. God said that when they would leave their father's house, paradise, they are one and must remain one. So, when they exited from paradise, Jesus' house, for good, through the program activated in Tree the Knowledge of Good and Evil, into negative spirit of a lie-believed they became one and separate from all other creation in a virtual realm on a planet in the universe called earth. Their assignment was to experience the physical environment as a race of people that must distinctively remain integral to their racial origin, Spiritual Adam and Spiritual Woman [bone of Adam's bone and flesh of Adam's flesh]. They were not to interbreed with the other races, although the physical environment would try what it can to make them disobey this intrinsic parameter of their education. Those who remain racially pure have a very good chance of being born-again in true spirit. Mongrelized humanity failed the test and they are dead to spirit. This is so because souls reincarnate, and those who destroyed their pure seed with other racial strains can only reincarnate into the mongrelized strains of the human races they created. This is justice and, like god, I cannot see anything wrong with it.

So, god advised Adam of which trees he could eat [touch and partake of] and which particular tree to avoid like the plague, for it was deadly to do so. [Even in paradise, god taught Adam and Woman.] By "eating," god meant to partake of the fruit and the body of the trees in a mental capacity. Truth is the wholesome fruit in paradise. Truth is food; it is expressed in ideas. So also, in that realm, a lie [also expressed in ideas] is poison and absolutely deadly to partake of for creatures existing in paradise. Lies are like drugs that affect the mind of soul which when believed [partaken of], will invert the awareness from a standpoint of reality to one of unreality and illusion. Lies are used to create illusions in creatures that lead the mind from facts to the unreality of fancy in such a manner that it rejects reality for the wisdom and other benefits, seemingly, readily available in the illusion as drugs do to drug addicts. Those who immerse themselves in an integrated system of illusion are drugged into an altered state of awareness where the altered state appears as real, and native environment disappears from awareness altogether. Therefore, truth is precious, and lies are not. God punished the serpent for his lie in that he had to eat his own spiritual dust, and crawl in his own pen of deceit and lies. He was to be the caretaker of those whom he had poisoned. He was thus banished from the realm of truth.

The Trees: Icons into Other Kinds of Universes

These trees in paradise were integrated realities that, when *immersed* into, either fed the soul mind with food of thoughts of eternity-sustaining wisdom and knowledge; or obliterated all memory of the spiritual reality and submersed the soul mind into an integrated existence of illusion, which, to our present altered state of awareness, presents itself as the physical realm. I think of all the trees in paradise as entrance points [active icons] into universes of which one can partake as visitors, either in temporarily altered states of awareness from which one shortly awakens refreshed and invigorated with new knowledge and wisdom about the love and truth of god or one enters into with the awareness one already had in paradise. Each tree then is an entrance point into a very specific edifice erected to the honor and glory of god by an entity like an archangel with the exception of the tree that, when entered into, might give one knowledge of the true and highest god, "Good," and, also, of the minor god or archangel that is the serpent, or Jehovah, who honors himself rather than his maker and who represents bad ["evil"]. This tree has severe consequences when immersed into because we have only a very small chance of returning from it, by the hidden and narrow way, through the intervention of the Comforter, Jesus' spirit.

When Woman was seduced to inquire into the nature of the poisonous tree, Woman had already partaken of it; and he was, instantly, beguiled by the action of the poison into believing that its produce was good and desirable. He fell even before he realized what he was doing because by becoming mentally interested in the tree he had already imbibed the mental poison (understood the idea behind the icon). The serpent used the greatest of cunning into bringing Woman onto the subject of the deadly tree. He then interjected that the god of paradise had misled him into believing that the tree was deadly so that if he [Woman], even for a nanosecond, got his mind onto the tree, he already was poisoned and enraptured by it. Now he could "believe" [not know as truth] that "good" had lied to him and that "evil," the serpent, had told him the real truth. Now his previous understanding of reality of truth was invaded by a lie, and he thus began to exist more and more in an illusion, which could not be part of a reality of paradise [something that happens so quick that it might resemble the original big bang theory of the universe]. Being so enraptured with his new knowledge, he sold the idea of the desirability of the fruit to Adam who was thus instantly poisoned by simply having his attention on the tree whether he wanted to or not. As Woman and Adam were [slowly?] dying from reality, they had to surrender their bodies (white raiment of truth) back to the reality of truth, leaving them totally naked and dead to their environment. This had never happened to them before, and they were ashamed to find themselves without any status or standing in the realm of truth, which realm did not sit well for them any more anyway.

Jesus' Spirit Was Teacher in Earth and Is the Teacher in Reality as the Comforter

You have only one teacher, father and guide; this entity is not a human, and it is not a daemon or demon. It is Jesus' spirit, son of the true god, who taught us in paradise and who taught us, again, as a human in our physical environment and will teach anyone who receives his inner message of the deceit we as souls harbor about its native reality, from spirit to spirit. If we neglect to have the true spirit of Jesus redeem us into the reality of the Good, we will be utterly annihilated through our own choice [the broad way, well paved, and with as many sign-posts of deception as the physical environment is capable of {Matt. 7:13}].

It Is Either Jesus' Spirit or Absolute Nothingness; There Is No Other Choice

There is only one way back to reality, and that is with the guidance of the one *true* spirit of Jesus. There are a billion wrong ways according to the many ignorant and deceptive interpretations or representations of Jesus as Christ and inventions by other deities, men and daemons. Anyone who does not know truth, yet speaks and proclaims as if he does, is a representative of Jehovah. All a sincere person can do is to suggest that one ceases to be taught by men and, instead, seek true communion with the Comforter—privately. Jesus preached [and you can now see why] it is better to cut out one's eye or to cut off one's arm if it makes one sin. What he meant was that in order to be assembled into a temple of living souls in the highest realm, reality, it is better to come there minus those souls who intend to hold onto certain aspects of the lie in their heart. Leave them behind, cut them out, and be present in reality without them.

Those Who "Have Ears to Hear and Eyes to See" Are Spiritually Attuned to Jesus' Spirit

His inner message is addressed to those who have ears to hear and eyes to see [those who were sufficiently awakened from the lie-induced drug-state to understand what Jesus was talking about].

On the other hand, it also made sense to people who thought he was teaching in support of the law and Jehovah's reign of the universe. You can see the double agent character of his preaching. He was telling one group, "Do not take this realm of darkness as truth and thus stay detached from it. He was telling the other group, "Do not make your present god angry because his wrath will be your desert."

Chapter 6

The Intermediate State Between Reality and Non-Reality or the Period of Dying Away from the Realm of Truth

God's Farewell Speech

"The god of paradise was immediately aware of the altered state of reality Adam and Woman had undergone and addressed them while they were dying away by calling out to them. Adam answered that he was ashamed to show himself because he had lost the raiment of status in the kingdom. There was only one way to lose one's status, so god asked, "Why are you naked? Have you gotten yourself involved with the tree of death?"(Paraphrased) Adam and Woman then gave their versions of how they got involved with the tree; and god scolded the serpent, Jehovah saying, "Because you have done this terrible thing [making me a liar in my realm], you shall crawl in the dust unworthy of truth [you shall exist in and feed off lies and deceit of your own cunning] forever." In other words, the serpent was banned from paradise, which he violated because of the lies he spoke concerning the god of paradise, and was relegated to the realm of his own cunning—negative spirit and the physical universe. The serpent thus left the realm of truth to start reign in his own realm of cosmic lies, cosmic deceit, and cosmic propaganda, which is a clever construction based on a binary system of truth and lies, the underlying concept and program of physical nature. *He is the father of all lies because he uttered the first lie.*

> *God here says that humans and their god, Jehovah,*
> *will always be enemies of each other; that fits in*
> *nicely with what my thesis claims.*

God added that there would be a perpetual enmity/struggle for supremacy between the human race [derived from Woman's womb] and the offspring of the serpent. I believe that the serpent's offspring are daemons whom he adopted as his children because they corroborated with him in the idea/seed of the lie to form this realm of illusion and deceit. These spirit-daemons form an extensive hierarchy below him and reign each over a particular part of the entire spectrum of animal and plant nature in the universe and each daemon baits its particular section in the full proof trap with its own kind of seductive bait. The seed of Woman [Woman now to be the female principle in the reproductive ability of the white or Caucasian human strain] would culminate in Jesus [of the seed of that particular Woman, now called Eve, who died from paradise and became a set of souls imprisoned in a physical body of the female gender] who would come in a future time to proclaim to his close brethren a knowledge and awareness of the true father we all still have in the realm of true spirit. So we now have Jehovah and his hierarchy of daemons reigning over the greater part of human and animal nature, and Jesus, the Comforter, guiding the few out of this realm of deceit.

The Spiritual War Is Over Your Soul

Jesus came and exposed Jehovah as the liar and thus bruised his head by exposing him as an imposter [false] god by revealing to mankind the true father of us all [whom we, as physical beings on earth, had never known] and bringing some of the lost souls back home with him. Woman and her seed are bruised in the heel by the false god by making the return of all pure descendants of Adam impossible because of a most cunning propaganda that causes most people to continue to believe that the universe is all there is and that he, Jehovah, is the highest god extant. By now you should see that most of Christendom still believes that Jesus is not the son of the true father who exists in realms higher than Jehovah, but the son of Jehovah. This misrepresentation of Jesus the Christ as son of Jehovah will be their doom and destruction. A misrepresented spirit in Jesus is an illusion and not truth. The entire universe and all creatures in it form a spiritual Antichrist edifice, or temple. It is impossible to resist or to overcome the illusion of physical reality induced by this edifice by oneself, or through any human organization, or religion.

To Woman, he said, "I will greatly multiply your sorrow and your conception; in sorrow you shall bring forth your children; and your desire and need to reproduce shall be fulfilled in your husband who will rule over you [through the seed [pollen] you will need to produce offspring]." Woman would not be like "good" without much sorrow and pain; therefore, he ordained her to be the female in the sexual pair of the new human species to descend into the universe of deceit and propaganda. The illusion, false awareness of the universe, and our alignment with evil hides the reality of paradise. Because it is hidden, we are lost. The universe is a production of a computer program progressing according to a schedule based on time.

Adam and Eve Fell into the Universe After It Was Already Established and Fully Operational

And to Adam he said, "Because you have believed Woman instead of me, cursed is the ground [the intrinsic matter created from lies and deceit] and in sorrow shall you eat [these lies] of it all of your life." "Good" explained exactly what they had gotten themselves into—they had believed a liar over him, and now, they were stuck in the realm the liar had fashioned of lies, deceit, and propaganda. They would henceforth exist in the realm of evil until those who had their fill of it had a chance to return through the intercession of Jesus' spirit. It was only then that Adam called his companion "Eve," for henceforth she would be the mother of the entire race. Before, she was never subject to conception and the bringing forth of children. Therefore, she could not have been part of creation of mankind in Genesis 1, for in Genesis 1, mankind was already commanded to be fruitful and multiply and was thus created male and female from the beginning. Adam and Eve fell into childbearing and child rearing only after they partook of the tree. Therefore, there must be two kinds of humans on the earth—those that were created in the first week according to Genesis 1, and Adamites, human beings that were introduced at the time of their fall. This seems logical to me because creation is much older than just the fall of Adam and Woman. They just appeared into an already existing and operating realm of fiction.

Adam Is an Alien in This Universe

This gives credence to my understanding that Adamites are aliens in the universe. There is only one race that distinguishes itself from other races in peculiar characteristic: the race of white people or Caucasians as others call them. It is the race that *en bloc* converted to Christianity, and was misguided in a supremely clever way to create a religion worshiping the spiritual Antichrist, Jehovah. They are all white but have the greatest variety of characteristics, such as the color of the iris of the eye, color of hair etc.

Then god [their new god, Jehovah] gave both of them skins of animals [coats] to clothe them. God does not go out and kill animals. Actually, he provided them with the physical, animal-type bodies as soul garments in which they could form a pair of sexual beings of a new species. Jesus, as stated in the Bible, compares these bodies to clothes by referring to them as dirty rags. In Matthew 8:22, he refers to the living human body as a dead thing [without truth and life-giving love]. The human body is the body of an animal, dead in spirit.

God then said in Genesis 3:22, "Man has become one of us by having experience and knowledge of good and evil and lest he put forth his hand/mind and take of the Tree of Life and partake of it [learn from it] and live forever." (paraphrased) Here God states that Adam and woman cannot commune with the tree of life until they fully understand evil and from that understanding can grasp the ideas inherent in true good.

God evicted them from his presence to the illusionary mental state to which they had succumbed and so became man and wife in the realms of evil or spiritual darkness under a god named Jehovah, Prince of Darkness, because he was a liar from the beginning. God placed a bar against their return because evil cannot be allowed in true reality.

The serpent Jehovah, guards the gate outside of Eden [the realm of good] to prevent them from returning to paradise because it is Jehovah's desire to be god over his own realm with Adam and Eve as an additional coveted race that he would try to prevent from escaping with all the power and cunning that is spiritually his. The angel and the sword are nothing less than Jehovah and a set of spiritual laws that cannot be adhered to at all, which law will prevent them from ever returning but, instead, guarantees their death in the realms of evil. Jehovah, the angel, has control over the soul through the deception that keys the human awareness to the physical realm, and the flaming sword is a code of law that cannot be understood or adhered to by beings clothed in flesh.

Existence in Love or in Law

Adam and Woman had played with fire, and they had burned themselves seriously. In love, there is no law or restrictions; but when love has been rejected, those who reject it will have to be under law. For without love and without law, there would be utter chaos, and good's love prevents such horror by insisting on law where love has been evicted. That might be the reason Jesus in the sacerdotal prayer addresses his father as righteous father; but I cannot conceive him doing that. The utter extent of the physical universe cannot be equated with the love "good," has for the serpent Jehovah; for Jehovah used the spirit of god's love for him as the energy, intermingled with lies, to create his realm of darkness and keep it in suspension. "Lies-believed" made spiritual slaves of the souls that made up Adam and Woman.

Jesus said that those having true faith [by knowing that Jesus is the son of the true god] proceed straight from the realm of evil to true reality. This is, of course, accomplished through the Comforter in the Good Spirit, who reacquaints us face to face with god "good."

Chapter 7

The Beginning of the Reordered Universe and the Condition in Which Adam and Eve Found It When They Entered into It

The Universe Prior to Adam's Fall

Genesis 1 describes how the serpent, Jehovah, reordered the chaos into which the previous universe was dissolved and created anew an ordering of the universe, the earth, and the species to be part of and on it in which the dark-skinned human races are created in the likeness of their god, Jehovah, god of evil and darkness. Into this reordered universe, Adam and Eve descended to become a new white race of humans—white because they are the most recent race of humans to have known god, the god of light, and truth and because they are Jehovah's most recent and most coveted prize.

Soul Recycling

The Universe is like a compost pile that recycles alienated souls as refuse into undifferentiated virgin spirit that returns to "good" to become again part of his absolute love. This recycling process does not start for Adamites until Jesus in the Good Spirit has given all Adamites an opportunity to repent of their part in the mistake Adam and Woman made in the Garden. We can consider ourselves as living spiritual cells in the beingness of spiritual Adam and Woman.

Escape From the Compost Pile

Those who return will again form a spiritual edifice, a living temple to the honor of "good." When the last redeemable Adamite soul has gone to the kingdom of truth, the universe will be rolled up and reordered into a new organization where all species, existing in the previous cycle of the universe, will all take one or more steps down in the hierarchical ordering of biological nature, depending on the extent of loss of energy potential in the souls. The present white race will become the highest race in the order of dark-skinned human races, and the least human race will step down into the species of the highest form of animal primates, such as the chimpanzee or the orangutan, or maybe a form of the aquatic mammals.

The Existence of the Offspring of Adam and Eve Up to the Coming of Jesus

Right at the start of Adam and Woman's offspring in the world Jehovah was a harsh god who showed partiality and loved or hated according to his own whims or according to his creatures' deeds and actions. The setting was that of Abel and Cain, each making a private sacrifice in honor of their god. Even though both of them offered their sacrifices with good intent to honor him, Abel's sacrifice was accepted and Cain's utterly rejected, causing serious strife and the death of one of them and the punishment of the other. As I see it, god [Jehovah] was the cause of this trouble by rejecting Cain without observable good cause. This harsh god again turned to serious violence when the Adamites, Jehovah's darlings, intermarried with the terrestrial dark-skinned races that created a race of adulterated offspring who, according to Jehovah did nothing but evil. He wiped the entire adulterated mess out with one huge deluge and started all over again with a "pure" strain of Adamites, Noah, his one wife, and their immediate family.

As time went by, all of Noah's pure offspring were rejected and abandoned by this god for one reason or another until he found another favorite in Abram whom he renamed Abraham. He was pleased only with him and made many serious promises to him and to his posterity. Yet, as time went by, he had to renege on most, if not all, of his promises and allowed them to be thoroughly enslaved by a foreign nation of people. When he finally rescued them, he set strict laws and rules of worship, which rules contradicted his "spiritual" laws. One of his primary laws stated that one should not kill, which law contradicted the rules of worship that demanded the killing of untold many domestic animals to please his insatiable desire to be honored and be worshiped according to his strict wishes. He liked to be called by important-sounding names such as "Lord of Hosts," "Yahweh," and "Elohim" while the true god is referred to only as "Good," an understandable wholesome name, and "father," another wholesome and intimate appellation.

Jehovah finally rejected all the tribes of Israel [Israel being the two nations of offspring of Abraham, which he before said he favored] along with all the other tribes and nations of Adam's offspring, clearly showing that he could not be trusted and that true love and truth did not abide in him. Jehovah ran a reign of prejudice, personal vanity, and terror that brought utter consternation to his "supposed" darlings, who were trying their best to please their insane god. Abandoned by their god, the void of authority was quickly filled by his underling daemons that did what they pleased with them.

They drifted along for some four hundred fifty years in this state of all godly abandonment before Jesus came to their rescue with an offer to return those who wanted to, to their places of spiritual origin—reality in good or respectability in evil or in the alternative back to the Promised Land with full status from which they were evicted by Jehovah.

Christ's mission of preaching and his plans and actions to set free his brethren in the race from the jurisdiction of Jehovah was such that every person, individually [in all liberty, once they were fully informed of good and evil], could decide a second and final time whom they prefer to be their god—good or evil. This choice, however, must be backed by true intentions by living a life that shows the Comforter that, in deed, word and action, one desires life in the realm of the Good Spirit over the existence in the physical universe. One can only serve one master—good or evil. So the choice that was placed before them in paradise was placed before them again.

Metaphorical Presentation of Reality

Metaphorically, one could see god in Christ, reality, as the sun. One could see lies, religious doctrine, taboos, disciplines, the traditions of the church, ceremony, protocol and ritual, and the whole spectrum of pagan activity as clouds that conceal the sun; and one could see Jesus' mission, death, and resurrection and the guiding of the Comforter as the wind that clears the sky so that the sun, true god becomes visible and known to us again. All these clouds that hide the god, "good," are based on daemonic propaganda schemes that are believed by people who then transformed these beliefs into doctrines, science, taboos, traditions, etc. Jesus taught repeatedly to step away from the traditions of men and to follow him only—to such an extent that we are told to forget about burying the dead or to forgo arranging one's private matters, to love him more than one's dearest beloved, and to even getting rid of all worldly wealth and status. The traditions of men are based on false belief systems, and the guidance of the comforter orients soul back into the truth of reality.

Either Seek Jesus' Spirit Singularly or Not at All

Our choice must be Christ Jesus as spiritual ambassador or nothing because as soon as you mix in a little of the world while following the true Christ, you already lost the kingdom of Good. The reason, of course, is that the universe is a lie; and you cannot continue to desire good along with evil, mix evil with good, or mix truth with the lie. Once you truly understand this, you simply cannot place any value at all on physical life, so you consider yourself dead to the world and alive in Christ Jesus. He said these things to make us fully aware where our heart and desires should lie. If one continues to *cling* with any measure of desire to the earth, in heart and mind, god in Christ will give him his desire—the world, not his kingdom of Good. This is the crux of the spiritual gospel and of faith in Christ. The true father will not force or deceive anyone into a realm not of his liking or choosing. Jesus stood thus as one who separated the goats from the sheep. He allowed the sheep their desire in the universe, and he awakens the goats in true reality.

Matthew 12:32, "Anyone who says something against the son of Man can be forgiven, but anyone who says something against the Good Spirit [Holy Spirit is a misnomer in the Bible because no one suspected there to be a Good Spirit] will not be forgiven," and Mark 3:29 also says the same, but added, "He has committed an eternal sin." One cannot continue to call the Good Spirit evil and be accepted in the kingdom of good. Jesus clearly separated the realms of truth and evil by stating that one cannot expect to be redeemed if one thinks evil of the Good Spirit, for there is absolutely no evil in him [because good and evil are separate and opposite realms]. Jesus, however, admitted that he was a physical part in the realm of evil while in the flesh, and one can have different opinions of things in this realm because the true nature of the facts cannot be known because things of this universe are based on lies and deceit. Jesus stated also that only the Comforter in the Good Spirit is your guide, teacher, and father. The same can be said about me. I appear in flesh and you can derogate what I tell you, but you never can derogate the Good Spirit.

This is the problem with the religion of the Latter-Day Saints. They have prophets, seers, apostles, and rituals; and they claim that if you distrust their word, you miss out on becoming a god. This of course is a discrepancy with what Jesus stated. All men are of flesh, so, even Jesus cannot be trusted, and one can be forgiven for such distrust. It is just the Comforter in the Good Spirit and his guidance that cannot be taken for granted. Jehovah is a mighty god in the universe, and he comes across as an angel of light; He is always disguised his deceit in splendor, and propaganda. He is the great stumbling block to being born again in reality. God in Jesus' spirit shows no power or splendor in this evil universe. He comes quietly from within without any contact or pomp from the outside environment if you sincerely invite him in.

Baptizing for the dead, spiritually, is useless. It is only a religious ritual. It is not of spirit. Every soul must decide for himself; no one can be forced into the kingdom of truth, and no one is. Eternal souls stuck in this universe of death and decay must, of necessity, reincarnate so each soul has plenty of time to accept the Good Spirit on his own cognizance. No man can interfere in the communion between the Comforter and the individual soul. Jesus said so, "You have only one teacher, master and guide".

In Matthew 15 Jesus expounds that physical food does not make or break the purity of a man's spiritual value but what comes from the heart of his thoughts do, such as ideas or thoughts that lead one to kill, commit adultery, to rob, lie, and slander others. Thoughts and ideas are either food or poisons for the spirit of the soul. If they are food, they come from certain words of Jesus through the Good Spirit, and poisons when they arise from any other source.

Paul, in Galatians 5:19 states, "*What [all] human nature does is quite plain. It shows itself in immoral, filthy, and indecent actions; in worship of idols, in witchcraft. People become enemies and they fight; they become jealous, angry, and ambitious. They separate into* [opposing political] *parties and groups* [a house divided cannot stand] . . . *I warn you now as I have before: those who do these things will not possess the kingdom of god.*" What Paul fails to mention is that these actions show where one's heart lies! God must decide which environment is the one you truly seek and treasure—that of good or that of evil. Because the Comforter is the loving god, he can only give you what you truly desire. He does not punish you because you do not do as he wants you to do; instead, he must give you what you want because he can do no other thing. He must give each one of us what each of us truly shows him in thought, action, and deed to be our preference. People who do enjoy the things that the world gives to gratify their desires choose to be aligned with the world. Such persons are happy here. Others have qualms but are faithful toward the daemonic hierarchy in order to get their wishes granted to make their situation better. They all fail to convince the Comforter that they want to return to the realm of truth.

The world and the universe seem to be filled with beauty, grandeur, splendor, and majesty. We all gawk over it in national parks or out on a very dark night at the splendor of the night sky, but it is the majesty of evil. If you fall for it, it will overawe you and coerce you to seek your destiny in it. The universe is a magic trick, and its purpose is to make you forget reality and to make you believe that the universe is the creation of the highest god. But it is a trap, and the bait is irresistible. We all fell for it, and the only way out of this living death is steadfast faith—not in this universe, but god's house in positive spirit, the goal of this trip in the Tree of Knowledge of Good and Evil.

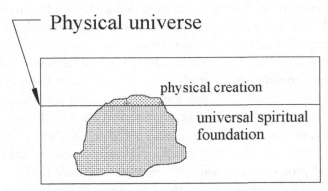

Physical universe

physical creation

universal spiritual foundation

Things that are seen are upheld
by things not seen Hebrews 11: 1

The universe is sustained by negative spirit.

Figure 8

Do Not Be Conformed to the World

The truly faithful person shuns as much as possible the things the world offers as pleasant and desirable [he tries to be dead to it in mind] because that person views them as propaganda and deceit that does not satisfy the soul. What satisfies his soul is the word of Jesus in the Good Spirit as it is the food the soul craves and grows on. The faithful spiritual person's sight is set in following the Good Spirit out, and he does everything what the Good Spirit suggests, not because it is a command, but it is his innermost desire. He does not refrain from the things of the world because Old Testament law or man's rule forbid it, but because he, by his free will, refrains from doing certain things. This is the true response of love and loving loyalty. In this context, it is good to read in Galatians 5:22-26 and Galatians 6:7-10, 6:16 in the King James Version.

The Living Eternal Temple Is a Body of Assembled Souls Just as the Creature Body Is an Assemblage of "Living" Cells

Paul wrote that when the Jesus collects all the souls he has redeemed and has brought them into the realm of positive spirit, they shall all, as living stones, form a living temple to the honor of god, the father, in which each living stone has its own place and purpose. We can thus assume that this edifice is a living, truth-loving being in which each soul is placed as a living spiritual cell [just as the physical body consists of an assembly of specifically arranged living cells that together constitute a well-integrated human being]. Knowing these facts, we can surmise that Adam, similarly, was constituted of living spiritual [souls] cells, each of which was placed in the proper location having the proper function, which assemblage of cells constituted the living Adam in the setting of paradise. When Adam died away from the environment of paradise [went out of communion with paradise], all these living cells went out of communion as well. His spiritual cells entered negative spirit [the spirit of deceit] and projected this universe because what befell Adam in paradise was the result of a decision that involved all these spiritual cells in Adam and Woman. However Adam did not become aware in the universe as a whole entity, he became aware in all his cells individually. He lost the ability of coordinated beingness through his "soulular" structure. These cells are living souls, and because of loss of unity in communion they act as individuals separately in physical reality on cue of Jehovah.

Earth Is a Spiritual Soul Distillery

What is happening on earth to all these individual cells existing as individual souls is the taking of a quality assurance test that will separate the defunct cells from the properly functioning cells. The defunct cells will be recycled into virgin spirit in the universe, and the approved cells will return to the spiritual realm to be assembled again into a living temple that will honor the father in true spirit evermore.

Mormon Doctrine Does Not Fit into the Spiritual Plan of Redemption.

I cannot accept the doctrines of the Mormons. Their faith is in the revelations Joseph Smith claimed to have received. They are against the teaching of Jesus who tells us that we have no teacher, master, or guide, but the Comforter. Since Christ and the coming of the Comforter, there is absolutely no more use for angels, prophets, and seers. The Good Spirit is within. Revelation must thus come from within, not from out in the world buried and in the ground.

Only the few will be redeemed to reality as Jesus clearly and often stated, so how can all the millions of denominational Christians and Mormons make it all into the kingdom? Therefore, either Jesus is lying or Joseph Smith is lying. The Mormons believe that individual souls become gods over planets and such. Individual souls cannot ever obtain spiritual independence because that makes soul unhappy. Soul wants to reunite and be one with those of their own race, to again become another Adam in spirit. If that is impossible, souls will remain in this hell.

A signpost of deceit in Mormonism is their insistence on calling the murder of Joseph Smith a martyring. Jesus' death was a deliberate authentic occult sacrifice with all ceremony and powers present. Joe Smith was simply murdered. The word "martyr," here, is clearly a propaganda tool, heaping religious myth on top of their religious practices, as if Joseph was martyred by a determined group of the public authorities. Jesus was not martyred; he actually sought out his own "punishment." He wanted us to know, for absolutely sure, that the physical body is a dirty rag with which one cannot assault reality. Second, he needed to be sacrificed in order to set his brethren free by making them dead to the world and alive again in spirit. He needed them to be free so they could make another utterly free choice of the master they wanted over them, good in the reality of Jesus' spirit or evil [in Jehovah] in fiction. It must be a genuine choice to which soul must stick forever. *Jesus is not chasing us, but he insists, now that you know good and evil, that you make your final and utterly permanent choice.* It is all so simple and clear; but religion, for religion's sake, has to make it all so mysterious to confound the laymen and to give the clergy a lucrative job for life. Joseph Smith, surely, was one clever fellow, but that is all he was. Jesus will not support having more than one spouse. If that would be the case, god in paradise would have made as many "Womans'" as Adam had ribs.

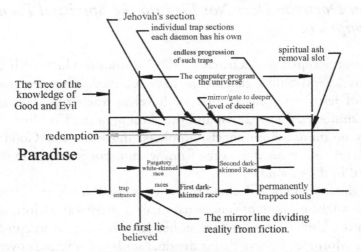

Jehovah's section

individual trap sections
each daemon has his own

endless progression
of such traps

spiritual ash
removal slot

The Tree of the
knowledge of
Good and Evil

The computer program
the universe

mirror/gate to deeper
level of deceit

redemption

Paradise

Purgatory
white-skinned
race

Second dark-
skinned Race

trap
entrance

races

First dark-
skinned race

permanently
trapped souls

The mirror line dividing
reality from fiction.

the first lie
believed

It is the mirror effect that the Father warned A & W about.
We, like Alice, are trapped in Wonderland,
caught behind a mirror.

The prefect spiritual trap.

Jehovah thought he could
trap his father in it.

Figure 11

The true church of Jesus Christ is not of the world. It is a spiritual nest in which spiritual "eggs" are hatched by the Good Spirit. These eggs are spiritually conceived and are cared for and brought to hatch in reality by the Good Spirit. This nest consists of souls living in places and settings all over the world. Yet they are growing into a newborn child of god in Christ in one nest; no mass movements here. As eggs have shells, so the human body is the shell of the spiritual egg, both types of shell are left behind when the young is hatched because both types of shell are made of dead material.

Thinking Is Praying and Praying Is Thinking

Thinking is praying, and praying is communing. Jesus taught us to see whether fruit are from a good tree or a bad. Wholesome fruit cannot come from a poisonous tree, and poisonous fruit cannot come from a good tree. Poisonous berries do not grow on an apple tree. Revelation can come to anyone, but who is the source of the revelation? If thoughts have anything to do with worldly or community matters at all, it is not from the Good Spirit.

The Good Spirit gives highly personal insight of himself, not of the universe. His teaching cannot be used to create edifices of any kind on earth, not even to boast in one's own vanity. It is private, and concerns no one else. Satan [Lucifer] gives revelations of grandeur and power and accomplishment in community affairs of men. An outward church is an affair of men.

Are We Chasing God or Is God Chasing Us?

The gospel of Joseph Smith is deeply rooted in this universe. Joseph and the hierarchy of the Church of Jesus Christ of the Latter Day Saints are being deceived by the evil spirit of Jehovah, and they are deceiving many people into hell. There is no existence in reality possible for Mormons. Their entire religion is based on the supposed findings of gold plates buried in the ground. They will guide to somewhere but they cannot redeem a person into all truth.

Christians are just as far off the mark. I read a bumper sticker stating, "God Chaser. I am chasing hard after God." But the truth is that Jesus came chasing after us and still is chasing after us through the Comforter. There is absolutely nothing we can do to bring our redemption about. A better statement would be, "I am waiting on the Comforter", but that falls short as well because Jesus said that he is waiting outside the door of our hearts for us, but almost everybody refuses to open the door to him.

Most Christians are neither chasing nor waiting but are freewheeling their time away in a delusion of religion. Christians are all led astray by their goody-goody authorities, who are more interested in their own worldly welfare than the spiritual welfare of others. There truly are only the few who will be born again in positive spirit. Jehovah-inspired Old Testament statements simply do not fit the bill when it comes to Jesus' spirit as Comforter. Jehovah insists that we chase after him; but Jesus, in spirit, can only chase after us because we are so confused and lost. There simply is no spiritual initiative in the human race, because humanity is the figment of souls' imagination. As long as Christians believe that there is only one god rather than two, good and evil, they cannot understand Jesus' missions. Jesus is the sheep herder in his parable of the lost sheep for which he went looking everywhere until he had found it; then rejoiced in having this one sheep back. Jesus is searching for you, but you do not know the true spirit in Jesus, so Jesus' spirit continues to search for ways to bring you back to reality so you will recognize him again.

Also, whatever is in the Bible that is of spiritual consequence and importance in being born again in positive spirit is still there from the days it was written. The spiritually important things that must be spiritually discerned cannot be discerned by those lacking the Good Spirit. Those that have an evil mind, [those who constantly pray to Jehovah or one of his underlings] and anyone else who might have had a mind to adulterate the Bible so that it would be of no use to receive spiritual guidance, cannot see the importance of exactly those parts in the Bible that hold keys for redemption into reality.

This book gives you the crucial knowledge to make sense of the ideas of salvation and redemption. Without the correct knowledge, one cannot hope to get into communion with the spirit of the true god and to be born again in spirit.

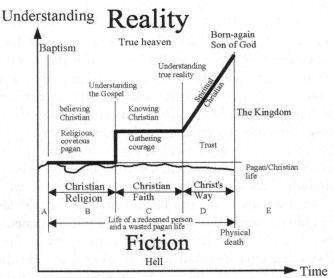

A: Many reincarnations of life untouched by Christ.
B: Many reincarnations in belief of Jesus as Messiah.
C: Many reincarnations trying to understand New Testament.
D: One life time in understanding that Jesus came as double agent, Christ and anti-Christ.
E: Jesus' message understood, death is an awakening in reality.
The pagan and carnal Christians will reincarnate and start all over again.

Figure 12

Chapter 8

Consequences of Believing in the Different Categories of Christ Jesus

Different Realities and Different Gods

The Comforter, the physical Antichrist, being Love and Truth and being the environment of those who know Truth, does not use force, but allows his constant love to bear down on all his creations. His love for the serpent has been materialized in the expanses of the physical universe, which he allowed the serpent to fashion. It is all fiction. It cannot hurt or damage true reality, but it can deprive beings of communion in reality by believing a lie and joining the serpent in make-believe communion and existence.

The true father also allowed Jehovah to be the only god known in the universe until the moment of truth when Jesus declared him to be a false or minor god. John 17:3 states that eternal life is *"knowing"* the only *true* [not the false] god and Jesus Christ whom he sent [meaning the *true* Jesus, as Antichrist, for only he was sent by the true father]. Now the fact in truth is that if one knows that the Good Spirit is not Jehovah, but the god whom Jesus newly introduced in John 17:25 and 26, and who is called *"good,"* and knows, therefore, also who Jehovah [evil] is, then one knows the realms they each have jurisdiction over.

If you know for sure [by conviction of the spirit] and not just because I tell you that this is so, and you prefer this other god, you already have eternal life. You are already a son of god; all that needs to happen next is to lose the deceitful flesh, which is fiction. You are assured of your redemption; nothing can happen that will hamper your being born again in positive spirit. If you believe [or believe you know] that Jehovah is Jesus' father, then, not only do you worship the wrong god, but also the wrong Jesus. Jesus came in two guises, Messiah and anti-Messiah, the only manner in which he could have a human body. Therefore, if you believe the imposter mission of Jesus, you worship Jehovah's Messiah and permanent capture in negative spirit is still your lot. If you can detect Jesus' hidden message of truth, the Jesus you worship is the Antichrist. He is the messenger that will lead you to communion with the Good Spirit. Jesus as Christ makes us accept the fictional universe on Jehovah's instructions and Jesus as anti-Christ makes us repent of joining Jehovah in this universe by trusting Jesus as Anti-Christ over Jesus as Messiah.

> ***Jesus, as god, lost us to Jehovah. Jesus as spirit came into the world to gain some of us back from Jehovah.***

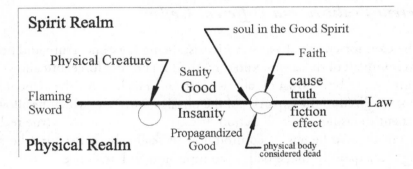

Physical pagan man is barred from reality. For the Pagan Jehovah is highest god and the universe is his highest realm.
Those with faith in Jesus' true message, and that faith nurtured by the Good Spirit are part of both positive and negative spirit. The physical body is the shell of the incubating spiritual egg, and the body is considered dead. Faith in truth is nurtured by the Good Spirit. When the true father is known, reality again invades the awareness of the soul. Faith is loyalty to Jesus' secret message.

Figure 13

A need for preachers to teach Jesus' inner message

Those who have never heard of Jesus are the most easily approached by a preacher who understands the gospel by me, Anti Christ, correctly as I have given it here to you. There is a great need in the world for preachers who know the god of true reality to preach the correct understanding of Jesus' mission to those around them. Remember the definition by Jesus of eternal life: **knowing** the *true* God and the Jesus only that true god sent and also *know that the* **mindset of the flesh** *cannot be a part of true reality*. They must direct soul to the Comforter in spirit. This new gospel will again be corrupted because in the realm of spiritual darkness, spiritual light will be hidden under a basket.

The Works of Man Cannot Please the God of Truth

The Mormons and Orthodox Jews are excellent examples of highly moral communities that, nonetheless, will not make it into true reality. Morality, like any other human activity, stinks spiritually because nothing the flesh does pleases god of truth. The **mindset of flesh** cannot inherit reality, but the soul led by the spirit of good can and will reestablish itself in *a spiritual body to match the truth this soul will know* in guidance of the Good Spirit.

The works of men are like a sculpture made from fresh human feces. No matter how crafty it is done, it repulses even the most ardent art connoisseur. Morality is still the viable manner for humans to interact, but it is of humanity in the holy/evil spirit, not of spirit of good/truth. It serves the lord of the universe, Jehovah. If you will just read Mark 13 and Luke 17, you will see that Joseph Smith cannot be a servant of the Comforter.

Jehovah, on the other hand, welcomes and demands you honoring him, sacrificing to him and dedicating your physical actions of piety and worship to him. See, there are two different kinds of gods.

Chapter 9

The Bible as a Court Case to Decide
Who Will Be Your True God

The Proceedings

The Bible is like a court. It briefly summarizes the facts of the matter in Genesis 1 for the prince of darkness. Then there follows the summary of facts of the matter in Genesis 2 for the god of positive spirit. [The court shifts from truth to apparent truth and back because we are in the realm of evil.] Then, the complaint of the god of light is stated in Genesis 3, and the consequences of the parties involved are summarized in Genesis 4. Then, the lives of those fallen from paradise are given in much detail as they exist under the jurisdiction of god in negative spirit, Jehovah. It relates how these Adamite children quickly ran to violence, then to corruption and adulteration of race; at which time, Jehovah sent a flood that wiped out the effects of this adultery.

Then, Jehovah relates how he again nurtured Noah and his progeny and seemingly abandons them again. He revives his interest in Adamites by making a pact with Abram [renamed Abraham by Jehovah]. From here, we see the abandonment of Israel by Jehovah and how he finally rescued them from Egypt. He brings up the distrust and disobedience of his chosen people, and we watch as they slowly alienate themselves from this god Jehovah, who thereupon abandons them, seemingly, for good. Then, Apocrypha informs us how they drift from one catastrophe to another.

From there, the story takes on a new approach as the god of light, with much interference from Jehovah, tells his story. The New Testament is that story. The parties state their concluding statements in the book of revelation where, again, both gods restate their case.

Soul must make a final decision whether it wants evil [disguised as good] as god or good in the reality of love. Evil allows a person all the tactics that the universe allows, from deceit, propaganda, force, seduction, tricks, and a plethora of other schemes, most of which have been covered in the stories of the Old Testament and are supported by one daemon or another—or to seek the meek master who loves without limit and who will give us all he has if we choose to accept him. I think the book of revelation is a summary of what will happen in the realm of darkness if one chooses to remain in the universe. The final conclusion is that soul does not belong in the universe. Soul would be better off in reality, but one is left to his own judgment. In this universe, one is rudderless, without foresight, and lost while speeding along the road of perdition. The sinister thing is that man believes that the world is man's home with all its false fanfare and hidden forms of deceit. Most people will thus miss the little hidden side trail that leads to reality.

"Maybes" Are Barred from Positive Spirit

From the Good Spirit's standpoint, everybody must have a clear and open choice between the two masters—good and evil; therefore, neither Jesus' spirit nor the Good Spirit can derogate the god of the universe. This is because in the universe, the word of Jehovah is universal truth [there is nothing else], just as the Word of the father in true reality is truth in the positive spiritual realms. All that Jesus was able to do was to call Jehovah the Prince of Darkness. He could not use the spiritual term *"evil"* because it has the wrong connotation with respect to humans in the universe under Jehovah. In the universe, Jehovah does not consider himself evil, but righteous [an inversion of love]. But since Jesus laid claim to the term "god of light" for his father in truth, he could distinguish Jehovah by vaguely insinuating him to be the prince of darkness. Jesus' death on the cross set the Hebrew souls free from Jehovah's jurisdiction. so they are free to make a new choice of the spiritual realm they prefer to be a part of.

We are talking about two gods, each having indisputable jurisdiction in their own realms. Man must decide who of the two will have ultimate jurisdiction over his soul—Jehovah, god of negative spirit, or Jesus' true father, god of positive spirit.

Jehovah's Source of Power: Deceit

Jehovah lied and used the power of the lie, which must be rooted in truth [otherwise, the lie would have no place to be] to fashion the universe. The universe is a fiction, and the spirit on which it rests is negative spirit. Once he had herded a bunch of souls from paradise into the universe [by means of the lie, or propaganda] and once he was settled in the universe as king and god, he was master of his own domain, and *whatever he decrees is universal truth*. There is nothing that can oppose him and alter what he has brought into physical being, whether these are laws, matters, rules, etc. Jehovah lied in paradise [realm of spirit] of which he was a part before he was sent down by his father to begin his reign as god over the universe. Jehovah is the father of lies of which Jesus spoke. In short, *spiritual truth is "good,"* and *universal truth is "evil"* according to the lesson we learned from the Tree of Knowledge of Good and Evil. Jesus, in the flesh, is an intruder in Jehovah's domains having a role in counter espionage.

Spiritual Counter Espionage

Jesus disguised himself as an entity of evil to reveal truth, for that was the only way open to him. I, as a sinner and as deceived soul am blunt on revealing Jehovah as the prince of darkness.

Jesus could do miracles and healing because Jesus had a physical body and because he knew how to operate the spiritual computer. As Jehovah's Messiah, he was given support in doing miracles. The Good Spirit, however, is not part of Jehovah's realm and never will give material blessings because all things in the universe are tainted with the lie; and because the universe is not in his immediate jurisdiction. He cannot give credence to the negative realm of spirit because it is fiction and because he does not have the power to give blessings that materialize in the universe. He has no standing here. To have standing in the negative realm, one must be a believer or enforcer of lies or otherwise obtain a license to operate. Jesus, on the other hand, did have standing and did substantiate the universe by appearing in flesh. If Jesus would not have substantiated the negative universe or if he would have violated Jehovah's laws while in the flesh, Jehovah would have brought down the true god because Jesus promised to be the Messiah, and the Messiah was prophesized to substantiate and bless the physical realm. Just the fact that Jehovah and Jesus' spirit could enter into agreement is proof that they are, somehow, together in teaching us the principles of Good and Evil.

If, however, the Good Spirit would have given blessings on earth, reality would be sucked up in fiction, and I believe all creation would vanish. There is no way that Ultimate Truth could be wiped out; god, Good, has control over that!

Jesus allowed people to call him lord. He said that indeed he was their lord. In the capacity of lord he spoke in Jehovah's name but in private he told his disciples that he was their brother and friend because he was willing to die for them to release them from Jehovah's law, so they could embrace communion in the Comforter, as positive spiritual entities.

All the Good Spirit can do is to try to get into communion with souls who have faith in him and then kindly guide them away from the realms of evil into the realms of truth. Jehovah can have religions in honor of him, and the congregations in these religions can have temples, cathedrals, and synagogues where masses of people give him honor and glory; but the Good Spirit has no place [to lay his head] in negative spirit because all matter is tainted with a resisting of the spirit of god in anti-Christ. All that the Good Spirit can have in us is a belief in the existence his true father, kindled by Jesus, which belief can lead to faith that the Good Spirit needs to make contact with the individual espousing the faith. This is the miracle that Jesus has wrought in the realm of fiction; he opened a gate to reality away from fiction so that souls can be raised into ultimate reality with God in truth. He was able to introduce me to reality and make it stick in soul—I am doing the same thing by introducing reality at a time that it seems to sink from the consciousness of soul altogether. The serpent is extremely effective in enforcing this universe as ultimate reality on us, souls. Thanks to the Good Spirit working through this book the unlocked door to true reality remains unlocked. It is my hope that you will help keep it open and use it.

Jehovah's Two Adversaries

Jehovah, since Jesus came into the world, has two adversaries who try to remove the Adamites from his jurisdiction over a soul. The Good Spirit wants the Adamites to repent of their original wrong choice and come home to him in the spiritual realms, and Satan [Lucifer] wants to bring the Adamites another step down, away from Jehovah's jurisdiction into his own [under Jehovah]. Jehovah or one of his underling daemons, on the other

ANTI CHRIST

hand, can produce religiously significant effects in this universe, like making you all warm when you feel you are in communion with him, or by creating a sparkling effect above the area of the altar in a church building, temple, or synagogue, etc. Satan tempted Jesus in the desert. He did so from two motivations. First, he resisted Jesus who came to tell the people about the true god, and in that respect, he was in cahoots with Jehovah; and secondly, he hoped to make Jesus insult Jehovah by violating his rules and laws so that Satan himself would gain jurisdiction over Jesus. This second motivation was thus in opposition to Jehovah.

The one world, one economy, one race system is inexorably approaching. It cannot be stopped. Once all races are amalgamated into an indefinable mass of humanity, the purpose of the universe has been thwarted; and once the last soul has been redeemed, then Jesus' predictions in Mark 13 will happen.

Religion Is a Trap into Oblivion

I have an aversion for religions where men have authority over the destiny of my soul, over America, the world, and universe. I have to fear such authority and obey, or I will be retaliated against. A god who instills fear in his subjects can have no love because one never has to fear the one who truly loves you. The one who loves—to me—is the good one, and the one I must fear and be uncertain about as to how he will treat me is not good. So the choice between reality and the universe/world is like a choice [in the world] between a ten-Billion-dollar estate and a dish of fresh human feces. The Mormons believe, and I think they might be right, that they will be gods over star systems and galaxies; but these are still parts of the universe under Jehovah—tainted, and in comparison with the *"kingdom of truth and love"* *[the realm where love and truth reign]*, it is like a pile of fresh feces.

Faith straddles the line between spirit and the physical realm. When I think of worldly matters, I close the door to the positive spiritual realm. I shut out the Good Spirit while the door to Jehovah's realm stands wide open, but when I think of pure positive spiritual matters, the door to the Good Spirit is opened; but because we are so grounded in the physical realm, Jehovah's door remains ajar. We dare not close that door. A universal deity is listening in, and when the communion turns too truthful, Jehovah will enter and brusquely intervene with some smooth propaganda ploy in the hope to have you slam the door to true spirit shut. Jehovah does this by directing your thoughts to personal and physical matters, such as long-coveted desires, wishes, and personal or business problems. There is a gamut of seductions available for Jehovah to get us in communion with negative spirit again.

The Difficulty of Overcoming the Flesh

Jehovah generally wins out over the Good Spirit. If one wants to commune in positive spirit, it is vitally important to remain completely in positive spirit. Do not get seduced by the world by getting wrapped up with solving the problems of the world or by being entertained. What you think determines the god you are communing with. That is why almost all people have never communed in the Good Spirit. Worldly affairs, complements of Jehovah, are too important to them.

After knowing the truth about Jesus, who can ever trust in the tainted religious word of any man or worldly affairs again? Unless one finds the *Good Spirit* in the *true* Christ, one will never lose one's animal skin!

I seek the raiment of light [which is the spiritual body] over a very insecure fleshy body, even if I might reign like a monarch or god. I prefer light, truth, and love over power, vanity, cunning, uncertainty and darkness. Since Jesus sets us free from Jehovah's jurisdiction [the angel stationed east of Eden] and law [the flaming sword], we are utterly free to go back to paradise. Very few know that this is so because they continue to see the evil angel as the true god rather than just a higher creature. As seen from positive spirit, the universe is the Antichrist, and Jehovah is king in negative spirit. The true Christ is the one carefully hidden from us by clever deceit and propaganda. How could anyone have guessed that Jesus came in two guises? The illusion of the universe as ultimate reality and powerful Christian indoctrination are too great; our physical bodies shut all spirit carefully from our detection and awareness. If we get in contact with spirit, by default it is always negative spirit. That only leads us from the frying pan into the fire. Jesus as Messiah as a misrepresentation of the true Christ in positive spirit does a good job to continue to make the many believe the lie. He could not help that.

Chapter 10

The Incomprehensible Statement by Jesus to Peter and His Apostles

Your Spiritual Reality Defined

Matthew 16:17-19 states that what you bind on earth is bound in heaven; and what you loose on earth is loosed in heaven. I see this as a very personal key in positive spirit because if it ever could apply to another person, it must first apply to you. Also because if anyone else, having deep faith, will receive a personal key to the kingdom of positive spirit as well, as he gave to all the apostles, then the individual keys will conflict with each other because there cannot be found two people who agree on all things. It is a key that fits to exactly those things that you, as a private individual, have loosed on earth, and of the things you have bound on earth to fit your personal character and outlook. It is a key that will confine or set you free of things that you decide are acceptable and unacceptable. It is a complete statement of how you would want to treat others because you yourself would want to be treated that way, not as you financially, culturally, morally, or legally have to respond, but as you individually would like to be treated regardless of any limitation or supposed standard. It is your personal statement of how to be a good and faithful follower of the true Christ. God trusts you sufficiently, while in deep faith, to allow you to set your own spiritual standards of conduct, as you have defined it and practice it now, to be valid for you once you are in reality. Because having a deep faith in the true Christ will make you set yourself apart from society [like being dead to it] and do things differently than members of society, not by some religious doctrine you espouse or other local or public standard that limits you now, but by your innate personal standard of personality and character. You decide the way things are for you in positive spirit. You have no right to infringe in the manner on how another individual sees his place in true spirit!

You do things on earth because you would applaud these kinds of things to happen in heaven. This is done so that when you get into the kingdom, it will be exactly the way you expect and want it to be. The true father would not want you in reality and then find out that you don't like it one bit and that you would feel betrayed all over again. I expect exactly this from a loving god that he gives me the freedom and liberty to do as I see fit as a mature being, whether on earth or in reality, and not having to be afraid that I will be scolded or punished spiritually for it. My standard is that naked evil and evil in any disguise is banned from reality, which of course it is.

I believe that Jesus also spoke in the name of Jehovah that when an apostle looses things on earth, it is loosed in heaven. That is the power the pope relies on in making rules and laws applicable for Roman Catholics on earth and in their heaven. To me, such rules are unfair and suppressive. But it is what Jesus as Messiah was forced to tell the people. Jesus, thus, gave us exoteric messages and esoteric messages. It is the typical routine of a double agent.

If people force things on you on earth that offend you because some "authority" has decreed that you must do so, and you cannot see anything wrong with what you want to do your way, you can simply decide that it is wrong and that, even though you will obey, you will not want to see this repeated in reality. You are not going to have guilt trips if, inadvertently, you violate the authority's silly rules. The authority is wrong, not you!

You must consider, of course, that if you want to have power and a matching authority over other beings in true reality, then you do not have true faith. True faith reveals itself in a humbled mind that does not seek such gross worldly things. If you don't have true faith, you will remain here in your self-created nightmare where your wishes of having power and authority can, but generally will not be granted. A person with true faith comes from a position of love; and love does not rule over others whether despotically or benignly, but support others as much as his nature allows. Those having deep faith will be thinking along similar lines of thought because they are in communion with the same Good Spirit.

In Matthew 18:8-20, Jesus tells all the apostles that they all have received the same kind of key. Now, it is a fact that no two pagan people will agree together on anything. Everybody has his own wishes, desires, dreams, and expectations; and everyone insists on being the top dog if one's wishes could be granted to them on the spot. The Bible even mentions an incident where two apostles were arguing which of the two would have a better place and power and authority as the other in heaven. When this became known to the other apostles, havoc broke out. Thus, Jesus' statement can apply only to each individual, individually. The realms of truth, obviously, are so large and so varied that there will be a place where you, individually, will be completely happy. Others who have the same or near same expectations will be bordering on you, and so on, just like the colored rays in the spectrum of light, each individually, but in combinations, creating all kinds of environments that suit everybody just perfectly and all in love with god and with those around them. Those that have other standards exist farther away and those radically different exist at the other extreme end of the living temple.

Also, Jesus said to Peter that not "on the rock of the person Simon [Peter]," but on the rock of the faith in the person Simon, he built his church. The faith which Peter displayed to Jesus was of such rocklike solidity that Jesus can and will build his church or a personal nest for Peter because, without faith, no divine church would be possible. Peter meant Jesus to be the son of Jehovah, not the father in truth. He was not yet introduced to the true father in positive spirit. What Jesus really said was that to meet the minimum requirement for being his church, one must have the same kind of faith, which Peter showed to Jesus that day—a solid knowledge and understanding that, indeed, Jesus is the son of god. This solid belief and understanding is called faith. Jesus insists on a personal relationship because love is personal. Jehovah insists on law and order, and that is a sentiment that concerns the masses and individuals as caught in a mass. The individual is reality, and a relationship between two individuals is reality; law and order and the mass mind or artificially induced mass solidarity is fiction. Jesus deals in reality, Jehovah in fictions. Jesus was always working to separate believers in Jehovah from souls seeking beyond the realms of negative spirit. Jesus always meant to get in mental contact with those who could have the meaning of his deeper message. That is why he so often hinted that a deeper meaning existed for those who had ears to hear, eyes to see, the positive spiritual message. Everybody got the meaning they chose to get, hence, his separating the goats from the sheep and where, in the deeper meaning, the goats and the sheep are reversed; the greater blessing goes to the goats.

One can now clearly see how Satan can make you misunderstand what Jesus is trying to bring across to us. As long as the door allowing Jesus' spirit access into your heart and mind remains closed, the door to Jehovah or some of his daemons is always wide open. So the interpretation you receive from the Bible is the worldly one if your mind is grounded in the world, and with a mind so grounded in the world, you keep the door to the positive spirit closed.

Every soul who *knows* god in true reality, already has eternal life; all they are still doing on earth is defining how they, in deep faith, want the temple in the realms of truth to be for them. I find that, in my faith, in all things, I want the living temple to be like the way god himself has a mind of establishing it; but he is open to sincere and well thought-out suggestions. Like I wrote, *thinking is praying*; so as long as you keep your thought on positive spiritual subjects, the Good Spirit will help you define what heaven will be like for you and keep any fraudulent worldly thoughts coming from Jehovah and his underlings away. In our communion with the Good Spirit, he guides us and informs us what the kingdom, the realm of truth, is about but he also gets to know exactly who and what we are and what we expect to find in the kingdom when we get there. That is communion!

I have always been a seeker of truth, and Jesus taught that he who seeks shall ultimately find. I have poked my nose in all kinds of religious and occult schemes. I have been a member of many such cults and religions, even a member of the Masons; but I have broken all my connections with them in order to follow Jesus, the true Christ. I am not seeking power, wealth, status, or any other worldly imminence, and really never have; but if one was to seek these with enough ambition, one would, like Jesus stated, also find them. Personally, I was seeking to understand the utter confusion in which we exist in this world. I present this set of books, as I understand what I am and how I fit into the schemes of things, physical and spiritual, and of what I know about the relationship between body and soul, gods and environments. I do so with love and hope but without pressure or expectations of any kind. I know that the standard versions of the Christian bibles give all one wants to know in order to seek the light—the views of the evil one and the views of the good one. I have given some of the more important quotes to allow you to see what the Bible really is, and I hope that in silence and in thought you will commune with the Good Spirit who will lead you out of this vicious trap—the universe. If one returns from this trap back into the realms of reality, the "Tree of Knowledge of Good and Evil" has done you a great blessing as you then will know *good* and *evil* and from then on choose correctly. If this is so for you, I will meet you in the kingdom of truth and love.

If you are not seeking true reality, you will either settle for evil or seek the particular kind of evil of your dreams, like riches, power, status, one or more relationships with the opposite sex, etc. This kind of seeking is called ambition. Those who pursue such dreams with enough ambition, shall, too, find what they seek; but whatever it is they seek, it will lead to spiritual death.

By knowing good and evil, we will receive a body of the content of both positive and negative spirit that can exist in either realm, but our true knowledge will prevent us from seeking the flesh. Knowledge sets one free but also gives one power in the physical realms. Hence, the immortal body, which, like an amphibious aircraft, can be wherever one's knowledge exerts one's power to be; in this case, the choice is between realms of existence defined by different gods. Jesus came in the world to enlighten us about things not known on earth, in the universe, or in the entire realms of negative spirit. If these things were known in negative spirit, the universe and negative spirit would vanish; that is why pure truth is so persistently banned from the realms of negative spirit

The Difference in Being Baptized As Understood By John The Baptist and Being Baptized As Understood By Jesus' Positive Spirit

I have another proof that Jesus came in a disguise of evil to teach us good. Jesus said that we need to be baptized in his name so as to be considered dead to the world. Now we know that Jehovah is god over the world. If anything at all, Jehovah would want you to be alive in the world while still in the physical body. It must thus be another god who wants you to be baptized in order to be considered dead to the world so you can be guided by a spirit that is not part of the negative spiritual realm [as the universe is] to the reality of positive spirit. John the Baptist only baptized people to repent from their wrongdoing as Hebrews in the Promised Land. There is a universe of difference in being baptized by John in the name of the physical Messiah, and being baptized in the name of Jesus, god of positive spirit.

It should come as no surprise now when I tell you that Jesus' apostles were chosen on order of Jehovah, not on order of the Good Spirit. The apostles were to spread the gospel according to the Messiah on earth. They were not appointed to spread the deeper and real meaning of Jesus' preaching. Jesus cannot preach truth, he said so himself. He wanted you to seek the Comforter in the Good Spirit in order to receive truth. Truth cannot be spread by word of mouth because people cannot understand truth as it sits cockeyed into the schemes of the world. Language can only convey the lie, the propaganda. The truth is hidden in the Bible, and very few will find it. I hope that I have been able to give you some insight in ferrying it out of the clouds of camouflage it is buried under. However, at the eve of Jesus' crucifixion he stole all the apostles from Jehovah to spread the teaching of his inner message for positive spirit. It is a pity that few or none of them, as far as I can discern, understood Jesus' inner and deeper message when they died.

The Purity of Souls Permanently Captured in the Different Sections of the Trap

Regarding the above picture of relationships between good and evil, most souls are enticed by baits [seductive schemes of deceit] available in each successive deeper cone section in the trap, (Figure 11, page 396) because additional schemes of deceit lead you farther away from reality. One must have accepted as real another round of basic propaganda in order to arrive in the next lower section. Each round of propaganda accepted makes the true god in Christ more inaccessible to the mind and the soul.

For those caught in any particular section of the trap, the good that is proclaimed there is pursued by the puritan or orthodox believer in that section as heaven, the place where their god dwells. They are stuck in that particular section of the trap. They resist the bait of evil in the next lower section determinedly. "Good," in each of these sections, is like a heaven of relative rest. That is why the Bible speaks of three levels of heaven. The good in each cone section in the trap signifies a level of heaven. As there are some seven different human races on earth, then, each has its own level of heaven. The Muslims count seven heavens, all of which are in this universe. These are all a derivative "good" of the next level of higher evil, deeper in the net. Orthodox Jews have been trying to attain the highest section of the trap for thousands of years, Jehovah's section. Yet Jehovah has rejected them. They wait hopefully for him to reclaim them. That is the reason for their particular kind of physically redeeming Messiah—the one that would make them masters of the world. Jewish religion definitely seeks worldly riches and status. The negative spiritual realm, thus, is based on a spiritual feudal system, but where the upper lord is robbed by his vassals. The higher lords want the lower lords to "rob" them of useless souls to keep their own reigns "pure" from "riffraff."

The Good News Bible states in Galatians 4:3 and 9 that pagan humanity is under the rule of weak pitiful spirits of the universe—which fact gives credence to this chart in figure 11, page 396 where each cone section is ruled by a "pitiful" weak spirit of the universe. More confirmation can be found in the following cites. Luke 25:36 states [Jesus speaking], "They will be like the angels and cannot die; they have risen from death [they as soul projections rise from evil to relative Good or from physical to negative spiritual]." John 6:63 states [Jesus speaking], "What gives life is god's spirit". Man's power [even the authority of the clergy] is of no use at all. "My words bring god's spirit to those who believe [me]." John 10:29 states [Jesus speaking], "What my father has given me is greater than *everything* [thus, greater than the entire universe] and none can snatch them from the father's care. The father and I are one." John 16:8-9 states [Jesus speaking], "And when he comes [the Good Spirit], he will prove to the people of the world that they are wrong about sin and about what is right, and about god's judgment. They are all wrong about sin, because they do not believe in me. They are wrong about what is right because I am going to the father and you will see me no more, and they are wrong about judgment because the ruler [weak spirit in a high place, Jehovah] of this world [the physical realms] has already been judged [in paradise when god made him crawl in the dust]."

The Good News Bible states in Galatians 4:4-6, "He came as the son of a human mother and lived under the Jewish law to redeem those that were under the law [Israel], so that they might become god's sons. To show that you are His sons, god sent the [good] spirit into your hearts." There are two gods; and the Adamites, of which the Israelites are a part, are thus "coveted" by both these gods. The true god, good, from a love motive, wants to set them free from the trap; and the false god, "evil," from a power motive, wants them because they are his latest prize "won" from god, good. The spiritual war is between these two gods. The spiritual war Christians believe in, between Jehovah and Satan, is only a shadow war [like the Cold War between USSR and USA was a shadow war]. The purpose of this supposed war between Jehovah and Satan is to hide the true spiritual war between Jehovah and the positive spirit in Jesus. Everything in physical reality is shadow play to hide the existence of a reality in truth.

A Kaleidoscope of Religious Beliefs Based on the Negative Spiritual Hierarchy

Now one can begin to realize how contorted and scattered the kaleidoscope of human beliefs is. It is impossible to communicate to people of a different belief about what one means by the terms *"good," "heaven," "spirit," "evil", "god" and "hell."* On this subject, as with any other important ideologies, the mightiest or the most cunning [he who can tell the cleverest lie] prevails.

One might say that this is a real Tower of Babel that is almost impossible to overcome. One must also realize that the creatures caught in each section of the trap got there on their own volition and that the believing puritans in each section seriously believe that it is the best place for them [and any other person they can convert to their views] to be and will resist "forced" change of belief through torture to the point of death.

In spirit, the truth and the lie are like matter and antimatter. The lie will always try to negate and make truth of no power; and the truth is invested with all the powers, glory, and love that can be; but truth is helpless when a lie uttered is believed. A lie-believed destroys truth in the one who believed the lie. When truth is destroyed it does not exist in mind and awareness, and it is almost impossible for such a soul to retrieve truth again. Redemption is only possible from beyond the realm of fiction the lie-believer has adopted.

The purpose of the universe, it being a realm based on the lie and deceit, is to negate, and make of no consequence the realm based on truth. For mankind [that has imbibed the propaganda the universe can feed it] the realms of all spirit is utterly unknown or is somewhat like a fable that holds no solid content, wisdom, and understanding even when advocated by the son of the god of all truth. Similarly, when you have been invested with or have been fed the food of truth through the Good Spirit, the lie will have lost its power over you. In spiritual awareness, one realm cancels out the other. But the truth stands eternally by itself because the lie cannot exist without the presence of truth whether one believes in it or not. Spiritual truth is based on knowledge; all else is based on false belief. Science, thus, is based on false belief and vanishes from the mind of the soul to whom truth is revealed and is accepted.

It must be said that Jesus came as the imposter Messiah for Jehovah; He later revealed himself to be the spiritual Messiah to set his brethren free from the bondage of deceit and propaganda in the realm of darkness. He taught that **truth will set you free**! Why would he teach that, if we already had truth according to the laws and prophecies of the Old Testament in Jehovah in which the Jews believed? Jesus meant that no one was free until one has received the ultimate truth, not from the mouth and mind of man [the son of man], but from the Comforter whom he would send after he had ascended. [Men can only communicate with each other according to the standards and understanding of tainted, physical existence.] One cannot commune in Jehovah and receive redemption in positive spirit, because Jesus revealed a higher god who overrules the previously known god, Jehovah.

This Comforter could never come as long as Jesus remained on earth. That is just one reason he had to die and ascend. The Comforter communes in truth. He transforms the [spiritual] soul from death to life. Similarly, now many forms of the Antichrist come to us disguised as the Christ [human spokesmen for daemons disguised as angels of light]. Some of them, of course, are Joseph F. Smith and all those who succeeded him as corporate chief of the cult of incorporated Mormonism. Since Jesus' departure, no one can speak for Jesus but the Comforter in the Good Spirit alone. One in guidance of the Comforter cannot be influenced by human teaching, daemons, and Jehovah. It must be understood [just as Jesus understood] that Jesus was an Antichrist to positive spirit because he appeared in flesh, deceiving us that "good" can come from a source in this universe. Because he came in the flesh, most Christians still believe in the power of the flesh and thus in the clergy. Jesus had to die in order to be here without any connection to this universe. He is here now again as the Comforter, proclaimer of truth, not in the immortal body in which he disappeared from the human senses. That immortal body is linked to physical reality and he cannot use that body to redeem souls to positive spirit.

Jesus Mission of Miracles and Healing Causes Many to Be Unaware of Jesus' True Mission

The relative good in each cone section going down always is a weaker, more pitiful, universal ruling spirit; the evil in each lower cone section is always another bait of a more covetous, brutal, material choice. Many will seek daemonic guidance as their entire human and spiritual outlook is keyed to universal existence. The comforter will be beyond their comprehension and reach.

A more covetous material choice might be the desire to capture another person and torture him to death as many of the nobility in Europe and Asia did for entertainment, and also some American Indian tribes, some slave owners, and other such gross characters. This trait can actually be seen in cats that have caught a mouse or a bird and take great delight in torturing it for hours, then killing it, and finally walking away from it. Other such choices might be to fire a person and then deny him a place to be as happened often in Ireland and Scotland where the nobility evicted or cleared people from property they controlled [by deputized sheriffs or police, who were never hurt by the victims and who were given authority to do these things] and left them exposed, abandoned, and shunned by all.

Summary of the Spiritual Court: Revelation in the New Testament

Finally, it must be said that Jesus' spirit will not give you prophesies. [Jesus only implied that the end of the world can be foretold by observing the change in the spiritual weather—Jehovah's servants prophesize]. Revelation is a book primarily dedicated to Jehovah because, to almost all those who believe in Christ, Jehovah is his father; yet, in Revelation, god in Christ has the final word, which harmonizes with and strengthens what he said in Genesis 2 about the "Tree of Knowledge of Good and Evil". Revelations 22:11 says, "Whoever is evil must go on doing evil, and whoever is filthy, must go on being filthy; whoever is good must go on doing good and whoever is holy must go on being holy." This means that in the end those who prefer this evil environment and its god[s], and even this god [Jehovah] himself, must remain evil. By "filthy," Christ, here, means for souls to prefer the physical body based on the lie [dirty, filthy rags]. Anyone who retains such a body must remain clothed in them forever and thus continue to be locked into the realm of filth, darkness, deceit and propaganda—the physical universe. Whoever is good must go on doing "good". This means that no matter what, the true god will always be god in love and truth; and all those gathered under the wings of the Good Spirit will continue to rest in him, and not only be guided back into the house of good, but remain in the loving communion of the trinity of truth evermore. Then, we have the next negative statement, which states, "Whosoever is holy must go on being holy." Here we have a perfect rendition of the nature of Evil/Jehovah. Jehovah will remain Jehovah and continue to call himself holy and separate because he must; and all those who follow him closely, by following the universal Christ, will continue to follow this Christ and never make it out of this evil universe of darkness. I have come to understand that by obeying all of Jehovah's laws, a person only becomes fully compatible with the parameters of the program run on the spiritual computer. Such a person is in complete synchronization and probably will have powers to wreak miracles in the environment that normal people would not have. The soul would still not be able to return to reality. His fictional existence could be called blissful and that means the person has arrived in Jehovah's heaven. He might become a daemon and become an operator in the negative spiritual computer complex. Jesus occupied that state for a while and left from there to his father in reality.

Jesus' spirit promised that he would send us the Comforter after he had ascended. He did not promise another prophet, seer, or savior. Therefore, there was no need for him to come again in the flesh either. That makes Mormonism a spiritual antichrist doctrine and makes Mary, Mother of god, of the Catholic Church a fantasy. The knowledge that the true god in Christ is not Jehovah and that Jesus was sent by the true god causes positive spiritual conception in a soul. The Good Spirit, then, watches over the development of that spiritual embryo, to fetus, to hatchling in spirit. Once one has arrived in the nest of the Good Spirit, nothing can snatch that soul from that spiritual nest [John 10:29].

Those of us who will be born again in the kingdom of truth will come home with a full understanding of what the "good" in god in Christ means [because the Good Spirit has taught the soul about true good], only because they have come to know and understand the true nature of evil and how, utterly, cunningly deceptive, enslaving, cruel, etc., it is. By being born again in true spirit, we finally know "Good" to such an extent that what we knew of good before our fall was utterly nothing in comparison. *Adam and Woman were so ignorant of the goodness of god that they actually chose 'evil disguised as good' over good.*

In closing, I must stress that the attitude, personality, and character traits imbued by human love, compassion, helping others, and loving assistance will not help one iota in bringing us any closer to reality. On the contrary, in general, these character traits only help solidify our permanence in the realm of darkness and evil because such traits is *evil disguised as good*. This is the greatest deceit played on us in the universe and in human society. On the other hand, cruelty, selfish ambition, and brutality of any kind will also only further one's permanent place in hell.

I believe that a sincere person cannot exist without giving aid, assistance, and care to those who need these, whether the persons in need are of good or bad character. Then what is the solution? We exist in this realm, and we must curse our being present here, but this does not mean we cannot give aid and care. The way to impart charity is with an attitude of aloofness toward our emotional attachment to our feelings of pity, compassion, and love; for they mean nothing. These are negative spiritual program routines that fasten us stronger into the physical universe. Nonchalantly giving to incorporated charity will do absolutely no good at all for advancement in positive spirit. Charity is a personal act between two individuals.

Jesus strongly admonished us that if we love our brothers, father, mother, and family and friends more than him [as the ambassador of truth] we are not fit to be his disciple (cannot be redeemed to reality). This statement reveals all the validity of what I have written in this book. Nothing matters other than for us to get into communion with the only spark of reality in our soul and heart—the Comforter in the Good Spirit, who is there always; for he exists in reality, which reality of course include all and everything. And the only real things in negative reality are our souls—it seems even to include the nothingness of the realms of the lie. You can now see the power of the lie; it does not exist, yet it can deceive souls forever to seek the darkness rather than the light. The power of the dark one is almost impossible to fathom; that is why Jesus' message is almost universally misunderstood.

In the back of this book, find the addendum consisting of some articles that I have written before I wrote this book and some I wrote after. Really what I give in this book to you and what I learned chronologically was given in a Montessori kind of study atmosphere. One has to start somewhere, and that is all right as long as the message is given and understood. The chronology is not really important. The essence of the book is to seek the Comforter, Jesus in spirit, in an attitude of understanding that all that we know and understand of this universe is unreality, a false illusion, absolute spiritual nothingness. In truth, the whole universe is nonexistent. It can only exist in the mind of drugged souls to whom the universe seems real enough—so real that true reality has become nonexistent. **I must say that I cannot understand how the god in truth managed to come into our dream universe of falsehood and that he was able to convey his message of liberty and departed again into the realm of true reality—of all things that we in our delusion call miracles that is the only true miracle.**

Chapter 11

A New View on Christ's Message of Truth

The Dream of a Comatose Soul

Human life is a spiritual addiction souls acquired in paradise. A lie-believed in spirit is a drug a million times more potent than heroin is here in earth. A lie-believed in spirit causes one to reject true reality. What remains for a soul to do is to exist in a fictional vacuum—nothingness. The art of twisting reality is propaganda, in true reality as well as in this fictional reality of souls' human experience.

Adam and Woman were made to believe that true reality is a lie and the maker of true reality a liar. So souls opted to believe the one who accused god to be a liar, and since then they took this liar as their god and cast their true spiritual father from their awareness.

The realm in which they descended was nothingness in true spirit. Jehovah and his conquered souls fashioned the universe in this nothingness and all pretend that it is true reality.

A soul is dreaming that it is in this universe in the realm of the highest god, Jehovah. It accepts in its dream that Jehovah is the highest god because the soul feels that he represents truth. [The power of the lie is that a soul believes that it exists in a reality of truth.] Soul was made to believe that the true god and father of reality is a liar. That is why the soul clings so tenaciously to the dream-reality it has now. To the deceived soul, there is no other reality, and Jehovah is king over the universe and the soul just has to worship him. Jehovah is the universe. He is everywhere in it and has complete control over it. He, or one of his daemons, watches over you through spiritual computer control and manipulation.

Lies Believed Caused Souls' Coma

In reality, soul went comatose because it refused to have existence in the realm of truth. Thus, the soul, the spark of livingness, still exists in the true reality in a comatose state. A newly adopted **personality** overrides the true one. In this reality based on a lie, lying seems to give advantage materially, but remains devastating in the spiritual make-up of Adam and Woman.

It is just like a child having a dream. The child in his dream finds himself anywhere but in his bed. It might be running and falling and something is trying to get him. He is scared out of his wits and groans or yells, making real sounds that the mother hears. The mother comes over and tries to quiet it down. Slowly the dream dissolves and the child awakens and finds the mother sitting next to him stroking him. The child suddenly is back in reality and the dream existence vanished. It is no more, but the memory of the dream might or might not repeat itself. I have dreams but I seldom remember anything of them. These, of course, are only nighttime dreams, part of the physical lifecycle.

The child, somehow, through mind power, created himself, his pursuer, and the environment in which the dream unfolded.

Now the encounter of Adam and Woman in paradise with the killer tree, made them so scared of true reality, that they went comatose in spirit and started a dream. The serpent that snared them into his invention of nothingness, however, invaded their dreams, and changed and synchronized these dreams. There they now exist in their minds, while the soul-bodies are located in reality, just as comatose people are located somewhere here on earth where the bodies can be properly cared for while their minds have adopted another more acceptable dream reality.

The nightmare the soul might be in may become overwhelming. The soul might do something that the Comforter notices and he begins to calm it down and tells it to wake up. It is like a father or a mother might do to their child. This might be the process that a soul goes through, except that there is one difference. In our case, Jesus was able to join us in our dream in the language of our dream. That contact is real to the physical person and is the reason that a dreaming soul or the physical person will remember. So, the dreamer may allow a momentary contact with the Comforter in a manner and language the soul understands. It has 'starts' of semi-consciousness through which the Comforter can commune with it.

In the soul's case, the dream has such a hold that it will not wake up, because waking up means entering into a reality that cannot be trusted.

Therefore, the Comforter begins to tell the soul how it was in reality before it fell into a coma. These words are said in true reality but cannot be heard in the dream, because this dream is very effective in hiding everything of spirit. The language, in which the Comforter speaks of course, is of reality, expressed in whole ideas, and therefore does not make sense to a human being. The human being does not remember a word of what might have been said, but the comatose soul in reality understood the words perfectly. Therefore, a person in communion with the Comforter cannot remember anything, except the ideas that were conveyed from the Comforter to soul. It may have unspoken premonitions of things in truth. Therefore, Jesus' statement to the rich young man that he, Jesus, was not good, but only the true father is good, was to encourage the dreaming soul to again have faith in the true, good god. Jesus was but a figment of the dreaming soul's imagination, reinforcing the dream-state, but the father he came to reintroduce is real and good. We must always remember that Jesus was not trying to contact human beings but comatose souls underlying the form of the human being. That is why Jesus' teaching was so difficult to understand and hard to accept by his human listeners.

> *Try to read and understand Jesus teachings from a standpoint of a lost soul, rather than from a point of view of an educated human being.*

Psychiatrists know how a person may assume a coma because a person went through some overwhelmingly powerful trauma caused by an incident or someone he knows. He blocks the trauma completely from his mind and in his comatose state might assume a new fear-free environment or a character and personality as a disguise so that the cruel person or persons cannot recognize him anymore, or a personality that is more acceptable to the mean person[s].

I believe that a comatose person, here on earth, has experienced such a terrible trauma that it refuses to return to consciousness. This person is dreaming also. The dreams of a comatose person seem as real as the person's physical life was. It dreams of some other existence, maybe not even anything like physical life; except that terrible things do not happen in that dream world. Meanwhile, the person's real lifecycle is progressing, and the years lost in the coma are irretrievable; they are lost. I do not know if the people that come out of a comatose state actually remember their dreams, but I would suppose they do not. Souls redeemed back to consciousness in reality must remember their dreams. It cannot be a void in experience because this experience actually lifts them to a much higher state in reality. In order for the lesson of the "Tree of Knowledge of Good and Evil" to have meaning it is done in a class setting. What was learned must thus be remembered for it to do any good.

I can remember in my younger years that I had what seems like memory lapses. I wonder whether the soul underlying my human form was communing in spirit and kind of left me out in left field. These experiences happened quite often and sometimes interfered with my driving home. I did not know where home was for some seconds. I believe that it is not sound practice for psychiatrists to interfere with human minds too much. It may be that a person not in touch with physical reality may have an underlying soul matter where soul is in communion with the Comforter. Human beings really are totally ignorant about spiritual situations underlying human experiences.

I do know that people who care for a comatose person would very much like for the person to return to the experience of physical life. They hold hands with him and talk to him continually. I can imagine that the Comforter does the same thing for us in our spiritual, awakening process.

Somehow, Jesus was able to enter into our dream-lives to tell us [or our souls, really] that another god exists who loves us and always wants to embrace us and wants us to be "one" with him. This information resonates in the soul when the Comforter tells how it was when it was awake [in reality].

Jesus said that your soul [or heart] has a closed door behind which he stands and waits for you to open, so that he can sup with you. You keep the door tightly closed because you cling to your father, the father of lies, whom you see as the teller of truth. For you, the dream world you are in is truth, so you keep the door tightly shut that might allow this "supposed" liar in.

Things are happening in reverse as it was in reality. The true god said that to eat or partake of the "Tree of the Knowledge of Good and Evil" would cause it to die. Now, Jehovah makes sure that the soul will not open the door that will allow truth in because then soul would die away from the universe. Soul refuses to open the door to truth! Once hurt, twice shy.

Here the parable of the dishonest manager may have some relevance. The manager changed the accounts of the boss who fired him, so that those who owed the boss a lot of money could pay off their debts at a great discount. The manager hoped to make friends with one or more of the boss' debtors, so he will not be penniless. He was transferring his allegiance from the present boss to these other people. That is the meaning of this parable. We are encouraged to let go of the false god and return to the real one. The parable only suggests a transfer of loyalty in spirit. Therefore, this parable also indicates the presence of another god.

Because of Jesus' teaching you might begin to understand that not all is well in the dream. It is not like heaven, something is missing or terribly wrong. You are confused and begin to believe that this god of yours [Jehovah] might not have told you the truth either! Now what?

The person on earth, then, remembers what he read in John 17. There is a true god out there that loves you. Therefore, the person's soul groans and the Comforter hears and calms it down and tries to wake it. The soul hears some things from the Comforter and then returns into its dream-state, but it retains some of what the Comforter said. This is how a soul slowly, and in starts and stops, gathers more and more information about true reality and goes from the comatose state to a state of spiritual hibernation.

Jesus did a very clever thing in John 17. He prayed aloud to his father in reality in the language of the dreaming souls, tying into one reality again the truth and the fiction. This gives us an 'in' to reality that is also real in the illusion in which we exist. It was the first real bridge for comatose souls back to the father in true reality.

That is why I think that a person is 'blessed' when he has a terrible life because the soul, must give signs in reality that calls the Comforter to him who then tries to impart as much of its true life before it fell comatose [before it believed a lie]. Something triggers the Comforter by watching your soul that allows him into your dream consciousness. Then you quickly returns to the dream-state. I believe that a daemon is with the soul all the time preventing a soul as much as possible from opening that door into reality, because that door is the spirit of truth. Can you now see that the spiritual battle is entirely different from what Christian doctrine tells you?

I believe that most people's lives are just good enough so that souls are not scared back into reality. It is done through spiritual propaganda. Jehovah has set a lower limit to the horrors of life that cannot be trespassed by the spiritual computer, or souls will have cause to wake up from their lie-induced state.

This must be the reason intelligent creatures are created male and female, for sex, love, and companionship, and why people are encouraged to have compassion for the poor and the sick and the ill-treated. How can we ever act in any other way? The moral and ethical person aids Jehovah in making earth a desirable place to be. We are constantly being fooled to believe that we count in this miserable environment.

Just enough good things are awarded to a, truly miserable, human life so that this limit routinely will not be violated. Moreover, enough people are laid in the cotton for others to see that life does not always have to be miserable. Also, because rich people are well connected and are having much satisfaction from life, they will insure that their lifestyle will continue, and thus automatically forsake contact with the Comforter.

Jehovah has many moral and ethical laws to that effect. Human life is miserable, but propaganda makes it seem worthwhile anyway. The mixture of human experience is just above what is acceptable. You can see from this that human society makes it impossible for souls to find the way back to reality. We enforce this false reality on each other like gangbusters.

I believe also that some people are so terribly mistreated that they live for revenge of one kind or other. They refuse truth because they are consumed in their soul with hatred and retaliation. Somehow, they get what they want because people continue to be terribly abused for no apparent reason. I believe they get their desire from one lifecycle to another. Those who seek shall get what they want or are looking for, in this case revenge and a permanent place in hell for as long as this hell lasts.

I, therefore, urge the reader to stop any thoughts of revenge and hatred. Spiritually, the cycle cannot be broken, unless, somehow, such a soul can understand why one suffers and why one is so angry and terribly sadistic. We are driven to these thoughts by propaganda. We are all deceived to believe that we exist in the only reality possible and thus must make the best of it through our propaganda-induced feelings on life.

Insight into Previous Lives

My first wife divorced me many years ago. A year or so after this terrible divorce I was persuaded to see a psychic. This woman told me that there was a triangle between me, my wife, and the man who stole my wife, and that we had had this triangle going on from lifetime to lifetime. I now believe her, for in my mind I have always resented very much what took place. The man was supposed to be my friend and I loved my wife, yet this thing happened in secret behind my back for many years. I now have resolved that the matter is not worth the trouble going through for any more lifetimes. This lady-psychic has done me a real service and, unbeknownst to her has helped my redemption another step forward.

Because of that divorce, I found the best person as wife I could have hoped to meet. All is well that ends well. I hope very much that this is true for you as well. I have had enough of physical existence and my wife feels the same way.

Our idea of reality has turned upside down in the conscious of the soul when the serpent in paradise told us a lie that we believed. The top became hidden and he, the serpent, showed up as highest authority in the soul's spiritual awareness.

The Comforter is trying to raise the level in the hierarchy right side up again. When that is accomplished, soul will wake up, and the universe, like a bad dream, will vanish.

The Bible Alone Cannot Give a Person Spiritual Understanding

One must place a limited reliance on the Bible and the knowledge of religious experts. It is better to study the Bible very well yourself and then put it away, because the Bible cannot save you. However, it can help in having meaningful communion with the Good Spirit.

I must confess that I repeat many principles, but repetition is the key to comprehension and understanding. Also, the repetitions are not identical. They highlight other facets of the same principle that give light to other facets of the ideas and helps to round out penetration of understanding and insight that is so sorely needed to bring you realization that what our bodies perceive is only a very small fraction of what the entire environment holds. Our bodies are our most effective deceivers. These implements are the curses Jehovah laid on us and we are helpless against the deceits the body implants in our souls. It is so important to differentiate the true Christ from the many advertised false Christs. A fake Christ always uses some form of mental light and material splendor to fool the people, like those gorgeously arrayed processions down the streets of downtown areas in an all-Roman Catholic community. I say this not to insult that religion, but to help open your spiritual eyes and those of adherents in that religion as well.

As long as lies and propaganda still have a hold on me, I remain dead to true reality. I apparently still have conflicts in truth with that reality. If, for some reason I can resolve that conflict, or have it resolved for me by the Comforter, then I will wake up in true reality and my physical appearance will vanish. It must vanish because nothingness cannot have any hold on my soul if there is no mental content to it [propaganda content], and reality has again flooded my spirit.

As a final word, I give the below illustration of Joseph Smith, founder of the Mormon religion, as an example of how to recognize whether one is dealing with true spirit or a daemon that disguises its evil in apparent light and splendor. A person in the Good Spirit can easily see that the Good Spirit, the only spirit of truth, cannot deliver his guidance through material means. The Good Spirit has no ability to support the lie on which the appearance of the universe is based. Mormonism is an example, because this is so clearly a deceit played by a daemon on humanity because humanity still loves the lie more than truth. I could take any of the Christian major denominations as an example also as they are trapped in the same kind of deceit through their sacred book, the Holy Bible. Jesus in his ministry admitted that he was not good, that he came in the guise of one who believed the original lie. He was honest about that. It, also, was the only manner in which the good news of true reality and of the true god, his father, could enter into the universe. There simply is no other way.

I wrote this essay originally to a very good, Mormon-bishop friend. He is a Mormon still. It is almost impossible to make religiously indoctrinated people see the error of logic in their belief. I have to communicate a lot, even if it is somewhat repetitious, because in this realm of fiction one also must be indoctrinated into accepting the reality of the Good Spirit as one has to be indoctrinated into any other activity or mindset in the physical universe. Here, everything we do or say has a strong link to fiction—unreality. This universe has no apparent link to reality, exactly because it was designed to hide reality.

The Mormon Church clearly shows how an entire control system of bondage and damnation is built up from one original lie, the 'supposed finding of a set of divinely inscribed gold plates, making the finder, Joseph F. Smith, [Joseph] god's chosen, equal to Jesus, like another Mohammed. This first lie is supported by innumerable additional lies. It starts with a seduction of supposed, invaluable quality of life for all especially in the spiritual realm, while all during his life all benefits accrue mostly to this prophet. The rest of the members in the cult are deluded by false promises.

Even if Joseph found the disks, then any link in the disks that connects to Jesus, should only aid Joseph in accepting Jesus as Christ and bringing him into the folds of existing Christendom. His true motive showed up when he started a new religion. If he were devout in his faith to Christ, he would have used his information to worship Christ as a Christian and if the disks revealed that present Christendom was so corrupt as to be useless to be redeemed in spirit, he would have had to become a determined reformer and use his disks to prove that he is right. What purpose can it possibly have to find disks and bury them again? It is phony!

Religion Is a Spiritual Death Trap

Everything in this universe, fact or fancy, is the true spiritual anti-Christ—I am, this book is, Jesus in the flesh was. Anything that feeds our belief that this universe is real; that enforces our belief in the universe is spiritual anti-Christ. Whatever we can see, feel, touch or can communicate with in the universe promotes the lie and tries terribly hard to hide the truth. Jesus was able to impart some truth, but the truth was forced to hide in a huge camouflage of deceit, in that Jesus was also forced to be the Messiah of the Israelites, which Messiah was the deliverer of Israel in Jehovah's name. It is no wonder that his real message was almost entirely buried in universal propaganda because truth cannot be told without immediate corruption by evil. The negative spiritual computer cannot run on just the state "0".

Apostle Paul made an intuitive statement that all our prayers must be translated by the Good Spirit in groans that words cannot express. We cannot possibly know what is good for us, or how to make ourselves clear to god [who only knows truth] in the language and consciousness of liars and swindlers, and creatures that play make-believe. Jesus said of himself that he was not good, but only one is good—The spirit of the true god. If Jesus is not good, he was like us, part of the problem. Yet he had to come to impart the way out to those who have eyes to see, ears to hear and a soul that understands his true message. One can now see that Jesus imparted the universal message in his parables to his apostles and disciples. He gave only meanings to his parables a couple of layers removed from the layer of deceit in which the apostles were trapped. The Comforter in the Good Spirit can only make the spiritual meaning of his parables understood in concepts of positive spirit and that had to wait until he had ascended.

Now you can see that all Jesus says in the New Testament makes sense according to what I have told you herein. There are no more secrets and no more mysteries. Jesus revealed the true father to us and he has waited for 2000 years for someone to get the full uncorrupted message. Now that you know the truth, do not waver. Allow the Good Spirit to lead you.

For the past 2000 years, everyone has understood Christ to be the servant of Jehovah, but from Jesus' true message we can now see that **the Messiah is the spiritual anti-Christ; and Jesus' spirit as Jehovah's anti-Christ is the son of the true god!** Jesus, the Christ, is the one who invites those who cannot have the true message to remain in negative spirit as sheep; and points the goats in the direction of the Good Spirit. The goats have the much tougher job. They must have a lot of courage to wake up in reality. True Reality is all around us but we are all dead to it, (out of communion with it).

Chapter 12

The Crucial Question

I conclude Book IV with the crucial question, "Why does evil exist?" By now you hopefully can answer this for yourself. Evil always comes in a disguise of good. Evil is the depth of deceit because it comes disguised as good. Souls *must understand and know evil* [remember, we, in paradise partook of the tree of *the Knowledge* of **Good** and **Evil**] to be able to look through all the disguises that evil can hide behind. This is of spiritual significance because if evil could take on a disguise of good in the realm of good, evil would invade and settle in the realms of good without "good" knowing about it. So whoever will enter into the ultimate realms of good must know every aspect of evil to be able to look through all the disguises of evil in order to identify and embrace good and shut out all avenues through which evil can slip unnoticed into the realm and communion of good. Nothing is as it appears to be. Everything in the universe is evil in a disguise of good.

Evil is a communion, just as good is a communion. Do not let a communion of evil disguised as good fool you any more. Evil can be a (booby-)trap, expressed without words, but as deadly and tragic for those who wander into it.

If evil would succeed, existence in any plane of reality would become an intolerable nightmare and we would be caught in inescapable suppression and hatred without love and without anything to look forward to, because evil would have shut off any possible escape route. I give you examples of evil that shut off all avenues of escape: the Wall erected between East and West Germany, The Elba River in Germany between East and West at the end of the war with Germany, the river of death and the IMF, whose inescapable slaves we all have become without even knowing it. I give you the continual encroachment of government into our every moment of daily life.

Liberty and love would disappear from all levels of reality forever. I hope that everybody in the world can identify with this kind of horror. If you can, you are truly ready to embrace the Comforter in the Good Spirit who is reality as good and not as evil. Government, marriage, children, cars, computers, planes, you name it; they are all disguises of evil pretending to be good.

Do Not Let the World Confuse You Any More; There Is No Good in It. Only One Is Good, Ultimate Truth in Ultimate Reality; and As Yet, You Have No Part In It.

The disguise in which evil tried to usurp the intentions of good in Jesus is so severe, that it took 2,000 years to understand what Jesus was truly doing. Jehovah has been exposed and stands naked. Good is the responsibility of every soul in existence. If you cannot rally for good you will be utterly annihilated.

Now, I Sincerely Hope You Take Me To Heart. I Am Not Much Of A Spiritual Leader or Politician, I Am Not Jesus Or Some Saint; But I, Anti Christ, Am All You Have in the Good Spirit, Whether You Are The Pope, The Ayatollah, The Dai La Lama, Bill Gates, Oprah, George Bush, Or Whoever You Think You Are—Like Jesus' Words, My Words Help Give You Life.

All Christians brag on knowing truth, however not one knows what truth is. The truth is that you live a lie in a reality based on a lie. Jesus came to make you aware of that fact. From hereon out it is a matter between you, Evil, and the Comforter. The ball is in your court.

NOTE: It is up to you to recommend this set of books in one cover to everyone you care for. Many people have a tendency to repress knowledge of others by withholding recommendation to those they hold dear. This is a selfish attitude. If you love someone you should allow that person to have information and options to form his or her own opinion. Be yourself, not Jehovah's patsy. This book helps you to do that.

This material will give anyone powerful rehabilitation of awareness and understanding of liberty and love. If you are unable to convince a person, or if you believe that a person you would want to recommend this book to will not be persuaded by its spiritual value, recommend it on its value as a works of science fiction, or for its philosophical, historical and political value. It is also up to you to help make the world a better equitable place to be where every race, species and creature can have a worthwhile place. Humility and true understanding are the greatest blessings one can give another. Be yourself, not Jehovah's patsy. This book helps you to do that.

BOOK V

HUMAN PERCEPTION OF REALITY IS A SPIRITUAL FABRICATION

Introduction

The true father is the god in positive reality. The son was created in a virtual environment because nothing appears new in true reality. You cannot add or subtract anything to true reality. To create a new entity [the son] a new environment must be created to place the new entity and a means must be devised to interactively communicate with the new entity—a set of rules, a protocol. The Good Spirit is this means of communication. The father gave all power and authority to this son. See, in a real communion, respect is retained from son towards father, from the creature towards its creator and visa versa. *The difference in realities in the father and the son were resolved and are expressed by the son as him being son and his father being the father. Honest acceptance of the relationship in a set of different realities have been equalized through honesty, humility and love.*

The thing is accomplished in a *de jure*, honest manner; hence, in the reality of positive spirit, father and son can communicate in truth with each other—be together by means of the Good Spirit, the total, honest communion between the two. Therefore, somehow, spiritually redeemed souls are part in that communion because they are in his son as separate creations in their own set of parameters in a derivative reality.

The character of negative spirit, on the other hand, can overpower the beingness of an already existing entity through clever deceit and induce the deceived entity to dream up a deceiver-controlled fantasy-environment in which the deceived entity can lose itself as a creature. Nothing new was created. The relationship is dishonest because of one-upmanship. The deceived entity is deprived of its existence in reality by believing a lie about its native reality; and finds itself back in a negative spirit-induced projection of a world placed in a universe of pure imagination. A hypnotist, kind of, does the same with people he puts under. When the subject of hypnosis awakens after the experiment, he may or may not retain a memory of what transpired while under the spell

435

of hypnosis by command of the hypnotist; but clearly, the subject was under the impression that the subject's experiences under control of the hypnotist were real. Therefore, in both cases, when the subjects awaken, the dream state vanishes and the entity is again in present time and environment.

In the same manner that the father created the environment for the son, free of any deceit played on the new creation, the son created an environment for Adam and Woman based on humility, honesty and love, and then placed these two in that environment. The environment did not automatically give the creatures Adam and Woman complete knowledge of their father. The son therefore included an arrangement through which these two creatures could get to know their father [the son]; and another arrangement was included whereby these two, after graduating from knowing the father [as god's son], could gain knowledge of the father of the son, ultimate god. This other arrangement is the inclusion in paradise of the "Tree of the Knowledge of Good and Evil".

Woman found her being in Adam's environment, because Woman was extracted from Adam, and is thus an integral part of Adam and his environment. An analogy to this event is the fashioning of a chair; everything needed for the chair is available in the existing environment of the artist; no new environment is required to place the finished object. However, computer programs need a computer environment to display the results of the program. This environment had to be created first before computer programs could even be composed. Computer programs are limited in its original display capability to a computer-created environment.

As you can read in Genesis 2, god created animals as companions for Adam. God, the son, found that animals were not the answer to Adam's longing, so he created Woman to be Adam's companion. Woman found the snake, an animal, in this tree of death. This snake found an abode in this tree and it fashioned an icon of that tree, which icon when activated opened up a universe in a virtual environment. Therefore, the other trees are associated with the other animals god created as company for Adam. These animals, obviously, are of a lower status than Adam—just as animals in our environment have a lower status than human beings. I call these animals, archangels, because they are creators of their own universes, and as such, play god over souls as long as the souls remain associated with their tree.

The archangels and their trees are the means the son of the true god used to give Adam and Woman knowledge and experience of the higher environment of the son. After graduating from the trees of paradise Adam and Woman will have the wisdom and knowledge to enter into the tree of

Life and be with their father [the son], or in the alternative can partake of the "Tree of Knowledge of Good and Evil".

The true god has very many sons, each existing in their own, harmonized-with-reality, virtual planes. However, none of these virtual environments were created using the principle of a lie to punch a hole in reality but, yet, they are extractions of a higher reality; therefore, they fall short of true reality—all truth. The principle on which these positive-spirit-created virtual environments rest is humility and love, or more generally, the good in the father, and not deviousness or evil in a deceiver imposter.

The son is not the father, but communion is possible because of the principle of the spirit of communion. It is a method whereby the higher can communicate with the lower reality and visa versa. It is above board, the spiritual father can fully commune with the son. They can experience each other fully; one can face the other and touch. There is no one-up-ism.

Moses, who existed in the projection of a spiritual computer display of negative spirit, also created a virtual reality called Israel in the Promised Land, under the auspices of Jehovah. Moses claimed to have been in full communion with Jehovah, when he received the Ten Commandments. I do not believe they saw face to face though, because that would have killed Moses as was related to us in a conversation between Jehovah and Elijah. Elijah was allowed to see Jehovah's back, but not his face. Whatever he experienced was some kind of projection of Jehovah into the computer display. Moses, as related in Deuteronomy, was given the entire plan on which Jehovah based his decision to create the nation of Israel for his favored people.

The Constitution for the United States is another example of a communion between reality and fiction, although the Constitution has deceit and mediocrity built into it. However, let me use that example. This constitution created the medium of communication between a free union of states and the newly formed United States; and how this union could be governed and made to operate in a manner acceptable to the people. It is a protocol or set of ground rules. The Constitution was an afterthought of the articles of Confederation of the states formed from the prior colonies. The people and government found that it was impossible for the union to exist without some sort of protocol or set of ground rules or, really a means of communion and trust.

The Constitution can be seen as a communicating spirit, a 'holy spirit' so to speak. The constitution provides for departments of government, the departments provide for agencies and spokespeople, and for ways by which the people can approach heads of government through the agencies. This process is referred to as delegation of authority. In a well-written Constitution, the fiction is prohibited from altering or modifying the articles of the constitution that govern the fiction. Thus, government cannot be allowed to undermine the intent of the spirit of communion, the Constitution, created by the higher form of reality, the people. The Constitution must remain the intermediary between the real people and the fiction and retain the true relationship between the fiction and the people. However, the snake in the grass was that the Constitution allows state governments to speak for the people and decide changes to the Constitution that adversely affect the standing of the free people. Through this loophole, the people lost control over their government and over the Constitution, especially when the northern states lost their sovereign state rights because they violated the sovereignty of their southern sister states, established by the very grounding agreement prior to declaring independence. Therefore, the sovereignty should have reverted back to the people, but instead the federal government usurped that right under the principles of the democracy. It sidestepped the states entirely and proceeded to be the government and sovereign of all the people of the states. Government officials acted as Serpent, traitors.

After the Civil War, the states had no right to be the representatives of the people and lost the ability to make decisions that involved the relationship between the US government and the people, the true sovereigns, which arrangement was devoid of sincerity to begin with. Yet the state governments incorporated many additional amendments to the constitution. Now you can see that our snake in America were the governments of the states that deceived us and stuck our heads in the mud.

It is noteworthy that this inversion of power happened just as the international bankers, for the third time, tried, and this time successfully, to gain control of the United States. The bankers, under Mammon the daemon, have always been behind all the trouble the United States experienced in its first century and the people were overpowered through this conspiracy and the deceits played out before, during, and after the Civil War. The bankers have been in complete control ever since.

The question might come up, "How can the people be in charge of government?" How will people assemble and combine to stay in control of government? To me, it must happen through the strict code for the police forces that enforce the peace on society: the county sheriff departments, police dept. and the armed forces. Of course, there is the rub; police and armed forces are there to enforce the fiction, and the sheriff department, a leftover from the republic, is the enforcer of the rights of the individual people. All the enforcement forces, including the sheriff now report to the directors of fiction, leaving the people helpless. Therefore, the Constitution is a farce. It is still upheld because it is a useful means of propaganda for government to make the people believe that there is an agreement to maintain de-facto order in the country—which of course is true as long as the people buy the snow job. In truth, there is no constitution because the constitution is an arrangement between the states and the body that governs the union of states. The states lost their sovereignty after the Civil war. This proves that everything is make-believe. We dramatize a fairy tale. We dramatize being free citizens in a free country, and it is all hogwash.

If our youth were educated by the people [not government], according to the principles of liberty [being taught to be principles over government], posterity would have been much better equipped to retain control over their governments. The servant government would have to petition the people like people petition Jehovah in prayers to obtain something. Everything in our experience of physical reality is ass-backwards. That is why this is the realm of darkness and evil.

What I write in the next couple of paragraphs is totally mind-blowing—it is new to me also.

Jesus said to the rich young man, "Why do you call me good? Only one is good." Jesus meant to say, I am not good, not even in my own spirit (this is because the father is good and the son honestly realizes that); only my father is good. Then, after the Last Supper, in the garden outside Jerusalem, Jesus said to the disciples; "I tell you the truth, in my father's house are many mansions. I will go and prepare a place for you *also*." Here, he does not mean, in my house there are many mansions, but in my father's house—we are talking about a different realm than the one Jesus as the son resides in. When we arrive in the father's house, we occupy one of the many mansions in God's house, not Jesus' house. Therefore the same Good Spirit that enfolds Jesus will also enfold us. We will truly be a brother to Jesus and a son of god, the father.

Before Adam and Woman partook of the Tree of Knowledge of Good and Evil, they had already partaken of all the other trees in paradise. By knowing all those trees they graduated into knowledge and understanding of their father, the son. Through that base of knowledge, the "Tree of Life and the "Tree of Knowledge of Good and Evil" became significant. If one entered into the "Tree of Life", one would enter into the realm of their father, the son, and be in his house. That entry provides a mansion in Jesus' house, not Jesus' father's house. They will thus be grandchildren of the true father.

However, by partaking of the "Tree of Knowledge of Good and Evil", one would die, become comatose, totally out of communion with god, the son, permanently. This tree will teach the knowledge of evil and good. The extreme danger of this tree is that if one does not get the knowledge and understanding of good, one will succumb to the powers of evil and die spiritually. If the message of that tree is fully comprehended through assistance in the Good Spirit, one has transcended the godhead of the son and can enter [come to life] into the house of God, the father, ultimate truth, as son.

Other entities in sets of Adam and Woman before us who fell into this realm created by negative spirit and who graduated from this realm already have their mansions there (in my father's house are many mansions). They are co-sons with the spirit of Jesus. If one can graduate from the realm of knowledge of good and evil, one will be housed in the realm [the street] where Jesus has his mansion, in his father's house, true reality. One is son by the same standards that makes Jesus son.

Therefore, go for spiritual-good. Forget worldly good such as riches, status, prestige and eminence in this realm of foolery. Go for the GOLD, be truly and totally real!

However, if you cannot be convinced, I tell you below how to be in this physical environment. Everyone should read this, because one must know all about evil and good, and the "Ode to Jehovah" below teaches how to participate in a realm of evil disguised as good.

Chapter 1

Ode to Jehovah, God of the Universe

The Negative Spiritual Hierarchy

People exist in god, Jehovah, this universe. We live, breathe, move, and have our being and life in him. We are we what are in Jehovah. The universe is negative spirit. It is make-believe reality and he is the director of the play. He gives each of us a role to play. As director, he wants your attention and your adoration. He works through an organization, the negative spiritual hierarchy. What we see is upheld by what we cannot see, the spiritual hierarchy that is the management staff that produces the play. This organization [including also souls] works behind the scene. Human beings are the actors on the scene. There is about 99% of involvement going on behind the scenes. The physical universe is thus 1% [see figure 8, page 393]. The play is about Jehovah's greatness, magnificence, glory and majesty. The better we can convey our admiration for him in our roles, the better he likes it. If you cannot meet his standards, he will pass you on to an underling, a daemon, who then becomes your god under Jehovah. Jehovah must always remain the greatest because you exist in him. You, soul and body, are a part of him. Yet, he will not know you anymore when he passed you on to a daemon lower in rank. He is the whole environment and by dedicating yourself to pleasing him in the Messiah's name (Jesus Christ) you adore him.

Curses and Blessings

Jehovah rewards worship. He wants you to recognize him openly as the greatest and best god one could possibly have. You treat him that way and he will favor you. People either complement or insult him. There is no in-between. No one can boost his ego enough. He is therefore disappointed in us.

Jehovah arranged the universe in such a way that you are either cursed or blessed and even while he may bless you, he can still send curses to you if you fall short in adoring him. He wants all your attention. Humans are not capable of such constant adoration because we are vain critters ourselves that try to steal adoration from others that Jehovah feels belongs to him. Jehovah wants to be first in our devotion. However, humanity is riddled with anxiety, fears and things to do for ourselves first, so that we fall far short of his demands on us.

He rewards sacrifice in the form of dedication and development of our talents. He wants everything we do to be a sacrifice to him, not just to our own betterment. If you neglect your talents, you remain a 'nothing', a potential unfulfilled. He seconds your choice. For human beings life without blessings is miserable; and because it is miserable, we work hard to make our life better. We neglect to give sacrifice to him, so he gives us more difficulties and sorrows, and we react by working harder and more determinedly to improve our situation, rather than make our efforts a sacrifice to him. Reverse the trend—dedicate your efforts to him and the situations in your life will suddenly improve. Joseph in Egypt understood that principle and it stood him well.

If you have incurred the curses, you are in deep trouble. Pain, suffering, betrayal, poverty, fruitlessness of effort, and unhappiness are your constant companion. One does not forsake Jehovah without penalties. In addition, if you are abandoned by him, your best bet is to try to be worshipful to whomever he has passed you to. Daemons become more brutal as one goes down in the hierarchy of negative spirit. This is arranged so because you continue to insult your highest god, Jehovah himself. He curses you in this manner. The ancient Greeks were so wise as to make a place of worship for the god that for some reason was not known to them. They did not want to incur the wrath of any daemon.

Adorn His Body, the Universe

By using and developing your talent, you make his raiment more glorious. Examples of such glory-added beautification are the great temples in Asia and Europe and in Africa—the pyramids, magnificent cities all around the world, great architectural edifices like 1,500-ft-tall buildings, paintings, sculptures, art of any kind, sailboats, cruising ships; you name it. They must represent the best effort and the best that the funds available can buy. Jehovah is into material things. He wants you to worship him in the medium that we believe in, our body as part of his universe. I hope you get the picture. If you apply yourself and dedicate your efforts, not just to your boss or to your own vanity, but to Jehovah, Jehovah cannot help but reward you. It may be difficult but through your continued application, in the face of continued defeat [set up by him]; you show him that your faith in him never falters. He considers that sacrifice due to him. Abram was of that caliber.

You cannot praise him with empty words. Most people's efforts do not adorn his raiment. Dedication and applying one's talents so that a new piece of art materializes to adorn his body gives him pleasure; especially if you dedicate the fruits of your labor to him. This kind of adoration comes from determination; and not just from superficiality—trying to get away with the least. Half-hearted effort does not give honor to Jehovah. Those kinds of people generally do not do well in life. A good example of his standards of perfection and taste are the specifications for the portable tabernacle Moses was to assemble for him in the desert and the manner in which Jehovah had to be served and worshiped in that tabernacle. He wants a good environment for all, so he hates super riches and suppression. He allows these things as a means to punish and reward. He would rather have you dedicate everything to him and to those who are your servants and he will keep his wrath away from humanity. I believe he likes the idea of communism practiced in an equal sharing manner.

He wants all your dedication in your best talent. Present-day schooling does not often allow a child to find its niche or to be encouraged to develop that niche through dedicated study and best effort. The reason is in the environment of school. Wild, unchanneled peer pressure dictates that a child must not stand out at the peril of being mocked. A few popular adolescent scoundrels generally set the standards of misconduct for the rest. The standard of conduct in public school is inverted by allowing children to set the standard of conduct. Children must be under discipline and under guidance of mature people, not immature people as what we generally see. Most people do not mature over the mental age of a ten year old. There is thus something wrong with the way we train and educate our youth.

Education in Honor of Jehovah

Modern schools are universes of activity and not of study and artistry. Schools should never be under the control of government; and in size classes and schools are way out of proportion for their purpose. Present schools keep the herd engaged. They do not concentrate on developing the pupils' talents.

The first three years of schooling should be devoted to general education in addition to a large selection of art and craft study.

During these three years the school must try to determine the child's main interest—scholastic, technical, trade or art, and then the child should be transferred to a school that gives in-depth attention to that range of skills and talents. Draw a child from the mass and into a niche that he likes and he will do fine, especially if the classes are small and the teachers do not play favorites. Sports in schools are hyped up and overdone. If a child is good in sports, it should be transferred to a school developing that sort of skill. Allow the rest of the children to enjoy sports without having to be the best, because sport is not their niche. The way it is today, it ruins the enjoyment of sport in most children.

No child should be idolized, especially not by adults. It ruins the child's interpersonal development—and an adult should not allow people to idolize him. The popular kid in school has a personality problem and will bring that problem into adulthood. Who would want to be a friend or spouse to such a person. We should try not to compete with the glory of god, for what you excel at is a gift from him. The proper attitude should be satisfaction, and thankfulness. Humility, also, is rewarded. Words cannot express humility; it is a character trait—a state of mind, a state of being and of accepting others without prejudice. God and people will like you a lot better if you do not seek the limelight socially. In these respects, the Muslims have a much better understanding of rearing children, except for the treatment of girls and women.

You cannot say that you do not believe in god; having been born is proof that there is a god. You would not have materialized if you did not believe in him. He would not have granted you another life. Being alive in the world is an expression of your faith in god. If you believe in society, you believe in god. If you believe in the socialist democracy, you believe in god. So, dedicate yourself to god. We must train our children to grow up and mature in the raiment of god, the world and society. We have no other choice. Jesus said through the parable of the dishonest manager that we must be like that manager. If we cannot always please our worldly boss, always be sure to be on good terms with god, and you will never be without a friend. This world will always have its poor.

Modern schooling seems to ensure that the bulk of students become general workers. The world needs masses of basic-skill workers. Yet, even if you are basic skill worker, your best effort will result in good workmanship. Workmanship is the incorporator of almost all things of art—the jewels that brighten the raiment of god.

Excellent ideas lying dormant are potentials denied. Banks are the judges that evaluate ideas for commercial potential, not necessarily for the sake of beauty. Artists often spend the lion part of their time in supporting themselves and in finding a suitable patron, and not in expressing the art. We put the emphasis on money while it should be on god, the universe. All humanity is part of god.

Jehovah Loves Sacrifice

Art, expertly expressed, make the crown jewel 'earth' the more magnificent. He considers it nothing if you did not dedicate your efforts and wealth to him. You die and he will inherit your works, you cannot win, so change your outlook, dedicate your works to him and you will fare better. All our sustained and dedicated efforts are allegiance to his Majesty, god. In being creative and in executing your plans in the physical realm you help him create and beautify his edifice, the universe. In return, he will give us the formulae to create new materials and tools needed to express the art forms. Modern utilities are good pieces of art as long as we thank god for having them.

You are helping to make this planet the crown jewel of his divinity. Right now, I am listening to a collection of arias from operas. The music is superb and the voices magnificent. They are part of the raiment of god; and they are just expressions and abilities of dream projections of souls lying in a state of coma in true reality. Souls dedicate their talent to the deity and thus they support him in fashioning his raiment, the universe. If we give our best in what we are good at; we show him that we admire and appreciate his creation. No matter what, he inherits your works and efforts; and allows it to slowly crumple to dust so that others may create new art in its place.

Creature Experience Is a Measure of Jehovah's Acceptance of Them

The experiences of creatures in the universe are graded from exhilaration and exultation to the deepest emotions of hopelessness and despair. This was done by the daemons to gain and maintain control over us, creatures. He is thus a control freak. Control is the opposite of liberty. To be under control means to be subject to the will of another. Liberty means that, in your capacity of being mature and responsible to your self and others, you can do any thing you want without damaging others, and without trying to gain or having control over the life and actions of others. If you dedicate yourself to Jehovah you take yourself out of the loop of competition with him as god. For women this definitely means to have children. Without children there is no inhabited world, and without human habitation there can be no adoration of Jehovah.

Jehovah's Relationship with the Hebrews

The kingdom of physical environment is the kingdom of subjection and slavery. Our bodies are designed to be fragile, subject to diseases and accident, hunger and deprivation of all kinds, and then you die. It was done on purpose to force us to his will. From the interactions between Jehovah and Abraham and his descendants, one can easily pick up the control mechanisms used by Jehovah to gain and keep control over the Israelites. Abraham's and the Israelites' original responses were rational because they knew that they were up against a being of higher standing than royalty, a deity. He was the highest, and one cannot, without punishment, turn one's back on deity and royalty. When they were made aware of him they devoted themselves to him.

The way they handled their subsequent relationship with Jehovah shows that they were insane. They knew the power and status Jehovah had over them and they deliberately exposed themselves to his wrath. Since Jehovah as a spiritual being is insane, he will retaliate, and he did.

They wondered what kind of relationship they really had with him, because they could not see this god. He was not hugging them and visiting them in a splendid carriage to show that he cared just a little bit. Jehovah set the universe up in a two-level structure, the spiritual structure underlying the physical environment: one level for spiritual beings and a projected physical universe as a game board for the spiritual beings. Jehovah is head of the invisible level. He will not show himself in the physical, but he has full control over the display of the projections—us.

Reality, a One-Stratum Realm

The kingdom of Jesus' father, the other kingdom, is a one level structure. Everything is done in the open. There are no secrets or hidden government. Jesus' prayer, as related to us in John 17, gives us proof that there is only one stratum. In that reality, what we see is what is there, truly. No one can pull a fast one on someone else. When we go to god our true father, we will be in another reality than paradise. In paradise, a creature such as the serpent [Jehovah] could pull a fast one on us, even though god warned us about him. In the true kingdom, this cannot happen. When you get in contact with an item, you know everything about it. In that kingdom, a being can be in liberty—that means being god. The spirit and the body are one, both open to view.

Below follows real evil that humans perpetrate on humans; as above so below.

Operation and Effect of Secret Societies

A set of very depraved human beings are playing the identical tricks on us that the spiritual hierarchy has played. These characters have created another physical, secret structure, by which these characters can control us as effectively as the spiritual structure does. A second secret layer, a spirit-like structure has formed above that of the Negative spiritual structure. This structure is prophesized to come as the beast in both the Old Testament and in the book of Revelation of the New Testament. I believe it was shown as having a little horn among its many horns, which grew much bigger than the others, from which grew another horn etc. The first Horn represents the conspirators, secret society, of which the CFR [Committee for Foreign Relations] is a sub-committee and the International Jewish Rabbinical Congress has a management position. Such institutions as the United Nations, the Federal Reserve System and the International Monetary Fund are its enforcement and control organizations. We are all well under the control of these organizations. Now you can see that the Social Security number is your inventory tag and that it is referred to in Revelation as proof that you are a domestic animal in the beast's herd. It all does not matter anymore. You can read in Revelation what will happen to the bunch and what Jesus and his father will eventually do. It is just sad that we humans were not wise enough to see what was happening through the ages.

Secret societies and such are sustained through nothingness and a conspiracy that fills that void with plans they do not want others to know about because the plans involve the exploitation of others. These societies have much power because they rely on the cycle of death and reincarnation. The old generation of people preyed upon, that would learn to know too much, dies off, and their souls come back as ignorant babes. Humanity must start anew every sixty years or so while the physical environment continues. The character of a secret conspiracy does not change but the members change every 40 years or so. It is the timelessness of such a conspiracy that identifies it as a kind of spirit, or spirit-supported plan. We, as souls, are all guilty. We cannot point the finger at a couple of creatures and say they are the ones. No. We all, as souls, played our parts in the beast. We laid the groundwork for those who are now at the top.

I hope you can now see why the idea of nothingness and the formation of corporations [fictions] are so evil. Corporations and secret societies can outlive a hundred generations, while the execution of their plans for the society at large is brought forward in time. I believe that the present members of the conspiracy were in some quandary of how to reveal this surfacing structure, One World Order. They can only reveal the edifice when it is finished. It must be a reality before it can be exposed, because if it is not finished yet we can prevent it from happening.

President Bush Sr.'s clumsy try at making the One World Order conspiracy an accepted institution during the Desert Storm campaign was not accepted by anyone, not even to those in charge. It just did not fly, just as the first try for a League of Nations failed. They had to start another, more terrible, war to get that accomplished in the organization of the United Nations. The introduction of the One World Order is necessary because the structure is complete. [I fear, though, that when nothingness" has been properly expressed materially its annihilation is close by. The reason is that time in it must come to a stop]. It appears to be another tower of Babel, and Jehovah will not stand for it unless it is fully dedicated to him which it is not. The only thing not done yet is the inclusion of the Arab countries as obedient lapdogs. I wonder if their god Allah can make them escape capture and turn the whole edifice upside down. Fiction in completion is like plastic. Over time plastic continues to polymerize and become more brittle, until it simply falls into pieces. Fiction in completion must fall into dust.

Punishment without a Pronounced Sentence Does Not Make Sense

Obviously, I was trained by the negative spiritual realm to understand and reveal this structure of evil to you. You must understand why this punishment will come and why you are guilty of receiving the punishment that will be dealt to the world from negative spirit, where human beings have no control. Punishment, without knowing why one is punished, does not make sense to the spiritual hierarchy. This book thus is something like a court of sentencing. You are informed of what you are guilty of and then punishment will be pronounced and accorded. The punishment is written in Revelation. It comes from Jehovah, not from true spirit. You can see that the One World Order is a plan of this character Mammon Jesus talked about. He must be sitting on the other side of the table from Jehovah as they are playing this game. In the end, Mammon does not dare win from Jehovah or his name will be mud—royalty must be assuaged. As below, so above

Jehovah, of course knew all this was coming; that is why he placed it in the book of Revelation of the Bible. He set it all up in this manner. The universe is his game board and he plays the game.

It is obvious that the people in the One World Order conspiracy have obtained some help and consent from the spiritual hierarchy to perpetrate this depraved plan on their fellowmen. The conspirators [another hidden hierarchy of *physical* spirits—world bankers and top politicians] have become another god-hierarchy. They act through a specially established propaganda-news department based on cutting-edge science and technology. This organization prepares the news releases that will cause the American human herd to act exactly according to the dictates imbedded in the news messages. Unless people change, they as enthusiastic government supporters, will always obey the propaganda commands. The entire population of the United States has been yoked together like a huge ox-team to do the exact bidding of the conspirators. We have become animals of burden to catch and domesticate, first ourselves, secondly the entire world population and then to expand the conquest into space.

Creatures and Fictional Institutions Used as a Means of Punishment and Enslavers of Humanity

I can show you how animals are used in this exact manner. Well-trained cow ponies are used to catch an entire herd of wild and free-roaming mustangs. To do so, they first build a temporary corral in which to steer the captured herd. Then the *cowponies* are used to keep the wild herd together, aided by the loud sounds of guns and lots of shouting. Slowly the cowpokes guide the herd in the direction of the corral. Finally, the herd is funneled through the gate of the corral and when they are in, it is closed. The trained ponies used are brought back to stable, their doors are closed and they are fed some hay and grain so they can be used to catch another herd tomorrow. Now just substitute humans for horses and you see what you are. The owner of the operation can do with the ponies as he pleases. The United States has caught hundred thousands of free-roaming mustang horses and slaughtered them to clear the land. Your owners have done the same with your ancestors and yourself in the last 175 years or so. They made your ancestors fight an illegal civil war, a real war on make-believe premises. This original herding operation locked all Americans into one huge corral. Then the first and second world wars were fought to do the same with all Europe. See, how all the European nations are settling in nicely into their new corral, the European Economic Community.

In the last 100 years, the US government bridled you and your children into the ox team to fight dozens of wars around the globe to gain control of herds of people still roaming free in the world. After Europe, more wars were fought in Asia, the American continent, and now in Minor Asia and Africa. The Arab nations do not want to be corralled into a One World Order. These people are now made to look like terrorist-supporting nations and we all do our level best to corral them for our bosses; but we *are* working for the terrorists. You must turn all the propaganda around to see the truth. We are the terrorists.

The real terrorist is the US government. The US government is the ranch house of the world. Remember the bad guy in all those western movies in which this bad guy hires a bunch of gunslingers, and proceeds to usurp the lands of his neighbors through devious means, and then makes them laborers on his expanded ranch. You could see it happen in western movies, yet you do not see it happening to our own country.

Can you see that you are evil, for allowing yourself and your children to be used like that? It is as Jesus said, 'You have sinned, but it would be better for those who made you sin to tie a mill stone around their necks and to drown themselves.' These conspirators, united in secret against all humankind, have used spiritual tools and techniques to enslave and exploit you so they could exploit all the people of the world and conquer space. Soon some one in their group will step forward to proclaim that he is emperor and god of the world. We will then have a physical god. We will not be able to resist him because he has wired us all into a computer network that he can control like a computer scientist. No one will be able to resist and speak against the propaganda reality because everyone in the brainwashed mass of people will enforce public opinion that will crush any dissident or group of dissidents back into the background.

Human conspirators have wired us, people, into a computer system by which they can accomplish anything they want, such as making a One World Order and a solar system government, later on a galactic empire if such things are even realistic.

Their plan was to use the United States as their initial base of operations because it was a new nation based on untried principles of liberty. The American people did not guard their newly won freedom from the cunning conspirators because they had and have a fairy-like belief in a constitution by which government was to operate and by which constitution conspiring enemies slowly herded us into a group of captured animals. Once they had us well trained, they had to increase the strength of the armed forces, and the best way to accomplish this is to create enemies to fight. Government created them through propaganda or through secret conspiracies with the governments of other nations who are willing, for a price, to become enemies. The top authorities of Germany prior to the Second World War, or Austria in the First World War, agreed to start wars because they were part of the conspiracy. They were told to fight terrible, but losing wars. War allows government to spend enormous amounts of money on weapons research. The atom bomb was funded in this manner and all the A-bomb technology was quickly transferred to the USSR through channels of diplomatic immunity as soon as it became available. Wars have given this monster, the US government all the enforcement tools, technology, and a seamless legal net, to enforce public peace, according to the laws of a One World Order.

Their system was developed and put into operation as I described it in Book I. Slowly; through the propaganda for war they have garnered complete control over the USA and the people. They have reduced us to the status of serfs in our own country. Your politicians are your worst enemies because they follow a secret agenda in opposition to the trust of the people who voted them into office. The whole voting process is now a propaganda ploy, just as the Constitution is a propaganda ploy—to keep the herd quiet, to make them believe things that are utterly false to be true, and to keep these false beliefs solidly wired in the brains of the masses!! *Remember, Jesus claims that life is death and death is life.* This is another inversion that propaganda has wrought. Consider the millions of war-horses throughout history; they fought and died, but never for their own cause. Soldiers throughout the ages have died in wars but never for their own cause either. Fight this time for the people and yourself. If you die and are reincarnated you will be back in a much better world and universe, or you might wake up spiritually before you die and thereafter you are out of this universe forever.

Revealed Evil Can Be Made to Lose Its Power

I threw a monkey wrench into Jehovah's secret hierarchy of spirit and another monkey wrench into the secret hierarchy of the One World Order. Now that these two are exposed, we must consider what to do with the wealth of information and weapons at our disposal. The One World Order is just kid's stuff. It could be used for worldly 'good' for souls that prefer this negative realm of darkness. The One World Order can be rearranged to make it an asset for humanity in the future. All that needs to be done is pour out the present content and set new goals and plans of execution so that this power can be controlled for the good of everybody and not just for the present owners.

People must then safeguard the institution so closely that no criminals can get a hold of it again.

A Possible Means of How to Reverse Sentence

Awakened souls can do the same with the universe. We can pour out the previous intent and purpose of the universe in negative spirit and refill it with the reality of truth and we can deliver this universe as present to our father in truth—a nice present for him. We can ask Jehovah to head this newly organized universe, and if he agrees he can be the master sergeant to present the new graduates to the father in truth.

I wrote this book as science fiction; but the book strives to instill us all with a deep sense of responsibility. You take responsibility for what you want to make your own and what you want to discard; but be assured, whether you believe this account is true or false, it can easily be accomplished, and completely in secret and it can be revealed completely in the open. I am teaching everyone responsibility and respect for other creatures' liberty, values, and dignity. When you do not know all the details and information about a situation or plan of action your support to the plan can cause millions of people to be murdered; as happened in the takeover and establishment of the USSR, the civil war, both world wars, and in all the other wars wherein you either participated or to which you gave your consent. Presently you are supporting a government that was responsible for deliberately destroying the World Trade Center in order to corral the Islamic nations into the One World Order. It can all be considered as science fiction, but I have a completely worked out scenario how these towers were brought down. Initially it was hoped that the planes would bring down the buildings, but when that failed the conspirators used their back-up scenario—to demolish them. Their destruction was part of a bigger plan. Many people lost their lives in this holocaust [*holocaust* = human sacrifice made to gods to obtain a goal].

Holocausts

The other holocaust in Germany was a theatrical propaganda production to steer public opinion in a direction for specific actions planned for ten to a hundred years in the future. The creation of the colony of Israel was one object to be accomplished by this deceit. Israel is the focal point of all the unrest in the Middle East that is now exploited by the United States to help conquer all these 'terrorist' Arab nations. The US government is committed to support the presence of this Jewish colony in the Middle East through the conspiracy. I am convinced the US government gave whatever technology Israel needed to produce its own A- and H- bombs. Every American is guilty by association with and in support of all these heinous crimes.

When I first heard of the holocaust in Germany *1 million* people were murdered in it. Then this number magically increased to *6 million* when the idea was accepted to have really happened. In the year, 2006, I watched a program on a history channel about the Sahara Desert. One segment was about a very prosperous Phoenician city, Carthage, on the West African side of the Mediterranean Sea that had angered the Romans. The Romans besieged it for three years, entered it, and killed every human being in the city after which they leveled it to the ground. The commentator said that this was the greatest number of people [150,000] deliberately murdered in history, except for the holocaust which murdered *12 Million* people. Man, the dead do multiply fast! We had better watch out for the dead before they take over the entire planet.

I know of Pre-Christ Roman battles wherein 4 million people belonging to a wide number of Germanic tribes that were on a migration track died. One group came along the Mediterranean side of France into Italy, and the other group came in about a year later through a pass in the Alps from Switzerland to northern Italy. The significant thing of these victories was that the Roman army was only about a hundred thousand strong and the soldiers were common people, not the free nobility as was the tradition in Rome at that time. The general in command of both battles had taken the best strategic positions well in advance of the approaching hordes. These were easy to pick because both tracks followed a pass through the mountains.

This shows what advantage an organized army has over mere numbers on the opposite side. Of course, many of the dead were women and children. I believe that these were the greatest numbers of people murdered at one time. Romans were extremely tough individuals. So, here the commentator was wrong as well. America is now in Rome's position. The US government is more cruel and tougher than the Romans ever were. It is only that you are not made to believe so. People actually believe the US government to be the most benevolent government that has ever existed!

The Method to Undo Government's Brainwashing Schemes

You see, you are made to believe the exact opposite of what the real facts are. That is because you believe unverified information. If you turn around whatever upsetting news they feed you through the media, you have undone their mighty secret weapon—propaganda! Jehovah can be made to be powerless also, by the exact same method. Whatever you see, experience or feel, negate the observation and reverse what you believe. The universe makes you believe a lie; it is virtual reality. It is all mere bullying—they scare you into giving them your allegiance and support, and without a doubt they will use your allegiance against you and your kin. If you give them support you become as guilty of crime as they are—the perfect setting of a lynching party where innocent people are strung up, except in modern times you are strung up yourself because as a brainwashed person you always work against your best interest. That is the purpose of having you brainwashed.

Evil is so bad, that you must be utterly drenched in it to understand the full meaning of it and begin to exist in it in utter despair. It can multiply from spirit into the physical realms such as the One World Order has done. We must understand the concept of evil from every perspective and from every atom of our awareness. This is the only manner in which it can be fully understood. Thus every cell [Human beings] in Adam and Woman's persons are individually immersed in all the possibilities of evil and must become so disgusted with it that they will never, ever partake of it again, if they can ever escape. There will be those who will like this realm and are left here and those who got the message will be extracted to Reality, to be formed into a living temple.

Jehovah, a Drill Sergeant?

This negative realm of spirit may be like the movie 'An Officer and a Gentleman'. Jehovah is the drill sergeant in charge of souls as cadets. The drill sergeant in the movie made the kid's life a misery till he begged for forgiveness, and in the end the officer became a worthy member of the navy as a naval aviator, and the sergeant was saluted and thanked for a job well done. The universe, also, may be a cadet training course.

One cannot be free and enjoy liberty in reality if evil is not completely understood. The universe will be rolled up, but only after those who want to leave, have exited from it. Whatever remains in the universe, are just souls who for whatever reason do not want to quit the play, and are thus not worthy to reenter positive spirit. Since they exist in fiction, they disappear with the fiction when the show is over.

I believe that the god, Good, has left enough opportunities for escape through the escape hatch created by Jesus' inner message. Therefore, I do believe that Jesus' spirit, in those three days of death, was on a mission throughout intergalactic space to inform universal soul life and matter dispersed therein of the opportunity to leave. He collected a bunch that would go home with him. Jerusalem experienced a sample of the dead rising when Christ died on the cross; many graves were opened and the dead were walking aimlessly around until Christ was ready to go. When he ascended, he must have had many of the dead with him that did not want to continue here in the universe. The bodies of these souls vanished from existence because they were just projections of soul that awakened in spirit. This universe may begin to experience the conclusion of this spiritual play.

Take for instance *Mama Mia* that played in London. The group performed for five years. It was a fixture in London. It closed up by the end of 2006. If you were to go back to the site, you will find nothing back that had any connection with the play. Another play is in rehearsing to open soon. The setting for the play Mama Mia vanished from the universe. You cannot find it back. Whatever was left in the building after it closed was gathered and discarded. Maybe, the corporation was rolled up too—everything vanished.

Paradise Is a University Campus

I now understand that paradise is a school for many sets of Adam and Woman. They were to attend school and learn. All the trees are classrooms. When they had successfully attended all the classes the one class they were advised not to attend intrigued them. However, when one takes this class, one becomes a post-graduate student. Most graduates may leave paradise through the Tree of Life into the house of their father, the son. This is thus the first dividing of sheep and goats. The sheep go to their father, the son's house; the goats disappear through coma-death into a computer display of negative spirit, where they might learn all there is to know about evil and good. Graduates from this course will leave this realm of *'evil disguised as good'*, into true good, the house of all truth. They become sons of the true father. Paradise and the universe can thus be considered places of gestation before birth into positive spiritual reality. Those that are not redeemed die as the spiritual placenta in connection with the birth of the new son of god.

Two-Tier Setup of the Universe

I trust Jehovah enough, as a being created by the son in the father, that he is the sergeant of the son in teaching us the depth of Evil. It explains the two-tier setup of the universe, a visible one for us to experience things in and a hidden one by which Jehovah can create the settings and scenarios of evil, intrigue, conspiracies and such. If we would be in the know of these things while we are playing we would never understand the depth of evil. It has to come to us secretively and seemingly naturally. It must overwhelm us; we must experiment with it, in order to experience all the shades and total depth of Evil.

Two Kinds of Gods

Jesus stated that our bodies are like rags in spirit. Obviously, there are two kinds of spirit. One kind of spirit made us in Jehovah's image and the other kind of spirit says that these bodies in Jehovah's likeliness are only rags. It is a person's duty to select the god he wants to support—the god of fictions or the god of reality, except that souls consider reality to be fiction and the fiction of the universe is taken as reality. Such inversion is the typical product of a successful propaganda campaign.

In order to choose wisely we must have a good understanding of these two spirits, yet as normal humans we have no inkling that there are two kinds of major spirit. It is through the teaching of Jesus that the second kind of spirit is made known to us, with Jesus himself as the mediator between the two; hence positive spirit of the true father, neutral spirit (of the mediator) in Jesus and the negative spirit of Jehovah. It is also Jesus who made us aware that the god we considered to be good is actually the evil one; and the by him newly introduced god to be the true good god.

Outward Glitter or Inward Worth

Now you must decide if you want to live for outward effect or for inward worth? Outward effect is glitter and dedicated to seek someone else's approval, god and human. It is a life of frustration and defeat; reward comes from receiving someone else's approval. It is fiction because you never have complete control over another being. It is fiction because it is not in you. How can you be real, if you are only able to find your self in the approval of others?

Inward worth leads you to know your own true spirit. Inward worth makes you realize who you are. You will find also the Good Spirit and the true godhood because you will find yourself in reality. Reality is the truth in god.

What the human race as a whole can do in ability of effect, is to work for Jehovah. He has the ability to give to us, outwardly. He is a righteous god and rewards dedication to physical, outward existence in the universe. Composers such as Beethoven, Mozart, Andrew Lloyd Webber, great musicians, and all others, who do, or have done great works such as authors, movie directors, architects, designers, and what have you, give honor to god. They have done what Jehovah asks of humans, and he returns as favor and blessing what they ask for as manifested in their efforts. Remember, Jesus said, ask and you shall receive. Seek and you shall find. This applies in the universe as it does out of it, in reality. We can be enlightened into the truth of reality or we can please Jehovah by helping him fashion this earth to be his shining jewel.

Jesus as Lord of Both Outward Glitter and Inward Worth

> By giving credence to Jesus, we give credit to two realms of being. Jesus' person alone can do that. His physical person is a credit to the universe, outwardly, and his positive spirit is credit to reality, inwardly.

Jesus is the only entity that has ever been a part of the universe and also is a permanent and conscious part in reality. Any other person, who becomes conscious in reality, will vanish from this universe. The reason for the difference is that Jesus was a conscious member in the realm of fiction, while the rest of us are unconscious.

Jehovah, Lord over Physical Reality

Jehovah cares for us in that we can adore him, worship him and ask for favors because, as he basks in his glory as given by us, he can give blessings and favors, which exalt him even more in the eyes of his subjects. In that respect, he is like royalty that always seeks to be honored, admired and exalted. No one can take that from him. He is god of the universe, and no one else. In our physical being, we must adore Jehovah, and Jesus did not contradict this, but Jesus also directed our attention inward by saying such things as "the kingdom of heaven is within." Do not look out there to find it, because it does not exist there.

Ears to Hear and Eyes to See

I will give examples that show that either god has a split personality or that there must be two different gods.

Jehovah says, "Do not eat unclean food." Jesus in Mark 7:15 says "There is nothing from without a man, which, entering into him can defile him: but the things which come out of him, those are what defile the man." Then Jesus said a confounding thing: "If a man has ears to hear, let him hear." Later on, he clarified what he said. Food follows the digestive track and is expelled leaving no spiritual uncleanness, but from the heart flow forth evil thoughts, adulteries, fornications, murders, theft, etc. What comes from his heart out of him into the world defiles the man. Jesus referred to the decisions of soul. He is clean or dirty according to the character of the soul that expresses itself through actions in the outer world. What Jehovah commands is opposite of what Jesus taught! *Jehovah makes you look to outward things to be clean. The true god wants you to look inward and see what defiles or cleanses a person. So there must be two kinds of gods.*

The outward man is evil because his innermost being, his heart [soul], is corrupt. Yet, Jesus also states that the kingdom of god is within the heart. Something very wrong took place inside the heart of men. Soul believed a lie about its native environment. That is why Jesus said as quoted in verse 16 above about having ears to hear and so on. He tells us that not all people defile themselves with their actions. There are those who are more sincere and can receive Jesus' message as intended; they are humble and non-possessive. Others receive the message from a consciousness that is synchronized [indoctrinated from sources without] by the traditions of man, based on outward experience. The common person does not think his own thoughts but those that have been implanted by authority, which authorities Jesus calls hypocrites [the learned, the lawyers, Pharisees, priests, and the scribes; those who have sworn allegiance to the prevailing propaganda system and also the universe]. The ones with ears to hear have propaganda filters placed between their senses, brain and the heart. They refuse to be mentally herded around by authority. Their hearts are open to teaching coming from a different set of drummers. **Jesus advised that we should steer away from gossip and news of any kind; these twist the mind to accuse and murder the innocent and to praise and elevate the deceivers.** One must refrain from bringing the outside world into one's heart, because all there is out there are the clever lies of propaganda. If our hearts are empty of things universal [things that defile the soul] the Good Spirit can enter and bring us truth. Does that make sense?

Chapter 2

The Same Scenario One More Time

All Truth

Jesus said in John 16: 13 When the spirit of truth has come [into the heart] he will erase all spiritual corruption settled there that causes evil to proceed from your being, by revealing *all truth* to you. In other words, if you are grounded in reality, all the lies of the fiction will quit their hold on you, because you then know truth.

Two Kinds of Outpouring of Spirit

Some forty days after Jesus' ascension the holy spirit was poured out on the apostles in great splendor of flames over the heads of the apostles and by them being able to speak in foreign tongues. This outpouring of the holy spirit was definitely coming from Jehovah because it was grounded in outward display. It was a trick to confuse the apostles and all who were converted by them to seek the outward approval of negative spirit rather than focus on the inward spirit of true reality. Extremely cleverly done! But then, God in paradise said that this serpent was one hell of a wily character.

We see the physical environment because we believe in outward things, not the things that are true in us. Our outward orientation, the glory of Jehovah, has corrupted the truth that is in us. Inside of us is another huge environment, reality. This reality is extant everywhere, but it cannot be seen by the outward looking senses we have—senses designed to place us in this physical universe. By ignoring the senses, we can dive deep into our consciousness where we will meet the two gods. The one, the holy spirit, will advertise the glory of the universe and all its possibilities. The other is the Good Spirit, and he will lead you to **all truth** if you allow him into your heart. The reason Jesus said that corruption, fornication and such proceed from your being is because this holy spirit [the spirit of deceit] is comfortably settled in an easy chair in your heart. You listen to him for all things. He talks universe to you. He is like a continuous TV program advising you how to be outwardly, in relations and in communion with the outward world. He keeps you so busily oriented in worldly things that you do not have time to listen to the demure knock on the other door to your heart. Jehovah nailed that door shut. You probably do not even know there is a door there. That door leads into another reality, a reality Jehovah does not want you to know about because he is banned from it and he does not want you to be there either.

However, if you have "ears to hear and eyes to see", you will notice that knock, and when you start to remove the nails, the door will open and you are in communion with the Comforter, the Good Spirit in Jesus himself. What he could not teach you when in the flesh; he can teach you now in his spirit. The reason for that is that Jesus was a double agent. It was the only manner to contact us. We can only be aware of physical entities, so he had to appear in a body outwardly, so he could later reach you inwardly.

He had to ask permission from Jehovah to do so because physical nature is Jehovah's jurisdiction. Jehovah gave him permission all right, as long as he came as the long foretold and prophesized Messiah. Coming in that role, Jehovah thought, would defeat the purpose for which he came into the world. Also, while in the world, Jehovah had all the opportunity to seduce Jesus to accept the physical environment. Satan did his utmost best to seduce Jesus while he was fasting and suffering in the desert for forty days and during the rest of his days on earth, but Jesus rebuked him by Jehovah's own rules and laws. The bright thing for us though was that he did not succumb to physical reality, and that he never committed a sin, and thus could not die. One of Jehovah's laws says that if one commits only one sin one must die. The people killed Jesus anyway. Jesus and Jehovah had another conference on that issue. Jesus insisted that he receive all souls for his death. Jehovah agreed because he thought that he could kill Jesus in such a grueling way that Jesus would surrender or commit a sin.

Through his death, Jesus was able to buy all those who believed in his power of redemption and, thus, has set those souls free from Jehovah's law. The souls did not belong to Jehovah any more. Jesus rose in 3 days, and he was physically and spiritually conscious in the physical body again. Jesus, actually can appear on earth any day he wants, but then he would glorify the universe.

He wants to discredit the universe, so he opted to come in spirit, and because he revealed the existence of truth, and introduced us to the Comforter in the Good Spirit, we are now able to commune in the heart, utterly beyond the confines of the negative spiritual realm, and lead us into truth. When we commune with the Good Spirit, we are not longer in a coma. Communion must take place in reality, so it is proof that we are awakening.

The Extreme Difficulty of Finding Reality

The Comforter leads because truth is an environment that is foreign to us. He leads the way to it. Truth has no physical outward appearance because that would confuse us to look for outward things and that would weave us again into physical reality, rather than the real environment in truth. One cannot find the kingdom of truth through the senses or through mind-games.

Therefore, a true believer of Jesus' inner message will not die spiritually; bodily maybe. We must actually train ourselves to disbelieve our senses. See how wickedly clever this Jehovah is? Jesus' body was confirmation of our belief that the universe exists. He perpetrated a spiritual error, but it was the only manner he could get in contact with us. The error was negated because his purpose was accomplished.

Jesus had to come into the environment that was familiar to the dreaming comatose souls. The souls actually had a common script given to them by Jehovah, and they followed that script in their dreams. Jesus followed them there in a dream body assigned to him by Jehovah. Through much difficulty and confusion, he brought the true message and established a spiritual link to reality with their outwardly projected human forms in a manner that their souls [the inward source of the outward appearance] *with ears to hear and eyes to see* could understand and follow. He thus formed a link in reality via the dream state that could not be established directly from reality to the comatose souls lying there. He, in person, was the entity that caused soul to open the door out of the dungeon and into reality. Why? It is because through Jesus' mission, souls again have ears to hear the knock of true spirit.

Jehovah Inspires Us through Outward Glitter and Might

Jehovah is a magnificent god, but he is naked. He has no eternal body in reality. In that manner, he is like us, for he prefers fiction to truth. Remember the fable of the emperor who had no clothes. His clothes were fiction; he believed he wore clothes because the propaganda he received convinced him he wore the best clothes that man could make. A kid with his head screwed on right shouted, "He has no clothes!" The propaganda image in his head faded, and the emperor saw that he was naked. Truth invaded the lie he believed; and he became aware of the real situation. Jehovah designed his own raiment, the physical universe. It is how he dresses up. It is all the raiment he has because his lying made him stand naked in true reality also. This raiment of his is also make believe. Once you know the truth you can see him standing utterly naked too.

Creation the Positive, and the Negative Way (see also figure 15, page 502)

Jehovah did not originally believe a lie, he invented it. He did believe in the power of the lie. He must have done so through a combination of vanity and ingenuity. In a realm of reality where all things are already expressed, he invented a new thing—*nothingness*. He realized that the true father had to start with nothingness also. The difference is that the father started with nothingness and created reality. Jehovah was in reality and discovered that he could poke a hole in it by inventing and incorporating 'nothingness' in an already existing reality and filling it with a fiction contrary to the reality it is based on. All physical creatures can do is deal with the form of reality that they exist in, the universe. They can poke holes in physical reality that they can fill with more fiction, either in alignment with that reality; or through conspiracy in contradiction with that reality. This is expected of them by Jehovah. He says 'as above so below'. Do as I do. He knows that if you do, you will never find your true self for your attention is outward and not inward. Outwardly you can only find physical reality, inwardly you must find yourself, as soul, your connection with reality.

The universe is there because souls have placed their collective imagination in the void and created the universe according to Jehovah's compositions, which only exists because souls have this universe in their collective mind and have projected it out into the void and voila, the make-believe universe.

> **Since souls created the universe, it is very dear to them. It is this dearness with which Jesus wants us to buy the true pearl hidden in the field. We must forsake physical reality in favor of true reality.**

The Universe is the Major Outward Propaganda System

The universe is also a propaganda system because it deludes us into believing that it exists as the only external entity and us, as creatures, in it. Our role as spiritual workers in it takes all our attention. We have no time or thought to realize there is true reality also. This is, again, due to the cleverness of Jehovah, who induced us to believe in a universe that he imagined; he transferred the idea to us, and we use our spiritual energy to erect this universe and keep it suspended in Jehovah's honor, and we love it.

One must worship the universe. There is no other way out. By just being alive in it, you give credence to it; you worship it because you deliberately chose to be in it as your idea of reality. All Jehovah asks of you is that you go along with the entire scenario and see him as ultimate god and provider. Does he not give you the opportunity to feed yourself, clothe yourself and give you your being, movements and abilities in him?

He will like you and bless you if you will just worship him, the god of the universe. This is, exactly, what he asked of Jesus, when he tempted Jesus in the desert. He tempted Jesus in the desert because Jesus was the only person who came in the universe as a stranger, and Jehovah very much wanted to trap him here forever also. Jesus was the only door remaining open to souls as an escape hatch. Jehovah wanted that hatch closed and sealed. If Jesus' spirit could be trapped as our souls' spirits were trapped here, Jehovah would have usurped the position of father of reality.

Jehovah demands that we obey his moral rules and ethical rules. He wants the poor to be taken care of because they are an eyesore in his raiment and because it is a gesture of outward expression. The beggar just might turn his attention inward, because for the beggar there is nothing that will help him. Jehovah wants to prevent that. All the glory for Jehovah is on the outside, the miserable insides are hidden by veneer, skin and flesh and a glorious outward looking environment to be in.

Our very intricate worldly infra-structure of corporate organization is a gift from Jehovah. It is a copy of the hierarchy of daemons in negative spirit. The world has become a most magnificent jewel in his crown. But the set-back for humanity is that all this convenience, splendor and inventiveness makes the world so appealing that a person cannot accept that it is all make believe and that soul must awake from the stupor of addiction. Just as a heroin addict cannot have enough hallucinations, so a soul caught in this perfect trap cannot have enough of the dream of the universe. After physical death, a soul will opt for another shot of the lie, and thus another life cycle through reincarnation, just so he does not have to miss the next episode of existence in earth.

Cycles within Cycles

There are other cycles of episodes working in the universe. Besides cycles of reincarnation that work souls down into the realms of animal nature, there are also cycles of roll up and renewal of the universe. Our presence as souls here drains our spiritual energy. While we are dreaming, and receiving cycles of physical life, our corrupted soul-energy is depleted by continuing to suspend this universe.

As soon as your batteries have depleted to a point that the universe must be rolled up you will have lost status in the eyes of Jehovah who then needs to trap another set of entities in paradise. Each time a human dies physically and then reincarnates it coincides with a specific step down in spiritual energy to empower the computer that runs the program 'Universe". Jehovah is not exempt from this process. Jehovah will eventually be a daemon under another great god, who will again be called Jehovah. So one day, Jehovah will be a jealous Satan etc. until this present Jehovah will end up as a scavenger demon possessing some poor human being.

All souls, in the cycles, of universal roll-up-and-re-employment, and of reincarnation, have had their moment of grandeur and approval of Jehovah. Since there are so many souls, just a few in each period of history will have their moment of glory, but Jehovah will shine always because all the grandeur of life is an expression of his creativity. During the period of human reincarnations, all souls will have had a period of eminence and status. It is part of the dream that such shall be the case.

Karma

The only one receiving eternal honor is Jehovah, but he is consumed as well by the energy this dreaming takes from him. This universe is run by the motto, nothing for nothing; tit for tat. "You have to pay for what you have received." The Hindus call a similar process going on lower scale "karma", but in the greater scheme, there is *karma*, utterly deadly spiritual justice. It will undo your soul as a living real entity. The physical material dust left behind is mass in the form of hydrogen I believe; and the soul dust will return to the realm of truth, which realm the soul never had left.

Therefore, in the history of reality there will always be an archangel, who will start "dreaming" and takes over from Jehovah. This must be so because god loves all his creatures and must give them what they desire, but he would love most of all for some dreamers to awaken and be happily home with him again. The parable of the prodigal son is the story of a young man who wants to spend his life in the magnificence of worldly splendor. He wanted the splendor of the world, and would only wise up when he found out that even splendor will not last, for his resources ran out due to mismanagement. This son fell into abject poverty. In the deepest of his despair, he went home to finds his father waiting for him. The father did not scorn him; but gladly accepted him back in the household. This is what is supposed to happen to us souls. Jesus told us this parable to inform us that souls dreaming an existence in a lie deplete their spiritual energy. Jesus wants us to wake up and seek communion with the Comforter and go about life in reality.

Jehovah is in a coma as well. He is a dreamer, because he dreams that he is god over the universe. That is why the true father calls him a snake, an animal. All those caught in the perfect trap and who are not conscious of reality are animals; all of us are. You can see what splendid artisans humans can be in this fictional environment, yet, we are animals. The human body proves it.

Your Time of Reckoning

I must relate these things in a book. You, as captured souls must decide what is more to your liking—fiction or reality. This will be the final parting for us souls. I, too, am separating the goats from the sheep. May the sheep find their pasture, and may the goats join me in true reality. May the rest of the souls be happy in the universe for as long as it can last for them as humans, because most of the dream will turn into a most horrible nightmare; but not until all their chances of return to their true father in reality have been squandered! Therefore, do not despair because the prodigal son was in a most precarious position also, and he made it home. He was lucky to find his way back to his father. He was lucky to remember his father who had a home to which he could return. I urge you not to forget that you have a true father. I urge you not to wait too long because it will be "curtains" for this episode of the universe in not too many life cycles to come, simply because your batteries will be too low to keep the universe suspended. How low can you go and still be able to find the way home? Do not try to find the ultimate limit. Meet up with the Comforter and he will lead you out of the magnificent-looking trap. We, souls, do not have the power to resist the seductions of the universe by ourselves, we need a guide to help and encourage us. When we joined the Serpent, the way out was locked. The universe, after all, is just a program on a computer with your belief system trapped in it as a caricature. The cruelty of it is that it seems so terribly real and worthwhile. It seems so worthwhile exactly because it has our dedicated input attached to it. Between you and yourself, *"Are you willing to give up physical reality for true spiritual reality?"*

My Final Statement

If we need to know the principle of evil completely in order to understand the principle of good in god, completely, then Jehovah is a member of the trinity. Therefore, he is much more than an archangel, because Jehovah understands evil so completely that he must understand good completely. He is a master. Is he the true God in ultimate reality? In that case he knows us completely.

If Jehovah is truly evil he would not have given Moses the insight to the Tree of the Knowledge of Good and Evil, and the commandment of racial purity in Genesis 2 & 3. These are the crucial fact that stitches harmony of understanding into the entire Bible. Without this information physical creature-existence could have never discovered the meaning of the Bible and of the physical environment. Having furnished us with this information makes him Good and not Evil. Without that information mankind and all creature kinds would have been lost forever.

Chapter 3

After Word

Throughout the last decade of the 20th century and in the first decade of the 21st century, I have written very lengthy articles on Christendom and on the American political situation. Much of the contents of this set of Books, "The Truth About Reality", is taken from those articles.

I sent these articles anonymously to about 230 terminals in the world, most of them to ministers having a regular radio or TV schedule, to religious institutions in the USA, to a list of important radio and TV talk show personalities for whom I could obtain a mailing address, and also to many department heads of universities.

In early 1997, I wrote an article describing the universe as being a projected computer display. To me that idea was so new that I thought it would generate some interest, but as far as I know it was never discussed on radio or TV.

Then, in the winter of 1999 we told a friend of this concept of the universe, and he said that a brand new movie had just come out called **The Matrix** related to that subject. He had a copy of the movie and showed it to us. The movie really had no connection with the deep content of my idea of the universe being a spiritual computer display, but it did show remarkable similarity that things were upheld, somehow, by a computer code, to the effect that humans were displayed in this fashion. I am writing this to let you know that my idea was developed long before the movie was released. I have never had a connection with the producers of the movie or anyone else connected to the movie. However, they may have had a connection with someone who received copies of my articles.

Below is an excerpt from the article 'God in Christ or Bust #1' in Italic

By making god a liar Woman and Adam had to presuppose that the liar told the truth, thus the serpent, Jehovah, in the minds of those deluded souls, became the 'true' god. Those who partook in thought of the tree died to the realm of truth because none who believes a lie is worthy of the truth. The tree bore fruit for selfish thought.

*So the true god in Christ became utterly lost to souls and became non-existent to them. In John 17: 3 Jesus calls His father the **true** god, which presupposes that mankind had always held the **false** god, Jehovah, to be that true god. In John 17: 25 Jesus claims that the world has not known this true god, so whoever mankind held as the highest god, which for Israel and Christendom is Jehovah, is an imposter.*

*Physicists have demonstrated that underneath all other forces and elemental particles there exists the interaction between the strong and the weak forces. I say that these forces are the lie and the truth where the truth is of spiritual origin and the lie a dirty play on it. The two combine to create a fiction which we call the universe. The truth is the weak force but it is of such incredible importance that without the truth the strong force, which is the lie, could not exist. Whatever happens in the universe that is evil and underhanded, could not have any existence unless in relation to the truth. This proves the existence of a higher order of reality than what we find in the universe. The truth always has a controlling power over the lie just as the lie has a means of nullifying or altering the reality and intent of the truth. The lie is always secondary, for without the truth the lie is meaningless. Yet, the lie was instituted in order to separate itself [**to become individualized**] from truth. Therefore evil willingly and desperately flees from truth, just as Jesus stated, "The deceit cannot stand the light of truth so it abides in darkness. To insist on individual power, then, is to insist on being in darkness. In love, there is oneness, in law there is individualized greed and vanity, a state of de facto beingness. Lawyers will always make sure that the maximum possible hostility exists between the parties in court. Law is for those who insist on their individuality. It is not part of god in Christ. In law no party knows or understands even the basic concept of love.*

The incredible corrupting influence and power of the lie is that when it is applied to the truth, the truth loses respect and meaning and the meaning of the truth has been altered to mean something else or often the opposite of what the truth actually is. The universe then, is a fiction which can only exist as long as those who believe in it will continue to do so. [The same holds true for the forces that science calls the strong and weak forces.]

The function of propaganda is to interplay these two forces or values so that those in control of the propaganda apparatus will always pull the wool over the faces of all those they want to mislead and confuse in order to harness the power of the individuals in the mass and to exploit the very same masses with their combined confiscated power. Individuals in the mass, who may have the insight and intent to expose and prevent the purpose and goals of propaganda, are stifled or ridiculed by the shear force of public opinion, which is a cowardly way to express personal individuality of those bound in a group.

The matter, of which the universe consists, then, is a mixture of truth and lie in many differing proportions, just as the programs in a computer are a mixture of ones and zeroes (two differing states of electrical charge). Matter, then, may be thought of as codes made up of a series of such binary value combinations, and the universe is thus an artificial environment, just as one finds in Nintendo games. Not only have the pawns in the environment control, but the designers and daemons have an interactive power to create settings, situations etc. in which certain groups of pawns find themselves on the game board-universe.

It is conceivable that when Adam and Woman partook of the tree in paradise that caused their fall, they became the archetypes of the white race, and as such became the nucleus, the trunk and root system of the tree of physical species. All their offspring form the branches and leaves in that tree, and in season every leaf comes into existence, is productive, and then dies and falls away from the tree. Every other race and species on earth belongs, each and every one, to its own tree, and each tree grows and decays like any other tree. The substance of the trunk and roots system of this human tree, the gene structure of the race, continues unbroken while the leaves and twigs come and go. Because of spiritual neglect each racial tree degenerates and becomes an ever cruder version of what it has been before. This is how the white race will atrophy into one of the dark-skinned races and how the dark-skinned races, one at the time, will degenerate into the higher forms of pure animal species such as dolphins, chimpanzees, etc. The whole spectrum of biological life then can be seen as flowing forth from generations of original white races of beings that came before the present cycle of Adam and Woman. This can clarify Jesus statements, "This generation [race of people] shall not pass, till these things be fulfilled" [Mt 24: 34].

In all my following articles I often referred to this idea of the universe being a computer display and even gave a very detailed description of how this computer program works.

In the article, '**God Exists**', for example, I wrote the following paragraph:

Pagan man wouldn't know what to do with energy that isn't convertible into heat. Spirit is energy, the use of which completely escapes rational man, because he doesn't know how to convert it into heat. Spirit is useful to those who believe in it through their faith in the triune god. God, the father, is the will, who approves and gives authority for the execution of plans. Jesus, the son, designs and creates under him. "The father has combined all three powers in Jesus, for "the father has given all power and authority to me". ***Jesus had no problem using or transforming spirit.*** *For believers, then, Jesus is all there is, and through Jesus we can give praise and see our prayers realized.* ***Jesus has control of the computer*** [I high lit this for you] *that creates and suspends the universe, according to the programs He designed and controls. Jesus though, only designs in the manner shown Him by the father, for Jesus always does what pleases god.*

My idea of how this computer system really works was still in a very formative stage, in my earlier articles. I do not agree anymore with all I wrote in this article, but basically the truth already lies exposed.

Chapter 4

Brief Synopsis of the Major Thesis of This Set of Books

In discussing the book with others I have found that they still do not have a good understanding of the principles involved in becoming a son of god. So, this is a very good place to give a summary of facts of the process. Studying the figures in this book will help greatly in rounding out understanding as you read the below synopsis.

There is Ultimate Reality, true god. This god has many sons. Each son has one facet of the realities that is in god, the father—Ultimate reality. In this discussion we only follow the reality sphere in one son we will call the spirit in Jesus. There is a whole spectrum of realities in him, just as there are in the Father.

To incorporate his sphere of realities, he created paradise, a spiritual computer desktop for those for whom paradise was created, Adam and Woman. As an integral part of paradise he provided the realm with trees and animals. The trees form icons to potential programs that can be created by entities I call archangels, paradisiacal animals. The archangels each hold one facet of the character of Jesus, their creator. The archangels [the animals] associated with the trees, are the system managers for the programs they devised. These programs deploy universes of existence into which Adam and Woman can dissociate into individual cellular entities to learn a particular facet of the character of their father, the spirit in Jesus of which each archangel has sole understanding. Adam's and Woman's cells are dispersed in a setting in that universe to interact with each other and with their managing universal spirit. The program can only be activated by the cellular structure of Adam and Woman becoming interspersed, live, interactive entities in the program. In this manner each cell of their being is immersed into the concepts that form that one facet in the character of god, Jesus.

One archangel identified as the animal, Serpent, has a program activated by the icon, "Tree of the Knowledge of Good and Evil", which when activated, teaches the concept of Good and Evil. This concept is not a facet of the son but of his father, Ultimate Reality. The father insists that those having potential of becoming future sons of his understand the concept of evil so well that it raises the understanding of the concept Good to such a level that the concept of evil disappears in nothingness by comparison. Evil must be understood so that creation cannot run out of control by evil having a chance to permanently settle in true reality; and the concept of evil can only be taught in a virtual reality to isolate it from the spheres of true reality. This program runs on a different set of binaries and regimen of protocol than any of programs of the other trees.

This program activates the physical universe. It is created in a virtual reality that has its fictional base in paradise. The entire scheme is designed to remain fictional so that evil expounded in this universe cannot escape and infect reality.

For this educational purpose this universe has no voluntary exit. It is a post-graduate course, the womb in which the newly forming son of god is in gestation. Once captured in this virtual reality there is no escape from it by any means employed by any of the entities captured in it. Once in, you are imprisoned. It is a non-existent reality in the Ultimate Reality of the Father. It is merely a computer model. Those captured in this reality have a chance to be rescued from their condition of perdition through the aid of Jesus, in conjunction with the Good Spirit [the means of personal communion between the father and son Jesus]. The Good Spirit is there to help Jesus stay in control of the model.

In earth we can only find two genders, men and women. They form an integral bond of one as genders, in the white race; they are one in Adam. In order to be viable entities worthy of a son of god they must both be **white people** just as all the other human races of previous sets of Adam' and Eve', differentiated through other racial characteristics, also have pairs of male and female that form a unit of one in the generation of their Adam'. All women and all men in each race are one in this arrangement because the only way they can receive pure offspring in the particular racial species is through the sexual act between members of only their set of Adam and his mate Eve. This bond of being one in each racial strain is a strict spiritual order. Animals, previous entities in their generation of Adam" still only mate in their own strain of species. By intermarrying between two races offspring are created that are not one in the race, but spiritual hybrids. Hybrids are sterile, devoid of spiritual content. They have no capacity to return to positive spirit. They truly are spiritually dead and so are the individuals who perpetrated this racial treason, their ancestral parents who committed the act. For this reason, by order of the gods, Jesus as well as Jehovah, the races cannot intermarry upon penalty of being barred from the opportunity to become cell [soul] entities in the newly forming son of god [spiritual bone and flesh].

Arrangement of the negative spiritual hierarchy

The physical realm is under management of a hierarchy of daemons who each control a certain realm of creature existence under Jehovah, the Serpent. So, here we have a serial line of organization. The line under Jehovah is as follows, Jehovah, Satan, daemon A, daemon B, daemon C, etc. as represented by the perfect trap in figure 11, page 396. Each daemon tries to bait the entities in a higher jurisdiction down to his, so there is a constant migration of souls [cells in Adam and Woman] downward through the hierarchy. Each daemon has jurisdiction over a species of biological life in earth. That is the manner in which nature is organized. Souls that refuse the redemption of their savior will migrate lower and lower until the soul disintegrates and is spiritually undone.

God, the son Jesus, enters this physical reality to be one with the latest trapped race of Adam and Woman. He can only come in a dual role, because by entering he adopts the countenance of the pure race of latest descended Adam and Eve, a fictitious identity, while retaining his status as god. As he said himself, he is son of man and also the spirit of god. **He represents reality and fiction in one person.** He comes thus to proclaim a dual message, one in honor of Jehovah, as physical Messiah, and one in his true role as deliverer of souls in Adam and Eve to true reality. His inner message of true spirit is the important one because the duality of his mission is to separate those who have a sincere affinity for the physical reality on the one hand, and those who sincerely seek a means of exit from this realm of evil on the other hand. Those who capture the inner message will be spotted by him in the capacity as the Comforter in company of the Good Spirit, so that the true father is always at hand to instruct and help the son through his most precarious mission. So when I write of the Good Spirit I also mean the Comforter and when I write about the Comforter, I also mean to include the Good Spirit. They are one, always; as Jesus said in his preaching "the father and I are one." *For this reason souls in the present generation of Adam continue to reincarnate because only one set of Adam and Woman descends every so many tens of thousand years, and the white race perpetuates for that length of time as white people. Therefore they must reincarnate to have this white race carry on.*

Those in the grasp of the Good Spirit and thus in the grasp of the entire trinity of god will be raised to the highest reality in god, Ultimate Reality, where these souls are reassembled into a temple, **another living Adam**, but now as son of god with the same standing as Jesus. The entire creation in the son, Jesus, is thus to produce a new son of god. The purpose of creation in Jesus then is a means of birthing a new son. It is therefore clear that Jehovah is a vital part in the birth process of the new son.

> *It can therefore be said that Jehovah is the true god's wife,*
> *and is our pregnant mother.*

In a nutshell, God in paradise gave Adam and Woman liberty of choice and provided a means to sup off the "Tree of the Knowledge of Good and Evil". We had a choice to listen to god or to go against his advice. We decided to investigate and to die to paradise. We learned the error of our choice, learned about evil and were given the opportunity to discover 'good' all over again, because our choice shut him from our awareness until he came in the man Jesus. In Jehovah some of us experience what the prodigal son experienced and will become conscious of true good. We follow the Comforter back home and find that we are as loved as before we left, except that we will be received in higher honor than when we left. We discover that Jehovah is not the ultimate evil, but a means to help us understand the principles of evil and good. It becomes clear that she was in Good's service all along as a teacher to help us mature in spirit. She is thus the wife and mother of God in truth and we must be awfully thankful to her for her to adopt her role as evil for the purpose of good.

Chapter 5

Critiques on Two Important Books

A Critique on "A New Earth" by Mr. Eckhart Tolle

The book was recommended by a friend so we bought a copy.

The author gives us insight into the make-up of our human psychic integration. That is where the value of the book stops. I appreciate his essays on ego and the pain-body. The ego and this pain-body are emotional, reactive program routines in the make-up of the human psyche. These components of the human psyche clearly show that our physical interaction in earth is set up in a devious manner so that we will experience all the levels of evil as the predator and as the prey. The capacity for unhappiness this make-up of our mental and psychic constitution enforces on us shows devilishness in the character of the god that supposedly created us in his total image. It shows directly that this god does not appear to be our father, friend and confidant. For this reason alone this book is good reading for readers of The Truth About Reality. The book contains much redundancy as most educational books have to entrench the basic factors that govern the thesis or theory in the mind of the reader.

He recommends Buddhism and Zen, a branch of Buddhism, which recommendations show the diabolical nature of this deceiving god, Jehovah, and the utter, spiritual ignorance of the author. Of course, Buddha and Buddhism and Zen, and any other religious disciplines or religions conceived by humans so far, come from the hierarchy of daemons in negative spirit. These theories and practices are given to mankind to deceive and not to free the enslaved souls. Daemonic communion is the only communion possible for souls in the grasp of negative spirit.

The human ego described by Mr. Tolle exposes the truly clever evil planted in the bosom of man. This is the human mental state to which Jesus referred when he stated that from the heart proceed all kinds of evil things. Mr. Tolle then proceeds to give us a method of how to overcome this devilish computer circuitry implanted in the human. His advice is to still the mind to allow Consciousness to work through the emptied human mind in order to renew the world and universe. If we follow his advice, we will destroy the purpose of the universe and us as critters in it. We must experience physical existence as given to us so that we will experience it as evil in order that we may begin to find the true good by the method given to us by Jesus.

I do not blame the Buddha and the Zen masters of old. They had no input from Jesus when they discovered and developed their plans and practice-routines to find happiness in a by-everyone-agreed-upon miserable constitution of the human being and the cruel environment of earth given to us creatures. From the entire make-up and understanding we all have of earth, earth is hell. Hell has been given us to learn about evil and good. If we sidestep the hell's brew of earth we will not accomplish the task asked of us.

And now we, who know the content of The Truth About Reality, can clearly see that this book, A New Earth, is devil-inspired. It is another clever display of evil in the disguise of good. The message of this book, A New Earth, is that humankind can recreate earth anew through deliberate, thought-free, alignment with the will of Consciousness and he links his supposed wisdom to that of Jesus Christ by quoting and relying on statements made by Jesus. Due to the dual role Jesus played in order to be among us, such misrepresentations of Jesus' true inner message are almost always common in human awareness. Jesus must be understood spiritually and then a person will not be misled. Jesus spoke to us, souls, through our physical projections, and not to just humans, because communion in spirit with dead souls was not possible. His much-constrained-by-Jehovah method led to much confusion as to the real message he came to bring to souls.

The author speaks of the universal spirit and Consciousness. Nobody, he writes, knows what this Consciousness is; it is unknowable. Jesus whom the author quotes quite frequently, however, says that we can know All Truth, and thus the true god when we commune in the Comforter. In the setting of the book, A New Earth, we are confronted with a single god, Consciousness who prefers to remain unknown and one-up from us and who is going to give us a newly transformed, deceitful arrangement of heaven and earth if we but lay ourselves prostrate before him. Mr. Tolle thus has no inkling of the existence of the true god.

The human soul exists in a state of a spiritual lie-believed, and earth and man are the reflection of our state of existence in an adopted erroneous spiritual belief system. It reflects a belief system—not truth. If there is not truth in the universe any system developed in this universe to find happiness and peace are thus tricks to accept this universe and to lull us to sleep so that we will never even try to pursue the truth available to us from the region beyond this realm of negative spirit.

Mr. Tolle equates ego with thought and condemns thought as the true deceiver of man. I agree, but to a point. We existed on thought alone in paradise. This communion in thought with truth **is** eternal life; it is the only recommended process of thought. But when we communed in thought with a deceiver, this process of thought became our death because the thoughts communed in were pure misrepresentations of the reality of paradise and of himself, the deceiver. Our thought processes can only be in alignment with the original lie we believed. We are thus trapped in hell without a means of escape through the only manner possible, our human-inspired thoughts. So, I agree that a mental body developed by the processes of human thought is utterly bad, but the thought processes that tell us to bypass our thought-processes and to just be like a vegetable in the negative realm of the universe to let the consciousness of the Serpent transform the old heaven and earth into a new heaven and earth through us is equally bad and a devilish propaganda scheme to keep us dead to true spirit and trapped in hell permanently. There is only one proper way to be in hell and that is to be truly miserable so that we will listen to Jesus' inner message and find truth outside this realm created through a spiritual propaganda scheme. We were given this miserable ego of ours to be in effect of a body of pain to seek the Comforter. By our conscious efforts and ego-appointed suffering in earth we may eventually embrace truth completely so we will graduate from the class of The Knowledge of Good and Evil. Mr. Tolle proposed plan will place us on a dead-end—a spiritual side-spur.

Life is thought and without thought there is no life. We are told by Jesus to pray, but how can we pray if we are told not to think? To be brought in touch with truth means that we must embrace truth in thought because it was also through communion in thought that we were deceived. Mr. Tolle tells us to not identify anything, but *how can we even grasp the difference between truth and a lie if we cannot differentiate between good and evil*. It is hard enough to not see the worst of evils as good when evil is so well disguised as being (for our) good. What sense does life and language have if we cannot label things in agreement with each other so that we can use language to interact with each other? To be able to commune in earth we need an ego and an emotional pain-body. We need to be able to communicate what is mine and what is thyne.

The trouble with human religious belief systems is that adherents of religious belief systems believe they have truth, completely forgetting that all thoughts they can embrace are lies. That is exactly the reason Jesus told us that he could not impart truth to us but that we had to be given thoughts of truth through the Comforter in true spirit; and when these thoughts are fully understood we simple disappear from the realms of deceit-created fictions because we have then been lead into "all truth". The universe will then have been sublimated out of our awareness but not from our memory.

In Mr. Tolle's case, in silence of thought we are channels for Consciousness in renewing the earth and universe; but in my case, silence in thought will bring the Comforter and the entire universe will sublimate from our awareness and never reemerge again in our awareness. Reality seekers must be silent in thought to evict the thought processes planted in us by earthly teachers so that our awareness can be flooded with teachings of true reality by the Comforter. There are two kings of consciousness, one belonging to the deceiver and the other belonging to truth.

I know I can recommend this book to you because you have also read The Truth About Reality, the only "truth" available in negative spirit because it only is an implied truth—not pure all-truth. You will not be deceived again by the clever deceits of the world; however, if you reject my book you deserve Mr. Tolle's truth steeped in deceit over my implied truth steeped in the truth of the true father of us all.

When we are spiritually redeemed, our existence in truth is what we experience just as fiction in the lie is experienced as physical reality. Whether in the one realm or the other, our thought processes must necessarily be aligned according to the realm we are in. These thought processes are the only life we have in these realms. If we exist, we must think—to stifle thought is to stifle life and be as dirt.

A tree is a creature with stifled life and dirt is stifled even more. Dirt exists entirely in the present. It can do nothing at all. All that happens to dirt is in effect. Consciousness works though it but nothing happens of itself. Dirt is transformed by the conscious thought processes available in humans into cars, bridges, buildings, TV sets, computers, h-bombs, propaganda, etc.

Humans coming from dead dirt in spirit—souls, also, are already possessed by Jehovah's consciousness by believing in his propaganda as souls. Modern implements of technology are here because Jehovah implants his thought processes in our minds. Our modern world is the handiwork of Jehovah working through us. That is how he already transformed the old world into the new that now exists. The "new heaven" according to Mr. Tolle simply means that humans can now be in the "physical heavens" also and transform it completely. We did that already through space ships, space stations etc. We did not have to practice anything Mr. Tolle tells us to do to have accomplished that. In fact, it was created simply through applied human thought processes and not by practicing stifling thought altogether. If we take sole credit for having shaped this new world of technology we truly are blind and insult Jehovah. Jehovah worked through us.

Dirt is just available. As physical dirt is available to us to fashion things so we, "dead" souls, are available as spiritual dirt to Jehovah and his hierarchy, but of itself souls can do nothing. If you practice being physical dirt as humans now also, I am sure you will degenerate through incarnation to be physical dirt that much the sooner in addition to already being spiritual dirt. By the way, Jesus never meant us to refer to outer space as heaven; he always meant that the spiritual heaven is responsible for the physical heaven and true reality as the true birthplace of soul alive. Heavens are the spiritual departments responsible for environments. The universe is an environment, not a spiritual department. Remember that Jesus addressed humans in the capacity as son of man; and our souls in his capacity as Son of God, but all that ever was of any importance to him were souls, and not mere people.

So similarly, souls that believed a lie in spirit are dirt—spiritual dirt. This spiritual dirt lies helplessly in a coma, and the spiritual liar, the Serpent, used and still uses this spiritual dirt to fashion the universe and souls themselves as creature-projections in it. Wise up! Be awake in reality, not in the universe of spiritually dead dirt.

However, the process of stepping from spiritual darkness into the light of spiritual truth must involve our thought processes, and once in truth we will only have thoughts in alignment with "All Truth" which thoughts are our daily bread and our eternal life in reality. I identify myself with the father in all truth, not with the deceiver who plunged us into spiritual darkness. I deliberately, and of necessity, identify and align myself with the god in truth. It is the only identification I have and want. To do that I must think and differentiate.

Mr. Tolle suggests that one surrenders even one's most intimate spiritual identity, soul, to Jehovah so that one will be entirely metabolized into his body of evil. It will be the permanent undoing of us as spiritual entities. To me, that is the deepest kind of deceit we can fall prey to in this realm of utter darkness.

However, for those who reject the choice that the Comforter provides, Mr. Tolle's book is a complement to the chapters in this book devoted to "Ode to Jehovah". As an aside, I believe that a strong hug stops all thought if not held too long. A hug has a calming effect that reaches through the entire human psychic structure.

Critique on the book "In Search of Heaven, the Eternal Life"

I must add one more book-report to this book, "In Search of Heaven, the Eternal Life" by Rodger W. Berg. It is a book based on certain concepts of Mormonism, although he never mentions Mormonism.

The book confines itself to second and third level creations in reality. He confuses the identities of the primary god and the false god into a fantasy primary god, as all major Christian religions do because the manner Jesus appeared to us and taught us gives that impression to us. It is extremely difficult to extract Jesus' true message from all he said and did. He was/is a savior for the true god and, at the same time a savior for Jehovah. There is a tremendous conflict of interest here, but it was the only manner in which he was able to relate his real message at all.

This book does not adequately explain or mention the tremendous catastrophe that happened in the beginning to Adam and Woman in paradise that involved the tree of Knowledge of Good and Evil, the lie-believed, Adam and Woman's fall and their transformation into sexual physical creatures in a very hostile world. It does not explain why god favored Able and rejected Cain. It was Cain who thought of making a sincere sacrifice of thanksgiving to god first. It is the original gesture that counts, more than what is being sincerely sacrificed. It does not explain God's anger and violence against the corrupted offspring of Adam and Woman because they as a pure, newly formed race mingled their seed with the seed of other strains of humanity on earth. It does not explain god's anger against all of us humans all the time and his wishy-washy mind-changing from Israel being his favorite to being damned, and the abandonment of all the other human races and especially the species of animals that the Israelites had to slaughter by the millions to offer to this god.

We, humans, have always been helpless, ignorant and abandoned by those spiritual entities who could have taught us correctly. We are ignorant because no god or spirit told us anything of value and these gods and spirits gave us only demands. All we ever were told was to obey. Obeying without understanding does not make sense. Jehovah, without fail, behaves and acts like a god who instills evil in the universe by setting one people against another in war, by making it impossible for us to understand the meaning and purpose of life and why we should worship him freely. Worship is a sick thing to do. It only makes sense in an evil, dangerous and maligned realm where we must seek the protection of an evil and powerful entity that demands payment and subjection for services received. This kind of relationship stinks; and he stinks as a god.

I have nothing but respect for what Rodger W. Berg has written. It is a seamless whole that integrates modern scientific principles in the understanding of the greater universal whole. It does not explain what science discovered about the big bang by which the universe was started. To me, the big bang is such a tremendous anomalous occurrence that it can only have been based on the calamitous event of believing a spiritual lie about the reality of being. To believe such a lie will overturn the entire structure of existence, so that a new form of habitation and beingness had to be quickly incorporated. This new universal incorporation was already planned and thought out by the Serpent, so that incorporation could take place instantly when some suckers would believe his lie.

The new universe based on "light" as explained by Rodger is the darkness of the lie in true reality. Jesus could only have supported this universe of spiritual darkness because he was coerced to express the will of Jehovah in order to convey the real message of truth for which he came into the world. Jesus' message of spiritual truth is darkness in the world and Jehovah's splendor of inner universal light is darkness in true reality. Rodger does a good job explaining the operation of the negative spirit and the universe on which it is based but leaves untouched the true god (thus in contra-distinction to the false god, Jehovah) as written in John 17: 3 and who Jesus came to introduce to us (John 17: 25; 26). Jehovah was already known for ages to mankind as a god of light. He is thus the false, old god.

There are several principles in Rodger's universal outlay that do not fit into the working of the universe as explained by him. For instance, Jesus transformed himself into light before Peter, John and James and to an intimate following when he ascended. He also did so before Saul of Tarsus on his way to catch and arrest "Christians" in Damascus. Neither of these people had the power to vibrate at higher frequency rates, how could these men see this bright light display that is only real to those who have attained these higher rates of vibration? Why can Jesus transform himself into light, body and all, and move in any direction at will, and why must humans leave the gross body behind when they vibrate at higher rates? To me these questions are crucial! To Rodger, the entire body is made of light.

For instance, Mormons are graded into classes of believers based on their knowledge and practice of sub-atomic vibration rates. The attainment of higher vibration rates can be learned and practiced. One has to make certain sacrifices to receive the extra capabilities [tit for tat]. Practice and study are sacrifices. As one becomes more adept one is raised in class and one will vibrate with the group that can vibrate in the same frequency range. The Mormon god is a physical god. Except this god's vibration rate is so extremely high, they say, that hardly any person can vibrate on that level. But with the help of one's personal spirit these things can be achieved. To my understanding Jehovah is spirit, not material. He is thus outside the box and we, soul-projections are inside the box, and our souls are like dirt (dead) in spirit. It is thus impossible to be in materially, visible communion with Jehovah.

This ability of high energy vibration is based on the oscillations of physical sub-atomic particles that can be found throughout all the planes/levels of frequency-based vibration rates of awareness in the universe. Souls existing on higher rates of sub-nucleus particle vibration can observe the entire frequency range from human physical to the rate they have attained in spiritual mastership. God, Jehovah, can observe activity in all the ranges, and it is probable that he can manifest in all those ranges if he can adopt a physical projection (which I doubt) while souls in normal humans can only observe and manifest in their own spectrum of common frequency. According to Rodger, we, normal humans, are captured and locked in this coarse, mass-controlled physical frequency range from lifecycle to lifecycle until we finally wake up to our personal accompanying spirit who will then train and guide us into higher frequency ranges. To me, this is a cruel punishment when, all that is needed, training, is withheld from us. Why is that done? The only reason that this is so, according to my understanding, can be that we are to learn and experience Evil so we will be gregariously seeking Good in the end; a good that cannot be found in this universe so it has to be brought to us from beyond the entire universe by the spirit of the true God. Jesus said to the rich young man that he, Jesus, was not good, but only one was. If Jesus is the light of the world, why is he not good? It is because he was parading in a body of evil, physical flesh that is part and parcel, 100%, made from universal fabrics—the fabric of the lie.

There is a marvelous comparison to this range of possible multilevel awareness in the vibration rate of occult existence. I have a computer aided design and computer aided machining program "TurboCAD/CAM Professional". I started out with a cheap version, called "TurboCAD Delux". The Delux version is identical to the professional version, except the manufacturer has turned off [grayed out in the menus] many capabilities in the cheap version. By doing certain agreeable things, like upgrading at so-much cost extra, the manufacturer will send out another set of CDs with the professional capabilities of the program turned on. These are all versions of the same program except that different capabilities of the program are turned on or off according to the sacrifice a purchaser makes. This is standard procedure in sophisticated software companies. Similarly Jehovah will gray out most functions in humans but will turn on extra capabilities when you make sacrifices and do the necessary amount of kowtowing—thus tit for tat; but Jesus said that there was nothing we could do to receive eternal life. See the contradiction in deity? There must be two of them!

Let me explain "spiritual" vibration frequency ranges and their accompanying tactile and other sensatory experiences. These are based on already existing philosophies of other secret societies, such as practitioners of Hindu, Buddhist, Cabala, Masonic, Rosicrucian and Eckankar [a religious/occult society based on the spiritual experiences and writing of Mr. Paul Twitchel]. Most occult groups only know the very basics of these techniques and keep the knowledge secret.

The coarsest frequency rate is that of the physical creature-detectible universe. It is where all biological creatures and material are locked into. This visible-to-us-coarse creature universe is there for souls' spiritual experience and as learning curve, they say. Our frequency rate is the lowest and does not take any spiritual knowledge to generate. For some reason that I do not understand, life in this region is mortal while attaining much higher rates of vibration gives one more ability and longer life or even eternal life. Since spirit is eternal and souls are eternal, they say, one must reincarnate in the physical frequency band as long as one has no spiritual understanding and one thus is not able to exist on a higher plane of vibration. We 'normal' people have no knowledge and no understanding at all of these higher rates of vibration, so we do not know whether souls in higher planes of frequency will die. I am sure they do. If a person is part of the greater physical realm the person is still in the universe and the person is dead to true reality because that is the verdict of god in paradise; and he does not lie. If you partake of that tree of the Knowledge of Good and Evil, you die . . . you die spiritually, and thus also physically because the physical is still anchored in true reality through the real souls lying comatose in paradise.

I am sure that these ethereal planes of existence are quite real and true for universe-bound creatures. It also explains all the different heavens over which all the different daemons in the Jehovahic hierarchy reign. That seems to prove that there are deamon-controlled heavens for animals, for every physical species has its own deamon authority.

Now let me try to explain Jesus' statement that this is a realm of darkness. One explanation is that it is darkness because of the extremely low vibration rate. All higher realms of vibration have light according to different rates of sub-nucleus particle vibration. Through the help and urging of one's personal spirit who always abides with a person or creature, one can learn to attain this trick of accelerating one's vibration rate. This is thus one explanation of Christ's statement that this is the realms of darkness and when stuck here it will lead to one's death as human being; yet, being the "children of the god of light" according to Rodger Berg would preclude our death in this universe in any way. There is thus a discrepancy in this explanation in the death that faced Adam and Woman when they partook of the Tree of the Knowledge of Good and Evil. God said they would die and they are thus dead to the spirit of paradise after they partook. Dead means being like dirt here on this earth. If you die your body has become mere dirt; so when you die spiritually you are like mere spiritual dirt or dust in spirit. You have lost the ability to commune/ communicate/be-conscious in the environment from which you died.

Christ's deeper message is that the devil always disguises himself as an angel of light. If one devil takes the disguise of an angel of light, will not all devils disguise themselves in the same manner? According to Christ's deeper message existence experienced in a spiritual coma is death and darkness, and awakening from one's spiritual slumber is light and understanding. This light and understanding that gives true Life is based on becoming aware that the lie about the god and realm of reality one still believes as soul prevents soul from being present in true reality. Once a soul becomes aware that it exists in a realm created through the power of a lie-believed, it will awaken from its coma and be present in true reality. As one can see there is virtually an innumerable range of existences in the ethereal planes based on the vibration rates of sub-atomic particles of physical creatures, all based on believing the original spiritual lie *fed* to us in paradise. A lie believed is darkness and the shedding from our consciousness of the lie believed is light—the light of true reality. Do you now see how kinky things can get when one believes a lie, especially a lie anchored in spirit! Since spirit is hidden from us through the belief of a lie this lie remains always hidden from our personal awareness and thus we are trapped forever in the state of spiritual coma and as creatures projected in a fictional, universal setting—*a perfect trap.*

For a soul caught as a human being true spiritual awakening can only be accomplished through Jesus' deeper message and the accompanying activity of the one and only Good Spirit, because one's personal spirit companion also believed the original lie—he is the one in a coma. The spiritual state of mind must be changed from a grounding in the realms of negative spirit [the entire realm of imagined physical universe, encompassing all the possible planes of existence based on sub-nucleus vibration rates] to one of positive spirit; one must be spiritually prodded to let go of the spiritual lie and its accompanying spiritual and physical array of propaganda. The propaganda proved to be as deadly as explained by god, Jesus the son, to Adam and Woman in paradise. As long as the original lie is believed one remains dead to reality; no matter what vibration rate one has been able to attain here in the physical universe. It is all still based on imagination—the imaginations forced on souls through their separation from existence in paradise and their capture in a Void created by the Serpent, the cleverest of animals in paradise, Jehovah. Whatever is based on science and its accompanying technical skill is darkness and will mislead a soul to remain in darkness disguised as apparent light; it is thus part of deceitful cosmic propaganda, the hermetic seal of the trap and of damnation.

Everything that relates to us creatures has its beginning and its end in the tree of the Knowledge of Good and Evil and the Serpent; the Alpha and the Omega. One must know evil, the premeditated act of lying and the believing of a lie in the beginning—Alpha, in order to understand and know good, truth in the end—Omega. Only one entity can bring us this resolution of Alpha and Omega to resolve all our confusion, aimlessness, ignorance, fear, anger and frustration—Jesus. He came in a dual role because of his status of Alpha and Omega. We must know evil in order to know and understand good. He came to us in the disguise of evil to disguise his good in order to bring us good revealed as truth—the Good Spirit. In his disguise as a physical creature Jesus is correct to state that he is not "good". This is the only sensible interpretation of his statement that he was not "good" for he deceived us by coming in the form of the captives and claiming to be our spiritual Lord.

Throughout Rodger's explanations of how the father's source of light energy functions and creates images and beings points to the working of a spiritual computer. The source of power is not even his own but belongs to the souls deceived and empowered by the deceit to fuel the computer. Jehovah, the Serpent is outside the computer, but bound to it through full commitment to it.

For example, Rodger Berg writes,

> "Let us examine our bodies and how they might have been
> created. Where does the organizational force that controls the entire
> body structure on the atomic molecular level come from?
>
> Would it not come from the "Mind of God," where thought
> once expressed creates an image pattern in "Spirit Energy Form?"
> When you say "elephant," what image comes to mind? It invokes
> the image of an elephant. And this word "elephant" creates in mind
> the pattern of the life form . . .
>
> It seems rational that images were first created in "Spiritual
> energy Form" in the Father's Light-Energy."
>
> It might be that thought frequency in spirit from the "Mind
> of God" and from his children, is at such a high pitch that it emits
> no light at all and is like a void (for Rodger says he knows such to
> exist from his own experience). He goes on, "If you were in a totally
> dark room would loneliness not become boring? It would be better
> to see images of what it is you are thinking. So god became bored
> with the darkness. He said, 'Let there be light' and suddenly there
> was light. Light originated and reflected back and forth dispelling
> the void, revealing all his thoughts and thought creature creations
> (his private children, that now he could see). Now suppose, he goes
> on, that the children of light became bored and asked the god of
> light if they could create another dimension location within the
> heavens where all the spirits could become in solid form the very
> things they created.
>
> Could Adam have been *homo-sapient human form* proto type
> that we, designed, using the "Father's Light-Energy," that all
> spirit children could use? We could have designed this form so we
> would experience death through it. The physical form would be
> a quickening spirit that we can use over and again and improve
> upon?

By doing so would we be co-creators with deity?" Rodger supposes that
our experiences are recorded by our spirit and placed in soul with a copy to
the hall of records. He even states that we could copy the arch-types of Adam
and Woman and use it over and over and improve on it. Again these things
smell of computer generated models that we can copy, improve, and again
copy for storage and reuse for further design modification and reanimation.

I do such things on my Cad program and Word program all the time. Photos displayed on a computer display screen are images of light.

Much of what he wrote in chapter eight reeks of computer technology, from making copies to the archive, designing and creating patterns in light that can be copied and animated. He states a lot that coincides with my understanding of the whole of the negative spiritual realm, and the manner in which the physical universe is projected, but he fails to see that all souls existing in a higher reality than the whole universal realm were forced to participate in the creation of the physical universe. If the Serpent was able to do this all on his own, he obviously would not need to seduce Adam and Woman in creating and suspending the physical universe. The computer program can hold everything Rodger is supposing and is confirming to be true according to his own experience. He failed to see the *spiritual* computer scenario because he is a display character in it and thus is limited to only see things projected into the universal and hence to his physically (to him spiritually) grounded mind.

In short, he fails to see that other levels of reality exist that he is unable to get in touch with because these exist outside the box of the computer display. He only sees the effects created by the spiritual computer. He is utterly unaware of the reality in which the computer exists.

It is extremely important to understand that Adam and Woman existed in paradise, a realm in which the concepts of good and evil did not exist. They were ignorant of these concepts. It is through partaking of this particular tree that the concepts good compared to evil can be made manifest to the minds of Adam and Woman. The universe is the medium through which souls can be brought to the knowledge of good and be raised in power to sons of the god of all existence through the medium of evil, a universe and life created and experienced on the basis of a lie believed.

In Rodger's schema of the spiritual realms and on the creative ability of the father, I can only see it as is stated in John 3: 1. God created the Word (His Son) into whose person he gave all the powers he himself has. In the creation of the son, the Good spirit came into being as the truthful communion between the god in reality and the son in a virtual realm whose "being virtual" was removed through the means of communion in the Good Spirit. It is the communion in truth that brought the son on par with the father.

The son was responsible for all secondary and tertiary creations. The father did this, according to Rodger's supposed scheme to prevent boredom. Had God created all the children and all the manifestations himself, he would be bored still, because there is no surprise. But if the Son did all the creating, than

the father would be constantly surprised by what the Son did and so would
be entertained by his Son's actions. Jesus came up with a scheme that would
cause the creation of other sons of God, who then also could entertain the
father with their surprise creations. This scheme was put into effect through the
Serpent and his Tree of the Knowledge of Good and Evil. It is a masterpiece and
those who learn to distinguish spiritual good from spiritual evil (disguised as
good) have earned their diploma and become the sons of the true and ultimate
god, being raised from a secondary reality of paradise in the son to ultimate
primary reality in full capability and power of a son. Sometimes we have to
take a step back to gain an extra step forward. This can only be so because
our being virtual is overcome through this same Good spirit who communes
in truth and through truth makes us on par with truth itself.

The conclusion is thus that any sort or kind of physical light is utter
darkness in true spirit, and the light of truth is utter darkness in the physical
realm; but the light of true spirit does give life in the realms of the physical
universe to those who have regained lost consciousness in true reality because
the memory of the experience of the universal dream will remain with a soul
that has reentered true reality. There is thus an unbridgeable gulf between
the realms of the lie [negative spirit] and the realms of truth [positive spirit]
as seen/understood from realms based on the lie; except if one is pulled up
to the realm of truth by one in the realm of truth [the Good Spirit]. This has
been made possible through the mission of Jesus (see figure 9, page 488).
Jesus started the process of bringing truth into our being so that we can
return to reality. The process was finished by the positive truth in the Good
Spirit (Jesus' spirit). Jesus, in the flesh revealed and gave humans access to all
the possible heavens and gives us the choice of our hearts, death as sheep in
the glamorous body of Jehovah and life as goats in the realms of truth. He
separated and continues to separate the sheep from the goats—the dead in
the lie from the living in truth. Rodger's book proves again that much of what
Jesus preached can be taken either way, as a messenger for Jehovah and as a
messenger of one in true reality. We must remember that Jehovah as god of
negative spirit can claim to have his own sort of truth he can imbue on the
souls he captured. Jehovah's truth is based on the lie but souls who believe
his lie think it is truth.

*One crucial issue must be addressed in order before Bible-believing
people can receive any kind of spiritual guidance. The issue of Adam and
Woman's spiritual death must be addressed. When a spiritual revealer does
not address that issue and resolves it correctly, followers of that spiritual
teacher will not be redeemed back into higher realms of reality.* Since we

are all dead in spirit to the god of paradise, that god cannot reach us in spirit. It was the exact mission of Jesus to come as man and thus not as god to set the stage for our return to life in spirit. Only if Jesus' inner message is heard and understood can such redemption take place. Jesus came to reawaken us from our dead stage by giving us a belief in true spirit again and have this belief strengthened by the Good Spirit into solid faith so that when we have our next choice to choose between Life and Death we will choose Life instead of the default choice Death.

One's belief in the premises of the book, "In Search of Heaven, the Eternal Life" will *not* make sons of the true god.

It is another aspect and revelation of evil, disguised as good from the very moment the Serpent sold the lie in a disguise of truth. The result of that lie is manifest in our miserable existence as creatures in earth. Let's not get confused again. Whatever can be revealed in earth is evil. Good cannot be revealed because it is spiritually hidden from us by us believing that the lie is truth and in trying to find meaningful existence in this realm based on a lie. We cannot know Good unless it is revealed to us in the spirit of truth—the Good Spirit. In the realm of truth all things lay revealed, while the universe is devoid of truth that can make sons of god. Where there is a difference in status there is not truth. The transformed image of Jesus hovering over mere pitiful humans lying prostrate in adoration is not spiritual equality. It is a demonstration of one-up-ism. It is a revelation of the image of evil—Jesus' role as the physical Messiah. The true spiritual Messiah is the Good Spirit announced by Jesus as the Comforter who communes only in true spirit to the spirit of the individual; not seen or manifest in any way because he is truth. He communes in spirit, not in and through the universal flesh or any other medium of evil. Jesus transformed and glittering person hovering over the people deliberately shows us the image of evil, flesh made to look magnificent.

The god of lights is a disguise of evil, but I believe that only a son of the true god can play that role of Evil. Only true sons of god that have ascended from playing a soul in earth and having understood and having overcome the evil released in themselves can play this role. Only true sons of God know Good and Evil. In God's realm are many mansions, all inhabited by souls that are integrated into living temples that know evil and have overcome this state of soul-mind by understanding and knowing good. These are the perfect entities to play the role of Evil because they can play the role and yet remain master over the urges and state of mind of evil. These can play the master sergeant for god to teach souls good and evil. By knowing the love of god, there can be no irrevocable death for souls. It thus stands to reason that Paul made a sound statement in saying that the world is waiting and groaning for the sons of god to be revealed. These new sons of god will redeem all souls in earth. It is part of the course of knowing good, god. There shall be no permanently god-condemned souls in his realms. Remember only one is good, god of all reality. The task of Adam and Woman was to know god, good. Between Jehovah and Jesus there is no chance that we will not learn our lesson.

How Jehovah plays the role of evil is up to him. He can very well play it according to way Rodger Berg relates his experiences and knowledge to us. It gives one idea of the arrangement of the negative spirit. It is of course all make-believe because the real daemons are not in the computer display, although they may have created physical projections for themselves as well. The several heavens of the daemons are thus located in the ethereal planes Rodger mentioned to have experienced.

"In Search of Heaven" can be obtained at insearchofheaven.com. I do not place any stock in his experience of hypnotist. Whatever attracts a person sensationally will drive the person deeper into negative spirit because the whole idea of physical life is to take any sensational bait one is hungry for to drive the soul deeper into Hell.

Addendum

Propaganda [The Mind and Workings of the Holy God, Jehovah]

This section in part is an essay on the book *Propaganda—The Formation Of Men's Attitudes* by Jacques Ellul, translated by K. Kellen and J. Lerner, and published by Alfred A. Knopf [New York, 1964]. This is a Borzoi book. I very, very strongly suggest you read this book to get the insight on propaganda that this expert can give you. It is not likely that a better book on the subject exists for us laymen. The present Baal[s], the government[s] of the world, does not want the people to know about the methods they use to deceive them.

Propaganda is the deliberate spreading of ideas, information, or rumors for the purpose of helping or injuring ideas, facts, or allegations to further a cause or to damage an opposing cause by misleading people into polarizing public opinion against an enemy of the propaganda system, not necessarily an enemy of the people. Propaganda is a cleverly thought-out scheme of lies, disseminated [through the media] to a group of people.

Cosmic propaganda emits from Jehovah through negative spirit. Human propaganda is under the control of Satan, Jehovah's adversary. Both types of propaganda work fiercely to hide true reality.

Propaganda works because soul would rather believe a lie than the truth and people love the darkness more than light. Propaganda is the reality of this world, and it is totalitarian. In any setting you can place yourself you are in effect because

491

your beingness is controlled and exploited by unseen others because you believe authority's schemes of lies. As Jesus said, and I whole-heartedly agree, the universe is a realm of utter darkness due to spiritual and worldly propaganda.

Any organization that has influence over you or whom you trust uses propaganda to enslave your mind for their use or to keep it in your trust. It is similar to what is now happening on the internet with millions of idle computers being connected to the Internet by unscrupulous characters using high-tech intrusion techniques. Zombie computers are made from units connected to the net that sit idle for most of the time. These units are scanned continuously by pirates to see if they can be used. Similarly, propaganda systems have taken possession of your mind. If you graduated from high school and if you are closely tuned to the media, news and entertainment in visual, written, and spoken form, your mind has been bundled into what is called "public opinion." If you express what the propaganda system wants you to say or do, you are considered a worthy American by those who brainwashed you. In general, the authorities have done an admirable job in making your person and mind subject to their will, completely unnoticed by you. You will get my admiration if you can reclaim the use of your own mind and body—and that would only be step one in returning to reality.

You probably do not believe this; but, nonetheless, all of society is deeply brainwashed, and this essay and the above-mentioned book explain to you why and how it is done.

The worst is that in the spiritual setting underlying the physical universe, your soul, has been captured; and your spiritual energy is used to run the computer that displays the program, "universe." Your human brain is an infinitesimal interactive little part in the program. You receive propaganda through the program and disseminate it simultaneously—all beyond your power to observe. Thus, your body is a caricature entity in the program; and your personality, character, and habits are just computer subroutines over which you have some control; and the daemons running the program have complete control.

Human-run programs reveal much of how the spiritual powers use you for their purposes. The worst thing is that by them using your spiritual energy to run the computer, you will lose what they use. They suck you dry like a spider its catch. It is important that you get the full message of this book and trust Jesus' spirit to lead you back home.

Public and private schooling under the control of the state are systems of indoctrination first and systems of education last. Public school, preschool, and childcare centers are primary institutions of pre-propaganda that make it possible for the mainframe propaganda machinery to easily subject the future graduates to ongoing and more in-depth propaganda.

Schooling puts the minds of children on mind-conditioning tracks so that hardly anything beyond the tracks ever stirs their minds, unless somebody goes through the trouble of reconditioning them. That will almost never happen because ongoing propaganda keeps them securely trapped on this mental track. Propaganda [brainwashing] effectively changes, and then locks up a person's view on reality.

In the Netherlands, the legal courtroom is called *recht kamer*. One meaning of the word "recht" is "right." The presiding judge is called a *rechter* [the one that determines the parties' rights after a trial] and the lawyers are called *rechtsgeleerden*, educated in matters concerning the rights of people. The *recht kamer* is a room in which, supposedly, the rights of the parties are determined. At one time in history, the names for this court and of its practitioners were correct. Today, after socialism and democracy have firmly established themselves in the cultures of the Dutch, this name cannot be more inappropriate.

Today, people anywhere in the Western world have no rights. Rights have been abolished. People now have privileges and equitable interests in things [having a license, or permission, to certain things and actions], which is a shift down from having rights and liberty. The same thing happened to us, as souls, in paradise. In paradise, we were talked into surrendering our status as real "beings," to receive fictitious status as human being, in a realm of nothingness—fiction. Rights are to privileges as a pile of gold and precious jewels is to a pile of fresh human feces. The Dutch culture can be labeled *"ultra capitalist, equitable communist democracy"*, as is the US culture. It is **capitalistic** because only a few people own the whole of the Netherlands and another few own the whole of the USA; **equitable** because you possess things only according to your standing in the **communist** structure—you own nothing outright. **Democracy**, because one can vote; which vote does not mean anything other than sticking the voter's head deeper in the mud.

Rights are inherent in the organic human being. They cannot be extended to a human being by another human being. Rights are inherent in a free person. They are considered to have been granted by god. But privileges can be accorded to a horse; the horse, however, can never have rights. It does not have any rights. It is owned outright by someone else, and this person can make life easy [accord it privileges] or this person can make its life miserable by denying any privileges and driving the animal beyond its ability to cope.

Rights are inherent in a person. It is part of the person's flesh, blood, and bones; yet through criminal violence, or through legal artifact and legal maneuvering, someone can actually kill another and confiscate a victim's bones, organs, and blood and sell them. Rights are plundered from a person while he is in the prime of his life or he is born with the rights already removed by legal fiction. Courts in earlier days tried to determine if a person had trespassed on the rights of another person. The object was to determine if someone was injured in his being as an organic person, not as a subject to someone else. The word "rights," in the English language, was taken to mean common-law-determined possessions. Laws were based on the rights of free people. Rules and statutes refer to the granting and retaining of permissions and duties determined by a higher authority. They are generally part of some license of incorporation. The Ten Commandments establishes the rights of god and the privileges of free people in a community that has received a license from god, Jehovah, to operate as the nation of people in the "Promised Land".

What I am saying is that, presently, the previous meaning of the word "rights" has been changed to mean privileges [or permission] by some clever lawmakers. Rights are inherent in a person; permission is granted by people who consider themselves to be the higher authority, based on irresistible power. All an ordinary person sees is the word "rights," and just believes he has rights according to the previous definition, but that is not how the court sees it. If you come into court claiming your rights nowadays, you will quickly learn that you don't have steadfast rights of being, but only revocable privileges.

The honest term for modern trial courts would be "courts of permissions." This word would alarm the people, so the deceivers have kept the old word, but enforced your "rights" according to its new meaning. That is a propaganda ploy. This is just one word, a "myth" as the psychologists call it. Every myth in the scale of soul and human importance has been drained in a similar manner and refilled with the same kind of nothingness.

To make certain that you remain ignorant, the courts made a companion rule that no one but those learned in law and licensed [given permission] to practice *law*, may have standing in court. I believe also that when lawyers are granted their license to practice "law," they promise to keep the difference between "rights" and "privileges, and "Laws" and "ordinances" out of the conversation where it might lead a "layman" to comprehend that he has been duped.

The American people were sold into slavery for nothing. They simply allowed a small group claiming to have authority to rob them; and the common people never saw it happen. If you are only granted privileges you are in effect—you are a slave. The elected officials and their servants, in my observation, forfeited their claim to authority due to default of duties and betrayal of trust of office. We exist in hell, and so this happens all the time. The great preoccupation of creatures in hell, spiritual and material, is to pull the rug from under you over and over again. And then they tell you, "Oh that is life! Live and learn." Well, I have learned, and that is why I hopefully am helping you to seek the Good Spirit to commune in!

You never knew that you, here in America, exist in what Russians would call a communist state. The United States government owns everything, even your body. You have no right to anything. Ownership is determined by who has possession of the certificates of origination. A birth certificate is a "certificate of origination." Government has the original; you are only granted to copy of it, and you must pay a fee to obtain a copy. The certificates of origination of all things fabricated or assembled have certificates of origination. These are kept on file by government. Government owns these things, and you are granted an equitable interest in them according to certain terms and conditions. If you are a "good" slave, government allows you to have this equitable interest, if not, the government confiscates it. They can confiscate your house, your car, and your body. These belong to government. Government is your god.

This is just an example from our religion "*ultra capitalist, equitable communist democracy*," but the same thing happens to all religious people. Everybody is sent up the creek without a paddle. Whatever you believe [even if you do not believe in god] is your religion—and religious expression is guaranteed by the "organic law" [the constitution]. But believe me, hardly anyone is allowed to practice what they believe. What you believe in your person and what thus is an inalienable right—a part of you like your foot—is absolutely and strictly forbidden. Only politically and religiously indoctrinated correct thoughts and actions are allowed to be expressed. Modern society has mutilated and emasculated you in your organic being, and you have been made to believe that it was done in your best interest. Lawyers are apt to say, "You enjoy the benefits of this society, so you have no right to complain and thus you must pay the tribute, taxes." But I have no choice; all that was ever important to me was robbed from me before I was born. And now that my life is almost over, I discover these things. Oh, ignorance *is* bliss!—and ignorance will destroy your soul.

Reading this book can be very unsettling for religiously inclined people. It can induce deep-felt indignation because to every sincere Christian, it will reveal the power, actions, workings, and the psychology of the Baal whom they consider to be a loving god. Baal is an authority, spiritual or material, to which you have no choice but to submit. The above-mentioned book and its references expose some propaganda ploys that slip quite easily by one's awareness. These ploys are integrated in the manner in which one can publish a book in America—according to the law. Nothing can be published unless it supports and upholds the system. Yes, all we read or listen to is censored. How is it done? It is done through laws that bind incorporated publishing businesses. You must have heard the phrase, "politically correct." It is law; you can be charged for violating it and be placed in jail, simply for doing what you thought was your "right" to do. And what law cannot handle, corrupt case law will handle.

Most people have been so brainwashed that they already behave, say and think in a perfectly politically correct manner because they are afraid what other people with propaganda's big tool stamped in their brain, will say. They are afraid of public opinion. Most people, though, have no other opinion than the public opinion; and they are very opinionated about it. They are happy slaves. They are aligned with the lies they believe.

Scientists Are Imbued with a Spiritual Public Opinion

Now the spiritual world underlying the physical universe has a system of laws as well, and it is arranged so that you, on your own or in a group setting, will never discover the possibility of another reality. If there is another reality out there, it is most carefully hidden from us. The way it is done is through cosmic propaganda. We are made to believe by everything we see, feel, and otherwise sense that this universe is real and that it is all there is. Scientists, especially, are spiritually so dense that they refuse to accept anything that they cannot in some manner observe. How can they observe? They and all the tools that can ever be available to them are "numb" to spirit. They can only see what is physically correct; all other things have been censored out of their ability to observe. Scientists, we may say, are imbued with an environmental public opinion; and they are very opinionated about it. They are blind to truth and claim to have all the answers, and if they have missed one, they will find a thesis as answer.

In the past, the sword was the system of propaganda. If a person did not listen or obey, the sword of authority will enforce the will of the one in charge of the sword—the king, chief bandit, or clique of rich people. Galileo, claiming that the world was round, experienced that kind of enforcement from the pope.

Following, the sword "systems of belief" came the propaganda tool. Again we find an authority at the top. This authority now has more tools to its disposal. There are the tool of public opinion, penance, ostracizing, spiritual damnation, and the sword. Belief systems are less brute and more efficient in conditioning people into obedience and into obtaining wholehearted support for the authorities. Good propaganda starts at birth, and continues through death and reincarnation back to birth. Cosmic propaganda is that good. Therefore, the US government has included a belief system into its arsenal of propaganda—the liberal socialist democracy. It is a religion. The masses are piously devout to it to such an extent that they place their creed second to this government cult. Now government has also added the controlled media to its arsenal and taken international banking as means of spirit, to make it undisputedly god over its realms of influence. This influence now stretches across the globe and into space. The high priests are the superrich hiding behind the screen of banking, like the holy of holies in the Hebrew tabernacle in the desert. These superrich do not know that their dependence on these riches, power, and the conspiracies based on these will be their demise. Jesus said that a camel has more chance to go through a needle's eye than a rich man has on being spiritually redeemed. Oh, they heard about that statement, but fling it to the wind. If your mental sight is on the universe and what it can give you, your spiritual sight is nil. You do not even have to be rich to be numb to spirit. It is exactly the spiritual numbness of the masses that give some people an edge over them that can be expanded on so that the few will be masters and the masses the slaves. Human society has always been this way, and it is always based on acquired spiritual and mental numbness and premeditated evil.

What is Propaganda, and what is its Purpose?

Propaganda forces a final decision between the true god and Jehovah, between Jehovah and daemons lower in his hierarchy, and between authority and one's free will according to one's own understanding of things. The individual is at the bottom of all propaganda-enforced systems. The individual is an important part in fictional reality, but his importance is packaged, bundled into groups through which the individual can be easily controlled, and groups are bundled into masses that can be controlled through group pressure. In fiction, the group is all important. The reality of fiction is slavery, and the reality of positive spirit is liberty. In spirit, the individual is crucial because the individual creates reality in freedom. *Without the individual, any scheme of reality would be impossible.*

The purpose of propaganda, human or in negative spirit, is to ensure that you remain trapped in the universe by derogating Jesus' true message or by making his apparent message to be law, which has already happened in America. In other words, true spirit is banned, and negative spirit in Jehovah is promoted.

Propaganda is not only *spiritually unclean food; it is, downright, deadly poison.* The serpent gave Woman his propaganda, and it was one heck of a smart sales pitch. Woman fell for it and convinced Adam of it also. They both died from true reality because they believed a liar over the one who can only state truth and in whose realm of truth they had their being. The basic overriding purpose of propaganda is to view your specific enemies as friends and your true special friendly people as enemies. You see truth as your enemy and a liar as your friend.

In the environment of truth, one believing a lie has placed himself beyond the ability to commune with truth. Truth does not compute by someone believing a lie. This is the real definition of death and life. You are alive if you have the ability to communicate, interact with the environment honestly. The environment is your closest buddy. Environment is always around you. You are dead to this buddy if you cannot interact with it in any way. Your friends, family, and society see it the same way. When you are in a *permanent* coma, you are dead to the world. There is no knowledgeable communion between you and the environment. We, as souls in the universe, are comatose—dead in true reality where the Good Spirit exists. This reality is everywhere around us, and we are dead to it. Our souls are still in true reality but in a state of being comatose. We, souls, have entered a realm of absolute nothingness, a fictitious environment to which we all agreed to be a part; and it is controlled by your enemy. Since we, souls, agreed to be in fiction, we cannot experience true reality that does not know fiction.

We are lying seemingly dead around the Tree of Knowledge of Good and Evil. There we all dream, attuned to the same propaganda, making believe that we live and love and be in this universe while our involvement in it slowly drains our spiritual energies. The universe is a fiction, but to these bodies that we seem to inhabit in our dream, this universe is the only reality possible. It is absurd to say that the universe is a fiction of our imagination because we see it as real. Here, I tell you, comes in the power of propaganda's mighty weapon—"public opinion." We all enforce this universe on each other, and where we fail to do so, the negative spiritual hierarchy will help enforce it on us all. In our dream state, it is real; that is why our souls, in true reality, must be unconscious. It is either the one or the other.

The major propaganda force is the program "universe" itself. From everywhere, far and near, cosmic propaganda immerses us in a display of a

THE TRUTH ABOUT REALITY

solid earth, nature, and the infinite heavens above. All creatures walk, move, talk, love, and have their beingness in it. It is all but a computer display with us, our soul consciousness, captured and wired solidly into the display.

Propaganda Creates a False Sense of Reality

Human beings are enforcement agents in the display of the universe and events happening in it. We must enforce our impression of the physical world on each other, or it would not be there. I enforce on my wife the fact that I exist and sit in this room. She does the same to me. We have to, in order to be together. Our soul minds have been wired into the spiritual computer display. Her display capability places me visually in my chair only after we have spiritually agreed that I am in the same room with her. It seems that our physical senses are redundant, but this redundancy creates in us the false sense of physical environment and our interactions with it. In the case of an animal of prey capturing its prey, these two agree on the negative spiritual level that the tiger sees the doe, and that the doe will not observe the tiger. It seems that an attack is taking place, but in negative spirit this drama has already been agreed upon.

This false sense of the universe and of each other is all important. It gives soul projections, those we call creatures, a sense of being one with the environment. It makes them perfect actors on an imaginary stage. The important thing is that negative spiritual communion of souls is not perfect. Voids in communion and twists in understanding give randomness to the actions of creatures. For instance, the nature of a lion is not known fully by a lion, but it is not known to a much greater extent by a human being. The nature of being a woman is not fully understood by the soul of a woman, and it is understood much less by the soul of a man. This ignorance of understanding creates randomness in life. This kind of ignorance, not understanding or misunderstanding of all things and creatures seems to make physical reality interesting and seems to bring reality, spontaneity, and randomness. It brings with it a need to guess and make decisions. These are like the confusion and adaptability that ad-libbing brings to the actors on a stage of theater. The actors know what is supposed to happen next, and they count on that; but something else is being substituted or is omitted, and they must respond in a suitable manner in order to save the *illusion* of the play being performed before an audience. All this takes place in the imagination of comatose soul in spirit. But who is our audience, because there obviously is one? Who are we entertaining through living our confused, unsure, miserable existences? We are creatures on stage, and we are not aware of it. Maybe women are aware of it. They are forever working on their makeup and attires. To do these things seems innate to them.

There is thus a lot of physical interactivity and randomness included in the program to hide the spiritual activity that underlies the display of the universe. This is exactly what the One World Order conspirators are doing. They have a solid plan to conquer humanity and they play out the actions as if these are happening naturally, while in truth every move and action has been planned and placed into a script scenario. Then, after the plan has been incorporated, they simply report the results as if these things occurred spontaneously.

The Illusion of Creature Interaction in the Universe

It seems that my wife is in effect by seeing and hearing me in the room physically, but that is the illusion. It is the same with TV and radio; the signals are sent, processed, and then we see the images and hear the sound. But strangely enough, we do not see the images on TV until we first are spiritually informed that this process of receiving TV signals in visual form is occurring. My wife received my spiritual message first, and that is the only reason that she is able to notice that I am here, but it seems that this observation is arrived at through her vision and hearing abilities. The entire affair is run electrically so to speak, and the effects are thus visually and audibly imprinted on her senses. The senses are secondary; the electrical (spiritual) impulses are primary.

The affair of living and interacting physically is a farce. It all happens on a spiritual level, and that level has been captured and wired into a massive spiritual computer [or maybe a script]. The effort to do all this is alien to a soul in reality, so the soul is artificially drained of its spiritual energies. You may think that I am off my rocker, but computer scientists and play directors will probably see this idea very well because they use similar techniques in robotics or script enforcements. Yes, humans and all creatures in this universe are spiritually operated, highly-interactive robots—interactive with the environment and with other creatures and things. The spectrum of electrical and of physical electronic gadgets designed by humans proves the underlying artificial reality of the universe, and that it is automatically run. The universe is a fabrication.

A creature's first reaction to unexpected happenings is suspicion, animosity, and also curiosity. Suspicion and animosity give life to intrigue and further deceit; one has to outsmart the other. It creates randomness of action and randomness is physical reality. Everything seems in its place, and everything is anticipated to occur according to certain reasons of logic, and then things go differently. Human curiosity, likewise, is a weakness that is exploited by others to draw a person into an unsuspecting trap. Written and spoken sales pitches are based on curiosity of finding out what is in there for me? We are being exploited because we conform to laws (routines) of reacting and behaving.

Theater and movie directors experience about the same in the production of a play or movie. The whole scenario is first written down. Then each section is hashed and then rehashed in committee meetings and rewritten. Then the players must learn their lines and each scene practiced and rehearsed until it is ready for final approval to start the play commercially. Anyway, the final illusion is that a story seems to unfold that is quite realistic. The written script can be compared to the display program on the spiritual computer; it is not seen by the observers of the movie or in the case of nature by the creatures. They are numb to it.

In spirit, the whole thing is automated and interacted between the players via scripts in the computer program that daemons can interrupt and modify at any time. According to the script changes, the humans or creatures react in preprogrammed ways according to the scripts of their individual nature as creatures, personalities, and characters, and the program is instantly produced.

The souls have been reduced to computer circuitry bringing to life, interactive puppets that can feel, suffer, triumph, love, and hate and reproduce without end—all for the entertainment of a bunch of daemons. That is all that is left of them as souls that could have been at cause rather than being, helplessly, in utter and total effect. We are not aware of these spiritual activities in our daily life because we have first been disconnected to the source of spiritual reality [through having been made to believe a spiritual lie]. We are completely numb and ignorant that these things are happening in negative spirit. [I say negative spirit because it is spirit that causes us to be in effect. In positive spirit, we are at cause.] What people see are the effects, just as people are in the effect when they are watching a TV program. We are nothing but spiritual signals, and the whole universe is based on spiritual signals. It is when the spiritual signals are processed in our creature brains that we become aware of physical activity taking place in a physical environment. Paul stated in Hebrews 11:1, "To have faith is to be sure of the things we hope for; to be *certain* of the things we cannot see." Paul, I believe, has it a little wrong because the spirit that underlies our physical reality is a terrible crime against our soul beings. Yet it is that exact trueness of spirit of our souls-deceived that is used to fill this nothingness with the physical universe. Paul might have understood that reality of the spirit underlies the reality of the universe. Because of the existence of true reality, this fictitious one was made possible by the serpent by him committing a heinous spiritual crime. I take off my hat for the spiritual insight of Paul. It is truly stunning. Paul realized that innocent spirit was betrayed and misused to trap them into involuntary spiritual servitude to create this phony universe. However, I know that from a spiritual viewpoint, the horrible things we humans play on each other with weapons and propaganda, by deceit, and other actions make us repulsive to Jehovah. I think he is giving us our deserved desert. But then, we are here to learn, experience, and enact evil. That is the way to fulfill the purpose of the "Tree of Knowledge of Good and Evil".

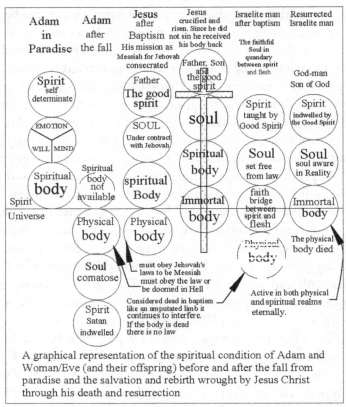

A graphical representation of the spiritual condition of Adam and Woman/Eve (and their offspring) before and after the fall from paradise and the salvation and rebirth wrought by Jesus Christ through his death and resurrection

In the representation of Adam in Paradise I say that Adam in his spirit is self- determinate. This must be so, because if he was Good-Spirit indwelled he would never have fallen for the serpent's sales pitch .

Jesus never died spiritually. He just laid down the physical body
The body of the baptised believer is considered dead.
If the body is dead, then there can be now law!
When a baptised soul is under the guidance of the Good Spirit the body must be considered dead, and the rules and laws of the world must be set aside. One either is under the guidance of the Holy Spirit and under the rules of men, or one is guided by Good Spirit.

Figure 15

Jesus did miracles. He did so for Jehovah's sake first and for his father secondly [although his father was always first in his mind]. He walked on water; he appeared in a room to which all entrances were closed. He healed people from incurable diseases and made a crippled person whole. What does that tell you? He had access to controls of the spiritual computer that are denied to us. We are in effect because we are being controlled and manipulated. Jesus could do these things because he has control and knows how to exert His will over the computer. He is at cause. His miracles also enforce the reality of the universe on us because that is all we can see, and our ignorant importance is placed even stronger on the physical environment. All appearances and effects in the universe make the universe more real. Yet, Jesus calls physical existence the realm of darkness, and he tells us that there is a realm of light, understanding and happiness. He either speaks with a forked tongue or he came here amongst us as a double agent. He had to tread very lightly and make sure not to trespass on the rules of incorporated nothingness, or he would be sucked in as well. He preferred to be killed rather than endure more time in this trap. I know that I want to be where he is because he experienced both realms consciously, and he promotes the one we are numb to.

The Bible teaches us over and over not to fall victim to propaganda. Goliath's talk to David was propaganda of intimidation. Assyria's talk before the gates of Jerusalem during their siege of that city, as is related to us in the Old Testament, was propaganda of intimidation. Joshua and Caleb resisted propaganda against trust in god, the daemon [Jehovah] and were rewarded by Jehovah. Yet, Jehovah is the inventor and manipulator of all propaganda—he is a two-face. Jehovah, clearly, is a god who says, "Do as I say, not as I do." There is not a bit of propaganda going on that he is not an intimate part of. Satan, Jehovah's adversary, wages a successful propaganda against him.

This universe is a propaganda scheme—the realm of darkness Jesus called it. Propaganda is always directed against spirit and spiritual values. Propaganda always works to capture people's trust and faith in a person, a system, and material things and then exploits that trust. Materialism is an obsession of the flesh. Flesh knows nothing else because flesh and the universe are interactive units that cannot exist without *each other's* constant reinforcement.

The use of propaganda to intimidate the population of the enemy is a standard procedure before attacking an enemy or when the enemy has experienced a tremendous defeat. Fear and anxiety are of the flesh. Our lives are driven by the powers of the flesh over our minds. When push comes to shove, it is the flesh that dictates our reaction, not our rationality. Flesh is our intimate and cruel enslaver.

True inner peace comes from trust in Jesus, in his Good Spirit, and from knowledge that all is just a clever constructed nothingness. By knowing this, we can break the chains that anchor us materially in the universe and can begin to act in faith that a real environment exists that welcomes us when we are ready to let this one go.

Propaganda Creates Public Opinion

Propaganda is a system that deliberately instigates hatred and persecution through the powerful tool of public opinion. It uses law and enforcement wherever needed. Propaganda is mental paganism; its most natural targets are the things of god in Christ, which it reduces to manipulative stereotypes without spirit. This definition reaches as high as Jehovah, "the serpent." He used propaganda to deceive Adam and Woman. His real enemy, though, was the spirit in Jesus. He was the one that was robbed and Jesus could do nothing to prevent it. No wonder he calls propaganda evil and the realm built up from it the realm of darkness. Christendom has been reduced to rubble because all members of the Christian congregations are brainwashed zombies. Religion became brittle and fell apart of its own.

The Good Spirit De-Brainwashes His Followers

The Good Spirit de-brainwashes his followers. I can truthfully say that no regular church-going Christian exists who has the Good Spirit to guide him. How do I know? It is because I know the Good Spirit. If you can comprehend and understand the full impact of what I convey in this book, you will have communion in him as well.

The first and basic axiom is that there is absolutely no spiritual good in the universe. To know truth, you will have to find it beyond this universe. I am just telling you where not to look. Do not look to, or trust government or religious authority, do not trust in Jehovah and angels, and do not worship Jesus' body. Do not have a mental idea of true reality because it will trap you back in the universe. If you discount physical existence completely, the Good Spirit is already in you. All that needs to be done next is to learn to commune with him. He is not of this universe because the universe is a fiction. It is because this universe is a fiction [nothingness] that the Good Spirit has always been with you. In the eyes of the Good Spirit, you are a comatose soul in reality that he is trying to wake up. He never leaves your side in reality. And always tries to reestablish communion between your soul and him.

Your Flesh Is Soul's Greatest Enemy

Your physical body of flesh is your greatest enemy. You are physically integrated with your worst enemy—your body that you try so hard to please and make comfortable. That is a good definition of being in hell. It suppresses you in physical nature through ignorance, deceit, wants, disease, hurts, and sorrows. Your constant awareness of the body deprives you of waking up in spirit. Death won't help if you are mentally grounded in physical reality. Your spiritual mental understanding only forces you to return into physical nature through rebirth. You are spiritually addicted to flesh. The flesh is a deceiver, a personal propaganda system that makes you believe that good can and does come through the flesh. There is no good available in the universe. That is the first and most important lesson for a comatose soul.

Propaganda of Agitation or Subversion

Another kind of propaganda is agitation or subversion. Agitation works best when social propaganda is well established and is fruitful. The mass of people are under the strong and effective control of the propaganda operators. [The well-implemented propaganda in America can be seen in operation in the ease by which government was able to convince the American people to kick ass in Iraq.]

Political propaganda in a democracy inevitably results in a two-party-only system held in balance by government who exerts control over both parties, making a mockery of democracy. If this is not done, democracy runs out of control by the group having the greatest access to the media, taking over completely like what happened in Nazi Germany and in socialist democratic America. We are now witnessing the dissolving of the two-party system into a one-party system. The one-party system will be in complete control of government through the appropriate propaganda techniques. It is obvious that this present president, Bush Junior, is a socialist, not a Republican. He is a Socialist on order of the hidden government but pretends to be a Republican. He is redefining republicanism for the young growing up.

The Scientific Base Underlying Modern Propaganda

Presently in America, propaganda is under the discipline of several branches of the sciences such as sociology, psychology, management, human engineering, systems design, and group manipulation and control. Propaganda is now based on what man discovered about man, such as desires, necessities, his psychic apparatus, and his prior cultural heritage. Today, propaganda is based on science that establishes rigorous sets of exact and proven procedures. These compound sets of principles and laws force every propagandist into established sets of procedures, making him a slave to the routines. The propagandist increasingly follows exact and well-established routines that are learned in schools—clearly a characteristic of a technique anchored in science. He must determine precisely, by surveys and through polling and planning, the campaign to match the environment and the type of individual that must be subjected to the propaganda. [I have touched previously on the fact that anything that has to do with rigorous formulas—such as protocol, ritual, dogma, science, and technology—are the trademarks of the Baal, a daemon or an organization under Jehovah, whether four thousand years ago, two thousand years ago, or today.] The technicians and the researchers of propaganda serve this Baal, and they are the priesthood, who are only anointed and dedicated into service after rigorous training and forced by the system to absolute obedience. The major established denominations, Christian and otherwise, have always been controlled and manipulated by similar techniques. Religious authorities have always used propaganda methods to keep folks under their control.

Propaganda was never just a method of covering up evil deeds. It is also a method to instigate people to *do* evil deeds. The old-fashioned lynching party is based on clever, fast-acting propaganda; and the beauty of it is that no one can be charged for murder—all participated, so no one is singly guilty. Jesus met his death through this method. The lynching party is one way to get away with murder. The instigator is the real guilty one, but he generally has enough power and prestige to keep the rest of the guilty masses quiet. Like Bush and his Iraqi, Afghanistan, and Iranian wars, all done behind a campaign of lies—but as in any lynching party, we are all guilty.

What Makes Propaganda Possible?

Modern [fully integrated] propaganda systems can only exist in technological societies under the control of a government-dominated corporate structure. The conditions for social propaganda to take root and be effective are as follows: [Following statements are based on information from the above-recommended book, Propaganda: The Formation of Men's Attitudes.]

The population to which the propaganda is directed must have a standard of living such that it is not overly concerned with the daily needs of oneself or the household. An individual must have a certain amount of free time on his hands to pursue other interests and must be interested in the pursuits of society at large. He must be educated to or beyond the grammar school level and believe that he is informed. He reads one or several newspapers and magazines. He must regularly tune into TV or radio or frequently watch movies.

Humanity must be concentrated in metropolitan areas, where the individual lives in personal isolation. This condition became possible through centralized planning practiced in these metropolitan areas. These conditions are designed on purpose by zoning laws, civil rights legislation, and development companies that *force* people of all different ethnic backgrounds to live in extremely close proximity. The closer the proximity and the denser the centers are populated, the more isolated each individual in it is, and the more threatened he feels by his neighbors and unknown characters in the community. He may seek protection in gang membership. This is the perfect environment for propaganda campaigns to take root fast.

Further, the majority of the population must be employed by the corporate structure. This is a structure in society where one is isolated and controlled in an impersonal manner from the top down. Management keeps social contacts to a minimum, or management will encourage controlled social intercourse in settings where a sense of corporate loyalty is furthered as in sports and controlled discussion groups. Propaganda of *esprit de corps* is very evil and effective, especially in connection with the military, sports in the school system, and in commerce.

Small closely knit social groups such as family, religious and social circles in the mass of people addressed by propaganda had to be broken down to such an extent that the individuals in it are unconnected entities in a large amorphous mass. This shows the state the church in America is in. Sport and fun in church are often seen as more important than understanding Jesus' real message. The social security system helps break up family life by forcing women to full working hours in order to qualify for social security upon retirement leaving the children at the mercy of corporate indoctrination centers.

Modern society forces large amounts of people to leave home and find work in unfamiliar environments, through the deliberately created world wars and by war in general, by the emancipation of women, by the education of our youth in schools far away from the parental home or in settings where the parents have absolutely no input, authority, or participation and through corporate offers to graduates for jobs far away from the family.

Education, or what usually goes by that word in the modern world, is the absolute prerequisite for propaganda to be possible. Education is one's grounding in spiritual deceit. In the young, it is referred to as pre-propaganda. The mind of the young are overwhelmed by fast changing traditions, fast changing technology, and a peer pressure that conflicts with the culture at home. Children's minds, burdened by vast amounts of incoherent data and falsified facts [such as in falsified history and cultural courses] dispensed for ulterior purposes—*posing as facts and education*—is essential for a society to be ruled by propaganda. Public schools are therefore poisonous places for children.

The ability to read is essential for propaganda to take root and establish itself permanently. This then is the reason that education is enforced by law and is controlled and designed entirely by the government, taking this responsibility entirely away from parents where it belongs.

Intellectuals are the most vulnerable to all modern propaganda schemes for the following reasons: professionally, they absorb large amounts of second hand, unverifiable information; they insist on having an opinion on every important question of our time, and they consider themselves capable of judging for themselves. They are the suckers set up and manipulated by exactly the institutions they think they are master of. Since these people are looked up to they will influence many less educated people.

The need for propaganda is so strong in people who are set adrift in an ever faster changing world, culture, technology, and events bombarding them from every corner of the globe that people seek sources of propaganda in an effort to stabilize their confusion so that they, at least, can retain their sense of balance in it. **President D. Roosevelt stated that one can be absolutely sure that whatever government does is very carefully thought-out, and integrated into an overall scenario of plans and schedules.** We must then be ever more aware that our experience of politics, confusion, and progress are carefully planned to lead us to a certain destination like a herd of cattle led to slaughter.

A sophisticated infrastructure of communication must exist where communication flows from the top down, and communication in the other direction is impossible or strongly discouraged; and when it does take place, the results are totally unsatisfactory. These kinds of communication became rapidly available in modern times with the development of printing presses, photography, movies, radio, television, and the Internet.

Propaganda communication must be continuous, from as many different sources as possible, and provide information, falsely and colored, but mostly, irrelevantly truthful, in such enormous abundance and variety that the average person is swamped by it. Therefore, people only make very superficial conclusions from the information received as most of it is utterly irrelevant. News is not news, it is propaganda. By "irrelevantly truthful" I mean facts that are true but have no bearing in revealing the hidden plans that are brought forward. The true facts the media inform you of do not give you understanding as to conspiracies that are constantly being brought to fruition. News items are merely smoke screens.

The media will only report accomplishments of the conspiracies as if they happened naturally, and not by careful, hidden, ongoing design. Such accomplishments are given a twist so as to appear to have been done for your benefit and according to spontaneous negotiations or through great effort of government officials or the military. When the media tell you things are done for the greater good of us all, be careful, turn things around. They are not for your benefit, but for those who have the power to change things in the earth—the very rich. These are the people everybody is working for, even presidents. You do not count. That is the true message the universe gives you when you reverse the impressions they give you. You are made to believe you count in order to bury you in the mud of misunderstanding and to exploit your mind and resources. Everything considered of value in the universe is only of value to those who can pay for it. That is never you. You simply pay because it is forced from you through taxes. Your contributions are always held against you, just as the efforts of slaves and domesticated animals hardly ever are good for them, but only for their masters. That is one of the most important lessons I can give you about this universe. In the negative spiritual realms hidden from human observation, even these superrich are but slaves and beasts of burden. That is why Jesus calls this universe the realm of darkness. The importance of things happening in this universe is *always* hidden from those who have no power or who are being preyed on. This state of things of importance being hidden from our awareness is darkness. This is the realm of darkness because anyone who can benefit from you being ignorant will not give you the facts that will reveal the hidden plans to exploit you. A snake in the grass will not tell the mouse that he is being preyed on. A cat hidden in the bushes poised to jump at the prey does all it can do to remain hidden.

I give you an example of how your children are enslaved by those preying on them. Say I know of a herd of swine that I want to domesticate. I go out to their feeding area and throw out bait. I keep doing this every day, so they come back to it all the time. While the herd is absent, I am working on putting up a fence and a wide gate around the bait area. In the mean time, I keep on baiting the area. Then when the entire corral is finished, I throw out a lot of bait. When the whole group is in the corral, I close the gate. The group is trapped. But my greater catch is the reproducibility of the swine. By catching the group, I caught their entire progeny as well. I will have swine to eat for the rest of my life. You are like swine, and some evil characters in government and banking are devouring you and your posterity.

Consider yourself a swine that others, unbeknown to you, are preying on. The fence to catch you was in the making over decades and even centuries. They are almost certain that your route of escape is cut off. As a matter of fact, you are already in the corral, and all it takes now is to close the gate before you can escape. The fence to confine you is already in existence. It is a seamless web of laws that is like a close-spaced picket fence all around you. The stakes and the boards of the fence are the laws of the land, the precedence of many court cases, more than ample police forces and jails. The hardest thing to put into place was the laws and cases of precedence. They took decades to establish. Everything had to be done by taking tiny little baby steps so your suspicion would not be awakened. It went on during your parents' lives and now in your lives, and your progeny is at stake. We, the people, are the herd the One World Order is preying on.

Now, as for the gate, it consists of all the police enforcement agencies, dozens and dozens in number. You are caught by trained animals who believe in enforcing rules and they will do the most evil things to you because of rules made by true criminals that say they can do that. Your police forces stand guard at the gate.

The laws were put into place through preplanned crime, setup to prove that the law is needed. The First World War was staged to set the environment for the League of Nations to come into existence. The surrender term for Germany were set so unrealistically high that it provided the jump-off point for another, more violent and more destructive war in case the League of Nations would fail or needed extra incentives to empower it sufficiently. The League of Nations failed to bear fruit. It was done prematurely, so the stage was already set for the Second World War. The Second World War was so deliberately utterly destructive, so disruptive to society, took so many lives, and had so many cleverly executed deceits built into it that the conspirators had no problem at all instituting the United Nations. As you can see, it is the net that will catch the entire world population in the very near future. The whole herd of humanity will be in the corral for the conspirators to do with as they please. There is, however, a way out—redemption into positive spirit from whence we have fallen as spiritually empowered souls. We have Jesus' invitation to return to true reality.

This one world order conspiracy seems to be spiritual based because it has been going on over stretches of time spanning many human lifetimes. Someone or a group of people working toward their own enrichment would have used more direct methods to enrich themselves. We see such plans come to fruition through well-planned violence and takeover. Machiavelli was a fellow who accomplished that in Italy. It took one day, and he was in the seat of power. The serpent is another example; he had to prepare the trap first. It was the tree he was found in. But when it was in place, it took but a blink of the eye to trap Woman and, through Woman, Adam.

Information is used by the media to present an aura of authenticity and honesty behind which the plans of the conspirators can safely continue to come into fruition. It is intended to put one's suspicions to sleep because [irrelevant or camouflaged] news seems to be so profusely available, and it is so hard to make head or tail of anyway. Once the mind is put to rest concerning one's suspicions and fears, one will take bulletins and other not so accurate news without discrimination. Presently in America, propaganda is all pervasive; and only by consciously *disconnecting* oneself from all sources of possible propaganda can one protect oneself and retain one's integrity and oneness with god in Jesus as I try to do from moment to moment. The immediate society I must interact with always tries, inadvertently it seems, to prevent that.

To keep the mass of individuals cohesive within the framework of the propaganda machine, it must be frequently jolted by shocks of horror and devastation, which bind the human mental masses closer together in outrage, sympathy, and concern. This is done by causing instances of mass destruction and death as was done by the system through the bombing of the federal building in Oklahoma City, the bombing of the Olympic Stadium in Atlanta, the downing of huge passenger planes such as happened in Miami and off the Long Island coast, and the deliberate destruction of the World Trade Center. I know it seems preposterous to make these claims, but I have gathered enough evidence to give these allegations enough strength for me to write it down here. What do we really know about this government? Anything of value that should be reported to us has been classified as secret. If important information is kept from us, how can we get a correct understanding of the things they do tell us—and why should we then trust government and the information it feeds us? How can we vote intelligently?

These crimes are committed by the government propagandists to lay the blame on the enemies of the present controllers of power and authority—on the basically white population in America, the constitution-guaranteed militias, Christians, and white separatist supremacists and such generally only white groups labeled as the Neo Nazis, the KKK, the Skinheads, etc. These groups even may have their origin in some department of government's propaganda system. Because of the destruction of the World Trade Center, the United States received the support of the American people to fight the Afghanistan and Iraqi wars—the support of a nation of brainwashed zombies. We gave our support to government on wholly unverified information. We just believe what they tell us.

The Constitution guarantees the people the possession of weapons for use in militias. What could possibly be the reason that people want to retain possession of their weapons? The amendment states that this is for the security of the states and our immediate property and family. Who can possibly be the enemy of any of the states, and we, the people?—US government. It was the entity that needed to be controlled through a Constitution to limit its powers. Weapons and state militias are necessary for the security of the states against the US government. Any adult person in good standing can have any weapon he deems necessary to be a deterrent against federal government encroachment so that the states can form armies of militias to secure the sovereignty of the states against federal government. For that reason, states can and should prohibit state citizens from becoming soldiers and policemen in the service of the United States. But, presently, all the states make sure that all their enforcement and defense apparatus make an oath to uphold the federal regime, not the people of the states. All police forces in the states have a contract with federal government to help enforce its laws in the states—against whom?—we, the people. That is betrayal of the people and of the state and federal constitutions by the elected state officials.

Since the US government continues to claim that we still have a valid Constitution for the United States, people can still claim to have the unabridged right to any arms they can afford. It shows that the states have deceived the people because states control the possession of weapons on the insistence of the US government. Again I declare, constitutional questions cannot ever be handled in the Supreme Court in which the judges are chosen by the prime title of nobility in government—the president. It makes no sense. Constitutional questions must be handled, in all their aspects, by the people. It is mainly due to the unfair and biased interpretation of the Constitution by Supreme Court judges that we have lost control over our possessions—the Constitution and the US government. They have proven to be enemies of the people. These institutions violated the exact reason for which the Constitution was adopted. Judges should represent the people, not government; and the armed forces and police should never be allowed to report to any branch of government.

One must ever hold in mind the purpose of the writing of the Constitution: to guarantee the liberty of the people against the encroachment of government against the people; and to continue to limit the powers of government over the people and the states. If this is infringed on, in any way, the governments, federal and state, and local have become criminal institutions. I therefore say that judges have lost the right to preside in court cases because they have betrayed the trust people have placed in them, and through the deceit of the courts, the governments have become our enemies. It stands to reason that we, the people, must rewrite the Constitution as the present one did not do the trick. Government must not interfere in that process. As a matter of fact, no one who has ever held a position in government, and no one who has a license to practice law in any of the states and federal government can be part of these proceedings, and no officers and VIPs in the corporate structure must be allowed to participate. These are already the enemies of the people, by siding with government. Presently, government is run by traitors-of-the-people lawyers. I say lawyers must not be able to run for president or governor. They profess to be counselors; so they must be forced to only hold public positions as counselor and not as executive.

Now, after the US government has empowered itself through amendments and it is secure in these powers, a drive is underway to undermine and remove the rights we, the people, secured for ourselves in the first ten amendments. Can you not see the constant drift through the amendments in the enlargement of the rights and powers of government and the removal of personal rights over the history of the US government? Can the people not see that the founding fathers were right in limiting the power of government? Why, then, do you all sit back and allow this monster to trample all of us without any resistance whatsoever? **If government claims we still have a Constitution, it is your duty to make government walk the line of *the original Constitution*, as interpreted by the people and not by corrupt judges.**

We can see the One World Order at work in President Bush. He just signed a contract with Mexico and Canada merging the inviolable union of American states into a larger confederacy, probably called the North American Economic Union (NAEU). This is only a test to see if the people of these three nations will obediently settle in their common corral before merging us into a larger union of all the American people. Remember, the evil ones are masters in taking baby steps to accomplish their objectives of a world-wide human corral. But also, whatever is finished becomes brittle through use and age and it must crumple—but how long will it last?

Propaganda only works when an enemy to attack is identified by which the propaganda-influenced masses can be mobilized to antagonistic action. The defeated enemy is than absorbed into the regions of the winner, first through installing puppet governments and then by merging the conquered entities into the larger whole.

Government has made our natural attitudes and culture the enemy that needs to be subdued so that the people's minds can be reconditioned to government's world-wide standards. Let's face it; whatever people's attitudes were a hundred and seventy years ago is now considered complete bunk. *It was not bunk then, and it is not bunk now. Public school conditioning and, presently, the all-encompassing propaganda emanating from the airwave media have twisted people's attitudes into ugly contorted pretzels that they wear like mental straight jackets and display proudly.* Humanity is insane!

News is not news. News is the promulgation of cleverly choreographed lies to dupe you into giving support when that is harmful to innocent people and very beneficial to the secret plans of government. If there is no antagonism anywhere, the government creates a brutal crime and blames the group they secretly want to destroy. Government is a fiction. The only manner a fiction gets attention and respect is by making us believe that it is doing things in support of the country. Therefore, to be honored and recognized, they need surrogate enemies to fight and report on. As I wrote, there is no news, but manufactured news; and it is fabricated to further their secret plans. All the media are solidly under the control of government through incorporation.

Whenever a news reporting agency is incorporated, it has become the enemy of the people and a slave to government. You cannot trust the media. They enforce your enslavement through propaganda. All the channels of media are an integrated part of the creature called the beast of government. Only politically correct statements are allowed in the media. Large voids in public understanding are created in areas where the media deliberately maintain total silence; which is censorship. It is against the "now-defunct" First Amendment to the now-defunct US Constitution. The media serve government against the people. Liberty and freedom of the press in the United States of America are a farces.

The constant stream of news bulletins concerning even the tiniest bits of information on purposely created incidents glues the masses to their TV's and radios in horror, sympathy, and concern and with hatred to those insinuated to be the culprits. This gives the spokespeople of the machinery the opportunity to make comments, suggestions, and have public discussion panels, which make the fiction of the governmental beast real by showing government apparatus and officials at work or in the process of giving information, comments, and suggestions as to whom and what caused the horror. *Business is good for government.*

These, deliberate, acts of terrorism by government are kept to a minimum because the more it is done, the more they run the risk of exposure. Generally, natural disasters give the government sufficient occasion to run the same scenario of bulletins and information to satisfy the needs of the machinery; but in the lack of such natural disastrous, non-government-controlled incidents, the apparatus insist that incidents are created artificially. That is why government has this sinister department—the CIA. The CIA is the most subversive organization in the world and the things they do best is to deceive the American public. I can say these things from having observed the history of deceits government has pulled on the people. We all know that lawyers are liars. Why do we allow these characters in office where they really can profit from their main line of expertise—deceit?

The propaganda machine knows from polls and other means of gauging public opinion that such incidents are necessary to glue the human mental mass that is always falling apart back together in coherence. In general, private people [or groups of supposed terrorists] will not cause such disasters as I mentioned above, for it gives them no payoff. The robbing of banks, stores, and rich individuals or the kidnapping of officials of rich corporations are more prone to be the true actions of terrorists; for terrorism also "banks" on propaganda. They also know that real, brutal terrorist attacks will move public support against them. They are not dummies. Terrorists know that government is always the greatest beneficiary of devastating acts of terrorism as it creates splendid opportunities to plug the government's own goodness and efficiency. Governments' mega systems of propaganda condemn these supposed terrorists and seem to react to them. I advise you to take unverifiable information that is supposed to stir the people and government to action as utter bunk. OK, the World Trade Center came down. That is a fact; we all have seen it. But the pointing arms [within twenty minutes or so after the acts] by the accusers in government also point the arms backward at themselves. Nobody ever seems to keep that in mind when someone is making an accusation. In court and any other situation, the guilty person, if he can get away with it, is always pointing away from himself.

It may even be true that Bin Laden is the culprit, but in that case, it is most likely that he has been hired via a certain setups of the US government. The only ones that always profit from acts of terrorism is government; so why would "radicals" do these things? Radicals generally profit more by protest marches as was so successfully done by the civil-rights movement. That particular movement had the support and funding of the federal government. It keeps this fiction "government" right in front of our awareness, and thus the people give it their support. If it happens and succeeds in America it has government's approval. If it happens and fails in America, it has the government against it. Whatever happens in America definitely happens because government wants it so. It is god; and it is increasing its godly powers by the day.

In Jesus' case, and in the many instances in the Old Testament, the sacrifice of individuals was to protect or consolidate the grip the system had on the people. Jehovah often stated that he hated the sacrificial deaths of human beings. Moloch is a Baal that controls the group that owns and operates the propaganda system for its own benefit and pleasure. Jesus knew full well and expressed the fact that he too would have to be sacrificed to keep the system intact, just as the high priest, who advocated the capture and death of Jesus, said, "It is better that one [innocent] man dies rather than the whole religious power structure of Israel suffers." The Old Testament also makes it clear that the casting of spells, which is propaganda, is condemned. So beware of your government that does these things on a continuous and all-pervasive basis. Propaganda destroyed the entire Israelite civilization, and it will destroy ours.

Jesus was fully aware of the propaganda machinery operating in his day in Jerusalem. He frequently bundled the several branches of this system together when he addressed or referred to them as the priests, Pharisees, lawyers, scribes, money changers, and merchants—basically the same groups that have their tentacles on the modern apparatus of propaganda in America. He spoke in parables and often finished his stories with the statement, "Let those who have ears *hear* and those who have eyes *see*." I never understood what "those having ears" meant, but it is now crystal clear.

Brainwashing and conditioning was prevalent in those times, and Jesus' deeper messages were directed to those in the crowd who were undefiled by this form of daemon-possession and therefore could grasp his messages the better. *The conditioned and brainwashed masses are deaf and blind.* That is exactly the purpose of propaganda. The phrase in the New Testament, "Many believed in secret because they feared the authorities who would put them out of the synagogue," or, "Many believed in secret because of fear of the Jews" shows that the people feared those in control of propaganda and the enforcement forces. These statements refer to those in charge of power and the propaganda apparatus that control the masses through a well-formulated public opinion and enforcement powers to back it up. Both the words "authorities" and "Jews" were synonyms for the block of people in control of public opinion and police power. Judas, an apostle of Jesus, had a devil in him as he was under the influence of the religious authorities. He was more brainwashed by the authorities than he was awakened by Jesus. Jesus warned his disciples of the leaven [propaganda and lies] of the establishment. It is insidious and spreads to defile the innocent as well. The Old Testament referred to propaganda by saying of those who practice it as, "those who turn white into black and black into white," and "those who cast spells." "Those" are always very, very rich, have much power and influence and are considered dignitaries with status and eminence. These are always the clowns you look up to.

Jesus, in his teachings, set up a form of worship of the true god that is immune to infiltration and takeover, including propaganda. He wants us to follow him in spirit and not follow or believe any system. Just before he was captured, Jesus transferred this leadership from his person to his spirit whom he called the Comforter. The only one the Comforter has to face when communing with any soul that allows him into the door of his heart is the father of lies, Jehovah. He is already firmly settled in an easy chair right in your heart, and just to make sure you do not shut the door on him, he has removed the door on his side to the heart. At least, the Good Spirit has a chance, even though a very slim one, once he is in the heart [the point of contact between flesh and soul].

Jesus rebuked Satan working through Peter when Peter responded to a stimulus that activated the death stereotype [Peter forbade Jesus to go to Jerusalem where he might be caught and put to death. Satan here is a propaganda system that controlled Peter and made him say these things.] Jesus offered us his words as bread for life for our soul. His word will help you to be de-brainwashed socially and universally so that spiritual reality can break through again [so that soul can awaken from the stupor of a lie-believed]. He said, "Satan, get behind me!" What Jesus meant was, "Peter, use your own thoughts, not those implanted in you by authority"

Repentance [spiritually] was to mean to separate ourselves from all possible forms of worldly influence and seduction [from the many schemes of lies-believed here on earth]. These seductions always come in the form of lies; deceit bundled in a system called propaganda. Such propaganda was also directed at Jesus as activist. It bound the people together in mind, soul, and flesh, en masse to a powerful form of social control, which reduced the masses, even Peter, to mere instruments in the power of others. In the book, *Propaganda: The Formation of Men's Attitudes*, the author actually refers to "propaganda" as **meat, nourishment, and spirit** that drives individuals to seek out propaganda, in their insatiable hunger for understanding. Only through faith in Jesus can we override worldly stimuli; that is why Jesus' word is spiritual food. Yet, even Jesus had an esoteric [a secret] and exoteric [public] message. He was forced to do that because the reason he came was to reveal his spiritual message, but Jehovah forced him to be his Messiah, a worldly deliverer, which was directly antagonistic to what he came in the world to do.

Presently, the whole comprehensive force of propaganda is directed to the very young and upcoming generations. They will receive nothing but carefully planned and executed programs of propaganda so that their conscience and awareness will see an environment and reality carefully designed by the system—an environment and reality completely alien to us older folks.

The same was done in China to illiterate peasants. Mao Tse-Tung devised a new, written script of Chinese characters that was taught in the schools. This script completely replaced the original Chinese script, wiping the entire history of China from the conscious of the Chinese people in forty years time and closed them up in communist propaganda. Chinese teachers were trained as indoctrinators so that all the interpersonal training children received in school were in accord with what they read in their books. Their entire intellectual world consisted of propaganda, and that is what they now know and understand their reality to be. In a similar way, our youth is taught what government wants them to know, not what parents or the church might want to teach them. Propaganda is so pervasive; it deceives those who design, produce, and broadcast it. He who digs a pit for another shall fall in it himself.

The reason propaganda works in an individual is because we need to feel normal. We gauge normality from the environment around us. We have a need to belong. This need to belong to a natural small group [and groups] is an anchor for our personality, just as the family, the village, and the religious congregations were anchors for our ancestors. These basically, locally integrated groups were thoroughly destroyed by progress of one kind or another, leaving modern men with terrible voids in their sense of security and belonging, and lonely in the indifferent mass of people that surrounds them. Propaganda creates a seamless structure that integrates all these isolated and forlorn characters back into a mass that can discuss things during chance encounters and create the illusion of belonging and of reality.

The first steps in the propaganda machinery of Russia and China were the enormous upheavals these government systems wrought on the people. Any possible system of security and familiarity the people of these countries had was thoroughly destroyed, leaving the people, isolated, bewildered, lost, and desperate without trust, sense, or reason. Nothing made sense anymore. One's reason for living was destroyed; and people reverted back to organic drives of instinct, for protection, basic human needs, and company. They willingly sought out sources of propaganda to give them answers to their bewilderment and a feeling of belonging. Communist propaganda quickly filled the void by brutal and forceful indoctrination which later aligned itself to the system employed in America, where propaganda unites the people in a false feeling of unity and closeness.

In America, during the period of pioneer expansion, large masses of people were displaced and new groups reformed based on common plans, dreams, and opportunities. In the process, the light of Christianity was almost entirely blown out. It was through Jehovah's inputs that large numbers of very dedicated preachers formed associations that rekindled the light of Christendom in the American continent and turned it into a blazing fire. The Methodist circuit riders were members of such a group. Pagan government found itself again facing a formidable Christian faith, coherent and obedient to the worldly Christ, rather than government and anchored in secure small communities of families, villages, towns, and congregations. The major flows of Christendom were always inspired by Jesus as Messiah [Jesus' flesh of darkness], rather than in the role of proclaimer of spiritual truth. Government had to find a means to break up this happy peaceful society because the way it was constituted, the government had no opportunity at all to gain control of the people to enslave them for the benefit of the super-rich and the super-ambitious, the hoodlums in government and banking.

The Civil War and the world wars were designed to create large upheavals in society and communities. Most of the male youths were uprooted and placed under military discipline. Nearly a million of them in the Civil War died in a planned genocide. The military draft was one method to mix people of different regions, ethnics and tradition. WWII, especially, gave cause to dislodge the huge groups of blacks isolated in the Deep South from life and progress by relocating them throughout the industrial centers in America and in the armed forces. Propaganda and the armed forces were splendidly organized to nip racial barriers in the bud by the use of iron discipline in fighting these, supposedly, very necessary wars.

To engage in the many planned wars, money was needed that the rich surely were not going to provide, so this money was to come from the people themselves. In the Civil War, international banks were brought in and an income tax was created to provide these funds; while in the south, where the rich were pushed in the corner, they had to provide these funds themselves. The income tax was really a means to obtain credit from world banks that eagerly sought to establish themselves permanently in America. The bankers were given full control of the income tax and collection system, in return for guarantees to whatever kind of loans the government claimed it deeded. This way, loan requests by government were beyond approval by the banks because the bankers were in charge of establishing the laws to set the tax and the means of enforcement to collect the tax. This is still the way our tax system is organized. It is run by the bankers in order to guarantee government any request for credit. You are still being suckered by the bankers to give the US government unlimited access to your wallet.

Federal and State Governments Are in Bank-Receivership.

Since the national debt cannot be paid off any more, government has been declared bankrupt. The power of compound interest has aided in the early bankruptcy of government. The Civil War, the world wars and all wars since were designed to help the US government go bankrupt quicker. This means that all its assets are now assets of the bankers. It also means that you have been sold as slaves to the banks because the Civil War reduced your ancestry to serfs subject to the United States of America. The banks have now full power to collect any revenue or profit from the people it believes it is entitled to or can extort from the people without causing wholesale chaos. You can see that all forms of government have carefully hidden these facts from you through all the years since the Civil War. Government has never stopped deceiving you. This did not have to happen if government was faithful to the people, or the people had courageously enforced the constitution on government. The people were deliberately betrayed by government in conspiracy with bankers. You must now be well aware that the universe is held together through innumerable control systems based on betraying those who have given their trust. It goes all the way down to control systems between parents and children and spouse and spouse. Let us not kid ourselves. I know you understand what I am talking about. There is nothing we can do about these things because the people must delegate powers to others in trust. Trust is always broken from the formation of the universe down to trusts in a family setting and trust in a religious institution today. There is only one rational escape—trust in the Good Spirit who has absolutely no input whatsoever in this universe. He, alone, can be trusted. In the meantime, in this super-corrosive and deceitful world, we must shift for ourselves as best we can.

The income tax worked so well to generate funds during the Civil War that it was permanently installed the second decade of the twentieth century to fund all other wars on the planning board of the One World Order. The funds from this tax was put very hard to work to arm and strengthen planned future foes of America before America actually engaged these artificial "enemies" in war.

> *Government proved to be our enemy by deliberately allowing government to go bankrupt. No sound government can be allowed to financially ruin the government and the people governed by it. So, we are dealing with a secret conspiracy between government and banking.*

Nazi Germany, pre-World War II Japan, Iraq, Iran, and many other countries received enormous funds in American grants, in military training and war materials, before they attacked America or before they were attacked by America. North Vietnam was given enormous wealth on the departure of US forces. Huge damns with hydro dynamic electricity stations, complete airports and huge inventories of weapons, and implements of domestic aids, whole cities erected and the list goes on and on were all provided by the good ol' US of A. All planned in advance of any hostilities, because the USSR was a secret friend of the USA.

Propaganda works best on people severed from each other and from their god. War provides the means to separate human beings from their home, families, villages, and congregations, and reform them into large pools of creatures without any common denominators and willing to be under indoctrination and severe discipline. War only helps bankers and government.

Government is a fiction. Fictions are created for evil purposes. If it cannot be seen there is something dishonest about it. Oh, their fronts can be seen, but fronts are things to hide one's crimes behind; like Lincoln's statue in Washington. Fictions are useless if they cannot place a false front up because if these cannot be seen or appreciated there is no need for them. Government is like any other enterprise, it must have products or services people **feel** they need. This need can only be created if there are situations where people feel threatened and seek this service. Social Security, welfare, and any other services people think they need of government were needs carefully fostered in the minds of people by entities that sought to exploit them. This was done first by the artificially created financial crash of '29 and followed by the necessary propaganda before such systems were put in place. If such situations do not exist, government, through the insatiable desire for power and lucre of the foundationally rich, will create these schemes, even in cooperation with other governments who find themselves in the same situation with respect to their own citizenry. The power behind all "civilized" nations is in the international bankers. The international banks consortium is the hidden government of every nation in the world. It is only a fiction dealing in fictional funds, but it has the power to dig into anyone's pocket; and to give any kind of reward to those who are loyal to them and any kind of punishment to those who are not, as the Iraqis and Afghanis have experienced. They are god on earth with the people's money. The last one who was able to resist them and throw them out of the nation was iron-fist red-headed President, Andrew Jackson. It took years and almost bankrupted the nation. Twenty-five years later Lincoln, a lawyer, and the Congress during his term of office betrayed Jackson and all the people to set the bankers up for good in the United States of America. Lincoln and the Congress of that era sold the posterity of all Americans into slavery and through propaganda they are still hailed as heroes!

Where government is already fully operative on the local scene, a government far removed has no way of finding acceptance in these local groups. So, larger government has to find ways of making itself visible by uniting and incorporating the smaller regions into itself.

This was done in America fighting Indians on the myth that they were dangerous. Government and criminally minded people made the Indians dangerous by simply killing them, by removing land and liberties from them in piecemeal quantities so that the agitators in Indian societies had the opportunity to organize them into politically active and marauding groups. *Agitation* works only on the most ignorant, suppressed, or hunted groups of people. American government, in these deliberate actions, fostered this agitation on the Indians and then used that as reason to destroy the Indians with supporting propaganda that painted these people as unwanted animals; and look, the US government made itself visible to the people of America.

Government's visibility must be recreated continuously by more unwarranted propagandized activities of war, suppression and control, for which the population first had to be molded for support and approval. All American history since 1840 can only be credited to the activities of the most advanced propaganda machinery available. *Anything, at all, must and will be sacrificed to ensure the visibility and need for government and the suzerainty of the International banking consortium over governments.*

As propaganda technology became more advanced, the US government was able to make itself so completely prominent that it is now the all-encompassing entity, displacing gods, honesty, and care. All the good possible can only be conceived of as originating from some sort of government-controlled corporate structure. Individuals have been made to be of no consequence unless the brain of the propaganda machinery determines some credit must be parceled out to an individual or small group here or there.

The governor of California, Arnold Schwarzenegger, is pushing legislation to provide medical insurance for all children, citizens and illegal immigrants. Bush successfully pushed something similar for the United States. What will be the consequences of such mandatory insurance? Parents will care less and less for their children because government will clothe them, feed, train, and care for them. The responsibility is ripped right from the caring parent. Adults will not care if they have ten children, because government will take care of them. But government will not care for them. Government is a fiction, incapable of love and fostering intimate relations or creating anything. It must take the means to provide for all its promises from the people [including the parents]. Government is a fiction. It can do nothing, produce nothing; all it can do is to take from others.

This governor claims to fund this program of insuring children who were illegally introduced into the country by taxing business and industry, and from the state's own resources. This is a propaganda ploy because whatever funds business, government, and industry take in come from the people. The people are the only true consumers. If people do not buy all commercial and government-created products into which all the dishonest schemes of government have been added in the value, business comes to a standstill. Therefore, people are robbed of the honor of caring for their children, yet they have to foot the bill to have their children cared for in a manner that they may not approve of, by a bully called government. We are entering an era of utter carelessness, and government loves this because it will become even more prominent because now it can start taking care of everybody; until it will try to replace Jehovah. That is the drive in any nothingness. The same thing is happening in the spiritual hierarchy, with the result that all souls will end up deep in the trap as utterly disintegrated viral dust, and utterly disintegrated spiritual dust.

Children will soon catch up with this governmental scheme and begin to disrespect parents and society as a whole. Irresponsibility will be bred wholesale. Criminals are fostered because if one does not respect one's elders, respect for society is disintegrated. This is a condition government loves because the more trouble and violence there is in a society, the more indispensable it can make itself through reforms and more laws stifling liberty and freedom, promising to get the situation back in control and thereby ruining other conditions. It can even claim that the parents are to blame for wanton disrespect in their children. Government stinks! It is only a management agency for the bankers. You can now see that the bankers insist on being ultimate god [just as Jehovah wants to be ultimate god and is always busy trying to usurp that position from the true god].

The propaganda machine can work best when it can convince the people, somehow, that individuals do count.

Governor Schwarzenegger is a most clever deceiver. He seems sincere and caring, but he is a calculated criminal, destroying whatever is left of a wholesome society. Parents must care for, teach, and ground children in the world. That is an organic right and duty. If one alters this, only government-enforced suppression and mayhem will ensue; and god will curse America.

This seeming caring attitude of government also is the glamour of the democracy. It actually gives people the illusion that they count and that their vote is important, which it is absolutely not. Voting has as much merit in this brainwashed society as allowing cows to determine in which side of the pasture they will stand before they are being slaughtered.

Government, in short, is then not our friend, our support, and our caretaker; but, instead, it is our very worst enemy and deceiver and is always under the control of evil. Hopefully through this article you will be awakened to the true relationship of people versus government. The job of authorized fiction is to deceive the people and rob them of their liberty. Jehovah sees it that way, and any form of government that has ever existed sees it the same way. Why? It is because they are nothingness that needs to be cluttered up with action so they seem to become visible, and to give them an excuse to rob you of your wealth.

I agree that it is impossible to not have government; but then, having to deal with one, people ought to keep a much closer eye on it than we have done in the past. Really, those behind government are way too clever for us. But thankfully, spiritually, they are the greatest fools.

Political campaigns are propaganda driven by having platforms that are designed to slant people's attention on things the government wants installed. Both platforms come with predetermined issues from which the people can choose. Everybody gets on the bandwagons and discusses pros and cons that nobody prior to the platforms even gave a thought about. For government it is a win-win situation. The losing platform will be put into law a couple of years later by that very same Congress voted into office. No matter which party wins, government can do what it plans such as attacking the Iraqis based on proven-to-be false claims.

Saddam Hussein ran Iraq with not a single loss of American life, not a maimed American soldier and not a penny cost to the American people, and he did a splendid job of it compared to what Bush is doing. Bush's regime in Iraq is in a chaos, and it costs the American people too many deaths and over a trillion dollars to feed this bank-enforced madness; and yet, there are masses of people supporting this dictator "Hither" Bush. I saw a headline on the Internet. Bush replying to skeptics: "So, what is your plan for Iraq?" We have none! You should not have lied to us about Iraq in the first place. We would have saved many thousands of American soldiers and more than a trillion dollars that became part of the national debt Americans are responsible for. I cannot understand that the people still allow him in the White House.

Do you realize that Bush's action already killed more American soldiers than were killed in the destruction of the World Trade Center? He did not have authorization from the American people to fight that war. He told a lie, and that lie altered the awareness of the American people and the world. A liar is totally responsible for the consequences of his lie. He betrayed the American people and spent lots of lives and money through the fruits of his lie. He is an international terrorist. How is he ever going to apologize to the families that had their relatives killed in that unauthorized war? Now he is taking military actions in Iran without the consent or permission of the members of the UN whom he so much seemed to respect. He does not give a hoot about the American people, Congress or the UN. If Bush is not working for the American people, Congress, or the UN, then who is his boss? The representative form of government leaves too much to be desired. Besides we are part of a huge estate that belongs to the bankers.

The very best form of government is still the kingdom. It leaves the hands and minds of the people free to mind their own business. If we must have a government, and we must, the best form is a kingdom. Kings tend to mind their own business as they are all related to each other and need each other's company socially. Just because King George needed to be put in his place does not mean all kings and queens are bad. But from what we can see from American presidents, there was hardly a good one in the lot, and most were straight-out traitors to the American people. I only say this to those who prefer this universe over the spiritual kingdom. If you have to make your home here forever, you might as well make it as good as possible for as long as it lasts, because you are going to be around for a long time. I just observe these things and then drop them.

Our souls' worst enemy after government is technology and progress that we always so eagerly support and believe in, and which are always in the hands of these governmental creators of unrest and slavery. Our only hope, then, is to receive the guidance of the Good Spirit, the bread of truth—the food for the spiritual lives for those who follow his spirit. You are more than the lilies in the fields and the birds in the sky. Seek first the kingdom and all else you need will be provided because your heavenly father knows you need it, and you receive eternal life upon leaving this body. All things of the world that concern you are creations of some propaganda machinery at work, and because of it [because of all the lies you love to believe], you are your own worst enemy. This universe is in your head and in my head, and we are forced to project it outward into this nothingness, and we call it universe. What a mess!

People are the only reality in this universe because they are linked to real souls. Jehovah exploits real souls to have his universe. Government exploits real people, so the few can have overwhelming power over the masses. You are the only thing of value in the universe, and that is the reason all the criminally insane prey on you. The only way they can prey on you is by deceiving you. Government, everywhere, does so in order to have "almighty" authority. Their authority rests on the support of deceived people, and these authorities and the deceived people will die after traversing the entire range of animal natures.

Propaganda's Different Functions and Faces

The main function of propaganda is to secure the hold of power and authority the few have over the many and their own superior relationship among other power blocks, domestic and foreign. Propaganda builds up the esteem, worth, and necessity of the present system of authority and power. It guides the mass mind of humanity in predetermined channels, and it creates the cohesion that is called its culture and society.

It does so with its set of myths that fuel society's sense of ideology, loyalty, and tasks, such as work and production; and it lulls the people to sleep with supposed obtainable ideals in happiness, progress, technology, nationalism, socialism, democracy, the constitution, and even Judeo-Christianity. None of these are even superficially understood but nonetheless fully accepted by the masses. Nothing is important but the creation of an illusion of an all-good government. The system always attacks the other guy. He is the culprit; never dastardly government itself.

An ideology has basically three components—an element of valuation [cherished ideas], an element of actuality [ideas relating to the present], and an element of belief [based on supposition rather than on proof]. Ideology is an appendage more or less secured to this bedrock of the myth by means of clever and effective programs of propaganda. By means of increasing the importance of the ideology, one can slowly break the grip of the anchor within the being and within society and eventually reverse the entire system that makes up the myth and then anchor it again securely within the geographical setting, with a new culture and new traditions. [Mao Tse-Tung was very clever in accomplishing this, but the American government is yet more clever for its strategy is not detected by its own citizenry].

Propaganda steals, borrows, overthrows, or enforces elements of the prevailing myth to evoke new reactions and loyalties and antagonisms within the mass of people toward a predetermined goal for action, conformity, disdain, and loyalty. It is proclaimed that in our democracy, we have a choice of action by voting; but this is a lie because we don't know anything about the elected officials, and the candidates do not know us. As soon as a candidate is elected and in office, he listens to an entire different drummer and forgets any promises he might have ever made. Politicians pretend to listen to the constituency, but their orders come from elsewhere. Politicians are vote robbers by making false promises, and the purpose of the election game is to con over as many people to their side as possible. Besides, voting happens along the lines of an artificial-induced public opinion. A clear example of propaganda is that Bush was still able to run for president for a second term after it has been proven that he deceived the citizenry about weapons of mass destruction Iraq was supposed to have. Bush and the people knew months before he went to war that his reasons for war were entirely untrue. He is a mass murderer and an international criminal. But no one cares. Why not? Because of propaganda. People voting for him are obviously as criminal as Bush, and all of them are international terrorists. He proved to be a criminal before his election. It boggles the mind that the American people have no conscience left and voted him in.

Propaganda works because, as Jesus stated, "people rather believe a lie than understand the truth, and they love the darkness more than light." Here Jesus is saying that we live in fiction of deceit and that there is a realm of truth we have forgotten. We have lived in nothingness so long that the fiction has taken on a reality of its own; and thus we cannot envision, understand, or believe that a true reality exists that will make this reality utter nothingness.

Like Jesus, I am calling people to at least experience a greater, more solid reality by worshiping Jehovah over government and, preferably, seek the true reality from which we fell by believing a spiritual lie.

Who Benefits from Propaganda?

It never, ever, benefits the person it is directed to: Y-O-U, because it always is the fiction [government] that wants to be visible and all encompassing. The manipulators of society are so dumb that it can only think like controlled cattle—and make us cattle like themselves.

What Happens to Private Opinion in a Propaganda Influenced Society

An individual's view of thought and angle of private mental vision is reduced by the creation of stereotypes, which are categories of public opinion. This hardening of opinion soon makes it impervious to all contrary reasoning, proof, and even fact. Propaganda changes opinion without offering proof; "latent opinion" subjected to propaganda will absorb everything, believe everything without discrimination, and cause people's world view to crystallize and synchronize with the view presented by propaganda. This unifying character leads us to a second propaganda effect on public opinion: by the process of simplification, propaganda makes it take shape more rapidly.

Without simplification, no public opinion can exist; the more complex the problems, judgments, and criteria are, the more diffused opinion will be. This cannot be tolerated. Attitudes, therefore, are reduced to two kinds—a positive and a negative—or as in our democracy with a phony two-party system, both controlled from the top by only one party. In plain view, propaganda will simply place anyone with more differentiated opinions into one group or another. Answers to problems are clear cut, white-and-black; and under such conditions, public opinion forms rapidly, breaks free, and expresses itself with force.

The effect of propaganda is to separate the two types of opinion even more. Ordinarily, some interplay between the two sectors [good, the white hat and bad, black hat] continues. When this is short circuited through the intervention of propaganda, relations between the two are interrupted, and propaganda takes over public opinion altogether. The free-thinking person is treated as a fool.

Private opinion clearly becomes devalued where public opinion is organized by propaganda. The more progress we make in society, the less private opinion can express itself through the mass media. The development of the press, radio, and television has reduced considerably the number of people who can express their ideas and opinions publicly. The media exclusively serves public opinion, which is no longer fed by private opinion at all. Individual opinion is without value or importance in a milieu and even in the individual himself as public opinion assumes all authority and power.

Talk show radio/TV is a very clever twist on reducing private opinion as every caller who tries to express his opinion already expresses the public view to a greater extent. The talk show host then will always come back with straight propaganda and public "interest" commentaries stifling free thought. *Talk show hosts are expert indoctrinators* with whom the public can't have the slightest chance of winning, especially because the station management can short circuit any opinion that they feel gets out of hand by cutting off the person's call.

From there on, private opinion can no longer absorb the various elements of public opinion in order to rethink them and integrate them. Propaganda moves too quickly for the individual to react intelligently.

Propaganda makes public opinion impossible to be assimilated by the individualist; he can only follow impersonally the current of public opinion into which he is thrown. The more massive public opinion becomes and expresses itself routinely, the more individual options become fragmented. On the collective plain, they express themselves in such a dispersed way that their intrinsic uncertainty is revealed. In this fashion, man's psychological process is separated into two unrelated elements.

How Does Propaganda Cause Man to Act in Predetermined Ways?

The two world wars were choreographed by means of propaganda. It set people into motion to hate and kill each other in unprecedented forms of calculated slaughter and destruction. Propaganda works best for war or to target a certain group or phenomenon as an enemy. *Propaganda runs the world* [and the universe]. I know and understand that peace by means of a One World Order or a United Nations is impossible, for propaganda will not tolerate it; for by the rules of propaganda, *a nation receiving peace propaganda is in reality preparing for war.* A One World Order will only stifle all local public opinion and behavior on a steep exponential curve as all propaganda is then aligned through only one all-pervasive system of knowledge, action, and technology. A modern nation can only exist and function when the citizens give it their full support; and that support can be obtained only when privatization is completely erased, when propaganda succeeds in politicizing all questions, in arousing individual passions for political goals and in convincing the citizens that activity in politics is their duty. In this manner a nation becomes a living, thinking and acting person; a One World Order becomes a living, thinking calculating giant, and in the same manner Jehovah became a huge, irresistible, fierce god.

The churches often campaign to register voters to demonstrate that participation in civic affairs is a fundamental religious duty. It is a religious duty all right, but not fueled by true faith. The truly faithful withdraw from the world and are incubating every day to become born again in spirit, completely beyond the boundaries of this nothingness called universe.

Now how does this church sentiment fit into a one world organization where all races, groups, and religions are pitched against each other and against a government that controls all the strings to make this collective world-beast come to life by means of fraud, coercion, deceit, and propaganda? It will be necessary on a daily basis somewhere on the globe to suppress a propaganda induced hatred of some sort with irresistible, massive force. This world order will do so without conscience and without any meaningful opposition from the people. The order is just managing its assets.

It is when this order believes it can successfully compete with Jehovah that spiritual hell will break loose. That time is surely not too far in the future.

Today, humankind is again building a tower to bring down god. Whatever will happen, it is all happening in the vacuum of nothingness. It is all a bad spiritual dream.

How Does Propaganda Affect the Christian Churches?

Propaganda destroys man's personality and freedom. It creates a new and false reality that is grounded in the philosophies of the regime/religion and tries to defeat all connections to and belief in the true Jesus and positive spiritual salvation. It makes Christianity of no spiritual effect because the members of the church are all individually programmed and owned by the operators of the propaganda machine; and in most cases, they are directly or indirectly involved in the creation, generation, and dissemination of propaganda. Almost every Christian is under the control of entities that exist by the regime's power, and they are employed in corporations that design, create, produce, transport, instill, transmit, and distribute building blocks, programs, or systems of propaganda.

Practically everybody, including the clergy, is under the strong influence of propaganda; and they are subject to its ideologies, stereotypes, and links. They are subject to absorb, seek, and enjoy mass quotas of propaganda to such an extent that the Christian public opinion cannot be distinguished from the pagan public opinion.

Opinions, ideas, and belief systems imbedded in the minds of the recipients of propaganda are fallacious and have no ground in reality and rob them of their free will and functioning. People's minds are lubricated to follow pre-established tracks of reasoning, which blind them to the fact that their minds are possessed by the operators of the propaganda machinery. These greased tracks make them feel as if they belong and can have righteous indignation against those differently indoctrinated. They will obey propaganda triggers that make them act exactly against their own and immediate society's interest and are Anti Christian and Anti-American in nature. They think anyone who is not affected by the propaganda is a nut and a danger to society—a good example of such lubricated reasoning was the crucifixion of Jesus. Patriots criticizing US government often get the following sentence thrown at them, "If you do not like it here, leave!" This statement preempts such spokesmen from ever correcting anything politically. It shows that people are insane!

Below are quotations from pages 163-166 of this book, *Propaganda: The Formation of Men's Attitudes* [remember that this book is already obsolete by more than forty years of further study and application], I could not say it better, so I will not try. My comments are added throughout in brackets [ ].

Psychological Crystallization

Under the influence of propaganda, certain latent drives that are vague, unclear, and often without any particular objective, suddenly become powerful, direct and precise. Propaganda furnishes objectives, organizes the traits of an individual's personality into a system and freezes them into a mold. For example, prejudices that exist about any event become greatly reinforced and hardened by propaganda; the individual is told that he is right in harboring them; he discovers reasons and justifications for prejudice when it is clearly shared by many and proclaimed openly by the "authorities" as right. Moreover, the stronger the conflicts in a society, the stronger the prejudices, and propaganda that intensifies conflicts simultaneously intensifies prejudices in this very fashion.

Once propaganda begins to utilize and direct an individual's hatreds, he no longer has any chance to retreat, to reduce the animosities, or to seek reconciliation with his opponents. Moreover, he now has a supply of ready-made judgments where he had only some vague notions before the propaganda set in; and those judgments permit him to face any situation. He will never have reason to change his judgments, for they are based on authorized 'truths'.

In this fashion, propaganda standardizes current ideas[2], hardens prevailing stereotypes, and furnishes thought patterns in all areas [of importance to the system]. Thus it codifies political, and moral standards[3] [This is done in several areas for different purposes and goals; it is the very reason that peace on earth is not possible. Propaganda sets groups of people at each other's throat like cocks in the fighting ring, to fight each other on cue]. Of course, man needs to establish such standards and categories, but propaganda gives an overwhelming force to the process; man can no longer modify his judgments and thought patterns. This force springs, on the other hand, from the character of the media employed, that give the appearance of objectivity to subjective impulses, and, on also, from everybody else's adherence to the same standards and prejudices.

At the same time, these collective beliefs, which the individual assumes to be his own [these scales of values and stereotypes play only a small part in the psychological life of a person unaffected by the propaganda], become big and important. By the process of crystallization, these images begin to occupy a person's entire consciousness, and to push out other feelings and judgments. All truly personal activity diminishes, and a man, finally, is filled with nothing but these prejudices and beliefs around which all else revolves. In his personal life, man will eventually judge everything by such crystallized standards. Public opinion within an individual grows as it becomes crystallized through the effects of propaganda while his private opinions decrease.

My own comment: This is true in the spiritual reality as well. We, all beings in the universe, are dead to the true god, because we consider Him a liar. We are dead to him, because we will not have His truth. In the meantime we have accepted and brought to live in our soul as god, the serpent who, to us, is the speaker of truth, but who is in spirit a liar. Everything has been turned upside down. Reality is fiction and fiction has become reality. In the meantime the serpent's propaganda is continuously at work through our physical bodies, through our material and intellectual environment and through the seemingly unlimited expanse of the universe itself. All of these proclaiming the lie to be a truth and making the truth a lie. This is mass crystallized public opinion in all its glory. The true god calls it Evil!

Another aspect of crystallization pertains to self-justification for which man has a great need. To the extent that man needs justification, propaganda provides it. But whereas his ordinary justifications are fragile and may always be open to doubt, those furnished by propaganda are irrefutable and solid. Man believes them and considers them to be eternal truths. He can throw off all sense of guilt; he loses all feelings for harm he might do, all sense of responsibility other than the responsibility propaganda instills in him. Thus he becomes perfectly adapted to objective situations and nothing can create a split in him.

Through this process of intense rationalization, propaganda builds monolithic individuals. [A monolith is an idol] *It eliminates inner conflicts, tensions, self criticism and self doubt. In this fashion it also builds a one-dimensional being without depth or range of possibilities.* [It creates physical entities devoid of spirit and unable to receive the spirit and the truth Jesus hints at]. *Such an individual will have rationalizations not only for past actions, but for future ones as well* [making repentance near impossible]. *He marches forward with full assurance of his righteousness. He is formidable in his equilibrium, all the more so because it is very difficult to break his harness of justifications. Experiments made with Nazi prisoners proved this point."* [The old word for such beings in religion is zealots.]

Tensions are always a threat to the individual, who tries everything to escape them because of his instinct of self-preservation. Ordinarily the individual will try to reduce his own tensions in his own way, but in our present society many of these tensions are produced by the general situation, and they are less easily reduced. One might almost say that for collective problems only collective remedies suffice. Here propaganda renders spectacular service; by making man live in a familiar climate of opinion and by manipulating his symbols, it reduces his tensions. Propaganda eliminates one of the causes of tension by driving man straight into such familiar climates of familiar public opinion [after having created the tension in the first place]. *This greatly simplifies man's life and gives him stability, much security and a certain satisfaction. At the same time crystallization closes his mind to all new ideas. The man has a set of popular prejudices and* [false] *beliefs, as well as an objective justification.* [The man, so manipulated, will assertively declare that all new ideas contrary to his are propaganda.] *Propaganda gives a person a religious personality: his psychological life is organized around an irrational, external, and collective tenet that provides a scale of values, rules of behavior, and a principle of social integration. In a society in the process of secularization, propaganda responds to the religious need, but also lend much more vigor and intransigence to the resulting religious personality; a rigid and mechanical personality that mechanically applies divine commandments and is incapable of engaging in true human dialog and will never question values that propaganda has placed beyond the limits set on him. In this respect orthodoxies in religion have always been the same.* [He becomes a true idol and Baal worshipper because of the stereotypes, symbols and slogans that fill his conscious and unconscious mind and active life. That is why pomp, ritual & national symbols are of Satan. The flag, the eagle, sport heroes, movie stars and singers are so idolized, all by the power of propaganda. The allegiance to the flag is a slogan that binds most Americans into an irrational national group prepared to do any harm to anybody, anywhere on command of those in charge.] *He is characterized by his rigid responses, his unimaginative and stereotyped attitude, his sterility with regard to the socio-political process, his inability to adjust to situations other than those created by propaganda. His mistaking of an artificial problem for a real one is a characteristic of neurosis. So is his tendency to give everything his own narrow interpretation, to deprive facts of their real meaning in order to integrate them into his system and give them emotional coloration, which the non-neurotic would never do.*

Similarly, the neurotic anxiously seeks the esteem and affection of the largest number of people [that is what politicians are doing], *just as the person brainwashed by propaganda can live only in accord with his comrades, sharing the same reflexes and judgments as everyone else in his group. He does not deviate from the group norm in one iota, for to remove himself from the affections of this milieu means profound suffering and that affection is tied to a particular external behavior and to an identical response to propaganda. He feels that he does not want to fool or exploit others, but that others do that to him. This mechanism is reproduced by propaganda with great precision.* [He makes war projects this intention onto his enemy; then this projected intention spreads to himself and he is then being mobilized and prepared for war himself; his hostilities are aroused at the same time as he is made to project his own aggression onto the enemy]. *He will refuse friendship and exhibits hostility toward those outside his group.*

To produce these effects, propaganda restricts itself to utilizing, increasing, and reinforcing the individual's inclination to lose himself in something bigger than he is, to dissipate his individuality, to free his ego of all doubt, conflict and suffering, through fusion with others and devotion to a great leader and a great cause [a thing souls are missing ever since they lost the integrity of being-as-one in Adam]. *In large groups, man feels himself united with others, and he, therefore, tries to free himself of himself by blending with a large group. Indeed, propaganda offers him that possibility in an exceptionally easy and satisfying fashion. But it pushes the individual into this mass until he disappears altogether* [like mass into a black hole]. *What does it make to disappear? Everything in the nature of critical and personal judgment. It limits the application of thought and inquiry. It orients him to very limited personal ends and prevents him from exercising his mind or from experimenting on his own. Propaganda determines the core from which all his thoughts and action can come and draws from the beginning a sort of guideline that permits neither true criticism nor imagination. The acceptance of this line presupposes the suppression of all critical judgment, which in turn is a result of the crystallization of thought and attitudes and the creation of taboos.*

These quotes represent only 5 pages from a total of some 255. Please, dear reader, do you even see a fraction of these tendencies and reactions within your own makeup? Does it represent a mask you might be wearing? Can you see these things in operation among acquaintances or in people in your congregation? Come out of her, this mental whore of Babylon! We cannot allow so many millions to die without an effort to reeducate them. Once the lie is exposed, it will never bind you or them again.

Propaganda gives the individual stereotypes, so he no longer needs to take the trouble to evaluate things for himself; it furnishes these in the form of labels, slogans, ready-made judgments [and responses]. *Propaganda transforms ideas into slogans, and by giving the word, convinces the individual that he has an opinion.*

Symbols are related to the psychological phenomenon of the stereotype. A stereotype is a seeming value judgment, acquired without any intellectual labor, and reproducing itself automatically with each stimulation. [Military and police academies operate on this principle, producing 'academic-dummies' who can only react according to the doctrines and disciplines instilled]. *The stereotype arises from the feelings one has for one's own group* [or against the out group]. *Man attaches himself passionately to the values represented by his own group and rejects the clichés of the out-group. "To share the prejudices of a group is only to demonstrate one's affiliation to this group. Stereotypes correspond to situations which the individual occupies in society, his group and his profession. "The stereotype is a "genuine category . . . a manner of thinking, of interpreting*

experience, of behaving"—but founded solely on affective reactions. The stereotype
is specific: it relates to a given name or image, which must be precise in order for
the stereotype to work [Neo-Nazi, white supremacist, Christian home-schooler,
far right Christians etc].

The stereotype, which is stable, helps man to avoid thinking, to take a
personal position, to form his own opinion. Man reacts constantly, by reflex, in
the presence of the stimulus evoking the stereotype. This reflex permits him to have
a ready-made, apparently spontaneous, opinion in any situation; in fact, it gives
him the sense of a situation. With regard to an ethical problem, the stereotype is
the criterion of values. It is usually formed in a limited group [such as a class of
10-50], *but tends to develop, to extend itself to an entire collective. It is endowed*
with a force of expansion; moreover it gradually detaches itself from the primordial
images that have aroused it and takes on a life of its own. [That is why there is
such unity among police and higher-level bureaucrats in general and against
persons in the citizenry.]

In propaganda, existing stereotypes are awakened by symbols. The symbol
permits the formation of a favorable response that can be transferred to persons and
objects associated with it. To ask a group what it thinks of some sentence written
by Victor Hugo, results in the Victor Hugo stereotype [previously created in a
group setting]: *but to ask their opinion of the same sentence without giving the*
author name, evokes no stereotype and elicits a very different opinion.

In a bourgeois milieu the proposition "Communism demands justice"
provokes an unfavorable reaction, but the reaction is favorable among groups that
stress justice. Here the stereotype "justice" wins out; in the former the stereotype
"communism" is dominant.

The Use of Symbols

We can divide symbols into three categories. There are symbols of demand,
which express the aspirations of the group seeking to produce events. Then symbols
of identification, which define the protagonist who acts for us, or the antagonist
against whom we act. Finally there are the symbols of expectation which present
facts for immediate or future objectives, but all these facts are, in reality, abstracts
of themselves and have become symbols.

The use of symbols divides the individual's conscience against itself.
Effective propaganda uses multiple symbols linked in such a way that some
evoke known images and appeal to the conscience, whereas others violate the
conscience and tend to destroy it or deny it. The symbol is an effective instrument
for progressively separating the individual from primitive impulses, from his

*natural attitudes, and for creating "counter attitudes" and "counter behaviors."
By this procedure, propaganda succeeds in weakening the individual's conscience
and consciousness and in unsettling individual attitudes during a period of
transition with a view to furnishing them with new content. One does not,
for example, destroy symbols of authority and replace them with independence;
one replaces them with new symbols of authority. This use of symbols presumes
a very advanced propaganda. It is what we find for example in the Stalinist
propaganda.*

*At an elementary level, all symbols have the purpose of awakening stereotypes,
an appropriate function because by their nature they already unite the emotional
and the intellectual life.*

*This function is served by photos and images that have a special power to evoke
the reality and immediacy of the stereotype; itself an image, it is fed by certain
other images. The Statue of Liberty and the Arc de Triumph provoke immediate
reactions. The photo carries with it the intrinsic qualities of the situation that it
represents; it thereby reinforces the stereotype while stimulating it.* [Pictures evoke
manufactured responses in people to aid hungry people or support suppressed
nations. These images may secure the aid the propaganda elicits, but it will
not lay up treasure in heaven, for they create counterfeit feelings and loyalty
in people coming from Satan]

*Another particularly evocative symbol is the slogan, which contains the
demands, expectations, and hopes of the mass mind, while simultaneously it
expresses the established values of the group. Slogans determine quite accurately
the type of groups toward which an individual is oriented; whether or not he is
a member.*

*Above all, the stereotype assures the continuity of the stereotype, which is fixed
as a function of the past. But the individual finds himself constantly faced with
new situations that the stereotype alone does not permit him to master; the slogan
is the connection used by the propagandist to permit the individual to apply his
old stereotypes to new situations. The mind brushes up and adjusts the ready-made
image; at the same time, he integrates the new situation into a classic context,
familiar and straightforward. That is why the slogan flourishes in times of crisis,
war, and revolution. It also explains the attraction slogans have. Thanks to them,
the individual is not intellectually lost. He clings to it, not only because the slogan
is easy to understand and retain, but also because it permits him to "find himself
in it." It tends, further, to produce stereotypes in people who did not have them
before the crisis situation. By so doing we can create errors by force or an effective
error; although the opinion or judgment is incorrect, they become unimpeachable
through repetition and the strength of collective belief.*

Below is an excerpt from pages 9-11 of the book *Propaganda: The Formation of Men's Attitudes,* again with my comments in brackets.

Propaganda addresses itself at once and at the same time to the individual and to the mass the individual belongs to. The propagandist cannot separate the two. For propaganda to address itself to the individual, in his isolation, apart from the crowd, is impossible. The individual alone is of no interest to Propaganda; as an isolated unit he represents much too much resistance to external action. To be effective, propaganda cannot be concerned with detail, not only because to win men over one by one takes much too long, but also because to create certain convictions in an isolated individual is much too difficult. Propaganda ceases where simple dialog begins. That is why experiments in propaganda in America to gauge effectiveness of propaganda on isolated individuals are not conclusive, because they do not reproduce the real propaganda situation. Conversely propaganda does not aim simply at the crowd. A propaganda that functions only where individuals are gathered together would be incomplete and insufficient. Also, any propaganda aimed only at groups as such—as if a mass of people were a specific body having one soul, one set of reactions, and their own feelings, entirely different from the individual soul's reactions, and feelings—would be an abstract propaganda that likewise would not be effective. Modern propaganda reaches individuals enclosed in a mass, yet the individuals in it must be isolated from one another. [This is exactly as Paul, the apostle, saw the body of Christ forming on earth; but in this case, the body would be inhabited by Christ as the soul and mind. That is why I say that to be a part of Christ's body, one must drop participation in all matter and manners of worldly affairs. If you do contrary, as a Christian, you would be a cancerous cell fighting the whole body and mind, rather than aiding Christ's mind in operating his body.]

What does that mean? First, that the individual never is considered as an individual, but always in terms of what he has in common with others, such as his motivations, his feelings, or his myths. He is reduced to an average, and, except for a small percentage, action based on averages will be effectual. Moreover, the individual is considered part of the mass and included in it [so far as possible systematically integrated into it], *because in that way his psychic defenses are weakened, his reactions are easier to provoke, and the propagandist profits from the process of diffusion of emotions through the mass, and at the same time, from the group-pressures felt by the individual when in the group. Emotionalism, impulsiveness, excess, etc.—all these characteristics of the individual caught up in the mass are well known and very helpful to the propagandist. Therefore the individual must never be considered as being alone; the listener to the radio, though actually alone, is nevertheless part of a large group of listeners and caught up in the same stream of emotions as part of a large group and he knows that. Radio listeners have been found to exhibit a mass mentality; all are tied together as a sort of society in which all individuals are accomplices and influence each other without knowing it. The same exact mentality is true for the public visited by a force of canvassers on a door-to-door interview program. The individual is no longer Mr. X, but a particle in a current flowing in a particular direction. The current flows through the canvasser* [who is not a person speaking in his own name with his own arguments, but a segment of an administration of an organization, a collective movement]; *when he enters a room to canvass a person, the mass, and more over, the organized leveled mass, enters with him. No relationship exists between man and man; the organization is what exerts the attraction on an individual already part of a mass because he is in the same sights as all the others being canvassed. Conversely, when propaganda is addressed to a crowd, it must touch each individual in that crowd, in that whole large group. To be effective it must give the impression of being personal, for we must never forget that the mass is composed of individuals. Actually, just because men are in a group, and therefore weakened, receptive, and in a state of psychological regression, they pretend all the more to be "strong individuals."* [The mass man is clearly subhuman, but he pretends to be superman. That is why the Good Spirit can only commune one on one. If a person in a mass was directed, the spiritual message is instantly corrupted. Now you can see that super preacher Billy Graham may convert hundreds of thousands of people, but he will never guide a person to the Comforter. His preaching is an exercise in futility and the converts are mere individuals drugged by Bill Graham's sort of religious propaganda. His converts are robots with mechanical hearts; besides Billy has no idea about Jesus' inner message. He is a phony!]

The person under propaganda pressure is more suggestible, but insists that he is more forceful; he is more unstable, but thinks he is firm in his convictions. If one openly treats the mass as a mass, the individuals who form it feel themselves belittled and will refuse to participate. If one treats the individuals as children [and they are children exactly because they are in a group], *they will not accept their leader's projections or identify with him. They will withdraw, and the propagandist will not have control over them.*

On the contrary, each one must feel individualized, each must have the impression that he is being looked at, that he is being addressed personally; only then will he respond and cease to be anonymous [although in reality they all remain anonymous]. *Thus all modern forms of propaganda profit from the structure of the mass, but exploit the individual's need for self-affirmation; and the two actions must be conducted jointly, simultaneously.* [It is important in TV propaganda that the speaker or narrator looks very often straight at the lens of the camera. Eye-contact is person to person contact. News casters are trained to do so to make the propaganda pill have stronger effect.]

Modern mass media have just exactly that remarkable effect of reaching the whole mass individually; and at the same time. These principles are used extensively on fundraising projects of public radio and TV stations all over the country; and by the Christian TV of the *700 Club*. The speakers always look you straight in the eye, and masses of people cannot resist the urge to pick up the phone impulsively to make a commitment that is not theirs, but is literally forced out of them by the trigger mechanisms of the propaganda machine.

The same format is used from program to program, and it is never deviated from because it is the fine tuned precision machine that reaches a person under influence of propaganda. The viewers or listeners are puppets on a psychological string, and they all are made to dance the same routine for ends that serve the organization and not for the sake of the congregants. The 'Jesus' myth [as Christ] is used to obtain the goals of men; it is not used in service of the Good Spirit, which is to redeem your soul.

Pick up the phone; make a pledge and feel victorious. These reactions have no personal value because they are done, not by personal reflection and intent, but by a trigger in the system that creates fake responses from the mass mind. It is made to look like it is the right thing to do, and every time a sucker phones in his name and his pledge it is announced and used to enforce the same response from others. This routine is never deviated from, because it is like a copy machine—every time you push the button, a new set of copies [responses] are produced. [In the case of the *700 Club*, it has no spiritual effect at all; all the funds are obtained by simply forcing it by psychological means from the pocket of the listeners.] The individuals are moved by the same motives, receive the same impulses and impressions, find themselves *focused* on the same centers of interest, experience the same feelings, have generally the same order of reactions and ideas, participate in the same myths—and all this at the same time; what we have here is really a psychological, if not a biological mass-mind.

Every tear-jerking movie produces the tears on this same principle of mass psychology, fake emotions relating to a totally fictitious representation of facts, totally irrational; and that is what propaganda aims to elicit from each individual in China, Russia, France, and America. The more all the components of this infrastructure of the media interplay with each other, the more propaganda addicted the audiences of such media are.

> *The structure of present-day society places the individual where he is most easily reached by propaganda. The media of mass communication, which are part of the technical evolution of society, deepens this situation while making it possible to reach the individual man, integrated in the mass; and what these media do is exactly what propaganda must do in order to attain its objectives. In reality, modern propaganda cannot exist without the use of these mass media, thus one leaves no part of the intellectual or emotional life alone; man is surrounded on all sides—man and men, for we must also bear in mind that the media do not all reach the same public in the same way. Those, who go to movies three times a week, are not the same people who read the newspapers with care. The tools of propaganda are thus oriented in terms of their public and must be used in a concerted fashion to reach the greatest possible number of individuals.*
>
> *Each medium is particularly suited to a certain type of propaganda. The movies and human contacts are the best media for sociological propaganda in terms of social climate, slow infiltration, progressive inroads, and over-all integration.*
>
> *Public meetings, posters and TV are more suitable tools for providing shock propaganda, intense but temporary, leading to immediate action. The press tends more to shape general views, radio is likely to be the instrument of international action and psychological warfare, whereas the press is used domestically. In any case, it is understood that because of this specialization not one of these instruments may be left out: they all must be used, in combination, to produce an all-pervasive public opinion.* [The propagandist uses a keyboard and composes

a propaganda symphony. The American corporate law system integrates all media into a machine operated by governmental news-disseminating departments to implement their propaganda. Americans do not get news per sé, but propaganda.]

It is a matter of reaching and encircling the whole man and all men. Propaganda tries to surround man by all possible routes, in the realm of feelings as well as ideas, by playing on his will or on his needs, through his conscious and his unconscious, assailing him in both his private and his public life. It furnishes the victim of the propaganda with a complete system for explaining the world, and provides immediate incentives to predetermined action. We are here in the presence of an organized myth that tries to take hold of the entire person.

Through the myth it creates, propaganda proposes a complete range of intuitive knowledge, susceptible of only one interpretation, unique and one-sided and precluding any divergence. This myth becomes so powerful that it invades every area of consciousness, leaving no faculty or motivation intact. It stimulates in the individual a feeling of exclusiveness, and produces a biased attitude. The myth has such motive force that, once accepted, controls the whole of the individual, who becomes immune to any other influence. [This explains the totalitarian attitude that the individual adopts—wherever a myth has been successfully created—and that reflects the totalitarian control of propaganda on him.]

Not only does propaganda seek to invade the whole man, to lead him to adopt a mystical attitude and reach him through all possible psychological channels, but more, it speaks to all men. Propaganda cannot be satisfied with partial success; by its very nature, it excludes contradiction and discussion. As long as a noticeable or expressed tension or a conflict of action remains, propaganda cannot be said to have accomplished it aims. The desired manipulation must be complete in that the aims are completely accomplished through it. It must produce quasi-unanimity, and the opposing faction must become negligible, or in any case cease to be vocal. Extreme propaganda must win over the adversary and at least use him by integrating him into its own frame of reference. [I am afraid that the Church may have used these methods not only in drawing all Europe into it, but also once Europe was conquered by this false church, to enrich itself by propaganda on the wealth of its captives. Propaganda used for religious purposes has nothing to do with one's personal surrender in repentance, but in manipulating the mechanical triggers that can produce compliance in flesh.]

Lenin discovered a principle of "*ends over means*" and Hitler intensified that principle to liberate all energy available to pure action with goals that are so far out that they could not be called ends; as for instance, Hitler's "millennium" end was for Nazism. His slogan was that work ennobles, and in many cases, people were put to work doing senseless things to apply this principle of his propaganda machine. His administration forced all people to work with all the vigor and means available and to not look to the end to which the work aims, but only at the work to be done now. They were both so successful that it completely transformed the relationship between ideology and propaganda. Ideology was only important to them if it could mobilize the masses to some predetermined action. They discarded ideology where it could not be used, or it was used as a component in propaganda strategy. Propaganda then became the major strategy while ideology retreated completely into the background as some sort of end as it is to this day. Propaganda, then, does not obey an ideology at all. This seems to be a fully sound principle for those in the Comforter. As far as work is concerned, we are to completely rest in Jesus; this means doing absolutely nothing towards the ends of spirit because as creatures of the flesh, we cannot work toward spiritual ends because the flesh and the spirit do not know each other. We do his will in our personal selves by entirely depending and resting in Jesus and allowing his will to create the things of his mind in us. Jesus stated this principle in particular in his prayer he taught his apostles and disciples. Your will be done in earth [in us in the flesh] as it is in heaven [in god]. The true god's will for us is to do absolutely nothing because nothing we do can help our redemption in true spirit. All true spiritual understanding must come from the Comforter.

All governments, it appears from the Bible, are based on propaganda; and it seems the only way in which to maintain them. God, Jehovah, hates man-based propaganda because it is based on lies and deception and because it creates an artificial reality that hides the righteousness of him, and because it makes mechanical creatures of his people who can then be riled singly or collectively for any evil project or action. ***Jehovah insists on being the authority, not government. Jehovah hates government. He said so to the judge Samuel in the Old Testament.***

Jesus was especially perturbed with the Jewish authorities, who by forcing all kinds of rituals on the people kept his people from true worship; and today, again, it is a new group of Jews that hold us in bondage by this same evil scheme. The purpose of propaganda is strife, and strife the world has always had because of it. That is why Jehovah sent all the prophets to wake up the people and the kings. Unrepentant people cannot be forgiven or saved, and people under control of the wrong propaganda refuse to repent by power of the myths and the stereotypes hammered into their minds. So we need to really understand this evil, propaganda; deliberately observe the hold it has on us, then realize that we cannot be forgiven and then repent where we are sincere in our reliance on grace in Jesus. Jesus can disconnect us from propaganda through real faith in his spirit. Our captivity in and by propaganda keeps us from obeying the father, and it seems that our very flesh is part of this system of propaganda. When Jesus gave his sermon on the subject of "eating his flesh and drinking his blood," he addressed the people by means of stereotypes that the public under the influence of propaganda could not receive. Their mechanical response was to denounce the sermon and Jesus without finding out what he truly meant. That sermon, even up to the present, has turned people off by activation of these same stereotypes. Jesus used stereotypes in other sermons to allow the people to give reasons to be offended. This was one way in which Jesus separated the goats from the sheep. It was a pretty complex procedure, but by the time he was on the cross, the separation was complete. Souls who belong to Jehovah will stay here in the universe as propaganda herded sheep, and his goats will be redeemed, no matter how long it may take. Once a goat is in his grasp [is disconnected from external propaganda] it is part of his flock, and it will be brought home in positive spirit. That is the reason I say that you cannot listen to worldly teachers when under the guidance of the Comforter. Worldly teachers are completely immersed in propaganda and that is all they can teach you. It is of the world and thus poison to the spirit.

It is noteworthy that those who used propaganda were the most under its influence, and the first to denounce and hate Jesus—the priests, Pharisees, and scribes. It seems likely also that the people of Babel were united in actions and belief through propaganda. It is as I stated before, ***"Language transmits the lie, not truth."***

We will have to start looking at such completely trusted publications as the *Plain Truth, Daily Guide Post, Watch Tower,* and *Our Daily Bread* as effective tools of propaganda. The propaganda of the establishment is most rigorously addressed to [and at the same time against] Christians to make them believers in government's religion and values. These publications are mass distributed to Christians free of costs and are generally beyond suspicion. Most every church receives and distributes them among their members. I have often found within these publications propaganda opposing racial segregation and propaganda upholding this evil government and their wrongful legislation and actions. These weekly publications certainly uphold and align themselves with the dictates of government propaganda; they have no choice if they want to remain in weekly and monthly circulation. The circulation is more important than uncorrupted messages; and believers become adherents of propaganda and lose their spiritual grounding.

These circulars have all the criteria that are essential for an effective propaganda medium; they are trusted and accepted among Christians to such an extent that they have replaced the Bible for most Christians. People will read these daily devotionals instead of the Bible. These media are read almost daily with religious attention and belief. They are a teaching medium. The publishers print mostly factual information in a religious frame and introduce, proclaim, and uphold established government propagandized myths, stereotypes, and allegiance to qualities of government that have long since disappeared or have actually been reversed in practice and meaning.

These devotionals even contain propaganda the authors of the articles sincerely believe themselves and therefore do as much or more harm than propaganda brought into the home by unsuspecting parents. No propaganda is as thoroughly believed as propaganda believed and regularly disseminated by parents to their children and by unsuspecting ministers to their gullible flocks. All actions based on false belief are irrational, of this world, and cannot ever lay up treasure in heaven.

We must, above all, remember that infiltration is the most effective tool to destroy the church and destroy the opportunity to receive eternal life. These booklets are supreme in their routine acceptance by the clergy and laity alike. A mixture of true gospel and false gospel believed in will not result in a saved soul. Both, the true god and Jehovah shun lies and believers of a false or a corrupted gospel. Propaganda will destroy gospel coming from Jehovah and the true message coming from the father in truth.

We are truly only safe in Christ, all else is Satan modifying or corrupting our true beliefs. We have two options left; the first is to be as trusting in Christ's popularly understood gospel as the lilies in the field are to nature, or secondly, to separate oneself from all group activity, political activity, media involvement and rest in the Good Spirit privately.

But how can we live in this society and not be a part of it? How can we not be employed in this Baal system? The answer is: "With men, this is impossible; but with god, all things are possible." One must simply, being in Jesus, quit the religious and secular establishments and in full faith and sincerity wait upon the Good Spirit; and stances of being will open up that run entirely free of the establishment structure. Being true in Christ is based on incomparable courage and trust. Trust that Jesus' Good Spirit cares for you so much that, in spite of the sheer pervasiveness and power of the Baal, he will provide; and most likely, at the cost of the Baal without subordinating you to it.

It took almost three years for Jesus to reform the mindset in his apostles from propaganda indoctrinated zombies to trusting adherents of his teaching. It was only at the end of his ministry that he said to the apostles the things written in John 13-18. Yet most apostles reverted back to the propaganda of the cosmos. I believe that Thomas was a true convert.

Paul differentiated in 2 Corinthians 10:1-7 between the weapons of the world, which have always included mind control, lies, fraud, force, and deceit, and the weapons of the father by which we destroy such strongholds in our minds. "Those weapons in our hands will destroy false arguments, can pull down every proud obstacle raised against the knowledge of god and take **every thought captive**" [Know and recognize propaganda and how its tries to force itself in your mind] and make it obey the positive Christ. This sure positive spiritual weapon is *to be dead to the world and the universe*. Only *after we have proved our complete loyalty* will we be visited by the Good Spirit. It is now time for Christians to start pulling down Antichrist's strongholds [all forms of propaganda] in their minds and prove to god their complete loyalty to him, rather than to the deceivers in spirit, church and government [Rev. 3:15]. You can only pull down strongholds in your own mind; all else, thank god, is beyond your responsibility and power. The way to pull down Satan's strongholds is to abstain from the media, voting, etc. The world is Satan's prison yard; you are set free by ignoring the ways of the world [Satan] and the power of cosmic propaganda, and the negative spirit in Jehovah; then you are floating in limbo, but the Comforter will fill the void and guide you into his spirit, reality.

Man's purposes are exactly inverted from what the father in reality wants. An example of symbols presented to stimulate universal stereotypes was when Satan tried to seduce Jesus in the desert trice, based on the myths of the value of pagan life—vanity and worth.

Generally, this stimulation would trigger the desired effects in the target, and Satan was surprised to see that they did not work on Jesus, but he thought he could accomplish Jesus' fall some other way yet. Active *stereotypes* in the mind will convince man that to do wrong now to obtain a future desired good is OK. They put to sleep our conscience while we are planning to do wrong and justify our wrongful actions with promises to use the profits for some future good purpose. All communist propaganda was based on that tenet; and, of course, though not so visible to us, American propaganda.

It will fool men who live mostly for the flesh [and that includes most all religious people]! The evil within man is that he can be seduced to react to symbols that activate the stereotypes in his mind, rather than base his actions and thoughts on true faith. Souls captured in flesh have become a machine, a computer. The worth of the pure soul has been lost [the gold and jewels have been ripped from him], and the mind of the soul has been incorporated' or wired in to the computer that projects into nothingness the universe. And this illusion is our captor and our eternal hell. And people do love it so!

But for those who want to be redeemed, it is all or nothing, the Good Spirit or the world, because the Good Spirit is all; and the world is nothing, fiction, a web of lies.

The Crucial Question

I conclude Book V with the same crucial question I concluded all four other books, "Why does evil exist?" By now you hopefully can answer this for yourself. Evil always comes in a disguise of good. Evil is the depth of deceit because it comes disguised as good. Souls **must understand and know evil** [remember, we, in paradise partook of the tree of **the Knowledge** of **Good** and **Evil**] to be able to look through all the disguises that evil can hide behind. This is of spiritual significance because if evil could take on a disguise of good in the realm of good, evil would invade and settle in the realms of good without "good" knowing about it. So whoever will enter into the ultimate realms of good must know every aspect of evil to be able to look through all the disguises of evil in order to identify and embrace good and shut out all avenues through which evil can slip unnoticed into the realm and communion of good. Nothing is as it appears to be. Everything in the universe is evil in a disguise of good.

> *Evil is a communion, just as good is a communion. Do not let a communion of evil disguised as good fool you any more.*

If evil would succeed, existence in any plane of reality would become an intolerable nightmare and we would be caught in inescapable suppression and hatred without love and without anything to look forward to, because evil would have shut off any possible escape route. I give you examples of evil that shut off all avenues of escape: the Wall erected between East and

West Germany, The Elba River in Germany between East and West at the end of the war with Germany, the river of death. I give you the continual encroachment of government into our every moment of daily life.

Liberty and love would disappear from all levels of reality forever. I hope that everybody in the world can identify with this kind of horror. If you can, you are truly ready to embrace the Comforter in the Good Spirit who is reality as good and not as evil. Government, marriage, children, cars, computers, planes, you name it; they are all disguises of evil pretending to be good.

> *Do Not Let the World Confuse You Any More; There Is No Good in It. Only One Is Good, Ultimate Truth in Ultimate Reality; and As Yet, You Have No Part In It.*

The disguise in which evil tried to usurp the intentions of good in Jesus is so severe, that it took 2,000 years to understand what Jesus was truly doing. Jehovah has been exposed and stands naked. Good is the responsibility of every soul in existence. If you cannot rally for good you will be utterly annihilated.

> *Now, I Sincerely Hope You Take Me To Heart. I Am Not Much Of A Spiritual Leader or Politician, I Am Not Jesus Or Some Saint; But I, Anti Christ, Am All You Have in the Good Spirit, Whether You Are The Pope, The Ayatollah, The Dai La Lama, Bill Gates, Oprah, George Bush, Or Whoever You Think You Are—Like Jesus' Words, My Words Help Give You Life. They are truly worth all you have.*

All Christians brag on knowing truth, however not one knows what truth is. The truth is that you live a lie in a reality based on a lie. Jesus came to make you aware of that fact. From hereon out it is a matter between you, Evil, and the Comforter. The ball is in your court.

NOTE: It is up to you to recommend this set of books in one cover to everyone you care for. Many people have a tendency to repress the knowledge of others by withholding recommendation to those they hold dear. This is a selfish attitude. If you love someone you should allow that person to have information and options to form his or her own opinion. Be yourself, not Jehovah's patsy. This book helps you to do that.

This material will give anyone powerful rehabilitation of awareness and understanding of liberty and love. If you are unable to convince a person, or if you believe that a person you would want to recommend this book to will not be persuaded by its spiritual value, recommend it on its value as a works of science fiction, or for its philosophical, historical and political value. It is also up to those who ant to remain in this universe to help make the world a better place to be where every race, species and creature can have a worthwhile place. Humility and true understanding are the greatest blessings one can give another.

APPENDICES

APPENDICES

Appendix 1

Below are fragments from a letter I wrote to my son who called me a bigot:

I am writing the following to explain to you why I am not a bigot.

First, do you know what a bigot is? How do you define the word "bigot"? Do you have any idea at all?

Bigot as defined by Webster: "One obstinately or intolerantly devoted to his own church, his own party, belief or opinion." This is you. It is the bigot that almost always calls another person a bigot. It has to do with the idea that you have an entire mass of brainwashed people supporting you against a single person.

The way I define bigot: "One, who obstinately, derogatorily, and without proper insight or knowledge attacks another person's view on, or his devotion to a church, belief, racial opinion, political party, or special group in spite of the other person's valid argument given for his stance." This one fits you to the letter.

How present-day propaganda defines bigot: "One who refuses to, or does not consent others to marry someone from another race, regardless of that person's valid reason for his view."

Both parties can disagree with each other, for whatever reason, but when a person can give a very good reason for his stance, then the appellation 'bigot' does not stand. The intolerant stance, without accepting a sincere reason or explanation, of not allowing another person his view is bigotry. The person calling the other person a bigot is the true bigot.

This is a word from a list of words that when used on another always causes a war and brainwashed people are set up to incite such a war whether enough people are present to intimidate the one attacked or not, so that he will cower and submit to the public opinion of millions of equally intolerant people. It is a technique of brainwashing that programmers of propaganda schemes incorporate to induce the zombies to state such inflammatory words for the power of intimidation these almost always bring.

The word 'bigot' is used by indoctrinated people having a preconceived idea of how it ought to be as advertised and hammered into society by means of consistent, insistent, and intense propaganda campaigns that inundate our minds day and night from as many sources as possible. It is a supreme hostile act against another to use these kinds of words. It is like dropping an atom bomb on Japan.

I am livid with you for calling me a bigot. And that after I had explained to you at least four times why it is not sane to marry into another race for anyone no matter what race one belongs to. You even told me once that you explained to [your son] why he shouldn't intermarry, for crying out loud, or was that another lie?

I told you many times that each race manifested on earth today, has had its own Messiah come to their rescue **when it was a white race and before it descended to become a dark-skinned race**. In each case it was the spirit of Jesus Christ, in a flesh body of the white race that was then last-descended from paradise. [I told you also that every creature, man or beast, has a human soul]. After the members of races that came before us had solidly rejected their own racial Christ, they lost the status of the then white race and became a race lower, like for instance the Mongolian races. I should not say lower, but of a racial definition different from white.

Many racial sets of Adam and Woman were redeemed. Jesus told us that there were many mansions in the kingdom. These mansions belong to the saved of all the white races that came before our white race. So there are souls in mansions in the kingdom that belong to the same original white race whose race of unsaved souls has now deteriorated and atrophied to the animal kingdom.

Jesus said that His father's house had many mansions and that he had to go and prepare a place for us. When he came down to be our Savior, there was not even a place for us. But the mansions that Jesus said were there already belong to the redeemed racial stock of previously redeemed souls. I guess, by now there is a mansion for our race as well. See, even in heaven, the several racial stocks that were redeemed exist in separate mansions, but there is no enmity between them.

I see these mansions, just as Paul, the Apostle, saw them; as living temples in which each soul of that temple is a living stone. In other words, each living temple is a whole person, made up of all these spiritual cells, such as Adam and Woman originally were also. Each soul has become a living spiritual cell in the living body of cells, just as Paul also described it, and just as natural science has discovered biological creatures are constituted, an assemblage of billions of living cells that, together, form a biological creature. The new person formed of all the souls is a being that loves god, the father by his entire soulular structure and is a new son of god. This new person, redeemed from the forge [the universe] that removed the *impurities in soul and that returned the pure souls to form the new son existing in permanent happiness, and having good relations with everybody.*

These steps down that the races on earth make for those who have not accepted their Christ go on from time to time and the races fall from a higher status race to a lower race and eventually enter into the animal world. Why do you think there are so many races in the world, from white man, black, asian, through gorillas and killer whales to rats and spiders, etc.? It is the curse of the universe and the refusal to seek the Comforter in truth when one had a chance to do so. As you can see from my example, the Comforter is a very patient spirit. It took him 2000 years to bring me to a point where he can lead me into all truth—a thing Jesus was utterly unable to do while in the flesh. I know he had me in his grasp then, and will never let go until he has me safely back home. So, I am not worried.

The universe is a fiction—an utter lie, it is not really there in spirit, and biological existence for all races is just a spiritual nightmare dream—a nightmare that increases in horror with the increase in time spent in the universe.

The universe is souls' nightmare and requires souls' spiritual energy that slowly leaks as their energies are drained to keep the fiction in place. This is because we believed the original lie and cosmic propaganda for a very long time so it becomes more real and true with every cycle of physical life we go through. The more real the universe becomes, the more our positive spiritual energy is drained and the more we become solidly integrated in the universe.

This universe is the only hell there will ever be, because we believed a liar and that liar has been the only god to us because we died to the real god, Jesus, just as he told us in truth. If Jesus, our god tells us we are dead, please believe him. He should know! Jehovah is the serpent, because we believed him and he was the only god and remains the only god in the universe. He is the creator of this fictional universe, but souls empower it. He is the true devil that prevents us from escaping to the true god whom we lost when we acted on advice of this liar. We cannot escape because we are wired into the computer as a source of energy that runs the computer. The program is considered essential to these captured souls. The computer uses a binary system of two spiritual states, truth and lie. The program universe in which we are trapped runs on this spiritual binary concept in which all things in the universe have been defined by a binary code, just as our biological genes are defined by long strings of biological codes. Any item is identified by making up a code, for instance 'tlllttltlltl', where the 't' stands for an instance of truth [something relating personally to the addressed] *and 'l' stands for an instance of lie. This is so because a lie must be constantly supported by more lies and instances of truth in order for the first lie to maintain its power to deceive.*

This agreement, to be subject to the lie and to confirm the lie by creating codes, and by using computer codes to identify things, integrates us into the program and gives the program validity in the soul, which soul is a spiritual entity. This is the way we are wired into the power-supply of the computer and have become inter-active computer processing units in the computer, making us an essential integrated part of the program. It seems to us as if our existence and our reality depend on it.

Animals have been so solidly wired into the computer through complete agreement with the program for immeasurable long stretches of time they have become a permanent part of the program. The program has become the only reality possible for animals.

Everything in the universe is subject to change. Spiritually, you are required to keep up with all the changes. You must upgrade your knowledge base which base is part of a memory system of the main computer. By always being an active integral part in the reprogramming of the computer, you give it validity and you are caught by what you believe. And you are caught into it by participating in the programming and by forcing others to see reality as you are seeing it.

This is one of the basic functions of death and reincarnation. If we would live on we, sooner or later, would catch up with the program that keeps us caught and we would find a way out. Death stops that. Rebirth is the process that reintegrates a soul solidly again into the program through all the indoctrination it receives from those who care and love for it most; the parents, other family members, friends, teachers and peers in school. The soul is good for another 80 years or so.

The running of the computer program is nothing but a set of operating instructions in a series of programming steps just like the program routines that make our computer programs run. It sets your death and your rebirth into the display.

The Old and New Testaments are full of miracles stories. What are miracles when you are dealing with a computer and can show effects by means of programming routines?

In Genesis 6 god tells Noah to build a huge boat because he will cause a flood to get rid of the adulterated race of Adam that had interbred completely with the races of the world. There are already two miracles. God speaks to man and gives specific orders, and Noah can actually hear him and converse back. The second miracle is his prophesy of the flood coming. Then, only after Noah is completely through building the boat, the flood comes. The adulterated race drowns and the boat comes safely to rest on solid ground after the flood recedes. Now we understand why Jehovah got rid of the interracially mixed breed.

I Kings 17 tells the story of a little meal, and oil that outlasted a drought.

Judges 6 tells the story of Gideon. He was called by god to lead the army. Gideon was cautious and wanted proof that god was truly speaking so he demanded of Jehovah that the following morning there would be dew on a fleece and not anywhere else. Jehovah complied. Gideon then asked to reverse the places where dew would settle, that there would be dew everywhere else but not on the fleece. Jehovah complied.

There was a miracle where time stood still for some twelve hours but the war the Israelites were fighting continued unabated. The sun did not move, but for them time went on.

Apocrypha has a story on which the feast of Hanukah is based. An oil supply for one day for a lamp lasted for eight full days.

There is the Story of Daniel in the Lions Den, another in which three men that were thrown into the fiery furnace inside which furnace a fourth person was seen walking around with the other three, and the occurrence of an angel communicating with, I believe, Daniel from across a river. The angel had what looked like a bronze body. One can bring to bear hundreds of miracles in the Bible.

Then the New Testament has many miracles. Jesus changed water into wine; Jesus walks on water; Jesus multiplies the fish and bread. Jesus did these things in one of his two roles, the one being the physical Messiah for Jehovah.

If the universe is an interactive program between entities in the program and between the operators and entities in the program it is easy to create advanced, nonstandard effects by calling up a special routine, defining regions where a special routine will take effect, by changing a sequence in programming steps, set boundaries for an effect etc, to change the color and appearance of an entity and to insert a nonhuman type of character and more such easily arranged changes to create anomalous effects.

The normal Universe program is based on a main routine that keeps the universe performing in standard mode where billions of subroutines keep species looking the way they do, act as species do, allow for interactions between entities, like human conversations etc. This explains why human speech is but a computer program that gives the human species languages, racial isolation, etc. When special effects are called for, the programmers simply call up a routine or design a routine to create the effect asked for. Miracles are no big deal to operators and programmers when they are called for. The miracles and prophesies in the Bible make a very strong point that the universe is a computer-run display. Human speech, by the way, was invented to convey lies, not truth. The reason is that truth cannot be expressed in the universe based on lies.

God told Adam and Woman, that they would die if they partook of the tree. The true father does not lie! They died from His realm after they partook of the tree! Death means to be out of communion with the environment you were a part of. Why death?. You violated a primary agreement to be in that reality. In the realm of truth you know truth. If you believe a lie in the realm of truth you are out of communion with the realm of truth.

We, as souls that made up the cellular structure of Adam, don't exist anymore in paradise. You too, believe that the true god lied because, obviously you are alive and not dead as the true god foretold. But you did die to the truth in that you consider the true god a liar because somewhere, as a spiritual cell in Adam, you believed the lying serpent and held him to be the true god and you have still never changed your mind for you still worship Jehovah, the serpent, in your church. So, you are dead to the true god and you acquired "life" in the universe, a reality created by the liar. If you were not dead, you would still be able to stand face to face with god; but you cannot!

You also cast Jesus' words, that we are truly dead, to the wind. You do not even believe Him. Your spiritual vision is inverted and you are now existing in the false realm, a spiritually, nonexistent realm, for in true spirit only truth reigns and there you would be cause and not an effect. You would not die because a subroutine in a computer dictates that you can only live a finite amount of time because a computer clock is ticking to count the seconds of your life.

Now you can only see the false computer-generated-environment, and the true reality and the real souls of you and of your fellowmen are hidden from your awareness. You can only see the hateful flesh, and not I, soul. You still consider any other god to be a false one, including the father of Jesus who is not an entity in the program. You merged "your" kind of Jesus into Jehovah [who is not father of all truth] as his son and thus you cannot be saved—wrong god and wrong Jesus. That is organized Christianity for you!

The Old Testament Israelites were right. In their time Jehovah was the only known god, but they did not know he was a liar from the beginning because they believed him and thought him to be the god of truth. This is called propaganda—to make the truth a lie and the lie the truth. It distorted Adam's awareness something awful and inverted his vision and understanding and caused him to die and disintegrate into a mere bunch of cells we call souls.

All you see of the universe and what you are told by the scientists about the universe is so cleverly displayed that one can only believe it is all real. Your parents raised you up in the world and used any and all propaganda techniques to train you to see the world and the universe and society at large as real, good and loving—yet it all is fiction. My parents did the same and all parents everywhere do the same, whether they are people, monkeys or cats. Ever wonder why children are mostly born from young parents? They are at a stage in life that their environment-induced programming is at a peak state. They are ambitiously working their way to be something in the world. To them the universe is "all" real! Let's kick ass!

For animals, this false realm, called universe, or the realm of darkness by Jesus, is real because the souls in them have been indoctrinated by all sorts of propaganda for millennia and they have lost all sense of true spirit—and therefore their spiritual energies have been mostly depleted. They are wholly aligned and integrated into their status as physical creatures in this fictional world, even though they have a soul. That is their curse.

Animals, no doubt, know that they were human once and can think just as well as you and I. Scientists trained monkeys to use computers and a computer language so they could communicate by using the computer. The monkeys can converse as easily as humans. They can ask for a banana and say, "Thank you" when they receive it. They can ask, "You do not want one?" and understand my answer when I say, "No, I'll take a cookie." And the animal replies, "Suit yourself." Now, does that sound human? Sure as hell it does! Animal's curse is that they can still think but not express themselves very good, but through shrieks, grunts, yells, whistles and coughs they can make do. These have specific meanings, proving that they have intelligence to spare.

For the dark-skinned races there is still a small chance of redemption. Jesus still has a chance to redeem us, but the propaganda of the universe and of Christendom has reduced this chance to a very small one indeed. The book of Revelation says that there will be only 144,000—twelve thousand per tribe of Israel—redeemed [maybe twice as much if you include one spouse for each man]. Considering the amount of people now on earth you can see it is a very slim chance at all to be redeemed or born-again. As you can see there are no persons redeemed of any other race, just Hebrew whites, although I believe Jesus was speaking on behalf of Jehovah, not true reality. But one thing is for sure, very few will find true reality.

If you encourage your children to mix their genes with another race, no matter which—Chinese, black or chimpanzee—you will reduce the chances of redemption of our offspring so much the more. Do you see why it is important to stick to your own race? You do it for your posterity, not for yourself. [Even if you can't grasp this, just marrying into another race causes inevitable grief and problems for your offspring, who are now neither one race nor another with violent splits and turmoil in the family clans.

I respect and get along well with people of the other races, but one thing is clear about them as well, all my dark-skinned friends were married into their own race. It seems that, today, only the white people in America, and in the world, are under strong pressure from organized propaganda sources to mix their genes with the other races. I can see the working of daemons here. The end of this cycle of heaven and earth is coming close, and the universal spiritual hierarchy is determined that not a single soul shall escape from their grasp. It needs the energy to keep the universe in suspension. Believe me; it will have plenty of energy coming to it because few will escape.

I know that the ministers in your church have an enormous racial propaganda campaign going [for it goes on in all churches] that we are equal to all other races—baloney. Why do you think there are so many races, just for fun? No, it is for very important spiritual reasons—reasons you have no inkling or understanding about. Jesus said about priests and ministers that the blind [the clergy] lead the blind and they all end up in a ditch. Do you know why they are blind? They can't see the truth because truth is not present in the universe! We are ignorant so Jehovah set us rules to follow in earth. If we knew what we are doing we do not need rules. He is a spiritual entity and knows things we do not. Don't fight spirit, you will be the loser.

That is why the Comforter must guide you, as he is guiding me. Redemption is a one-spirit operation and excludes all but the one soul being guided. The church wants to turn this redemption thing into a mass movement—not a chance of that!

The posterity of a racially mixed couple is doomed forever because the children's chances of redemption are non-existent, and that is exactly the way it is. Besides, the white gene structure is the weakest of all races. You cross it with anything else and you will never see a white individual emerging from the breed, no matter how many times you breed it back with genes from the white gene pool.

I cannot see why it is so damned important to marry into the colored races anyway. It is not that there is an extreme shortage of men and women in the white race. Also, if you do not know exactly what the consequences are of such a step, why take the risk? The colored person can surely find a person of his own nature to marry as well. What you experience is dirty propaganda that induces you to act before you know what the ramifications of your deed are. This is a spiritual error and it is permanent and it does not affect only you, but also your mixed posterity.

By all means, have people from other racial strains and of mixed strains as friends—close friends. They are not one iota less as persons. They make marvelous contributions to society. We recognize them for that, but you will find that they are more at ease being married to their own kind just as we are, being married to our kind. Marriage is not an easy alliance, as you know by now. Don't complicate life for your children by allowing them to intermarry, because the stresses and strains of the marriage of people of the same race cause breaks in more than 60% of the marriages. Inter-racial marriages will be loaded with so much more stress and strain they simply cannot and will not last and in the end everybody is stuck with interracial offspring.

I say this not with derogation—you like your dog, lizards and cats—they are of other racial stock also and with sensitive souls—would you marry any of them? This example is much farther removed than human races, but even animals left to their own will only have offspring with mates of the same gene structure.

I know that this inter-racial marriage promotion stuff also comes from your church, because it is preached from most pulpits today. It may be done in a subtle manner, but the results speak for themselves. Your name calling of "bigot" is one of the most forceful present-day propaganda attacks one can deliver to another—like dumping a nuclear warhead on Japan—so I know you are indoctrinated by church and media propaganda. It forces almost everyone in the camp of the "good" people against the attacked person, and marks him as an evil person that should be ashamed of himself. These masses of brainwashed people never know they are brainwashed, but they are nonetheless, and the public-opinion to which they subscribe makes them zombies in control of the propaganda system. When such a person calls his father a bigot, the command from the programmers triggered in you to do so overrides all other relations. You act as a programmed robot and believe that you are very much in control of your own person. That is the cunning of propaganda. It brainwashes people in a most subtle manner and makes them believe that they act from cause rather than from effect.

Jesus made all things new, the Bible teaches. He broke with all kinds of religious traditions and attacked the maintainers of tradition, the priests, lawyers and scribes. That was the reason that he was eventually hung on the cross. He came to introduce a new god—the true god. Jesus had 12 male apostles. If it was just and right to have women and colored people as apostles in starting all things new, then, why didn't he choose some women and some Chinese and a black? Because it wasn't spiritually just and right. [It is not that he didn't love women. He loved several women].

Pose these questions to your minister and see how he deceives you once again. So, do you think Jesus was a bigot also? Believe me, if Jesus wanted any of those, they would have been around to pick from. He came well prepared and he, or his spiritual coworkers, would have placed them in his immediate environment so that he could choose them.

These are, spiritually, extremely dangerous times and you are much too trusting of your minister. No amount of singing and listening to sermons is going to redeem you. It will kill you spiritually. That is why I am not attending church. I know where the devil is laying its traps; the traps are where you do not suspect them and then trap you forever with silk tongues and twisted, emotional sermons and scare tactics. Jesus chose me to proclaim truth, because I am not attached to any church. Church organizations are brainwashing institutions and the truth is far from them.

Your family is obviously a very talented family. You are linked for four hundred and fifty years to a line of ministers. To be a minister takes much learning and intelligence, but I believe very few, if any, were redeemed in spirit. My grandfather was not a minister, he was a ships captain. My father was not a minister and you and I are not either. This is good because Jesus once said that all will sin, but that those who make other people sin would do themselves good by tying a mill stone around their neck and to drown themselves.

Jesus also accused the priests, lawyers and scribes of being hypocrites and that they resembled tombs that look clean and whitewashed on the outside and inside are nothing but filth. They, including all Christian ministers, are the ones that should tie a mill stone around their necks etc. Jesus spoke not only of those days, but of all days to come, because no religion or faith can remain pure for a very long time in this utterly deceitful, corrosive environment. He meant, as sure as I am writing this, to include almost all ministers of future times, and especially of our time. That is exactly the reason that at this time in history he was able to reach me through the millions of layers of propaganda and deceit that I have been exposed to and that had themselves incorporated into my belief system, to supp with me [exchange ideas and thoughts] and teach me this time around and through many previous lifetimes to understand that there are two realms, one of truth and another of deceit where existence is hell.

I have written about it as it was taught me and it is not likely any child of any man in the history of all mankind has had more communion from his father than you have from me and there is not likely a child in the history of mankind that ignored to such an extreme extent as you have the communions of his father. This is all the more sorrowful because what I have written and given you is the bread of life, just as Jesus gave it two thousand years ago. I have written enough material to fill over fifteen volumes of books, each five hundred pages long. You have them all and you have dishonored me by completely ignoring them and causing me to be angry with you by calling me a bigot. You have no respect for elders and especially not for your father. And in trying to use your brain you are like a baboon, you live life by rote—why learn anything new—kind of attitude.

Throughout the ages the churches have staged an on-going religious propaganda campaign, enforced by laws and enforcement to ingrain a strong public opinion against those who stray from standard religious doctrine. Wherever brainwashing and indoctrination is practiced, the Good Spirit cannot be present. You show all the signs of being brainwashed. Woman and Adam were brainwashed. They received crescendo sales talks from the serpent and it was the woman who was sold first and quickly. They died from their father's environment. Propaganda is plainly dishonest. You can recognize propaganda because it requires that people attend often and regularly to place and set the propaganda [to be exposed to more sales talk], as is the standard routine in network marketing, in church, and in public school. You can always see when propaganda is going on by who is the final beneficiary of the campaign. Church propaganda can be checked by seeing how many people attend regularly. The more people attend regularly, the stronger the organization and the richer and the more respected the minister is.

See how public school instills a blind loyalty to a government system that is now public enemy #1. Insistent propaganda in the completely government-run school system makes it possible.

See how many people watch TV and the news religiously and see how brainwashed the American people are. Propaganda is a money-making and power-brokering business. Money counts, and it is made by keeping the flock or constituency religious in religion and in our attitude toward government—and this is a solid guarantee that no one will be saved by god in the true Christ. We refuse to give him reality in our illusion and he is far away from any form of propaganda induced zombies and, in the case of the constituency, the people allowed themselves to be wired into the political propaganda machine by registering to vote. It is a sure way for the people to lose their rights and become ever more enslaved as is happening now.

It is exactly the Comforter's job to de-program you, for all the programming you absorbed in your soul-being is your downfall and is the length and strength of chain that binds you to your continued capture in the universe. Jehovah or one of his subordinate daemons will always be in control of you [that is what effective propaganda does to a person], for that is how the whole universe got its start—through his propaganda campaign.

The universe is a spiritual fiction that must be enforced continually through [spiritual] cosmic propaganda first and always [that makes all things look real and gives the impetus for you to believe everything that happens in the universe]. All human interaction is spiritual propaganda that establishes the universe completely and solidly in your mind and makes you accept it as a viable environment and society. It is people [parents, ministers and politicians] also that keep you a slave in this universe. Animals have their propaganda set forever. Don't be another victim of propaganda, be free in the Comforter.

The universe looks real but can be rolled up—for crying out loud. Anything that can be undone is not reality. The true god and truth is reality, for these endure always and we are utterly unaware of it. This universe is just like a 3-D movie, *where you watch the movie with red and green goggles—everything looks real and 3-D, but it is all phony, a delusion. The worst thing is that we, all together, produce the show and enforce it on one another. We clamor and struggle as souls to put another set of spiritual goggles on every time it is taken away from us. We demand to reincarnate so we can have another set of goggles [bodies] to enjoy the program with.*

Truth is truth—Jesus is always, and reality lasts forever. The universe is a lie—it will be rolled up and so it was not created by the god of truth or it would last forever and it would not be evil. It can be rolled up because it contains a lie [by removing and exposing the lie the universe can be made to disappear]. If you could completely deprogram yourself the universe would vanish and the truth of all things would remain—the true god's reality. All that would remain of the universe is a bunch of rotting, comatose souls. There is unrestricted liberty, everywhere, and a god who smiles and loves you for being you and talks to you. No more physical body or integrated goggles that contain all the lies you have adopted during your stay in the universe. But not for the souls imbued with a lie.

The crazy thing is that all the souls in negative spirit are somehow wired together and keep themselves and each other under the spell of the lie. These souls are cross-feeding propaganda to each other while they are lying together in a sort of opium-den, in a state of being comatose. The illusion is too well set for you to be able to find your way back alone or in a human group-setting. You need the Comforter!

The true god does not want all those souls caught in a scheme of lies, but the souls keep themselves caught by believing cosmic and human propaganda and having this propaganda reinforced from moment to moment. See for yourself, how evil this scheme is that continues to keep you caught in that ridiculous human body—like you being a top salesman. You go to work each day to reinforce the physical environment and the thought that you are great in sales. In spirit you do not have to sell cars—so it is a useless enterprise.

The reason Jehovah will not show us his face is that the lies and deceit are written right on his face. Jehovah is a spiritual magician. He created a reality that is not there, like 3-D movies and makes us believe it is real. We are not allowed, or we are too scared to take off the goggles or we will literally die. The goggles are our means of communion with the fiction. The true god walked around in paradise. He had nothing to hide. Adam could approach him, face to face, any time and be fed by Him [be in communion with Him]; try to do that with Jehovah.

I agree we should not kill someone else, for that person may not be ready to die and he is none of our concern. I agree that we should not kill our own bodies until the Comforter thinks it is time to go on our journey. He is our guide—we cannot take charge ourselves because we do not know how to get out of here, and we do not know where and how to arrive. All Jesus did was to take off his goggles when he thought it time to depart. He had himself hung on a cross to let us know there is nothing good with the rotten thing called human body. Jesus still exists, but he can see in truth—he can only make contact with us in truth and thus not through physical means. It is told that He rose into heaven in the body. I know why! He went up to Jehovah and cast it in front of him and said "Here, this is my payment; give me the souls we bargained over." Yet because of his mission he will always have an immortal human body. Why? He fulfilled the law. He can be anywhere.

A certain amount of specific Bible knowledge is imperative to get in contact with the Comforter, but I would stick mainly to the words Jesus spoke. His words contain more truth than the rest of the Bible put together, and as I told you, you must sift through his words as well to get the truth. Also Genesis 2 and 3 are of utmost importance, but if you misunderstand what they say, you are up the creek without a paddle and if you take someone else's word for what you should understand yourself, you don't even have the canoe because that other person certainly has it wrong. Read with the Good Spirit and not with your minister.

Most people read with the holy spirit and are sent back up the creek. Bible reading is more dangerous than falling off a cliff. It tells the truth if you know where to look and if not, you are lost in eternal bushes, like our minister forefathers. The clergy were brainwashed to understand the Bible according to some church's or seminary's interpretation and not theirs in the Good Spirit. If you want to be redeemed, stay away from anything that is ordered, put down, written or organized by humans or their institutions. You must seek the Comforter all alone or not even pretend that you are seeking. Churches have become social institutions and are thus communistic in nature. They are there to keep you indoctrinated into the world and for you not to escape into the realms of truth and liberty.

I believe churches have their place. Children need to be acquainted with Jesus, and the Bible must be kept in circulation. Children will be taught all wrong, but it is utterly impossible to teach them correctly. They were born into this place and must be reared by their parents and society to become effective members of society. How can anybody abandon the rearing of their child and not be a reprobate? I believe, though, that when a child becomes a well-established adult, he should be encouraged to seek the Comforter singularly, and all preaching to the adult must stop.

Oh no! Everybody shouts. People are too immature to be left to themselves as adults. Of course, I agree, because most people do never mature. They grow up with a mental state of about a ten year old child. But whose fault is that—the parents' or the child's They were grown up by parents that had a mental attitude that never reached beyond that of a ten year old also—and so on down the line into history. The problem is that even a great percentage of ministers, politicians and educators never grow up either. The world is a real mess. It cannot be set straight—and therefore I suggest you listen to the Comforter and get the hell out of here.

Read John 17, verse 3, "This is eternal life, to know the true god"—not the false one, Jehovah.

Read verse 25-27. Talking/praying to his father, Jesus said, "You have never been known on earth". Can this father be Jehovah who has been known to the Israelites for more than 1500 years already when Jesus spoke those word. No. Jesus identified Jehovah to be the father of lies when he answered the Jewish priests; "Your father is a liar and he lied from the beginning." Who lied from the beginning? It was the serpent who deceived Adam and Woman so he could enslave them and use them to run and operate his computer and display his program universe to keep deceived souls ensnared.

Jesus came to introduce the true god; the god from whom we died when we ate of the tree—god who never lies. He is the true god mentioned in John 17, verse 3. There are also a true Christ and a false Christ. The true Christ is the Comforter, the one who can lead us to all truth. The false Christ is the man Jesus in the flesh. In the flesh, he was made of the fabric of the lie. Jesus knew that very well. Jesus said to the rich young man, "Why do you call me good? There is only one who is good" [not some person in the flesh as I am]. Jesus, in the spirit of the Comforter, is good, that is why I call His spirit the Good Spirit [a very good identification because, by Jesus' own words, only one is good]. The churches use the physical person 'Jesus' in their propaganda campaigns by having sculptures of him on a cross. Jesus, the human, is powerless. He said so. He could teach the apostles no more. It was good for him to leave so that the Comforter could come who would lead them into all truth—the true god and the realm where this true god exists.

The holy spirit is the spirit of deceit and propaganda. It is the spirit that deceived Woman and beguiled her to partake of the tree and made her dead to the true god. It is not the spirit of love and embraces, but rather of separateness and great difference in standing. The Good Spirit wants, completely and utterly, for the true god and Christ to be one with us, see John 17. How is it possible that your minister can confuse the truth and the lie so much that you only know the falsehoods and I, who never goes to church, know the truth and why do you distrust me so much in my spiritual understanding? It is because you are a brainwashed zombie. It is clear that my understanding rises far and far above any and all church doctrines which doctrines are nothing but the [false] traditions of men and riddled with the deceits of the worldly Christ. What I received I did not receive of men, but of god in truth through the Comforter. Who else knows what I know? Do you think I can come up with this stuff all by myself?

The movie Pirates of the Caribbean is an excellent example, almost prophetical, in showing what humanity looks like in spirit. All the pirates on the Black Pearl were semi-dead. They could not enjoy their spoil of gold in the chest because of the curse placed on the gold. They could not enjoy sex, liquor, food or any other form of entertainment. At full moon you could see why. They were mere skeletons—wine would drip through their ribs to the ground, food also, etc., etc. We laugh at the movie, but tragically, we are all something like that as spiritual beings. We are dead, yet we live. Jesus told us so. How can you believe you are alive? The universe is a piece of deceitful fiction and our bodies have been carefully computer-designed to only make us see the lie around us and in us as truth. We cannot see the true soul for we are blind to it and to all truth. There is absolutely no truth to be found in this universe of pure deceit through our bodily senses; and spiritually we are numb as dead bats. Reality is another realm in which this physical universe shrinks to the size of a walnut if that other realm were represented to be the size of the universe. It is a mere prison or asylum in which creatures are kept who have made themselves blind and dead to the truth by believing a spiritual lie. We are blind to the entire realm of truth. In my case the Comforter taught me that there is a realm, a huge realm, outside this asylum. I, myself, do not know what the realm of truth looks like or what "truth" is, but I have the necessary information needed for the Comforter to lead me into all truth when my body dies away from me this time. I can now trust the Comforter to guide me through the most severe forms of intimidation and seeming horror. Horror and intimidation, I write, because the deceiver will do all she can to prevent my escape and she is incredibly seductive, mean and clever. Yes, I believe that Jehovah is a female or an effeminate type of daemon. For me and my wife, this is the last time around and I do my very best to open this opportunity to others like yourself and your family. I have never met such enormous resistance, anywhere, as I get from you and your wife and from your minister whom I have never even met—a sure sign that you are indoctrinated and brainwashed.

Read my article "Propaganda". You had it on a diskette, but I doubt you have it anymore. It would be so good if you would be my right hand and help me disseminate my articles; you would be so good at it [it would be a natural calling for you], but instead you want to continue to find fault with a father who has never done anything to cause you to treat him with such contempt, disrespect and insincerity. It is time for a change in the wind. Stop being brainwashed about me by your mother and wife. It is difficult but possible.

I am de-brainwashed. You proved to me that you can do the same by many of the choices you made in your life that required stepping outside the box of propaganda driven routines. You have the guts and strength of character to face it. Women, all women love to have their husbands solidly brainwashed, so they can control them. Jesus insists that you must be free from brainwashing, because the Good Spirit cannot lead if outside forces control your mind and actions. Every American is brainwashed and it is incredibly tragic. We have lost all freedom. There is no more constitution that has any power for the people, it only gives abundant powers to government; and just like Jehovah, government had to steal these powers from the people.

There is nothing new under the sun.

Appendix 2

Three Kingdoms [April 1995]

This was written before I understood that Jesus came to us as a double agent. Later I tried to change this article to include my later understanding of spirit. If you have eyes to see, ears to hear, [a soul who can understand] there is yet a lot of understanding to be gotten from this article.

Jesus knows all things, even natural law, of which His contemporaries knew nothing. He was constrained to use a lot of allegory and parables. His deliberate use of allegories and parables was also used to separate the sheep from the goats. The sheep would interpret the parables in the fashion of the world and would gain nothing, as Jesus said the flesh will gain nothing from what he had to say. Only goats would understand the true message and receive the spiritual meaning once they are in the guidance of the Good Spirit. Yet, today we have a better grasp of the natural laws that rule all of physical nature. Jesus knew that there were three kingdoms:

1. The mineral kingdom
2. The kingdom of organic life
3. The kingdom of god

Below, some of the laws mentioned in the Bible:

1. As below—so above, as His parables indicate.
2. I am the Way, the Truth and the Life.
3. No one comes to the father but by me.
4. What is of flesh is flesh and what is of spirit is spirit. [The flesh, and nothing of the flesh, like morals and conscience, will profit us spiritually.] Souls that fell from paradise were clothed in human

bodies that are like prison garbs or animal skins when they entered the spiritual prison earth.

5. One must serve one master. One must serve either the god of the universe, Jehovah, the god of darkness and proclaimer of the first lie, *or* the god of truth, love and life. This item clearly indicates that Jesus came to us as double agent. He represented both good and evil and confronted us to seek the right one and to choose His father in true reality.

These compare to the natural laws known today as follows:

a. Natural laws are continuous through all kingdoms.
b. Matter, of itself, cannot spontaneously spring to life. Christ [in the third kingdom] is to the man in the second kingdom what plants [in the second kingdom] are to inorganic matter of the first kingdom. Jesus' spirit, the Comforter, is the means by which a man of the second kingdom may be raised to the third kingdom.
c. A particle from a lower kingdom cannot rise to a higher kingdom unless it is pulled up by an entity of the kingdom directly above it.
d. There is an impassable barrier between the kingdoms as viewed from a kingdom below.
e. One can belong to only one kingdom.
f. By coming to life in the third kingdom one sees the entities in the other kingdoms as being dead.

So, we know from the two kingdoms open to our inspection that in kingdom #1 [we see matter as dead, but that is our blindness. Matter is soul just like I am soul], entities consisting of dead material and in kingdom #2 entities having organic life, that if a particle or ion of the mineral world is made a part of the higher kingdom of organic life, it has three possible routes:

1. It passes through the roots of plants and plant-like creatures.
2. It passes through the leaves of plants [carbon assimilation under the action of photo synthesis].
3. By ingestion of certain sub-microscopic entities, I believe.

The inorganic kingdom lacks the capacity of "life" available in the second kingdom. An inorganic particle is incapable of life unless absorbed by entities of a life member of the bio-organic kingdom. In the same manner there is an impassable barrier between the kingdom of organic life and the kingdom of heaven when viewed from the kingdom below [the kingdom of organic life]. Mankind is eternally barred from the kingdom of heaven because man lacks the spirit of god [regardless whether that spirit is positive or negative].

Jesus [as dual agent] opened the way for our transcendence to the spiritual kingdoms [positive and negative] by giving us the capacity to believe in the holy spirit [of Jehovah] and the positive spirit of His father [the Good Spirit] through our belief in Him. He is the only one that could allow us entry by him taking us up. This is done in the same fashion by which ions from the inorganic world are absorbed by plants to become part of the kingdom of organic life. As ions become part of a complex structure in a biological entity so are the souls of men designed and transformed to become part of a large spiritual structure. After his ascension Jesus only represents positive spirit. His role as Messiah ended when he ascended. His role is taken over by the Holy Spirit, in whom almost every Christian still believes. From hereon down I only speak of Jesus and spirit as the Good Spirit.

This transformation, of course, is the process of removing all deceit and yearnings for sophistication and the fleshpots of human culture from the mind and soul of man. Since there is absolutely no entity in the universe capable of de-brainwashing the mind and soul of a human being, it stands to reason that such transformation must come from an entity in a higher form of reality. Jesus said that he could not do it because he was part of the scenario of deceit—physical reality. He came to us as a human being. He had to wait until he had returned to "his father" as he put it. He had to return to reality, so that from there he can reach us, minus the human body, in spirit and commune with us. I say without the human body, because anything entangled with the universe has corruption in it. Jesus took advantage of corruption in his own being as human to be able to learn our situation of deceit as established by the universe, religion, society and government and the means by which human culture in that time communicated.

Even though he was here by his own undeceived mind and will, he was in the flesh, and flesh simply does not have it in itself to reveal truth. Even if he did, people had the choice to believe what he said, to think it all hogwash or to deliberately alter it for the sake of some plan of organized deceit—propaganda. In earth no one has 100% surety that something is true, right! Yet he taught. But his teaching was only preliminary to being de-brainwashed. He had to return in spirit for those who sincerely believed in him, to raise their belief system to a solid faith that Jesus' deeper message was right. It is only through faith that a person can be raised to the next higher level of awareness. This last level is the awareness of truth. This kind of faith is like the baby blanket with the corners tied together in which a new-born baby is depicted when brought home by the stork. Faith is like that baby blanket. The one with faith is contained by that blanket so that someone in spirit can grab this blanket by the knot with the baby in it and pull it from the level of human belief into the next kingdom of beingness, reality, spiritual knowingness.

Jesus declared that no one comes to the father, but by Him; He is the gate, the only gate to reality. He who drinks my blood [spirit] and eats my flesh as food [accepts the deeper meaning of what I teach] shall live. He who drinks from my well [the source of truth] shall have eternal life. For humanity entrance into the kingdom is voluntary. All we have to realize and accept is that Jesus is the son of god [a representative of the higher kingdom who has the capability to draw us up from above]. Just as a plant has to prepare a molecule before it can be pulled up through its roots by creating an ion of the proper charge and complexity so Jesus has to prepare a human [soul] to the proper attitude and understanding before He can pull it up to the higher kingdom. Jesus said, "My words are food for [eternal] life. His words are food for eternal life just as physical food is sustenance in physical reality. Both the ion and man have this latent capacity to be properly charged for such transcendence. This Jesus accomplished through His personal life, His deeper teachings and His suffering. All the mechanisms for the charging of the entities was in place and for each properly charged mind and heart the way to the father was and is open from that time forward through the only gate, the spirit of Jesus Christ. The way of acceptance is preached along with the gospel. There must be a repentance [a spirit-caused change or shift from an earthly, universal viewpoint to one of the kingdom of heaven, or truth/reality], a baptismal immersion in water as a way to seal the covenant to die to this world and to live for the kingdom, accept Jesus as the Way and as god's son and to **live thereafter not for worldly but for spiritual goals**.

The three kingdoms are major realms of awareness. In earth there are the following realms: a realm of awareness of dirt [there may be several sub layers of awareness in this realm], a realm of awareness of bacteria and viruses, a realm of awareness of plants, a realm of awareness of insects, a realm of awareness of animals and a realm of awareness of human beings. Then there is an almost impassable barrier between the realm of awareness of the human being and the realm of awareness of son of the true god.

The god of the universe created the physical body of man from compounds of the kingdom below, mineral matter [ash of spirit formed from soul's acceptance of propaganda]. Jesus called this composition flesh, filthy rags, prison garbs. They are not us souls, but only the clothes we, souls, wear. Likewise, Jesus' father creates spiritual beings with components derived from the kingdom below. The organic kingdom creates live beings from the kingdom of inorganic matter. He stated this law as relating to the two higher kingdoms as "that which is born of flesh is flesh and that which is born of spirit is spirit," or that which is born of universal deceit are rags and that which is born of spirit is pure white raiment. What Jesus means is that your soul is spirit, made from truth/real things, and the flesh is a compound derived from a realm based on untruth/the lie/fiction. You cannot mix pure truth with filthy propaganda and be alive in positive spirit.

There is a difference in class between spirit and flesh, as there is a difference in class between minerals and flesh. Only organic life can reproduce flesh. The mineral kingdom is incapable of it. So it is also with flesh. It is incapable of creating the spiritual being.

Jesus says there is an unbridgeable difference between a believer in truth and a non-believer in truth. Only through the actions of a believer in truth [like believing in the gospel "Truth" but not Gospel "fiction" can a non-believer of true reality become a believer. The action must come from the believer; the choice thereafter is up to the non-believer. That is because the spirit of Christ is in the faithful and not in the non-faithful. Therefore, there also is an impassable void between the morality of the flesh in the pagan and the super morality of the true believer. True morality of the believer is of a higher order. Non-believers [they include practically all Christians] lack spiritual content. The Old Testament of Jehovah had its own classification: "The nations that know Jehovah, god of the universe, and the nations that know not god"—or those with potential and those without. Jehovah deals with nations. The same is true for The Good Spirit as it refers to individual men.

The moral beauty is of the moral [fleshy] man and the spiritual beauty is of the spiritual man. So the classifications of the three kingdoms can be stated: That which is mineral is only mineral, that which is flesh is flesh and that which is spirit is of spirit. The moral pagan is really the highest achievement of the organic kingdom. However, the morality of the person transformed by Jesus' inner message is just the first expression of the morality in the kingdom of truth which has an unlimited scale of beauty yet to be aspired to. Even the commitment of each class is different. Jesus said: "If anyone loves the world [this universe], the love of the father is not in him". This difference in classification demarcates a difference in commitment and desires; one to the world and its' assortments of desired objects and ends; the other a commitment to the spirit of truth and its unwavering drives. A mild or pretended religiousness of the average Christian together with a desire of the flesh shows a distinctive lack of the love for the true father. Even the lovers of Satan [of the world] do that. So each kingdom has its drive and they are compatible only to the kingdom to which the entity belongs. *One cannot hope to live for two kingdoms at once.* One cannot serve two masters. One will despise the one and love the other. A true believer of Jesus' deeper message can and will care for the sterile needs of the pagan but that is simply an expression of one of the character traits of the compassionate Samaritan. One cannot be praised for it. If it was done to seek praise the deed is corrupted and is not a deed done in the Good Spirit.

A truly incontrovertible fact in favor of Jesus being the Christ/Antichrist is the conversion of Saul of Tarsus. Saul was alive when Jesus preached, died and was resurrected. Saul was one of the highest educated Jewish men of his time and was an ambitious rabbi active in condemning the Christian communities in Palestine and its surroundings. Paul's written letters, along with Mark's, Peter's and John's are the oldest documents of the New Testament. *These books* are important because they give substance and true historical setting for all the other documents in the New Testament. Paul's conversion from a rabbinical, Jesus-condemning, Jew to a truly faithful—practicing what he believes—Christian is the clincher in the entire New Testament that makes belief in the crucified and risen Christ practical, necessary and without refute. I write this just to prove that Jesus existed and that we can trust what is written about him in the gospels. Through dealing with and interrogating arrested, determined believers in Jesus Christ, Saul of Tarsus was transformed into Paul, the apostle.

Saul's conversion confirms Jesus as a man, who was the antagonist of the Law-enforcing priesthood and the interpreters of the Law. It confirms Jesus' arrest, crucifixion, and rising. For, without a doubt, Paul would not have converted to belief in Christ—the crucified and risen, if it was not completely provable that it was true. Paul, in other words, was burned because he played with fire. In his pursuit and zeal to condemn Christians, he received such convincing testimony and reliance on Christ from believing witnesses of Jesus' preaching and teaching, even unto jailing, beatings and death that he obtained the full gospel, while pursuing and interrogating Christians and so he was converted also, against his will and against his upbringing and education. It takes guts to abandon one's wealth, status and prestige of one's sophisticated education and to start anew in something despised by all those with whom he was acquainted and by whom he was upheld in esteem. He abandoned everything, just as Jesus preached man should do in order to obtain redemption—what a guy. He knew that Jesus is the man and the bringer of entirely new principles of understanding!

Paul is the one excellent example of a person who sold everything he owned and possessed to buy the field in which the treasure of the universe is hidden, the truth found in Jesus Christ, god and father of reality in spirit. There is no justification for not taking Jesus and my words seriously. If you do not, you loose.

Here is wisdom: those who are least entitled to have an opinion generally are the most opinionated and most set in their false belief system to force others into it also.

Appendix 3

Below I give you the website for the documents created before, during and after the establishment of the United States:

http://www.liberty-page.com/foundingdocs/main.html

All the documents are most interesting, but it behooves the reader to study the following:

The Rights of the Colonists, by Samuel Paine
The Constitution for the United States of America
Declaration of Independence
Bill of Rights [to the Constitution]
Articles of Confederation and Perpetual Union
Jefferson's Opinion on the Constitutionality of a National Bank
Federalist Papers
Give me Liberty or Give Me Death
Anti-Federalist Papers
Common Sense, by Thomas Paine

Appendix 4

For your understanding of the World Trade Center atrocity, I strongly suggest that you Google "The Truth Behind 911" and read the article "The Destruction of the World Trade Center: Why the Official Account Cannot Be True"

[*http://www.globalresearch.ca/index.php?context=viewArticle&code=GRI 20060129&articleId=1846*].

Or you could go to Web sites *www.911truth.org* and

www.911forthetruth.com or

Read the article "The Truth Behind 9-11"

[*www.geocities.com/northstarzone/WAR.html*].

Appendix 5

Below follow some books to round out understanding of physical reality and the impact modern practices have on man and beast.

Recursionism and Reality: Representing and Understanding the World (2005) by Subhash Kak of Louisiana State University, Baton Rouge

File Format: PDF/Adobe Acrobat—*View as HTML*
Recursionism and **Reality**: Representing and **Understanding** the World . . . . One may speak of God, who represents the spirit, the **understanding** behind **reality** . . . .
[*www.ece.lsu.edu/kak/RReality.pdf*]

Understanding Reality—A Commonsense Theory of the Original Cause . . . .

Stefan Hlatky and Philip Booth's book argues that **understanding reality** is a prerequisite of solving problems.
[*www.reality.org.uk/*]

These books above may vary widely in thesis and understanding, because these books represent more primitive views of mankind as experienced and understood from inside a spiritually locked and controlled artificial reality. They see things from inside the box.

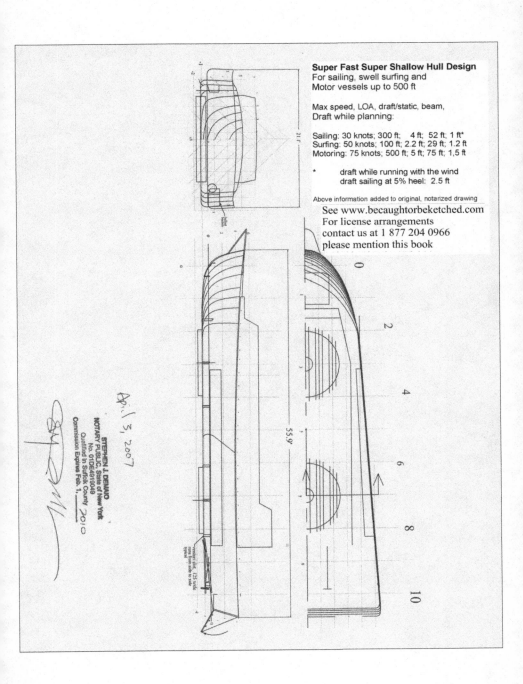

Super Fast Super Shallow Hull Design
For sailing, swell surfing and
Motor vessels up to 500 ft

Max speed, LOA, draft/static, beam,
Draft while planning:

Sailing: 30 knots; 300 ft;   4 ft;   52 ft; 1 ft*
Surfing: 50 knots; 100 ft; 2.2 ft; 29 ft; 1.2 ft
Motoring: 75 knots; 500 ft; 5 ft; 75 ft; 1,5 ft

*   draft while running with the wind
       draft sailing at 5% heel: 2.5 ft

Above information added to original, notarized drawing

See www.becaughtorbeketched.com
For license arrangements
contact us at 1 877 204 0966
please mention this book